Adam Smith

The International Library of Critical Essays in the History of Philosophy
Series Editor: Tom Campbell

Titles in the Series:

Hume – Moral and Political Philosophy
Rachel Cohon

Adam Smith
Knud Haakonssen

Grotius, Pufendorf and Modern Natural Law
Knud Haakonssen

Kant, Vols I & II
Heiner F. Klemme and Manfred Kuehn

Hegel, Vols I & II
David Lamb

Marx
Scott Meikle

Locke's Moral, Political and Legal Philosophy
John R. Milton

Hume – General Philosophy
David Owen

Bentham
Gerald Postema

Hobbes
Robert Shaver

Descartes
Tom Sorell

Mill's Moral, Political and Legal Philosophy
Chin Liew Ten

Leibniz
Catherine Wilson

Rousseau
Robert Wokler

Adam Smith

Edited by

Knud Haakonssen

Department of Philosophy, Boston University

Ashgate

DARTMOUTH

Aldershot • Brookfield USA • Singapore • Sydney

Published by
Dartmouth Publishing Company Limited
Ashgate Publishing Limited
Gower House
Croft Road
Aldershot
Hants GU11 3HR
England

Ashgate Publishing Company
Old Post Road
Brookfield
Vermont 05036
USA

British Library Cataloguing in Publication Data
Adam Smith. – (The international library of critical essays
in the history of philosophy)
1. Smith, Adam, 1723–1790
I. Haakonssen, Knud
330.1'53

Library of Congress Cataloging-in-Publication Data
Adam Smith / edited by Knud Haakonssen.
p. cm. – (International library of critical essays in the
history of philosophy)
ISBN 1–84014–031–3 (hardbound)
1. Smith, Adam. 1723–1790. I. Haakonssen, Knud. 1947– .
II. Series.
B1545.Z7A22 1998
192–dc21 97–52283
CIP

ISBN 1 84014 031 3

Printed and bound by Athenaeum Press, Ltd.,
Gateshead, Tyne & Wear.

Contents

Acknowledgements

The editor and publishers wish to thank the following for permission to use copyright material.

American Political Science Association for the essay: Edward J. Harpham (1984), 'Liberalism, Civic Humanism, and the Case of Adam Smith', *American Political Science Review*, **78**, pp. 764–74.

The Aristotelian Society for the essay: D.D. Raphael (1972–73), 'Hume and Adam Smith on Justice and Utility', *Proceedings of the Aristotelian Society*, **72**, pp. 87–103. Copyright © 1972–73. Reprinted by courtesy of the Editor of the Aristotelian Society.

Cambridge University Press for the essay: Donald Winch (1992), 'Adam Smith: Scottish Moral Philosopher as Political Economist', *The Historical Journal*, **35**, pp. 91–113.

Centre for Independent Studies for the essay: Donald Winch (1988), 'Adam Smith and the Liberal Tradition', in Knud Haakonssen (ed.), *Traditions of Liberalism*, Sydney: Centre for Independent Studies, pp. 83–104.

Cornell University for the essay: Peter Stein (1979), 'Adam Smith's Jurisprudence – Between Morality and Economics', *Cornell Law Review*, **64**, pp. 621–38.

Duke University Press for the essays: Ronald L. Meek (1976), 'New Light on Adam Smith's Glasgow Lectures on Jurisprudence', *History of Political Economy*, **8**, pp. 439–77. Copyright © 1976. Reprinted by permission of Duke University Press; Ronald L. Meek (1971), 'Smith, Turgot, and the "Four Stages" Theory', *History of Political Economy*, **3**, pp. 9–27. Copyright © 1971. Reprinted by permission of Duke University Press.

Samuel Fleischacker (1991), 'Philosophy in Moral Practice: Kant and Adam Smith', *Kant Studien*, **82**, pp. 249–69. Copyright © 1991 Samuel Fleischacker.

Historical Reflections/Reflexions Historiques for the essay: Henry C. Clark (1993), 'Women and Humanity in Scottish Enlightenment Social Thought: The Case of Adam Smith', *Historical Reflections/Reflexions Historiques*, **19**, pp. 335–61. Copyright © 1993 Historical Reflections/Reflexions Historiques.

Imprint Academic for the essays: John Robertson (1983), 'Scottish Political Economy Beyond the Civic Tradition: Government and Economic Development in the *Wealth of Nations*', *History of Political Thought*, **4**, pp. 451–82. Copyright © 1983 Imprint Academic;

John Salter (1992), 'Adam Smith on Feudalism, Commerce and Slavery', *History of Political Thought*, **13**, pp. 219–41. Copyright © 1992 Imprint Academic.

John Donald Publishers Ltd for the essay: Knud Haakonssen (1982), 'What Might Properly Be Called Natural Jurisprudence?', in R.H. Campbell and Andrew S. Skinner (eds), *The Origins and Nature of the Scottish Enlightenment*, Edinburgh: John Donald Publishers Ltd, pp. 205–25.

Johns Hopkins University Press for the essays: Norbert Waszek (1984), 'Two Concepts of Morality: A Distinction of Adam Smith's Ethics and its Stoic Origin', *Journal of the History of Ideas*, **45**, pp. 591–606. Copyright © 1984 Journal of the History of Ideas Inc.; T.D. Campbell and I.S. Ross (1981), 'The Utilitarianism of Adam Smith's Policy Advice', *Journal of the History of Ideas*, **42**, pp. 73–92. Copyright © The Johns Hopkins University Press; Christopher J. Berry (1974), 'Adam Smith's *Considerations* on Language', *Journal of the History of Ideas*, **35**, pp. 130–38. Copyright © The Johns Hopkins University Press.

Journal of the History of Philosophy Inc for the essays: Eugene Heath (1995), 'The Commerce of Sympathy: Adam Smith on the Emergence of Morals', *Journal of the History of Philosophy*, **33**, pp. 447–66; Richard A. Kleer (1995), 'Final Causes in Adam Smith's *Theory of Moral Sentiments*', *Journal of the History of Philosophy*, **33**, pp. 275–300.

Kluwer Academic Publishers for the essay: Charles L. Griswold Jr (1996), 'Nature and Philosophy: Adam Smith on Stoicism, Aesthetic Reconciliation, and Imagination', *Man and World*, **29**, pp. 187–213. Copyright © 1996 Kluwer Academic Publishers.

Michigan State University Press for the essay: T.D. Campbell and I.S. Ross (1982), 'The Theory and Practice of the Wise and Virtuous Man: Reflections on Adam Smith's Response to Humes' Deathbead Wish', *Studies in Eighteenth-Century Culture*, **11**, pp. 65–74.

Jeremy Shearmur (1973), 'Adam Smith's Second Thoughts: Economic Liberalism and its Unintended Consequences', *The Adam Smith Club Kirkcaldy Paper No. 1*, 1–13. Copyright © 1973 Jeremy Shearmur.

University of Chicago Press for the essays: Richard B. Sher (1989), 'Adam Ferguson, Adam Smith, and the Problem of National Defense', *Journal of Modern History*, **61**, pp. 240–68. Copyright © 1989 The University of Chicago; Lawrence Dickey (1986), 'Historicizing the "Adam Smith Problem": Conceptual, Historiographical, and Textual Issues', *Journal of Modern History*, **58**, pp. 579–609. Copyright © 1986 The University of Chicago; Richard Teichgraeber III (1981), 'Rethinking *Das Adam Smith Problem*', *Journal of British Studies*, **20**, pp. 106–23.

Valparaiso University Law Review for the essay: Neil MacCormick (1981), 'Adam Smith on Law', *Valparaiso University Law Review*, **15**, pp. 243–63. Copyright © 1981 Valparaiso University Law Review. Reproduced with the permission of the publisher and author.

Every effort has been made to trace all the copyright holders, but if any have been inadvertently overlooked the publishers will be pleased to make the necessary arrangement at the first opportunity.

Series Preface

The International Library of Critical Essays in the History of Philosophy is designed to bring together, in an accessible form, the best journal essays in English on the history of philosophy. The series makes readily available, in a systematic manner, the most important essays in the history of philosophy, selected and presented by volume editors who are highly respected in their fields. The original essays are reproduced in full which helps to make the series an invaluable reference tool for all scholars interested in the history of philosophy. It is of particular assistance to advanced undergraduate and graduate students in the history of philosophy as well as those who research in this area. The series focuses primarily on the philosophical traditions of Germany, France, Britain and the United States.

The dominant approach of the series is philosophical in that the essays are primarily accounts and critiques from the perspective on the philosophical issues of the time. Some essays trace philosophical influences and elucidate the context of the major philosophical writings. Other essays offer commentary on the texts in the light of current theories of interpretation and historical understanding.

The overriding criteria for the selection of essays are their quality and importance. The essays overall are chosen to ensure a systematic coverage of all important scholarly debates but they also reflect the interests and perspectives of the individual editors which gives each volume a distinctive flavour. I am very grateful to all the editors for the enthusiasm and experience they have brought to the difficult task of selecting essays which bring out the central controversies over the interpretation and understanding of the work of the enduring figures and schools in the history of philosophy.

The International Library of Critical Essays in the History of Philosophy complements the highly successful International Research Library of Philosophy, edited by Professor John Skorupski, which now runs to over 20 volumes and is widely used throughout the world.

The series owes much to the vision and persistence of John Irwin and the great work done by Valerie Saunders, Sonia Hubbard and the Ashgate editorial team.

TOM CAMPBELL
Series Editor
Faculty of Law
The Australian National University

Introduction

The literature on Adam Smith is enormous. Although most of it is devoted to his allotted role as the father of modern economics, the subject of this volume – Smith's philosophy – has also attracted a great deal of scholarly and critical attention. Even a generous presentation, such as the one which follows, has to be selective. This task is made difficult not only by the sheer volume of the literature to choose from but also, and not least, by the fact that Smith's 'philosophy' is a less than straightforward concept. Like his contemporaries, Smith had a much broader idea of philosophy than that current in the twentieth century. Furthermore, the many different parts of Smith's inquiry are, arguably, systematically connected. While acknowledging a certain, inevitable arbitrariness in the borderlines chosen here, I have tried to strike a compromise between Smith's and our concept of philosophy, although in cases of doubt Smith has had the upper hand.

The development of Smith scholarship can be divided in many different ways, but it is indisputable that the latter part of the 1970s constitutes a watershed. It was during this period, and associated with the bicentenary of the publication of the *Wealth of Nations*, that most of the *Glasgow Edition of the Works and Correspondence of Adam Smith* appeared.[1] This was the first complete edition of Smith's work; it includes the first attempt at a full edition of his correspondence; and it includes a set of student's notes from Smith's *Lectures on Jurisprudence* that had never been published before and which significantly changed the understanding of Smith's work as a whole. While there is much valuable work on Smith prior to the Glasgow Edition, the general lines of Smith interpretation have been permanently transformed by its impact. This assessment has informed the selection of essays for this volume. Nearly all of them have appeared during the past 20 years, and the few that are older were written by scholars involved in the Glasgow Edition and thus peculiarly informed about the 'new' Smith. In other words, this volume is more a reflection of the current state of Smith scholarship than an 'historical' collection.

The volume mainly comprises essays from the periodical literature. I have excluded material from readily available and well known books. This means that some very important essays cannot be found here: my aim has been to supplement, not duplicate. Furthermore, during the past 20 years more than 30 books on Smith have appeared.[2] A brief introduction, such as this, one, cannot hope to present this range of literature. Instead I provide a general background to the subsequent essays by outlining a few major themes from that literature.

The Coherence of Smith's Work

Ever since German scholars in the late nineteenth century 'discovered' that the author of the *Wealth of Nations* had also written a work of moral philosophy, the so-called 'Adam Smith problem' has haunted Smith scholarship. It seemed that the *Theory of Moral Sentiments* (*TMS*) suggested that sympathy was natural to man, while the *Wealth of Nations* (*WN*) worked out a grand socioeconomic theory on the assumption that human nature was essentially self-interested. This interpretation forced scholars to propose that Smith had changed his basic moral outlook between the two books (published in 1759 and 1776, respectively). However, there were formidable obstacles to such a view of Smith. He continued to revise and reissue the two works during his lifetime without ever hinting at any discrepancy between them. With the discovery and publication (in 1896) of a set of student's notes from his lectures at the end of his Glasgow professorship, it became clear that Smith saw both the published works as parts of a larger whole. Scholars such as D.D. Raphael and A.L. Macfie suggested that the *TMS* provided a general theory of moral psychology in which self-interest was only one feature and that, in *WN*, Smith developed the social and economic implications of this part of humanity's moral motivation (Raphael and Macfie, 1976; Macfie, 1967, pp. 59–81; Raphael, 1985, pp. 89–90). This conclusion was undergirded by several others who looked at Smith's apparent systematic intentions or provided a more detailed analysis of Smith's concept of sympathy, showing exactly how it functions as a 'value-neutral' medium of social intercourse and, more particularly, that it has nothing to do with positive attitudes, such as benevolence (see, for example, Lindgren, 1973; Winch, 1978; Skinner, 1979; Haakonssen, 1981). Even so, the 'Adam Smith problem' remains a feature of the literature, mainly because interpreters identify the self-interested character who reigns in the *WN* with 'rational economic man' who, however, was the invention of later political economists, especially Ricardo and James Mill. As a consequence, the complex motivations which Smith unravels to explain even simple economic relations are not properly understood.[3] Furthermore, only on a more comprehensive view of human nature than that of neoclassical *homo economicus*, can we make sense of Smith's concern in Book V of *WN* with the need to ameliorate the effects of the ever-deepening division of labour and the associated specialization.

While I find these differences between the two works, at best, a minor puzzle that might be explained by the very different audiences Smith was addressing, it has nevertheless led to some interesting work on the more substantial question of what exactly it is that binds Smith's two works together. In one recent contribution (Brown, 1994), *TMS* and *WN* are seen as harbouring two entirely different textual ethics, and the idea of trying to re-create Smith's system is rejected as an unwarranted use of authorial intention to guide interpretation. A full discussion of this interesting suggestion would take us too far into purely hermeneutic issues, including that of the interpreter's ability to keep consistently to her principle, but I should point out that one has to draw a distinction here. It is one thing to try to guess Smith's frustrated intentions by means of students' notes from his lectures. Quite another concern is to re-create the argumentative coherence of a complex of ideas that we can discern if we put the published works and the students' reports together, allowing for the obvious uncertainties and imperfections inherent in the latter.

If the two main works can be reconciled, the question remains, how are they connected? My view is that Smith's systematic 'science of a legislator' could be reconstructed as follows. Based on the moral theory in *TMS*, Smith wanted to develop a theory of law and rights that could form the basis for a theory of government, including the theory of 'police, revenue and arms' that he presented in *WM*. The connecting link between morals and 'police' – the theory of natural jurisprudence – was discernible in outline from the lecture notes published in 1896, but it was the more recently found set (published only in 1978) that allowed a detailed reconstruction of this part of the system (Haakonssen, 1981; cf. Brühlmeier, 1988).

The Basis for Smith's Normative Ethics and Jurisprudence

A recurring theme in the literature is Smith's attempt to develop a moral, political and legal theory in which explanatory and normative functions are closely related. The former had been analysed in an important study by T.D. Campbell but to the exclusion of any serious normative concern in Smith (Campbell (1971). Campbell supplemented this thesis by suggesting that Smith might be said to subscribe to a purely 'contemplative utilitarianism' according to which what is good and right ultimately is what has the best results for all concerned, but that this is not a criterion for human behaviour, only for contemplating the meaning of it all – namely, God's meaning (see Campbell and Ross, Chapter 6 in this volume). Ultimately, an assessment of this view comes down to a question brought into question by recent critics who suggest that we have to take Smith's use of teleological language more seriously than many commentators, including myself, have been inclined to.[4]

This is a complex question and, in the end, it may be impossible to find a clear answer in the texts, but we have to keep trying. One reason why it seems impossible to consider that Smith would accept a conventional deistic and teleological view of the world is that we must then assume that he had not understood one of Hume's most central arguments, namely the following. If we want to explain the connection between *x* and *y* as one that is intended by some agent, then we need some evidence of such intentionality independent of (beyond) the fact that *x* and *y* are connected. To suggest that the elements of *x* (such as human nature) are exactly 'fitted' to produce *y* (the moral world) is, in itself, no more than a restatement of the causal connection. The point that has often been made is that Smith does very well in his causal explanations of 'fitness' without assuming anything in addition to that 'fitness': 'fitness' evidently *means*, 'leading to certain effects'. I find no evidence that Smith operates with a superhuman intentionality that has any explanatory role *independent* of the 'fitness' of causes (human nature) to bring about their effects (the moral system). This leaves two problems. First, why then does Smith often insist on redescribing his causal explanations in intentionalist terms? Second, does he not need God's intentions as the ultimate justification for the validity of morality?

First, it should be pointed out that Smith never denies the existence of God. Nor does Hume. What is more, even Hume – though to a much less degree than Smith – uses conventional language about religion which, if read in ignorance of its author, could naturally be taken to imply that there is a divinity. Hume's whole concern was with the epistemic question: can we know anything about a divine realm? He never considers the ontological question: is there a God? To understand Hume, it is therefore important to distinguish between agnosticism and atheism, as we term these concepts today. In fact, he was certainly an agnostic but never declared himself to be an atheist. In this, I think, Smith followed him. At the same time, both Hume and Smith were, of course, well aware that religion was as much part of the human imagination as science and common-sense knowledge and that this was reflected in the common linguistic tools used to account for everyday life. On such a view, the same event may be described in both causal and intentionalist terms, and the inclusion of the latter – of religious language – would be entirely a matter of consideration for your audience. If you could stimulate both the explanatory and moral imagination of your listeners and readers and, at the same time, dull the imagination of potential clerical critics who might disturb your philosophical tranquillity, why not.

Here, we should remember that the *TMS* originated as lectures and, even after five revisions, the book retained many legacies, other than religion, of its pedagogical provenance. Furthermore, Smith evidently held much more positive views than did Hume about the secular benefits of popular religion, not only in terms of the moral 'decency' of society but also in terms of the literacy that religion might promote. Finally, there is no reason to deny that this sort of agnosticism might be accompanied by a certain anxiety and uncertainty that could lead Smith to bouts of that religious wistfulness which he saw as a common feature of the human mind. Having acknowledged these points, we should not lose sight of the fact that, when Smith talks about religion, he is not concerned with the divinity but with human imagination about the divine. We should never forget the depth of his sceptical distance not only to all great claims to knowledge, but to his own ability to maintain the sceptical distance to such claims! Thus, in a famous passage, after showing how the great Newtonian system excelled over Cartesianism and all other systems, and having heaped praise upon its seeming ability to explain everything, Smith pours this bucket of cold water over us and himself:

> And even we, while we have been endeavouring to represent all philosophical systems as mere inventions of the imagination, to connect together the otherwise disjointed and discordant phaenomena of nature, have insensibly been drawn in, to make use of language expressing the connecting principles of this one <Newtonianism>, as if they were the real chains which Nature makes use of to bind together her several operations. Can we wonder then, that it should have gained the general and complete approbation of mankind .... (Smith, 1980, p. 105)

It is, inevitably, in this light that I approach the second question mentioned above, concerning God as the ultimate foundation for morality. The common suggestion seems to be that, without God's sanction, all moral imperatives would remain hypothetical – in other words, dependent on our desire for happiness – and that Smith would ultimately be a relativist inasmuch as the good and the right would vary with our conceptions of happiness. But this is a false dilemma since it does not exhaust the possibilities. I know of no clear evidence that Smith himself saw the choice as one of relativism or deism. And if the sort of agnosticism outlined above is at least a possible reading of Smith, then it may be prudent to reconsider this question.

Smith never explicitly declares any discomfort with moral or cultural relativism, but he does make a number of statements that are incompatible with a complete relativism. In a nutshell – which suffices for Smith's purpose – we have three kinds of moral phenomena that seem to rule out relativism. First, the negative virtue of justice – essentially the regulation of violence – is as close to universal as we are likely to achieve in human affairs, for, without at least a guiding ideal of minimal justice, human togetherness, beyond momentary intimacy, seems impossible. Second, the positive virtues that regulate people's love of each other – broadly conceived – while varying so widely according to time and place that they cannot be made into a universal system, nevertheless have a more or less universal family resemblance that allows empirical comparisons and enables us to establish transcultural understanding. Third, there is what we may call the procedural 'virtue' of impartiality. Wherever two or more persons are together, there will be 'spectating', mutual observation. This reveals the gulf between subjective standpoints and accentuates the need for a common standpoint in cases of conflict. In the search for such commonality of standpoint, the human mind has a universal tendency to make impartiality an ideal. Impartiality has a special status inasmuch as it is involved in explaining the other virtues and their rules. I have tried to provoke attention to this feature by saying that there is an elementary similarity with Kant here: given morality as we know it in any human circumstance, what must be assumed as its precondition, apart from the faculties of the human mind? And the answer is that impartiality as an argumentative procedure is at least a necessary precondition (Haakonssen, 1996, ch. 4).[5] Put differently, the first two points indicate that, as a matter of fact, human morality as hitherto known has not been entirely relative to time and place; it has had certain stable features. And the third point, concerning impartiality, indicates that this is for a good reason – namely, that anything that we recognize as morality has an underlying pattern of reasoning which it seems impossible for anyone to reject while also wanting to engage in moral debate – whether literally or metaphorically.

I can find no evidence to suggest that Smith commits himself to a more extensive anti-relativism than this. And this conclusion is very much in tune with the fact that all his moral, legal and political criticism is, as it were, internal to an historically given situation (country, period, institution, and so on); he never conjures up eternally right answers; he has virtually nothing to say about what to expect of the future; and his few prescriptions are all 'internalist', piecemeal and hedged with qualifying doubt on all sides. Altogether, it is very difficult to see Smith as a subscriber to the Divine Corporation view of the moral life of the species.[6] For Smith, life is a matter of contingency and uncertainty – which we often cope with tolerably well, as experience shows and philosophy accounts for.

Historical Materialism and *Laissez-faire* Liberalism

While deism and teleology would present a hindrance for those, such as myself, who see a *pure* spectator theory of morality in Smith, the idea that Smith was an historical materialist was in conflict with the activist role of law and government that some interpreters have ascribed to him in recent years. By the 1970s the interpretation of Smith's theory of social development and historical change in terms of changes in productive conditions had been developed with great sophistication in an extensive literature. This was, at least in inspiration, an antidote to the still widespread view of Smith as the father of *laissez-faire* liberalism. Both lines of argument received a fatal blow with the publication of Donald Winch's *Adam Smith's Politics* – a book which, more than any other, changed the common perceptions of Smith. Winch showed how Smith in fact had a 'politics' – that is, a theory of the nature and conduct of government in all the stages of human society, including that of commerce. I developed a further dimension – already present, of course, in Winch's account – namely, the role of law and legal institutions in all organized social life. In order to drive this point home, both Winch and I criticized the materialist interpretation. This argument has in turn recently been criticized (see John Salter, Chapter 20 in this volume). It is suggested that, while deterministic historical materialism cannot be attributed to Smith, this does not mean that there is no form of historical materialism in his work. To the first part of the charge, I readily plead guilty; I concentrated exclusively on materialism as a form of historical determinism, because this was the interpretation of Smith that was being offered. But I never meant to deny that material causes are *necessary* factors in explaining major socio-political change.

Natural Law and Republicanism

On Smith's view, both the deities and history have left scope for humanity to formulate moral, legal and political norms. Furthermore, such moral activities, while profoundly changeable, have formal elements of universality (the impartial spectator) that enable us, at least in principle, to transcend our particular circumstance through critical assessment; and one of the most important results of such moral judgements is our notion of simple natural rights which define us as moral persons. This was, in simple terms, the basis for what Smith saw as his theory of natural justice or his natural jurisprudence.

Duncan Forbes in his book, *Hume's Philosophical Politics* (1975), had indicated the importance of natural law for an understanding of these two thinkers, and I reached the same conclusion from a purely internal analysis of the Humean and Smithian texts. These tentative suggestions were made at a time when scholarship on modern natural law, had been moribund for a generation or more – at least in the English-speaking world. At the same time, interest in the history of early modern political thought was being renewed by attention to neorepublicanism and associated civic humanism. In particular, John Pocock's magisterial study of the peculiar longevity – the Machiavellian moment – of this line of thought in the Anglo-American, or Atlantic, realm inspired a great deal of new and original work (Pocock, 1975). 'Natural jurisprudence' and 'Republican civic humanism' were immediately seen as rival 'paradigms' for the interpretation of political thought, not least in Scotland, and this discussion is still an important feature of the scholarly debate.

The neat dichotomy between natural jurisprudence and humanist republicanism is difficult to accept. Whatever one's view of natural law and republicanism within the classical and pre-modern tradition, it seems obvious to me – as it did to Pocock himself and to others – that the two coexisted throughout the Enlightenment in Scotland (Pocock, 1983, pp. 250–51; cf. Lecaldano, 1992, pp. 13–40). The question was, and remains, how did the two traditions interact? In order to get anywhere with this question, one has to look more carefully at the natural law tradition in order to differentiate its various strands and their influence in Scotland (see Haakonssen, forthcoming; 1990; 1996).

After Smith

Although Smith was a great moral philosopher and social theorist, he is today principally seen as the father of modern economics and the patron of free market economics. This distortion of Smith was largely accomplished a generation after his death. Smith was partly a victim of the success of *The Wealth of Nations* (1776) which completely overshadowed his *Theory of Moral Sentiments* (1759), and which Henry Buckle in 1861 saw as 'probably the most important book which has ever been written' (Buckle, 1894, vol. 1, p. 214). But he was also needed as a victim for Romantic and other forms of idealism in their search for identity through contrast with the preceding age. Indeed, the notion of the 'dismal science' of economics as a product of the eighteenth century, and especially of Smith, is the epitome of a distortion of history that began early in the nineteenth century and which is known today as the 'Enlightenment project'. The recovery of a more authentic Smith has been a major feature of scholarship during the last 20 years, and one of the most fruitful approaches has been to dissemble the constructions that were put upon the Scot during the first 50 years after the *Wealth of Nations* (see Collini *et al.* 1983; esp. Winch, 1996).

Notes

1. *Glasgow Edition of the Works and Correspondence of Adam Smith*, (1976–83). Each of the six volumes has separate editors.
2. See the Appendix to this Introduction which includes only works in English. There is a significant recent literature on Smith in German, Italian, and Japanese, as well as much in other languages.
3. This is clearly explained in Winch (1996, pp. 104–9).
4. In addition to Campbell (1971) and Campbell and Ross (Chapter 6, this volume), see especially Kleer (Chapter 8, this volume). For a vigorous but overstated rejection of any religious interpretation of Smith, see Minowitz (1993).
5. For more detailed discussions of the relationship between Smith and Kant, see Fleischacker (Chapter 1, this volume) and Fleischacker (1996).
6. Cf. J.B. Schneewind's outline of his view which he does not ascribe to Smith (Schneewind, 1984).

References

Brown, V. (1994), *Adam Smith's Discourse: Canonicity, Commerce and Conscience*, London/New York: Routledge.

Brühlmeier, D. (1988), *Die Rechs- und Staatslehre von Adam Smith und die Interessentheorie der Verfassung*, Berlin: Duncker & Humblot.

Buckle, H. (1894), *The History of Civilization in England*, (new edn), 3 vols, Edinburgh.

Campbell, T.D. (1971), *Adam Smith's Science of Morals*, London: George Allen & Unwin.

Collini, S., Winch, D. and Burrow, J. (1983), *That Noble Science of Politics: A Study in Nineteenth-Century Intellectual History*, Cambridge: Cambridge University Press.

Fleischacker, S. (1996), 'Values behind the market: Kant's response to the *Wealth of Nations, History of Political Thought*, **17**, pp. 379–407.

Forbes, D. (1975), *Hume's Philosophical Politics*, Cambridge: Cambridge University Press.

Haakonssen, K. (1981), *The Science of a Legislator: The Natural Jurisprudence of David Hume and Adam Smith*, Cambridge: Cambridge University Press.

Haakonssen, K. (1990), 'Introduction', Thomas Reid, *Practical Ethics: Being Lectures and Papers on Natural Religion, Self-Government, Natural Jurisprudence, and the Law of Nations*, ed. K. Haakonssen, Princeton, NJ: Princeton University Press, pp. 1–99.

Haakonssen, K. (1996), *Natural Law and Moral Philosophy: From Grotius to the Scottish Enlightenment*, Cambridge: Cambridge University Press.

Haakonssen, K. (ed.) (forthcoming), *Grotius, Pufendorf and the Modern Natural Law Tradition*, International Library of Critical Essays in the History of Philosophy, Aldershot: Dartmouth.

Lecaldano, E. (1992), 'Paradigmi di analisi della filosofia morale nell'Illuminismo scozzese', in M. Geuna and M.L. Pesante (eds), *Passioni, interessi, convenzioni: discussioni settecentesche su virtù e civiltà*, Milan: Franco Angeli, pp. 13–40.
Lindgren, J.R. (1973), *The Social Philosophy of Adam Smith*, The Hague: Martinus Nijhoff.
Macfie, A.L. (1967), *The Individual in Society*, London: George Allen and Unwin.
Minowitz, P. (1993), *Profits, Priests, and Princes: Adam Smith's Emancipation from Politics and Religion*, Stanford CA: Stanford University Press.
Pocock, J.G.A. (1975), *The Machiavellian Moment: Florentine Political Thought and the Atlantic Republican Tradition*, Princeton, NJ: Princeton University Press.
Pocock, J.G.A. (1983), 'Cambridge paradigms and Scotch philosophers: a study of the relations between the civic humanist and the civil jurisprudential interpretation of eighteenth-century social thought', in I. Hont and M. Ignatieff (eds), *Wealth and Virtue: The Shaping of Political Economy in the Scottish Enlightenment*, Cambridge: Cambridge University Press, pp. 235–52.
Raphael, D.D. (1985), *Adam Smith*, Oxford: Oxford University Press.
Raphael, D.D. and Macfie, A.L. (eds) (1976), 'Introduction', *Adam Smith The Theory of Moral Sentiments*, Oxford: Clarendon Press, pp. 59–81.
Schneewind, J.B. (1984), 'The divine corporation and the history of ethics', in R. Rorty, Q. Skinner and J.B. Schneewind (eds), *Philosophy in History*, Cambridge: Cambridge University Press, pp. 173–91.
Skinner, A.S. (1979), *A System of Social Science: Papers Relating to Adam Smith*, Oxford: Clarendon Press.
Smith, A. (1976–83), *Glasgow Edition of the Works and Correspondence of Adam Smith*, 6 vols, Oxford, Clarendon Press.
Smith, A. (1980), 'The Principles which lead and direct Philosophical Inquiries; Illustrated by the History of Astronomy', in W.P.D. Wightman and J.C. Bryce (eds), *Essays on Philosophical Subjects*, Oxford: Clarendon Press, pp. 31–105.
Winch, D. (1978), *Adam Smith's Politics*, Cambridge: Cambridge University Press.
Winch, D. (1996), *Riches and Poverty: An Intellectual History of Political Economy in Britain, 1750–1834*, Cambridge: Cambridge University Press.

Appendix: Recent English-language Publications

Brown, V. (1994), *Adam Smith's Discourse: Canonicity, Commerce and Conscience*, London: Routledge.
Camic, C. (1983), *Experience and Enlightenment: Socialization for Cultural Change in Eighteenth-Century Scotland*, Edinburgh: Edinburgh University Press.
Campbell, R.H. and A.S. Skinner (1982), *Adam Smith*, London: Croom Helm.
Campbell, T.D. (1971), *Adam Smith's Science of Morals*, London: Allen and Unwin.
Copley, S. and K. Sutherland (eds) (1995), *Adam Smith, The Wealth of Nations: New Interdisciplinary Essays*, Manchester: Manchester University Press.
Evensky, J. and R.P. Malloy (eds) (1994), *Adam Smith and the Philosophy of Law and Economics*, Dordrecht: Kluwer Academic Publishers.
Fitzgibbons, A. (1995), *Adam Smith's System of Liberty, Wealth and Virtue: The Moral and Political Foundations of the Wealth of Nations*, Oxford: Clarendon Press.
Foley, V. (1976), *The Social Physics of Adam Smith*, West Lafayette, IN: Purdue University Press.
Fry, M. (ed.) (1992), *Adam Smith's Legacy*, New York: Routledge, Chapman and Hall.
Glahe, F.R. (ed.) (1978), *Adam Smith and the Wealth of Nations*, Boulder, Col: Colorado Associated University Press.
Haakonssen, K. (1981), *The Science of a Legislator: The Natural Jurisprudence of David Hume and Adam Smith*, Cambridge: Cambridge University Press.
Haakonssen, K. (1996), *Natural Law and Moral Philosophy: From Grotius to the Scottish Enlightenment*, Cambridge: Cambridge University Press.
Hollander, Samuel (1973), *The Economics of Adam Smith*, Toronto: Toronto University Press.

Hont, I. and Ignatieff, M. (eds), (1983), *Wealth and Virtue: The Shaping of Political Economy in the Scottish Enlightenment*, Cambridge: Cambridge University Press.
Hope, V. (1989), *Virtue by Consensus: The Moral Philosophy of Hutcheson, Hume and Adam Smith*, Oxford: Oxford University Press.
Jones, P. and Skinner, A.S. (eds) (1992), *Adam Smith Reviewed*, Edinburgh: Edinburgh University Press.
Justman, S. (1993), *The Autonomous Male of Adam Smith*, Norman: University of Oklahoma Press.
Lindgren, J. Ralph (1973), *The Social Philosophy of Adam Smith*, The Hague: Martinus Nijhoff.
Miller, R.D. (1990), *An Interpretation of Adam Smith's 'Theory of Moral Sentiments'*, Harrogate: Duchy Press.
Minowitz, Peter (1993), *Profits, Priests and Princes: Adam Smith's Emancipation of Economics from Politics and Religion*, Stanford, CA: Stanford University Press.
Mizuta, H. and Chuhei, S. (eds) (1993), *Adam Smith: International Perspectives*, New York: St Martin's Press.
Muller, J.Z. (1993), *Adam Smith in His Time and Ours. Designing the Decent Society*, New York: The Free Press.
O'Driscoll, G.P. (ed.) (1979), *Adam Smith and Modern Political Economy: Bicentennial Essays on 'The Wealth of Nations'*, Ames: Iowa State University Press.
Pack, S.J. (1991), *Capitalism as a Moral System: Adam Smith's Critique of the Free Market Economy*, Aldershot: Edward Elgar.
Raphael, D.D. (1985), *Adam Smith*, Past Masters series, Oxford: Oxford University Press.
Reisman, D.A. (1976), *Adam Smith's Sociological Economics*, London: Croom Helm; New York: Barnes and Noble.
Ross, I.S. (1995), *The Life of Adam Smith*, Oxford: Clarendon Press.
Shapiro, M.J. (1993), *Reading 'Adam Smith': Desire, History and Value*, London: Sage Publications.
Skinner, A.S. (1979/1996), *A System of Social Science: Papers Relating to Adam Smith*, Oxford: Clarendon Press.
Skinner, A.S. and Wilson, T. (eds) (1975), *Essays on Adam Smith*, Oxford: Clarendon Press.
Teichgraeber, R.F. (1986), *'Free Trade' and Moral Philosophy. Rethinking the Sources of Adam Smith's Wealth of Nations*, Durham, NC: Duke University Press.
Werhane, P.H. (1991), *Adam Smith and His Legacy for Modern Capitalism*, New York: Oxford University Press.
West, E.G. (1976), *Adam Smith: The Man and His Work*, Indianapolis: Liberty Press.
West, E.G. (1990), *Adam Smith and Modern Economics*, Aldershot: Edward Elgar.
Wilson, T. and Skinner, A.S. (eds), (1976), *The Market and the State: Essays in Honour of Adam Smith*, Oxford: Clarendon Press.
Winch, D. (1978), *Adam Smith's Politics: An Essay in Historiographic Revision*, Cambridge: Cambridge University Press.
Winch, D. (1996), *Riches and Poverty: An Intellectual History of Political Economy in Britain, 1750–1834*, Cambridge: Cambridge University Press.
Wood, J.C. (ed.) (1983–84), *Adam Smith: Critical Assessments*, 4 vols, London: Croom Helm.

Part I
Ethics

[1]

Philosophy in Moral Practice: Kant and Adam Smith

by Samuel Fleischacker, Williamstown/Massachusetts

Let me state at the outset that my concern in this essay is not merely to bring out an historical connection between two eighteenth century figures: if I can show that Adam Smith was an important influence on Kant, I will be in a position to re-interpret the purpose of Kant's moral philosophy. But the historical connection is interesting in its own right, and curiously overlooked by most scholars. I shall take this scholarly oversight as an excuse, in section I, to survey the hard evidence for Smith's influence on Kant. In section II, proceeding on the assumption that mis-interpretation of Smith has helped draw attention away from his importance for Kant, I shall present my understanding of the central point, and main contribution, of the *Theory of Moral Sentiments* (= *TMS*). I will attempt to show in section III what we can gain by reading Kant's *Groundwork* in the light of *TMS*. And in section IV I will discuss where Kant differs from Smith, and why.

I

That Kant read the *Wealth of Nations* is clear from a reference to the work in the *Doctrine of Justice*.[1] Smith's economic masterpiece was translated into German in the year it was published (1776), and it particularly impressed a community of academics and political advisors in Königsberg, many of whom were friends and/ or students of Kant.[2] More difficult to establish, but more important for our purposes, is whether Kant read the *Theory of Moral Sentiments*.

In 1877, August Oncken published a book entitled *Adam Smith und Immanuel Kant*,[3] in which he suggested that Smith's moral theory may have influenced Kant, and that in any case there were remarkable verbal and philosophical parallels between the two systems. As far as he was aware, however, there was no clear evidence that Kant had actually read *TMS*. Since he refers to the *Wealth of Nations*, it may be reasonable to assume he had also read the moral theory, but Oncken did

[1] Academy edition (= Ak), VI, 289.

[2] For instance, C. J. Kraus, Theodor von Schön, Friedrich Leopold von Schrötter, and Johann Gottfried Frey. For a full discussion of the *Wealth of Nations*' impact on Königsberg, see Carl William Hasek, *The Introduction of Adam Smith's Doctrines into Germany*, Columbia Studies in History, Economics, and Public Law # 261 (New York: Longmans, Green, 1920), pp. 84 – 86, 119 – 124.

[3] August Oncken, *Adam Smith und Immanuel Kant* (Leipzig: Duncker & Humblot, 1877).

not want to go beyond calling the connection he drew a "Vermuthung," albeit one that "nähert sich der Gewißheit."[4]

Fifty years later, Walther Eckstein provided a little more textual evidence for this *Vermuthung* in the introduction to his translation of *TMS*.[5] Eckstein considered Oncken's parallels rather forced, and pointed instead to a reference to "the impartial spectator" in the *Reflexionen* and a 1771 letter to Kant from Markus Herz that mentions Smith.[6] In the letter, Herz says he has heard from David Friedländer that "der Engländer Smith" is Kant's "Liebling" (presumably among recent writers on the passions). Since the *Wealth of Nations* was not to be published for another five years after 1771, the letter presumably refers to *TMS*, which had just been translated into German in 1770.[7]

This comprises the sum total of what such prominent current writers on Smith as A. L. MacFie and D. D. Raphael take to be the "hard textual evidence" for Kant's awareness of and interest in *TMS*.[8] In the face of the fact that Kant wrote no known response to the Herz letter, and in the main body of his work nowhere specifically addresses Smith – the way he addresses, for instance, Hutcheson and Hume – this is of course not *very* hard evidence (perhaps Friedländer was wrong? or Herz misunderstood him?), and MacFie and Raphael leave the possibility as a tantalizing suggestion, but one that, as Eckstein admitted, ultimately cannot be proven.[9]

After all this cautious speculation, it may come as some surprise to find Susan Meld Shell casually and confidently remarking that "the categorical imperative seems to have occurred to Kant as, among other things, a solution to the problems posed by Smith's [impartial spectator]."[10] She accompanies this claim with a wealth of citations, some of which go well beyond Eckstein's. On the other hand, not every

[4] *Ibid.*, p. 97.

[5] Walther Eckstein (ed. & trans.), editor's introduction, *Theorie der Ethischen Gefühle* (Leipzig: Felix Meiner, 1926).

[6] *Ibid.*, p. XXXIII.

[7] By Christoph Rautenberg, as *Theorie der Moralischen Empfindungen* (Braunschweig, 1770): see Eckstein, p. XXXII, for a full discussion of the translations into German. Scholars may want to note that the Rautenberg translation was based on the third edition of *TMS* – we cannot assume that Kant was aware of any of the material added in the considerably altered sixth edition. In this essay I occasionally quote from the sixth edition, but only when the passage in question seems to me a more eloquent version of an idea that had already appeared in the third edition. (All references to *TMS* will be from the MacFie and Raphael volume cited in note 8. Passages omitted from the sixth edition will be marked by page number as well as section number.)

[8] See MacFie, *The Individual in Society: Papers on Adam Smith* (London: George Allen & Unwin, 1967), note 23 on p. 91, and MacFie and Raphael (eds.), editors' introduction, *The Theory of Moral Sentiments* (Indianapolis: Liberty Classics, 1982, re-printed in paper from the Oxford edition of 1976), pp. 30–31.

[9] Eckstein, p. XXXIV, note 1.

[10] Susan Meld Shell, *The Rights of Reason* (Toronto: University of Toronto Press, 1980), note 6 on p. 102. See also p. 80.

reference she gives is equally useful. Since she passes over the whole matter in three brief comments and an extended footnote, moreover, and since she is the only Kant scholar, as far as I am aware, to mention this material at all,[11] I think it will be worthwhile to lay out carefully just which documents explicitly show *TMS'* influence on Kant. I offer the following annotated list for that purpose:

(1) In *Reflexion* 1355, Kant regrets that no German writers have dealt with the "moralische Kenntnis des Menschen" with the insight of Smith.[12] Adickes places this note in one of three possible groups of writings, two of which date before 1776,[13] but there is reason to refer it to *TMS* quite independently of its date: no-one would describe the *Wealth of Nations* as an examination of human *moral* thought.

(2) In *R* 6864 Kant writes, "In Smiths system: warum nimmt der Unparteiische richter (der nicht einer von den participanten ist) sich dessen, was allgemein gut ist, an? und warum hat er daran irgend ein wohlgefallen?" Berger dates this comment between 1776 and 1778, but the reference to *TMS* is unmistakeable: the "impartial spectator" is not a part of Smith's system in the *Wealth of Nations*. Indeed, the phrase does not appear. As for Kant's use of "impartial *judge*" rather than "spectator," this reflects more a considerable familiarity with *TMS* than otherwise, for Smith, unlike many of his commentators, frequently replaces "impartial spectator" with alternative expressions, such as "indifferent spectator" or "impartial bystander,"[14] and on one or two occasions speaks of an "impartial judge."[15]

(3) Eckstein correctly describes *R* 767 as employing the phrase "unpartheiische Zuschauer" in what clearly seems to be a technical capacity. It occurs in the midst of a discussion of taste, which Kant already views as a communicated and communal form of pleasure ("Der Geschmack macht, daß der Genuß sich communicirt; er ist also ein Mittel und eine Wirkung von Vereinigung der Menschen"), and he uses it to clarify what he calls observing "from a

[11] Among those who conspicuously say nothing about a connection between Kant and Smith are H. J. Paton, in *The Categorical Imperative*, Ernst Cassirer, in *Kant's Life and Thought*, L. W. Beck, in *A Commentary on Kant's Critique of Practical Reason* and *Essays on Kant and Hume*, J. A. Bernstein, in *Shaftesbury, Rousseau, and Kant*, John Rawls, in his Lectures on Kant at Harvard University, and, most surprisingly, Paul Schilpp, whose *Kant's Precritical Ethics* (Evanston: Northwestern University Press, 1938) is considered by many the definitive work on Kant's relationship to his British predecessors. Beck does mention the Herz letter in *Studies in the Philosophy of Kant* ((Indianapolis: Bobbs-Merrill, 1965), note 5 on p. 7), but only in passing, and he says nothing about the other material. As far as recent scholarship is concerned, Manfred Kühn says nothing about the connection in *Scottish Common Sense in Germany, 1768 – 1800* (Montreal: McGill-Queen's University Press, 1987), while Howard Caygill begins the long overdue discussion of Smith's influence on Kant's aesthetics (see below, p. 267, n. 61), but only in a fleeting and very general paragraph: see *Art of Judgment* (Oxford: Basil Blackwell, 1989), p. 85.

[12] Ak XV, 592.

[13] Adickes' dating system can be found in his introduction to Ak XIV, pp. xxxvi – xliii.

[14] See T. D. Campbell, *Adam Smith's Science of Morals* (London: George Allen & Unwin, 1971), p. 134 – 135, for an extensive list of these alternatives.

[15] *TMS* II.ii.2.4, and, in editions 3 – 5, III.2.37 (p. 130, bottom, in MacFie and Raphael); see also III.1.2 and III.1.6. Rautenberg tracks this shift in translating the first of these passages (202: "dieses angenomenen unpartheiischen Richters"), as does Kosegarten in his 1791 translation (*Theorie der sittlichen Gefühle* (Leipzig, 1791), p. 151), although Eckstein (127) does not. In translating the second passage, Rautenberg substitutes "seinem Charakter" for "the character of this impartial judge" (284), but he uses "unpartheiische Richter" on another occasion, where Smith himself only has "equitable judge" (271, translating III.1.2).

communal point-of-view." The connection of Smith to Kant's *aesthetic* theory,[16] a subject we shall touch on briefly in section III, here becomes obvious.

(4) *R* 6628 also uses the "unpartheiische Zuschauer" in a technical way, this time in the context of moral theory. After asking, "Welches ist die Regel der Anwendung ... auf ein object der diiudication," Kant notes in a parenthesis, "sympathie andrer und ein unpartheiische Zuschauer." Berger takes this to be a clear reference to Hume and Smith, and indeed the contrast between sympathy and impartial spectator nicely encapsulates the contrast between what Hume and Smith respectively consider central to ethical judgment. (When Berger guesses, by-the-way, that this note belongs either between 1764 and 1768 or between 1769 and fall, 1770, the first dating at least is surely too early. Although *TMS* was originally published in 1759, it was translated into German only in 1770.[17] On the generally held assumption that Kant did not read English, it is unlikely he would mention Smith before 1770 at the earliest. In fact, I take Herz's remark about Smith being Kant's "Liebling" as a sign that in 1771 Kant was going through the enthusiasm of his first acquaintance with *TMS*.)

So much for the clear documentary evidence. With it safely in hand, we can return to some of the weaker claims, including Oncken's supposedly forced parallels. In particular, there are one or two striking references to the impartial spectator in the body of Kant's main work. On the very first page of the first chapter of the *Groundwork*, Kant says that a "reasonable and impartial spectator" (*vernünftige und unparteiische Zuschauer*) could not approve of the prosperity of a being that lacked a good will, while in the Dialectic of the *Critique of Practical Reason* he writes that "impartial reason" must judge that the highest good for virtuous human beings will involve happiness. Now the addition of reason to impartiality in the line from the *Groundwork* is an unsurprising Kantian emendation, and it will indeed be Kant's main criticism of Smith (implicit already in *R* 6864) that the device of the impartial spectator makes no moral sense unless it is grounded in reason rather than the mechanism of approbation that Smith himself provides. But note, on the other hand, that Kant does not just say "rational spectator," even though one might have supposed reason, for Kant, to imply impartiality. Since the phrase "impartial spectator" is unique to *TMS*,[18] I think we can fairly take this as a deliberate nod to Smith – though for what purpose is not entirely clear.

[16] MacFie and Raphael note that Lessing, Herder, and Markus Herz were all interested in *TMS* for the purposes of aesthetics, but they consider it unlikely "that Kant's own regard for the work will have been thus confined" (p. 30). "Confined" or not, Kant's interest in Smith as a theorist of judgment is evident, and would reward thorough research.

[17] See above, note 7.

[18] I take this opportunity to point out that the phrase "impartial spectator" clearly seems to have been coined by Smith. MacFie and Raphael suggest that the phrase may have been borrowed from Addison's dedication to the first volume of *The Spectator* (editor's introduction, p. 15), but even if so, the extremely casual use of it there has only the most accidental connection to Smith's development of it as a tool for moral philosophy. As for the presumed philosophical antecedents of Smith's spectator theory, none of the passages I have seen cited as foreshadowing Smith (for instance, the passages from Hume and Hutcheson mentioned by Campbell on p. 127) modify "spectator" with the adjective "impartial" (or "indifferent," or any of the other terms Smith uses). Clarke comes strikingly close to Smith at one point (L. A. Selby-Bigge, *British Moralists* (Oxford: Clarendon Press,

The passage in the second *Critique* raises altogether greater difficulties. In the first place, for all his many ways of describing the impartial spectator, Smith never speaks of "impartial reason."[19] He does use "reason" as a term for judgment, and draws important and deep connections among judgment, impartiality, and spectatorship, but the second *Critique* passage might still be a remote and unlikely echo were it not for two things: 1. the apparent superfluity, again, of "impartial" as a modifier for "reason," and 2. the fact that "impartial reason" clearly serves as a spectator/judge here. My guess is that in both passages Kant uses the word "impartial" and the position of observer to gesture towards the feelings and capacity for imagination (in all senses)[20] in Smith's figure. A being that has both reason and imagination will still have to recognize a good will as the only absolute good, but it can also acknowledge that the highest good for creatures with feelings will necessarily include happiness. I do not want to make too much of these brief passages – only to indicate by means of them that Smith's work seems to have interested Kant for many years after he read it in 1770 or 1771.

Finally, consider some of the remarkable verbal parallels Oncken points out between the accounts Smith and Kant give of conscience and moral laws. In the first place, both frequently compare conscience to a judge or court of law. Kant calls it the "innerer Gerichtshof," Smith the "inferiour tribunal."[21] In the second place, Smith moves from conscience to the role of general rules in morality, and winds up the latter discussion by arguing that moral laws "are justly regarded as the laws of the Deity."[22] Kant, in the *Doctrine of Virtue*, closes a discussion of conscience or moral self-knowledge, as the faculty for scrutinizing one's own ability to follow moral law, with a reference, in quotation marks, to the duty "of recognizing all our duties *as if* (*instar*) they were divine commands."[23] Considering the striking

1897), vol II, § 496), but without using the term "spectator," and in the course of an argument about moral epistemology (he is defending rational intuitionism) rather than moral practice. How well Smith knew Clarke is also debatable: the discussions of him in *TMS* and the *Essays on Philosophical Subjects* are brief and extremely perfunctory, and the only work he owned by Clarke was an edition of Homer (Hiroshi Mizuta, *Adam Smith's Library* (Cambridge: Cambridge University Press, 1967), pp. 82, 103 – 104).

[19] Clarke does (Selby-Bigge, vol II, § 501), but there is no reason to think Kant was familiar with Clarke's ethical writings. The *Personenindex* to Kant's works (K. Holger *et al.* (Berlin: de Gruyter, 1969)) gives three references to Clarke, all of which concern the Leibniz – Clarke correspondence about Newtonian space. Schilpp writes that Kant must have known Clarke's moral writings (p. 23), but the source he gives again concerns the Leibniz – Clarke correspondence rather than the *Discourse of Natural Religion*.

[20] MacFie (*Individual in Society*, pp. 49 – 50, 88) rightly notes the emphasis Smith places on imagination in the process of moral judgment. To approximate the feelings of the participants, the spectator must imagine their situations as fully and realistically as possible.

[21] Oncken, p. 92. Quotations can be found in Kant, *The Doctrine of Virtue*, trans. Mary J. Gregor (Philadelphia: Univ. of Pennsylvania Press, 1964), p. 103 (Ak VI, 437), and *TMS*, third edition, III.2.32 (MacFie and Raphael, p. 128, bottom).

[22] Oncken, p. 95 (referring to *TMS* III.5, chapter title).

[23] *Doctrine of Virtue*, p. 110 (Ak VI, 442).

similarity in structure and language, Oncken claims we have good reason to regard the unattributed quotation as from Smith.[24] I would add that viewing moral laws *as if* they issued from God – rather than, with rationalists and natural law theorists, as *in fact* issuing from God, or, with most empiricists, as having little or nothing to do with God[25] – was highly unusual in the eighteenth century, and that it is precisely in the matter of rules, conscience and judgment that Smith most deeply looks forward to Kant. But the parenthetical word "instar" in the Kant passage, which Oncken conveniently omits, throws doubt on the purely verbal echo. The Latin word indicates that Kant may be thinking back to the Roman Stoics, many of whom could well have argued that moral rules, while actually products of our reason, should be regarded as though they issued from the Deity. Stoic notions may well lie behind the Smith passage itself, which serves as the title to an especially Stoic chapter in *TMS*.

Whatever the merits of these last points, there is enough clear documentary evidence of a connection between Smith and Kant to justify a philosophical comparison of their work. I turn to that in the remainder of this paper, but before doing so, let me say a few words about why there may have been so little mention of a tie between these two crucially important eighteenth century figures. On the side of Smith scholarship, the answer to that question seems to be fairly simple. When Eckstein published his translation in 1926 (and, *a fortiori*, when Oncken wrote in 1877), the nineteenth volume of the Akademie Kant edition had not yet come out, so *R* 6628 and 6864 had never been published. (That he missed *R* 1355 is less excusable, but without Martin's comprehensive Kant index of the 1960s and 70s, such obscure Kant references must have been very hard to find.) And MacFie and Raphael, although they wrote on the Kant–Smith connection as recently as 1976, seem to have relied almost entirely on Eckstein for their information.

As for the Kant scholars, with the lone exception of Shell, I imagine their ignorance of Smith simply reflects the more general lack of interest in Smith's moral philosophy in the academic community. Gilbert Harman, a recent reader of *TMS* who, like the present author, found it unexpectedly exciting – "I believe that the ... *Theory of Moral Sentiments* is one of the great works of moral philosophy"[26] – ends his article on the book by speculating as to why Smith's moral theory has been so neglected in comparison with Hume's: "Is it that Hume also had a metaphysics and an epistemology and that Smith did not? Or is it that Smith was a more important economist than Hume? And why should that matter? I do not know."[27] The easiest answer is probably that Smith's economic theory has eclipsed his own ethics, and

[24] Oncken, p. 97.

[25] Shaftesbury argued that belief in God could be an aid to moral action, but he certainly did not tie this belief especially to moral *rules*.

[26] Gilbert Harman, *Moral Agent and Impartial Spectator* (Department of Philosophy, University of Kansas: The Lindley Lecture, 1986), p. 13.

[27] *Ibid.*, p. 14.

indeed has removed him out of the proper "domain" of philosophers altogether. The loss, for both philosophers and economists, testifies to the folly of academic compartmentalization.

II

Smith was a student of Hutcheson and close friend of Hume. Like them, he believed that our fundamental perceptions of right and wrong must be a matter of feeling rather than reason – "the first perceptions of right and wrong ... cannot be the object of reason, but of immediate sense and feeling" (*TMS* VII.iii.2.7) – but unlike them, he does not take this as a significant issue. On the contrary, he says that moral epistemology "is of no [importance] in practice ... To examine from what contrivance within, [the] ... notions [of right and wrong] arise is a mere matter of philosophical curiosity" (*TMS* VII.iii.intro.3). And moral philosophers, he believes, should contribute to moral practice: "To direct the judgments of [the man within the breast] is the great purpose of all systems of morality" (*TMS* VII.ii.1.47).[28] His own intended contribution is a theory of how to make specific moral decisions. The theory relies on the famous device of the impartial spectator and an account of moral rules, which together make up the richest and most outstandingly original part of his work.

We will better appreciate the uniqueness of Smith's impartial spectator if we first consider the role of the spectator in Smith's predecessors and peers. Hutcheson draws a firm distinction between spectator and agent, but he does so only to buttress his case for the existence in human nature of a moral sense. Trying to persuade his readers, against Hobbes, that not all of our feelings are egoistic, Hutcheson appeals to the feelings we have about events to which we must be spectators rather than participants (in the past, at a great distance from us, or in fictional narratives).[29] It is in the heat of action, he maintains, that our natural benevolence gets clouded by other passions, or misled by bad judgment and foolish systems.[30] To recognize our capacity to feel pure benevolence for mankind, we need to withdraw from action to the cooler position of the spectator.

Hume, like Smith a student of Hutcheson, allows his teacher to pursue the case against Hobbes while marking out as his own territory an argument more directed at Clarke: that sense, rather than reason, must be the basis of moral knowledge, and that a construction of sense (utility), rather than an ideal of reason (fitness), must be the object of moral knowledge. A distinction between spectator and agent, and a fleeting reference to a "judicious spectator" (in the mouth of a presumed

[28] This particular line appears only in edition six, but one can find the same idea at VII.iv.33 (MacFie and Raphael, p. 340). (See note 7.)

[29] See, for instance, Hutcheson, *Inquiry into the Original of our Ideas of Virtue* (Charlottesville: Ibis, 1986), pp. 75 – 76, 78, 80 – 81, 156 ff.

[30] *Ibid.*, pp. 130 – 132, 134 – 137, 152, 156.

opponent to Hume's position), appear in *Treatise* III.iii.1, as part of a defense of moral sentiment theory against the critic who suggests that the difference between the feelings we have towards people close to us (physically or emotionally) and people far from us shows that sentiment does not adequately map the realm we normally think of as "moral approval." Hume argues that, much as we correct our sense-impressions of physical objects for distortion by fixing some "stable ... steady and general" position reflecting an average of our various actual impressions, so we may correct our moral impressions by seeking some more or less stable average of our actual moral impressions. The spectator thus serves an argument about the nature of moral knowledge – not, as for Hutcheson, about human nature, nor, as for Smith, about moral practice.

Smith, as we have seen, for the most part eschews moral epistemology, and seems to feel, like Hume, that his teacher Hutcheson did an adequate job of refuting Hobbes' egoistic account of human nature. Nor is he particularly interested in what we might call moral metaphysics: the nature of the Good, the goal of the good life, etc. Not that he has nothing to say on these subjects. After remarking on the unimportance of the subject, he sides with Hume and the moral sense theorists against Clarke and Cudworth (although he also allows much more room for "reason" in ethics than Hume had done); he tells us, albeit with no particular stress or elaboration, that the object of moral action is to achieve an Aristotelian "harmony of sentiments and passions" (*TMS* I.i.5.5; see also VII.ii.1.11 – 12); and he embraces various views on the nature of the good in an eclectic summary of the bases of moral approval in section VII (*TMS* VII.iii.3.16). But the territory Smith cuts out for himself is the nature of moral action, and he develops the impartial spectator to meet a particular problem in moral practice, rather than in moral epistemology or the theory of human nature.

This problem is the pervasiveness of self-deceit. Smith is practically unique, among eighteenth century British thinkers (and perhaps all Enlightenment moralists, with the important exception, I shall argue, of Kant),[31] in making the dishonesty of the self to itself a prime issue of moral philosophy. Having joined in Hutcheson's rejection of egoism, Smith finds an entirely new reason to take a dark view of human nature: its apparently ineradicable moral blindness. "He is a bold surgeon, they say, whose hand does not tremble when he performs an operation upon his own person; and he is often equally bold who does not hesitate to pull off the mysterious veil of self-delusion, which covers from his view the deformities of his own conduct" (*TMS* III.4.4). While acting we are too caught up in the passions moving us *to* action to see our situation fairly. And afterwards we are too afraid of facing the real structure of our character to admit to our real motivations: "Rather than see our own behaviour under so disagreeable an aspect, we too often, foolishly and weakly, endeavour to exasperate anew those unjust passions which

[31] Clarke does discuss self-deceit (see note 18), but in passing, and, as I have noted above, not in the context of an argument specifically about moral practice.

had formerly misled us" (*TMS* III.4.4). Smith sees the blindness of motivating passions as inevitable (*TMS* III.4.3), the "preference which every man has for his own happiness above that of other people" as "natural" but morally unacceptable,[32] and the moral feelings that Hutcheson and Hume so relied on as weak and susceptible of easy corruption (*TMS* III.6.10). At several points he reminds us that we often do not know the contents of our own hearts,[33] and implies that if we try to know we risk "disgust," "shame" and "horror" (*TMS* I.ii.1.3, II.ii.2.3, and II.iii.2.5). Repeatedly, he compares shame and remorse to the Furies (*TMS* I.iii.3.8 and III.2.9), which suggests not only that they torment us but that we fly from them, and at one point he gives what amounts to a psychoanalytical reading of the *Oresteia*, as an analogy for the universal human experience of trying to hide from one's own wrongdoing and of finding solace for the shame and horror of that self-condemnation only in an acquittal by the judgment of humanity as a whole.[34]

There is more than a touch of the Christian Fall here,[35] but, as the reference to the *Oresteia* indicates, Smith is not strictly *pessimistic* about human nature. For there is a way out, he believes, from our ugly passions and our tendency to hide from them. Metaphorically represented by the judgment of humanity as a whole, this remedy for self-deceit is ultimately an internal form of judgment: the judgment

[32] *TMS* II.ii.2.1, from which the last quotation comes, goes on to say, "Though it may be true ... that every individual, in his own breast, naturally prefers himself to all mankind, yet he dares not look mankind in the face, and avow that he acts according to this principle ... If he would act so as that the impartial spectator may enter into the principles of his conduct, ... he must ... humble the arrogance of his self-love, and bring it down to something which other men can go along with."

[33] *TMS* III.2.15: "... scarce any man can know perfectly what he himself is capable of doing. What the peculiar constitution of his own mind may or may not admit of, is, perhaps, more or less a matter of doubt to every man." Cf. also III.1.2 (in edition 6 only) and III.4.6.

[34] "The violator of the more sacred laws of justice can never reflect on the sentiments which mankind must entertain with regard to him, without feeling all the agonies of shame, and horror, and consternation. ... He ... regrets the unhappy effects of his own conduct, and feels at the same time that they have rendered him the proper object of the resentment and indignation of mankind, and of what is the natural consequence of resentment, vengeance and punishment. The thought of this perpetually haunts him, and fills him with terror and amazement. He dares no longer look society in the face, but imagines himself as it were rejected, and thrown out from the affections of all mankind. ... Every thing seems hostile, and he would be glad to fly to some inhospitable desert, where he might never more behold the face of a human creature, nor read in the countenance of mankind the condemnation of his crimes. But solitude is still more dreadful than society. His own thoughts can present him with nothing but what is black, unfortunate, and disastrous, the melancholy forebodings of incomprehensible misery and ruin. The horror of solitude drives him back into society, and he comes again into the presence of mankind, astonished to appear before them, loaded with shame and distracted with fear, in order to supplicate some little protection from the countenance of those very judges, who he knows have already all unanimously condemned him." (*TMS* II.ii.2.3. Compare also I.iii.3.8 and III.2.9.)

[35] In connection with which, see also the passage on atonement in *TMS*, editions 1–5, II.ii.3.13 (MacFie and Raphael, pp. 91–92, bottom. Cf. also Appendix II, pp. 383 ff.).

of our internalized figure of humanity, our "inmate within the breast," our "impartial spectator."

Now, to clear up some common confusions, the "impartial spectator" is not identical either with the empirical fact of "sympathy" or with the rational principle that some contemporary thinkers call the "ideal observer." Raphael and MacFie rightly correct those who say that Smith uses sympathy as the basis of moral action, but they go on to claim, equally misleadingly, that he does use it as the basis of moral judgment.[36] Rather, sympathy[37] functions as the mechanism by which the impartial spectator can operate, but it is only the sympathy *of the impartial spectator* that provides a standard for moral judgment. Smith's insistence that sympathy be impartial would by itself be at least a shift of emphasis from Hutcheson's and Hume's theories of moral approbation.

But one must be careful, on the other hand, not to idealize or idolize impartiality as an end in itself. In the first place, as T. D. Campbell has excellently shown, Smith's impartial spectator is an empirical tool, subject to feelings and cultural influences, and not a perfectly informed, perfectly rational position like Roderick Firth's "ideal observer."[38] The impartial spectator is not supposed to lack feelings, only to lack *partial* feelings, the feelings of the "person principally concerned."[39] In the second place, Smith does not unequivocally praise the impartial spectator. He introduces that device immediately following a discussion of "propriety" as the attainment of a *concord* of feelings between the spectator and the person principally concerned. "[T]he spectator must, first of all, endeavor, as much as he can, to put himself in the situation of the other, and to bring home to himself every little circumstance of distress which can possibly occur to the sufferer" (*TMS* I.i.4.6). While Smith does not expect this effort fully to succeed, and the person principally concerned will have to modify his or her feelings accordingly, it remains a virtue, and indeed the foundation of all the "soft, the gentle, the amiable virtues, the virtues of ... humanity" (*TMS* I.i.5.1), for the spectator to enter as much as possible into the feelings of those involved. Spectator and participant react to each other's reactions in what one might call, by analogy with Smith's economic theory, a "marketplace of feelings," until they find a mutually agreeable standard of judgment.[40] The position of choice for moral judgment is thus one of a balance between impartial and partial feelings, not one of impartiality alone.

[36] "Sympathy is the core of Smith's explanation of moral *judgment*." Editor's introduction, p. 21.

[37] Which for Smith as for Hume means simply "feeling with," not pity or compassion – *TMS* I.i.1.5.

[38] Campbell, pp. 127 – 141.

[39] *Ibid.*, pp. 127, 135 – 136. Campbell tends to identify the "person principally concerned" with the "agent" (see, for instance, pp. 96, 164), but I prefer Smith's own phrase, which reminds us that we sometimes seek to have the "right" feelings and reactions in situations in which we are not, strictly speaking, agents.

[40] I owe the analogy with Smith's economics, and the marvelous phrase "marketplace of feelings," to Amy Reichert. (But Campbell also notes the comparison: p. 139, note 1.)

So why does Smith write in later passages as though the sympathy of the impartial spectator were in itself the touchstone of moral judgment? Perhaps because he understands the feelings of the participants to be built into the notion of the sympathy of the impartial spectator. But perhaps also, we need to bear in mind that those passages, unlike the ones we have so far considered, are not talking about *actual* spectators. In a move that a number of commentators have likened to Freud's theory of the superego,[41] Smith tells us that we eventually come to internalize the reactions of actual spectators, and to judge of our own conduct in each situation by what we think an impartial spectator *would* recommend. I think we must understand Smith to assume that there could not possibly be a problem of excessive impartiality in these internal judgments. We already have the feelings of the person principally concerned, since we are in fact that person. To achieve the proper balance for moral judgment, we simply need to take cognizance of the impartial spectator's view as well. Hence Smith can speak of the impartial spectator's view as if it were itself the standard of judgment. The spectator within ourselves is so heavily biased in our own favor that, as Aristotle would have said, we cannot possibly err by leaning towards the excess of impartiality.

Only with the distance of the impartial spectator, moreover, can we compensate for the overwhelming blindness we have toward our own actions. Smith eventually defines "conscience" as the impartial spectator within the self, and he builds up to that definition by stressing the impossibility of seeing our own characters directly. "We can never survey our own sentiments and motives, we can never form any judgment concerning them; unless we remove ourselves, as it were, from our own natural station, and endeavour to view them as at a certain distance from us" (*TMS* III.i.2). What enables us to attain this distance is the fact that we naturally take other people's words and actions as a "mirror" for ourselves:

> Were it possible that a human creature could grow up to manhood in some solitary place, without any communication with his own species, he could no more think of his own character, ... than of the beauty or deformity of his own face. ... [T]hese are objects which he cannot easily see, which naturally he does not look at, and with regard to which he is provided with no mirror which can present them to his view. Bring him into society, and he is immediately provided with the mirror which he wanted before. It is placed in the countenance and behaviour of those he lives with, which always mark when they enter into, and when they disapprove of his sentiments ... (*TMS* III.1.3).

In less flowery language, Smith tells us that we begin with an original desire for praise, and an original tendency to praise and blame others ("our first moral criticisms are exercised upon the character and conduct of other people" – *TMS* III.1.5), and later translate that desire into a desire for praise-worthiness, and that tendency into a capacity for scrutinizing and judging our own behavior. The resulting

[41] Campbell, pp. 149, 165; Harman, pp. 11–12; and D. D. Raphael, *Adam Smith* (Oxford: Oxford University Press, 1985), pp. 41–43. We can probably see an incipient version of the id, as well, in Smith's view of the passionate self as something that often or normally causes us more "shame" and "disgust" than we can directly face.

internal judge should, like any other judge, be impartial, and it learns from experience that it can achieve impartiality only if it takes on the aspect of a spectator rather than an agent:

> When I endeavour to examine my own conduct, when I endeavour to pass sentence upon it, ... it is evident that ... I divide myself, as it were, into two persons; and that I, the examiner and judge, represent a different character from that other I, the person whose conduct is examined into and judged of. The first is the spectator ... The second is the agent, the person whom I properly call myself ... (*TMS* III.1.6).

The internal judge can thus equivalently be called the "impartial spectator," or simply, as the faculty that tells or reminds us what we ought to do, "conscience." Smith distinguishes conscience radically from the sentiments it judges:

> It is not the soft power of humanity, it is not that feeble spark of benevolence which Nature has lighted up in the human heart, that is thus capable of counteracting the strongest impulses of self-love. It is a stronger power, a more forcible motive, which exerts itself upon such occasions. It is reason, principle, conscience, the inhabitant of the breast, the man within, the great judge and arbiter of our conduct. It is he who, whenever we are about to act so as to affect the happiness of others, calls to us, with a voice capable of astonishing the most presumptuous of our passions, that we are but one of the multitude, in no respect better than any other in it ... It is from him only that we learn the real littleness of ourselves, and of whatever relates to ourselves, and the natural misrepresentations of self-love can be corrected only by the eye of this impartial spectator (*TMS* III.3.4).

But even this impartial spectator does not entirely suffice, in Smith's opinion, to combat the temptations of self-deceit. Even conscience needs a guide, and this turns out to be Smith's explanation of the origin and purpose of moral rules. For Hutcheson, rules served as a check on precipitate passions;[42] for Hume, they were simply a means of preventing social strife.[43] For Smith, rules have no such utilitarian function. Instead, they are nature's remedy for "self-deceit, [the] fatal weakness of mankind" (*TMS* III.4.6). We naturally come to form general rules about human conduct out of our observations on the behavior of our neighbors:

> Our continual observations upon the conduct of others, insensibly lead us to form to ourselves certain general rules concerning what is fit and proper either to be done or to be avoided. Some of their actions shock all our natural sentiments. We hear every body about us express the like detestation against them. ... We resolve never to be guilty of the like ... We thus naturally lay down to ourselves a general rule, that all such actions are to be avoided, as tending to render us odious, contemptible, or punishable ... Other actions, on the contrary, call forth our approbation, and we hear every body around us express the same favourable opinion concerning them. ... We become ambitious of performing the like; and thus naturally lay down to ourselves a rule of another kind, that every opportunity of acting in this manner is carefully to be sought after (*TMS* III.4.7).

Out of a process that looks suspiciously like gossip (what "every body" is saying), Smith says that we fashion rules for our own conduct. Once fashioned, moreover, those rules become "fixed in our mind," imbued with "authority," evocative of

[42] Hutcheson, p. 171 (section VII).
[43] Hume, *Treatise*, III.II.II – VI.

"reverence," "awe," and "respect" (*TMS* III.4.12). Through these associations they come to be "of great use in correcting the misrepresentations of self-love concerning what is fit and proper to be done" in each particular situation in which we find ourselves (*TMS* III.4.12). Revulsion at (or approval of) the behavior of others, in specific circumstances, translates into a rule against (or for) such conduct in all similar circumstances, and these rules then give our internal spectator a way of preventing the misinterpretation of our circumstances that passion alone might have urged. Smith gives an example:

> The man of furious resentment, if he was to listen to the dictates of that passion, would perhaps regard the death of his enemy, as but a small compensation for the wrong, he imagines, he has received; which, however, may be no more than a very slight provocation. But his observations upon the conduct of others have taught him how horrible all such sanguinary revenges appear. Unless his education has been very singular, he has laid it down to himself as an inviolable rule, to abstain from them upon all occasions. This rule preserves its authority with him, and renders him incapable of such a violence. Yet the fury of his own temper may be such, that had this been the first time in which he considered such an action, he would undoubtedly have determined it to be quite just and proper, and what every impartial spectator would approve of (*TMS* III.4.12).

Note that impartiality, or at least the position of the impartial spectator, is not enough here. In order properly to make use of that position, we need first to interpret each situation according to fixed rules, because even our faculties of moral judgment tend to be tainted by self-love and are best informed not by our immediate opinions and feelings but by our observations of others. In suggesting that even our moral faculties can be corrupt, in telling us that general rules inspire reverence, awe and respect, make the agent "hesitate" and "tremble," and "are justly regarded as the Laws of the Deity,"[44] Smith lets us know that their function is to humble us, to break the passions and self-conceit that blind us. Regard for these rules "is what is properly called a sense of duty" (*TMS* III.5.1), and Smith insists that it, rather than benevolence, ought to be "the ruling and the governing" principle of our conduct (*TMS* III.6.1). Earlier, as we have seen, he remarked that conscience, not the "feeble spark of benevolence," was the best force to counteract self-love. Here he appears to warn as well against the excesses of misguided conscience. If the harsh and ascetic judge of our "inferiour tribunal" is not subjected to the sacred general rules of conduct, it may serve selfish anger rather than true righteousness. Duty, the regard for rules, thus forms the apex of Smith's system of moral judgment, directing "reason" or "conscience," which in turn encourages or restrains our immediate selfish and benevolent passions. And it is this placement of duty, and this conception of rules, that comes so startlingly close to Kant.

[44] *TMS* III.4.12 (tenses slightly changed), and title of III.5.

III

In talking of "duty" as a central ethical motivation directed towards rules, and in describing conscience as a judge in an interior "tribunal,"[45] Smith clearly looks forward to Kant. In fact, there is a "doubled-self" passage in Kant uncannily similar to the one from *TMS* III.1.6 quoted above (p. 16):

> The man who accuses and judges himself in conscience must think of himself as a twofold personage, a doubled self who, on the one hand, has to stand in fear and trembling at the bar of the tribunal which is yet entrusted to him, but who, on the other hand, must himself administer the office of judge which he holds by inborn authority. ... I, the prosecutor and yet the accused as well, am the same *man* ...[46]

And when Smith talks of reverence for law as that which best restrains selfish passions (*TMS* III.5.2, III.6.10), and of regard for conscience as something "capable of astonishing the most presumptuous of our passions" (*TMS* III.3.4), he foreshadows Kant's analysis of reverence as the feeling that defeats all other feelings.[47] They share, on these matters, a deep sense of the hiddenness and unreliability of the everyday self, and of the need for something independent of its immediate passions to correct for their blindness.

We can find such a conception of the self in Kant when he tells us that actions not done for the sake of duty will usually conform with morality only in a most "contingent and precarious" way (*Groundwork* 58/viii), when he speaks of the burden of our inclinations and the constant struggle against them that virtue entails,[48] when he attacks benevolence theorists like Hutcheson for "flattering themselves with a spontaneous goodness of heart,"[49] and, above all, when he insists that there is no empirical self-knowledge:

> In actual fact it is absolutely impossible for experience to establish with complete certainty a single case in which the maxim of an action in other respects right has rested solely on moral grounds and on the thought of one's duty. ... [Even when it seems that nothing except the moral motive of duty could have moved us to a given action], we cannot infer from this with certainty that it is not some secret impulse of self-love which has actually, under the

[45] *TMS*, third edition, III.2.32 (MacFie and Raphael, p. 28, bottom: cited in note 21 above). See also III.1.2 and III.1.6, and compare *Doctrine of Virtue*, pp. 61, 105 – 108 (Ak VI, 399, 438 – 440).

[46] *Doctrine of Virtue*, p. 104 n (Ak VI, 438 n). Compare also, from the *Doctrine of Justice*: "When ... I enact a penal law against myself as a criminal, it is the pure legislative reason (*homo noumenon*) in me that submits myself to the penal law as a person capable of committing a crime, that is, as another person (*homo phaenomenon*) along with all the others in the civil union who submit themselves to this law." *The Metaphysical Elements of Justice*, trans. John Ladd (Indianapolis: Bobbs-Merrill, 1965), p. 105 (Ak VI, 335).

[47] Kant, *Groundwork of the Metaphysic of Morals*, trans. H. J. Paton (New York: Harper Torchbooks, 1964), pp. 68 – 69 and note (Ak IV, 400 – 401), and *Critique of Practical Reason*, trans. L. W. Beck (Indianapolis: Bobbs-Merrill, 1956), part I, chapter 3.

[48] *Practical Reason*, pp. 122 (118) and *Groundwork* 95 – 96 (428). Page-numbers in parentheses are those of the academy edition. On virtue, *Practical Reason*, pp. 32 – 33 and 87 (32, 84).

[49] *Practical Reason*, p. 88 (86).

mere show of the Idea of duty, been the cause genuinely determining our will. We are pleased to flatter ourselves with the false claim to a nobler motive, but in fact we can never, even by the most strenuous self-examination, get to the bottom of our secret impulsions (*Groundwork* 74–75/407).

For Kant, however, hypocrisy and self-deceit are more than mere empirical facts, features of the natural history of mankind. Having accepted Hume's epistemological critique of the self, Kant can claim that the empirical self is *necessarily* elusive: "Consciousness of self according to the determinations of our state is merely empirical, and always changing. No fixed and abiding self can present itself in this flux of inner appearances."[50] But just as, in response to Hume, he uses precisely this point to argue that knowledge must depend on an *a priori* cognitive self and *a priori* epistemic rules, so, in response to Smith, he will argue that morality requires an *a priori* moral self and *a priori* moral rules. Smith was more deeply aware of our inability to perceive our selves in our moral deliberations than any other empiricist, and he set up his impartial spectator, as we have seen, in order to get at the self indirectly. But he saw this as an empirical problem, while Kant understands it as a necessary consequence of the structure of experience. The observer, in order to observe at all, cannot perceive its own role in observation; self-reflection *must* be indirect, given the role of the self in making reflection possible. It is with this deep insight that Kant explained and overcame Hume's scepticism, and it is with this insight as well that he can advance from Smith. For Kant, the internal judge of our passions will not be merely an empirical product, and the rules it follows will not be merely generalizations we have derived from our experience. Given the (necessarily) amoral nature of the empirical self, they will have to have an *a priori* necessity.

But that Kant grounds his moral rules differently from Smith does not mean they serve a different purpose. Recall that Smith's self came up with moral rules in order to tell *itself* not to do the kind of thing it had abhorred in others. They were means by which the self beat down its own pride and distorted vision. In each of Kant's examples in the *Groundwork*, an agent debates with himself about his own conduct. Never does Kant take as the paradigm moral question, "what should all people do?," or "what should so-and-so over there do?" The question is always, "what should *I* do?," or, more strictly, "how can I *convince* myself of what I ought to do?" For the agent in the examples is never really in doubt as to the nature of the appropriate moral laws, even in those cases Kant calls contradictions of will rather than conception: "If we now attend to ourselves whenever we transgress a duty, we find that we in fact do not will that our maxim should become a universal law ... but rather that its opposite should remain a law universally: we only take the liberty of making an *exception* to it for ourselves (or even just for this once) to the advantage of our inclination" (*Groundwork* 91–92/424). The categorical imperative

[50] *Critique of Pure Reason*, trans. N. Kemp Smith (New York: St. Martin's Press, 1965), A 107. See also B 133 & A 381.

is not so much a moral rule itself,[51] as a principle that I ought not to exempt myself from whatever the moral rules happen to be. It reminds me that those rules, which I most often affirm in their application to others, also and necessarily apply to myself.

Thus the categorical imperative, like Smith's conscience and moral rules, seems to function as a remedy for self-deceit. We may want to remember here that Kant tells us he intends the *Groundwork* to aid ordinary people in the day-to-day struggle of moral practice (*Groundwork* 73/405), and that even in the second *Critique*, a more strictly theoretical work, he condemns alternative moral positions because they fail to "humble my pride," to "morally educate the soul," to "strike down all arrogance and vain self-love."[52] Kant writes to instill humility, and he praises duty primarily because, as Smith had pointed out, it is a supremely humbling principle. If he disagrees with Smith, he does so not over the need for moral philosophy to defeat self-deceit, but over the adequacy of Smith's own mechanism for the battle.

One interesting implication of this reading is that Kant, by making the categorical imperative demand universality, may be trying not so much to found a morality that will embrace or transcend all empirical differences between people, as to cast a moral net wide enough to entangle the empirical self in the strictures it would rather apply only to others. Exactly one case in the universal application of the agent's laws arouses Kant's interest, in his examples and in the way in which he exhorts us to understand and make use of his moral philosophy, and that is the agent him or herself. Kant thinks that only the necessity of the moral law, only its non-empirical character, will give it sway over the agent's slippery and deceptive desires, and necessity for him always implies universality, but the claim to universality is not meant to wipe out differences between sets of circumstances, only to remind us that we may not exempt our actual set of circumstances from the laws that properly apply to it.[53] Contrary to the impression of many of Kant's readers, the categorical imperative is not intended to be a recipe for the invention of a universal morality. This opens up the possibility, which I hope to explore elsewhere, that Kant's moral views are not as incompatible with at least some versions of cultural relativism as they are often taken to be.

I therefore disagree with Susan Meld Shell's claim, in explication of how the categorical imperative might solve the problems posed by the impartial spectator, that Kant's "critical guide to moral judgment is based in universal self-legislation, rather than in a neutrality fostered by non-participation, [that it] is not the negation

[51] Here, as, I think, on much else, I agree with Barbara Herman: "... the Categorical Imperative ... is not itself a moral rule – it is an abstract formal principle" (*The Practice of Moral Judgment*, Journal of Philosophy 1985, p. 415).

[52] *Practical Reason*, pp. 80, 88 (78, 85, 86). Verb forms slightly altered.

[53] Indeed, the question of what we might be permitted to do in other circumstances is itself often an invitation to the casuistry of self-deceit. Kierkegaard discusses this wonderfully in *Either/Or*, vol II (trans. W. Lowrie & H. Johnson (Princeton: Princeton University Press, 1972), pp. 267 – 270).

of interest but its universalization that yields results in touch with the interest of all men."[54] Kant's central revision of Smith is to base self-legislation not in universality (*tout court*), but in reason or freedom. That reason and freedom reciprocally imply each other is a view I shall accept and defend. That reason entails universality is certainly one of Kant's claims, but not, I think, a particularly clear or satisfying one, either in his ethics or his epistemology. What he does reject with good reason is any form of empirical grounding for moral law or moral action, and it is in that respect, as we shall see, that he most importantly disagrees with Smith.

IV

Kant most explicitly seems to be criticizing Smith on the subject of whether upright people constitute some sort of aristocracy. Rawls rightly says that Kant has no room for a moral aristocracy.[55] Smith definitely does have such room. The mechanism of approbation that shapes moral character takes note only of remarkable acts, not the behavior of the everyday. "Approbation, mixed and animated by wonder and surprise, constitutes ... admiration," so only something surprising, "something uncommonly great and beautiful, which rises far above what is vulgar and ordinary," will be admired, even in the realm of "virtue" (*TMS* I.i.5.5). Virtue is excellence, Smith says, adopting Platonic and Aristotelian terminology, and excellence cannot consist in "the common degree of the moral" (*TMS* I.i.5.5; see also II.ii.1.6). For Kant, this is a moral flaw in Smith's system, a moment of unfaithfulness to the ideal of humility:

> ... to teach a pupil to *admire* virtuous actions, however great the sacrifice these may have entailed, is not in harmony with preserving his feeling for moral goodness. For be a man never so virtuous, all the goodness he can ever perform is still his simple duty; and to do his duty is nothing more than to do what is in the common moral order and hence in no way deserving of wonder. Such wonder is rather a lowering of our feeling for duty, as if to act in obedience to it were something extraordinary and meritorious.[56]

Kant says that he learned the importance of regarding human beings as equal from Rousseau:

> By inclination ... I feel a consuming thirst for knowledge ... There was a time when I believed this constituted the honor of humanity, and I despised the people, who know nothing. Rousseau corrected me in this. This binding prejudice disappeared. I learned to honor man,

[54] Shell, p. 102, note 6.

[55] "Kant's basic moral conception is that of an aristocracy of everyone, each a free and equal person. It is not an aristocracy of nature, or of social class, or an aristocracy of intellect and beauty, or of unusual achievement. Nor is it, as one might carelessly think, an aristocracy of moral character and moral worth," in his lectures on Hume, Kant, and Leibniz at Harvard University (unpublished): Kant IX, pp. 13 – 14.

[56] Kant, *Religion Within the Limits of Reason Alone*, trans. T. M. Greene and H. H. Hudson (New York: Harper & Row, 1960), p. 44.

and I would find myself more useless than the common laborer if I did not believe that this attitude of mine [as investigator] can give a worth to all others in establishing the rights of mankind.[57]

I take this as a lesson in humility. It is not enough to humble one's desires before the moral laws if one raises oneself above them again by regarding them as especially designed to honor oneself. But in what respect *do* people equally deserve honor? Certainly not as regards their intellectual or physical abilities, or even their emotions or character. Only in their freedom and their capacity for reason are all human beings equal. So moral practice, as well as moral epistemology, demands that we regard people as essentially rational and transcendentally free.

But there are deeper grounds for these assumptions, which we can better understand, in their contrast with Smith, by examining more closely the notion of "reason." We have seen that Smith's use of such terms as "duty," "reverence" and "conscience" closely resembles Kant's. When he calls conscience "reason," however, and speaks of a role, albeit a limited one, for reason in our moral thought, he is not using "reason" in the Kantian sense.[58] "Reason," he says, is "the judging faculty," the faculty by which we "judge of the propriety or impropriety of desires and affections" (*TMS* VI.ii.1.3). In the same passage, he praises Plato for considering this "judging faculty" to be the "governing principle" of the soul. If we recall, in addition, his rhetorical identification of "reason" with "principle" and "conscience," it will be clear that "reason" for him is analogous to what Kant would call "judgment," specifically "determinant judgment":[59] it determines which specific situations or feelings belong under which general rule of propriety.

Elsewhere, we find that it also performs what Kant would call "reflective judgment." Smith says that "[i]t is by reason that we discover those general rules ... according to which we endeavour, as well as we can, to model our conduct" (*TMS* VII.iii.2.6), and makes clear that these general rules "are ultimately founded upon experience of what, in particular instances, our moral faculties ... approve, or disapprove of. We do not originally approve or condemn particular actions; because, upon examination, they appear to be agreeable or inconsistent with a general rule. The general rule, on the contrary, is formed, by finding from experience, that [we approve or disapprove of] all actions of a certain kind ..." (*TMS* III.4.8).[60]

57 Ak XX, p. 44, and quoted, to show how Kant differs from the British moralists, by Beck in *Studies in the Philosophy of Kant*, pp. 9 – 10.

58 MacFie seems to miss this point when he writes that Smith gives a "rationalistic turn" to moral sentiment theory (*Individual in Society*, pp. 51, 87 – 88).

59 "Judgment in general is the faculty of thinking the particular as contained under the universal. If the universal ... be given, the judgment which subsumes the particular under it ... is *determinant*. But if only the particular be given for which the universal has to be found, the judgment is merely *reflective*." *Critique of Judgment*, trans. J. H. Bernard (New York: Hafner Press, 1951), p. 15 (introduction, § IV).

60 See also III.4.9 – 11 (and IV.2.2), where he insists that ultimately moral judgments are always particular (as are aesthetic judgments: V.1.4,7), and are not made "by considering first the general rule, and then, secondly, whether the particular action under consideration fell properly within its comprehension." The generality of the rule only comes into play, apparently, when we apply it to our own projected actions.

Smith details wonderfully how we come up with general rules out of specific cases, in aesthetic as well as ethical matters, arguing in advance of Kant for something very like "disinterested satisfaction" (in the sympathy of the impartial spectator itself) and "purposiveness without purpose" (in his notion that what we find beautiful is not utility itself, as Hume had said, but an apparent *suitedness for* utility that might in fact not be useful – *TMS* IV.1.3).[61] In addition, by using "reason" for both this process and that by which the self applies moral judgments to itself, Smith implies that determinant and reflective judgment necessarily belong together, a point in the theory of judgment that Kant himself never properly explored. In these ways he anticipates, and at times even surpasses, Kant's account of judgment. But judgment is not what Kant calls "reason," and the faculty that develops and applies specific rules in experience is by no means the faculty, necessarily beyond the experience it shapes, that determines the very nature and legitimacy of all rules.

Now one of the things for which Kant has been frequently criticized is the separation of his theory of judgment from his moral philosophy.[62] In the light of the comparison with Smith, one response to this complaint might be that he felt *TMS* had already supplied an adequate account of moral judgment and that he was therefore free to pursue a rather different project. Another response, however, might be that he felt that judgment was the *wrong* faculty to supply the highest principle of morals, and that he deliberately set reason against judgment as the foundation of ethics. (This is not, of course, incompatible with regarding Smith's theory as valuable once the ground of ethics is laid elsewhere.) For judgment is defined by its relationship to specific situations, and is guided by empirical imagination; it cannot soar free of empirical determination. We have only to look at Smith's proposed genealogy for the internal spectator, as a necessary consequence of our

[61] There is, in addition, a hint of the *sensus communis* in IV.2.2, and there are two passages that anticipate Kant far too closely for the resemblance to be a coincidence: IV.1.8 (p. 182), which looks forward in both thought and language to *Judgment* § 41, and V.1.8, which anticipates *Judgment* § 17 down to the juxtaposition, when giving examples, of Africa, Europe, and China, and human beauty with the beauty of a horse.

[62] See, for instance, H. G. Gadamer, *Truth and Method*, eds. G. Barden & J. Cumming (New York: Seabury Press, 1975), pp. 31 f. Paul Dietrichson, Barbara Herman, and John Rawls would all like to maintain that Kant does have an account of moral judgment, but they each admit at one point or another that their proposed reconstructions of that account may be an addition to Kant rather than a reading of him (Dietrichson, *When is a Maxim Fully Universalizable?*, Kant-Studien 1964, p. 170; Herman, *op. cit.* in note 51, pp. 414, 435–436; and Rawls, *Themes in Kant's Moral Philosophy*, in: *Kant's Transcendental Deductions*, ed. Eckart Förster (Stanford: Stanford University Press, 1989), p. 85 and note 4 on p. 254). I would like to add here that when Hannah Arendt was casting about for a source onto which to graft her theory of political judgment (in *The Crisis in Culture*, *Truth and Politics*, and *Lectures on Kant's Political Philosophy*), she would have done much better to pick *TMS* than the third *Critique*. Kant seems quite deliberately to have kept judgment away from moral theory, while Smith reads as if he had consciously anticipated Arendt's views.

natural and necessary desires for approbation, to see that he has no room for the possibility of free choice, or for the absolute good which, according to Kant, can only be posited on the assumption of free choice.[63]

One might say that the entire point of the first *Critique* is to show the freedom of reason. Reason demands that empirical phenomena be fitted under the category of cause-and-effect, but precisely *in* that demand recognizes that it cannot place its own workings, its own very establishment of causal determinism, under that determinist framework. The process that establishes the framework cannot intelligibly be considered a part of it. Kant writes in the *Groundwork* that because Reason "mark[s] out limits for understanding itself," a rational being must regard itself, insofar as it is rational, as beyond the limits of the understanding (*Groundwork* 120/452) – hence as beyond the categories, including the category of cause-and-effect. In the second *Critique* he tells us that practical reason has primacy over speculative reason, which implies that our very pursuit of empirical science and its principles depends originally on our freedom.[64] In this way, Kant argues himself entirely out of the empiricist approach to moral thought. According to that approach, all accounts of morality had to provide a mechanism for both action and judgment, which led inevitably to the question, "why should this mechanism be of *value*? why, if I can, may I not ignore it, or defy it?" Kant replaces Smith's mechanism of approbation and internalization, like Hume's apparatus of sympathy, with *no* mechanism, with an insistence that morality not only needs no mechanism but cannot exist unless it is rooted in an unexplained and inexplicable freedom.

Consider, once again, Kant's stated purpose for the *Groundwork*: to aid "the common reason of mankind" in the struggle he calls the "natural dialectic" – "a disposition to quibble with [the] strict laws of duty, to throw doubt on their validity or at least on their purity and strictness, and to make them, where possible, more adapted to our wishes and inclinations; that is, to pervert their very foundations and destroy their whole dignity" (*Groundwork* 73/405). This disposition arises out of our inclinations, which form a "powerful counterweight to all the commands of duty." Now any empirically based theory of morality, whether it sets as our goal "utility," the harmony of the passions, or the approval of an impartial spectator, must play to the inclinations' claim that their side of the dialectic is the whole story. In practice, even a follower of Smith may be tempted to ask, "why should I obey the impartial spectator if I don't feel like it?" and the only answer he could receive would be a lame, "Well, if you've been raised properly, you *should* feel like it." Or perhaps, "your desire for approval ensures that you *will* feel like it." (And why

[63] See *Groundwork* 95–96 (427–428), where he argues for the absolute value of human beings as a condition of reason's having a principle of action, and *Practical Reason* 65 ff. (63 ff.), where he argues for the priority of the concept of freedom over the concept of the good.

[64] *Practical Reason*, p. 126 (121). Compare the argument at *Groundwork* 121 (453–454).

should I value approval, or being raised properly ...?)[65] It follows that to establish the possibility of absolute value we must step beyond the infinite regress of empirical explanation and justification, and this Kant does by seeing in the very process that grounds and defines empirical thinking both an absolutely valuable way of acting and an absolutely valuable being (the first and second formulations of the categorical imperative).

If practical reason has primacy over speculative reason, and all interests are ultimately practical,[66] then we may ask what moral purpose Kant's own moral philosophy serves. I suggest that even in his examination of such epistemological and metaphysical issues as the proof and nature of freedom, or the role of reason rather than imagination in moral judgment, he is guided by the questions that concern Adam Smith in *TMS*. Certainly, he deals more deeply with moral epistemology than Smith does, but not as an issue in its own right, in the manner of Clarke or Hutcheson or Hume. Rather, he grounds moral rules in reason instead of emotion as part of a strategy to defeat the self-deceit by which we evade our responsibilities. In the course of defending this position, he does give an answer to the philosophical challenge of moral empiricism, but such empiricism is just one of the many ways in which the everyday self deceives itself, and Kant answers the challenge in order to help the everyday self, in its everyday practice, meet the demands of morality. In this – as, I have suggested, in much else – he shares the direction of his work, if not its destination, with the moral philosophy of Adam Smith.

[65] In addition, someone might say, keeping in mind the empirical nature of the impartial spectator, "any impartial spectator raised in my circumstances or culture would approve of action x," and thereby excuse behavior that ought to be culpable.

[66] *Practical Reason*, p. 126 (121).

[2]

Man and World **29:** 187–213, 1996.

Nature and philosophy

Adam Smith on stoicism, aesthetic reconciliation, and imagination *

CHARLES L. GRISWOLD, JR.
Department of Philosophy, Boston University, Boston, MA 02215, U.S.A.

> First, it is clear that all human affairs, like the Sileni of Alcibiades, have two aspects quite different from each other. Hence, what appears 'at first blush' (as they say) to be death, will, if you examine it more closely, turn out to be life; conversely, life will turn out to be death; beauty will become ugliness; riches will turn to poverty; notoriety will become fame; learning will be ignorance; strength, weakness; noble birth will be ignoble; joy will become sadness; success, failure; friendship, enmity; what is helpful will seem harmful; in brief, you will find everything suddenly reversed if you open up the Silenus.
>
> Erasmus[1]

"Nature" is perhaps the most crucial term in classical Western ethical and political theory. It seems that virtually all the ancient schools, whether philosophical or anti-philosophical, appealed to it as a way to ground their ethical and political theories. What was meant was, first, human nature (as distinguished from human beings as convention has shaped them), but that understood in some way within a larger whole, a larger ethically relevant framework. Book X of the *Laws* contains one of Plato's strongest statements to the effect that nature, i.e. the whole, is governed by reason (personified by the gods) and not by chance or any human art (i.e. convention). We are enjoined, indeed required, to live according to nature, that is, to subject our self-love to the perspective of reason or "the life of the whole" (903c). Cal-

* Earlier versions of this essay were delivered at Yale University, Trinity College (Hartford), and at Boston University as part of a symposium on "Philosophies of Nature" held in honor of Erazim Kohák (the symposium was sponsored by the Boston University Center for Philosophy and History of Science).

licles forcefully appeals to nature (as opposed to convention) in arguing that the strong should rule (*Gorgias* 483a–e). In the *Protagoras* Hippias speaks of a natural brotherhood that transcends conventional boundaries (337c–d). In Aristotle's work, the appeal to nature in book I of the *Politcs* is perhaps most striking. The Stoics, Epicureans, Sceptics, and even Sophists all appealed to the same notion. Only some of these ancient appeals to nature amount to appeals to teleology.[2] In one form or another the centrality of the notion of nature continues down through Cicero, Augustine, Boethius, Aquinas, among many others, through Hobbes, Spinoza, and Leibniz to parts of the 17th and 18th centuries.[3]

I say "parts" because already in Hume, Smith's immediate predecessor and close friend, the notion comes under attack. Hume wrote to Hutcheson: "I cannot agree to your Sense of *Natural*. 'Tis founded on final Causes; which is a Consideration, that appears to me pretty uncertain and unphilosophical. For pray, what is the End of Man? Is he created for Happiness or for Virtue? For this Life or for the next? For himself or for his Maker? Your Definition of *Natural* depends on solving these Questions, which are endless, & quite wide of my Purpose."[4] This does not prevent Hume from using the term constantly, though perhaps in quotation marks.

With Kant, of course, the traditional usages of the notion come under severe attack. In the Preface to the second edition of the *Critique of Pure Reason* Kant famously tells us that "reason has insight only into that which it produces after a plan of its own, and that it must not allow itself to be kept, as it were, in nature's leading-strings, but must itself show the way with principles of judgment based upon fixed laws, constraining nature to give answer to questions of reason's own determining" (B xiii).[5] It is only because of this injunction, Kant teaches, "that the study of nature has entered on the secure path of a science," whereas all traditional, metaphysical appeals to nature are dogmatic and unwarranted (B xiv). The second *Critique* continues the attack, this time on the ethical relevance of the notion of "nature" as distinguished from that of freedom. Most of Kant's successors carried on in the same vein. Mill and Sidgwick, for example, find the notion incomprehensible or useless so far as ethical theory goes, and this in good part because "nature" is understood as the factual, the non-evaluative brute "given."[6] Since even the "unnatural" is natural, the term seems useless. Contemporary moral and political philosophers tend either to ignore the notion – there are two relatively unimportant entries under "nature" in Rawls' most recent book, for example – or to view the notion of natural teleology as intelligible but no longer credible – as remarks by Nagel and Williams show.[7] The exceptions are those who argue in conjunction with religious views (I have in mind appeals to nature in Catholic teaching), and those who argue for a "naturalized ethics."[8]

The end result, in any event, is that the term "nature" and its cognates have virtually lost all meaning for us in ethical and political discussions, to the point that notions such as "natural right," or "the laws of nature and of nature's god" (Jefferson's phrase in the Declaration), begin to sound like mysterious relics from a bygone era. Yet while the vocabulary may be atrophied, I suspect that many of us feel a need to articulate the place of humans in nature, as well as the grounding of "values" in something other than our contingent customs or wishes. So far as the contemporary public stage goes, the first issue lies at the heart of environmentalism, the second at that of discussions of civic religion, public morals, and the like.

Adam Smith seems to occupy a defining moment in the history of "nature." On the one hand, he shared with Hume a scepticism about teleology and about any "metaphysical" senses of the term. Understood as the "essence" or "substance" or "form" of a thing, "nature" is already dead in Smith's philosophy. Smith seems to say that moral norms arise not from nature but from the impartial spectator, that is from a principle that seems closer to Kant's "categorical imperative" than to some notion of natural moral perfection. On the other hand, Smith uses the term and its cognates with extraordinary frequency throughout his work. It occurs in the title of one of his two published books, viz. *An Inquiry into the Nature and Causes of the Wealth of Nations*, and in crucial passages Smith clearly implies that it serves as a standard. For example, in the *Wealth of Nations* he defends what he calls "the obvious and simple system of natural liberty," criticizes the inefficacy of state interventions to modify the course that the flow of capital and labor would "naturally" take (IV.ix.50–51), and sets out a theory of the "natural price"(I.iv.17).[9] In the *Theory of Moral Sentiments* he says of all previous ethical systems that "as many of them are derived from a partial and imperfect view of nature, there are many of them too in some respects in the wrong," whereas his, by implication, is right because in accordance with nature.[10] He concludes his moral philosophy with references to the "natural sense of justice," "rules of natural justice," and "natural jurisprudence," and these are explicitly meant to be distinguished from the merely conventional (VII.iv.36). There may even be a role for teleology in his system. Smith would thus seem to be one of the last major philosophers whose work is a defense of nature, even as he has dropped some of its traditional meanings.

I cannot here offer a comprehensive discussion of his use of this crucial term. Rather, I shall focus primarily, but not exclusively on one of the uses to which he puts it, viz. as meaning "the whole," "the world," "the universe." This use links up strongly with that of the classical school whose reliance on the term was decisive, viz. Stoicism, and whose influence on modern philosophy down through Kant is important and complex. This use also allows me to examine what I think are very interesting questions Smith's moral philosophy points to, questions still with us today.[11] Smith is an unusually dialectical thinker, and writes at a variety of levels simultaneously. My paper will be correspondingly dialectical. Each section will seek to excavate successive layers of the discussion, both going over the same ground and going deeper.[12] Or to switch metaphors to that suggested by the passage from Erasmus quoted above, my discussion resembles a series of Sileni, one nested inside the next, but all resonating with one another in a sort of *pros hen* or focal meaning way.

The underlying issue in this paper concerns the relationship between nature and philosophy, as is indicated by the first part of the paper's title. I shall frame the first part of my discussion in terms of Smith's appropriation of Stoicism.[13] The influence of Stoicism on Smith is frequently underlined, but his critique of it is rarely grasped. It amounts to a rejection of a whole notion of "living according to nature," and thus of a conception of philosophy. In section II, I address problems Smith's alternative to the Stoic view encounters, i.e. problems in the view that we live according to moral and not philosophical reason, or with a view of a part of nature and not nature as a whole. These include that of the presence of natural evil and conflict, and seem to require something like unnatural intervention if reconciliation with nature is to be possible. In section III I examine Smith's notions of harmony, beauty, and purposiveness, for these "aesthetic" notions pervade his thought and seem to explain how reconciliation with nature is to be understood. The aesthetic language may at first strike us as Platonic, but in fact is deeply anti-Platonic at several levels. Seeing how that is so helps us both to grasp the problems internal to Smith's "aesthetic" solution to the problem of reconciliation, and the importance of the next step of the analysis, viz. the doctrine of the imagination. In the concluding section of the paper, I examine this doctrine, and argue that Smith's notions of nature, harmony, and philosophy are predicated upon a view of the imagination as fundamentally "productive" or "poetic." Consequently Smith's "defense" of nature actually exemplifies the turn, crucial to the Enlightenment and so to modernity, from "nature" as the paradigm to be imitated by the human soul, to "nature" as that "something" which the imagination seeks to make whole according to its own demands.

1. Living according to nature: Smith's critique of stoicism

Of all the philosophical schools preceding him, Smith accords Stoicism by far the most attention. He struggles with its teachings throughout the *TMS*, and not just in his review of the history of moral philosophy at the end of the book. In the repeated revisions of the *TMS*, the passages on Stoicism were rearranged and repositioned a number of times; clearly Smith gave them and their place in his book a great deal of thought. Stoicism is the first school identified by name in the *TMS*, and this occurs early on in the book (I.ii.3.4). Smith writes:

> The ancient stoics were of opinion, that as the world was governed by the all-ruling providence of a wise, powerful, and good God, every single event ought to be regarded, as making a necessary part of the plan of the universe, and as tending to promote the general order and happiness of the whole: that the vices and follies of mankind, therefore, made as necessary a part of this plan as their wisdom or their virtue; and by that eternal art which educes good from ill, were made to tend equally to the prosperity and perfection of the great system of nature. No speculation of this kind, however, how deeply soever it might be rooted in the mind, could diminish our natural abhorrence for vice, whose immediate effects are so destructive, and whose remote ones are too distant to be traced by the imagination.

Smith's first reference to this school is critical. What exactly is the criticism?

This discussion is part of a chapter in which Smith explains what he calls the "unsocial passions" of hatred and resentment which, he claims, are at the root of our judgments about justice and injustice. The passions of hatred and resentment are themselves extremely useful in that they are the "guardians of justice"; but we do not evaluate them in light of that utility, so much as in respect to the specific context in which they manifest themselves or with which they are associated. We seem irrational in our refusal to focus on the question of utility, i.e. of their role or function within a whole. Smith is arguing for what one might call the contextuality of the moral sentiments. And it is just at this point that Smith makes the statement about the Stoics I quoted. For the Stoics adopt what one might call the standpoint of reason, that is, a synoptic, comprehensive, or simply a philosophical standpoint. It is crucial to note that Smith does not deny that one could take a synoptic standpoint, or that doing so would amount to philosophizing about the phenomenon in question. On the contrary, he frequently connects philosophy with just this sort of synopticism, and at times himself "speaks" in just that voice.[14] As he states, from that standpoint it appears that even our irrationalities ("follies"), even our "vices," have their place in promoting the "general order and happiness of the whole." He seems to agree that from the Stoic's elevated standpoint, there is no real distinction between virtue and vice; "every single event" serves "equally to the prosperity and perfection of the great system of nature."

In other words, from the standpoint of nature or the whole, moral distinctions disappear. In the passage quoted, Smith refers to "that eternal art which educes good from ill." Probably Smith's most famous phrase is the "invisible hand," and that metaphor expresses just that process by which good is educed from ill. The Stoic background of the "invisible hand" is undeniable; and correspondingly when Smith uses the metaphor, he is adopting the standpoint of the philosopher who observes things synoptically. The *TMS*, and especially the *WN*, are full of examples not just of unintended consequences, but of good consequences arising from bad actions, passions, or situations. That the term "nature" occurs in the title of the *WN* is perhaps indicative, then, of the removed "speculative" standpoint on human life political economy generally assumes.

The conclusion of the passage quoted is that moral distinctions reappear when perceived in context, and moral perception is the work, on Smith's account, of sentiment and sympathy. Differently put, moral distinctions show themselves from standpoint of the part, not of the whole. Smith is here asserting that no philosophical "speculation" could diminish our hatred or resentment of vice or, we may infer, our appreciation of virtue. The speculative pronouncements of reason cannot obviate the moral judgments of sentiment. Consequently Smith is here urging on us the importance of recognizing the differences between the standpoint of the moral actor and that of the theorist or philosopher. He invites us to join in his harsh condemnation of "stoical apathy" that results from confusing them.[15]

As the book unfolds, however, the picture becomes more complicated; we come to see that a person schooled in Stoicism, i.e. in the view that philosophy ought be a "philosophy of life," as we are given to calling it, will shape his or her moral sentiments accordingly (VII.ii.1.47: "That the Stoical philosophy had very great influence upon the character and conduct of its followers, cannot be doubted"). And this Smith clearly thinks is a generally bad thing, for it amounts to an erosion of the basis for moral distinctions. He will therefore argue not just that we ordinarily do not confuse standpoints of part and whole, but that we ought not. We may be Stoics in theory, as it were, but ought not be in practice.

The underlying issue in Smith's discussions of Stoicism concerns the relationship between philosophy and ordinary moral life, and his repeated discussions of Stoicism are a sign that the just mentioned issue in fact pervades the *TMS*. It is just because he accepts the Stoic view of the kind of standpoint philosophical reason would adopt, viz. that of nature or the whole, and because he accepts the Stoic view of what morality would look like if viewed solely from that standpoint, that Smith is both deeply attracted to and critical of Stoicism. He commends a sort of moral imitation of philosophical synopticism, viz. the standpoint of the impartial spectator. For the Stoics had something right when they urge us to diminish our natural affection for ourselves by viewing ourselves from a detached perspective. In the second through the fifth editions of the *TMS* Smith wrote that "the stoical philosophy, in this respect, does little more than unfold our natural ideas of perfection" (p. 141). But the Stoics push our natural ideas too far when they insist that "man . . . ought to regard himself, not as something separated and detached, but as a citizen of the world, a member of the vast commonwealth of nature" (III.3.11). Stoicism thus supplies Smith with a case study of how natural moral sentiments become distorted when pressed philosophically. We begin to see why Smith has an ambivalent attitude towards Stoicism.

In the course of his long discussion of Stoicism in part VII of the book Smith quotes Epictetus' crucial question: "in what sense are some things said to be according to nature, and others contrary to it? It is in that sense in which we consider ourselves as separated and detached from all other things . . ."; as a human being you are "a part of a whole, upon account of that whole" (VII.ii.1.19; *Discourses* II.v.24–26). The passage Smith quotes concludes with a recommendation of the famous Stoic apathy, and ties that emotional stance to the Stoic Sage's insistence on viewing himself from the standpoint of the whole. The Sage's happiness consisted, Smith says, "in the contemplation of the happiness and perfection of the great system of the universe" and in "discharging his duty," that is in discharging with absolute propriety whatever role in the universe God had assigned him. His passions completely under control, with indifference to what fortune might bring, and with no attention whatever to the consequences of his actions – these being out of his control and under the administration of the "Superintendant of the universe" – the Sage was assured tranquillity. If his situation for some reason became unbearable, he could always escape it through suicide.

While Smith paints a sympathetic and extended portrait of this doctrine, it culminates in an important criticism already implied by a point made much earlier in the book to the effect that the doctrine of "stoical apathy" was a result of "metaphysical sophisms" (III.3.14). At the end of the *TMS*, Smith characterizes the Stoic doctrine of suicide as "altogether a refinement of philosophy" (VII.ii.34). In order to substantiate the charges against the Stoics Smith appeals to nothing other than nature, but now in a somewhat different sense of the term. "Nature, in her sound and healthful state, seems never to prompt us to suicide"; nor does nature lead us to approve of suicide even when it is performed so as to avoid some deep "melancholy" or "distress" (VII.ii.1.34). As Smith says here: " . . . no natural principle, no regard to the approbation of the supposed impartial spectator, to the judgment of the man within the breast, seems to call upon us to escape from it [distress] by destroying ourselves." On the contrary, suicide strikes "us" as moral weakness, and by way of proof Smith provides one of his favorite examples, viz. the "American savage." Smith notes that these courageous people endured torture not just without attempting to commit suicide, but with contempt for their tormentors (VII.ii.1.34).

In sum, Smith denies that the Stoic's conception of what it means to live according to nature can be entirely correct. It is correct insofar as it enjoins us to examine our motives and conduct from a general point of view, i.e. from the standpoint of an impartial spectator. Stoicism rightly emphasizes the importance of self-command, of checking self-love, of having a perspective on self (III.3.44, III.3.11; III.3.22 and context). Further, Smith cites with evident approval the notion that "every man . . . is first and principally recommended to his own care," and "is certainly, in every respect, fitter and abler to take care of himself than of any other person" (VI.ii.1.1; presumably Smith is alluding here to the Stoic doctrine of *oikeiosis*). He also approves of the Stoic notion that true happiness "consists in tranquillity and enjoyment" (III.3.30).

But Stoic doctrine is misleading insofar as it assimilates that standpoint to one which is properly speculative or philosophical, and which consequently requires us to see ourselves as mere cogs in "the whole machine of the world" (VII.ii.1.37).[16] It is just from that confusion that all the "paradoxes" of Stoicism are derived, including those of *apatheia* and of suicide, or so Smith explicitly argues (VII.ii.1.38–39). He maintains that we act in accordance with nature when we impartially evaluate our *local* situation, the "little department" over which we have some management and direction, and when we are guided by the moral passions – including that of self-love – which nature furnishes us. The passions as well as detached perspective on them focus on the requirements of the specific situation. The impartial spectator does not consider "propriety" with an eye to our place in the whole or the absolute standard of benevolence appropriate to god, but with an eye to how we are placed in this part of the whole, here and now. For it is to that place that our emotions are chiefly tied, and from the emotions functioning in specific situations ethical distinctions arise. The whole is not a "situation" or "place" with which one could empathize, and reason is not empathetic. Smith's critique of the Stoics is thus the flip side of his "theory of moral sentiments."

Natural religion does of course supply us with a view of the whole as God's creation, and Smith commends it as nature's way of supporting morality. This does not contradict his critique of Stoicism, however; for this view of the whole is really a "sense of propriety" concerning the level of gratitude or reverence or even fear we imagine we ought to feel towards the Deity understood as a benevolent designer (III.5.12). Thanks to the "natural principles of religion" we reinforce our "natural sense of duty," and that sense is always responsive to a specific context unless "corrupted by the factious and party zeal of some worthless cabal" (III.5.13). Hence natural religion provides us with a holistic context which increases our sympathetic attention to right character and conduct here and now, and thus has an influence opposite to that of Stoicism (as Smith construes Stoicism). Smith explicitly protests against the metamorphosis of natural religion into a religious teaching that insists that "all affections for particular objects, ought to be extinguished in our breast, and one great affection take the place of all others, the love of the Deity, the desire of rendering ourselves agreeable to him, and of directing our conduct, in every respect, according to his will" (III.6.1).

Smith concludes that "the plan and system which Nature has sketched out for our conduct, seems to be altogether different from that of the Stoical philosophy" (VII.ii.1.43). Nature does offer us Stoic philosophy in a moment of consolation of our misfortunes; but "Nature has not prescribed to us this sublime contemplation as the great business and occupation of our lives" (VII.ii.1.46). Nature, then, bids us to view the whole from the standpoint of the part; in reversing this natural order the Stoic makes a mistake characteristic of philosophers, namely that of transforming into a governing principle that which was merely one element in experience. For nature also bids us to view the part impartially, from outside itself; and this is an imitation of a philosophical stance. But the Stoics understood nature's teaching far too ambitiously, and substituted the imitation for the original. All of their "sophisms" and "paradoxes" arose from one basic mistake, namely that of holding that nature ought ideally be coordinated with philosophical reason.

Smith might agree that we should live in accordance with the impartial spectator, the "great inmate, the great demi-god within the breast" (VI.iii.18). It is not so much nature, but our attitude towards it, that should guide us. Stated somewhat metaphorically, Logos is prior to Being. Perhaps Smith's deepest debt to Stoicism consists in just that point. It is a matter of emphasizing the priority of the standpoint of the spectator, and this runs all the way through Smith's philosophy (including his teaching about the passions "derived from the imagination"). In the final section of this paper, I will return to this crucial point to the effect that our view of nature is prior to nature itself. Smith's break with Stoicism consists in his determination of what the appropriate attitude is. The Stoics confused, on Smith's account, levels of spectatorship.

In the Moor-Hutcheson translation of Marcus Aurelius' *Meditations* (V.9) Smith would have read: "Don't return to philosophy with reluctance, as to a severe tutor. . . . Remember that philosophy requires no other things than what your nature requires."[17] This is a proposition Smith could not have accepted without qualification. Morality guided by nature will not then be a matter of pursuing philosophical ideals – for again, the point Smith is making by means of Stoicism holds, for him, of philosophy altogether. While we have such ideals and while Smith contrasts our actual goals and conduct with them, he does not generally urge us to shorten the gap between the two. Rather, as we will see, he gives us reason to accept the gap as itself natural. But here we get ahead of ourselves, for we are again speaking of a philosophical reconciliation with the whole or nature, but in a still different sense.

2. Natural conflict and unnatural intervention

To summarize a crucial result of the preceding section: we cannot or ought not live in accordance with a view of nature as a whole, that is, with philosophical reason. We are to live in accordance with right perspective on nature as a part, that is, with moral reason. Let us now proceed to excavate the next layer. When we act in accordance with "the dictates of our moral faculties" we "co-operate with the Deity" and "advance as far as is in our power the plan of Providence." Smith immediately complicates this cheerful assessment; for we are also capable of acting against those dictates, in which case we "declare ourselves, if I may say so, in some measure the enemies of God" (III.5.7). The phenomena attest to our ability to act in both ways; yet Smith declares that both a consideration of God's "infinite perfections" and an "examination of the works of nature" lead us to the belief that the "Author of nature" intended the happiness of mankind (III.5.7). Obviously, there lurks here the old theological problem of evil. And things get more complex as Smith develops his point.

For human experience amply testifies that the workings of nature, and of our "natural sentiments" (III.5.9), are sometimes at odds with one another. Smith himself insists on the point in a passage that very much bears on the connection between his political economy and the moral theory. He takes the examples of an "industrious knave" who cultivates the soil, and "the indolent good man" who does not. Of these two, "Who ought to reap the harvest? who starve, and who live in plenty? The natural course of things decides it in favour of the knave; the natural sentiments of mankind in favour of the man of virtue." Non-human Nature is absolutely rational and fair in her judgments, Smith says (also III.3.27); yet human nature will not and ought not accede, and demands a quite different proportion between virtue and reward, vice and punishment. "Thus man is by Nature directed to correct, in some measure, that distribution of things which she herself would otherwise have made," and "like the gods of the poets, he is perpetually interposing, by extraordinary means, in favour of virtue" (III.5.9–10). It thus seems that nature is self-contradictory, and the problem is driven home by what Smith says next: "The natural course of things cannot be entirely controlled by the impotent endeavours of man"; we not only fail to humanize nature, but as

Smith especially emphasizes in the *WN*, our efforts to do so sometimes have the perverse effect of making things even worse.

Smith assures us that "the rules which she [Nature] follows are fit for her, those which he follows for him: but both are calculated to promote the same great end, the order of the world, and the perfection and happiness of human nature" (III.5.9). Yet he has just shown us how that this view begs our credulity. Indeed, with literary deftness he casts doubt on what he has himself just asserted by quoting, out of the blue, the "eloquent and philosophical bishop of Clermont." The lines Smith quotes are as poignant and direct as any on the subject: "does it suit the greatness of God, to leave the world which he has created in so universal a disorder? To see the wicked prevail almost always over the just . . . ? From the height of his greatness ought God to behold those melancholy events as a fantastical amusement, without taking any share in them? Because he is great, should he be weak, or unjust, or barbarous? . . . O God! if this is the character of your Supreme Being . . . I can no longer acknowledge you for my father . . . You would then be no more than an indolent and fantastical tyrant . . ." (III.5.11). Smith neither prepares us for this outburst nor has a word to say in response to it. The paragraphs immediately preceding it suggest that we turn to God for comfort in the face of the injustices of the "natural course of things." The two paragraphs that immediately follow it simply reassert the importance, for a coherent moral life, of trust in an "All-powerful Being," even though it is precisely that which the Bishop's lament has just called into question. The Bishop's "philosophical" words disrupt rather than confirm Smith's narrative about natural religion as the appropriate response to the opposition between our moral sentiments and the course of nature.

We could conclude from Smith's quoting of this passage that we find ourselves in a hopeless situation. On the one hand, we cannot live in accordance with nature as a whole, for to do so is to abstract from moral considerations. On the other hand, we cannot live in accordance with nature as it shows itself to us in our individual lives, because our lives are so frequently dominated by a "course of nature" we are unwilling to accept and impotent to control or understand. We are left with the Bishop's rebuke to a God who would structure things thus; but a denunciation is not a philosophy of life or a comfort to the afflicted.

Let us back-track for a moment. Smith has made it clear that we need morality in order to protect us from nature; for without the moral sentiments we are reduced to cogs in that "machine of the world." And just as we need morality, so too does our survival depend on the intervention of *techne*, from the art of agriculture to the system of law to the intellectual artifact of political economy. Moral reason, intelligence, and in some instances theoretical reason are needed to guide human affairs. But further, Smith argues that these inventions are themselves natural developments, and thus stresses the beneficence of nature. We have not been abandoned by nature. This is so even where the aims dictated by human nature are simply not defensible on their own grounds or in comparison with what human experience teaches. The most striking case of this sort mentioned by Smith is nothing other than the pursuit of wealth, which he argues is fueled by a "deception" imposed on us by the imagination. We are profoundly deceived in our belief that by achieving wealth and therefore prestige, we will be happy. A simple trick of the imagination, in combination with the passions and what Smith calls "sympathy," are responsible for changing "the whole face of the globe" and completely shaping our individual lives, for thanks to it we force ourselves to work, create, compete, strive. This "deception" is in fact a good thing. "It is this deception which rouses and keeps in continual motion the industry of mankind" (IV.i.10). While each seeks to better his own condition, thanks to a mistaken view of what betterment amounts to, he labors ceaselessly, and unintentionally contributes to the mastery of nature, to the generation of increased supplies of food and material goods, and of course to the wealth of nations. But the wealth-lover does not achieve the happiness he desired; "the beggar, who suns himself by the side of the highway, possesses that security which kings are fighting for" (IV.i.10).

It is in this passage that the *TMS*' one reference to the "invisible hand" occurs. The metaphor is introduced as a way of explaining how the unequal accumulation of wealth in fact benefits the whole of society. Thus nature, precisely in its dividedness of whole from part, seems harmonized with itself. Not just our inability to live in accordance with a view of the whole, but both our inability to control the natural course of things and our illusions about how best to advance our individuals lives, are themselves conducive to the improvement of nature considered as a whole. As he says when considering the "irregularity" in our judgments of justice, "every part of nature, when attentively surveyed, equally demonstrates the providential care of its Author, and we may admire the wisdom and goodness of God even in the weakness and folly of man" (II.iii.3.2).[18] Nature's plan is being fulfilled even as we reject it. The conflict between the whole and part is not itself to be corrected; it may be lamented at a moral level but need not be at a theoretical level. It is a natural conflict that embodies an underlying harmony. *Sympatheia* governs the orders of nature. This resembles Smith's comment that a "fallacious sense of guilt . . . constitutes the whole distress of Oedipus and Jocasta upon the Greek, of Monimia and Isabella upon the English, theatre" (II.iii.3.5). The guilt is deeply felt, but "fallacious" because these characters are not responsible, and it is a good thing that we should be subject to this fallacious guilt. Similarly, the "world" (or "nature") is like a tragedy which has no tragic ending.

But this is spoken from the standpoint of the philosopher and does not obviate lament at the level of the actor. Smith seems to think that the lament itself becomes destructive, as it were, from the standpoint occupied by the "eloquent and philosophical" Bishop, and so ought not be brought to that level, and this is why immediately after quoting the good Bishop, Smith turns his back on him and continues, without any comment, to commend natural religion (as distinguished from philosophical religion) for supporting our "natural sense of duty" by reinforcing our trust that a wise Deity will reward the good and punish the wicked. Yet by quoting the Bishop, Smith shows that he understands the problem.

Theoretical reconciliation with nature, or the view that natural conflict embodies an underlying harmony, will be possible only when we understand that we are not to live in accordance with a synoptic perspective, that the natural course of things cannot be entirely mastered, that the deceptions of the imagination are not necessarily to be corrected. History is littered with misunderstandings of just these points, as Smith seeks to show not only in his treatment of Stoicism, but also in his discussions of, say, systems of political economy preceding his own. Hence not just any view or moral system people happen to hold is natural; and when it is not, our relationship to nature or human nature or both is conflict-ridden. It is here that a role for the philosopher shows itself. Philosophy will attempt to distinguish between unnatural and natural stances and conflict, and to guide us towards the later (by means of a book on the "wealth of nations," for example). One unnatural stance is that of a philosopher who intervenes in the wrong way in ordinary experience. Smith's insistence on this point makes his own moral philosophy seem not like a moral theory (i.e. a normative theory that postulates principles of action not already embodied in ordinary moral life) but a combination of phenomenology and metaphilosophy (that is, a view about what philosophy is and how it ought or ought not involve itself with practice). Similarly, moral reconciliation with nature will be possible only if "natural principles of religion" are not "corrupted by the factious and party zeal of some worthless cabal" (III.5.13). History is also littered with just such corruptions. Here too the philosopher can be of use in illustrating this point (by means of a book on the moral sentiments, for example).

But things are still more complicated; yet another figure must be extracted from that which we have been examining. For left to itself, nature seems to generate the unnatural – cabals, misplaced interventions by political utopians or misguided philosophers – and to fail in providing the antidote, viz. Smithean philosophers. Thus even if the philosopher succeeds in both cases, we are left with the disturbing suggestion that the need for the philosopher's intervention to help protect us either from misunderstanding nature's odd harmony or from corrupted moral sentiments testifies to the potential for a disharmony in nature that cannot itself be viewed, from either a theoretical or moral perspective, as a good thing. That is, the existence of the Smithean philosopher testifies to the need for what one might call an extra-natural human intervention in nature, like that of the "gods of the poets," as Smith says. This raises the possibility that since the human good does not seem in fact to be nature's principal object we need, as Mill remarked, not to imitate nature but to amend it.[19] Nature must be helped to be its harmonious self; which is precisely *not* to say, once again, that all corruptions or delusions or religion or self-love are to be extirpated and replaced by a Stoic "philosophy of life." Yet it *is* to say that at the end of the day, there does not exist some further, high altitude standpoint from which we can declare that nature is, after all, a harmonious whole. Conflict is natural to nature. The sheer contingency of the world, and the difficulty of introducing into it the harmony we so desire, only seems to make that harmony all the more important.

3. Harmony, beauty, and purposiveness

We can best pursue the connected issues of philosophy and nature by turning in a direction suggested by my use of the term "harmony," and by retracing our steps. For this and related notions are favorites of Smith. Beauty is in fact a pervasive theme in the *TMS*. The "fellow feeling with any passion whatever" that Smith terms "sympathy" (I.i.1.5) is a kind of "correspondence" of sentiments (I.i.2.2). We judge the "propriety" of the affections of others by means of their "concord" or "dissonance" with our own (I.i.3.1). "Propriety" is itself defined in terms of "proportion" (I.i.3.6), the moral beauty of which is judged in terms of its "harmony" with our sentiments. So that the agent's passions may "beat time" with the spectator's, the agent must adjust the "pitch," "flatten" the "natural tone," so as to obtain the "harmony and concord" with the spectator, that being sufficient for "the harmony of society" (I.i.4.7). From the start, Smith argues that we naturally take a disinterested pleasure in the situations of others and in a correspondence of our sentiments. Towards the end of the book, he remarks that the "great pleasure of conversation and society, besides, arises from a certain correspondence of sentiments and opinions, from a certain harmony of minds, which like so many musical instruments coincide and keep time with one another" (VII.iv.28). These musical metaphors pervade the book and express Smith's conviction that moral life is suffused with a spontaneous love of beauty.[20] From the first sentence of the book on, he attacks views that seek to interpret our approval of beauty or harmony in purely prudential terms. Correspondingly, he speaks of virtue as the "beautiful" (I.i.5.6) and of the "natural beauty of virtue" (VII.ii.2.13), of passions as "graceful" or their contrary (I.ii.intro.2), of the beauty that self-command has over and above its utility (VI.iii.4), of the "beauty of conduct" (V.2.1). He presents moral education as a process by which we come to see, step by step, what this beauty or harmony consist in. The "wise and virtuous man" is even "more deeply enamoured" of the "exquisite and divine beauty" of a high standard for human perfection, and in perfecting himself accordingly "he imitates the work of a divine artist" (VI.iii.25).

Smith's encomium to the force of beauty in human life goes considerably further. The word "beauty" appears in two chapter headings in Part IV of the book, this being literally the center of the *TMS*. This is the context in which the reference to the "invisible hand" occurs. Smith first argues that it is not the utility of "any production of art," that is, not the end for which that production is designed, that bestows beauty on them. We simply find immensely attractive objects that are ordered or finely made or exactly crafted, regardless of whether these properties allow them better to fulfill their goal (one of Smith's examples is that of a watch, but he also mentions palaces, gardens, clothes, "the retinue of the great," or even a room in which the furniture is well ordered). As in the case of the "harmony" of moral sentiments, we take disinterested pleasure in the purposeless purposiveness of things and, naturally, want to possess them.

Further, we imagine that in possessing them we would find "happiness and tranquillity," in part because we are aware that others will admire the possessor of these "trinkets of frivolous utility" (a phrase Smith uses twice here; IV. 1.6, 8). The admiration of spectators is itself a result, in part, of their aesthetic appreciation of the beauty or artfulness of the objects possessed by the rich (IV.1.8). Unless one is born rich, acquiring these objects entails "unrelenting industry." Thus our love of beautiful things conspires with our passion to be esteemed by others, as well as with our association of happiness with the possession of intrinsically satisfying things, to keep "in continual motion the industry of mankind" (IV.1.10). It is this imagined association of happiness or tranquillity with the "oeconomy of the great" that is the "deception" of nature I discussed above.

This striking account of wealth-getting is followed by still other observations of the influence of "the same principle, the same love of system, the same regard to the beauty of order, of art and contrivance." Smith singles out the effect of this love of beauty on public spiritedness, and argues that public benefactors (including legislatures) are often inspired not so much by sympathy with those in need of help, as the pleasing "contemplation" of so "beautiful and grand a system" of law or a constitution or economic measures. And thus public spiritedness may be improved by the "study of politics," i.e., "works of speculation" that exhibit the beauty of ordered complexity (IV.1.11). Heroic self-sacrifice may also be inspired by the "unexpected, and on that account the great, the noble, and exalted propriety of such actions" (IV.2.11). Thus the love of beauty has not only crucial moral and economic consequences, it also has decisive political consequences, though the point in each case is that we do not espouse beauty for the sake of their utility.

Smith takes all this one step further, noting that works in the "abstruser sciences" such as mathematics, also earn our admiration on account not only of their utility but of their exactitude, orderliness, and the like (IV.2.7). In his essays on the history of astronomy and of physics, Smith develops at some length the notion that good "philosophy" (in a sense broad enough to include what we call "science") grips us because of the elegance, conceptual fineness, systematic arrangement, and capacity to explain much on the basis of few principles. Theoretical intelligence too is attracted by the beauty of the "machine," regardless of its external purpose; and nature is one such machine or system, human nature another.

In his "Of the Nature of that Imitation which Takes Place in What are Called the Imitative Arts," an essay published posthumously, and apparently forming part of the projected "Philosophical History of the Liberal and Elegant Arts," the musical analogy reappears. Smith describes the "perfect concord or correspondence" of all the various instruments in a "well-composed concerto of instrumental Music," the "exact harmony" of all the sounds, the "happy variety of measure," such that "in the contemplation of that immense variety of agreeable and melodious sounds, arranged and digested, both in their coincidence and in their succession, into so complete and regular a system, the mind in reality enjoys not only a very great sensual, but a very high intellectual, pleasure, not unlike that which it derives from the contemplation of a great system in any other science."[21] This sort of "system" nicely describes the unity of the *TMS*, as well as that of the *WN*.[22] In other words, in contemplating the vast system of nature as though it were a well-composed concerto, the theorist imagines not the utility of the system for some further purpose, but rather enjoys the incredibly intricate internal order of the system. This is, in effect, what Smith thinks the Stoic philosopher does. Smith of course does so as well, and as I have noted often speaks in the voice of the synoptic philosopher who observes the perfect proportion nature has created between means and ends.

The much debated issue of "teleology" in Smith's philosophy should be seen in light of his account of our drive for a picture of the whole as harmonious, and his account of the beautiful as that which inspires human endeavor at all levels and thus as that which makes anything like "utility" possible. Teleology, understood as the doctrine of an ordered Nature or World, is here parasitic on an aesthetics, and not on some independent religious faith of Smith's or on an argument from design whose fallacies Smith had already learned from Hume. Teleology is not a description of how the world is, but a postulation of the harmony we yearn for it to have. It is therefore a sort of regulative ideal, and at the level of the theorist's demand for system, it does work. The doctrine of nature's unity is formulated at various levels, as is appropriate to the rhetorical voice Smith wishes to adopt. At times he speaks in a relatively conventional way of God's purposes; at other times, in a somewhat unconventional way about an "invisible hand" and nature's conflictual harmony; and at still other times, as in the essay on the history of astronomy, in a quite unconventional way about all "systems" as "inventions of the imagination" (below). All stem from Smith's teaching about nature and the beautiful, and all are themselves attempts to beautify.

In sum, we seem presented with a vision of one aesthetically pleasing order nested in another, from the harmony of moral sentiments on some particular occasion all the way up to the harmony of the parts of the universe as articulated in an elegant account of nature. The account sounds thoroughly Platonic, with Beauty serving as a continuous ladder from the sensual to the most abstract and philosophical. The natural whole is perfectly ordered, and even seeming disruptions of the sort articulated by the Bishop of Clermont are themselves part of the cosmic order.

Once again things are more complicated, however, for Smith's aesthetics is profoundly anti-Platonic, and in a way that does not seem to support the doctrine of a perfectly ordered natural whole. Beauty is both enlightening and deceiving on Smith's account, and this is so at all levels. At the level of sympathy, the "correspondence of sentiments" may lead to a mutually reinforcing system of vanity, and this too figures into our pursuit of wealth; "it is because mankind are disposed to sympathize more entirely with our joy than with our sorrow, that we make parade of our riches, and conceal our poverty" (I.iii.2.1). Our disposition sympathize with the "passions of the rich and the powerful" is the basis for our acceptance of social inequalities, and of this Smith remarks: "That kings are the servants of the people, to be obeyed, resisted, deposed, or punished, as the public conveniency may require, is the doctrine of reason and philosophy; but it is not the doctrine of Nature" (I.iii.2.3). While under the right conditions this "deception" is useful, Smith also terms it "the great and most universal cause of the corruption of our moral sentiments" (I.iii.3.1). For it leads us, as moralists have always complained, away from the path of virtue; to value appearances more than reality, the applause of the mob rather than real worth; and it leads us to corrupting ambition. Unchecked, nature seems to turn beauty into glamor, and thence to moral decay.

Similarly, that love of beauty that animates public spiritedness also animates political fanaticism, and Smith concludes his discussion of public spiritedness with a remarkable commentary on the "man of system" who is "so enamoured with the supposed beauty of his own ideal plan of government" that he is led to treat people entirely without sympathy, as though they were "pieces upon a chess-board" (VI.ii.2.17). Intoxicated rulers are certain "of the immense superiority of their own judgment"; drunk with beauty and sense of self, they are inhumane without even entertaining any overtly tyrannical thoughts (VI.ii.2.18). While Smith does not make this explicit, we may detect the same pattern in his account of religious fanatics, whose "false notions of religion" cause a "perversion of our natural sentiments." For their commendable drive for moral perfection leads to "erroneous conscience" – the insistence that every aspect of human life be regulated by a detailed system of duties or rules and not by sympathy and the moral sentiments (III.6.12). There is beauty and authority in such a system; but also fanaticism, inhumanity, and ugliness. Like the intoxication with system of the "political speculators," here too the love of beauty ignores the humanity of those we would perfect.

We have already seen, finally, that Smith thinks synoptic philosophizing also connected to the attraction of beauty, elegance, conceptual harmony, and how in ethics this tends to extinguish the very moral qualities it seeks to elucidate. In other ways I have not explored, Smith detects a distorting effect of the philosopher's love of system, as when he discusses the propensity of philosophers to account for the phenomena from as few principles as possible rather than being guided by the phenomena themselves (VII.ii.2.14). Thus here too, beauty is in one sense good but in another bad; it both reveals and conceals. Not only is beauty at each level both good and bad, the various levels either are not connected to each other by a continuous line, or where they are the connection is undesirable and conflictual. Smith presents us with no dialectical ascent from the ordinary yearning for sympathy to the philosopher's yearning for systematic explanation. As already noted, he does see a natural – or is it unnatural? – development of our need to observe ourselves from an impartial standpoint into the Stoic's demand that we view ourselves as mere parts of a vast universe; but this is a development to be resisted. Beauty is an unreliable, though indispensable, guide at any level.

The moral ambiguity of beauty, and the conflict among levels of beauty, recapitulates the problem of the unity of nature as a whole, though at first it seemed to promise a solution. The hostility of nature to humans seems reiterated even as nature offers the beauty of harmony at all levels. But there is a further step in this dialectic that remains to be taken, and it will bring us to what is perhaps the bedrock of his view of the matter. For Smith's aesthetics is rooted in a teaching about the imagination, and it is this to which we next turn. In the concluding section of this paper, the anti-Platonic dimension of Smith's teaching will become further visible as the combination of the precariousness of our mastery of nature, the fragility of beauty created by the imagination, and the ambiguity or power of the imagination, crystallizes.

4. Imagination, poiesis, and power

Some of the levels of beauty or harmony I have mentioned define our moral lives, and thus are central to what Smith calls "sympathy," which itself is a particular power of the imagination. It is that which allows us "fellow-feeling with any passion whatever" (I.i.1.5). Moral reflection on self is an exercise in a peculiar turn of the sympathetic imagination, thanks to which we see ourselves through the eyes of another (sometimes an imagined spectator not any actual one). Theorizing, whether about moral philosophy or a system of religious duties or in astronomy, is also a function of the imagination for Smith. By contrast with empathetic imagining, however, theoretical imagining does not require us to put ourselves in the situation of another human being, to grasp the passions that move him or her. Thus Smith argues at the start of the book that we have no "sympathy" with ideas or with the people thinking them; we either agree or disagree with them, but are not interested in them in the way we are in the emotions of others as well as moral evaluations thereof. We have no "sympathy" with the passion for knowledge because, on Smith's account, there is no such passion. Thus morality is not primarily a philosophical, theological, or scientific matter; and these intellectual pursuits are not primarily ethical. The detachment of intelligence from sympathy reveals the separation of the beautiful from the good, or perhaps we should say that it reveals the internal dividedness of the beautiful.

While sympathy and reason are distinct for Smith, both are also functions of the imagination. Smith makes it abundantly clear that the beauty apprehended by the imagination at the various levels I have discussed is not a passive assimilation of pre-existing form. The imagination is fundamentally creative or poetic. As Smith says at the conclusion of his grand narrative on the history of astronomy, "we have been endeavouring to represent all philosophical systems as mere inventions of the imagination."[23] The very notion of nature as a "machine" is an imaginative metaphor and led, on Smith's account, to the postulation of a Designer of the machine; thus nature imitates art.[24] That Smith should use a humanly created artifact – the machine – as the paradigm for unity natural or otherwise, rather than some organic whole, is itself indicative of the drift of his account.[25] Unity is an artifice. It is the demand of the imagination for order, harmony, in short for tranquillity, that drives our desire for both "correspondence of sentiments" and intellectual coherence.[26] But since unity and system are presented to us by the imagination's restless drive for order, we may say that for Smith the "world," as a unified "system," is given to us by our own imaginations. Thus all of the talk in the *TMS* about nature *as a whole* is itself an "invention of the imagination," and the Stoical view of self from the standpoint of the whole is, just as in the case of the view of self from the standpoint of an imagined impartial spectator, a sort of self-characterization within an imagined frame of reference. Underlying Smith's teaching about both practice and theory is a doctrine of the imagination as poetic, and thus of the limits of reason; for creativity stems from the imagination. Implicit in Smith's philosophy is thus a decisive turn in the history of "nature."[27]

Smith grants that at both moral and theoretical levels, the "inventions of the imagination" do not *feel* like inventions, especially when those inventions succeed in their task.[28] No doubt he believes that deception all to the better, as my remarks in the preceding section would suggest. But as a philosopher he recognizes that the inventions of the imagination, including moral ones, are just that – inventions. The imagination beautifies even its own work as it undertakes it. We saw something similar in Smith's account of the passion for wealth and power, a passion fueled in part by a "deception of the imagination" which only a philosopher sees to be a deception but which a Smithean philosopher thinks is a good deception. Our moral faculties "were given us for the direction of our conduct in this life. They carry along with them the most evident badges of this authority" (III.5.5). This is natural in the sense that they are not designed; thus nature is once again friendly to our illusions, within limits, though when we confront it without blinkers it seems hostile as well. The beautiful and the good, as I have remarked, are split from one another for Smith.

Smith's "poetic" aesthetics ultimately turns the imagination into poet; we might say that it is premised on the failure of the Platonic view that beauty is apprehended by reason, and so that nature is intrinsically beautiful.[29] We have listened to Smith say that "like the gods of the poets, he [man] is perpetually interposing, by extraordinary means, in favour of virtue" (III.5.10); and of the moral agent seeking perfection that "he imitates the work of a divine artist" (VI.iii.25). Nature, including human nature, is beautified by the imagination. Where does this leave us, then, with respect to nature?

We could conclude that nature is in itself indeterminate, neutral – a machine whose engine we may admire in a detached aesthetic way but whose purpose eludes us. Everything will depend on how we receive this rather frightening fact, and thus in part on the level and sort of spectating we adopt. Nature qua "essence" or "form" or as representative of "God's will" is not at stake for Smith; as already mentioned, he has dropped all such notions. Nature impresses itself upon us, it is that which is given and unavoidable, yet given in this strangely amorphous manner. To change metaphors, is rather like a force in the dark that we bump into; perhaps like the contours of a Platonic cave in which the fire has dimmed. The basic indifference of nature to us, so eloquently complained of by the Bishop of Clermont, consists in part in the irreducible divergence between what we picture as the harmony of the whole and the good of a part of the whole; in part in the unreliability of harmony at any level for the conduct of human life; and finally in nature's sheer opaqueness and contingency.

And yet nature also seems good in that it provides us with the ability to beautify it – in Descartes' oxymoronic simile, to open the windows so as to let some light into the cave, presumably so that we might better see and shape the pictures we have projected on the wall.[30] Smith's analysis of the synthetic role of beauty in our lives, that is, of the imagination's power to draw us to its harmonies, is also an account of our potential for defining nature, even if as a "system" or "machine." And this amounts to a potential for exercising power, for self-assertion in the face of an indifferent or hostile nature. This holds true at all the levels Smith's aesthetics touches, from our capacity to form social wholes and the "correspondence of sentiments," to our love of persuasion and thus of bartering and selling, to our drive to better ourselves through the creation of wealth and the mastery of physical nature, to our ability to examine ourselves through the eyes of an imagined impartial spectator, and finally to our ability to improve nature whether through scientific systems or poems. At all levels, our instinctual love of beauty can enlighten nature and improve it. But in every such case, it is we who enlighten ourselves. It may also lead to darkness; the ambiguous goodness of beauty itself stems from the imagination, whose power is thus itself morally ambiguous.

I have noted that Smith is fond of using the metaphor of the "machine" to characterize explanatory systems of thought whether religious or scientific. A machine is designed to accomplish a certain end, of course, whether it is the production of pins (*WN* I.i.3) or the explanation of the movements of the celestial bodies. It is a means to *production*, and thus captures the fundamentally poetic nature of the imagination. It is also an artificial thing invented by us for the satisfaction of our desires and, often, for the manipulation of external nature. In seeing varying sorts of organization as "machines," Smith points to the fundamentally "creative" nature of the human animal, even as he observes that we naturally deploy this machinery not for prudential reasons but because we find order and harmony immensely attractive. Production is the medium from which theory and practice both arise. I am suggesting that the pleasure of apprehending beauty is connected to the fact that the beauty is an exhibition of our own power and thus our freedom. This is the core of his teaching that beauty is prior to utility; the former, not the latter, attracts and empowers. Thus Smith does not write the *Wealth of Nations* primarily in order to make the world safe for the peaceful and cooperative pursuit of the demotic virtues and the accumulation of wealth. His new political economy demonstrates, as well, his own attachment to an exceptionally beautiful intellectual machine, a machine that articulates the beauty of the spontaneous order of the free market.

Nature is ordered by spectatorship inspired by beauty; beauty is ordered by imagination seeking tranquillity or equipoise; and that tranquillity embodies the ideal of self-empowerment. This "aesthetic" view of nature embodies the eclipse of reason by imagination, as well as the doctrine that we are active rather than rational beings.[31] It is also congruent with the split between theory and practice that pervades Smith's thought. Knowledge is power, so long as power is understood in its full moral and aesthetic dimensions, and acknowledges its own finitude. This ideal of self-empowerment is embedded in the "ethical" vision at the heart of Smith's philosophy and, in spite of all his criticisms of Stoicism, one still detects in it the Stoic themes of independence, freedom, and autonomy. This "ethical" vision underlying Smith's philosophy resonates with the passages quoted above in which Smith expresses his deep admiration of the well composed concerto, and helps explain why he commends pure instrumental music for not being "imitative" or a "copy" of anything. Since this system is not a copy, it is not measured by some standard independent of our own imaginations. Through this music whose "meaning, therefore, may be said to be complete in itself,"[32] we entertain ourselves with our own creation, and in doing so demonstrate our mastery. Smith writes that "No action can properly be called virtuous, which is not accompanied with the sentiment of self-approbation" (III.6.13). A theorist who could compose a comprehensive musical system would feel himself worthy of the highest self-approbation, for then "he imitates the work of a divine artist" (VI.iii.25). The *TMS* and *WN* are not imitations, but protreptic paradigms intended to help equilibrium establish itself.

Why does this not lead to a collapse of the polyphony created by a "system of natural liberty" into the monotone of a philosophical system? Not just any sense of self-empowering will do, not just any notion of beauty or imagining. To return again to Smith's paradigm of connectedness, the metaphor of the well-composed concerto: we ought not compose a system that reduces harmonies to monotones, or forces one instrument to play the sounds of another, or suppresses the demonstration of passion and the illusion of spontaneity, or pretends that the beauty can be appreciated without being heard and thus without the concerto being performed. The musical metaphor underlines the importance of our sensitivity to particulars, as well as the critical role of the sentiments in appreciating the production. Smith sees that the hybris implied in imitating the work of a divine artist must be appropriately moderated if it is to succeed, and be sensitive to the particulars and the context, and be accepting of each for what it can contribute. Recall Smith's powerful criticism of the misplaced love of system or beauty that would lead us to treat our fellows as "pieces upon a chess-board," as though each lacked "a principle of motion of its own" (VI.ii.2.17). Human society, Smith adds, "will go on easily and harmoniously" only if this is kept in mind. A philosophy of music does not replace music. They move in distinct spheres. This split between theory and practice, or on the one hand philosophy and Stoicism and on the other action and sentiment, is the basis for Smith's Enlightenment Liberalism in the economic and political spheres.

The complexity of Smith's thought derives in part from his recognition that we cannot just live against nature; nor live in accordance with nature without beautifying it; nor live without conflict if we beautify it in the wrong way; nor live happily if we beautify it knowing we are doing so. To do any of these is to live unnaturally. Smith's strikingly subtle and dialectical rhetoric is a function of the complex balancing act required of someone maintaining all of these propositions. By virtue of his attempt to maintain all these propositions, Smith occupies a defining moment in the history of "nature." In his constant use of the term, his reliance on prephilosophical experience and opinion, his speculations about the whole and our place in it, and his insistent attention to the problem of the relation between philosophy and ordinary life, Smith sounds much like a partisan of the ancients. But in his rejection of "metaphysical" notions of nature as "essence" or "form," as well as of teleology understood as the doctrine of the perfection of an entity, and in his gradual subordination of both theory and practice to an aesthetics based on the "poetic" imagination, he takes a distinctively modern turn. The persuasiveness and elegance of his writing beautifies both human nature and the whole, while at every turn embodying as well as praising a moderation that conceals the radicalness of his project. Smith's remarkable synthesis is testimony to the madness of an imaginative and philosophical nature aware of the limits that imagination and philosophy ought not transgress.

Acknowledgements

I am grateful to Klaus Brinkmann, Doug Den Uyl, Knud Haakonssen, David Roochnik, and this journal's anonymous reviewer for their comments on earlier drafts. This essay is drawn from chapter 5 of a forthcoming book on Smith's philosophy tentatively entitled *Philosophy, Virtue, and Enlighten-*

ment: a Study of Adam Smith's Thought. My thanks to the Earhart Foundation, National Endowment for the Humanities, and Woodrow Wilson International Center for Scholars, for their support of my work on various phases of the book.

Notes

1. *The Praise of Folly*, trans. C.H. Miller (New Haven: Yale University Press, 1979), pp. 42–43.
2. For an excellent discussion of the role of "nature" in ancient ethical theory see J. Annas' *The Morality of Happiness* (Oxford: Oxford University Press, 1993), ch. 2.
3. See Basil Willey's *The Eighteenth Century Background: Studies on the Idea of Nature in the Thought of the Period* (London: Chatto and Windus, 1940).
4. Letter of Sept. 17, 1739, quoted in D. F. Norton's *David Hume: Common-Sense Moralist, Sceptical Metaphysician* (Princeton: Princeton University Press, 1982), p. 3. In the *Treatise* III.i.2, ii.1, Hume discusses the different senses of the word. The problem of the relevance and sense of "nature," that is, was well established by the time Smith wrote the *TMS*.
5. Trans. N. K. Smith (New York: St. Martin's Press, 1965).
6. H. Sidgwick, *The Methods of Ethics*, 7th ed. (Indianapolis: Hackett, 1981), bk, I, ch. VI.2. Sidgwick sees appeals to nature as a way of moving from 'what is' to 'what ought to be,' and thinks that move impossible (p. 81). He concludes "On the whole, it appears to me that no definition that has ever been offered of the Natural exhibits this notion as really capable of furnishing an independent ethical first principle" (p. 83). Sidgwick attacks the Stoic dictum that we are to 'live according to nature' in bk III, ch. XIII.2 on the grounds that it is both circular and vacuous. The reference to Mill is to his essay "Nature" (published in 1874), reprinted in *John Stuart Mill: Nature and Utility of Religion*, ed. G. Nakhnikian (Indianapolis: Bobbs-Merrill, 1958), pp. 3–44.
7. For the references see Annas' *Morality*, pp. 137–141.
8. An example of the former may be found in J. Finnis' *Natural Law and Natural Rights* (Oxford: Oxford University Press, 1980). The quoted phrase has a variety of meanings. Some versions, such as that of A. Gibbard's *Wise Choices, Apt Feelings* (Cambridge: Harvard University Press, 1990), resurrect parts of a Smithean perspective within a "naturalized" framework. S. Hampshire remarks in *Two Theories of Morality* (Oxford: Oxford University Press, 1977), p. 54: "By naturalism I here mean the habit of representing judgements about the moral strengths and defects of persons as resembling in most respects judgements about the physical strengths and defects of persons, and of representing virtue as an excellent state of the soul or mind, and vice as a diseased state of the soul or mind, manifested in action, just as health is an excellent state of the body." This is a more classical, Aristotelian view of naturalism.
9. I advert to the Liberty Classics edition of the *Wealth of Nations*, ed. R. H. Campbell, A. S. Skinner, W. B. Todd, 2 vols. (Indianapolis: Liberty Press, 1981). Hereafter referred to as *WN*.
10. *The Theory of Moral Sentiments* (Indianapolis: Liberty Press, 1982), ed. A. L. Macfie and D. D. Raphael, VII.i.1. Hereafter referred to as *TMS*. Unless otherwise noted, all page references in the body of my essay advert to the *TMS*.
11. The sense of the term "nature" I will focus on is the central theme of E. Kohák's *The Embers and the Stars: a Philosophical Inquiry into the Moral Sense of Nature* (Chicago: University of Chicago Press, 1987): "By 'nature' in a similarly generic sense we shall mean the nature presented in lived experience, the primordially given cosmic context in which humans find themselves and to which they themselves belong in their bodies and

minds. . . . What is at issue between naturalism so conceived and its denial is not the nature of 'nature' but rather the place of the human in the cosmos . . ." (p. 8).

12. The "dialogical" or "rhetorical" dimension of Smith's writing is discussed in my "Rhetoric and Ethics: Adam Smith on Theorizing about the Moral Sentiments," in *Philosophy and Rhetoric* 24 (1991): 213–237.
13. I will not be discussing here whether or not Smith's interpretation of the Stoics is in fact accurate. He focuses mainly upon Epictetus and Marcus Aurelius, and to a much lesser extent Cicero and Seneca, and then in a rather selective way. He ignores Stoic logic, metaphysics, and epistemology, concentrating on what he takes to be its moral philosophy.
14. At III.5.7 Smith writes: "The happiness of mankind, as well as of all other rational creatures, seems to have been the original purpose intended by the Author of nature, when he brought them into existence. No other end seems worthy of that supreme wisdom and diving benignity which we necessarily ascribe to him; and this opinion, which we are led to by the abstract consideration of his infinite perfections, is still more confirmed by the examination of the works of nature, which seem all intended to promote happiness, and to guard against misery. But by acting according to the dictates of our moral faculties, we necessarily pursue the most effectual means for promoting the happiness of mankind, and may therefore be said, in some sense, to co-operate with the Deity, and to advance as far as in our power the plan of Providence." Shortly after this pronouncement, however, Smith observes that natural sentiments often reject the "natural course of things," and then provides us with the quotation from the Bishop of Clermont (discussed below) that calls into question the sunny optimism of the statement just quoted.
15. The reference is to Smith's discussion of familial affection, in which he notes that "the sense of propriety," far from requiring us to approve of a person who feels nothing, say, for his own children, leads us to blame his lack of that "extraordinary sensibility." He adds: "The stoical apathy is, in such cases, never agreeable," and that the "poets and romance writers" – he names Racine, Voltaire, Richardson, Marivaux, and Riccoboni – are "better instructors than Zeno, Chrysippus, or Epictetus" (III.3.14). For an excellent recent discussion of the differences between the standpoints of the moral actor and philosopher, a discussion particularly apposite to my remarks about Smith and Stoicism, see B. Williams' "The Point of View of the Universe: Sidgwick and the Ambitions of Ethics," in *Making Sense of Humanity* (Cambridge: Cambridge University Press, 1995), pp. 153–171.
16. We are reminded of Nietzsche's comment: "'According to nature' you want to *live*? O you noble Stoics, what deceptive words these are! Imagine a being like nature, wasteful beyond measure, indifferent beyond measure, without purposes and consideration, without mercy and justice, fertile and desolate and uncertain at the same time; imagine indifference itself as a power – how *could* you live according to this indifference? Living – is that not precisely wanting to be other than this nature?" *Beyond Good and Evil*, trans. W. Kaufmann (New York: Vintage Books, 1966), sec. 9, p. 15.
17. The translation is in *The Meditations of the Emperor Marcus Aurelius Antoninus. Newly translated from the Greek: with Notes, and an Account of his Life* (Glasgow: R. Foulis, 1742). The names of the translators (the Introduction to the book refers to "the authors of this translation") are not printed on the title page; but a letter from Francis Hutcheson (May 31, 1742) indicates that he and James Moor (eventually a holder of the Chair of Greek at Glasgow University) are the translators. For the letter see J. Bonar's *A Catalogue of the Library of Adam Smith*, 2nd ed. (rpt. New York: A. M. Kelley, 1966), pp. 13–14.
18. Much later in the book, Smith uses the same phrase when again discussing the influence of fortune on our moral judgments: "This great disorder in our moral sentiments is by no means, however, without its utility; and we may on this, as well as on many other occasions, admire the wisdom of God even in the weakness and folly of man" (VI.iii.30).
19. "The scheme of nature regarded in its whole extent cannot have had, for its sole or even principal object, the good of human or other sentient beings. What good it brings to them, is mostly the result of their own exertions. Whatsoever in nature gives indication of beneficent design proves this beneficence to be armed only with limited power; and

the duty of man is to co-operate with the beneficent powers, not by imitating but by perpetually striving to amend the course of nature – and bringing that part of it over which we can exercise control, more nearly into conformity with a high standard of justice and goodness." J. S. Mill's "Nature," in *John Stuart Mill: Nature and Utility of Religion*, p. 44.

20. Smith is of course picking up an old theme in the Scottish Enlightenment. Cf. Shaftesbury's *Advice to an Author*: "For harmony is harmony by nature, let men judge ever so ridiculously of music. So is symmetry and proportion founded still in nature, let men's fancy prove ever so barbarous, or their fashions ever so Gothic in the architecture, sculpture, or whatever other designing art. 'Tis the same case where life and manners are concerned. Virtue has the same fixed standard. The same numbers, harmony, and proportion will have place in morals, and are discoverable in the characters and affections of mankind; in which are laid the just foundations of an art and science superior to every other of human practice and comprehension. . . . For Nature will not be mocked. The prepossession against her can never be very lasting. Her decrees and instincts are powerful and her sentiments inbred." In *Characteristics of Men, Manners, Opinions, Times*, ed. J. M. Robertson (rpt. Indianapolis: Bobbs-Merrill Company, Inc., 1964), pp. 227–228.

21. "Of the Nature of that Imitation which Takes Place in What are Called the Imitative Arts," in Smith's *Essays on Philosophical Subjects* (hereafter abbreviated *EPS*) II.30, ed. W.P.D. Wightman and J.C. Bryce (Indianapolis: Liberty Classics, 1982), pp. 204–205.

22. In the paragraph preceding the lines quoted, Smith remarks "Time and measure are to instrumental Music what order and method are to discourse. . . . By means of this order and method it [our aesthetic enjoyment] is, during the progress of the entertainment, equal to the effect of all that we remember, and of all that we foresee; and at the conclusion, to the combined and accumulated effect of all the different parts of which the whole was composed" (*EPS* II.29).

23. "History of Astronomy" IV.76, in *EPS*, p. 105.

24. "History of Astronomy" IV.19, in *EPS* p. 66: intellectual "systems in many respects resemble machines. . . . A system is an imaginary machine." Also "History of Ancient Physics" 9, in *EPS* pp. 113–114: "As soon as the Universe was regarded as a complete machine, as a coherent system, governed by general laws, and directed to general ends, viz. its own preservation and prosperity, and that of all the species that are in it; the resemblance which it evidently bore to those machines which are produced by human art, necessarily impressed those sages with a belief, that in the original formation of the world there must have been employed an art resembling the human art. . . . The unity of the system. . . . suggested the idea of the unity of that principle, by whose art it was formed; and thus, as ignorance begot superstition, science gave birth to the first theism. . . ."

25. While Smith very often uses this metaphor, in one place he uses an organic metaphor. I refer to *WN* IV.ix.28, where he compares the ability of the "political body" to withstand the false prescriptions of political economists to that of the human body to withstand bad medicine. This fortunate fact is attributed to the "wisdom of nature." Cf. *TMS* VII.iii.1.2: "Human society, when we contemplate it in a certain abstract and philosophical light, appears like a great, an immense machine, whose regular and harmonious movements produce a thousand agreeable effects."

26. "History of Astronomy" IV.13, in *EPS* p. 61: Smith seeks to show that ". . . the repose and tranquillity of the imagination is the ultimate end of philosophy . . .," while wonder and perplexity provoke philosophy (a term that here includes science). At I.i.4.2 Smith refers to "the various appearances which the great machine of the universe is perpetually exhibiting, with the secret wheels and springs which produce them."

27. Smith's philosophy thus confirms D. Lachterman's thesis that "the 'idea' giving significant shape to the 'constellation' of themes ingredient in modernity, *in both its revolutionary and projective modes*, is the 'idea' of construction or, more broadly, the 'idea' of the *mind* as essentially the power of making, fashioning, crafting, producing, in short, the mind as first and last *poietic* and only secondarily or subsidiarily *practical* and *theoretical* . . .

making is *definitive* of the mind's 'nature' or better of its comportment in and toward the 'world'." *The Ethics of Geometry* (New York: Routledge, 1989), p. 4.

28. Smith concludes the "History of Astronomy" with the remarkable statement: "His [Newton's] principles, it must be acknowledged, have a degree of firmness and solidity that we should in vain look for in any other system. The most sceptical cannot avoid feeling this. . . . And even we, while we have been endeavouring to represent all philosophical systems as mere inventions of the imagination, to connect together the otherwise disjointed and discordant phaenomena of nature, have insensibly been drawn in, to make use of language expressing the connecting principles of this one [Newton's], as if they were the real chains which Nature makes use of to bring together her several operations." IV.76, in *EPS* pp. 104–105.
29. For further discussion of Smith's differences with Plato, see C. Griswold and D. Den Uyl's "Adam Smith on Friendship and Love," *Review of Metaphysics* 49.3 (1996): 609–637.
30. See Part VI of the *Discourse on the Method of Rightly Conducting the Reason and Seeking for Truth in the Sciences*, in *The Philosophical Works of Descartes*, ed. E. S. Haldane and G.R.T. Ross, vol. 1 (Cambridge: Cambridge University Press, 1972), p. 125.
31. Smith remarks that "Man was made for action, and to promote by the exertion of his faculties such changes in the external circumstances both of himself and others, as may seem most favourable to the happiness of all" (II.iii.3.3). Smith has nothing but contempt for systems of virtue produced by "monks and friars," systems which value "the futile mortifications of a monastery, to the ennobling hardships and hazards of war" and to the contributions of "all the heroes, all the statesmen and lawgivers, all the poets and philosophers of former ages; all those who have invented, improved, or excelled in the arts . . . all the great protectors, instructors, and benefactors of mankind" (III.2.35).
32. I quote from "Of the Imitative Arts" II.30, in *EPS* p. 205.

[3]

The Commerce of Sympathy: Adam Smith on the Emergence of Morals

EUGENE HEATH

IN RECENT YEARS, there have been several attempts to show how normative constraints can function so as to counteract the effects of limited altruism, self-defeating rationality, and scarce resources. In some accounts the discussion also focuses on whether or how norms could evolve without a centralized agency to implement them.[1] Although this aspect of the discussion usually takes place within the contemporary confines of game theory, the issue itself has an intellectual pedigree extending back to the seventeenth- and eighteenth-centuries. In one form or another, the English Common Lawyers, Bernard Mandeville, David Hume, and Adam Smith, postulate the gradual evolution of social and moral practices. Of the eighteenth-century moral thinkers, Smith adumbrates the most explicit and complex theory of the evolution of moral conduct.

In *The Theory of Moral Sentiments*,[2] Smith not only delineates a normative ethical theory but also proffers a descriptive psychology to account for the origins of our patterns of moral behavior.[3] Like twentieth-century game theore-

[1] Russell Hardin, *Collective Action* (Baltimore: Johns Hopkins, 1982); Robert Sugden, *The Economics of Rights, Co-operation, and Welfare* (Oxford: Blackwell, 1986); Edna Ullmann-Margalit, *The Emergence of Norms* (Oxford: Clarendon, 1977); and Viktor Vanberg, "Spontaneous Market and Social Rules: A Critical Examination of F. A. Hayek's Theory of Cultural Evolution," *Economics and Philosophy* 2 (1986): 75–100. See also the earlier work by David Lewis, *Convention* (Cambridge, Mass.: Harvard, 1969), 83–121.

[2] Citations from the *Moral Sentiments* will be indicated in the text using the paragraph numbers from the following edition: *The Theory of Moral Sentiments*, ed. D. D. Raphael and A. L. Macfie (Oxford: Oxford, 1976).

[3] Occupying much of his attention, the latter inquiry leads Smith to exclaim at one point: "the present inquiry is not concerning a matter of right . . . but concerning a matter of fact. We are not at present examining upon what principles a perfect being would approve of the punishment of bad actions; but upon what principles so weak and imperfect a creature as man actually and in fact approves of it" (II.i.5.10). One might also consider Smith's distinction, in *The Wealth of Nations*,

ticians, Smith endeavors to discover whether a common set of other-regarding principles can arise out of a situation in which individuals—motivated only by self-interest and limited benevolence—are not constrained by moral demands. In order to provide a motive by which individuals will arrive at an interindividual agreement on standards of moral approval, Smith appeals to the pleasure which accrues to each individual whose sentiments correspond to (or are similar to) those of another individual. This correspondence of sentiments is what Smith refers to as "sympathy."[4] Together the capacity for sympathy and the ability to place oneself imaginatively in the situation of another function in such a way that "even the ordinary commerce of the world is capable of adjusting our active principles to some degree of propriety" (III.3.7).[5]

Although some of the ablest commentators recognize that Smith has a theory of the emergence of morals,[6] there has been no attempt to elucidate the difficulties inherent in the psychology which Smith employs to account for the emergence of a uniform standard for moral judgments. I hope to show how this psychology leaves underdetermined the conditions by which such a uniform agreement could emerge. In the first place, although Smith's account hinges on the pleasurable emotion of sympathy, such sympathy is pleasurable only under certain conditions. Moreover, even if pleasure did arise from every act of sympathy, it is not obvious that sympathetic pleasure is a sufficient motive for engaging the sympathetic imagination. Finally, even when a spectator engages the sympathetic imagination the pleasure of sympathy may not be strong enough to motivate the spectator to assume imaginatively whatever facts or values are necessary to achieve sympathy. Despite these problems,

---

between the rules that emerge in common life and the systematic ordering and arrangement of these rules by moral philosophers. *An Inquiry into the Nature and Causes of the Wealth of Nations*, ed. R. H. Campbell and A. S. Skinner (Oxford: Oxford, 1976), II, 768–69.

[4] Thus, it is not sympathy which is the motive for such agreement but the pleasure which accompanies such sympathy.

[5] As Raphael points out: "No doubt Smith was predisposed to see a beneficent order in the natural running of human affairs. He probably acquired the idea from the ethical theory of the Stoics, which had impressed him deeply in his youth. Among other things, the Stoics believed in a cosmic harmony, which they described by the Greek word *sympatheia*, from which the modern word 'sympathy' is derived. . . . I have little doubt that the Stoic notion of a harmonious system is at the back of his mind when he describes the socializing effect of our feelings of sympathy" (*Adam Smith* [Oxford: Oxford, 1985], 73).

[6] See, for example, T. D. Campbell, *Adam Smith's Science of Morals* (London: George Allen and Unwin, 1971); Vincent Hope, *Virtue by Consensus: The Moral Philosophy of Hutcheson, Hume, and Adam Smith* (Oxford: Clarendon, 1989). See also Raphael, *Adam Smith*, who writes: "Smith's theory is primarily an explanation of the origin of moral judgment, something that nowadays would be assigned to psychology rather than philosophy" (37). A differing, but I think unsuccessful view, is suggested by George Morice who claims that the early chapters of the *Moral Sentiments* should not be construed as part of a "natural history" of morals but as an analysis of the nature of moral approval. See "Opinion, Sentiment and Approval in Adam Smith," in *Philosophers of the Scottish Enlightenment*, ed. Vincent Hope (Edinburgh: Edinburgh, 1984), 177.

however, it remains the case that Smith has not only outlined a schema by which the moral order, like the economic order, could be self-regulating, but, as I shall indicate at the close of this essay, he has done so in a way which mirrors the features of what are now called "invisible hand" explanations. For game theorists who are interested not only in the evolution of norms but in the historical antecedents of their enterprise, and for historians of ethics and political economy, Smith's theory offers a complex and intriguing account of how norms can emerge through a process of social interaction.[7]

1. A SUMMARY OF SMITH'S EXPLANATION

How does Smith propose that the choices and actions of independent individuals could be so coordinated that an interindividually uniform system of judgments of conduct emerges? A judgment of conduct is a judgment of approval or disapproval directed towards "the intention or affection of the heart" (II.iii.intro.3) or what Smith, like Hume, variously characterizes as passions, feelings, emotions, and appetites. A judgment of moral approbation occurs when a spectator comes to "perceive the harmony" (II.i.5.11) between the emotions he feels or conceives and the emotions felt by a moral agent. The desire for the pleasure of sympathy motivates both spectator and actor to modify and coordinate their sentiments so as to achieve a sympathetic harmony in both the content and intensity of their passions (I.i.3.1).[8] The pleasure of sympathy also motivates both spectator and actor to engage the "sympathetic imagination"[9] so as to understand how the other would feel if his situation were reversed. In this mutual act, the spectator endeavors to recreate the situation of the actor so that he, the spectator, might sympathize with him; the actor, in turn, modulates his passion so that he might better accommodate the sympathetic imagination of the spectator. If the two passions correspond, the spectator approves of the agent's passion; if they are dissimilar, the spectator disapproves. As this process

[7] Although I will not argue the point here, I would contend that Smith's account of the genesis of moral judgments is more complex and interesting than that of Hume, for whom, as Capaldi describes, "sympathy is . . . a social-psychological process which is instrumental in creating uniformities" (Nicholas Capaldi, *Hume's Place in Moral Philosophy* [New York: Peter Lang, 1989], 274). In his account of the seventeenth- and eighteenth-century moralists, A. E. Lovejoy concludes that the *Moral Sentiments* is "the most original and systematic eighteenth-century inquiry concerning the motivations of human behavior . . . " (*Reflections on Human Nature* [Baltimore: Johns Hopkins, 1961], 190).

[8] Elias Khalil contends that sympathy can be both a motive for and a criterion of conduct. See, "Beyond Self-Interest and Altruism: A Reconstruction of Adam Smith's Theory of Human Conduct," *Economics and Philosophy* 6: 255–73. However, Khalil's reconstruction of Smith's theory of conduct is not so much concerned with the descriptive psychology necessary for reconstructing Smith's conjectural account of the development of moral judgment as it is with reconstructing Smith's view of the structure of established moral judgments.

[9] Campbell, *Adam Smith's Science of Morals*, 96.

is repeated across society, the outcome is a uniform set of what Smith considers to be impartial moral judgments. Thus, given a motive for sympathy and a motive to engage in the sympathetic imagination, Smith assumes that the interaction of individuals leads to the crystallization of an imaginative point of view which is the impartial (moral) point of view.[10] Once individuals observe the regular occurrence of certain forms of approval and disapproval, they form, "from experience and induction," (VII.iii.2.6) rules of moral assessment. These rules conform to what the impartial spectator would approve and disapprove.[11] In sum, the impartial spectator is, in Campbell's words, "an average standard which emerges from the interplay of the reactions of ordinary spectators and agents; he personifies the results of a process of interaction whereby an agreed set of moral principles are evolved."[12]

As opposed to the "average standard"[13] of the impartial spectator, Smith

[10] In *The Wealth of Nations*, II, 793, Smith argues, similarly, that if religion is not subsidized or protected by the state, then the competition and interaction among the various religious sects "might in time probably reduce the doctrine of the greater part of them to that pure and rational religion, free from every mixture of absurdity, imposture, or fanaticism, such as wise men have in all ages of the world wished to see established. . . . "

[11] When we are motivated to act from these rules, we are acting out of a sense of duty (III.5.1). Indeed, Smith contends that the sense of duty is "the only principle by which the bulk of mankind are capable of directing their actions" (III.5.1). It is not at first clear why a reverence for duty is so important if it is sympathy and the sympathetic imagination which generates the rules for which there is to be such reverence. The answer to this problem may lie in the fact that the pleasure of sympathy diminishes in proportion to its frequency (see below, p. 456). Thus unless there were a reverence for rules, then as the pleasure of sympathy diminished so would the desire for moral agreement.

[12] Campbell, *Adam Smith's Science of Morals*, 137. Note that our judgments of conduct are so structured that they are either judgments of propriety or of merit. The former is a judgment as to whether a sentiment is the proper one to have—in either content or degree—in relation to the circumstances which caused the sentiment. The latter is a more forward-looking judgment which regards the effects which an agent's sentiment tends to bring about. To make a judgment of merit, the spectator must place himself in the situation of the patient of an agent, and by this act of imagination must come to feel (either actually or hypothetically) gratitude or resentment towards the passion of the agent which brought about a certain effect. However, judgments of merit are built upon judgments of propriety. Whether a spectator, who imagines himself in the position of a moral patient, will feel gratitude (or resentment) depends on whether the spectator first considers the sentiment of the agent to be proper (or improper) (II.i.3.1).

[13] In operational terms, the average standard is that standard which (almost) everyone expects (almost) everyone to employ in forming moral judgments. Thus, this standard will either underweight or exclude those valuations unique to a certain (minority) class or institution (note Smith's condemnation of the monkish virtues, III.2.35), just as it excludes the valuations of persons possessed of some "extraordinary delicacy or sensibility of character" (III.2.10). In effect, this average standard will be the standard of the common people: "That seems blamable which falls short of that ordinary degree of proper beneficence which experience teaches us to expect of every body; and on the contrary, that seems praise-worthy which goes beyond it" (II.ii.1.6). Consider also that in *The Wealth of Nations*, in the context of his discussion of religion, Smith writes that where church benefices are equally small, a minister "is obliged to follow that system of morals which the common people respect the most" (II, 810).

also adumbrates a more stringent standard, the standard of virtue. The distinction here is "between those qualities and actions which deserve to be admired and celebrated, and those which simply deserve to be approved of" (I.i.5.7). In addition, Smith notes a third standard, that of the *ideal* impartial spectator, which allows one to achieve some autonomy from the conventional standard of the (average) impartial spectator. The emergence of a standard of virtue or a standard of the ideal spectator presupposes that there has already emerged in society some prior consensus as to what is appropriate or required—the commonly expected qualities approved by the impartial spectator. Thus, any reconstruction of Smith's account of the emergence of morals must begin with a discussion of the generation of the minimum standards of moral practice. And so it is the emergence of those normative judgments, "commonly attained in the world, which the greater part of our friends and companions, of our rivals and competitors . . . have actually arrived at," (VI.iii.23) that is my concern.[14]

The original situation out of which these patterns emerge must be one in which there operate no moral constraints. Thus, an account of the development of moral conduct should attempt to show how uniform moral judgments arise from a nonmoral situation. However, how one chooses to examine this issue depends on which of the following questions one wants to emphasize: (i) from a nonmoral situation, how does a *uniformity* of our judgments of conduct arise? or (ii) from a nonmoral situation, how does a uniformity of *impartial moral* judgments arise? Although Smith does not separate these two questions, his inquiry, at one and the same time, attempts to answer both.[15] I, on the other hand, will not address the question of why (a uniform set of) judgments of conduct are impartial moral judgments. My concern is more basic: Can Smith's account demonstrate whether or how a uniform set of normative judgments (moral or no) could emerge out of individual interaction?[16]

---

[14] The above summary focuses on how uniform moral judgments arise within a society (or group of individuals). A separate question, which I do not discuss, concerns how an individual develops morally (within a society which already enforces uniform moral judgments). That there may be parallels between Smith's treatment of these topics, I do not deny. However, Smith seems to hold that the latter question is best addressed by appealing to the general rules—formed from the experience of a society (III.4.11–12)—which are "regarded as the commands and laws of the Deity" (III.5.6). Thus, the explanation of individual moral development, though not utterly divorced from the social processes out of which emerge moral norms, will also presuppose the educational and religious institutions which themselves feed off of general rules.

[15] As Hope points out (*Virtue by Consensus,* 89), Smith does not often distinguish between different kinds of approval—e.g., moral approval, approval of behavior, approval of manners.

[16] This question does not entail or imply that Smith is attempting to explain a universal moral code. Smith's account attempts to describe the psychological features which underlie any historical account of the emergence of morals. In this sense, his account is situated within a framework which is devoid of particular habits and customs. However, it is just such a framework that can, allegedly, explain the uniformity of moral judgment across some particular society or culture.

A set of normative judgments is uniform for a society only if almost everyone in that society who views an agent in circumstances C reacts with the same judgment towards the agent in C. Uniformity need not be absolute—there can be exceptions. If we assume with Smith that every passion is a response to some circumstance or event, then spectators will have uniform judgments of the passion of an actor only if there is interindividual agreement as to what passion is the appropriate response to some set of circumstances. Given Smith's view of the psychological uniformity of human beings, he finds that self-interest poses the major problem for the coordination of the passions. However, our reactions to some set of circumstances can differ not only because we may bear differing relations to the given circumstances but also because of our knowledge of or attentiveness to these circumstances (I.i.3.2). Thus, if everyone were an impartial, knowledgeable, and attentive spectator, then each person would react with the same passion to the same situation.

If this is the case, then what is required for the emergence of a uniformity of judgments of conduct? Since a judgment of propriety requires a sympathy between a spectator's emotions and those of an actor, such a judgment requires that the spectator know not only which passion he would feel if he were in the situation of the actor but also which passion the actor is actually feeling. Thus, in order for there to be uniformity between any two spectators' judgments of propriety, two conditions must be satisfied:

i. the spectators must have uniform judgments as to what passion an actor is feeling;

ii. the spectators must have uniform judgments as to how they would react in the relevant circumstances.

With regard to the first condition, Smith maintains a Humean view in which a spectator discerns another's passion by drawing an inference from the behavior of the actor (II.i.5.11; see also, I.i.3.1; III.1.3; and VII.iv.4–5). As to how an interindividual agreement arises concerning these inferential judgments, Smith provides no direct answer.[17] Since a discussion of this topic is

[17] Even if one individual infers from his own experience that passion P causes behavior B (as Campbell maintains, *Adam Smith's Science of Morals*, 97), another individual might make the inference that P_1 causes B or that P causes B_1. In at least one instance (III.i.3), Smith himself casts doubt on whether an individual could, prior to his introduction to society, construct associations between his passion and his behavior. This also explains why it would be difficult to invoke the sympathetic imagination as a means of inferring the passion of another. For in this case, an isolated individual would have to associate his passion with an (external) situation. If Smith is doubtful of whether an isolated individual can make inferences from behavior to passion, why would he be any less doubtful of the possibility of making inferences from situation to passion?

beyond the scope of this paper, I will assume that condition (i) is true—all spectators have uniform judgments as to what passion an actor is feeling.

2. SYMPATHY AND PLEASURE

Whether one is judging the merit or the propriety of an actor, one issues a judgment of moral approval because one sympathizes with the agent. Although Smith's words would indicate that approval "necessarily" follows sympathy (I.i.3.1) there is not so much a logical equivalence between sympathy and approval as there is a psychological relation.[18] It is the fact of pleasure which Smith believes is the psychological connection between sympathy and approval. It is in the pleasure of sympathy that "the sentiment of approbation properly consists" (I.iii.1.9). For Smith, the sentiment of approbation is ultimately the pleasure of sympathy in its particular coloration as the accompaniment of a sympathetic passion. What is not answered in Smith's account is whether the pleasure of sympathy is a distinct kind of pleasure. He claims only that this emotion is "always agreeable and delightful" (I.iii.1.9).

That the nature of the sympathetic pleasure is crucial was recognized by Hume, who advised Smith that the claim that sympathy is pleasurable or agreeable is "the Hinge of your System."[19] Once Smith supplies the hinge connecting sympathy and approval, it is not obvious that he achieves a squeakless swing. Hume, for example, contends that sympathy is not always agreeable. In his letter, he notes that sympathy is agreeable only when we sympathize with a *pleasant* passion or when we sympathize with an unpleasant passion of a friend. Hume's charge might even be extended to include sympathy with pleasant passions. For if we can sympathize with "any passion whatever" (I.i.1.5) and "upon such frivolous occasions" (I.i.2.1), then although the phenomenon of sympathy would occur frequently our experience does not seem to show that we are so frequently besieged by a pleasant emotion, even when we sympathize with a pleasant passion.

Given these preliminary doubts, it is worth asking why Smith hangs his system on the hinge of sympathetic pleasure. Unlike Hume, who had maintained that the act of sympathy was wholly governed by the natural associative principles of the imagination, Smith seems to launch his account of sympathy by assuming that the associative principles of the imagination may fail to bring about sympathy. And if there is no associative cause of sympa-

[18] Campbell, *Adam Smith's Science of Morals*, 92–93.

[19] Letter dated 28 July 1759. A portion of the letter is reprinted in an editorial footnote to the *Moral Sentiments* (I.iii.1.9). See also, J. Y. T. Greig, ed., *The Letters of David Hume*, I (Oxford: Clarendon, 1932), 311–14. For an account of Hume's criticism of Smith, see David Raynor, "Hume's Abstract of Adam Smith's *Theory of Moral Sentiments*," *Journal of the History of Philosophy* 22 (January 1984): 51–79.

thy, then Smith must appeal to a deliberate act—the engagement of the sympathetic imagination—in order to generate sympathy. How is this so?

Let us assume that a spectator has come to associate certain situations with certain preferences of his own. This spectator has a sentiment towards a certain situation only because he has certain preferences, interests, and values. Having these preferences (etc.), it is only natural that he has a certain sentiment towards a situation if he believes that the situation is related to the realization of his preferences. This association is *natural* in the sense that the imagination makes this association in a nondeliberate manner. As Smith points out, at times we know how we would feel in a situation merely by being confronted with the situation. When a spectator sees an actor in a situation, the spectator naturally associates this situation with the reaction which he would have (if he were actually) in the situation. Smith writes of how in the company of a friend, "we are immediately put in mind of the light in which he will view our situation . . ." (I.i.4.9; see also, I.i.1.3, III.3.23).

Clearly, however, sympathy and approval will not come about naturally if the preferences of the actor are sufficiently different from those of the spectator to cause them to differ in their emotional reactions to a situation. In this instance the spectator must, to one degree or another, consciously engage his sympathetic imagination if he is to sympathize with the actor at all. The spectator must remove himself from his natural association of sentiment and situation. The stronger the degree to which such an act is deliberate rather than purely reflexive, the greater the need for Smith to provide some motive for engaging in the act. Here Smith calls upon the pleasure of sympathy to motivate the spectator to alter his representation of the facts of the situation, pay closer attention to these facts, or assume the values and preferences of the actor whose conduct is under consideration. That the sympathetic imagination requires some motive can be seen in terms of the effort which, at times, can be demanded of the imagination: "the spectator must, first of all, endeavour, as much as he can, to put himself in the situation of the other, and to bring home to himself every little circumstance of distress which can possibly occur to the sufferer. He must adopt the whole case of his companion with all its minutest incidents; and strive to render as perfect as possible, that imaginary change of situation upon which his sympathy is founded" (I.i.4.6).[20]

---

[20] It should not be concluded from this discussion that the only motive for the deliberate exercise of the sympathetic imagination is the pleasure of sympathy. One can also be motivated to engage the sympathetic imagination from the motive of benevolence, in particular, that benevolence which manifests itself in duties and ties to family and friends. (When we do engage in imaginative sympathy out of a motive of friendship, this does not mean that the sympathy which results from our act is not pleasurable, only that the motive of our imaginative effort was not the probable pleasure.) It is, however, because such benevolence is limited that Smith must appeal to the motive of pleasure.

3. THE CONDITIONS OF PLEASURABLE SYMPATHY

Even though we have some idea of why Smith chooses to claim that sympathy is pleasurable, we are still left with the fact, as suggested by Hume, that such an unqualified claim seems false. It is not always the case that we feel an "agreeable and delightful" emotion on the discovery of sympathy. Most certainly, the problem here is complicated by the fact that it is not entirely obvious what it is that we are to look for when we look for the pleasure of sympathy. On the other hand, on some occasions of sympathy we do feel a kind of emotional satisfaction in the fact that our response to a situation is the same as that of another person. Perhaps this emotional satisfaction is what Smith would call an "agreeable and delightful" emotion. In any case, Hume's criticism points to the general question of what sort of conditions might be necessary for rendering Smith's claim more plausible.

Consider, for example, the case of two students entering college. Each is anxious about the semester which looms ahead, and each is relieved to discover that, yes, the other is anxious as well. On learning that the other shares the same reaction, each student feels an emotional satisfaction. One need not be guilty of finessing the matter in Smith's favor to say that this feeling of satisfaction is "agreeable," if not also "delightful." This emotion is produced not simply because one student recognizes that another feels the same as he does—it is not simply the similarity of reactions that pleases. This sympathy pleases because the recognition of shared passions provides an affirmation of an individual's own reaction to a set of circumstances, a reaction about which the individual is unsure. Thus, we can stipulate that one condition for the pleasure of sympathy is that we be uncertain about our own response to a situation.

Is there any evidence that this is an appropriate interpretation of Smith? Although Smith does not address explicitly the problem of uncertainty, he does believe that morality is constructed around opinion; in this sense, our uncertainty about conduct is a function of the degree to which there is an established opinion about conduct. As opposed to subjects of certain demonstration, such as mathematics, an uncertainty concerning our passions inclines us to be anxious about public opinion (III.2.18). The more certain we are about our judgments, the less relevant is the sympathy of another. Smith seems to acknowledge this when he writes: "The agreement or disagreement both of the sentiments and judgments of other people with our own, is in all cases, it must be observed, of more or less importance to us, exactly in proportion as we ourselves are more or less uncertain about the propriety of our own sentiments, about the accuracy of our own judgments" (III.2.16).

Prior to the achievement of a uniform standard for judgments of conduct, we will be anxious about public opinion simply because we are uncertain as to how others will view our own sentiments and judgments. However, once an interindividual agreement is reached on standards of conduct, then sympathy will be generally assumed as a matter of course, and its presence or absence need not occasion pleasure. Thus, at least one condition which distinguishes pleasurable sympathy from mere sympathy is whether one is certain of the standard for measuring one's response (or whether one is certain as to which standard will be applied in this instance). We can conclude that although it is false that any act of sympathy produces pleasure, a sympathetic pleasure is produced in some proportion to the desire for agreement that occurs when one is faced with uncertainty over one's response to a situation. If this is correct, then the pleasure of sympathy, insofar as it is a motive for the sympathetic imagination, is not uniformly of the same strength.

Uncertainty cannot be the only condition for sympathy being pleasurable. The pleasure which one receives from sympathy also seems to be dependent on the esteem which one holds for the person with whom one sympathizes. We can stipulate that sympathy is pleasurable only so long as the person with whom one sympathizes is not someone whom one holds in low esteem. Although Smith indicates (II.ii.3.10) that it is not impossible to imagine sympathetically the circumstances of an "odious" person, one may not be so inclined unless one's sentiments (and actions) have already been corrected by moral rules. (Even in this case, however, the resulting sympathy may not be pleasant.)

Finally, we must return to Hume's specific criticism. Absent the condition of friendship, Hume contends that sympathy with an unpleasant passion is itself unpleasant, for if not, "an Hospital would be a more entertaining Place than a Ball."[21] What this criticism would seem to show is that unless there is a significant psychological proximity (viz., friendship) between the two parties, then sympathy with an unpleasant passion will itself be unpleasant. And "in ordinary cases, this [proximity] cannot have place."[22] Smith responds to this criticism merely by distinguishing the sympathy between unpleasant passions from the sympathetic pleasure which results from this sympathy (I.iii.1.9). However, as Raynor explains, "it will not do to say that the observation of corresponding disagreeable sentiments is agreeable *by definition.*"[23]

One way in which Smith might reply to Hume is to argue that—in the case of unpleasant passions—the sort of psychological proximity necessary for producing sympathetic pleasure does not require that proximity which exists between friends. Instead, the relations requisite for some degree of proximity (and, therefore, for some degree of sympathetic pleasure) are the Humean

---

[21] Greig, ed., *The Letters of David Hume,* I, 313.

[22] Ibid.

[23] Raynor, "Hume's Abstract," 58.

relations of contiguity, resemblance, and causality. On this view, the degree of sympathetic pleasure would vary inversely to the degree of psychological distance between the spectator and the person with whom the spectator sympathized. This response might allow Smith to claim that when the degree of psychological distance is large, then the sympathetic pleasure is so small that the unpleasant sympathetic passion overwhelms it.

Another sort of response might also be available to Smith. This response would accept Hume's criticism at face value: sympathy with an unpleasant passion produces pleasure only when the two parties share a prior friendship. In accepting Hume's criticism, Smith would then have to show how the approbation which results from the pleasurable sympathy between friends can be extended to individuals who do not share such a friendly relation. In effect, Smith would have to answer the same sort of conundrum which Hume must answer at the end of his *Treatise:* "We sympathize more with persons contiguous to us, than with persons remote from us: With our acquaintance, than with strangers: With our countrymen, than with foreigners. But notwithstanding this variation of our sympathy, we give the same approbation to the same moral qualities in *China* as in *England.*"[24]

To render either of these analyses plausible (or even to combine them in such a way that a spectator's approbation is extended to another person who is psychologically distant from the spectator) is a task beyond the scope of this essay. However, even if Smith's claim that all sympathy is pleasurable is in need of significant qualification, the pursuit of these qualifications must, for the purposes of this essay, be set aside.[25]

4. THE MOTIVE FOR THE SYMPATHETIC IMAGINATION

If the conditions obtain for a pleasurable sympathy, is the prospective pleasure a sufficient motive for engaging the sympathetic imagination? That is, against any other preferences (and absent other inducements to engage the sympathetic imagination) is the pleasure of sympathy an effective motive? Although Smith writes that "nothing pleases us more" (I.i.2.1), it would seem more reasonable to conclude that the pleasure of sympathy may be sufficient when: (i) the spectator considers it probable that he will sympathize with the

[24] *A Treatise of Human Nature,* ed. L. A. Selby-Bigge, rev. P. H. Nidditch (Oxford: Clarendon, 1978), 581.

[25] If Smith's unqualified claim is false and if no qualifications can rescue it, then it may turn out that his explanation of the emergence of moral judgment is what Hempel would call a potential explanation. That is to say, an explanation which proceeds from a set of initial conditions and some lawlike statement (e.g., sympathy is pleasurable) is a potential explanation if either the description of the initial conditions or the lawlike statement is not true. See Carl G. Hempel, *Aspects of Scientific Explanation* (New York: Free Press, 1965), 273–78, 338.

passion of another; (ii) there are no competing preferences of a greater strength; and (iii) the sympathetic passion is not so unpleasant as to override whatever pleasure is gained through sympathy itself. Whether the pleasure of sympathy is sufficient depends on subtle changes in the degree of probability that one will sympathize, in the unpleasantness of the sympathetic passion, and in the strength of competing desires.

Smith does not adequately explain how these empirical problems are solved such that individuals do engage the sympathetic imagination in those cases in which there is no other motive (such as family ties or friendship) to do so. In this, as in other cases, Smith could simply reply that insofar as he is trying to explain the emergence of uniform judgments of conduct, all that is required is that the psychological mechanisms operate with a sufficient frequency. However, it is just this point that is at issue. It is simply not obvious that these psychological mechanisms would operate in the right sort of ways so as to bring about a uniformity of judgments.

For example, the expected probability of achieving sympathy (i) may depend on whether the spectator views the passion of an actor as an idiosyncratic passion or as a passion outside the range of the spectator's normal emotions (I.ii.2.1). Here the reluctance to engage the sympathetic imagination stems not from the perceived unpleasantness of a passion but from the psychological difficulty of coming to terms with the situation which might engender the passion.

It would also seem plausible (ii) that one could be disposed against engaging the sympathetic imagination simply because one holds preferences which override one's concern for sympathetic pleasure. Such a phenomenon occurs when envy prevents one from sympathizing with another's joy, and it also occurs in more innocent ways, perhaps because the other parties "are entirely unknown to us, or we happen to be employed about other things" (I.i.3.4).

Finally, (iii) it is more difficult to sympathize with unpleasant passions than it is with pleasant passions. Smith's explanation of this claim is ambiguous. That it is difficult to sympathize with unpleasant passions could mean either (a) a spectator is reluctant to enter into the sympathetic imagination in those instances in which he believes that he will entertain an unpleasant passion; or (b) a spectator who sympathetically imagines a potentially unpleasant situation psychologically resists the representation of those features of the situation which would give rise to the conception or actual feeling of an unpleasant passion.[26] Perhaps there is no practical difference between these two alterna-

[26] Smith's phrasing does not distinguish these two cases: "we often struggle to keep down our sympathy with the sorrow of others. Whenever we are not under the observation of the sufferer, we endeavour, for our own sake, to suppress it as much as we can, and we are not always successful. The opposition which we make to it, and the reluctance with which we yield to it,

tives. The difference here is on the order of the difference between the person who reluctantly visits a psychiatrist but speaks openly in his presence and the person who eagerly visits the psychiatrist but who resists speaking of certain ideas, desires, or feelings.

Whether the pleasure of sympathy has sufficient force to override the unpleasantness of a sympathetic passion might also depend on whether the sympathetic passion which results from exercising the sympathetic imagination is an actual or hypothetical passion. Smith provides no univocal answer as to whether the sympathetic passion need be actual rather than merely hypothetical (see I.i.1.2–3), but it does not seem to be the case that his theory requires one and not the other. Neither a correspondence between two actual feelings or between one actual and one hypothetical feeling undercuts the conditions necessary for an emotion of pleasure to follow upon sympathy. One might presume, however, that an act of the sympathetic imagination would more likely occur if the prospect of an unpleasant sympathetic passion involved a hypothetical rather than an actual passion.

5. THE SYMPATHETIC IMAGINATION

If spectators are to have uniform judgments as to how they would react in certain circumstances, then some account must be provided of the sympathetic imagination. Smith seems to view the sympathetic imagination as an operation by which we take on at least some of the character, values, and interests of the actor with whom we are attempting to sympathize:

> . . . this imaginary change is not supposed to happen to me in my own person and character, but in that of the person with whom I sympathize. When I condole with you for the loss of your only son, in order to enter into your grief I do not consider what I, a person of such a character and profession, should suffer, if I had a son, and if that son was unfortunately to die: but I consider what I should suffer if I was really you, and I not only change circumstances with you, but I change persons and characters. (VII.iii.1.4; see also, I.i.1.1)

When I imagine myself in the situation of another person, I may take on his qualities and talents, but I may or may not take on his values and preferences. It is important to note, however, that prior to the crystallization of a moral point of view, no moral constraints operate on the sympathetic imagination; one can engage the imagination without any obligation to assume the preferences of all relevant individuals or to provide equal consideration to each individual. Certainly, Smith assumes that given a motive to engage in the sympathetic imagination, the interaction of individuals leads to the crys-

---

necessarily oblige us to take more particular notice of it. But we never have occasion to make this opposition to our sympathy with joy" (I.iii.i.4).

tallization of an imaginative point of view which is the (impartial) moral point of view. Here again it is not at all obvious that Smith has sufficiently outlined the conditions that would allow the psychological mechanisms to operate in such a way that a uniform standard would emerge. In the case of the operation of the sympathetic imagination, the spectator does not consciously and deliberately strive to render his point of view impartial. What the spectator does aim for is sympathy.

As was noted earlier, when one naturally associates a sentiment with a situation, the sentiment which one conceives (or feels) is not necessarily the sentiment one would feel if one more closely examined the facts of the situation, paid these facts closer attention, or were impartial. When sympathy does not arise via natural associations, the prospective pleasure of sympathy furnishes a motive for examining the situation in one's imagination. This motive may cause one to change one's representation of the facts, pay closer attention to these facts, or to assume the values and preferences of the actor whose conduct is under consideration (I.i.4.2).

It has also been argued above that sympathy is pleasurable only if there is uncertainty about one's response to a situation, and the person with whom one might sympathize is not held in low esteem. Even when sympathy would be pleasurable, this pleasure is not necessarily a sufficient motive for engaging the sympathetic imagination. Pleasurable sympathy is a sufficient motive only if the spectator considers it probable that he will sympathize with the passion of another, there are not competing preferences of greater strength, and the sympathetic passion is not so unpleasant as to override whatever pleasure is gained through sympathy. Now, however, there is a further complication to add to the conditions which make sympathy pleasurable. This condition (or series of conditions) pertains to the way in which a spectator, who has failed to achieve sympathy via natural association, might choose to engage his sympathetic imagination.

In any deliberate engagement of the sympathetic imagination by a set of spectators in situation S, we cannot assume a uniform representation of S or a uniform attention to the features of that representation. Whether a spectator judges an actor impartially is determined by whether or how the spectator takes into consideration the actor's character, values, or interests.[27] Of course,

[27] Consider Smith's examples: "When we look upon the person who is the cause of his pleasure with the eyes with which we imagine he must look upon him . . . " (II.i.2.4); "In imagination we become the very person whose actions are represented to us . . . " (II.i.5.3); and in the case of sympathy with the insane, "The compassion of the spectator must arise altogether from the consideration of what he himself would feel if he was reduced to the same unhappy situation, and, what perhaps is impossible, was at the same time able to regard it with his present reason and judgment" (I.i.1.10).

if a spectator took on all of an actor's character, values, and interests, then the spectator would merely exchange his partial point of view for the equally partial viewpoint of the actor. Given a variety of characters, values, and interests no uniformity could be achieved. Is there any determinate answer as to whether a spectator will, in imaginatively considering an actor in some situation, (i) represent fully the facts of the situation, and (ii) attempt to take on or set aside whatever values are necessary in order to sympathize with the passion of the actor? (I ignore the less important investigation into whether there is a set of factors determining a uniformity of attention to the facts of a situation.)

6. IMAGINATIVE REPRESENTATION: FACTS

What the spectator envisages as an actor's situation is not subject to any norm or relevance prior to the establishment of a norm of conduct. If there is any intersubjective norm for what counts as a relevant fact of a situation, then that implies that there is an intersubjectively correct norm of behavior. That an assessment is correct in a certain situation means that certain facts are relevant to the consideration of the situation (and that if one takes these facts into account, then one will correctly assess the situation and prescribe the right conduct).

The problem of determining which facts are relevant to a situation is not easily solved. Of particular relevance here is the question of the generation of the two forms of normative judgment—propriety and merit. The propriety of an affection is determined by a judgment as to whether that sentiment, in both kind and intensity, is the right sentiment to have in relation to a preceding state of affairs. The merit of the sentiment presupposes its propriety in terms of a preceding state of affairs but also considers that sentiment in its intended effects on others (II.i.3.1). Occupying that middle ground between what comes before (situation 1) and what comes after (situation 2) is the sentiment or passion. A judgment of propriety assesses a sentiment in terms of situation 1; a judgment of merit assumes the propriety of a sentiment and then assesses that sentiment in terms of situation 2. Prior to the generation of a moral point of view, there are no constraints on the exercise of the sympathetic imagination. Even if there is a psychological uniformity in individuals' reactions to facts, the facts constituting any situation might be believed to include either the facts of the situation which provoked or caused the passionate reaction or the facts of the situation in which the reaction takes place. Thus it is not obvious why Smith believes that a judgment of propriety does not include a representation of the situation in which the reaction takes place. Why should a spectator represent the situation of an actor solely in terms of that situation which preceded his sentiment? Couldn't the propriety of one's reaction to situation 1 depend, at least in part, upon how one envisages situation 2? And if the propriety of a sentiment is determined in relation to situation 1, then why should the relation of a sentiment to situation 1 be a condition for approving that sentiment in relation to situation 2?

In order to show how this distinction evolves we would have to explain how self-interested individuals elect to represent certain facts of a situation (including the fact of who is affected by an action, to what degree, and whether this is a benefit or a harm) and how social interaction aggregates these considerations into norms of factual relevance. In order to accomplish this task, we would have to know the conditions which would incline a self-interested individual to either include or exclude certain facts when he engages his sympathetic imagination. One, if not the only, condition may be whether the spectator believes that if he considers a fact then he will achieve sympathy. However, whether that fact will be considered depends on whether the spectator finds it in his interest to sympathize with an actor. A complete explanation of the operation of the sympathetic imagination would not only specify the conditions under which certain sorts of facts are deemed compatible with the desire to gain (pleasurable) sympathy but would also indicate what sort of value reversal is compatible with this desire. We turn now to examine the latter in more detail.

7. IMAGINATIVE REPRESENTATION: VALUES

In great measure, sympathy is pleasing because we are anxious about our own reactions to a set of circumstances. And at least in those instances in which we do not disapprove of our own motives and passions, we want the opinions of others to confirm our sentiments. However, via the sympathetic imagination, a spectator can imagine himself in the situation of an actor. Is sympathy pleasing only if the spectator—having imagined himself in the situation of the actor—retains his actual values?[28] If a spectator views a situation only through the lens of his own values, then not only could he not examine the situation impartially but there would not arise any uniform point of view. In order to understand how a spectator might be inclined to take on (or to shed) values in order to reach sympathy, let us characterize the several ways in which a spectator's values might relate to the manner in which he engages his sympathetic imagination.

For each of the possibilities below we could determine whether sympathy would produce pleasure. If sympathy were pleasurable, we would still have to determine whether the prospective pleasure of this sympathy is sufficient to

[28] Although distinctions between values, preferences, interests, and desires may be relevant to a justificatory explanation of the sympathetic imagination, I assume that such a distinction is not necessary for an exploration of Smith's empirical model of the sympathetic imagination.

motivate a spectator to engage the sympathetic imagination. If sympathy were not pleasurable, then the connection between sympathy and approval is lost, and, presumably, such sympathy would not issue in judgments of approval.

If an actor perceives the facts of a situation S, the actor will react with passion P only if he has certain values (preferences, interests, etc.) V. Thus, if an actor has passion P, then the actor believes that value V is relevant to the situation S. When a spectator observes the behavior of the actor, the spectator infers that the actor feels a passion P. If the spectator believes he can achieve a genuine sympathy with the actor only if he assumes value V, then the spectator's relation to value V might be characterized in either of the following ways. (We will assume that V is neither a part of the spectator's actual values nor a part of the values which he would assume in situation S.) Where value V is different from but not in conflict with the values of the spectator, and the spectator believes V is necessary for sympathy, then the judgment of approval (of passion P) which would typically result from the inclusion of V in the spectator's imaginative representation of S will either (1) serve or (2) not serve to frustrate the desires and interests of the spectator.

In cases (1) and (2) we can reasonably stipulate that sympathy would produce pleasure only if the spectator could identify himself with the value which he takes on. An individual identifies with a value when that value is either a part of his conception of self or would become a part of his conception of self if he were in certain circumstances.[29] We could not feel pleasure in sharing sentiments if the sentiment which we shared was one which conflicted with our own identity. If the pleasure of sympathy derives from the commonality discovered between two persons, then it does not seem to be the case that any pleasure would be produced if the spectator achieved such sympathy by assuming preferences which he could not attach, even hypothetically, to his identity. In case (1), however, even if a spectator identifies with a value, it might not be the case that the pleasure of his sympathy would lead to a judgment of approval: For although a spectator might be pleased to see his own desires and values confirmed by another, he might be even more displeased to see that the value which he espouses will, in the present situation, serve to frustrate one of his desires. Perhaps in case (1), the spectator would not even take on values with which he could identify if those values would frustrate his own desires. (Although we can imagine ourselves taking on values the approval of which in another person would frustrate our actual desires, it does not seem correct to

[29] I will not elucidate further the rather elusive topic of "identifying" with a value or the equally troublesome "conception of self." On the former topic, see Harry G. Frankfurt, "Identification and Externality," in *The Identities of Persons*, ed. Amelie Oksenberg Rorty (Berkeley: University of California, 1976), 239–51.

assume that we would do so unless we valued the sympathy to be gained more than the value to be lost.)

In other cases, the value V may not only be different from a spectator's actual values but may actually be in conflict with them. Although there are complications even in these cases, let us stipulate that if (in order to sympathize) a spectator must take on a value which conflicts with the actual values with which he identifies, then any sympathy which results from this addition of values will not be pleasurable.

Instead of taking on values there will also be instances in which a spectator must shed a value in order to sympathize with an actor. If, in order to sympathize, a spectator must shed a value V, then the approval of passion P which would typically result from the exclusion of V in the spectator's imaginative representation of S will, once again, either (3) serve or (4) not serve to frustrate the desires and interests of the spectator.

In case (4), the sympathy which results from shedding a value with which one identifies cannot be a pleasurable sympathy. In case (3), a failure to achieve a pleasurable sympathy due to the shedding of a value with which one identifies may lead one to refrain from issuing a judgment of approval. And in this case, even if one sheds a value with which one does not identify, the pleasure which results may not be sufficient to lead one to a judgment of approval.

Whether the value one sheds is a value with which one identifies and which constitutes part of one's understanding of self (or whether the value one takes on is one which is incompatible with one's identity) is crucial to the question of whether one can pleasurably sympathize with another. The extent to which one is willing to consider another's point of view determines how the sympathetic imagination will operate. What our discussion has attempted to show is the difficulty of determining how the sympathetic imagination would operate if it were not subject to moral constraints. What our discussion also shows, however, is that individuals will not take on or shed whatever values are necessary to achieve sympathy. There are certain values which individuals will refrain from assuming when they engage the imagination.

8. CONCLUDING PROSPECTS

As was mentioned in the opening paragraphs of this essay, one way of understanding Smith's account of the development of morals is to view it as an anticipation of contemporary accounts of the emergence of norms. On this view, however, Smith's account suffers because the motive (sympathetic pleasure) by which other-regarding norms are to emerge operates only under certain conditions and is not always a sufficient motive for engaging the sympathetic imagination. We have also seen that in so far as one engages the sympathetic imagination, the possibility of achieving sympathy depends on which values one is willing to take on or to shed. Moreover, whether a spectator's sympathy will bring the spectator to issue a judgment of approval depends on whether or not such approval will frustrate the spectator's other desires or interests.

Although Smith's account, as I have construed it, is weakened by the underdetermination of the conditions sufficient to bring about a uniform set of judgments of approval, I believe that Smith's view incorporates a structure sufficiently interesting to warrant further research. In the first place, Smith could argue that the psychological mechanisms do operate in such a way that uniform judgments arise. However, to make this argument effective would require a more complete description than Smith makes available. This strategy is not, however, the point which I wish to emphasize. Rather, I want to suggest that Smith's account mirrors features of two sorts of "invisible hand" explanations.[30]

Despite their desire for sympathy, individuals will be selective in the sorts of facts and values they are willing to assume in the sympathetic imagination. In this sense, the sympathetic imagination effectively serves as a "filter device" which prevents our sympathizing with certain passions, namely, those passions whose objects are values with which we cannot identify. As Robert Nozick explains, two features of a filter device which help determine an outcome "are the particular nature of the filtering out process (and what qualities it selects against) and the particular nature of the set of alternatives it operates upon (and how this set is generated)."[31] Now the alternatives which the sympathetic imagination "operates upon" are those values which condition certain passions or sentiments. The qualities which the imagination selects against are precisely those passions with which one does not sympathize or with which one does not sympathize pleasurably: "And if we consider all the different passions of human nature, we shall find that they are regarded as decent, or indecent, just in proportion as mankind are more or less disposed to sympathize with them" (I.ii.intro.2). Unless, however, there is general agreement on which values (or facts) to assume imaginatively, the filtering effect of the sympathetic imagination will not eliminate towards uniformity. General agreement is encouraged, but not determined, by the fact that everyone has an original desire for approval and praise (III.2.6). Just as the imagination selects against certain senti-

[30] Smith's own view of the "invisible hand" is a functional one, in which the hand of God has so arranged things that every phenomenon has a beneficial function. In the sense in which I am employing this term, an invisible hand explanation is merely an explanation of how some pattern or order (functional or not) emerges without any conscious design or explicit agreement. See Edna Ullmann-Margalit, "Invisible-Hand Explanations," *Synthese* 39 (1978): 263–91.

[31] *Anarchy, State, and Utopia* (New York: Basic Books, 1974), 314.

ments, the desire for praise functions so as to encourage those values which condition those sentiments most likely to engender praise.[32]

This coordination is complemented by an equilibrating mechanism which insures that the similarity of the content of the passions is echoed by a similar intensity of the passions. "[I]n equilibrium processes each component part responds or adjusts to 'local' conditions, with each adjustment changing the local environment of others close by, so that the sum of the local adjustments constitutes or realizes P."[33] This equilibrating mechanism is the mutual sympathy which occurs when both the actor and the spectator engage the sympathetic imagination. Once the spectator has endeavored to place himself in the situation of the actor, he will "never conceive . . . that degree of passion which naturally animates the person principally concerned" (I.i.4.7). However, the actor who desires sympathy places himself in the situation of the spectator and recognizes that the spectator's passion will never be the same as his own. The actor then realizes that "he can only hope to obtain this [sympathy] by lowering his passion to that pitch, in which the spectators are capable of going along with him" (I.i.4.7). The similarity of passions reached through mutual sympathy will "have such a correspondence with one another, as is sufficient for the harmony of society. Though they will never be unisons, they may be concords, and this is all that is wanted or required" (I.i.4.7).[34]

State University of New York, New Paltz

[32] This point is emphasized by Raphael, *Adam Smith*, 31–33.

[33] Nozick, *Anarchy, State, and Utopia*, 21.

[34] I wish to thank two anonymous reviewers for this journal for their comments on and suggestions for an earlier version of this essay. David Drebushenko and Maria Elosegui provided helpful comments on an even earlier draft of this paper. I am grateful to the Social Philosophy and Policy Center of Bowling Green State University for granting me a Visiting Scholar Fellowship during the summer of 1991, at which time portions of this essay were completed.

[4]

VI*—HUME AND ADAM SMITH ON JUSTICE AND UTILITY

by D. D. Raphael

The subject of my paper is historical but the philosophical problem with which it is concerned is a continuing one. The chief difficulty that faces utilitarianism as a theory of ethics is to show that it can give an adequate account of the concept of justice. This was clearly seen and honestly faced by J. S. Mill, Sidgwick, and Rashdall. Mill and Rashdall thought they could accommodate justice within a strictly utilitarian theory, but to my mind their arguments are faulty. Sidgwick acknowledged that utilitarian principles alone are inadequate and added a separate principle of equity.

Most of us find an immediate attraction in utilitarianism. If we are later convinced that it does not account satisfactorily for the concept of justice, we are not quite sure which way to go. In the history of ideas the utilitarian tradition has been opposed to the natural-law tradition, and in general (though not universally) natural-law theory has gone along with a form of rationalism, while utilitarianism has gone along with empiricism. Rationalism is out of fashion, and so one is disinclined to talk about principles of justice evident to rational intuition. I do not know if this partly explains why Professor John Rawls, having decided that a utilitarian account of justice will not do, has put forward an account of justice in terms of social-contract theory. He says in one of his papers that the social contract is the traditional opponent of utilitarianism and so is the obvious alternative to it. I think he is mistaken. The theory of social contract was intended to deal with the problem of political obligation (why should a man obey the state?), not as an explanation of justice. However that may be, I find the contractual hypothesis in Rawls's theory singularly unhelpful, although his recent book, taken as a whole, is clearly an

* Meeting of the Aristotelian Society at 5/7 Tavistock Place, London, W.C.1, on Monday, 15th January, 1973, at 7.30 p.m.

important contribution to ethical theory. Nevertheless I am no more inclined than the next man to revert to intuitionism, even though the clearest-headed of the utilitarians, Sidgwick, did so. Like most people nowadays, I want to stick to empiricism as far as I can. The best empiricist approaches to the concept of justice that I know are those of Hume and Adam Smith. Hume is by and large a utilitarian. Adam Smith is an anti-utilitarian, indeed a natural-law theorist, but his natural law is natural law with a difference, a genuinely empiricist natural law.

Both Hume and Adam Smith were strongly influenced by Francis Hutcheson. Smith was a pupil of Hutcheson and shared his interests in ethics, aesthetics, law, and economics. Hume's relation to Hutcheson is more complex. Hume's ethical theory was a development of Hutcheson's, showing greater insight and greater subtlety. But that is not the whole of the story. Unlike Hutcheson and Adam Smith, Hume was more deeply interested in the philosophy of knowledge than in the philosophy of practice, and it was in the theory of knowledge that he displayed outstanding genius as a philosopher of the first rank. Kemp Smith[1] has shown, I think conclusively, that although Hume wrote and published Book III of the *Treatise of Human Nature* later than Books I and II, he began his philosophizing with ethics—Hutcheson's ethics—and was led by that to think he had the key to the problems of knowledge. Hutcheson treated beauty and virtue as partly projections of the feelings of spectators. What Hume did was to apply the same sort of move to ideas that were troublesome in the theory of knowledge. His genius lay in seeing that the move could be so applied more generally (as well as in the remorseless logic of his criticism of alternative accounts), and the greatness of his achievement is not diminished when we perceive that he took the initial idea from Hutcheson.

I do not know whether one can properly say that Hutcheson was the first utilitarian. A good case can be made for holding that Richard Cumberland, a traditional natural-law theorist of the seventeenth century, had a utilitarian theory of ethics. But Hutcheson was more explicitly utilitarian, and—what is

[1] *The Philosophy of David Hume.*

more to the point—he was the first thinker to produce a utilitarian theory from clearly empiricist foundations.

Hutcheson was of course also an exponent (as Hume was after him) of the moral-sense theory. In the hands of Hutcheson the moral-sense theory turned into utilitarianism in the following way. He began by insisting, against Hobbes and Mandeville, that there are disinterested factors in human psychology. There is disinterested love (affection, admiration) and disinterested dislike. We see these things not only in ethics, which some would dispute, but also in aesthetics, which is harder to deny. There is a disinterested motive to action, benevolence; and when a man acts from this disinterested motive, spectators naturally feel a disinterested approval analogous to the disinterested liking felt by spectators of natural beauty and art. The capacity to feel approval or disapproval is the moral sense. Virtue for Hutcheson is *benevolence approved*, not benevolence on its own, but benevolence as seen in the eye of the beholder (or, more properly, as felt in the heart of the beholder). That is the gist of the moral-sense theory.

But now: benevolence aims at giving happiness to others (or removing their misery), and while it does not always succeed it commonly does so. Therefore the tendency, and the aim, of virtuous action is the promotion of happiness for people in general (indeed for any sensitive creature). Although the feeling of the moral sense is an immediate reaction, not a calculated one, a wide benevolence is approved more than a narrow, and a universal benevolence is approved most of all. So on reflection we can see a correlation between the strength of approval and the degree to which the approved agent intends to increase and spread happiness. Hence Hutcheson concluded that "that action is best which procures the greatest happiness for the greatest numbers".

All virtue for Hutcheson is a form of benevolence, a natural motive to which there is a natural reaction. Hutcheson treated any virtue that aims at benefiting other people (*e.g.*, gratitude) as a form of benevolence. He denied that prudence is a virtue except to the extent that it enables us to exercise benevolence. He apparently did not feel any tension between benevolence and justice, and he defined rights in terms of universal practices that would promote or harm general happiness. Note that the account is in terms of *universal* practices. This is because Hutcheson was thinking of the rules of law when he talked about rights.

In Hume's development of Hutcheson's theory of ethics there are three things especially worthy of notice. (1) Like Hutcheson, Hume supported a theory of moral sense or sentiment by criticizing rationalist alternatives, but in Hume the attack on ethical rationalism was conducted with a battery of arguments as powerful as any in the history of philosophy. (2) Where Hutcheson had taken the moral sense to be a basic datum of human psychology, Hume explained it as an effect of sympathy. He thereby made it seem less mysterious and showed up more clearly the connexion between the moral-sense theory and utilitarianism. We feel a particular form of pleasure (approval) when we see a benevolent action, because we share by sympathy the pleasure of the beneficiary of the benevolent action; and likewise disapproval arises from sympathy with pain or distress caused by a vicious action. (3) Hume distinguished between benevolence and justice as 'natural' and 'artificial' virtues respectively, and recognized that the moral approval of justice requires further explanation. It is the third feature with which I am especially concerned here.

Hume's presentation of his view of justice differs markedly in the *Treatise* and in the *Enquiry concerning the Principles of Morals*. In the *Treatise* he stressed the thesis that justice is an artificial virtue, one that arises from human conventions. By denying that it is a natural virtue, Hume meant that the motive for acting justly is not a basic endowment of human nature, as *e.g.*, benevolence is. When Hume talked about justice he was generally thinking of rules about property. These are needed, he argued, because there is a scarcity in the supply of many goods that are wanted and because men are predominantly selfish with limited generosity. In a fictitious golden age or utopian state of nature, in which the supply of desired goods and the extent of human benevolence were unlimited, there would be no need for rules of mine and thine. As things are, however, we all find it advantageous to follow conventions of leaving others in undisturbed possession of goods so long as they do the same for us. And so there arise rules for 'stability' of possession. A man's first motive for joining in the conventions is self-interest. But how explain the fact that we morally approve of keeping the rules even in instances that do not benefit us? Hume's explanation was that we see that the system of rules as a whole is of benefit to society in general, and sympathy with the public interest gives rise to moral approval. In the *Treatise* Hume acknowledged that "a single act of justice is frequently contrary to public interest",[2] let alone private. But the whole system is advantageous, both to the public at large and to each individual considered by himself; and Hume argued that an essential feature of the system is that the rules be followed inflexibly in every instance. Without this rigidity, he thought, the system would collapse.

One may be sceptical of these last remarks, but the point to note at the moment is that in the *Treatise* Hume was aware of a problem in subsuming justice under utility. He recognized that on occasion (he himself said "frequently") particular acts of justice are contrary to public interest. He also recognized, at the beginning of his discussion, "that men, in the ordinary conduct of life, look not so far as the public interest, when they pay their creditors, perform their promises, and abstain from theft, and robbery, and injustice of every kind. That is a motive too remote and too sublime to affect the generality of mankind, and operate with any force in actions so contrary to private interest as are frequently those of justice and common honesty."[3] If I am not mistaken, Hume's view in the *Treatise* was that a moral approbation for the rules of justice arises from sympathy with the public interest that these rules normally serve, and that this feeling of moral approbation becomes attached by association of ideas to all instances of keeping the rules, even when their contribution to public interest is not obvious and so cannot produce sympathy.

In the *Enquiry* Hume's position was simpler, and to my mind less satisfactory. I suppose that his insistence in the *Treatise* on the artificial nature of justice was intended as a rejection of Locke's view that there is a natural right to property. Locke was to a large extent a rationalist and a traditional natural-law man in ethics. So in Hume's mind the general attack on ethical rationalism, with which the *Treatise* began, could be made

[2] III.ii.2; ed. Selby-Bigge, p. 497.
[3] *Treatise*, III.ii.1; ed. Selby-Bigge, p. 481.

more specific by an attack on the idea that property is founded on natural right. Accordingly, in Book III of the *Treatise* he first argued against rationalism and in favour of a moral sense; then in part ii he dealt with justice, stressing its artificial character; and finally in part iii he considered the natural virtues, including benevolence. When Hume came to write the *Enquiry*, he virtually dropped the thesis that justice is artificial, saying that dispute on this question was purely verbal; he relegated the dispute about reason and sense (or sentiment) to an appendix; and after an introductory section his order of treatment was to discuss benevolence first, to take justice and government next, and then to elaborate the relation of all the virtues to the useful and the agreeable. Either Hume had now lost interest in attacking rationalism, or he felt that rationalists could never be roused from their dogmatic slumber, or (the most probable hypothesis) he thought that he would get a wider reading public if he highlighted those parts of his theory that were more intelligible to laymen. At any rate the discussion of justice in the *Enquiry* was directed to show that justice is *wholly* founded on utility while benevolence is only partly so. The main argument for the conclusion was as before: relative scarcity of goods and limited generosity make justice necessary for the benefit of human life. In a utopia of plenty, or one of unlimited altruism, there would be no rules of justice because they would be useless. Again, in the converse conditions of extreme scarcity or of extreme self-regard (as in a Hobbesian state of nature or a state of war), the rules of justice are suspended because there too they are useless.

The writing is splendid and justifies, as a *literary* judgment, Hume's statement in *My Own Life* that of all his works the *Enquiry concerning the Principles of Morals* was "incomparably the best". But how does it stand philosophically? One is given the impression that justice fits a utilitarian account of ethics more completely than does benevolence. Can that possibly be true? Hume mentioned the difficulties but was too cursory with them. In appendix iii, noting that particular acts of justice may be harmful to the public interest, he said "it follows that every man, in embracing that virtue, must have an eye to the whole plan or system".[4] What price now the statement of the *Treatise*

[4] Ed. Selby-Bigge, § 257.

which I quoted earlier? "Experience sufficiently proves, that men, in the ordinary conduct of life, look not so far as the public interest, when they pay their creditors, perform their promises, and abstain from theft, and robbery, and injustice of every kind. That is a motive too remote and too sublime to affect the generality of mankind . . . ."

Hume's discussion of justice concentrated on laws of property, and on *civil* rather than *criminal* law (as we can see from his sections in the *Treatise* about the different methods of acquiring a title to property).

Adam Smith on the contrary had the criminal law chiefly in mind when, in an early part of the *Theory of Moral Sentiments* (II.ii.3), he considered the relation of justice to utility. (In his Lectures on Jurisprudence he touched on the question when discussing property rights as well as repeating the *Moral Sentiments* view about the justice of punishment.) In the *Moral Sentiments* Smith's account of justice followed immediately upon his account of merit. Like Hume in the *Treatise*, Adam Smith made sympathy basic to his ethical theory. But the concept of sympathy which he used is different from Hume's, indeed more subtle and having more explanatory power.

Smith began with the 'sense of propriety' (*i.e.*, the judgment that something is right). Hume held that moral approval and disapproval result from sympathy with people who are *affected* by the action judged. A benevolent action normally has the consequence of giving happiness. We sympathize with the beneficiary and so approve of the action. Smith instead looked in the first instance to sympathy with the feelings of the *agent*. As a spectator I imagine myself in the agent's shoes. If I find that I should be moved to act as he does in that situation, then my observation of the correspondence between his feelings ("sentiments") and my own hypothetical feelings is an observation of "sympathy". This observation of correspondence of sentiments causes me to approve of the agent's motive, to think of it as 'appropriate' or "proper".

But then, when I also note the feelings of the person affected by the action, there can be a second sympathy. Let us suppose that *B* (the beneficiary) is in need and that *A* (the agent) is moved to help him. As a spectator I sympathize with *A*'s motive of benevolence and I approve of it as proper. *B* feels grateful to *A*. I can imagine myself in *B*'s shoes too, and I find that I likewise would feel grateful; so I approve of *B*'s feelings as appropriate. The conjunction of the *two* sympathies gives rise to the 'sense of merit'. An impartial spectator will sympathize with *B*'s gratitude, and so think it proper, only if he also thinks *A*'s action is proper. When he does have this double sympathy, he judges *A*'s action to be meritorious, *i.e.*, to deserve the gratitude of *B* and the kind of action that gratitude motivates, doing good in return.

Contrariwise, if *A* harms *B*, *B* is liable to feel resentment. An impartial spectator will sympathize with *B*'s resentment only if he also thinks that *A*'s action was improper, *i.e.*, if he feels an antipathy instead of a sympathy for *A*'s motive. If he sympathizes with *A* because he thinks that *A*'s harmful action was justified, he will not sympathize with *B*'s resentment. But if he does think that *B*'s resentment is proper and *A*'s action improper, he will judge *A*'s action to have demerit, *i.e.*, to deserve resentment and the kind of action that resentment motivates, a retaliation of harm.

It was from this point that Adam Smith moved on to the distinction between justice and beneficence. Acts of beneficence, if done from proper motives, deserve reward, being the proper objects of gratitude. Harmful acts, if done from improper motives, deserve punishment, being the proper objects of resentment. Smith thought of justice as primarily requiring us to refrain from harming others. The mere lack of beneficence, so long as it does no positive harm, does not call for punishment. Beneficence differs from justice therefore in being 'free', *i.e.*, in not being enforceable by the threat of punishment. Justice is enforceable, attended by sanctions. Retaliation is a law of nature, both the returning of good for good, and the returning of harm for harm. Where resentment and the retaliation of harm for harm would be approved by an impartial spectator, there punishment is in order.

When Smith came to consider the relation of justice to utility, he conceded quite a lot to Hume, indeed perhaps too much. (I think there is no doubt that he had Hume chiefly in mind when he wrote this particular chapter of the *Theory of Moral Sentiments*.) He agreed that the social utility of justice is greater than that of beneficence in that justice is essential to the existence of society. But, he argued, this does not imply that approval of justice arises from the thought of its utility. To suppose otherwise is to confuse final and efficient causation, or (as people would put the point today) it is to confuse function with cause. Justice has the function of preserving society, but this does not mean that men establish, follow, and approve the set of practices called just because they see its utility. The thought of social utility is often a secondary consideration confirming our natural feeling of what is proper and merited. It is, however, seldom the first consideration. "All men, even the most stupid and unthinking, abhor fraud, perfidy, and injustice, and delight to see them punished. But few men have reflected upon the necessity of justice to the existence of society, how obvious soever that necessity may appear to be."[5] Our concern for an individual does not depend on a concern for the society of which he forms a part, any more than our concern for the loss of a guinea depends on the thought that it forms part of a fortune of a thousand guineas. On the contrary, our regard for a multitude is made up of particular regards for the individual members of the multitude.

Smith allowed that there are some exceptional instances where the application and the approval of punishment depend purely on social utility, and he argued that the exceptions prove the rule because our attitude is clearly different in the exceptional and in the normal instance. As an example of the exceptions he cited the case of a sentinel in the army who was put to death for falling asleep at his post. It was a real-life case, which evidently impressed Smith very much by the conflicting feelings to which it gave rise in him as a typical spectator. He referred to it in the *Moral Sentiments*, in a fragment of a lecture on justice which happens to be preserved in Glasgow University Library, and in his Lectures on Jurisprudence. A crime like that of the sentinel, said Smith, does not directly harm any individual, but it is thought to be actually or potentially harmful to society in its remote consequences. The severity of the punishment may seem to be necessary and for that reason "just and proper". Yet, although justified by utility, the punishment appears "excessively severe". "The natural atrocity of

[5] *Moral Sentiments*, II.ii.3, para 9.

the crime seems to be so little, and the punishment so great, that it is with great difficulty that our heart can reconcile itself to it." The punishment does not fit the crime in terms of desert. "A man of humanity" has to make an effort to approve of it. Things are quite different when the man of humanity contemplates a similar punishment for "an ungrateful murderer or parricide". There he readily applauds the "just retaliation". "The very different sentiments with which the spectator views those different punishments, is a proof that his approbation of the one is far from being founded upon the same principles with that of the other. He looks upon the sentinel as an unfortunate victim, who, indeed, must and ought to be devoted to the safety of numbers, but whom still, in his heart, he would be glad to save; and he is only sorry that the interest of the many should opposite it. But if the murderer should escape from punishment, it would excite his highest indignation . . . ."[6]

In his Lectures on Jurisprudence Smith preceded the example of the sentinel with another, which he evidently thought more telling. Because wool was considered the main source of national wealth in England, a statute in the reign of Charles II prohibited the export of wool on pain of death. "Yet though wool was exported as formerly and men were convinced that the practice was pernicious, no jury, no evidence, could be got against the offenders. The exportation of wool is naturally no crime, and men could not be brought to consider it as punishable with death."[7] When Smith said it is "naturally no crime", he meant it is not the sort of thing that naturally excites sympathy with resentment at injury.

I said earlier that Smith perhaps conceded too much to Hume in the *Moral Sentiments* chapter. He was too ready to agree that *justification* on grounds of utility makes an act *just*. He said that the execution of the sentinel is not only proper but also just. He did not say this, in the Jurisprudence Lectures, of the death penalty for exporting wool. Men were agreed that the export of wool was socially pernicious but they did not consider the penalty proper, let alone just. In the *Moral Sentiments* Smith said of the sentinel: "When the preservation

[6] *Moral Sentiments*, II.ii.3.11.

[7] *Lectures on Justice, etc.*, ed. Cannan, p. 136.

of an individual is inconsistent with the safety of a multitude, nothing can be more just than that the many should be preferred to the one." In the fragmentary manuscript of his lecture on justice, written earlier than the *Moral Sentiments*, he had similarly said: "Nothing can be more just, than that one man should be sacrificed to the security of thousands." But towards the end of the lecture he added something else which is inconsistent with this. "Improper punishment, punishment which is either not due at all or which exceeds the demerit of the crime, is an injury to the criminal . . . ." Now since, as the *Moral Sentiments* put it, the punishment of the sentinel "appears to be excessively severe", for "the natural atrocity of the crime seems to be so little, and the punishment so great", it is punishment "which exceeds the demerit of the crime" and is therefore "an injury to the criminal". That which does an injury is unjust. It may still be warranted as right and proper on the grounds of a degree of utility great enough to override the injustice, but *unjust* it remains. The sentinel is an "unfortunate victim" who must be "devoted to the safety of numbers". The example of the export of wool is simpler and less instructive, though in a sense more telling for Smith's case against utilitarianism, because in that example the refusal of witnesses to give evidence and of juries to convict means that they regarded the claim of utility as overridden by that of justice.

It is worth recalling two features of these accounts of justice given by Hume and Smith. (1) Both men conducted their discussions in the light of the actual working of the law. They were writing in a tradition in which moral philosophy included jurisprudence as a matter of course. But Hume thought chiefly of civil law, Smith of criminal. (2) They both talked about the *origin* of justice. They thought of themselves as giving causal explanation, in terms of psychology and sociology. Nevertheless, although they talked of origins, some of their evidence undoubtedly helps conceptual clarification. Hume's imaginary and real situations of utopia and of war point to limiting conditions in our use of the concept of justice. Smith's comparison of reactions to the sentinel and to a murderer highlights the difference between justification by utility and justification by desert.

Few people will deny Hume's contention that laws about property (or indeed any system of law) come into being because they are useful. And I think few people will deny Adam Smith's contention that the concept of punishment develops from feelings of resentment and the desire to retaliate. Hume and Smith were not really opposing each other here. The one was talking about the origins of civil laws of property, and was criticizing Locke's notion of a natural right to property. The other was talking about the origins of the *method of enforcing* a system of criminal law. But the Lectures on Jurisprudence show that Smith used his theory of sympathy and the impartial spectator to account also for the origins of the civil law of property. He said that the right to property by occupation depends on the sympathetic approval of an impartial spectator, and that the right to property by accession (*e.g.*, to the produce of land or animals acquired by purchase) "is not so much founded in its utility as in the impropriety of not joining it to that object on which it has a dependence".[8] I do not think that Smith's theory of propriety (sympathetic approval by an impartial spectator) has any real explanatory power when applied to property rights. For instance, he discussed Locke's example of acquiring property in the fruit that one has picked, and agreed that the right of ownership begins with the act of picking the fruit; but he did not follow Locke's argument that a natural right arises from having mixed with the earth the labour of one's body. Smith took the more customary view of natural-law jurists that property rights are all acquired or "adventitious", not natural. His argument for saying that ownership of the fruit begins with picking it was simply that an impartial spectator would sympathize with the fruit picker's resentment if some sly cad seized the fruit after it was picked but not if he darted in and snatched it while the first picker's hand was on the way. Smith's doctrine of the impartial spectator does no more here than repeat, in a roundabout way, that we think a right is violated in the one instance and not in the other. In the case of punishment, however, Smith is more impressive, both because

[8] *Lectures on Justice, etc.*, ed. Cannan, p. 110.

he made use of his account of the double sympathy that constitutes the sense of merit, and because he was alive to psychological differences in real-life cases that come before the courts.

What are the problems which the concept of justice raises for utilitarianism? I see them as follows: (1) It is difficult to dispose of the concept of desert in terms of utility when considering the justification of punishment, though not difficult in the case of reward. (2) The obligation to keep promises, and more generally to keep faith, does not seem to depend entirely on consequences. (3) A principle of equality, which is accepted by democrats (including democratic utilitarians—"Every one to count for one"), is an addition to, not a consequence of, the principle of maximizing happiness, and sometimes the two principles can conflict. (4) All three of the considerations referred to above, and others also, exemplify the general point that a major function of the concept of justice is to express and defend the value of individual persons rather than the value of pleasure or happiness as such.

Where did Hume and Adam Smith stand in relation to these four points?

(1) Desert. Adam Smith's case against the utilitarian account of justice rested largely, though not entirely, on the difficulty about punishment. I have suggested that he did not press the objection far enough and that he perhaps conceded too much to Hume. In making the latter remark I was thinking of Hume's general thesis that justice depends on utility. For if we concentrate on the justice of punishment, it is not easy to say where Hume stood. One passage in the *Enquiry*[9] suggests a utilitarian view but not unequivocally. A couple of brief passages in the *Treatise*[10] indicate some support for a view that is retributive, at least in part. However that may be, Hume's discussions of the relation of justice to utility barely glance at the justice of punishment.

(2) Promises. Hume is brilliant on the obligation of promises, and though nagging doubts may remain on the more general issue of keeping faith with other persons as a difficulty for

---

[9] *Enquiry concerning Morals*, III.i; ed. Selby-Bigge, § 148.
[10] *Treatise*, II.iii.2 and III.iii.1; ed. Selby-Bigge, pp. 410-11 and 591.

utilitarianism, nobody can complain that Hume did not face the problems raised by promises. Adam Smith on the other hand evidently saw no problem. The subject was not even mentioned in the *Moral Sentiments*. The Lectures on Jurisprudence criticized the social-contract theory of allegiance and of course dealt extensively with the law of contract; but on the obligation of promises Smith simply distinguished a promise from a declaration of intention and said that the obligation depends on "the reasonable expectation produced by a promise", which he defined as "a declaration of your desire that the person for whom you promise should depend on you for the performance of it".[11] Professor Neil MacCormick, at the end of his interesting paper presented to our last Joint Session,[12] noted that Adam Smith's view resembles his own theory that the obligation of a promise depends on the more general obligation that arises from having induced reliance. Professor MacCormick contrasted his theory with the now popular view of promises that is essentially derived from Hume. He also suggested (but not very convincingly and perhaps not with conviction) that his account could be accommodated within utilitarianism just as well as the popular view which we owe to Hume, J. L. Austin, and John Searle. Adam Smith's brief account does indeed look similar to MacCormick's. There is, however, no evidence that Smith criticized Hume's theory of promises, that he regarded his brief definition as an alternative superior to Hume's view, or that he had any thoughts at all about the consistency or inconsistency of either with a utilitarian theory of ethics.[13]

(3) Equality. In the *Enquiry*[14] Hume considered briefly the idea that one conception of justice calls for equality. He confined himself to the extreme suggestion of a *perfect* equality of goods and, not surprisingly, dismissed it as impractical. Earlier in the *Enquiry*[15] he said that in a famine people would

---

[11] *Lectures on Justice, etc.*, ed. Cannan, pp. 130-1.

[12] *Arist. Soc. Supp. Vol.* 46 (1972), p. 78, n. 9.

[13] A writer who did criticize Hume's account of the obligation of promises and argue for the reliance theory as a superior alternative was Henry Home, Lord Kames, in *Essays on the Principles of Morality and Natural Religion* (1751), Part I, essay ii, ch. 7.

[14] III.ii; ed. Selby-Bigge, § 155.

[15] III.i; ed. Selby-Bigge, § 147.

not think it "criminal or injurious" to make an equal distribution of bread without regard to property rights. Thomas Reid[16] fairly enough retorted that the equal distribution would be *required* by justice. Such an idea seems not to have crossed Hume's mind. He argued[17] that justice *presupposes* a measure of equality (of strength) in those to whom its rules apply, but this is not relevant to the notion that justice *calls for* equality where it does not exist—*e.g.*, between men and women; Hume was content to record the fact that in many societies women are virtually in the position of slaves. Adam Smith was no more sensitive than Hume to an egalitarian conception of justice. In his youth he wrote enthusiastically of our tendency to admire "the rich and the great". In his old age he modified his view. He still thought that admiration of the rich and the great, with contempt for the poor and the weak, was both natural and socially useful; but he also thought it corrupted the moral sentiments, which approve of admiration only for the wise and the good, and of contempt only for the foolish and the bad. That is to say, he became more sensitive to the tension between social and moral stratification, but he was always a stratifier, never a leveller.

(4) Individuals. Adam Smith showed some awareness of this point when he said that concern for individuals does not depend on concern for society. Hume said a little, in the last paragraph of appendix iii to the *Enquiry*, about considering the position of the individual. He held that *after* the laws of justice are fixed from a regard to general utility, a *secondary* consideration that causes us to blame breaches of these laws is disapproval of the harm done to individuals. It is bound to be secondary, he argued, because the idea of violating an individual's rights presupposes laws of property, and these must be established for reasons of interest, as he had previously explained. This argument of Hume's is faulty. In the *Treatise* Hume distinguished "three different species of goods, which we are possess'd of; the internal satisfaction of our minds, the external advantages of our body, and the enjoyment of such possessions as we have acquir'd by our industry and good fortune".[18]

[16] *Essays on the Active Powers*, V. 5.

[17] *Enquiry*, III.i.; ed. Selby-Bigge, § 152.

[18] *Treatise*, III.ii.2; ed. Selby-Bigge, p. 487.

Property concerns the third of these. But a man can be injured in respect of reputation and body as well as in respect of property.[19] In the simplest of societies laws protecting people from personal injury are at least as basic as laws protecting property. Adam Smith said that "the most sacred laws of justice" are those which guard life and person, followed in order of importance by those which guard property and then by those which guard the rights of contract.[20]

Some scholars nowadays seem to think that the difficulties which utilitarianism faces over the concept of justice are resolved by substituting 'rule-utilitarianism' for 'act-utilitarianism'. Hume's account of justice is a form of rule-utilitarianism, and a suggestion of such a view is found also in Hutcheson's definition of rights in terms of universal practices. Both Hutcheson and Hume were thinking of the rules of law, which are indeed applied universally even though the result in individual cases is sometimes absurd. 'Hard cases make bad law', they say. The justification commonly given is 'certainty', *i.e.*, of predicting what the courts will decide. It is a utilitarian justification in that the advantages of certainty are held to outweigh the injustice of applying the rules inflexibly to hard cases. Outside the law, however, nobody in his senses thinks that the utility of rules requires inflexible adherence to them in hard cases. A good administrator is not the man bound by red tape; he is the man who knows what rules to make and who also knows when to break the rules. Apart from Kant, no deontologist thinks that the rules of promise-keeping or truth-telling should *never* be broken in the interests of utility. A rule-utilitarian presumably does not want us to be less flexible than we are.

Hume's version of rule-utilitarianism was intended to give a genetic explanation of why people approve of keeping a rule even in instances where it is contrary to utility. He said it is because of psychological association. Hume did not raise the question whether it is reasonable to act on such a form of approval if one has the choice either of following one's psychological bias or of aiming at maximum utility. It seems to me

[19] *Cf.* Adam Smith, *Lectures on Justice, etc.*, ed. Cannan, p. 5.
[20] *Moral Sentiments*, II.ii.2.2.

that a utilitarian ought to say that the only reasonable and right thing to do is to aim at utility. Does rule-utilitarianism counsel otherwise, and if so, why? If it does not, are we to suppose that modern rule-utilitarianism, like Hume, is giving a psychological explanation of how people do in fact judge, and not a criterion of how they should? In that event it would do well to look at Adam Smith's improvement on the psychology of Hume. I agree with Westermarck that "Adam Smith's *Theory of Moral Sentiments* is the most important contribution to moral psychology made by any British thinker".[21]

[21] *Ethical Relativity*, p. 71.

[5]

TWO CONCEPTS OF MORALITY:

*A Distinction of Adam Smith's Ethics and its Stoic Origin**

By Norbert Waszek

"The amiable virtue of humanity requires, surely, a sensibility, much beyond what is possessed by the rude vulgar of mankind . . . Virtue is excellence, something uncommonly great and beautiful, which rises far above what is vulgar and ordinary."[1]

"The Stoics in general seem to have admitted that there might be a degree of proficiency in those who had not advanced to perfect virtue and happiness. They distributed those proficients into different classes, according to the degree of their advancement; and they called the imperfect virtues which they supposed them capable of exercising, not rectitudes, but proprieties, fitnesses, decent and becoming actions, for which a plausible or probable reason could be assigned, what Cicero expresses by the Latin word 'officia', and Seneca, I think more exactly, by that of 'convenientia'. The doctrine of those imperfect, but attainable virtues, seems to have constituted what we may call the practical morality of the Stoics. It is the subject of Cicero's Offices; and is said to have been that of another book written by Marcus Brutus, but which is now lost."[2]

The crucial claim of Smith's *Theory of Moral Sentiments,* first published in 1759, might be summed up as follows: Everybody can act or can be expected to act with complete 'propriety', determined by the 'sympathy' of an 'impartial spectator'. The description of social-psychological processes by which Smith elucidates upon the above concepts constitutes the originality and lasting significance of his ethical thought. Beside this main line of explaining how everybody can behave with propriety, another, more esoteric line is also discernible in Smith's thought, showing the praiseworthy path of 'perfect virtue' that is open to a small élite. The first purpose of the present paper is to clarify and emphasize the relevance of this two-level approach of Smith's moral philosophy.

Adam Smith, like many of his fellow-literati, felt strongly attracted by Stoic philosophy, an attraction which resulted in the pride of place devoted to "the

* This paper builds on the chapter on Smith in my unpublished M. Litt. Thesis: *Man's Social Nature: A Topic of the Scottish Enlightenment in its Historical Setting* (University of Stirling, Nov. 1979) and on a talk, "Stoicism as a Source of the Scottish Enlightenment", delivered at a 1980 meeting of the 'Seminar of Social and Political Thought', University of Cambridge. I wish to thank my old friend, Mr. David L. Simpson, M.A., for checking and improving the author's English style. His gratitude is also due to those who by their comments and criticism have helped to improve upon the previous versions of the paper. However, responsibility for all remaining failures rests entirely with me.

[1] Adam Smith, *The Theory of Moral Sentiments.* Henceforth cited as *TMS* and quoted from the first volume of the recent *Glasgow Edition of the Works and Correspondence of Adam Smith,* edited by D. D. Raphael & A. L. Macfie (Oxford, 1976) I.i. part V, 25.

[2] *TMS,* part VII.ii.I, 29lf.

doctrines of that famous sect"[3] in Smith's historical sketch "Of Systems of Moral Philosophy."[4] Such obvious external evidence was not overlooked by some Smith scholars—Professors A. L. Macfie and D. D. Raphael deserve a special mention in this context—but little has been done beyond these general comments.[5] Thus, the second purpose of this paper is to vindicate the general claim of a Stoic influence on Smith in a particular aspect: it will be shown that Smith's distinction (propriety of the multitude—virtue of the wise few), as well as most of the particulars in its wake, can be traced back to Stoicism. With regard to Smith's position within the Scottish Enlightenment, this affinity to Stoicism puts Smith's TMS closer to Hutcheson than to Hume.[6]

Finally, it may be appropriate to leave the question of indebtedness and influence on one side and to add something on the relevance of the issue. As any form of élitism is nowadays looked down upon, it is necessary to emphasize the real meaning of Smith's restriction of virtue to the wise few. In particular, Smith's account has to be defended against the sweeping and superficial charge of favouring class privileges. Smith's élite of the few virtuous wise has nothing to do with social classes, it rather is a *spiritual* aristocracy, a notion that may most easily be understood by recalling such sixteenth-century ethical formulas as "virtus vera nobilitas [est]".[7] Another way to gain an adequate insight into the nature and relevance of Smith's élitism is by an analogy with Dostoevsky—allowing for a moment the obvious anachronism and running the risk of being reckoned among those who "use Dostoevsky as a support for personal convictions"[8]. When Dostoevsky strove after the creation of the beautiful soul, after the convincing embodiment of the 'prekrasny' or morally excellent character, he was really in search of something very similar to Smith's perfectly virtuous and wise men.[9]

[3] *TMS*, Advertisement, 3.

[4] *TMS*, Title of part VII, 265-342.

[5] A. L. Macfie, "The Scottish Tradition in Economic Thought", *Scottish Journal of Political Economy*, II (1955), 81-103, here 82 & 86-88; an interesting attempt to relate Smith's account of virtue to Stoicism has now been made by D. D. Raphael and A. L. Macfie (Introduction" to *TMS*, 5-10). I am indebted to their presentation but will try to go further.

[6] The author hopes to follow up the present article with accounts of Hutcheson's indebtedness to the Stoics' *sensus communis* and Hume's criticism of the Stoics.

[7] "Virtue [is] true mobility". This is the motto of Trinity College and a crucial notion of stoically inspired Renaissance thought. I am greatly indebted to Quentin Skinner for a personal letter in which he sets forth the central rôle of this notion with reference to Sir Thomas More's *Utopia*, to Elyot's *Book of the Governor*, and to Bartolus's attack on Dante. Being convinced that Smith took his Stoic ideas from Roman sources rather than from the revival of these ideas in early British moral philosophy, I decided against adding this interesting material to the present paper.

[8] René Wellek, "Introduction: A Sketch of the History of Dostoevsky Criticism" in René Wellek (ed.), *Dostoevsky—A Collection of Critical Essays* (New York, 1962), 9.

[9] Dostoevsky's noblest heros (e.g., Sonya Marmeladova, Prince Myshkin, Father Tikhon, Father Zosima, and Alyosha Karamazov) are best understood in the light of this attempt. Dostoevsky's own formulation of this aim is to be found in the letters to Maikov (Jan. 12, 1868) and to S. A. Ivanova (Jan. 13, 1868) in which he informs them of the creation of Prince Myshkin. Cf. Konstantin Mochulsky, *Dostoevsky* (Princeton, 1971), 343ff.

I. The distinction between 'propriety' and 'virtue' is explicitly made by Smith himself:

There is . . . a considerable difference between virtue and mere propriety; between those qualities and actions which deserve to be admired and celebrated, and those which simply deserve to be approved of. Upon many occasions, to act with the most perfect propriety, requires no more than that common and ordinary degree of sensibility or self-command which the most worthless of mankind are possest of . . . [Whereas] The amiable virtues consist in that degree of sensibility which surprises by its exquisite and unexpected delicacy and tenderness. The awful and respectable, in that degree of self-command which astonishes by its amazing superiority over the most ungovernable passions of human nature.[10]

and modern scholars, like Prof. T. D. Campbell[11], have frequently underlined it. Likewise, Smith clearly distinguished—as Prof. H. Mizuta has recently stressed[12]—between the multitude, "rude vulgar"[13], or "bulk of mankind"[14] on the one hand and the wise few, "philosophers or men of speculation"[15] on the other hand. What seems to have passed unnoticed, however, is the close connection of these distinctions: Smith restricts 'virtue' to the wise few, while allowing for 'propriety' even among the vulgar. In order to vindicate this claim let us first consider the basic components of Smith's account of virtue: prudence, self-command, justice, and beneficence. In order to constitute the admirable standard of 'virtue' all these components have to be particularly marked; "in the common degree of the moral [qualities] there is no virtue."[16] As part of 'virtue' prudence "supposes the utmost perfection of all the intellectual . . . virtues"[17], self-command enables "to act with cool deliberation in the midst of the greatest dangers and difficulties"[18], justice preserves "a sacred and religious regard not to hurt or disturb in any respect the happiness of our neighbour"[19] even in the face of "the greatest interests which might tempt"[20], and beneficence extends to "the immensity of the universe"[21]. Let us now show

[10] *TMS*, I.i.5.7 & 6, p. 25.

[11] T. D. Campbell, *Adam Smith's Science of Morals* (London, 1971), 167f; Smith "uses the contrast between approval and admiration in order to distinguish two different moral standards . . . of virtue, that which is normally expected and that which is unusually virtuous."

[12] Hiroshi Mizuta, "Moral Philosophy and Civil Society" in A. S. Skinner and T. Wilson (eds.) *Essays on Adam Smith* (Oxford, 1975), 114-31.

[13] *TMS*, part I.i.5.6, p. 25.

[14] Adam Smith, "The principles which lead and direct philosophical enquiries; illustrated by the history of astronomy"; here quoted from Vol. III of the recent *Glasgow Edition of the Works and Correspondence of Adam Smith: Essays on Philosophical Subjects*, edited by W. P. D. Wightman, J. C. Bryce, & I. S. Ross (Oxford, 1980), II.11, p. 45.

[15] Adam Smith, *An Inquiry into the Nature and Causes of the Wealth of Nations*. Here quoted from Vol. II of the *Glasgow Edition* . . ., *op. cit.*, edited by R. H. Campbell & A. S. Skinner (Oxford, 1976), I.i.9, p. 21.

[16] *TMS*, I.i.5.6, p. 25.

[17] *Ibid.*, VI.i.15, p. 216.

[18] *Ibid.*, VI.iii.11, p. 241.

[19] *Ibid.*, VI.ii.Introduction.2, p. 218.

[20] *Ibid.*, VI.iii.11, p. 241.

[21] *Ibid.*, VI.ii.3.1, p. 235.

that this excellence is particularly characteristic of the wise minority. With regard to prudence, justice, and beneficence this is easily done: wisdom is a necessary part of them. Admired, as opposed to being approved of, is not the ordinary degree of prudence, but the "superior prudence . . . the most perfect wisdom . . . [which] constitutes very nearly the character of the Academical or Peripatetic sage."[22] Likewise, to be able to follow the path of justice and beneficence depends on knowing it, and who but a sage could always be sure of the rules of "strict justice"[23] and discern "the greater interest of the universe" to which, induced by universal benevolence, the "virtuous man is at all times willing . . . [to sacrifice] his own private interest"[24]? The connection between a high degree of self-command and wisdom is less obvious, but nevertheless discernible. To begin with, Smith certainly compares exceptional self-command with exceptional intellectual capacities.[25] And, more important, Smith's main examples of self-command—though he mentions the self-command of "the savages in North America"[26]—are taken from the little flock of philosophers, in other words, from the wise minority: he comments on Socrates and Sir Thomas More[27], and repeatedly on Cato Uticensis, that traditional prototype of the Stoical wise[28]:

Cato, surrounded on all sides by his enemies, unable to resist them, disdaining to submit to them, and reduced, by the proud maxims of that age, to the necessity of destroying himself; yet never shrinking from his misfortunes, never supplicating with the lamentable voice of wretchedness, those miserable sympathetic tears which we are always so unwilling to give; but on the contrary, arming himself with manly fortitude, and the moment before he executes his fatal resolution, giving, with his usual tranquility, all necessary orders for the safety of his friends;[29] . . . .

To sum up, Smith considered virtue to be excellence, an excellence which often depends upon and can always easily be associated with the wisdom of a small élite.

Such excellence cannot generally be expected, as Smith realistically points out, from "so imperfect a creature as man"[30]. Perfect virtue is rare, but propriety and decency, Smith insists, may be found among all men. Even the multitude is capable of "a mercenary exchange of good offices according to an agreed valuation"[31]. As the standard of propriety is generally traceable—even "the most worthless of mankind"[32]—Smith makes this level, rather than of perfect

[22] *Ibid.*, VI.i.15, p. 216.

[23] *Ibid.*, VI.iii.1, p. 237.

[24] *Ibid.*, VI.ii.3.3, p. 235.

[25] *Ibid.*, I.i.5.6, p. 25.

[26] *Ibid.*, V.2.9, p. 205.

[27] Ibid., VI.iii.5, p. 238 (Socrates); VI.iii.5, p. 239 (Sir Thomas More).

[28] Cp.: f. H. Sandbach, *The Stoics* (London, 1975) p. 143: "For later Roman Stoics of the upper classes he [Cato] became the ideal prototype, the man who lived and died as reason and conscience dictated."

[29] *TMS*, I.iii.1.13, p. 48.

[30] *Ibid.*, VII.ii.3.18, p. 305.

[31] *Ibid.*, II.ii.3.2, p. 86.

[32] *Ibid.*, I.i.5.7, p. 25.

virtue, his main concern. Consequently, questions like 'wherein does propriety consist? ', 'how can it be measured? ', and 'how can everybody achieve this level? ' take up plenty of space in the *Theory of Moral Sentiments,* whereas the account of perfect virtue is restricted to a few esoteric passages. In order to explicate the meaning of 'propriety' let us begin by considering Smith's general definition:

In the suitableness or unsuitableness, in the proportion or disproportion which the affection seems to bear to the cause or object which excites it, consists the propriety or impropriety, the decency or ungracefulness of the consequent action.[33]

According to Smith we judge upon this "proportion or disproportion" by imagining how we would have acted in a similar situation. If, for example, we could go along with that degree of indignation displayed by a man whose trust in a friend had been abused, we would call his indignation 'proper'. Our feelings were then in agreement, we 'sympathize' with him. If, however, his indignation would grow out of all proportion to its cause, e.g. if his indignation induced him never to trust again, our sympathy would falter and his reaction would be called 'improper'. But we not only imagine ourselves to be in the relevant situation, but also in the general circumstances and character of the person concerned, "we enter as it were into his body, and become in some measure the same person with him"[34]. The importance of this imagined change of person was emphasized by Smith himself:

When I condole with you for the loss of your only son, in order to enter into your grief I do not consider what I, a person of such a character and profession, should suffer, if I had a son, and if that son was unfortunately to die: but I consider what I should suffer if I was really you, and not only change circumstances with you, but I *change persons and characters.*[35]

It could further be clarified by the following example: If we only knew the immediate cause, a man's utter despair over the loss of a moderate sum of money would hardly seem 'proper' to us. However, if we take a closer look at this man and then imagine we had his psychological instability, his financial problems, and his bad luck in the recent past, we may well sympathize with his reaction. As we know friends and relations better than strangers, we find it easier to sympathize with the former than with the latter. In order to get a more objective measure, Smith introduces the concept of the 'impartial spectator'. The ultimate decision upon the propriety or impropriety of an action thus depends upon the granting or refusal of an impartial spectator's sympathy with the action. It is an old legal principle that no one should be judge in his own case. Smith accepts this principle: the propriety of an action is judged by a 'spectator' a word which implies, 'per definitionem', that the respective person is not involved in the action under consideration. The additional word 'impartial' guarantees that the spectator neither has any particular relationship to the agent, a condition best met

[33] *Ibid.,* I.i.3.6, p. 18.
[34] *Ibid.,* I.i.1.2, p. 9.
[35] *Ibid.,* VII.iii.1.4, p. 317-my own italics; N.W.

by a stranger, nor should he be affected, perhaps indirectly, by the outcome of the relevant action. In general, as Prof. T. D. Campbell has indicated,[36] the position of the 'impartial spectator' resembles the rôle of a juryman.

What behavior can now be said to constitute propriety or, to put it more precisely, what standards are used by the impartial spectator to identify propriety? As the 'impartial spectator' is an abstraction based on ordinary men, his standards of judgment are also determined by the normal feelings[37] and that ordinary degree of understanding[38] which is possessed by average men: "We are not at present examining upon what principles a perfect being would approve of the punishment of bad actions; but upon what principles so weak and imperfect a creature as man actually and in fact approves of it."[39] Therefore, in order to gain the sympathy of the impartial spectator the excellence of virtue is not required, a 'mediocre'[40] conduct is quite sufficient. In the place of rare wisdom, an "inferior prudence"[41] ("directed merely to the care of the health, of the fortune, and of the rank and reputation of the individual"[42]) will do. Constant universal benevolence is superfluous, but beneficence must not fall short of either the generosity towards friends and relatives or the love of one's native country. The justice of Solomon, the self-command of Cato cannot be expected, but to abstain from infringing upon other people's rights[43] and to confine the bodily appetities within the limits of modesty[44] is certainly required. In particular, the "social passions" (generosity, humanity, kindness, compassion, mutual friendship, and esteem)[45] are strongly approved of and thereby reinforced. The "unsocial passions" (hatred, anger, and resentment)[46] are disapproved of and consequently restrained. A moderate degree of self-love—best understood, perhaps, as an equivalent of the Christian '*ordinatus amor sui*'[47]—is positively valued,[48] but "the arrogance of . . . self-love"[49]—possibly an allusion to the psychological egoism of Hobbes—has to be humbled:

> In the race for wealth, and honours, and preferments, he [man] may run as hard as he can, and strain every nerve and every muscle, in order to outstrip all his competitors. But if he should justle, or throw down any of them, the indulgence of the spectators is entirely at an end. It is a violation of fair play,

[36] T. D. Campbell, *op. cit.,* 135.

[37] Which are subject to fortune, see *TMS,* II.iii.3.1, p. 104: "Fortune . . . directs in some measure the sentiments of mankind, with regard to the character and conduct both of themselves and others."

[38] As distinguished from the assessments of "cool reason"; *TMS,* II.iii.3.2, p. 105.

[39] *TMS,* II.i.5.10, p. 77.

[40] Cp. *TMS,* I.ii.Introduction.2, p. 27: "This mediocrity . . . in which the point of propriety consists . . ."

[41] *TMS,* VI.i.15, p. 216.

[42] *Ibid.,* VI.i.14, p. 216.

[43] *Ibid.,* II.ii.1.5, p. 79.

[44] *Ibid.,* I.ii.1.4, p. 28.

[45] *Ibid.,* I.ii.4, pp. 38-40.

[46] *Ibid.,* I.ii.3, pp. 34-38.

[47] 'Orderly' or 'legitimate' self-love.

[48] *TMS,* VI.ii.1.1, p. 219.

[49] *Ibid.,* II.ii.2.1, p. 83.

which they cannot admit of . . . they do not enter into that self-love by which he prefers himself so much to this other. . . .[50]

Let us finally show why, according to Smith, even the 'vulgar multitude' can achieve the level of propriety? The ultimate basis and principal motive of propriety is an inborn propensity of human nature, man's 'love of praise':

Nature, when she formed man for society, endowed him with an original desire to please, and an original aversion to offend his brethren. She taught him to feel pleasure in their favourable, and pain in their unfavourable regard. She rendered their approbation most flattering and most agreeable to him for its own sake; and their disapprobation most mortifying and most offensive.[51]

This motivating force, the love of praise, could be mistaken for vanity, had Smith not taken pains in preventing such misinterpretation: "The most sincere praise can give little pleasure when it cannot be considered as some sort of proof of praise-worthiness."[52] Before we can fully enjoy the approval and praise of our fellows, we have to be convinced that this praise is justified. Again, we have to consider our actions, not through the praise of a flatterer, but through the eyes of an 'impartial spectator', before we can be satisfied with them: "We must endeavour to view them [our character and conduct] with the eyes of other people, or as other people are likely to view them. When seen in this light, if they appear to us as we wish, we are happy and contented.[53] The 'love of praise' and the 'impartial spectator', we may conclude, complement each other in the most perfect way, the former providing the motivation and stimulus, the latter directing this stimulus towards its proper aim, the propriety of conduct.

II. The first objective of the present section is to introduce some Stoic terminology and ideas, to show how Adam Smith interpreted these ideas, and to argue that his distinction between the virtue of the wise few and the propriety of the multitude is indebted to these ideas. The second aim is to relate the elements of Smith's account of virtue to the Stoical system. Finally, a balance between Smith's indebtedness to the Stoics and the original aspects of his ethical thought will be sought.

Adolf Bonhöffer, the great German Epictetus scholar, once referred to the *katorthoma* (in English, though one cannot really translate the concept, perhaps best expressed by 'morally right action') and the *kathekon* (which, with the above qualification, we would call 'appropriate action') as being amongst the most difficult and still insufficiently clarified concepts of Stoic philosophy.[54] Even today, the *kathekon-katorthoma* issue is still a stumbling-block, a subject of controversy among classicists.[55] As is the case with many problems of Stoicism, the issue gained complexity through the sheer length of the period in which

[50] *Ibid.*

[51] *Ibid.*, III.2.6, p. 116.

[52] *Ibid.*, III.2.4, p. 114.

[53] *Ibid.*, III.2.3, p. 114.

[54] Adolph Bonhöffer, *Die Ethik des Stoikers Epictet* (Stuttgart, 1894) p. 193.

[55] Compare, for example, the opposing views of J. M. Rist, *Stoic Philosophy* (Cambridge, 1969) Chapter 6 and G. B. Kerferd, "Cicero and Stoic Ethics", in J. R. C. Martyn (ed.), *Cicero and Virgil. Studies in Honour of Harold Hunt* (Amsterdam, 1972), 60-74.

Stoicism flourished: the concepts underwent modifications which are difficult to document, more difficult to interpret, and most difficult to evaluate. We neither can nor do we aspire to solve these problems. For our purposes it is quite sufficient to make some basic points upon which a consensus may be taken as now established.[56]

From Zeno onwards the Stoics used two levels to judge upon an action. The first one is the absolute, 'all-or-nothing' level: an action either results from the perfection of the human soul, which may be defined as the full and true understanding of human nature coupled with the unerring will to live in accordance with this rational nature, in which case alone an action is truly virtuous *katorthoma* and only the rare representatives of wisdom are capable of this perfection, or it does not spring from this source, a shortcoming which would restrict the action, irrespective of its other qualities, to the realm of failure and sin, a *hamartema*:

> You must be one man, good or bad: you must develop either your rational soul, or your outward endowments, you must be busy either with your inner man, or with things outside, that is you must choose between the position of a philosopher and that of an ordinary man.[57]

"All imperfect men are bad men", as Prof. Sandbach sums up the Stoics' view,[58] and there is no doubt that their position is a radical one. The Stoics themselves were fully aware of this as may be taken from the instances when they looked for examples of those wise capable of the *katorthoma* and realized that there were only a handful of men (Socrates, Zeno, Chrysippus, Posidonius, Cato, Laelius, Tubero)[59] in the whole history of mankind; a few lonely stars amongst impenetrable darkness. And yet, in spite of its radicalism, their position is not an absurd one. For, first, this radicalism is mitigated by the function of those few capable of the *katorthoma*: they represent an ideal meant to help ordinary men in their own efforts and struggles:

> O felicem illum qui non praesens tantum sed etiam cogitatus emendat! . . . Elige itaque Catonem; si hic tibi videtur nimis rigidus, elige remissioris animi virum Laelium. Elige eum cuius tibi placuit et vita et oratio et ipse animum

[56] The following account is frequently indebted to F. H. Sandbach, *The Stoics* (London, 1975) and to Max Pohlenz's impressive *Die Stoa. Geschichte einer geistigen Bewegung.* In 2 vols. (Goettingen, 4th edition, 1970).

[57] Epictetus, *The Discourses and Manual.* Translated with introduction and notes by P. E. Matheson. In 2 vols. (Oxford, 1916) Book III, 16; Vol. II, p. 48—For a similar view of Zeno himself, see: Hans von Arnim, *Stoicorum Veterum Fragmenta.* In 3 vols. (Leipzig, 1902-5) Vol. I, pp. 192 & 230—Compare also: Diogenes Laertius, *Lives of Eminent Philosophers,* Book VII, 127 & Seneca, *Epistulae morales ad Lucilium,* Letters LXXII and LXXV.

[58] F. H. Sandbach, *op. cit.,* 47.

[59] This list is taken from Seneca's *Epistulae morales ad Lucilium,* Letter CIV. Quite often even fewer examples are given.

ante se ferens vultus; illum tibi semper ostende vel custodem vel exemplum.[60]

And, secondly, as both Bonhöffer and Pohlenz have emphasized,[61] a very similar position is indeed familiar to all of us, i.e. the radical challenge of Christianity, in the words of St. Paul: ". . . whatever does not proceed from faith is sin."[62]

Beside this perfection-or-failure level, however, the Stoics always had another way of considering an action. The theoretical position of dismissing indiscriminately everything short of the *katorthoma* has in practical questions been complemented by a more gradual system of evaluation. Even though an action is not perfect, it may still be preferred or rejected or considered indifferent:

Itaque cum esset satis constitutum id solum esse bonum quod esset honestum et id malum solum quod turpe, tum inter illa quae nihil valerent ad beate misereve vivendum aliquid tamen quod differret esse voluerunt, ut essent eorum alia aestimabilia, alia contra, alia neutrum.[63]

Let us illustrate this distinction and its relation to the *katorthoma-hamartema* level with the example—frequently used by the Stoics themselves—of a trust.[64] To breach a trust consciously and with a view to enriching oneself illegally is vicious (hamartema). To restore, on the other hand, a trust for its own sake, as a matter of principle and "with full understanding of why it is right to do so"[65] is part of the wise man's virtue *(katorthoma).* So far we have a simple clear-cut alternative: either acting in accordance with right reason or contrary to it. Obviously, however, there are other possibilities. A trust may be restored from a variety of motives and causes apart from right reason. It may be restored with the expectation of a reward or future advantages; it may also be restored from a sense of what is fitting, proper, or in agreement with the 'decorum'; or it may be restored merely as a result of custom. Whether this intermediate group of actions—as most scholars now believe[66]—may be considered a part of the total of proper actions *(kathekonta),* the perfect actions *(katorthomata)* being another rather special part of this total; whether this group of actions—as Zeller seems

[60] Seneca, *op. cit.,* Letter XI. My own translation: "Happy the man who improves others not only through his presence but even through their thoughts of him! . . . Thus choose yourself a Cato; if he seems too inexorable to you, choose Laelius, a man of more liberal character. Choose someone whose life, whose language and whose very face as mirroring the soul, has found your acclaim; always keep him in mind either as a guardian or as an example."

[61] A. Bonhöffer, *op. cit.,* p. 212; M. Pohlenz, *op. cit.,* I, 129.

[62] *New Testament,* Romans 14.23. Quoted from the *Revised Standard Version* (1946).

[63] Cicero, *De finibus bonorum et malorum,* III.xv.50—English translation by H. Rackham from the Loeb-edition (London, 1914) 269 & 271: "Accordingly after conclusively proving that morality alone is good and baseness alone evil, the Stoics went on to affirm that among those things which were of no importance for happiness or misery, there was nevertheless an element of difference, making some of them of positive and others of negative value, and others neutral." Cp. also Diogenes Laertius, *op. cit.,* VII, 105.

[64] Cp. A. Bonhöffer, *op. cit.,* 213.

[65] F. H. Sandbach, *op. cit.,* 46.

[66] For example: M. Pohlenz, *op. cit.,* I, 130; G. B. Kerferd, *op. cit.,* 62; F. H. Sandbach, *op. cit.,* 45ff.

to have thought[67]—may exclusively be called *kathekonta* or not at all—as Bonhöffer insisted[68]—are questions best left to the scholars of classical philosophy. To have shown that the Stoics had a second level of assessing actions is sufficient for our purposes. Although a trust, to come back to our example, has been restored from motives less sublime than the virtue of the wise, the Stoics still prefer the restoration to the embezzlement and likewise prefer the restoration from respect of the 'decorum', to mere custom or even the considerations of interest. And not only do they prefer the restoration, but would indeed expect it from any ordinarily decent man. Had Zeno really taught, to borrow a negative argument from Bonhöffer,[69] that restoring or breaching a trust and the various possible motives for restoring it were matters of complete indifference as long as the full understanding of the wise is lacking, the Athenians would presumably have put him to death instead of erecting a statue in his memory. How the two levels of the Stoics' evaluation of an action can go together is not always easy to see, but that does not mean they are incompatible. The lack of contradiction between the levels of absolute and relative value is, perhaps, best understood through another comparison with Christianity, for who would overlook the difference between the pagan and the convert even though both of them may be sinners?

The particular attention, if such a generalization is permissible, which Roman Stoicism paid to practical questions led to an increased interest in the group of imperfect but still acceptable actions. With regard to Seneca, Max Pohlenz has justly spoken of "the extension of the concept of *'kathekon'*, which leaves a wide space for the rules of social etiquette"[70]; Cicero devoted a whole book to the *medium* or *commune officium* (= ordinary duties)[71]; and both Epictetus and Marcus Aurelius, too, were far from diminishing the relative value of appropriate if imperfect qua unwise actions: . . . and do not, just because you have abandoned hope of being a thinker and a student of science, on this account despair of being free, modest, sociable, and obedient to God; . . . .[72] However, the greater interest among the later Stoics in the imperfect but 'proper' actions should not be interpreted as displacing the ideal of the perfectly wise and virtuous man. They insisted on this ideal as strongly as any of their Greek predecessors, and by painting it in the colours of the Roman *virtus* or *vir bonus* and by illustrating it with examples from Roman history, they even made it more appealing and convincing. That they devoted their special attention to what is 'proper' is not a radical transformation but merely a change of emphasis, reflecting the par-

[67] Eduard Zeller, *Die Philosophie der Griechen in ihrer geschichtlichen Entwicklung.* Part Three, Section I, 273f.—Our page reference is to the fourth edition (Leipzig, 1909), edited by Dr. Eduard Wellmann.

[68] A. Bonhöffer, *op. cit.,* 193-233, esp. 232.

[69] *Ibid.,* 209.

[70] Max Pohlenz, *op. cit.,* I, 310; my own translation.

[71] Cicero, *De officiis,* I.iii.8—Compare also the discussion of Cicero's Latin rendering of the *'kathekon'* in: Georg Kilb, "Ethische Grundbegriffe der alten Stoa und ihre Ubertragung durch Cicero," ed. Karl Büchner *Das neue Cicerobild* (Därmstadt, 1971) pp. 38-64.

[72] A. S. L. Farquharson (ed.), *The Meditations of Marcus Aurelius Antoninus.* Greek and English. In 2 vols. (Oxford, 1944) VII.67, Vol. I, 143.

ticular demands of Roman citizens on Stoic philosophy. This special emphasis of Roman Stoicism on the generally attainable level of decent conduct will become significant with regard to Adam Smith, for it was precisely the Roman Stoics (Cicero[73], Seneca, Epictetus, and Marcus Aurelius) with whom Smith was most familiar, as is testified by the many quotations and references in Smith's works.

We have shown so far that both Adam Smith, on the one hand, and the Stoics, on the other hand, clearly distinguished between the level of a perfectly virtuous conduct—of which only the rare élite of the wise are capable, those who have, according to the common stoical formula, "full understanding of all things both divine and human"—and the level of merely 'proper' conduct, in the sense of being in accordance with the 'decorum' of society, which can be expected from everyone.[74] However, the affinity of their ideas, taken on its own, does not manifest an influence. We still have to show that Smith knew and interpreted the Stoics' point of view in the same way as we have done. But this gap in our argument is easily filled. In Smith's historical sketch "Of Systems of Moral Philosophy"[75], it is clear that the 'true' Stoical doctrine[76] is presented as in our above account, namely as evaluating an action on *two* levels. Smith first explains the absolute, perfection-versus-failure level with two illustrations: morally imperfect actions are as indifferent "as the man . . . who was but an inch below the surface of the water, could no more breathe than he who was an hundred yards below it"[77], or "as in shooting at a mark, the man who missed it by an inch had equally missed it with him who had done so by a hundred yards."[78] Before going on to the second level, Smith emphasized that the first contrast should not be understood in the literal sense of excluding any further distinction between actions. Smith associates this type of misreading with the "dialectical pedant"[79] Chrysippus who "may very easily be supposed to have understood too literally some animated expressions of his masters [sc.: Zeno and Cleanthes]."[80] In the case of the majority of Stoics, as opposed to Chrysippus, Smith presumes a more gradual evaluation, "according to the degree of their advancement . . . to perfect virtue."[81] Thus, even imperfect actions may constitute propriety, fitness, and decency; and Smith refers to Cicero, Seneca, and Brutus as having dealt with this set of "imperfect, but attainable virtues."[82] Not only did Smith recognize and express the Stoics' distinction in his historical sketch, but the very same distinction, even in similar formulations, is also made in the presentation of Smith's own ideas, namely in the section on propriety:

[73] As far as Cicero can be considered either following Stoic ideas or, at least, transmitting them to Rome. In this context, his relevant writings are *De officiis* and *De finibus bonorum et malorum.*

[74] Cp.: F. H. Sandbach, *op. cit.,* 125.

[75] Title of Part VII of the TMS.

[76] As opposed to Chrysippus' misinterpretation; see below.

[77] *TMS,* VII.ii.1.40, p. 290.

[78] *Ibid.,* p. 291.

[79] *Ibid.,* VII.ii.1.41, p. 291.

[80] *Ibid.*

[81] *Ibid.,* VII.ii.1.42, p. 291.

[82] *Ibid.*

> ... when we are determining the degree of blame or applause which seems due to any action, we very frequently make use of two different standards. The first is the idea of complete propriety and perfection ... in comparison with which the actions of all men must for ever appear blameable and imperfect. The second is the idea of that degree of proximity or distance from this complete perfection, which the actions of the greater part of men commonly arrive at.[83]

We may therefore conclude that (a) we find the same two level approach—virtue of the wise, propriety of the multitude—in the ethical theories of both the Stoics and Adam Smith; (b) Adam Smith knew the ethics of the Stoics whom he interpreted as accepting the level of 'propriety' whenever 'virtue' could not be achieved; (c) it seems thus highly probable that the outlined distinction in Smith's own system is deeply indebted to Stoicism.

This conclusion finds further support if we consider the contents of Smith's account of virtue. In this respect, the first major parallel between Stoicism and Smith is the ultimate unity of virtue. Although Smith speaks of four individual virtues: "superior prudence"[84] or wisdom, self-command, justice, and beneficence, at bottom, he considered them but facets of the one and only virtue. Wisdom and self-command are the complementary preconditions of this virtue. The requirement of wisdom is a logical *conditio sine qua non.* To become virtuous, the path of virtue has to be known. The necessity of self-command, though less obvious, is equally strongly insisted upon by Smith: "The most perfect knowledge, if it is not supported by the most perfect self-command, will not always enable him [sc.: man] to do his duty."[85] The path of virtue, to keep to the metaphor, has not only to be known but also, to be followed with all the determination of a strong will. Neither self-command nor prudence do constitute virtue in themselves. Self-command may obviously be exercised in the pursuit of evil ends[86]; similarly, even the most perfect prudence is truly admirable only as an element of some other virtue, we thus praise the prudence of a great benefactor, or the wise judicature of Solomon. As the qualities of wisdom and self-command may be described as the preconditions of virtue, Smith's concepts of justice and beneficence or benevolence are best described as the negative and positive side of the one virtue. The virtuous wise knows through justice what he should not do and through benevolence what he ought to do.

The Stoics also regarded the cardinal virtues as nothing but different expressions or manifestations of the one indivisible virtue.[87] Characteristically, Zeno defined each virtue in terms of wisdom: "justice was wisdom concerned with assignment (or distribution), sophrosyne (self-control, temperance) was wisdom

[83] *TMS,* I.i.5.9, p. 26.

[84] *Ibid.,* VI.i.15, p. 216—As opposed to the common prudence which is "directed merely to the care of the health, of the fortune, and of the rank and reputation of the individual" (*TMS,* VI.i.14, p. 216) and which, "though it is regarded as a most respectable and even, in some degree, as an amiable and agreeable quality" *(ibid.),* is not really virtuous.

[85] *Ibid.,* VI.iii.1, p. 237.

[86] Cp. T. D. Campbell, *op. cit.,* p. 168.

[87] The following paragraph borrows material from Max Pohlenz, *op. cit.,* I, 126f.; F. H. Sandbach, *op. cit.,* 41ff.; A. Bonhöffer, *op. cit.,* 214, n. 2.

concerned with acquisition, bravery wisdom concerned with endurance."[88] His pupil Aristo went even further; according to him, the single virtue of the knowledge of good and evil can only be distinguished into different qualities by applying it to different objects. Other Stoics, like Chrysippus, were critical about this interpretation and upheld the view that virtues like bravery and justice were intrinsically different. All Stoics agreed however, and this is sufficient for our parallel with Smith, that the individual virtues form a unity and "could not exist separately."[89]

When we now turn to the possible sources of Smith's individual virtues or rather the different elements of the one virtue (prudence, self-command, justice, beneficence), it has to be emphasized that Smith is in the broad stream of the cardinal virtues issue in Western ethical thought with its origins in the Greek, especially Socratic tradition. And yet it can be argued that the particular manner in which Smith defined those traditional virtues distinctly echoes Stoic ideas and terminology. As this claim has recently been maintained by Professors Raphael and Macfie,[90] we may here leave it with a short summary. As for prudence, Smith's interpretation of "superior prudence" (= wisdom) as a precondition or necessary element of virtue has already been related to Zeno's attempt to express each virtue in terms of wisdom. A similar parallel can be found in the Stoics' and Smith's discussion of the elements of prudence. According to Smith, "the preservation and healthful state of the body seem to be the objects which Nature first recommends to the care of every individual."[91] This instinct leads to the desire for "the means of gratifying those natural appetites" and, consequently, man will look for "external fortune."[92] To satisfy this want, the prudent man will practise "real knowledge and skill in . . . [his] trade or profession, assiduity and industry in the exercise of it, frugality, and even some degree of parsimony, in all . . . expences."[93] Since he is also endowed with foresight, he will be "cautious in his actions"[94] and pay a lot of attention to his security. This method of deriving the elements of prudence, i.e. industry, frugality, caution, etc., from the instincts of self-preservation and well-being (esse et bene esse) is strongly reminiscent of Roman Stoicism:

Principio generi animantium omni est a natura tributum, ut se, vitam corpusque tueatur, declinet ea, quae nocitura videantur, omniaque, quae sint ad vivendum necessaria, anquirat et paret, ut pastum, ut latibula, ut alia generis eiusdem.[95]

Smith's emphasis on the virtue of self-command is also distinctly Stoic. For Smith, as we have already mentioned, self-command, in the sense of self-disci-

[88] F. H. Sandbach, *op. cit.,* 42.

[89] *Ibid.,* 43.

[90] D. D. Raphael & A. L. Macfie, "Introduction" to the *TMS,* 5-10.

[91] *TMS,* VI.i.1, p. 212.

[92] *Ibid.,* VI.i.3, p. 212.

[93] *Ibid.,* VI.i.6, p. 213.

[94] *Ibid.,* VI.i.8, p. 214.

[95] Cicero, *De officiis,* I.iv.11; my own translation: "At first, every sort of living creature is by nature directed towards the preservation of its own life and body, to avoid what seems to be harmful, and to look for everything that is vital, like food, shelter, and more of the like."

pline, is a necessary element of every other virtue. "Self-command is not only itself a great virtue, but from it all the other virtues seem to derive their principal lustre."[96] Thus self-command, as Profs. Raphael and Macfie have expressed it, "has come to permeate the whole of virtue,"[97] an emphasis which echoes the traditional aim of Stoicism: to dominate or even to abolish the passions and to acquire the wise man's 'tranquillitas animi', that peace of mind which alone can guarantee a perfectly virtuous conduct.[98] Again, when Smith discusses the virtue of universal benevolence (in Part VI.ii.3), his line of argument as well as his formulations clearly betray their origins in Roman Stoicism, especially the 'Meditations' of Marcus Aurelius to whom Smith once referred as "the mild, the humane, the *benevolent* Antoninus."[99] The very first sentence of the chapter, in which Smith widens the scope of benevolence from the services we render our country to the 'good-will' which embraces the immensity of the universe, echoes the Emperor's aim of benefiting not only his city and fatherland, but the universe.[100] Moreover, the basis on which Aurelius builds universal benevolence: his conviction of a society of all reasonable beings, with a benevolent God as its creator and sovereign, especially his imagery of a whole and its parts, a composition and its components, larger and smaller systems[101]—all this is consciously reasserted in Smith's presentation:

The wise and virtuous man is at all times willing that his own private interest should be sacrificed to the public interest of his own particular order or society. He is at all times willing that his own private interest should be sacrificed to the greater interest of the state or sovereignity, of which it is only a subordinate part. He should, therefore, be equally willing that all those inferior interests should be sacrificed to the greater interest of the universe, to the interest of that great society of all sensible and intelligent beings, of which God himself is the immediate administrator and director.[102]

If we finally consider the fourth element of Smith's account of virtue, i.e. justice, it has to be admitted that, in this respect, Smith's source can clearly be identified "with what Aristotle and the Schoolmen call commutative justice,"[103] defined in purely negative terms:

. . . we are said to do justice to our neighbour when we abstain from doing him any positive harm, and do not directly hurt him, either in his person, or in his estate, or in his reputation.[104]

Three of four elements of Smith's account of virtue, we may therefore conclude, strongly recall Stoical ideas and language.

[96] *TMS,* VI.iii.11, p. 241.

[97] D. D. Raphael & A. L. Macfie, "Introduction" to *TMS,* 6.

[98] Cp.: M. Pohlenz, *op. cit.,* I, 309f. & F. H. Sandbach, *op. cit.,* 59ff.

[99] *TMS,* VII.ii.1.35, p. 288; my own italics; N.W.

[100] Marcus Aurelius, Meditations, VI.44, Vol. I, p. 117.

[101] *Ibid.,* III.4 and IV.29 (for the society of all reasonable beings); II.11 (for the benevolence of the Deity); VII.13, VIII.7, and XI.8 (for examples of Aurelius' imagery).

[102] *TMS,* VI.ii.3.3, p. 235.

[103] *TMS,* VII.ii.1.10, p. 269.

[104] *Ibid.*

A final glance at Smith's account of propriety may help us to find the right balance between the originality of Smith's ethical thought and his indebtedness to Stoicism. The general meaning of Smith's 'propriety', to define a level of relative merit amongst the non-virtuous, unwise actions, certainly reflects the Stoics' allowance for a subdivision of the class of imperfect actions. Smith's emphasis on the generally attainable level of propriety, as opposed to the rare cases of perfect virtue, can also be seen as echoing the special attention which the Roman Stoics paid to the medium kathekon, convenientia or commune officium. The particular way, however, in which Smith decides upon the propriety or impropriety of any action—according to the sympathy or lack of sympathy which Smith's 'impartial spectator' shows—is doubtless independent of Stoic theories and has to be seen as Smith's own contribution to ethical theory.

III. After discussing the Stoic influence on Smith's distinction between the levels of the virtuous wise and the 'proper' multitude, a brief epilogue assessing the relevance of this distinction may also be in place. Its outstanding feature appears to be the far-sighted realism, expecting no more of ordinary men than to fulfil the level of propriety, whilst allowing for the saint-like supra-human qualities of the perfectly wise and virtuous. Smith's discussion of propriety contains an early and brave attempt to define a socially respectable standard of behavior and to explain how this level of behavior can be achieved by every one[105], an attempt which even the modern student of social psychology cannot fail to admire. Smith's allowance for a virtuous and wise élite is nowadays less readily accepted, as claims of superior qualities have too often been misused to justify privileges. But again, Adam Smith's distinction may well be defended, for firstly, his élite, like that of the Stoics, is an open one. The social rank has little or no bearing on man's chances of achieving wisdom and virtue. Secondly—and this is the place where the analogy with Dostoevsky, which was previously hinted at, may be helpful in spite of its anachronism—Smith's élite, like the long line of Dostoevsky's magnanimous characters from Makar Devushkin to Alyosha Karamazov, is an élite subject to increased duties and accumulated difficulties, requiring a heroic degree of virtue, rather than one which enjoys greater advantages and pleasures. Smith's high demands on the virtuous wise, especially the demand for self-sacrifice[106], is congenial with the enormous burden that Dostoevsky's heroes have to carry—a burden that may best be illustrated by Ernst Bloch's characterization, skilfully echoing Dostoevsky's own usage of the light-symbol[107]:

[105] T. D. Campbell, *op. cit.*, 238.

[106] *TMS*, VI.iii.3.3, p. 235.

[107] Dostoevsky frequently made use of the image of "light brought into the darkness" to characterize the rôle of his heroes. Katya Fyodorovna, for example, addresses Ivan Petrovich: "I am still, as it were, in the dark, I've been looking forward to you to bring me light." (Dostoevsky, *The Insulted and Humiliated.* Edited by Olga Shartse [Moscow, 1976], Part III, Chapter IX, 272). In *The Idiot* this imagery occurs more often, Prince Myshkin attempts to persuade Nastasya "to seeing light round her once more" (413), in turn, Aglaya to him is a "ray of light" (432); both references are to Constance Garnett's translation in the Random House edition (New York, 1935). Cp. M. Krieger, *The Tragic Vision* (Chicago & London, 1966), 217f.

. . . I am guilty not the others, and if they do not see, it is I who hasn't brought them light.[108]

Christ's College, Cambridge & The University of Auckland

[108] Ernst Block, *Geist der Utopie* (Munich & Leipzig, 1918), 347; my own translation.

Part II
Utility, Teleology and Religion

[6]

THE UTILITARIANISM OF ADAM SMITH'S POLICY ADVICE

BY T. D. CAMPBELL AND I. S. ROSS*

Man was made for action, and to promote by the exertion of his faculties such changes in the external circumstances both of himself and others, as may seem most favourable to the happiness of all.—TMS II.iii.3.3**

Adam Smith's works are primarily analytic and explanatory, but they also embody both general normative criteria for the assessment of the social, political, and economic systems he examines, and some guidance as to how the individual involved in these systems should conduct himself.[1] This distinction between general evaluation of systems and specific advice about individual action is important for the interpretation of Smith's normative ethics. While he is consistently hostile to utility both as an explanation for the origin of moral rules and as a principle to be applied routinely in everyday circumstances, it is to the criterion of utility—the maximization of human happiness—that he has recourse in his evaluations of practices, institutions, and systems (social, political, or economic) as a whole.[2] He may thus be regarded as a rule-utilitarian, or perhaps system-utilitarian, although, since he rarely recommends radical changes in the systems he describes, it would seem reasonable to emphasize the contemplative rather than practical side of his utilitarianism.[3]

* T. D. Campbell is grateful to the British Academy for a grant which enabled him to visit the University of British Columbia and work directly in Jan.-Feb. 1978 with the co-author.

** All quotations from Smith are taken from the Glasgow Edition of the *Works and Correspondence of Adam Smith* (Oxford: Clarendon Press, 1976-   ), whose system of references is adopted: Corr. = Correspondence: EPS = Essays on Philosophical Subjects; LJ = Lectures on Jurisprudence: TMS = Theory of Moral Sentiments; WN = Wealth of Nations. The numbers cited refer to book or part, chapter, section, and paragraph divisions, or to chronologically arranged letters.

[1] Cf. T. D. Campbell, "Scientific Explanation and Ethical Justification in the *Moral Sentiments*," *Essays on Adam Smith*, eds. A. S. Skinner and T. Wilson (Oxford, 1975), 68-83.

[2] Cf. TMS II.ii.3: "Of the utility of this constitution of Nature" and IV.1: "Of the Effect of Utility upon the Sentiment of Approbation"; WN I.ii.1, I.v.1.

[3] TMS IV.1.11: "The perfection of police ['regulation of the inferiour parts of government,' (LJ [B] 203)], the extension of trade and manufactures, are noble and magnificent objects. The *contemplation* [our italics] of them pleases us, and we are interested in whatever can tend to advance them. . . . We take pleasure in beholding

A failure to distinguish between the two levels of normative judgment, applicable to social systems and to individual conduct within systems, has led some commentators to argue either that Smith is in no sense a utilitarian or that the principle of utility is but one among several principles which he endorses.[4] In support of their view, it is possible to cite numerous occasions when Smith appears to give priority, for instance, to considerations of justice over those of utility.[5] However, in view of his insistence on the utility of justice and his express intention of demonstrating that the Author of Nature is perfectly benevolent and seeks to render human life as happy as possible, it seems right to interpret Smith's distrust of utilitarian reasoning at the practical level as justified ultimately by the tendency of such reasoning to diminish rather than augment the sum of human happiness.

Our essay does not seek to assess all the evidence for or against the view that Smith was at the bottom some type of utilitarian. Rather it discusses how far he departed from his own advice to eschew utilitarian calculations which neglect the less reflective guidance of immediate moral sentiments and thus turn his contemplative utilitarianism into a guide for practical judgments. To be sure, if we recall that Smith's philosophical interests were first aroused by the teaching of Francis Hutcheson, Professor of Moral Philosophy at Glasgow during Smith's student days there, it is natural to suppose that he would carry on the ideas of the man who reduced all virtue to benevolence and devised that stirring catch-phrase of utilitarianism: "the greatest happiness of the greatest number."[6] In fact, Smith was much more than a follower of Hutcheson, but the nature and source of his utilitarianism has been misconstrued perhaps by the habit of seeing in Smith the rebellious disciple of Hume rather than the follower (more or less faithful) of Hutcheson. For this notion of his

---

the perfection of so beautiful and grand a system, and we are uneasy until we remove any obstruction that can in the least disturb or encumber the regularity of its motions." For a discussion of Smith's contemplative utilitarianism, see T. D. Campbell, *Adam Smith's Science of Morals* (London, 1971), 217-20.

[4] Cf. J. R. Lindgren, *The Social Philosophy of Adam Smith* (The Hague, 1973), 82: "Smith argued for . . . changes on the basis of their utility not because he regarded utility as the sole criteria [sic] relevant to public policy decisions, but because he wished to persuade others . . ."; and A. L. Macfie, *The Individual in Society* (London, 1967), 48: "Utility for [Smith] was not basic."

[5] Cf. TMS II.iii.2.8: "There is a degree of negligence, which would appear to deserve some chastisement though it should occasion no damage to anybody."

[6] F. Hutcheson, *An Inquiry into the Original of our Idea of Beauty and Virtue*, Treatise II. "An Inquiry concerning Moral Good and Evil," 4th edn. revised (London, 1738), 181; see Robert Shackleton, "The Greatest Happiness of the Greatest Number: The History of Bentham's Phrase," *Studies on Voltaire*, **90** (1972), 1461-82.

philosophical relationships he is himself responsible to the extent that he was at pains to emphasize his disagreements with Hume more than his qualified acceptance of Hutcheson's utilitarianism. Thus, for instance, he repeatedly attacks Hume's account of the origin of justice, which makes it an artificial virtue with its source in social calculation of the utility of institutions such as property. Smith offers an alternative theory that justice is a natural standard originating in the unreflective resentment of those affected by what come to be regarded as "unjust" acts.[7] This tendency to highlight his differences with Hume has overshadowed Smith's claim that conduct and character are approved or disapproved of in proportion to their tendency to further or hinder human happiness[8]; it also ignores the fact that Smith uses the same criterion in evaluating moral, legal, and political institutions in toto.[9] Smith carried this procedure over into his economic theories, for here the playing down of utility as a motivating factor in economic behaviors[10] is combined with the assumption that it is the ultimate criterion for the evaluation of economic systems.[11] Further, Smith's frequent assertions that the system of natural liberty is just, as well as useful, must be seen alongside his equally frequent assertions that justice is a prerequisite of the physical security and economic progress on which human happiness depends.[12]

This combination of severely limiting the role of utility in explanations of and prescriptions for, individual conduct and then bringing it back for comprehensive evaluations (indeed, for "final" explanations in terms of God's purposes) is no mere accidental feature of Smith's

[7] TMS IV.2.3: "The same ingenious and agreeable author who first explained why utility pleases, has been so struck with this view of things, as to resolve our whole approbation of virtue into a perception of this species of beauty which results from the appearance of utility. . . . But still I affirm, that it is not the view of this utility or hurtfulness which is either the first or principal source of our approbation and disapprobation."

[8] *Loc. cit.*: "No qualities of mind, [Hume] observes, are approved of as virtuous, but such as are useful or agreeable either to the person himself or to others. . . . And Nature, indeed, seems to have so happily adjusted our sentiments of approbation and disapprobation, to the conveniency both of the individual and society, that, after the strictest examination it will be found, I believe, that this is universally the case."

[9] Thus, Smith writes: "All constitutions of government, however, are valued only in proportion as they tend to promote the happiness of those who live under them" (TMS IV.1.11).

[10] WN I.ii.1: "This division of labour, from which so many advantages are derived, is not originally the effect of any human wisdom, which foresees and intends that general opulence to which it gives occasion."

[11] WN I.v.1: "Every man is rich or poor according to the degree in which he can afford to enjoy the necessaries, conveniences, and amusements of human life"; and cf. WN IV.ix. 50.

[12] Cf. TMS II.ii.3.3 and WN IV.vii.b.2, 17.

work. His whole approach to social philosophy is summed up in the thesis that practices whose origins and supports lie in unreflective human sentiments, molded and harmonized by the socializing effects of life in a community, are admirably well adapted to the divinely planned end of human welfare. An apt illustration of Smith's thesis is his comment that approval of punishment for "unmerited and unprovoked malice" shows that "immediate and instinctive" feeling rather than the application of reason is the natural mechanism that best promotes human welfare (TMS II.i.5.10). Smith's theological form of functionalism is evident in the somewhat misleading image of the "invisible hand"; it appears, for example, in a famous passage in WN about the individual who employs capital in support of domestic industry out of self-interest, but in so doing is "led" to promote the public interest (IV.ii.9). Here, the end unintentionally promotes the maximization of happiness, whereas in TMS (at IV 1.10) in the passage mentioning the "invisible hand" the end is the distribution of the means of happiness.[13] In these passages, the "invisible hand" image carries no implication of ad hoc involvement in the ordinary course of events by an interventionist God. The phrase seems to be used to dramatize Smith's conviction that there is an "oeconomy of nature," whose discovery is the object of philosophical or scientific inquiry.[14]

One result of Smith's repeated attempts to demonstrate the unintended utilitarian consequences of non-utilitarian motivations is that it is not always clear how he copes with those situations—whose existence he freely acknowledges—when normally approved behavior does not maximize utility. The most striking case he cites is that of the sentinel shot for sleeping at his post: the offense does not seem to warrant the capital punishment which the safety of the garrison requires (TMS II.ii.3.11). Not only does Smith wish to minimize the seriousness of this problem, but also, for reasons connected with his appreciation of the complexity of social structures, he is unwilling to recommend that either the ordinary citizen or the run-of-the-mill politician should seek to improve the situation by indulging in their own utilitarian projections. He considers that they are liable either to get their calculations wrong or to produce unworkable schemes for social reform which ignore the inevitable conservatism of human

[13] Smith's approach to the explanation of a moral sentiment is to consider "first, the cause which gives occasion to it, or the mechanism by which nature produces it; secondly, the extent of its influence; and, last of all, the end which it answers, or the purpose which the Author of nature seems to have intended by it" (TMS II.iii.intro.6).

[14] A point made by the editors of the Glasgow TMS (1976), D. D. Raphael and A. L. Macfie, at p. 184, n. 7; see, also A. L. Macfie, "The Invisible Hand of Jupiter," *JHI*, **32** (1971), 595-99.

conduct.[15] It is clear, however, that the occasional outstanding statesman, guided perhaps by the insights of the academic student of human affairs such as Smith himself, should have recourse to consequentialist reasoning when pointing out the effects on human happiness of radical alterations in forms of government.[16] While this may appear as showing merely that Smith indulges in the occasional appeal to utility, if taken together with his doctrine of final causation, it strengthens the case that utility is for Smith, as for Hutcheson, the sole moral standard. However, since his utilitarian advice is usually to refrain from consequentialist calculations in practical matters, it is no wonder that interpreters of Smith have diverged in their assessment of the place of utility in Smith's philosophy.[17]

Our approach to the problem is to discuss instances we have selected from the biographical record of Smith when it presents key moral and political matters that elicit value judgments. To our knowledge, such a biographical approach to this particular problem about Smith's thought has not been attempted before, and we have the advantage of using the recently published correspondence as a source.[18] The issues we have selected from Smith's writings are as follows: the Union in 1707 of Scotland and England and the secession of the American colonies from Britain, two great political questions which Smith addressed; the monopolistic tendencies in trade and in professions about which his advice was sought; and finally Smith's attitude towards smuggling. Our claim is that detailed study of Smith's policy advice shows that it is indeed utilitarian in cast, and this result strengthens the view that this normative position is essentially a utilitarian one. In this connection, it is noticeable that, at least in his own case, he was prepared to support practical as well as contemplative judgments by a direct appeal to utility as the sole moral criterion.

[15] TMS VI.ii.2.17: "The man of system . . . seems to imagine that he can arrange the different members of a great society with as much ease as the hand arranges the different pieces on the chess-board."

[16] TMS VI.ii.2.12: "even a wise man may be disposed to think some alteration necessary in that constitution or form of government, which, in its natural condition, appears plainly unable to maintain the public tranquillity. In such cases, however, it often requires, perhaps, the highest effort of political wisdom to determine when a real patriot ought to support and endeavour to re-establish the authority of the old system, and when he ought to give way to the more daring, but often more dangerous spirit of innovation." We should note that Smith makes the general happiness the ultimate political norm (TMS IV.i.11)

[17] Cf. Lord Robbins, *The Theory of Economic Policy* (London, 1952), 48: "Adam Smith, who so frequently uses the terminology of the Naturrecht, but whose arguments are so consistently utilitarian in character."

[18] *The Correspondence of Adam Smith*, ed. E. C. Mossner and I. S. Ross (Oxford, 1977).

Smith commented on two great political crises of his time which involved "public discontent, faction, and disorder": the incorporating Union of Scotland and England in 1707 and the rebellion of the American colonies in the 1770s. Concerning the first event, he wrote to his publisher William Strahan on 4 April 1760: "Nothing . . . appears to me more excusable than the disaffection of Scotland at that time. The Union was a measure from which infinite Good has been derived to this country. The Prospect of that good, however, must then have appeared very remote and very uncertain" (Letter 50).[19] Noticeable, immediately, is the sympathy of the spectator with the resentment of those affected, for the next sentence runs: "The immediate effect of [the Union] was to hurt the interest of every single order of men in the country." Smith then presents a succinct analysis to show how the interest of the nobility, clergy, and merchants was hurt following the legislation. Smith passes next to the "infinite Good," which he presents in long-range utilitarian terms: "The views of their Posterity are now very different; but those views could be seen by but few of our forefathers, by those few in but a confused and imperfect manner." Such an historical, consequential analysis fits in with Smith's appreciation of the dangers of being led astray by short-term utilitarian calculations, but he is at the same time endorsing the judgment of those far-sighted statesmen who advocated the Union for, among other things, the benefit of Scottish commerce. Commenting further in WN on the effects of the same piece of legislation, Smith sticks to the same utilitarian theme, avoiding any appeal to presupposed political rights: "By the union with England, the middling and inferior ranks of people in Scotland gained a complete deliverance from the power of an aristocracy which had always before oppressed them" (V.iii.89). To be sure, Smith offers the palliative that the Scottish aristocracy (unlike that of Ireland, he claims) was "founded . . . in the natural and respectable distinctions of birth and fortune," but his arguments would seem to support the view that in the long-run the Union could be accepted as leading towards the "greatest happiness of the greatest number" and was certainly a blow against what Smith reckoned always to have been the "vile maxim of the masters of mankind . . . all for ourselves, and nothing for other people" (WN III.iv.10). Smith's "infinite Good," then, at least in respect of the outcome of one particular political crisis, refers to the maximizing of human happiness in one country.

In connection with the American crisis, Smith apparently does more than comment. In a letter to Smith of 8 February 1776 (No. 149), Hume alludes to his friend's discussions with influential men about

[19] See I. Ross, "Political Themes in the Correspondence of Adam Smith," *Scottish Tradition,* No. 5 (1975), 5-23.

American issues, and to the anticipated publication of WN, which another correspondent of Smith's, John Roebuck, thought "might have been of general use in influencing the Opinion of many in this American contest" (1 Nov. 1775, Letter 147). Hume continues his analysis of the American crisis by saying, "Our Navigation and general Commerce may suffer more than our Manufacturers. Should London fall as much in its Size, as I have done [Hume was in the throes of a wasting, terminal illness], it will be much the better. It is nothing but a Hulk of bad and unclean Humours." Bating Hume's views on London, Smith seems to have agreed with much of this analysis, and piecing together the evidence of Letter 158 addressed to Strahan, of 3 June 1776, and 159, from Alexander Wedderburn, of three days later, we gather that he took a gloomy view of the policy of military intervention by Britain, not so much as unjust as badly mismanaged and therefore likely to fail. Strahan, by this time an M.P., had originally favored the Americans in their dispute with Britain, but he was all for taking a strong line in 1775: "I am entirely for coercive methods with these obstinate madmen. Why should we suffer the Empire to be so dismembered without the utmost exertions on our part?"[20] Smith, by contrast, was cooler about the whole business: "The American Campaign has begun awkwardly. I hope, I cannot say that I expect, it will end better. England, tho' in the present times it breeds men of great professional abilities in all different ways, great Lawyers, great watchmakers and Clockmakers, etc. etc., seems to breed neither Statesmen nor Generals" (Letter 158). Towards the end of the American conflict, Smith wrote in a more general strain of utilitarian arguments to another correspondent: "The real futility of all distant dominions, of which the defence is necessarily most expensive, and which contribute nothing, either by revenue or military force, to the general defence of the empire, and very little even to their own particular defence, is, I think, the subject upon which the public prejudices of Europe require to be set right" (14 Oct. 1782, Letter 221). When the correspondent lamented that Britain would be ruined if the misfortunes of the American war continued, Smith is reported to have said: "there is a great deal of *ruin* in a nation" (Corr., 262, n. 3).

Equally utilitarian in cast, though argued more trenchantly and with a broad perspective of economics and politics, are the views on America presented in WN. The crux of Smith's argument over the retention or severance of the American colonies is that the monopoly control associated with retention is of benefit only to merchants—Hume's "general Commerce." That benefit, however, "a high rate of

[20] Quoted in Corr., p. 197, n. 3.

profit," is in fact corrupting, because it destroys the "parsimony" of the merchant, and "the capital of the country, instead of increasing, gradually dwindles away, [also] the quantity of productive labour maintained in it grows every day less and less" (IV.vii.c.61). Hence Smith's caustic assessment of the enterprise of trade following the flag: "To found a great empire for the sole purpose of raising up a people of customers, may at first sight appear a project fit only for a nation of shopkeepers. It is, however, a project altogether unfit for a nation of shopkeepers; but extremely fit for a nation whose government is influenced by shopkeepers" (para. 63). Though declining the task of prescribing how it ought to be done, Smith is resolute that relaxation of monopoly control of the colonies is the only means for saving Britain from precarious reliance, or perceived reliance, upon the American trade—"the only expedient which . . . can by degrees restore all the different branches of [Britain's industry] to that natural, healthful, and proper proportion which perfect liberty necessarily establishes, and which perfect liberty can alone preserve" (para. 44).

"Perfect liberty" looks suspiciously like an appeal to political rights per se, but Smith's formulation is thoroughly utilitarian, for these rights are based on their functional relationships to the happiness engendered by maximizing human consumption. At the same time it permits him to rehearse his theme that man must not play God; not even the sovereign may aspire to that role (WN IV.ix.51). Smith takes this position because he considers that the interest of society is, on the whole, ill-served by attempts to increase the wealth of a country by regulatory measures. His often-noted exceptions to this general prescription of governmental direction of the economy can be seen in a more positive light than is usually the case, if Smith's utilitarian outlook is fully appreciated.[21] However, these exceptions are not applied to trade with the American colonies, which Smith saw as a clear example of the pernicious economic effects on all concerned of trading restrictions.

Though Smith concedes that Britain's voluntary political withdrawal from her colonies is the least likely of all courses, since it would touch national pride to the quick and hurt the "private interest of the governing part of the nation whose power resides in patronage," he points out the real advantages of such a course of action (WN IV.vii.c.66). Such an utilitarian approach contrasts sharply with the tenor of contemporary debates in Parliament on America, which a modern historian has described as being transacted "to a disastrous

[21] This, together with the utilitarian characteristics of Smith's political theory, is discussed in T. D. Campbell, "Adam Smith and Natural Liberty," *Political Studies*, **25** (1977), 523-34.

extent, in terms of jurisprudence."[22] The conclusion of WN, indeed, could be viewed as a deliberate appeal to the legislators to leave aside their fantasies, the "golden dream" of a "great empire on the west side of the Atlantic," and instead of expending their energies on legalistic quibbling, to recognize that since the American colonies could not be made to contribute to the support of the empire, it was time that Britain cut the losses sustained both in war and in peace by maintaining these colonies. In this pragmatic vein, the very last words of the book counsel that Britain should "endeavour to accommodate her future views and designs to the real mediocrity of her circumstances" (V.iii.92).[23]

In addition to expressing his views on America in familiar letters to influential friends, such as the M.P.'s Strahan and Wedderburn, and addressing the reading public at large in WN on the issue of the economic considerations involved in the retention of the American colonies, Smith was apparently invited to write a pertinent memorandum for the Government. This was found among the papers of Wedderburn, who was then North's Solicitor-General and at the center of discussion on American policy. The memorandum is entitled, in Wedderburn's hand: "Smith's Thoughts on the State of the Contest with America, February 1778" (Corr. Append. B). The memorandum discusses four possible ways in which the "present unhappy war with the Colonies" might end: the complete submission of America; its complete emancipation; the restoration of the "old system" of links between mother country and colonies; and the submission of part of America together with the independence of the rest. Again it is noticeable that Smith never raises the question of irrevocable rights, of any ultimate justice in the dispute, but emphasizes utilitarian considerations against the background of politics and history.

The memorandum favors solving the American problem by the establishment of a "constitutional union" with representation in the British Parliament from the colonies, preferably arising from a treaty. Smith notes that such a plan has few adherents, but offers strong utilitarian arguments for it. Of interest is the fact that the model for the plan appears to be the Union between Scotland and England of 1707; "The Americans, I imagine, would be less unwilling to consent to such a union with Great Britain as Scotland made with England in 1707; than to the restoration, or anything like the restoration, of the

[22] Sir Lewis Namier, *The Structure of Politics at the Accession of George III* (London, 1960), 42-43.

[23] For other perspectives on Smith's analysis of the American problem, see A. S. Skinner, "Adam Smith and the American Economic Community: An Essay in Applied Economics," *JHI*, **37** (1976), 59-78; and Donald Winch, "The Present Disturbances," *Adam Smith's Politics* (Cambridge, 1978), Chap. 7.

old system" (Corr., pp. 383-84). What Smith reckoned to be the most probable, and at the same time the most destructive, outcome for Britain of the war was the retention of part of America. Once more the reasoning here is utilitarian: defense costs would exceed revenue, and the neighborhood of the part retained "would keep alive the jealousy and animosity of all the other provinces, and would necessarily throw them into the alliance of the enemies of Great Britain" (Corr., p. 384). Throughout Smith's comments on the American issue no mention is made of the colonists' right of rebellion. Smith's omission here may have been due, in part, to his rejection of that element of Hutcheson's theory of political obligation which stressed the significance of consent by the governed.[24] Smith does acknowledge, in principle, that there is a right of rebellion (LJ [B] 94), and his silence with regard to the exercise of that right by the Americans may have been due as much to prudence as to his preoccupation with the economic costs and benefits of the colonial link.

In writing about America, he may be said to have had two purposes: to comment on current events, and to develop a critique of what he called the "commercial, or mercantile System."[25] Arising from this critique the central message of the WN is to the effect that monopolies, restraints on trade, restrictions on the right of individuals to deploy their labor, stock, and land as they judged most advantageous to themselves, all these are to be condemned as unnatural in that they prevent people from following their instinctive propensity to truck, barter, and exchange, as well as their prudential desire to further their own economic interests. At the same time, the restrictions lead to inefficiency by removing the need for hard work and inventiveness and by interfering with the mechanisms whereby competition leads to an adequate supply of goods for sale at prices as low as the cost of production permits. Once systems of preference or restraint were taken away, according to Smith, "the obvious and simple system of natural liberty establishes itself of its own accord" (IV.ix.51). Students of Smith's thought have given much attention to this preferable "system" and it is now well understood that he allows, both in principle and in practice, such restrictions of economic liberty as are necessary for the legitimate purposes of government and the economic peculiarities of particular circumstances, but that, on the whole, he regarded economic freedom as beneficial to the prosperity of all countries. One argument strongly urged by J. R. Lindgren (*op. cit.*, 4) in this connection is that Smith presented utilitarian arguments for free trade for purely rhetorical reasons, and

[24] Cf. LJ, ed. E. Cannan (1896), p. 11, n. 2; LJ (A) v.114-19, 127-9; LJ [B] 15-18.
[25] Skinner *op. cit.*, 71.

that his real concern was with liberty for its own sake. We shall attempt to deal with this libertarian interpretation of Smith's thought by seeing what evidence lies outside WN concerning the motivating forces behind its author's economic liberalism.

In passing, we note that if Smith disguised in WN his real reasons for supporting free trading, then he must have followed this tactic from the beginning, for the *Early Draft* of that work (pre-April 1763)[26] presents six arguments against "unreasonable restraints imposed upon certain branches of Commerce" that are all utilitarian in character, having entirely to do with the economic disadvantages of such restraints. In the correspondence, moreover, we encounter the same kind of arguments directed against the injustice and folly of these measures as are found in WN, for example, restrictions on the wool trade, which he characterizes as being extorted from the legislature by "merchants and manufacturers . . . for the support of their own absurd and oppressive monopolies." Smith shows that these savage regulations have not affected the quantity or quality of wool, but they have hurt the interest of the growers of wool "for no other purpose but to promote that of the manufacturers," and he reasons that this "is evidently contrary to that justice and equality of treatment which the sovereign owes to all the different orders of his subjects" (IV.viii.17,30).

When he writes letters at some length on the restrictions on Irish trade, Smith takes the same approach. Thus, to Henry Dundas, he comments on 1 November 1779: "I perfectly agree . . . that to crush the Industry of so great and so fine a province of the empire, in order to favour the monopoly of some particular towns in Scotland or England, is equally unjust and impolitic. The general opulence and improvement of Ireland might certainly, under proper management, afford much greater resources to Government, than can ever by drawn from a few mercantile or manufacturing towns." Whereas in WN he displayed some sympathy with those who would be affected by the freeing of the colony trade (IV.vii.c.44), he tends rather to dismiss the effects of freeing Irish trade: "This freedom, tho in my opinion perfectly reasonable, will interfere a little with some of our paltry monopolies," and considers such an action justified for the greater good of the greater number; "It would help to break down that absurd monopoly which we have most absurdly established against ourselves in favour of almost all the different classes of our manufacturers"

[26] Text of ED in W. R. Scott, *Adam Smith as Student and Professor* (Glasgow, 1937), 322-56, and Glasgow LJ, pp. 562-81; discussion of date of ED in R. L. Meek and A. S. Skinner, "The Development of Adam Smith's Ideas on the Division of Labour," *Economic Journal*, **83** (1973), 1102-3.

(Letter 201). In a parallel letter to Lord Carlisle (No. 202), Smith argues further that the impediments to the development of Irish industry are the want of coal and wood, "two articles essentially necessary to the progress of Great Manufactures." There are more crucial lacks, however, for Ireland "wants order, police, and a regular administration of justice both to protect and to restrain the inferior ranks of people, articles more essential to the progress of Industry than both coal and wood put together, and which Ireland must continue to want as long as it continues to be divided between two hostile nations, the oppressors and the oppressed, the protestants and the Papists."

Besides being an acute political observation about the actual state of affairs in Ireland, Smith's comment is in line with the utilitarian thrust of WN, for example: "The natural effort of every individual to better his own condition, when suffered to exert itself with freedom and security, is so powerful a principle, that it is alone, and without any assistance, not only capable of carrying on the society to wealth and prosperity, but of surmounting a hundred impertinent obstructions with which the folly of human laws too often incumbers its operations" (IV.v.b.43). In the same vein, the letter to Carlisle continues: "As the wealth and industry of Lancashire does not obstruct, but promote that of Yorkshire; so the wealth and industry of Ireland, would not obstruct, but promote that of England." Though Smith is positive about "bettering our condition" as a result of political freedom, the skeptic Hume allowed himself to doubt "whether it be always true . . . that their riches [i.e., of the common people] are an infallible result of liberty" ("Of Commerce," cited in Glasgow WN, I, 540,n. 32).

In taking his stand on the injustice of economic restraints with respect to Ireland, Smith has in mind instances of what he regards as oppression and inequality. In neither case is justice opposed to utility: oppressive restraints such as the prohibitions on Irish exports cause great suffering by preventing sections of the people from earning sufficient to support themselves, and this is not counterbalanced by real benefits to British manufacturers. Similarly, he seems to have thought that the inequality in the duties imposed on goods from different countries was disadvantageous to all countries concerned. Nowhere in the letters can it be said that there is a suppressed libertarian rationale for free trade based on the principle that liberty is an end in itself.

We must acknowledge, of course, that the letters on free trade or on bounties and prohibitions are addressed to men of affairs such as Dundas, Carlisle, William Eden, and Sinclair of Ulbster, whom Smith may have thought susceptible to the utilitarian type of argument. Certainly, Dundas was enough of a utilitarian to write to Smith: "it has long appeared to me that the bearing down of Ireland, was in truth the bearing down a substantial part of the Naval and Military strength of our own Country," and he added that the defense of restrictions on the grounds of avoiding hurt to particular towns in England and Scotland was the "kind of reasoning [that] will no longer do" (Letter 200). There exists some evidence, however, that in his early lectures on economics at Glasgow (pre-1755), possibly even in the Edinburgh lectures of 1749-51, Smith used similar arguments concerning restrictions on trade. Dugald Stewart, Smith's first biographer, had access to a document presenting Smith's early teaching concerning political economy which included the following statement: "Little else is requisite to carry a state to the highest degree of opulence from the lowest barbarism, but peace, easy taxes, and a tolerable administration of government; all the rest being brought about by natural course of things. All governments which thwart this natural course, which force things into another channel, or which endeavour to arrest the progress of society at a particular point, are unnatural, and to support themselves are obliged to be oppressive and tyrannical" ("Account of the Life and Writings of Adam Smith," EPS IV.25). An important point here is that the restraints on trade in themselves are not "oppressive and tyrannical." These are characteristics of governments which resort to punitive measures to enforce such restraints, creating crimes that are "unnatural" and so arousing the resentment of the impartial spectator. This state of affairs adds further to the disutility of the legislation.

In the light of Smith's views on patriotism and the limited range of benevolent affections expressed in TMS, it is interesting to see how Smith in advising politicians does not try to get them to widen their horizons and look at issues from a more than national standpoint, except to stress that the prosperity of adjacent countries does nothing to hinder the prosperity of their own. Consistent with the outlook of TMS, in the letters and the American memorandum, he takes a national approach to strategic and economic problems. Despite his opposition to the British Government's policy in relation to the American colonies, his comments center on the question of military victory, which he thought (rightly) was remote, and on the minimization of economic harm to the mother country. On the general question of freedom of trade, the tone of his arguments is such as to suggest that, while national interest is best served by removing restrictions, if this were not the case, such restrictions would be justified. Thus, he thinks that an Irish demand for the freedom of "importing their own produce and manufactures into Great Britain; subject to no other duties than such as are equivalent to the duties imposed upon the like goods of British produce or Manufacture" would be the "most unreasonable" of all such demands, but he is prepared to advise that it should be answered positively because of the utility of competition in the British market (Letter 202). Smith clearly states to William Eden, one of the Lords of Trade, his general position on the economic aftermath of the American war: "every extraordinary either encouragement or discouragement that is given to the trade of any country more than to that of another, may, I think, be demonstrated to be in every case a complete piece of dupery, by which the interest of the State and the nation is constantly sacrificed to that of some particular class of traders" (Letter 233). Thus it is harm to Great Britain and her possible advantage that seem to be decisive factors in his policy advice, although this is a state of affairs which he would defend in terms of his declared position concerning the general utility of each group looking first to its own interests (TMS VI.ii.2.4).

One practical issue on which Smith's advice was sought elicited his most spirited, and possibly most doctrinaire, statement of opposition to monopolies. This issue was reformation of the system of conferring medical degrees at Scottish Universities. A memorial was drafted urging that candidates for these degrees must be personally examined and must submit certificates of pursuance of medical studies for at least two years. Smith opposed all this vehemently, also the proposal that failing Government action about the conferral of honorary medical degrees, a Royal Commission of inquiry be appointed.[27] On the latter point, he considered that asking for an inquiry in complete uncertainty about who would be the inquirers, and what they might recommend, would be "extremely unwise"; also, the alleged "abuse" seemed to him "not perhaps of great consequence to the public." With regard to regulations concerning degrees, he held that "the monopoly of medical education which this . . . would establish in favour of Universities would . . . be hurtful to the lasting prosperity of such bodies-corporate." He goes on to mention his studies concerning "several of the principal Universities of Europe," noting that he has satisfied himself "that the present state of degradation and contempt into which the greater part of those societies have fallen in almost every part of Europe, arises principally, first, from the large salaries which in some universities are given to professors, and which render them altogether independent of their diligence and success in their professions; and secondly, from the great number of students who, in order to get degrees or to be admitted to exercise certain professions . . . are obliged to resort to certain societies of this kind, whether the instructions which they are likely to receive there are or are not worth the receiving." Those causes of "negligence and

[27] For a fuller account of this issue, see Manfred S. Guttmacher, "The Views of Adam Smith on Medical Education," *Johns Hopkins Hospital Bulletin,* **47** (1930), 164-75, and David L. Cowen, "Liberty, Laissez-faire and Licensure in Nineteenth-Century Britain," *Bulletin of the History of Medicine,* **43** (1969), 30-41.

corruption" are at work in the Scottish Universities, according to Smith, to a lesser degree than elsewhere, and upon this fact is based their superiority. Professors' salaries are low; there are few bursaries; and their monopoly of degrees "is broken in upon by all other Universities, foreign and domestic." To be sure, their poverty has made them engage in the "disgraceful trade" of selling degrees, including medical ones, but Smith thinks this has been to the advantage of the public on two grounds: first, it has increased the number of doctors, and "thereby no doubt sunk their fees"; and, second, it has "reduced a good deal the rank and dignity of a doctor." Smith argues that Scottish doctors "are all made to feel that [they] must rest no part of their dignity upon [their] degree . . . and . . . must found the whole part of it upon [their] merit. Not being able to derive much consequence from the title of Doctor, [they] are obliged, perhaps, to attend more to [their] characters as men, as gentlemen, and as men of letters" (Letter 143).

Here the question of what might be called the injustice of conferring degrees "undeservedly" is given little weight, nor is Smith as concerned as he might well be for the reputation of the Scottish Universities engaging in the "dirty practice" of selling degrees. Of much more account is the utility of freedom of competition in medical education—Smith may have been influenced here by his knowledge of and friendship with Dr. William Hunter, who was a "private teacher" of anatomy and medicine, and also by a recognition of the utility of access to competent physicians. On funding education, the arguments of this letter we have quoted are in line with those of WN, for example, those directed against the system prevailing at Oxford whereby tenure and fixed incomes removed incentives: "the greater part of the publick professors have, for these many years, given up altogether even the pretence of teaching" (V.i.f.8). In Scotland, professors were largely dependent on class fees for their income and therefore the incentive existed to teach well so as to attract and retain students.

The last case of Smith's practical judgment that we are to consider brings us to his service as a revenue official. It has long been a matter for ironic comment that the supposed apostle of free trade should, in the end, enjoy a remunerative position as one of the Commissioners of Customs in Scotland, a post to which he was appointed in 1778 within two years of the publication of WN (Corr. Append. D). Smith himself does not seem to have felt that his tenure of this post involved him in any moral inconsistency or conflict. He was reasonably zealous in the application of the laws concerning smuggling, and he soon became deeply involved in giving advice to the Government on all forms of revenue raising, including the imposition of duties on imports and exports. Being a customs officer, in fact, was a family tradition, and he clearly manifested an intellectual interest in the relevant issues of public policy. His appointment as a Commissioner in part may have been due to the patronage of his former pupil, the Duke of Buccleuch, and in part it may have been a reward from North for help with the budgets of 1777 and 1778 (Corr. p. 378, n. 6). Smith certainly did not treat his Commissionership as the sinecure it could have been, and must have amply fulfilled any expectations about his usefulness to the Government as a taxation policy adviser. Moreover, the information and experience he gained during his period as a Commissioner left their mark in the revised third edition of WN (1784: see Letters 222, 227).

Smith can certainly be cleared of any charge of gross inconsistency in accepting that official post. He was never an across-the-broad advocate of *laissez-faire*, and stated flatly that there were not only reasons of state, such as defense, which required restrictions on free trade (WN IV.ii.24), but some purely economic considerations which could justify limitations on the natural liberty of each individual to sell his labor and his produce on the open market. Many of these restrictions, he assumed, should be applied only temporarily, notably in the case of prohibitions on the importation of certain types of goods, but he does not rule out relatively permanent prohibitions in circumstances where the system of natural liberty needs to be accommodated to specific economic factors, for example, in the case of regulation of small note issues by banks, on the grounds of defense of the stability of the monetary system (WN II.ii.90,106). We should realize, of course, that Smith did not have high hopes of the system of natural liberty prevailing in the economic sphere in his own country: "To expect, indeed, that the freedom of trade should ever be entirely restored in Great Britain, is as absurd as to expect that an Oceana or a Utopia should ever be established in it. Not only the prejudices of the public, but what is more unconquerable, the private interests of many individuals, irresistibly oppose it " (WN IV.ii.43).[28]

Smith's most characteristic position, however, on the matter of trade policy, was to advocate removal of all trade barriers, modified only by the need to raise revenue for the valid purposes of governing a country. To this end, he was prepared to recommend "moderate duties" on imports and exports. These should not be so high as to make smuggling profitable, for then much of the revenue is lost altogether. Moreover, these duties should be equal for different producers and importers so that their effect is not to the advantage of one group over another. These points are well summed up in a letter of 3 January 1780 addressed to William Eden: "The sole effect of a pro-

[28] See A. S. Skinner, *Adam Smith and the Role of the State* (University of Glasgow Press, 1974),19.

hibition is to hinder the revenue from profiting by the importation. All those high duties, which make it scarce possible to trade fairly in the goods upon which they are imposed, are equally hurtful to the revenue and equally favourable to smuggling, as absolute prohibitions.'' The letter continues with a reference to the prohibition on the export of wool as essentially a tax laid on the grower for the benefit of the manufacturer (No.203). To raise a moderate revenue in a non-discriminatory way does not seriously affect the process of price equilibrium on which economic efficiency depends and is, Smith thought, necessary for the provision of those political supports, such as the administration of justice, the defense of person and property, some access to education, and the creation and maintenance of public works such as roads, without which the economy could not operate. No doubt this awareness of the economic benefits of the political order is also sufficient to explain Smith's readiness to uphold the law even when he thought it inadvisable and unjust, as in the case of prohibition of certain imports and severe punishments for smuggling. He did not regard free trade as absolutely essential for economic progress, and he was prepared to accept in return for the benefits of a system of law some degree of rough justice and even actual injustice. It is not surprising, therefore, that there is no hint to be found in Smith's works or reported behavior which suggests that he actually condoned smuggling on the basis of the benefits of *de facto* free trade.

Nevertheless, it is evident that he did not regard smuggling as a genuinely criminal offense. To smuggle is not a natural crime like murder or theft for it does not raise the spontaneous resentment of victims and observers, but is a purely artificial misdemeanor based on the flimsy and temporary will of governments. In consequence, smuggling is imprudent rather than immoral. Thus, among the reasons Smith advanced for opposing restrictions on trade was that they lead to the punishment of smugglers, in his opinion, often perfectly moral people who, being labelled as criminals in this respect, move on to commit real crimes. Indeed, throughout WN smuggling is assessed entirely from the economic point of view. Smith notes that it is unprofitable for the smuggler because the normal profits of successful smuggling though high do not outweigh the risk of being caught, so that smuggling is the ''infallible road to bankruptcy'' (I.x.b.33). This observation arises in the course of the analysis of the possible employments of labor and stock, and the example is used to illustrate the tendency to equality in the profits to be made from various employments, no comment being offered about the conceivably immoral nature of smuggling.

This apparently amoral approach to smuggling is not adequately explained away by saying that WN is concerned with economics not morality, for Smith is always prepared to deal with questions of injustice as well as profitability. It is therefore surprising that as an official he had no qualms of conscience in superintending those who brought smugglers to book. Evidence exists, it is true, that he was aware of some oddity in his position because in the 1780 letter to Eden, quoted above, there is a whimsical passage about prohibitions failing to prevent the importation of prohibited goods:

> About a week after I was made a Commissioner of the Customs, upon looking over the list of prohibited goods, (which is hung up in every Customhouse . . .) and upon examining my own wearing apparel, I found, to my great astonishment, that I had scarce a stock, a cravat, a pair of ruffles, or a pocket handkerchief which was not prohibited to be worn or used in Great Britain. I wished to set an example and burnt them all. I will not advise you to examine either your own or Mrs Edens apparel or household furniture, least you be brought into a scrape of the same kind.

This friendly advice to the Edens not to examine their clothes or household effects with the same scrupulosity should not be taken, perhaps, as a very considered piece of moral advice, but together with the stated wish "to set an example," it indicates a certain ambivalence in Smith towards his duty of suppressing smuggling. Indeed, the episode might be interpreted as showing that his action in burning his prohibited possessions was motivated more by the prudential desire to safeguard his reputation and position as a Customs official, than by his desire to follow the "inner man" of his own conscience. Some weight to the opinion that the disposal of his smuggled clothes was not an action he would have taken as a private citizen is lent by a passage in WN casting ridicule on those who pretend to have a conscience about buying smuggled goods, as persons likely to be regarded as hypocrites and knaves (V.ii.k.64).

Smith would doubtless point out here he was talking of the conduct of the ordinary citizen and not of the public official. Still, the contrast between the attitude expressed in WN towards those who refrain from purchasing smuggled goods and his own action in disposing of his smuggled articles of clothing (albeit bought inadvertently) is enough to cast some doubt on his consistency in accepting a Customs post. The tension in his own thought on this issue, however, is manifestly located in the conflict between two utilitarian considerations: the first concerns the good or bad economic consequences of customs and excise laws; and the second, the serious long-term disutility of lack of respect for the law itself, even where there is disagreement about its content. But it is noteworthy that Smith was prepared, in practice, to judge his conduct by utilitarian considerations of one sort or another, and to take action against smuggling even though he did not regard it as a "natural" crime.

There remains, however, the fact that on the issue of trade barriers in general, he was ready to invoke justice as well as to make direct appeals to utility. Thus, he frequently comments on restrictions on trade as being both inequitable and detrimental to the progress of opulence, and he objects strongly to taxing the necessities of the poor, on the grounds of "oppression," although this is a utilitarian objection in so far as oppressing the vast majority of a society is acting in a fashion detrimental to that majority's happiness. But he also objects, on grounds of "equity," to taxing the products of one country more than those of another, and the connection of this, if any, with utility, is never spelled out, although it might be deduced, perhaps, from his general evaluation of the benefits of equal competition. Smith denounces, furthermore, the inequity of exempting from excise duty private brewing and distilling, and hence the alcoholic consumption of the rich, and leaving the poor man's drink to bear the burden of taxation (WN V.ii.k.45). While Smith recognizes the utility of saving the private family from the "odious visit and examination of the tax-gatherer," the exemption cannot meet the higher criterion of his first maxim of taxation: "The subjects of every state ought to contribute toward the support of the government . . . in proportion to the revenue which they respectively enjoy under the protection of the state" (V.ii.b.3.). But Smith shows no awareness that considerations of the justice and utility of taxation measures may conflict, remarking simply after citing his four maxims that their "evident justice and utility . . . have recommended them more or less to the attention of all nations" (para. 7). This accords with the tone of his letter to Dundas already quoted, in which he describes the restraints on Irish trade as "unjust and unreasonable" (No. 201), although in this particular instance the stress is on the assertion that free trade for Ireland would do little harm to Britain. A latent assumption seems to be that if removal of the restrictions did occasion real harm to Britain, then the injustices of such restrictions would not be an overriding argument against them. It is difficult to discern whether such an assumption for Smith would be based on considerations of general utility or of national self-interest. In sum, then, although Smith avoids discussing possible conflicts of justice and utility in the justification and application of trade restraints, it is the latter criterion which appears to have preoccupied him, and which seems to have been decisive both in his action as a Commissioner of Customs and as an adviser to Government.

We have not sought to present the full case for considering Smith to be a system-utilitarian. Rather our purpose is to see how far calculations of utility which are evident in his evaluation of economic and social systems as a whole are also at the heart of his practical judgments and dominate them. That they do so in very large measure is not in doubt: in his comments on the Union of Scotland and England, and in his anxious discussions of the rebellion of the American colonies, he openly and consistently argues in utilitarian terms, albeit from a British point of view, supporting and proposing, on such grounds, radical changes in political constitutions. And, in spite of some of the terminology involved in his attack on monopolies, the same can be said about his views on trade policy, the political question which is most clearly connected with his whole economic theory. Further, only utilitarian reasoning about the necessity of raising revenue for the useful purposes of government through the customs and excise laws could have enabled him to quieten his conscience, as he reflected on his share in organizing the suppression of the naturally innocent "crime" of smuggling. Moreover, in the matter of the granting of medical degrees by the Scottish Universities, he endorsed utilitarian arguments about improving the standards of medical practice with apparent disregard of what many would see as the more obvious point of moral principle: the dishonesty of issuing what were in effect bogus qualifications.

Still, it would be strange indeed if the author of TMS, whose express conviction is that the ordinary rules of morality are rightly regarded as the voice of God, neglected altogether appeals of a straightforward kind to the authority of the instinctive judgments of his own conscience, or to the immediate moral sentiments of mankind. Although we have argued against any simple opposition between justice and utility in Smith's work, something of this respect for the authority of relatively unreflective moral judgments is seen in his repeated insistence on the injustice as well as the folly of illiberal trade policies.[29] Considerations such as these, of course, cannot refute definitively the counter-claim that Smith's arguments as presented—even in his private letters—somehow screen his underlying convictions. Our thesis remains, however, that on the facts of the practical attitudes he reveals in his correspondence, as well as of the tenor of those parts of his major works where he addresses himself to the issues of his own time, Adam Smith must be viewed at the end of the day as both a practising and a contemplative utilitarian.

T. D. Campbell (University of Glasgow); I. S. Ross (University of British Columbia).

[29] A similar respect for an instinctive moral stand seems to be displayed in Smith's support for the Hamilton party in the Douglas cause, always assuming that friendship in this instance did not sway his judgment; cf. Letter 116 and, on the Hamilton-Douglas contentions, I. S. Ross, *Lord Kames and the Scotland of his Day* (Oxford, 1972), 133-40.

[7]

The Theory and Practice of the Wise and Virtuous Man: Reflections on Adam Smith's Response to Hume's Deathbed Wish

T. D. CAMPBELL AND IAN ROSS

In the sixth edition (1790) of the *Theory of Moral Sentiments*[1] Adam Smith added a new part (VI). There he included lengthy and elegant descriptions of the conduct of the perfectly wise and virtuous man which serve to indicate the direction of his normative ethics in the latter years of his life.[2]

According to this "practical system of Morality," as he described it (Letter 287), virtue is a combination "of perfect prudence, of strict justice, and of proper benevolence" (TMS VI.iii.1). Smith goes into some detail in depicting each of these elements of virtue in turn and seeks to bring them together through the use of his concept of the "impartial spectator."[3] In his exposition of this system of morality, two important and related issues are left obscure. The first is the circumstances in which benevolence ought to override prudence, and the second the role which consequentialist reasoning should play in the individual's determination of his duty. While the prime evidence relating to these questions must be his published work, some light may be shed on them by an examination of biographical material. We shall therefore examine Smith's response to a deathbed wish expressed by David Hume to the effect that Smith should see to the posthumous publication of Hume's *Dialogues concerning Natural Religion.* Although, as we shall see, it is doubtful whether Smith followed his own precepts in this matter, the arguments which he presents to justify his refusal to take on this task give us an example of his considered response to a practical manifestation of the issues which he left unsettled in his picture of the wise and virtuous man.

Since it is concerned with "perfect" virtue relatively little of Part VI is taken up with justice which is, for Smith, a purely "negative virtue," that "only hinders us from hurting our neighbour" (TMS II.ii.1.9). The virtuous man adheres strictly to the rules of justice and thus avoids inflicting injury on others by his positive actions. Injustice can never, therefore, be justified by an appeal to prudence or benevolence (TMS VI.11.intro.2). But for all its importance justice is a relatively straightforward and limited part of virtue. Moral perfection has more to do with the development of the two positive components of virtue, prudence and benevolence. Our problem arises from the fact that while Smith cannot and does not exclude the possibility of conflict between these two elements of virtue, he does not tell us how such conflicts are to be resolved, nor does he define with precision the proper range of our "good offices."

Smith does, however, provide a framework within which these two components of positive virtue can be brought together, for his ultimate normative principle is utilitarian in that he believes that each of the virtues contributes to happiness and that the moral system as a whole maximizes happiness. This, however, can only take us as far as what might be called "contemplative utilitarianism," for while Smith uses the principle of utility to vindicate the moral sentiments he analyses and describes, he does not think that the individual should attempt to apply the utilitarian principle for himself. Smith offers an approving description of the man of "sublime contemplation" who reflects on the "idea of that divine Being, whose benevolence and wisdom have, from all eternity, contrived and conducted the immense machine of the universe, so as at all times to produce the greatest possible quantity of happiness." This description, however, is followed by insistence that the administration of the "immense machine" is the "business of God and not of man," to whom is allotted a "much humbler department, but one much more suitable to the weakness of his powers, and to the narrowness of his comprehension; the care of his own happiness, of that of his family, his friends, his country" (VI.ii.3.5,6). Man is not to play God, and he must not so lose himself in contemplation of cosmic utilitarianism that he neglects his active duties. This echoes his earlier insistence that the individual should not attempt to calculate his duty by applying the utilitarian maxim for himself, since he has neither the necessary knowledge nor the necessary impartiality to carry out this enterprise successfully, and if he attempts to do so he is likely to reduce rather than increase the utility of his actions (TMS III.4.3).

There is no contradiction in Smith's position here, for he is not arguing that the moral sentiments *originate* in men's calculations of utility, but only that utility is their "final cause" in that it represents the end which the "Author of Nature" intended (TMS III.5.7). Smith's advice is, therefore, to serve the general happiness by following the dictates of the "immediate" moral sentiments. And yet an area of unclarity remains, for "perfect prudence," which Smith places firmly within the sphere of virtue, involves a substantial element of consequentialist calculation. Moreover, although Smith is clearly against the ordinary person attempting to apply the principle of utility to his own actions, he does envisage the possibility of the more knowledgeable and impartial members of society making some moral decisions on utilitarian grounds, so that it is not obvious how far the prohibition on practical utilitarianism applies to the "perfectly wise and virtuous man," particularly as Smith allows a sense of "prudence" in which is included wisdom in the pursuit of the interests of society as a whole (TMS VI.i.15). In the remaining part of this essay, we shall examine the way in which Smith appears to follow prudence rather than benevolence in his response to the deathbed wish by Hume,[4] and the extent to which he was prepared to acknowledge in a practical way that conflicts between prudence and beneficence should be settled by recourse to utilitarian arguments.

At this point it is necessary to turn from the published philosophy to the biographical record of Smith's correspondence. In general it can be observed that he was a dilatory correspondent: such letters as he did take the trouble to write are usually in response to specific requests for his advice, or concerned with the uncontroversial details of personal business, although several of these exhibit marked beneficence in his relations with his pupils or a willingness to be of assistance to those seeking positions or introductions. However, we find in his correspondence with Hume a glimpse of an altogether more personal aspect of Smith's life. Hume often chides him for failure to visit or write, and Smith's eventual replies are seldom fulsome. But there is no doubt that Hume was for Smith something more than one of those few "well-tried and well-chosen" companions cultivated by the prudent man. In WN, Smith saluted his fellow man of letters as "by far the most illustrious philosopher and historian of the present age" (V.i.g.3), and the well-known letter of 9 November 1776 to William Strahan, his printer as well as Hume's, describing Hume's steadfast composure and good humor in the face of death, demonstrates an intense regard and loyalty (Letter 178). It is therefore surprising to learn that during this terminal illness, when Hume was weak and in pain, Smith's letters reveal caution and even prevarication about Hume's request that after his death Smith should publish the *Dialogues concerning National Religion.* In LJ Smith had commented on the poignancy of a dying man's request: "We naturally find a pleasure in remembering the last words of a friend and in executing his last injunctions, the solemnity of the occasion deeply impresses the mind" ([B] 165).[5] How then are we to account for Smith's unwillingness to accede to the wishes of the dying Hume, and for the somewhat tortuous arguments to which he resorts to evade taking on an obligation?

One suggestion is that Smith was concerned about Hume's reputation. In defence of this, it would have to be assumed that the "Scruples" on Smith's part which Hume dismissed as groundless on 3 May 1776 (Letter 156) were to the effect that Smith feared Hume's reputation would be damaged by early posthumous publication of the *Dialogues,* and that Smith would be a dubious friend to Hume in overseeing such a publication. Now, Smith did not act invariably as protector of Hume's interests. To give one example of the reverse situation: when Hume was a candidate at Glasgow for the Chair of Logic in 1751, Smith did not stand up for him, but was swayed by the consideration that public opinion would be unfavorable and the "interest" of the University dictated acceding to that opinion (Letter 10). Additionally, the record of the friendship between Hume and Smith shows that Hume was the one who reached out again and again to maintain the friendship, and Smith seems self-contained (cf. Letters 87, 90, 121, 123, 129, 136, 140, and 149). In short, there is no prima facie case for thinking that Smith responded altruistically as a result of Hume's appeal concerning the *Dialogues.* Rather, it would appear that Smith's behavior in this regard smacks more of cold prudence than of warm friendship, or even common benevolence. It obviously caused Hume much trouble during the last weeks of his life, over a matter which was clearly of great significance to him. Having made Smith his literary executor, with instructions for him to publish the *Dialogues,* and added a small legacy for Smith to be paid upon publication (Corr. p. 195, n. 1), Hume came to realize that Smith did not wish to comply with this request. Accordingly, Hume added a codicil to his will ten days before his death on 25 August 1776, leaving the MSS to Strahan, and desiring him to publish the *Dialogues* within two years. A further codicil stated that if Strahan did not publish within two and a half years after Hume's death, the *Dialogues* were to be returned to a nephew (David Hume the younger), "whose Duty, in publishing them as the last Request of his Uncle, must be approved of by all the World" (Corr. p. 205, n. 1). Hume also wanted Smith to undertake to publish the book within five years of his death if the nephew had not done so by that time (Letter 165).

Smith replied by stating that Hume "should not menace Strahan with the loss of anything in case he does not publish your work within a certain time," and advised that there were no probability of Strahan not publishing the *Dialogues* (Letter 166). Smith communicated these facts to Strahan after Hume's death, adding: "I once had persuaded him to leave it entirely to my discretion either to publish them at what time I thought proper or not to publish them at all. Had he continued of this mind the manuscript would have been most carefully preserved and upon my decease restored to the family; but it never should have been published in my lifetime." He recommended that Strahan consult "some prudent friend about what you ought to do," and also that the *Dialogues* be published separately from *My Own Life*, Hume's brief autobiography, to which Smith proposed to add an account of Hume's last illness. He then stated flatly: "I am resolved, for many reasons, to have no concern in the publication of those dialogues" (Letter 172).

Now, what were those reasons that weighed so heavily with Smith? We have a clue in a subsequent, unsigned draft of a letter to Strahan, written in the October following Hume's death: "I am much obliged to you for so readily agreeing to [print] the life, together with my addition separate from the Dialogues. I even flatter myself that this arrangement will contribute, not only to my quiet, but to your interest. The clamour against the dialogues, if published first, might hurt for some time the sale of the new edition of [Hume's] works and when the Clamour has a little subsided, the dialogues might hereafter occasion a quicker sale of another edition" (Letter 177b). Since this is only a draft, and there exists an earlier one with the version of the paragraph just quoted struck through (Letter 177A), it would appear that this letter gave Smith some difficulty. Perhaps even to himself he could not state in a satisfactory way why he would not see to the publication of the *Dialogues*. For some reason Hume thought it necessary to make it clear to Smith that he considered the *Dialogues* among his best work: "On revising them (which I have not done these 15 years) I find that nothing can be more cautiously and more artfully written. You had certainly forgotten them" (15 August 1776, Letter 165). It seems likely that Smith may have expressed to Hume reservations about the content of the *Dialogues*, rather than their literary merit. In fact, Smith conceded to Strahan that the *Dialogues* were "finely written." We require therefore to have an eye to Smith's perception of the content of the *Dialogues*, to know what to make of the reference to his "quiet" and, to a lesser extent, his concern for Strahan's "interest."

We can take that word "quiet" in at least two ways. One of these would interpret it as Smith's concern for his reputation, the peaceful enjoyment of the esteem which his achievements as a philosopher and a man of letters had earned for him. It is certainly conceivable that he did not wish to be associated with publishing a work which, if Ernest Mossner is correct, he had read with insight as making a successful attack on religion both natural and revealed.[6] He may have shied away all the more violently from the role of overseer of publication because there was a question of monetary gain. He had elected to live in hidebound Scotland, and he may have remembered that his mentor Francis Hutcheson had clashed with the Glasgow Presbytery over heterodox views, also that his patron Lord Kames was excluded from the Commission of the General Assembly of the Church of Scotland for publishing such views, and could well have lost his judge's seat, at the time when Hume was threatened with excommunication for his alleged atheism.[7] Yet these events had taken place many years before, and by 1776 Smith was hardly vulnerable enough to warrant that such considerations should affect his decision in the matter of publication of a book.[8]

The other interpretation of Smith's reference to his "quiet" would take it to be concern for his peace of mind, his intellectual repose. Involvement in publication of the *Dialogues* may have been resisted because he had not come to grips with their content. Essentially, if he had no answers to Philo's demolition of the argument for a deity on the basis of the evident design of the universe, then Smith's own philosophy would be undermined. Theism was not, for Smith, a simple additional set of beliefs which could be added or subtracted from his own nontheological approach to social science: his philosophy of explanation involves final explanations, couched in terms of the purposes of nature or God, as an integral part of his approach to social phenomena. While he made a clear distinction between efficient and final causation, his whole functionalist approach centered on the attempt to show how the mechanism of efficient causation produced beneficial results intended by the utilitarian "Author of nature" (TMS III.5.7). Take this away and, Smith must have felt, his whole theoretical apparatus would be undermined. Possibly, too, his personal philosophy of contemplative utilitarianism or "universal benevolence" was deeply threatened by the *Dialogues*, if we can take as self-directed some sentences added to TMS at the very end of his life: "To this universal benevolence . . . the very suspicion of a fatherless world, must be the most melancholy of all reflections. . . . All the splendour of the highest prosperity can never enlighten the gloom with which so dreadful an idea must necessarily over-shadow the imagination" (VI.ii.3.2).

This second interpretation of Smith's concern for his "quiet" should not lead one to think that he consciously wished to suppress the *Dialogues* because the arguments conflicted with his own views. He seems to have been reconciled to Strahan publishing the book, offering prudential advice, as we have seen, about staging its publication after an edition of Hume's works to quicken sales of the latter. In the event, Strahan also declined to publish the *Dialogues*, and this task was carried out by Hume's nephew in 1779, to the accompaniment of no "Clamour." Returning to Smith's casuistic arguments to Hume about this matter, the "scruples" to which Hume refers and which he tried to counter (Letter 156), while these show a concern for propriety and offer no hint of duplicity, they reveal how far Smith was prepared to adapt the straightforward precepts of natural morality, when it came to applying them to protect deeply held beliefs and reputation. It may even be that in this affair of the *Dialogues* Smith failed to heed his own point about the importance of sticking to general rules of morality when one's own interests are involved, because of the danger of indulging in special pleading on one's own less-than-impartial account. Still, if we assume that here we have a genuinely moral stand by Smith – an effort to protect readers from the disturbing implications of the *Dialogues*, at least in the short run – then it demonstrates the considerable extent to which he was inclined to be influenced by the calculations of the possible consequences of different lines of action, rather than by the immediate moral sentiments of the impartial spectator. Had these been consulted in relation to this stand, they must surely have prompted Smith to speedy acquiescence in what Hume called, in referring approvingly to Mallet's publication of Bolingbroke's works, the "sacred Regard to the Will of a dear Friend" (Letter 156).

Putting aside the thought that Smith would not be flattered by the comparison with Mallet, it would appear that the successful avoidance of involvement in the publication of the *Dialogues* illustrates well Smith's preparedness to resort to a rather intricate type of casuistry, rather than to follow the obvious promptings of benevolence in a form he acknowledges to have the full backing of the impartial spectator. We can interpret this as Smith regarding the matter purely as a matter of prudence, in which case his consequentialist approach is in complete accordance with his normative ethical theory, although it is doubtful if the same can be said of his apparent failure to subordinate prudence to the duty of acting with benevolence towards close friends. Alternatively, if we consider that Smith's calculations were directed as much to the reputation of Hume, the interests of Strahan, and the welfare of the reading public as to his own peace of mind, then we can see this incident as demonstrating Smith's willingness to leave to the individual the task of finding a proper balance between prudence and benevolence in the light of the comparative utility of the alternative lines of action open to him. Or perhaps that he was prepared to allow the wise and virtuous man, at least, to modify the rules of common morality by reflecting on the utility of conduct in its particular context and arriving at an ad hoc balance between considerations of prudence and benevolence. This is probably how Smith saw the matter himself, and to that extent we can say that he was in practice prepared to turn his contemplative utilitarianism into a practical morality.

But in analysing his conduct from the biographer's point of view, it is the former interpretation that appears most plausible, for the fact that he had difficulty coming to terms with the argument of *Dialogues* seems to provide the best explanation for his failure to respond positively to Hume's request. We can therefore see the incident as an unconscious illustration of the dangers of partiality which, he thought, accompanied such "do-it-yourself" utilitarianism. Yet if this affair does not show Smith in his best light, his weakness is more in his practice than in his theory, for we may think that in responding to Hume's deathbed wish concerning the publication of the *Dialogues* he was too much the prudent man, and did not aspire enough to the character of his wise and virtuous man who, with strong self-control and refined sensibility, gives prudence its due but is swayed more by the claims of justice and of beneficence.

NOTES

T. D. Campbell wishes to record his gratitude to the British Academy for grants which enabled him to visit the University of British Columbia in January–February 1978 and work with the co-author of this essay on aspects of Adam Smith's thought and career, and to be present to deliver it at the annual meeting of the American Society for Eighteenth-Century Studies in San Francisco in April, 1980.

1 First edition, 1759. Hereafter referred to as TMS in line with the system of reference adopted for the Glasgow Edition of the *Works and Correspondence of Adam Smith* (Clarendon Press: Oxford, 1976–), from which all quotations have been taken. Corr. = Correspondence; EPS = Essays on Philosophical Subjects; LJ = Lectures on Jurisprudence; WN = Wealth of Nations. The numbers cited refer to book or part, or version (LJ); chapter, section, and paragraph divisions; or to chronologically arranged letters.

2 A simplistic view of Adam Smith presents him as abandoning the more humane as well as more complex subject of moral or social philosophy for the narrower and more reductive study of economics. As the biographical record makes clear, however, he seems to have maintained throughout his active teaching and writing years a lively interest in moral questions, both within and without the economic sphere. In another paper entitled "Utilitarianism in Adam Smith's Policy Ideals and Policy Advice," *Journal of the History of Ideas*, 42 (1981), 73–92, we document Smith's sustained attention to moral issues.

3 For a detailed discussion of Smith's Moral Theory see T. D. Campbell, *Adam Smith's Science of Morals* (London: Allen & Unwin, 1971).

4 Recalling that Hume revealed something of himself in his "characters" of the Stoic and the Sceptic (*Essays Moral and Political*, published late in 1741), it is natural to ask if Smith's disposition is reflected in Part VI of TMS. The answer lies, perhaps, in the picture afforded by the "practical system of Morality" of the man of prudence. Such a man is amiable and agreeable, but hardly an endearing and ennobling person. He takes meticulous care of his health, his fortune, and his rank and reputation, for these are the points "on which his comfort and happiness in this life . . . principally depend" (VI.i.5). He is simple, honest, sincere, temperate, steady, industrious, inoffensive, and decent, also unwilling to take on more responsibility than his duty requires of him. While he never tells a lie, he may sometimes omit to tell the truth. He is cautious and reserved but capable of friendship in the form of a "steady and faithful attachment to a few well-tried and chosen companions." At the same time, he has a cool attitude to "those convivial societies which are distinguished for the jollity and gaiety of their conversation. Their way of life might too often interfere with the regularity of his temperance, might interrupt the steadiness of his industry, or break in upon the strictness of his frugality" (VI.i.9).

5 The A version of LJ (Report of 1762–3) has a more extended comment on the "regard we all naturally have to the will of a dying person": "That period is of so momentous a nature that every thing that is connected with it seems to be so also. The advices, the commands, and even the very fooleries of the dying person have more effect on us than things of the same nature would have had at any other period. We have a great reverence for his commands at such a time; and after his death, we do not consider what he willed, but what if he was then alive would be his will: we think, as we say, what would be his will if he should look up from the grave and see things going contrary to what he had enjoined" (i.150–51).

6 E. C. Mossner, "Hume and the Legacy of the *Dialogues*,"*David Hume: Bicentenary Papers* (Edinburgh: Edinburgh University Press, 1977) at p. 1. As Smith very likely knew, his relationship with Hume was a puzzle to his friends among believers. Thus, the Genevan natural scientist Charles Bonnet wrote to Hans Bernhardt Mérian of the Berlin Academy on 2 September 1785 that he did not understand how "mon Ami Smith" in his account of Hume's last days could associate wisdom with this "Pyrrhon moderne." Bonnet claimed to have read little of Hume, and not to know the *Dialogues* at all, but he was prepared to forewarn his readers about Hume (Bonnet MSS, Correspondance, Bibliothèque, Université de Genève). We owe this reference to Professor L. L. Bongie of the University of British Columbia.

7 John Rae, *Life of Adam Smith* (1895; rept. with an introductory "Guide" by Jacob Viner, New York: Kelly, 1965), pp. 12–13; I. Ross, *Lord Kames and the Scotland of His Day* (Oxford: Clarendon Press, 1972), ch. 8, "*Brutum Fulmen*."

8 Besides, Smith was prepared to eulogize the quality of Hume's life and death in a way which was sufficient in itself to infuriate orthodox Christians. In particular, they were incensed by Smith's adaptation of the last sentence of Plato's

Phaedo for an epitaph to Hume: "Upon the whole, I have always considered him, both in his lifetime and since his death, as approaching as nearly to the idea of a perfectly wise and virtuous man, as perhaps the nature of human frailty will permit" (Letter 178). For the fury aroused, see the Reverend George Horne's abusive *Letter to Adam Smith, LL.D. on the Life, Death, and Philosophy of His Friend David Hume, Esq. By One of the People Called Christians* (Oxford, 1777).

[8]

Final Causes in Adam Smith's *Theory of Moral Sentiments*

RICHARD A. KLEER

1. INTRODUCTION

From its inception and for a long time thereafter, Adam Smith's *Theory of Moral Sentiments* was deemed to turn upon the concept of a benevolent divine author of nature. This view was perhaps put most succinctly by Wilhelm Hasbach, who claimed that the point of departure for all of Smith's theoretical investigations was "the tenet of a God whose most outstanding properties were the greatest possible wisdom and beneficence. His highest purpose in the creation of the world was human happiness. For the realization of his final purpose, he made use of mechanics. The Creator is to be compared to a watchmaker, who has so artfully assembled the gears of the world that it produces order, harmony, beauty and happiness without the gears knowing or willing this outcome."[1] However, in recent decades, the tendency has been to argue that teleological arguments, while present in *The Theory of Moral Sentiments,* may be excised without impairing the cogency of his analysis. I mention only those who have made that book itself the focus of study (ignoring the larger body of scholars who examined it merely as a stepping stone to the exegesis of *The Wealth of Nations*).

Alec Macfie claimed that, after reading *The Theory of Moral Sentiments* "with the sole and explicit aim of noting all the differing passages in which Nature, the Deity, or the invisible hand . . . occur," he found it "quite remarkable how little relation they have with the main sympathy-spectator argument. The

[1] Hasbach, *Untersuchungen über Adam Smith und die Entwicklung der politischen Ökonomie* (Leipzig: Duncker & Humblot, 1891), 7: "Ihren Ausgangspunkt bildet die Lehre von Gott, dessen am meisten hervortretende Eigenschaften größte Weisheit und Güte sind. Sein höchster Zweck bei der Erschaffung der Welt war die menschliche Glückseligkeit. Zur Verwirklichung seiner Endzwecke bedient er sich des Mechanismus. Der Schöpfer ist einem Uhrmacher zu vergleichen, welcher die Räder der Welt so kunstvoll zusammengesetzt hat, daß sie Ordnung, Harmonie, Schönheit, Glückseligkeit auswirken, ohne daß die Räder es wissen oder wollen."

latter indeed is self-sufficient on the level of moral philosophy."[2] The justification for this assertion was not made explicit but can be gleaned from his account of Smith's moral theory. He sought to overturn the opinion which had prevailed among earlier commentators, that in Smith's view moral distinctions are the result of sympathy or instinct alone.[3] He asserted, rather, that Smith actually assigns a large role in his theory to human rationality. Specifically, ethical distinctions are formed only through rational reflection upon the feelings experienced by individuals in their social interaction. Moreover, these distinctions evolve into a form suitable to social existence only over a long period of time, in which the process of reflection becomes ever more educated as past experience of feelings is accumulated.[4] The key role assigned to human rationality, in Macfie's view, gives Smith's moral theory an "inductive" quality and makes its teleological component dispensable. "In its inductive and descriptive arguments, *The Theory of Moral Sentiments* did give us a practical principle of moral discrimination, historically and socially as well as individually developed, and backed by the growing traditions of social experience. . . . It is in this system of inductive theory, not in the invisible hand, that his most valuable and original contribution was made."[5]

Other scholars have supported a similar conclusion. Hans Medick asserted that even if one conceives the "invisible hand" reference in *The Theory of Moral Sentiments* as "evidence for the preponderance of an optimistic deism in Smith's basic normative assumptions," one must nevertheless grant that such a concept has "no direct connection with Smith's empirically-founded statements concerning the social and economic actions of mankind." Rather, he claimed, "it symbolizes . . . the Smithian view of society as an objective causal nexus and a productive historical force *sui generis.* This force, on the one hand, generates the artificial needs of mankind and, on the other hand, at once is kept in motion by the dynamic of these needs and directs that dynamic to goals which are not intended by the individuals themselves."[6] For Medick,

---

[2] *The Individual in Society: Papers on Adam Smith* (London: Allen & Unwin, 1967), 12.

[3] Macfie ascribes this view to R. Zeyss, *Adam Smith und der Eigennutz* (1889), Hasbach, *Untersuchungen,* L. Limentani, *La Morale della Simpatia* (1914), and J. A. Farrar, *Adam Smith* (1881).

[4] *Individual in Society,* 89–92.

[5] Ibid., 125.

[6] *Naturzustand und Naturgeschichte der bürgerlichen Gesellschaft: Die Ursprünge der bürgerlichen Sozialtheorie als Geschichtsphilosophie und Sozialwissenschaft bei Samuel Pufendorf, John Locke, und Adam Smith,* Kritische Studien zur Geschichtswissenschaft, vol. 5 (Göttingen: Vandenhoeck & Ruprecht, 1973), 230–31: "Ob man sie als eine ideologische Rechtfertigung des 'Laissez Faire', als Ausdruck für die Präponderanz eines optimistischen Deismus in den normativen Grundannahmen Smiths oder lediglich als eine rhetorische Konzession des Verfassers der 'Theory' an den deistischen Zeitgeist ansah, meist ist ihr der Status einer philosophischen Annahme zugesprochen worden, die in keinem direkten Zusammenhang mit Smiths empirisch fundierten Aussagen über das soziale und ökonomische Handeln des Menschen steht. . . . Es symbolisiert am Beispel ökono-

that is, the invisible hand is only a metaphor designed to express that property of Smith's moral analysis which it was the principal aim of his own study of Enlightenment social theory to elucidate: the empirical reality of society as a power transcending individuals and not explicable as the simple product of individual actions.[7] Ronald H. Coase argued that, while Smith does allow "that particular characteristics of human beings which were in various ways disagreeable were accompanied by offsetting social benefits," he does not go so far as to state "that there was a natural harmony in man's psychological propensities"—i.e., "that any change in man's nature would tend to make things worse." Even though his analysis implies it, Smith resists stating such a conclusion because,

> in 1759, there was no way of explaining how such a natural harmony came about unless one believed in a personal God who created it all. Before Darwin, Mendel and perhaps also Crick and Watson, if one observed, as Adam Smith thought he often did, a kind of harmony existing in human nature, no explanation could be given if one were unwilling to accept God the creator. My own feeling is that Adam Smith was reluctant to adopt this particular explanation. His use of the term "Nature" and other circumlocutions was rather a means of evading giving an answer to the question than the statement of one. Since Adam Smith could only sense that there was some alternative explanation, the right response was suspended belief, and his position seems to have come close to this.[8]

Knud Haakonssen alleged of Smith's work in general that "[n]othing hinges on teleological explanations and thus on the guarantor of a teleological order. I think it is safe to say that wherever a piece of teleology turns up in Smith it is

---

mischen Handelns die Smithsche Auffassung von der Gesellschaft als eine objektiven Wirkungszusammenhangs und einer produktiven historischen Kraft sui generis, welche die künstlichen Bedürfnisse des Menschen einerseits schafft, andererseits durch die Dynamik dieser künstlichen Bedürfnisse des Menschen in Gang gehalten wird und diese zugleich auf Ziele hinleitet, die von den Individuen selbst nicht intendiert sind."

[7] Other scholars have interpreted the concept in a similar fashion. Glenn R. Morrow maintained that while Smith's reliance on the invisible hand concept was certainly "an expression of the eighteenth-century faith in the beneficent harmony and the ultimate rationality of things," it was also "an effort to think of the social order as a genuine organic unity, with principles of structure and functioning which maintain themselves independently of the wills of individuals" ("Adam Smith: Moralist and Philosopher," in John Maurice Clark et al., *Adam Smith, 1776–1926: Lectures to Commemorate the Sesquicentennial of the Publication of "The Wealth of Nations"* [Chicago: N.p., 1928; reprint ed., New York: Augustus M. Kelley, 1966], 171–72). Similarly, Louis Schneider concluded of Smith's invisible hand passage in *The Theory of Moral Sentiments:* "If we drop the teleological and theological vocabulary from all this, we are left with what many scholars have regarded as one of the most fundamental insights or perspectives in the social sciences" ("Adam Smith on Human Nature and Social Circumstance," in *Adam Smith and Modern Political Economy: Bicentennial Essays on "The Wealth of Nations,"* ed. Gerald P. O'Driscoll, Jr. [Ames, Iowa: Iowa State University Press, 1979], 51). The particular insight that Schneider had in mind was Robert K. Merton's concept of "the unintended consequences of purposive social action."

[8] "Adam Smith's View of Man," *Journal of Law & Economics* 19 (1976): 538–39.

fairly clear where we have to look in order to find a 'real' explanation in terms of what we may broadly call efficient causes."[9] And D. D. Raphael maintained that the use of theological language in *The Theory of Moral Sentiments* "does not mean that Smith abandoned explanation in terms of human nature, what we nowadays call empirical psychology." Phrases such as the "author of nature" were included only for rhetorical effect. "[B]oth for Smith himself and for most of his readers an account of natural process was more persuasive, as well as more vivid, if nature were personified or treated as the work of a personal God." But Smith's "account of natural processes can be read as a would-be scientific enterprise, with no need for an underpinning from theology."[10]

One commentator adopted an intermediate position. T. D. Campbell stressed that "the theological idea of God's purpose" is "one of the central organizing principles of Smith's social theory." For it "is a presupposition of Smith's whole theory that when men act under the direction of their immediate and short-sighted impulses, this works out to their own benefit, to the benefit of others and in the interests of the whole structure of society. To show this is the crowning aim of his explanatory endeavours." And Smith uses the idea of a divine intelligence to resolve this very problem. Nevertheless, Campbell himself posited a sharp separation between the efficient-cause and final-cause components of *The Theory of Moral Sentiments*, and ascribed to the latter a merely subsidiary status.

> [E]xplanations in terms of the will of God have no place in determining the efficient causes of behaviour, but enter at a later stage once the scientific investigation is completed. In fact, it is possible to remove the theological terminology and Smith's reflections about a benevolent Deity and not affect the empirical content of his work.

> The theological explanation is offered, not as a substitute for causal explanation, but as supplementary to it. Once the causal pattern of events has been exhibited, the end result or state towards which the pattern tends is alleged to have some benefit which was not foreseen by any human agent and on account of which it is intelligible and explanatory to say that the whole process exhibits a plan and therefore implies a planner. . . . This is not to introduce the operation of the divine will into the causal process; rather it adds to the causal explanation of events a different type of explanation, a teleological one. The last part of Smith's explanatory scheme is not, therefore, independent or self-sufficient but is supervenient upon his prior causal analysis.[11]

Campbell, accordingly, despatched the issue of teleology in two subsections in the introductory part of his book (Chapter Two, §iii, and Chapter Three, §ii);

[9] *The Science of a Legislator: The Natural Jurisprudence of David Hume and Adam Smith* (Cambridge: Cambridge University Press, 1981), 77.

[10] *Adam Smith*, Past Masters (Oxford: Oxford University Press, 1985), 36.

[11] See *Adam Smith's Science of Morals*, University of Glasgow Social and Economic Studies, New Series, no. 21 (London: Allen & Unwin, 1971), 61, 69–73.

it receives no mention in his long exposition of the actual content of Smith's moral theory.[12]

In this essay I will argue that the original view of the role of teleology in Smith's moral theory is the correct one. While the role I assign is the same one to which Campbell pointed, I draw upon the actual details of Smith's account in order to question Campbell's rigid separation of efficient and final causes and his relative devaluation of the latter. In Section 2, I sketch the basic structure of *The Theory of Moral Sentiments.* In Section 3, I proceed through its main parts in turn in order to demonstrate that the fundamental causes are a whole panoply of pleasures and pains innate to human nature. In Section 4, I conclude from the contingent nature of these elemental drives and aversions that the principle of a benevolent divine author of nature must be considered as one of the cornerstones of Smith's system of moral philosophy.

2. THE GENERAL STRUCTURE OF SMITH'S MORAL THEORY

In order to exhibit the general structure of Smith's moral theory, it is first necessary to sketch his conception of the nature and tasks of moral theory in general. Smith maintains that any theory of morals must answer the two questions: what is the nature of virtuous conduct, and how does this particular kind of conduct come to be distinguished from all others as right and proper?[13] Smith concentrates largely upon the latter question, the problem of moral judgments, addressing the nature of virtue only sporadically, as occasion arises.[14] He distinguishes four basic types of moral judgment, the permutations of two different pairs of possibilities. Moral judgments may concern the conduct either of other persons or of ourselves. They may also consider actions in relation either to their causes (propriety: whether the action was a proper or improper response under the circumstances) or their external effects (merit: whether the action, considered with regard to its consequences, deserves reward or punishment). This conception of moral theory defines the agenda for his book. Part One explains judgments about the propriety of

[12] He did mention it once more (in the last chapter), but only in a very limited connection: to help explain why Smith's moral theory failed to account for the authority of moral rules.

[13] *The Theory of Moral Sentiments,* ed. D. D. Raphael and A. L. Macfie, The Glasgow Edition of the Works and Correspondence of Adam Smith, vol. 1 (Oxford: Clarendon Press, 1979; facsimile ed., Indianapolis: Liberty Classics, 1982), VII.i.2. This work will hereafter be cited as TMS.

[14] This is probably why Part Six was inserted in the sixth edition. For in this Part Smith gives a more collected discussion of the nature of the several virtues, such as had been missing from earlier editions. I thank Dr. Raphael for drawing my attention to a recent article in which he argues this very point in some detail. See Raphael, "Adam Smith 1790: The Man Recalled; the Philosopher Revived," in *Adam Smith Reviewed,* ed. Peter Jones and Andrew Skinner (Edinburgh: Edinburgh University Press, 1992), 104–12. Raphael adds that even in the new Part Six, Smith's discussion of the nature of virtue is hardly thorough.

others' conduct. Part Two investigates the source of judgments regarding the merit of others' actions. Part Three inquires into the origin of judgments about the propriety and merit of our own actions. The essentials of Smith's moral system proper, therefore, are contained in only the first three Parts of the book.[15] However, even in these three Parts, only a portion of the text (generally the first Section of each Part) is given over to an account of the particular type of moral judgment under consideration. These elements of the book can be summarized in very short order.

Judgments regarding the propriety of actions are founded on the relation between two different sentiments: one that arises in the person originally experiencing it (agent) and the other produced, through the faculty of sympathy, in some other person (spectator) who, after the fact, placed himself, in his imagination, in the original situation of the agent.[16] The spectator approves of the agent's action when his own sympathetic sentiment is equal in degree of intensity to that expressed by the agent in his action. For when we feel the same about something as someone else does, we necessarily approve of that person's sentiment, and so of the action in which it is expressed.[17] Similarly, another's act is deemed meritorious (deserving of reward) when the spectator sympathetically experiences the same degree of gratitude (the basic emotion propelling us to reward another for his action) as was expressed by the person benefiting from the agent's action.[18] There is one caveat, however: the spectator will conceive no sympathy for gratitude unless he first approves of the agent's original beneficial action.[19]

Judgments regarding the propriety of our own actions Smith also explains by means of the principle of mutual sympathy.[20] That principle leads the agent, when he observes others' actions, to denominate some proper and others improper. In this way, over time, he comes to know within himself how an impartial spectator might regard his own actions. This knowledge is what informs his decisions regarding the propriety of those actions. He divides himself, as it were, into two persons—agent and spectator—and considers his

[15] The remaining Parts function largely to defend and bolster that system. In Part Four, he seeks to refute the competing account of moral judgments offered by David Hume. In Part Five, he introduces the influence of custom or habit upon moral judgment in order to account for the observed variety in moral codes across time and place. Part Six serves largely to demonstrate that his account of moral judgments does indeed serve to explain the nature of the several virtues. And in Part Seven, he surveys other competing moral theories in order to exhibit the superiority of his own approach.

[16] TMS, I.i.1 and I.i.3–4.

[17] TMS, I.i.3.1–2.

[18] TMS, II.i.1–2.

[19] TMS, II.i.3–5.

[20] TMS, III.1.

actions from these two different perspectives. He approves of them when the sympathetic sentiment experienced by this imaginary spectator is of the same kind and degree as that actually expressed by the agent; he disapproves of them when the degrees of these sentiments are unequal. Smith does not provide a separate, explicit explanation of judgments concerning the merit of our own actions. The missing demonstration should have come prior to the third chapter of Part Three, where it is clear that he shifts from the analysis of propriety to that of merit (since that chapter concerns the question of the effect of one's actions upon another). But his discussion of judgments regarding the propriety of our own actions makes it very apparent how the parallel issue of merit would be handled under his system.

With regard to the foregoing components of *The Theory of Moral Sentiments*, Smith's moral theory proper, teleology has no substantial role to play. The only properties which the system must ascribe to human nature are a capacity for sympathy and an inescapable tendency in the spectator to approve of those feelings which he shares with the agent. The latter principle Smith himself describes as perfectly necessary, so that the only element of contingency in the system is sympathy. Now Smith does elsewhere ascribe the presence of sympathy in the human constitution to the machinations of a benevolent Nature,[21] and the same view seems to be implicit in *The Theory of Moral Sentiments* itself. But the appeal to divine providence hardly seems necessary in this connection.

However, Smith's moral theory proper is not the only or even the predominant focus of *The Theory of Moral Sentiments.* In each of the subsequent sections or chapters of Parts One through Three, as well as in other places throughout the remaining Parts of the book, quite another theme dominates. He proceeds to show, namely, that the principle of mutual sympathy, operating in conjunction with certain other facets of human nature, causes individuals unwittingly to pursue actions with beneficial consequences and to avoid actions with the contrary tendency; alternatively, he exhibits the peculiar economy of that arrangement of the human constitution by which such effects are produced. To be specific, he explains how it comes about that: a) agents are led to perform actions good for themselves and society as a whole and are dissuaded from actions with harmful consequences; b) there is a natural tendency to a "distinction of ranks" by which political order is maintained; c) human beings are compelled by their nature to act with justice, but not to be benevolent—an

[21] Smith calls it "that fellow-feeling which Nature has, for the wisest purposes, implanted in man, not only towards all other men, but (though no doubt in a much weaker degree) towards all other animals" (*Essays on Philosophical Subjects, with Dugald Stewart's Account of Adam Smith*, ed. W.P.D. Wightman, J.C. Bryce, and I.S. Ross, The Glasgow Edition of the Works and Correspondence of Adam Smith, vol. 3 [Oxford: Clarendon Press, 1980, facsimile ed., Indianapolis: Liberty Classics, 1982], 136).

economical outcome in that justice is the "main pillar that upholds the whole edifice" of society, but benevolence only an "ornament which embellishes" it; d) scope exists for the performance of benevolent actions; e) people have a genuine desire actually to be, rather than merely to appear, virtuous; f) the expression of self-interest is kept within bounds suited to the maintenance of societal relations; g) the inability of the majority of mankind to form well-considered moral judgments is compensated by the emergence of an authoritative code of social mores; h) mankind has been induced "to cultivate the ground, to build houses, to found cities and commonwealths, and to invent and improve all the sciences and arts, which ennoble and embellish human life" and the rich "to make nearly the same distribution of the necessaries of life, which would have been made, had the earth been divided into equal portions among all its inhabitants"; i) agents tend to be benevolent toward those individuals and institutions whose happiness most depends upon their goodwill and whose interests their own situations best fit them, above all other people, to advance; and j) agents are induced to express that precise degree of every different kind of sentiment which is most to their benefit.[22]

It is evident from the text that Smith ascribes these outcomes to the purposes of a benevolent Nature; no commentator has ever denied this (though some have failed to recognize the connection of certain parts of the text with the concept of natural purposes). The question is whether such teleological references are a necessary or meaningful component of his analysis. In the next section I propose to examine in some detail the explanations which he supplies for each of these fortuitous outcomes. Specifically, I aim to show that in each case the fundamental causes are different innate, subrational desires and aversions embodied in human nature. From this I conclude in the final section that the idea of a benevolent divine author of nature is not mere window dressing, but an essential element of Smith's moral theory. I confine my study to the first three Parts of the book; this is due only to constraints of space, for the same exercise is perfectly feasible with regard to the other outcomes specified.

3. THE FUNDAMENTAL CAUSES OF SMITH'S MORAL THEORY

The thrust of Section Two of Part One ("Of the Degrees of the different Passions which are consistent with Propriety") is that the principle of mutual sympathy induces agents to perform actions with beneficial consequences and to avoid their contrary. Specifically, individuals are encouraged to give only restricted expression to bodily passions, as well as to those passions peculiar to

---

[22] These several parts of his argument occur, respectively, in TMS, I.ii, I.iii., II.ii, II.iii, III.2, III.3, III.4–5, IV.1, VI.ii.1–2, and VI.iii.

their own situation (e.g., love for a particular individual). Also, they are positively discouraged from acting upon so-called "unsocial" passions (anger and resentment), but are led to express the "social" (generosity, humanity, compassion, and friendship) and "selfish" (grief and joy) passions in high and moderate degrees respectively. In all cases the implied benefit is the same: that man is directed away from actions concerned with or peculiar to himself and toward those with a more general social reference. The question is how this result is established.

Smith's explanation turns on the fact that the agent experiences pleasure when he perceives that the sentiments to which he gave expression in his action are exactly matched in intensity by the sympathetically-conceived sentiments of the spectator, and also that he derives pain in proportion to the inequality between these two degrees of sentiment.[23] It is the pleasure of mutual sympathy which attracts all persons to the performance of "moral" acts (i.e., acts of which others will approve), and the pain of absent sympathy which repels them from "immoral" actions. Therefore, we must next examine why socially-oriented actions more readily receive approval than bodily, peculiar, "unsocial" or "selfish" ones.

Approval is not readily forthcoming in the case of actions oriented to the body simply because spectators have a limited capacity for sympathy with bodily emotions. The contemplation of another's hunger, for instance, does not tend to produce a like feeling of hunger in the spectator. Approval is also infrequent with regard to the expression of passions peculiar to oneself, since these arise from a transformation worked on the agent's imagination by habit, a transformation which has not occurred in the spectator. In both cases, the degree of sentiment forthcoming in the spectator is thus much lower in intensity than that experienced by the agent. In antisocial actions, the interests of agent and victim conflict. This divides the sympathy of the spectator and so permits only a low-intensity sympathy for the agent's sentiments. By contrast, because social actions benefit other persons, the sympathy of the spectator is redoubled—his sympathy for the sentiments of the recipient mingling with that for the benefactor's feelings. The expression of selfish passions receives a median degree of sympathy; since such passions refer only to one person, the sympathy of the spectator is neither divided nor redoubled. Restraint is thereby given to the expression of unsocial and selfish passions, and encouragement to the execution of social, i.e., benevolent, actions. There is one other reason that sympathy is more forthcoming for social than for unsocial emotions. The latter passions are disagreeable in themselves and as such prompt the spectator to shy away from any sympathetic contemplation of them; by

[23] TMS, I.i.2.

contrast, the agreeable nature of the former passions gives a positive inducement to the spectator to explore them in his imagination.[24]

In sum, agents are encouraged to the performance of actions with a social orientation, and are turned away from an exclusive concern with themselves, by the combined operation of a number of causes (beyond the omnipresent principle of sympathy itself): the association of pleasure with mutual sympathy, the "inflexibility" of the spectator's body, habit (i.e., the tendency of repeated exposure to a given set of circumstances to give a particular "turn" to the imagination), the conflictive and harmonious natures of unsocial and social passions respectively, and the fact that the former kind of passions are experienced as unpleasant while the latter are inherently agreeable.[25] Some of these causes may be conceived as perfectly necessary (for instance, the conflictive nature of unsocial passions). But prominent among them are certain instinctive pleasures and pains. And Smith conceives the latter as irreducible and arbitrary elements of human nature: "nothing can be agreeable or disagreeable for its own sake, which is not rendered such by immediate sense and feeling."[26]

In Section Three of Part One ("Of the Effects of Prosperity and Adversity upon the Judgment of Mankind with regard to the Propriety of Action; and why it is more easy to obtain their Approbation in the one state than in the other"), Smith focuses on the emergence of that "distinction of ranks" by which political order is maintained. Specifically, he is interested in the source of the respect and admiration accorded to the aristocracy, and of the great and natural aversion to injuring them in any way, by which they are able to retain power without challenge (at least from the lower ranks of society). In order properly to explain the origin of these moral sentiments, I must first introduce material from Chapter One of Part Four ("Of the Effect of Utility upon the Sentiment of Approbation"). By the term "utility" Smith understands "the fitness of any system or machine to produce the end for which it

[24] TMS, I.ii.3.4–5; I.ii.4.2.

[25] Campbell supposed that in Section Two of Part One, Smith is simply stipulating a few "laws," themselves just "empirical generalizations," upon which his account of moral phenomena in all subsequent Parts would build. But this is to miss the connection of the material in this Section with Smith's teleological theme. I suggest, rather, that in Section Two Smith is merely beginning his enumeration of the specific adjustments that had to be made to the human sentiments in order for the operation of the sympathy mechanism, identified in Section One, to produce beneficial effects. In subsequent Parts of the book, Smith does not so much build on this material as add to the list of deliberate adaptations evident in the human constitution that seemed designed to advance the beneficent purposes of nature. In short, his moral theory does not turn upon just a few basic "empirical laws," but in fact upon a whole array of discrete, contingent causes. Had Campbell interpreted it thus, he might have been led to alter his opinion of the importance of final causes for Smith's moral theory.

[26] TMS, VII.iii.2.7.

was intended."[27] He asserts it is common knowledge that the contemplation of a useful device gives pleasure to the beholder. He cites, approvingly, Hume's explanation of why it pleases: because the contemplation of a well-contrived machine continually suggests to its owner "the pleasure or conveniency which it is fitted to promote. Every time he looks at it, he is put in mind of this pleasure; and the object in this manner becomes a source of perpetual satisfaction and enjoyment."[28] But Smith immediately adds to Hume's account another explanation: that the apt adjustment of means to end characteristic of any work of artifice is pleasing to the human imagination for its own sake: "[T]hat this fitness, this happy contrivance of any production of art, should often be more valued, than the very end for which it was intended, and that the exact adjustment of the means for attaining any conveniency or pleasure, should frequently be more regarded, than that very conveniency or pleasure, in the attainment of which their whole merit would seem to consist, has not, so far as I know, been yet taken notice of by any body. That this however is very frequently the case, may be observed in a thousand instances, both in the frivolous and in the most important concerns of human life."[29] In other words, Smith stresses that the pleasure derived from "utility" is predominantly an instinctual component of human nature, rather than the product of a conscious recognition of the uses to which a given device can be put.

Now on Smith's account, admiration of the aristocracy is the combined result of the principles of utility and mutual sympathy. The innate pleasure of utility causes the imagination of the common man constantly to dwell upon the situation of the aristocrat, given the many useful articles which the latter generally possess. As a result, he becomes intimately familiar with the emotions which such useful objects may excite. "When we consider the condition of the great, in those delusive colours in which the imagination is apt to paint it, it seems to be almost the abstract idea of a perfect and happy state. It is the very state which, in all our waking dreams and idle reveries, we had sketched out to ourselves as the final object of all our desires."[30] Drawing upon Smith's earlier analysis, this means that the spectator possesses that "particular turn or habit of the imagination"[31] which makes him susceptible of a great sympathy with the wealthy; for he is in the habit of experiencing exactly those same sentiments which run through the minds of the wealthy in contemplating their possessions. But this "peculiar sympathy" for the wealthy disposes the

[27] TMS, IV.1.1.
[28] TMS, IV.1.2.
[29] TMS, IV.1.3.
[30] TMS, I.iii.2.2.
[31] TMS, I.ii.2.

286 JOURNAL OF THE HISTORY OF PHILOSOPHY 33:2 APRIL 1995

spectator to "favour all their inclinations, and forward all their wishes."[32] For "every injury that is done them, excites in the breast ten times more compassion and resentment than he would have felt, had the same things happened to other men." And in the same way, presumably, he conceives ten times more gratitude for actions which benefit the wealthy.[33]

Smith takes great care to refute any explanations which suggest that deference to the rich is the result of anything other than instinct. It is not founded upon the perception that, if he advances their ends, the agent increases the chance that they will bestow fortune or status upon him. For the benefits conferred by the wealthy are few, while the respect which they command is quite general. Nor is it a regard to the society's interest that motivates such behaviour. For even when the public interest requires that the monarch be deposed, the agent can scarcely bring himself to commit such an act. "That kings are the servants of the people, to be obeyed, resisted, deposed, or punished, as the public conveniency may require, is the doctrine of reason and philosophy; but it is not the doctrine of Nature. Nature would teach us to submit to them for their own sake."[34] On this view, accordingly, political order is the consequence of an elemental drive of human nature—the pleasure of contemplating well-crafted devices—not a deliberate contractual arrangement arising from a rational reflection upon the interests of all the parties concerned.

The focus of Part Two, Section Two ("Of Justice and Beneficence") is a certain economy evident in the arrangement of the human moral constitution. The spectator is disposed to reward beneficent acts but not to punish the agent who does not perform them. Similarly, he is inclined to punish injurious acts, but not to reward the agent who does not engage in them.[35] Consequently, the agent experiences pain when he commits injurious actions, but

---

[32] TMS, I.iii.2.2. It would appear that Smith has in mind here only the very wealthy, such as royalty. For only these individuals live in that condition which is "almost the abstract idea of a perfect and happy state"—a state of only moderate wealth not being that in which the spectator longs to imagine himself. Consequently too, it would only be the very wealthy whom the spectator would be inclined to assist, not just anyone possessing greater riches than he.

[33] Smith does not actually specify why this greater sympathy disposes persons to assist, and greatly to avoid injurious actions toward, the wealthy. But the logic of his principle of mutual sympathy demands something like the following account. The agent recognizes that all other spectators have the same high degree of sympathy for the rich. Consequently, he is conscious that any action which he undertakes to further the interests of the wealthy will easily obtain the approval of the spectator, giving him great pleasure. Similarly, he knows that the spectator's disapproval will be exceedingly great for actions which injure such individuals; the great pain which this lack of sympathy would cause him gives him enormous incentive not to commit such acts.

[34] TMS, I.iii.2.3.

[35] TMS, II.ii.1.

obtains little pleasure from avoiding them; on the other hand, he derives pleasure from the execution of beneficent acts, but is not subjected to pain if he abstains from these.[36] Now this adjustment is economical because beneficent acts, while they assist, are not indispensable to the maintenance of social relations. Such acts, accordingly, are encouraged by nature insofar as it links pleasure with their performance; but she did not positively compel them by attaching pain to their nonperformance. On the other hand, "the immense fabric of human society . . . must in a moment crumble into atoms" if unjust acts (i.e., actions which advance the interests of one at the expense of another) occurred with any frequency. Nature, accordingly, associated pain with the performance of such actions: a much more effective means of proscribing them than associating pleasure with their nonexecution.[37]

Closer examination of Smith's account shows that the references to the purposes of nature in this connection are more than just rhetorical. The priority of justice over beneficence arises from the fact that resentment is aroused by the nonperformance only of the former, not the latter:

> Resentment seems to have been given us by nature for defence, and for defence only. It is the safeguard of justice and the security of innocence. It prompts us to beat off the mischief which is attempted to be done to us, and to retaliate that which is already done; that the offender may be made to repent of his injustice, and that others, through fear of the like punishment, may be terrified from being guilty of the like offence. It must be reserved therefore for these purposes, nor can the spectator ever go along with it when it is exerted for any other. But the mere want of the beneficent virtues, though it may disappoint us of the good which might reasonably be expected, neither does, nor attempts to do, any mischief from which we can have occasion to defend ourselves.[38]

Resentment, that is, arises only when positive harm has been done, not when an opportunity for beneficence is foregone; in the same way, gratitude is conceived only for acts of positive benefit, not when an opportunity for injury is left unexplored.[39] Consequently, the agent experiences pain (in this case, from the consciousness that he is the proper object of punishment) when he fails to act with justice, but not when he neglects charity; he is accordingly compelled to be just, but has only an attraction to be beneficent (which he may

---

[36] TMS, II.ii.2.

[37] TMS, II.ii.3.

[38] TMS, II.ii.1.4.

[39] See TMS, II.ii.1.9: "There is , no doubt, a propriety in the practice of justice, and it merits, upon that account, all the approbation which is due to propriety. But as it does no real positive good, it is entitled to very little gratitude. Mere justice is, upon most occasions, but a negative virtue, and only hinders us from hurting our neighbour. The man who barely abstains from violating either the person, or the estate, or the reputation of his neighbours, has surely very little positive merit."

elect to forego in favor of the generally greater pleasures attainable from self-interested actions). But no mere physical explanation is available for the fact that resentment is not experienced by persons when others fail to act with beneficence toward them; it is only "by nature" that things happen to be so.[40]

In Section Three of Part Two, Smith explores "The Influence of Fortune upon the Sentiments of Mankind, with regard to the Merit or Demerit of Actions." This influence is evident in the fact that, even if a person has a clear intention to perform a beneficent action, the recipient is more grateful if this intention was actually fulfilled than if, by sheer accident, it was prevented from coming to fruition. This has a deleterious effect upon morality, for it may lead the spectator, upon occasion, to attach merit or demerit to actions undeserving of these judgments. But, despite these costs, such an "irregularity" was wisely ordained by nature. For if the human constitution had been adjusted so that moral judgments were formed on the basis of intentions alone, agents' disposition to perform beneficent deeds would have been hindered, for fear that a malevolent intention might nevertheless be suspected by the recipient.[41]

---

[40] Smith refers to Kames as the first author to have discovered this arbitrary arrangement of the sentiments as the source of the predominance of justice over beneficence. See Henry Home Kames, *Essays on the Principles of Morality and Natural Religion. In Two Parts* (Edinburgh: R. Fleming et al., 1751; facsimile ed., New York: Garland, 1976), 74: "Yet, as pain is a stronger motive to action than pleasure, the remorse which attends a breach of strict duty is, with the bulk of mankind, a more powerful incitement to honesty, than praise and self-approbation are to generosity. And there cannot be a more pregnant instance of wisdom than this part of the human constitution; it being far more essential to society, that all men be just and honest, than they be patriots and heroes." That Kames is referring here to a divine wisdom is clear from two sentences in the previous chapter: "And, in performing this task [viz. explaining the grounds for the distinction between what is obligatory duty and merely proper behavior], there will be discovered a wonderful and beautiful contrivance of the Author of our nature, to give authority to morality, by putting the self-affections in a due subordination to the social" (ibid., 58). "And, indeed, the more we search into the works of nature, the more opportunity there is to admire the wisdom and goodness of the Sovereign Architect" (ibid., 64).

[41] See TMS, II.iii.3.2: "Nature, however, when she implanted the seeds of this irregularity in the human breast, seems, as upon all other occasions, to have intended the happiness and perfection of the species. If the hurtfulness of the design, if the malevolence of the affection, were alone the causes which excited our resentment, we should feel all the furies of that passion against any person in whose breast we suspected or believed such designs or affections were harboured, though they had never broke out into any action. Sentiments, thoughts, intentions, would become the objects of punishment; and if the indignation of mankind run as high against them as against actions; if the baseness of the thought which had given birth to no action, seemed in the eyes of the world as much to call aloud for vengeance as the baseness of the action, every court of judicature would become a real inquisition. There would be no safety for the most innocent and circumspect conduct. Bad wishes, bad views, bad designs, might still be suspected; and while these excited the same indignation with bad conduct, while bad intentions were as much resented as bad actions, they would equally expose the person to punishment and resentment. Actions, therefore, which either produce actual evil, or attempt to produce it, and thereby put us in the immediate

Now it turns out that this fortunate priority of consequences (which are a matter of chance only) over intentions in the estimation of actions exists only because of a particular irrational and merely instinctive property embodied in human nature. Specifically, humans (and all animals) conceive gratitude and resentment directly for those objects which are the cause of their pleasure and pain, respectively—even if those objects are inanimate and so cannot possibly have any intention to do good or ill:

> We are angry, for a moment, even at the stone that hurts us. A child beats it, a dog barks at it, a choleric man is apt to curse it. The least reflection, indeed, corrects this sentiment, and we soon become sensible, that what has no feeling is a very improper object of revenge. When the mischief, however, is very great, the object which caused it becomes disagreeable to us ever after, and we take pleasure to burn or destroy it. We should treat, in this manner, the instrument which had accidentally been the cause of the death of a friend, and we should often think ourselves guilty of a sort of inhumanity, if we neglected to vent this absurd sort of vengeance upon it.
>
> We conceive, in the same manner, a sort of gratitude for those inanimated objects, which have been the causes of great, or frequent pleasure to us. The sailor who, as soon as he got ashore, should mend his fire with the plank upon which he had just escaped from a shipwreck, would seem to be guilty of an unnatural action. We should expect that he would rather preserve it with care and affection, as a monument that was, in some measure, dear to him.[42]

This instinctive gratitude and resentment also arises toward the agent insofar as he is the cause of another's pleasure or pain. But because the spectator too, through sympathy, involuntarily conceives such sentiments, a "shadow"[43] of merit or demerit, as the case may be, falls upon the agent's action, prior to and independent of any judgment about whether or not it was the actual intention of the agent to produce such an effect. Hence it is only because human beings are endowed with a knee-jerk reaction toward objects causing them pleasure and pain that fortune comes to have an influence (one which turns out to be beneficial) upon their moral judgments.

In Chapter Two of Part Three ("Of the love of Praise, and of that of Praise-worthiness; and of the dread of Blame, and of that of Blame-worthiness"), Smith attempts to explain why people are not content with merely appearing to be moral, but have a genuine desire actually to be so. This desire arises from the fact that the concord (or discord) of sentiments with the imaginary spectator "in the breast" produces pleasure (or pain) in the agent just as much as concord (or discord) with the sentiments of actual spectators. The agent always knows what

---

fear of it, are by the Author of nature rendered the only proper and approved objects of human punishment and resentment."

[42] TMS, II.iii.1.1–2.

[43] TMS, II.iii.1.7.

actions he has (or has not) in fact performed. Therefore, while pleasure will be produced in the agent when an external spectator approves of an action he mistakenly believes the agent performed, that pleasure will be offset by the pain of a discord of sentiment between the agent and his own internal spectator. Consequently, maximization of his pleasure requires the agent actually to perform the act in question. Now this new pleasure and pain are distinct from those identified in Part One, but they are equally arbitrary. There is as little reason, that is, why the agent should conceive pleasure or pain from a concord or discord of sentiments, respectively, with this internal spectator, as that he should from concord or discord with an actual, external spectator. Both are mere arbitrary properties of human nature:

> Nature, when she formed man for society, endowed him with an original desire to please, and an original aversion to offend his brethren. She taught him to feel pleasure in their favourable, and pain in their unfavourable regard. She rendered their approbation most flattering and most agreeable to him for its own sake; and their disapprobation most mortifying and most offensive.
>
> But this desire of the approbation, and this aversion to the disapprobation of his brethren, would not alone have rendered him fit for that society for which he was made. Nature, accordingly, has endowed him not only with a desire of being approved of, but with a desire of being what ought to be approved of; or of being what he himself approves of in other men.[44]

Nor is the later passion merely a derivative of the former. For the agent may approve of his own actions and derive pleasure from this even in the absence of the spectator's agreement; likewise, he usually will feel no delight in the applause of others that he knows he does not merit. "[S]o far is the love of praise-worthiness from being derived altogether from that of praise; that the love of praise seems, at least in a great measure, to be derived from that of praise-worthiness."[45] So the dedication to the actual performance of moral actions is ultimately the result of a second, independent pair of basic drive and aversion (pleasure and pain) embodied in the human constitution.

In Part Three, Chapter Three ("Of the Influence and Authority of Conscience"), Smith seeks to explain how the expression of self-interest is kept within bounds suited to the maintenance of societal relations. The agent naturally perceives his own interests to be of far greater importance than those of any other person. For instance, even a "man of humanity" would feel more real grief upon the loss of his little finger than upon receiving the news that "the great empire of China, with all its myriads of inhabitants, was suddenly swallowed up by an earthquake."[46] Why is it then, Smith asks, that individuals

---

[44] TMS, III.2.6–7.

[45] TMS, III.2.3.

[46] TMS, III.3.4.

generally are not willing to sacrifice the lives of myriad others in order to spare themselves some small pain (or attain some minuscule pleasure)? His answer is: the desire for mutual sympathy. For the impartial spectator within his breast experiences only a very small degree of sympathy for the agent's interests: no more than for the interests of any other person. Consequently, when the agent advances his own interests at the expense of someone else's, he is conscious that he does not have the approval of the spectator (that the degrees of their sentiments are unequal) and that he is therefore the proper object of resentment and punishment. In order to avoid the pain which this bad conscience brings him, the agent voluntarily restrains the pitch of his natural self-interest, expressing in his actions only that degree with which the spectator can concur. He is led, accordingly, to advance his own interests only so far as this does not entail injuring someone else in any way.

This chapter does not actually add anything new to Smith's analysis of the moral sentiments; it merely elaborates upon the analysis, in Sections One and Two of Part Two, of the origin of the sense of guilt. But it should be recognized that on Smith's view the sense of guilt is through and through the product of instinct. It is the consequence of the agent internalizing the judgments of demerit made by the spectator. In order to explain that internalized judgment, I first describe it as it arises in the external spectator. When someone injures another, the emotion of resentment is produced in his victim. This resentment is approved when the spectator, placing himself in imagination in the original situation of the victim, sympathetically conceives the same degree of resentment as that actually expressed by the latter. But when this degree of resentment is approved, so too is the action which it directs the victim to undertake, namely, the punishment of the offending agent. This is the basis of the spectator's judgment of demerit, i.e., his conclusion that the agent deserves punishment. This judgment comes to be internalized in the agent because he has experience, on other occasions, of having approved the punishment of certain actions by others. He therefore knows that when he commits similar actions, the spectator shares in the victim's resentment of him and approves of his punishment. This consciousness is painful to him. The pain is accentuated by the awareness that the spectator also did not approve of his original action: that in this regard his own and the spectator's sentiments about that action are not equal in intensity. Furthermore, after the fact, he even conceives a sympathetic pity for the person whom he has injured. These various pains together make up the sense of guilt.[47] Having experienced such pain upon the actual commission of some deed, or even having foresight that this would be the consequence

[47] TMS, II.ii.2.3.

of an unjust action, the agent resolves not to commit such acts in the future, so that such pain might be avoided.

Now at every point this explanation of the sense of guilt turns upon certain instinctive pleasures and pains variously experienced by spectator and agent. Certainly, one basic component of the process is the sentiment of resentment. Smith clearly conceives this as an instinctive passion that disposes individuals, without reflection, to visit retribution upon another for the harm that has been done to them; on three occasions he remarked that resentment is a sentiment which "immediately and directly prompts us to punish."[48] Notice, next, that the degree of resentment experienced (by victim and spectator alike) grows in proportion to the seriousness of the injury committed. Hence, for instance, the approval of punishment is most readily forthcoming in the case of murder.[49] But it is just as much beyond the pale of human control that this sentiment of resentment should be stronger for certain kinds of actions as that it should arise at all for any injurious action, i.e., this too is a perfectly contingent characteristic of human nature. And, finally, the sense of guilt itself is entirely instinctive in nature; it arises from the fact that certain pains are instinctively produced in the agent: a pain at being the proper object of resentment and punishment, the pain deriving from a discord of sentiment with the spectator, and the sympathetic pains conceived for the plight of the victim. Guilt, therefore, is a thoroughly instinctive phenomenon. Reason enters into the process only in the capacity to see that a given action is of a kind which, when the agent observed someone else committing it in the past, produced a judgment of demerit in him, and to recognize before the fact that he will experience pain if he too performs this action. And even in this case it can be argued that reason's role is limited. For on another occasion Smith argues that the association of pain with the commission of a given unjust action becomes habitual and unreflective.

Finally, in Chapters Four and Five of Part Three ("Of the Nature of Self-deceit, and of the Origin and Use of general Rules," and "Of the influence and authority of the general Rules of Morality, and that they are justly regarded as the Laws of the Deity"), Smith observes that the inability of the majority of mankind to form well-considered moral judgments (due either to indecision in the heat of passion or more commonly to a generally insensitive nature, i.e., a low capacity for sympathy) is fortuitously compensated by the emergence and rise to authority of a code of social mores. Smith explains their origin as follows. Morally refined spectators discover that certain actions strike them as particularly detestable—that they exhibit a degree of sentiment of

[48] TMS, II.i.1.1,2,7.
[49] TMS, II.i.2.5.

which they can never approve. They resolve, accordingly, never to commit such acts themselves, from the knowledge that they would otherwise be the proper object of others' contempt (a loss of sympathy that would be most painful to them). They observe other actions which inspire in them the greatest admiration. They resolve similarly to perform such actions whenever occasion arises, for they know that they will obtain great pleasure from being the proper object of others' praise. These resolutions, over the course of time, become established as general rules, as awareness grows that others share the same judgments.

Now inasmuch as these general rules are the crystallization of the judgments of moral agents and spectators, their emergence must depend upon all of the instinctual components of human nature catalogued above. But there are certain further instincts which help to give authority to these rules. In part, I grant, their authority does arise through the influence of reason; spectators form their resolve not to break such rules from the conscious foresight of the pain that is thereby avoided. But these moral codes are not exclusively enforced by the power of human reason. For, as Smith constantly emphasizes, the latter force is very weak, and is frequently overcome, at the moment of decision, by the intensity of the passions which drive individuals to act. The agent "changes his purpose every moment; sometimes he resolves to adhere to his principle, and not indulge a passion which may corrupt the remaining part of his life with the horrors of shame and repentance; and a momentary calm takes possession of his breast, from the prospect of that security and tranquillity which he will enjoy when he thus determines not to expose himself to the hazard of a contrary conduct. But immediately the passion rouses anew, and with fresh fury drives him on to commit what he had the instant before resolved to abstain from." But upon the thought of transgressing a general rule, a certain countervailing terror arises in the agent: "At the very time of acting, at the moment in which passion mounts the highest, he hesitates and trembles at the thought of what he is about to do: he is secretly conscious to himself that he is breaking through those measures of conduct which, in all his cool hours, he had resolved never to infringe, which he had never seen infringed by others without the highest disapprobation, and of which the infringement, his own mind forebodes, must soon render him the object of the same disagreeable sentiments. Before he can take the last fatal resolution, he is tormented with all the agonies of doubt and uncertainty; he is terrified at the thought of violating so sacred a rule."[50] This terror, which helps to offset the drive of the passions (though even it is not always sufficient for this purpose), is the product of "habit." By this Smith appears to mean that

[50] TMS, III.4.12.

the repeated observance of the disapprobation arising toward such an action itself creates in the spectator a kind of "reverence," or knee-jerk fear at the contemplation of the act. A similar "awe" arises in those who have merely been educated to the observance of the rule.[51] It is "very strongly impressed upon them" by parents and peers so that the same instinctive fear of violating it arises in them without their ever having experienced the actual disapprobation that first led the rule to be formulated.

This instinctive fear of violating general moral rules, as also the reflex pleasure of observing them, are further strengthened by the common belief that such rules "are the commands and laws of the Deity, who will finally reward the obedient, and punish the transgressors of their duty."[52] This belief too is a product of instinct. In primitive societies, certain objects of religious fear are commonly established (though by what process Smith does not state).[53] Savages naturally attribute to these gods "all their own sentiments and passions," because of the analogy between these "unknown intelligences" and their own intelligence. "They could not fail, therefore, to ascribe to those beings, for the excellence of whose nature they still conceived the highest admiration, those sentiments and qualities which are the great ornaments of humanity, and which seem to raise it to a resemblance of divine perfection, the love of virtue and beneficence, and the abhorrence of vice and injustice." In this way, "religion, even in its rudest form, gave a sanction to the rules of morality."[54]

The same belief also arises in civilized societies, though by a different course. Nature has endowed mankind, in regard to vices and virtues, with a "desire to heap upon them every sort of disgrace and disaster" and a "desire to see them crowned with wealth, and power, and honours of every kind," respectively.[55] But nature itself is more economical, in that the several vices and

[51] TMS, III.5.1.

[52] TMS, III.5.3.

[53] He does provide an explanation in the "History of Astronomy." Though the hunt for subsistence makes the savage too busy to discover the regularities of nature, he cannot overlook "[t]hose more magnificent irregularities" such as "[c]omets, eclipses, thunder, lightning, and other meteors. . . . His inexperience and uncertainty with regard to every thing about them, how they came, how they are to go, what went before, what is to come after them, exasperate his sentiment into terror and consternation. But our passions, as Father Malbranche [*sic*] observes, all justify themselves; that is, suggest to us opinions which justify them. As those appearances terrify him, therefore, he is disposed to believe every thing about them which can render them still more the objects of his terror. That they proceed from some intelligent, though invisible causes, of whose vengeance and displeasure they are either the signs or the effects, is the notion of all others most capable of enhancing this passion, and is that, therefore, which he is most apt to entertain" (*Essays on Philosophical Subjects*, 48).

[54] TMS, III.5.4.

[55] TMS, III.5.9.

virtues actually receive only that measure of punishment and reward necessary, respectively, to restrain and encourage them in the degree which the "perfection and happiness of human nature" require. Because their desires therefore are not usually realized, human beings are led to invent the idea of an afterlife, in which misdemeanor and self-sacrifice will receive their due reward. "When we thus despair of finding any force upon earth which can check the triumph of injustice, we naturally appeal to heaven, and hope, that the great Author of our nature will himself execute hereafter, what all the principles which he has given us for the direction of our conduct, prompt us to attempt even here."[56] Thus the rise of religion in civilized societies (and hence the authority of moral rules) can be traced to the merely contingent fact that the human beings actually affected by someone's behavior experience more gratitude or resentment (are disposed to bestow more reward or punishment) than does (is) the spectator (who is, after all, the arbiter of the "natural" degree of reward and punishment which all individuals receive). But just as it is arbitrary that a faculty for sympathy should at all exist, it is arbitrary that sympathetic emotions should be less intense than original emotions.

4. CONCLUSION

The foregoing summary of Smith's system shows that the common moral judgments of mankind support actions beneficial to both individual and society and restrain, as much as possible, those with the opposite tendency. In his own words, "[t]he prudent, the equitable, the active, resolute, and sober character promises prosperity and satisfaction, both to the person himself and to every one connected with him. The rash, the insolent, the slothful, effeminate, and voluptuous, on the contrary, forebodes ruin to the individual, and misfortune to all who have any thing to do with him."[57] The problem for Smith is to explain this fortuitous connection between moral judgments and human happiness. In Hume's *Enquiry Concerning the Principles of Morals,* it was ultimately traced to *human* reason; a sentiment of general benevolence disposes us to deem "moral" precisely those actions which reason informs us are useful either to ourselves or to others.[58] Smith expressly criticizes this view on two separate occasions in *The*

[56] TMS, III.5.10.

[57] TMS, IV.2.1.

[58] See *Principles of Morals,* ed. J. B. Schneewind (Indianapolis: Hackett, 1983), 82–83: "One principal foundation of moral praise being supposed to lie in the usefulness of any quality or action; it is evident, that *reason* must enter for a considerable share in all decisions of this kind; since nothing but this faculty can instruct us in the tendency of qualities and actions, and point out their beneficial consequences to society and to their possessor. . . . But though reason, when fully assisted and improved, be sufficient to instruct us in the pernicious or useful tendency of qualities and actions; it is not alone sufficient to produce any moral blame or approbation. Utility is only a tendency to a certain end; and were the end totally indifferent to us, we should feel the same

Theory of Moral Sentiments,[59] and his entire moral system tells against it. On his account, moral judgments arise independently of conscious human foresight of the consequences of actions. He envisions them rather as the merely mechanical outcome of certain basic instincts and drives of human nature, large in number and all of a perfectly contingent character. Consequently, at the level of efficient causes alone, there is no inherent reason why actions deemed moral should be the very ones which most conduce to human happiness.

It is in this very connection, I suggest, that the principle of a benevolent author of nature becomes highly serviceable. Specifically, it prevents Smith from having to ascribe to sheer accident the presence in the human constitution of the complete set of those sentiments which act to bring about human happiness. They may now be conceived as the means needed to achieve that very end, thus supplying a principle by which to explain why just they, and not other emotions equally possible, happen to be in place. Of course, this also obligates Smith to think of some intelligent being who adopted such ends, identified the requisite means, and constructed human nature accordingly. Such a conception is expressly formulated in *The Theory of Moral Sentiments:*

> With regard to all those ends which, upon account of their peculiar importance, may be regarded, if such an expression is allowable, as the favourite ends of nature, she has constantly . . . not only endowed mankind with an appetite for the end which she proposes, but likewise with an appetite for the means by which alone this end can be brought about, for their own sakes, and independent of their tendency to produce it. Thus self-preservation, and the propagation of the species, are the great ends which Nature seems to have proposed in the formation of all animals. Mankind are endowed with a desire of those ends, and an aversion to the contrary; with a love of life, and a dread of dissolution; with a desire of the continuance and perpetuity of the species, and with an aversion to the thoughts of its intire extinction. But though we are in this manner endowed with a very strong desire of those ends, it has not been intrusted to the slow and uncertain determination of our reason, to find out the proper means of bringing them about. Nature has directed us to the greater part of these by original and immediate instincts. Hunger, thirst, the passion which unites the two sexes, the love of pleasure, and the dread of pain, prompt us to apply those means for their own sakes, and without any consideration of their tendency to those beneficent ends which the great Director of nature intended to produce by them.[60]

The idea of a benevolent deity, far from being superfluous to Smith's moral theory at the level of efficient causes, is reciprocally connected with the contin-

---

indifference towards the means. It is requisite a *sentiment* should here display itself, in order to give a preference to the useful above the pernicious tendencies. This sentiment can be no other than a feeling for the happiness of mankind, and a resentment of their misery; since these are the different ends which virtue and vice have a tendency to promote."

[59] TMS, II.ii.3.6–12, IV.2.3–12. Hume's name is not mentioned in either passage, but there is little doubt he was the intended target of Smith's criticisms.

[60] TMS, II.i.5.10.

gent character of those causes. And it is needed to resolve the main explanatory problem of a theory which traces the correspondence of morality and happiness to certain basic yet arbitrary pleasures and pains embodied in human nature.

Mention should be made of one key paragraph in *The Theory of Moral Sentiments,* which some commentators have interpreted to mean that Smith himself recommended removing final causes from "scientific" analysis:

> In every part of the universe we observe means adjusted with the nicest artifice to the ends which they are intended to produce; and in the mechanism of a plant, or animal body, admire how every thing is contrived for advancing the two great purposes of nature, the support of the individual, and the propagation of the species. But in these, and in all such objects, we still distinguish the efficient from the final cause of their several motions and organizations. The digestion of the food, the circulation of the blood, and the secretion of the several juices which are drawn from it, are operations all of them necessary for the great purposes of animal life. Yet we never endeavour to account for them from those purposes as from their efficient causes, nor imagine that the blood circulates, or that the food digests of its own accord, and with a view or intention to the purposes of circulation or digestion. The wheels of the watch are all admirably adjusted to the end for which it was made, the pointing of the hour. All their various motions conspire in the nicest manner to produce this effect. If they were endowed with a desire and intention to produce it, they could not do it better. Yet we never ascribe any such desire or intention to them, but to the watch-maker, and we know that they are put into motion by a spring, which intends the effect it produces as little as they do. But though, in accounting for the operation of bodies, we never fail to distinguish in this manner the efficient from the final cause, in accounting for those of the mind we are very apt to confound these two different things with one another. When by natural principles we are led to advance those ends, which a refined and enlightened reason would recommend to us, we are very apt to impute to that reason, as to their efficient cause, the sentiments and actions by which we advance those ends, and to imagine that to be the wisdom of man, which in reality is the wisdom of God.[61]

From this paragraph, Knud Haakonssen concluded: "The tendency to take that for a motivating force of behaviour which is really nothing but the unintended, *de facto* result of such behaviour was very common, according to Smith, and it was the basic weakness of all teleological metaphysics. In this Smith simply applied Hume's general criticism of teleological explanations to such explanations of the moral world, and in doing so he also followed Hume's criticism of the theological versions of teleology."[62] Campbell thought it meant that the "general laws [of human behavior] must be discovered and

[61] TMS, II.ii.3.5.

[62] "What Might Properly Be Called Natural Jurisprudence?" in *The Origins and Nature of the Scottish Enlightenment,* ed. R. H. Campbell and Andrew S. Skinner (Edinburgh: John Donald Publishers, 1982), 211. See Haakonssen, *Science of a Legislator,* 77–79, for a similar, more detailed interpretation of this same passage.

explained in terms of efficient causes conceived in terms of constant conjunction; explanations in terms of the will of God have no place in determining the efficient causes of behavior, but enter at a later stage once the scientific investigation is completed."[63] And it led Milton Myers to remark: "It is evident from Smith's discussion about efficient and final causes that he plans to explore problems in moral philosophy largely in terms of what he considers to be their true causes, and these are their efficient causes. . . . He plans to avoid confusing sets of causes by concentrating mainly on only one kind."[64]

Such interpretations are unwarranted. Far from stating that final causes should be removed from scientific explanations,[65] the general thrust of the passage is to stress their importance. It may be paraphrased thus: "In both the physical and moral realms we see the apt arrangement of efficient causes for producing some end and rightly attribute this to the final causality of a benevolent Nature. In the case of physical phenomena, we always distinguish the efficient from the final causes. But in the case of mental phenomena, we confuse them, making reason, which in the grand scheme of things is only one of the efficient causes by which nature attains its ends, the final cause of all (by supposing it to be the efficient cause of our moral sentiments)." The implicit recommendation is that the human should follow the natural sciences in attributing to the wisdom of *Nature* the apt adjustment of efficient causes toward a beneficial end. Smith then immediately proceeds to *criticize* Hume for having fallen prey to this very confusion of final and efficient causes in his analysis of justice.[66]

---

[63] *Smith's Science of Morals*, 61.

[64] *The Soul of Modern Economic Man: Ideas of Self-Interest, Thomas Hobbes to Adam Smith* (Chicago: University of Chicago Press, 1983), 104.

[65] The only substantial basis for such an interpretation is the half-sentence: "Yet we never endeavour to account for them from those purposes as from their efficient causes." For this seems to imply that the natural scientist explains the organization of animal bodies by means of efficient rather than final causes. Granted, the phrase "from those purposes as from their efficient causes" is ambiguous. But the "as," it seems to me, is intended to convey a sense not of exclusion, but rather of hypothesis. In other words, Smith meant: when we give the teleological part of the explanation ("account for them from those purposes"), we don't proceed *as though* the purposes were themselves the efficient final causes. On this interpretation, the remaining part of the sentence is designed to reverse the contrast—nor do we argue *as though* the efficient causes were themselves the final causes: "nor imagine that the blood circulates, or that the food digests of its own accord, and with a view or intention to the purposes of circulation or digestion." Later in this passage, the term "as" is used in the same way: "we are very apt to impute to that reason, as to their efficient cause, the sentiments and actions by which we advance those ends." Here it clearly has the sense of hypothesis; we are apt to argue *as if* reason were the efficient cause of those sentiments, when actually their cause is the wisdom of God.

[66] TMS, II.ii.3.6–12. Hume's silence on the issue of final causes in his abstract of the *Theory* for the *Critical Review* presents a small puzzle. This is especially the case given that, on an earlier occasion, Hume had expressly rejected introducing teleology into his own analysis of morals. In a letter dated 17 September 1739, he replied to one of Francis Hutcheson's comments upon the

What of Smith's celebrated excision of the passage on Christ's Atonement (at the end of Section Two of Part Two) from the sixth edition of *The Theory of Moral Sentiments*? Its removal has led some to conclude that over the years Smith progressively abandoned the tenets of orthodox Christianity.[67] While such a view is plausible, it seems unlikely that Smith went so far as to surrender the principle of a benevolent deity. For in that same sixth edition there appeared some new passages in which the teleological theme of earlier editions is repeated and even amplified.[68] For instance, in Part Six, Section Two, Chapter One ("Of the Order in which Individuals are recommended by Nature to our care and attention"), Smith argues that there is a certain economy or "unerring wisdom" in the way that the moral sentiments have been adjusted. Specifically, the hierarchy in the agent's willingness to act for the benefit of others (from the top down: immediate family members, extended family, close acquaintances, those whose character he admires, benefactors, the very rich and very poor, and, last, everyone else) corresponds precisely to that order in which he is fitted to be of service to individuals. In other words, the agent is most inclined to be beneficent toward those whose happiness most depends upon his good will and whose interests his own situation best fits him, above all other people, to advance. While only detailed analysis can establish the point, I maintain that Smith's references in this connection to the wisdom of Nature are far from being mere window-dressing.

I am not claiming that *The Theory of Moral Sentiments* has an unavoidable logical dependence upon the idea of an "invisible hand." For it is always

---

manuscript of Book Three of the *Treatise:* "I cannot agree to your Sense of *Natural.* Tis founded on final Causes; which is a Consideration, that appears to me pretty uncertain & unphilosophical. For pray, what is the End of Man? Is he created for Happiness or for Virtue? For this Life or for the next? For himself or for his Maker? Your Definition of *Natural* depends upon solving these Questions, which are endless, & quite wide of my Purpose" (*The Letters of David Hume,* 2 vols., ed. J. Y. T. Greig [Oxford: Clarendon Press, 1932], 1:33). However, David Raynor has argued that Hume's foremost concern in writing the abstract seems to have been to forward Smith's career and that to this end he kept his misgivings about the book out of print (see Raynor, "Hume's Abstract of Adam Smith's *Theory of Moral Sentiments,*" *Journal of the History of Philosophy* 22 [1984]: 51–64). I would argue that Smith's use of final causes is one more repressed misgiving that should be added to Hume's list.

[67] See, for instance, Raphael, "Adam Smith and 'The Infection of David Hume's Society'," *Journal of the History of Ideas* 30 (1969): 225–48. Raphael went still further and suggested, on the basis of similar editorial changes in earlier editions, that Smith might already have held to a Humean view of religion in 1759.

[68] In a recent article, Raphael allows that the 1790 edition contains "certain revisions and additions on the topic of religious belief which afford evidence both that Smith had abandoned specifically Christian doctrine *and that he still retained an attachment to the fundamentals of religion*" ("Adam Smith 1790," 104; emphasis added). See also ibid., 116: "There is ample evidence that Smith abandoned a belief in Christian doctrine (while retaining a form of natural religion) long before 1790."

possible to argue, as has Coase, that the evolutionary principle of survival of the fittest can resolve the principal explanatory problem presented by Smith's moral theory. I am not as certain as Coase that such a solution is workable. No evolutionary theory, for instance, posits a connection between natural selection and human happiness; yet the latter is one of the purposes which Smith attributes to nature.[69] Furthermore, there are no textual grounds for supposing that Smith would have preferred such a solution; his commitment to a natural teleology seems omnipresent and genuine. In any case, the moment one argues that the theory of evolution has something to contribute to his analysis, my main point is already granted—that the principle of a divine author of nature cannot be removed without impairment to Smith's moral theory.

University of Regina

[69] Campbell recognized this problem, but proposed an alternative substitute: the modern biological concept of homeostasis. See *Smith's Science of Morals*, 75–79.

Part III
Jurisprudence

[9]

What Might Properly Be Called Natural Jurisprudence?

Knud Haakonssen

Author's Note: The argument of the present paper is closely related to some elements in my book, *The Science of a Legislator* (Cambridge, 1981), and some passages derive from the book.

I

HOW is legal criticism possible? This old question becomes a question to and about Adam Smith when we notice what he claimed for his system of natural jurisprudence, and when we remember the situation in which he made his claim: 'Jurisprudence is that science which enquires into the general principles which ought to be the foundation of the laws of all nations.'[1] This universally normative intention puts us beyond the pale of relativism in any of its forms — a fact with which any reading of the historical aspect of Smith's jurisprudence has to come to terms. But at the same time Smith did not want to take refuge in either the existing systems of natural law or in a positivistic command theory of law. He rejected the idea of external moral-legal verities of divine origin in both Grotius's, Cudworth's, and Hutcheson's versions. And he criticised not only what he considered to be Hobbes's theory of law, but also the utilitarianism which for later thinkers normally — although not necessarily — went with it. Our question was thus a genuine one for Smith, and his answer was an original doctrine of natural justice which formed the basis for his overall system of jurisprudence.

The theory of justice is part of Smith's general spectator theory of morals which he developed in response to the previous moral sense theories and in extension of Hume's spectator theory. The problem situation Smith wanted to meet with his theory was complicated. On the one hand he wanted to preserve an emotivist theory as part of the explanation of how people in fact evaluate. But on the other hand Smith's — like Hume's — secularism undercut the possibility that the emotive origin could be a divinely instituted and thus validating source of moral evaluation. It is well known that Smith, in response to this situation, developed his sympathetic theory of morals as a general framework for how a common morality emerges in any given society.[2] But this obviously takes us nowhere with the question which had been left wide open by Hume's bracketing off of the religious problem — an effort in which he was followed closely by Smith, as we shall see below. In view of his general claim about the nature of his system of jurisprudence, it would seem to be one of the most pressing — but also one of the most neglected — tasks in Smith scholarship to explain how he closes this gap. For although the central role of jurisprudence in Smith's thought has been stressed in recent work,[3] we are still missing an account of the philosophical argument which made this possible.[4]

Stated in general, abstract terms — which would have been foreign to Smith — his argument can be understood in the following way. Although it is not possible to find a body of moral-legal norms which are universally valid, there are a few, simple principles of practical reasoning which are universal. They are not universal in the sense that they have been and are being practised by everyone, but they are universal in the sense that it is impossible to deny their general validity as long as one wants to argue morally, and it requires special arguments to justify that they are dispensed with in individual cases.[5] This means that moral and legal argument primarily becomes a question of the application of these principles upon given moral and legal ideas, and the nature of the principles ensures that this application does not take the form of proof but of criticism. That is to say, it is impossible to deny that it is a valid point against any given moral or legal idea that it does not conform to the principles in question.

These principles are the ones embodied in the ideal impartial spectator. The most important is obviously that of impartiality, which amounts to a requirement of universality in moral and legal decisions. Only if anyone who is so properly informed as to be impartial is able to go along with the decision is it morally right — or at least not morally wrong: the two are by no means the same. The second principle, which follows from the first, is the requirement of consistency. The decisions of the impartial spectator must be mutually consistent in order for 'anyone' to be able to go along with them. The third and final of the more formal principles is the requirement of coherence which is also the loosest. It is not enough that the decisions of the impartial spectator are consistent, they must also lead to a coherent, or 'sensible', pattern of behaviour. This is particularly important when applied to legal decisions, for it provides for the connection between law and the wider moral ideas which guide our behaviour. Thus it would, for example, make little sense if a society generally respected and honoured the wishes of a newly dead person but did not legally recognise succession by testament.[6] Finally the impartial spectator will follow two further principles of a less formal kind, which I call the principle of the moral primacy of the negative (unhappiness, pain, injustice) over the positive (happiness, pleasure, justice), and the principle of the moral primacy of the individual over any collective. The latter, while important, needs no special attention here,[7] but the former we will have to return to, for it is Smith's means of distinguishing between justice and the other virtues and thus — in modern terms — between law and morality.[8] As for the three formal principles, they are simply meant as an explication of an important aspect of Smith's concept of the impartial spectator.

If we understood the impartial spectator as the embodiment of a set of universal principles such as these, then it becomes intelligible how Smith's moral philosophy, or at least the jurisprudential part of it,[9] could have a normative intention without being a body of substantive prescriptions. These principles are simply tools for testing and criticising whatever moral and legal ideas exist in a given society. At the same time this reading also gives the clue to an understanding of the relationship between the normative and the descriptive — especially the historical — aspects of Smith's thought. Since the critical principles can only be applied on given moral and legal ideas, an historical account goes hand in hand with any critical discussion. Furthermore, although the critical principles, Platonically speaking, are universal, the understanding of them is something well short of universal, and the history of morality and law and the attendant institutions is therefore also required to explain why and how they come to deviate from the ideal ones.[10] And in parallel with this it is an important feature of Smith's enterprise that just as the actual spectator introduces the impartial spectator in common life, so the study of the former is the necessary introduction to the study of the latter. Or, to put labels on it, Montesquieu's historical jurisprudence is the necessary complement as well as introduction to Grotius's natural jurisprudence. But in forging the link, both had to be transformed to the spectator mould — with far-reaching results for both. We get a view of the historical process as pluralistic and open-ended and a corresponding situationist historical method,[11] and we get a vision of jurisprudence as a critical tool rather than a set of positive doctrines.

Let me remark in passing that this turn from the hortative to the critical at the level of 'science', the 'science of a legislator', also gives *some* clue to Smith's transcendence of the so-called civic humanist tradition. The role of education and enlightenment amongst the classes which suffer most from the 'mental mutilation' arising from an extensive division of labour was not just to enable ordinary citizens to see themselves as creatures of civic virtues and public duties, but also — and, I suggest, quite as much — to enable them to see themselves as creatures of rights and interests.[12] The dramatic novelty of the modern attempt to live by commerce, as compared with the previous attempts, was that those whose labour made production and services possible were no longer put outside society by law, they were free-men. This meant that the viability of a society was no longer just, or mainly, a matter for those whose stake in the country was so tangible that traditional civic virtues at least in principle could appeal to them. It was also a matter for common folk whose sense of public duty was likely in the long run to be derivative from a respect for their rights and interests; and such respect could best be safeguarded if they themselves had an understanding of the rights and interests in question.[13]

Thus we see a parallel twist of the natural law tradition in a 'negative', critical direction and of the civic humanist tradition from an emphasis on virtue and duties to an emphasis on rights and interests. And one could say that Smith's point is that to the extent that notice of the former message at the institutional level is matched by attention to the latter at the social and educational level, to that extent a vital pre-condition for the continued viability of modern commercial society has been met. In both senses, at both levels, the modern experiment is an attempt to live by justice.

This is, of course, not overlooking that respect for rights in itself is a virtue. But Smith is careful to distinguish it as a very special virtue, the negative virtue of justice which, as we shall see, is fundamentally different from all the positive virtues. Nor does the suggested change in emphasis mean that Smith neglects the civic virtues.[14] My suggestion is rather that in a modern commercial society of free-men these virtues must for the bulk of the population be dependent upon a recognition of rights if they are to exist at all.

II

Before we further pursue my interpretation of the link between the impartial spectator and the system of jurisprudence, we have to consider what may look like a basic, structural difficulty for this interpretation. Smith's system of jurisprudence encompasses both 'laws of justice' and 'laws of police'.[15] The former arise directly from spectator decisions in cases of alleged injury,[16] but what are the latter and what is their philosophical status? This question is further complicated by the fact that Smith at the beginning of his *Lectures on Jurisprudence* says that the discipline deals with five areas of law: laws of justice, of police, of revenue, of arms, and of nations. Of these, international law is on the whole an analogical extension of the laws of justice, much as in Grotius.[17] But the laws of police, revenue, and arms, while in various ways separate,[18] have a fundamental structural similarity which sets them apart from the laws of justice and which justifies Smith in talking of them summarily as 'laws of police'. The laws of justice, as we shall see, are 'backward-looking' in that they are concerned with injury done, and they are general in that they deal with kinds of injury, as opposed to specific injuries at particular times and places. But the laws of police, revenue, and arms are all 'forward-looking' and particular in that they are instituted to achieve a particular aim, they have a specifiable and specific purpose. This does not mean, of course, that the laws of justice don't have a function and in that sense a 'purpose'; but it does mean that they are not instituted to achieve this, nor do they derive their binding character from this, nor can their full function — as opposed to their application — be individuated to particular persons at particular times and places.[19] In contrast to this, a law of police will typically institute and regulate a specific institution with a specific purpose, which for some reason is not fulfilled by the market,[20] and it will as such be directed to assignable individuals. Furthermore, it will derive its whole character as law from fulfilling its particular purpose. Similarly laws of revenue raise specific funds for particular purposes; and laws of arms are aimed at solving the problem of defence as it is at a given time and place.

The ideal foundation for these laws is thus a correct understanding of the needs, or the public utility, of the country in its historically given circumstances. Whereas the ideal foundation for the laws of justice is a sympathetic understanding of the standpoint of the impartial spectator. If one puts all the emphasis on the former aspect of Smith's jurisprudence and if one confuses public utility with private utility, in the sense of happiness-promotion, then one may succeed in seeing a proto-utilitarian in Smith. But if one takes a fuller view, it seems a strange utilitarian system that comes complete with commutative justice and retributive punishment amongst its main pillars.

These observations do, however, only raise in an even more acute way the question of the relationship between laws of justice and laws of police, revenue, and arms, and between natural justice and utility in Smith's system of jurisprudence. The fact is that Smith gave a clear normative basis for the laws of justice through his theory of the natural justice contained in the standpoint of the impartial spectator. But he never gave a general theory of utility which could serve the same function for the laws of police, revenue, and arms. As already mentioned, they derive their force from particular contingencies. But despite this, Smith's universal, normative claim, quoted at the beginning of this discussion, is made for the system of jurisprudence as a whole. The only way in which this makes sense is that the laws of police, revenue, and arms are appointed their role in the world of historical contingency by the laws of justice, for which Smith's claim applies in a straightforward manner. Or to put it bluntly, Smith's whole project only makes sense if the laws of police, revenue, and arms serve as supports for the laws of justice — speaking here of how things *should* be.

But we are now faced with the problem that Smith was as adamant as Hume that the one and only thing which could legitimately overrule justice was defence (or similar problems with the very survival of a society).[21] This objection is, however, more sophistic than many at first appear, for the point which both Hume and Smith were making was that without external security internal justice would be pointless.[22] Or in other words, in a particular conflict between a law of justice and a measure of defence, to opt for the former might well be a defeat for the system of justice of which it forms part. The social fabric which laws of defence should aim to protect in a would-be just society is thus exactly the system of justice.

As far as the laws of police and revenue are concerned, Smith's intention was explicitly that they should institute and fund institutions and services which are not supplied otherwise and which are necessary or desirable to secure or supplement the function of the laws of justice and arms and their attendant institutions.[23] Finally, in cases where there is no *conflict* with the purposes of justice or defence, there is obviously no reason why other, strongly felt values should not have some legislative effect. This is the background to Smith's suggestion that even *if* a minimum of basic education was not necessary both for defence and for the effective function of the system of justice, it would still be a *moral* duty arising out of basic human decency to supply such education.[24]

III

The background to Smith's distinction between laws of justice and laws of police is an implicit, very important distinction between two forms of human knowledge, with two different forms of evaluation attendant upon them. Somewhat inelegantly, but hopefully clearly, I call the two forms of knowledge, system knowledge and contextual knowledge. They are distinguished by their different objects in the following way. System knowledge is concerned with the relationship between the elements in some system or collection of elements, or with the system or collection as a whole. Contextual knowledge is typically of a particular event understood purely on its specific background. System knowledge is of functional relationships and has no necessary reference to time-sequences: it is concerned with things as well as events. But contextual knowledge is only of events and understands them as effects of or reactions to their immediate background or context and without regard to what they lead to. The two corresponding forms of evaluation are, respectively, in terms of functional efficiency and situational propriety or 'fittingness'.[25]

System knowledge is the basis for all science and technology, for metaphysics, for religion as a form of metaphysics and more generally for mankind's tendency to seek overall teleological explanations. It is in other words the form of knowledge involved in all attempts to understand things and events in terms of their 'utility', i.e. their function. The motivation for the search for this form of knowledge is a common human passion for orderliness which leads naturally to the kind of evaluation indicated, a mode of evaluation which either is aesthetic in character or closely akin to aesthetic appraisal.[26]

In contrast to this, contextual knowledge is our mode of understanding human behaviour in its individuality. This is conveyed by sympathy which is activated in any spectator in response to the real or imagined situation of another person, the 'agent'. It is the awareness of the inevitable difference in situation and hence in contextual knowledge in all cases of human behaviour[27] plus the basic human need for agreement which motivates the seeking of sympathetic understanding of other people. And since both the awareness and the need exist in agent as well as spectator — they are so to speak spectators of each other — the sympathy becomes *mutual.* In so far as the spectator's sympathetically created reaction to a situation is similar to the actual reaction of the agent, the consequent pattern of evaluation is one of approval of the reaction as proper; otherwise it is one of disapproval of impropriety. And since these evaluations follow people's sympathetic understanding of each other's situation, the mutuality of sympathy will adjust also the evaluation because it will lead one person into a quest for the other person's standard of propriety. This search for a common standard of propriety will almost inevitably lead to a search for an absolute standard of propriety, and in order to reach that the formal criteria of the impartial spectator have to be invoked.[28] This constantly ongoing attempt to settle disputes — explicit or implicit — about what should be the common standard by seeking out the standard of the impartial spectator constitutes the social selection-mechanism for behaviour at both the individual and the collective level.[29] In so far as the attempts fall into a definite pattern for different kinds of disputes, they will stand out as the general rules of morality. And in so far as people are convinced that the rules are expressions of the standpoint of the impartial spectator, they will regard them as morally binding.[30]

As long as the two kinds of knowledge are distinguished by the separate objects, the formula we have found here is engagingly simple: contextual knowledge as the basis for human morality; system knowledge as the basis for science, religion, and metaphysics. But problems arise once the moral world, the world of human behaviour, is made the object of system knowledge. How is a science of morals possible? Viewed historically, it was a long time, according to Smith, before people attempted to turn moral knowledge into systems, whereas the natural world was treated as a system very early.[31] Although Smith is not very specific in his brief essays in the history of science and philosophy, the reason for this is not far to seek. The driving force behind the growth of knowledge is the well-known surprise and wonder effect which sets in when our desire for order is somehow disappointed.[32] And as far as the natural world is concerned this can only lead to more and more comprehensive intellectual systems with greater and greater degrees of coherence. But the equivalent to wonder and surprise in contextual knowledge is disapproval of an adopted standard, and its effect is a process of practical adjustment conducted through the mutual sympathy mechanism. There is in other words a practical rather than an intellectual outlet for 'wonder and surprise', and consequently there is not the same pressure to create and develop systems of moral knowledge. Hand in hand with this goes another factor which is of much greater importance here. While a system of natural science has to satisfy the demands for comprehensiveness and coherence, as compared with any competing system, a system of moral science has a further and much more difficult requirement put upon it. Since it deals with people's contextual knowledge, it will have to be in accordance with this knowledge – and it is easy for anyone to check whether it is.[33] This is the real premise for Smith's stern criticism of all previous systems of morals. Whether they took the form of science, metaphysics, or religion, they all failed more or less in this regard.

IV

By far the most important attempt at a science of morals had been that of David Hume. But however impressed Smith was with it, and however much he learned from it, he still thought that it was deficient in its understanding of the basic mode of evaluation of human behaviour. In his view, Hume's concern with the difference between aesthetic and moral evaluation had not borne enough fruit, for the suggested structure of evaluation was still the same for the two. The central concept in both was 'utility', but according to Smith it was a mistake to think that people commonly did or could evaluate their own or others' behaviour under the forward-looking aspect of its utility.[34] This overlooked the fact that the basic mode of understanding human behaviour was what we have called contextual knowledge which refers the action to its immediate background and spontaneously evaluates it by this means. To take the evaluation beyond this is in some measure speculation, and to think that this is always done is to mistake philosophical speculation for human morality.[35] But of course evaluation in terms of utility can arise as a result of experience as a sort of typifying and generalising afterthought to the judgement of situational propriety.[36]

The tendency to take that for a motivating force of behaviour which is really nothing but the unintended, *de facto* result of such behaviour was very common, according to Smith, and it was the basic weakness of all teleological metaphysics. In this Smith simply applied Hume's general criticism of teleological explanations to such explanations of the moral world, and in doing so he also followed Hume's criticism of the theological versions of teleology.[37] It is important here to distinguish between what may be called moral theology and teleological systems of religion. Smith thought that it is a natural tendency in mankind to personify and idealise the impartial spectator as a divine being and to view men's attempts to apply the standards of the impartial spectator in this life as continued and completed in a life to come.[38] In this form religion may be seen as a simple and natural function of ordinary human morality. But the organised religions of the world have transposed this into speculative systems according to which people should act in this life for the sake of the standards of judgement in a supposed life to come. And this does as much violence to the basic mode of situational evaluation in moral matters as any other form of disregard for men's contextual knowledge. As such it is bad philosophy, and in so far as people attempt to follow it in practice it leads to the 'artificial lives' and 'monkish virtues' which Smith, like Hume, scorned.[39]

In the present context the most important aspect of Smith's criticism of common uses of system knowledge is, however, the political one. Smith's complaint about the 'spirit of system' in politics is exactly that it tends to overlook the individual citizen's own 'principle of movement' which is guided by his or her particular contextual knowledge. The imposition of systems of politics assumes that people could and should be acting for the sake of the system and its aim. But without violence or the deception arising from widespread 'fanaticism' this is only possible if the aims of the system are so broad as to be compatible with each individual's aims and the system consequently so loose that the word nearly becomes a misnomer.[40] Now if we look at the laws of police, revenue, and arms, which Smith either proposed or condoned, we see — as already mentioned — that their aims are subservient or supplementary to that of the laws of justice. And the 'aim', i.e. the function, of the laws of justice is to maximise the compatibility of individual persons' pursuit of their own aims. The tendency to political system building should therefore be checked and political enterprises kept to the concrete tasks at hand.[41]

This relative weighting of the laws of justice versus the laws of police, revenue, and arms and the consequent stress on a piecemeal approach to politics is further supported by Smith's principle of the primacy of the negative. This is, however, best understood through Smith's theory of the virtue of justice, of which the laws of justice are the institutionalisation.

V

Like Hume, Smith makes a sharp distinction between on the one hand justice and on the other all the 'positive' virtues, which are generally represented by beneficence. And he agrees with Hume that while all the positive virtues are an 'extra' which makes society flourishing and happy, social life is quite possible without them. But there can be no society without justice.[42] But as Smith reads him, Hume does — as we have seen — make this 'public utility' the basis for its morally binding force and that is a standpoint with which Smith disagrees, in keeping with his general rejection of consequentialist arguments.[43] Instead he argues that the public utility of justice is the unintended result of people's judgements in terms of situational propriety. But in order to understand this we have to look more closely at the unique character of justice.

The thing which struck Smith, as it had struck Hume, was that justice is so different from all the other virtues. It seemed to be more precise and it could therefore be formulated in strict and general rules which men always felt obliged to enforce. Now Smith did, I think, suggest a highly original theory of why justice is so precise and, in close connection with this, why it is enforceable. He observed that the difference between 'the happiness of the man who is in health, who is out of debt, and has a clear conscience', and 'the highest pitch of human prosperity', is 'but a trifle'.[44] In contrast to this narrow scope for happiness the possible depths of misery are 'immense and prodigious'. This fundamental asymmetry between happiness and misery is connected with the fact that

> Pain . . . whether of mind or body, is a more pungent sensation than pleasure, and our sympathy with pain, though it falls greatly short of what is naturally felt by the sufferer, is generally a more lively and distinct perception than our sympathy with pleasure, though this last often approaches more nearly . . . to the natural vivacity of the original passion.[45]

A spectator's sympathy with pleasure is lively, but fickle, while his sympathy with pain and sorrow on the contrary is unpleasant but more resilient.[46]

It is this 'primacy of the negative' which underpins Smith's distinction between justice and beneficence. While 'the mere want of beneficence tends to do no real positive evil', he argued, 'the violation of justice is injury: it does real and positive hurt to some particular persons'.[47] Consequently the former may be met with dislike and hatred, but the latter is met with the much stronger reaction called resentment.[48] Resentment is normally followed by punishment, a natural pattern of reaction approved of by the impartial spectator. Beneficence and justice are not only distinguished by our reactions to the neglect of them, but also by our reactions to the practice of them. Beneficence is naturally rewarded with gratitude while justice is judged to be nothing but proper:

> Mere justice is, upon most occasions, but a negative virtue, and only hinders us from hurting our neighbour . . . We may often fulfil all the rules of justice by sitting still and doing nothing.[49]

Moreover, Smith always insists that the fundamental rules of justice are precise, whereas the rules of beneficence are rather unclear and uncertain. As far as the rules of all the positive virtues are concerned, we go by their 'spirit', but with justice we follow the rules to the 'letter'.[50] The rules of justice are so accurate because they are derived from spectator reactions which are unusually 'universal' and 'distinct', namely the 'pungent' feeling of sympathetic resentment occasioned by 'real and positive hurt'. Smith's idea seems to be that clarity and accuracy is transferred in the following chain: the action (negative: injury), the reaction (resentment and punishment), the spectator reaction through sympathy (sympathetic resentment and support in punishing), the general rule arising from spectator-reactions.

The negative character of justice also implies that the general rules of this virtue arise somewhat differently from the rules of the other virtues. The latter stem from spectator-approval of the practice of those virtues, but the rules of justice emerge from spectator-disapproval of injustice, of the non-performance of the virtue. If nobody had ever been unjust, the rules of justice would never have been thought of, for they are but a specification of mere propriety.

We can now see that this principle of the primacy of the negative which distinguishes justice from the positive virtues provides a further support for the epistemological argument against utopian projectors which we considered above. The point of that argument was that it is impossible to ensure an accordance between political schemes and each individual's contextual knowledge unless the aim of the former is so broad and non-specific that it reduces the possibility of conflict with the aims of the individuals to a minimum. Further, that this is only achieved if the central part of the political scheme is the maintenance of a regular system of justice, to which other policy aims are subservient or supplementary. It has now become evident that this idea is not just based on the negative doctrine that each individual has his own more or less inscrutable 'principle of motion', but on the further notion that the way of justice is signposted by those elements in human life which we generally can know *most* about, namely the morally negative ones.

Political wayfarers who neglect this and aim to do more than 'remove the inconveniences and relieve the distresses immediately complained of', are always in imminent danger of getting lost in a wilderness which at its densest is 'the madness of fanaticism'.[51]

VI

The rules of justice have the form of protectors against injury, or injustice, and the areas thus protected are called 'perfect rights', whereas the positive virtues give rise to 'imperfect rights'. This distinction between perfect and imperfect rights stems from the modern natural law tradition,[52] but it obviously gets a new and distinctive foundation through Smith's elaborate theory of the distinction between positive and negative virtues. The dual concept of rights is only introduced at the beginning of the *Lectures on Jurisprudence* and it forms a connecting link between Smith's general moral theory in *The Theory of Moral Sentiments* and the system of jurisprudence of the lectures. The latter is only concerned with commutative justice, whereas the looser principles of distributive justice must be left to 'a system of moralls'.[53]

Smith's suggestion is that law is founded on the rules of justice, and that means founded on the spectator judgement of what constitutes injury. Further, that the foundation for punishment of the transgression of law is spectator judgement of what is the proper reaction to injury. The exact meaning of this idea does, however, depend upon whether we are considering positive law or ideal, 'natural' law. In the former case we have to look to the actual spectators; in the latter case to the impartial spectator. The positive law of a given society is formed by the actual spectators who are concerned with disputes over rights in that society. And they range historically from the *ad hoc* mediators in a primitive society, through the sovereign acting in a judicial capacity in early monarchical government, to the specialised, professional judges and legislators of developed society.[54]

This is the framework for Smith's history of law in society, which is the story of the multifarious factors which have influenced the actual spectators at the various stages of social development and in the particular circumstances of individual societies at given moments in time. This historically, sociologically, and psychologically descriptive side of Smith's jurisprudence is the one which has attracted the most attention and scholarly discussion. But while I disagree with one of the main lines of interpreting this aspect of Smith's enterprise — namely the suggestion that we here have '*a*, if not *the*, materialist conception of history'[55] — I do not propose here to engage in an argument about the nature of Smith's history of law. My concern is with the character of the ideal or natural law embodied in the impartial spectator, and with the relationship between the two sides of the system of jurisprudence.

The unique character of Smith's idea of natural law is the combination of the universal and the particular in the figure of the impartial spectator. The principles by which the impartial spectator reaches his decisions are the timeless, ideal ones outlined at the beginning of this essay. They are, as mentioned, not universal in the sense that they are everywhere practised, but in the sense that they ought to be everywhere practised. The disputes which the impartial spectator is to resolve are, however, greatly different from one period of history to another. Thus it must, for example, very much depend upon the notion of reputation in a given society, whether a man has been defamed.[56] Similarly there can hardly be disputes over property in land as long as a society has not got the idea that land is the sort of thing which can be owned;[57] and consequently even the most exemplary application of the principles of the impartial spectator will not by itself extend the law of property to land. Ideal or natural law must necessarily have reference to particular societies or particular epochs in the development of society, for it is a device for resolving disputes and the kinds of disputes which can arise must vary with the ideas and values a society or an epoch has.

It is this circumstance which provides the full link between Smith's idea of natural law and his history, sociology, and psychology of law and morality. The descriptive and explanatory disciplines not only provide an introduction to the attempts of mankind to reach the standpoint of the impartial spectator under various historical, sociological, and psychological circumstances, as mentioned earlier. They also serve to explain the situation in which the present generation will have to make their attempts. They explain the kinds of disputes which the would-be impartial spectator has to resolve and the situational factors which he will have to take into account in doing so. And hence it is that Smith goes to so great lengths to combine the analysis of contemporary law with the history of its genesis. The former shows the full extent of positive law and hence the range of legal disputes; the latter gives the factors which have deflected positive law from the principles of the impartial spectator and which may still be in their way. The set-piece here is, of course, the continued survival of feudal institutions and corporate privileges, but they are by no means the only ones.[58]

The full set of premises for a contemporary impartial spectator must therefore include not only an analysis of positive law, but also of the general moral values; of the institutions of law, politics, and religion; and of the economic, military, and international circumstances of the society in question. If we exploit Smith's concept of the science of a legislator with some deliberate anachronism, we can say that it is these elements which make his jurisprudence into a *science*. But it is the fact that this science provides the factual premises for the normative argument of an impartial spectator which makes it into that of a *legislator* — a point to which we will return.

If we read Smith in the way suggested here, it becomes clear why he rejected as incomplete and imperfect all previous attempts at natural law, including the best of these, that of Grotius. Natural law had to have reference to the stage of social development, and hence jurisprudence had to combine the historical with the natural. But at the same time Smith's idea of jurisprudence could preserve the all-important feature of being a natural weapon for criticism of all positive law which falls short of its standards:

> In no countries do the decisions of positive law coincide exactly, in every case, with the rules which the natural sense of justice would dictate. Systems of positive law, therefore, though they deserve the greatest authority, as the records of the sentiments of mankind in different ages and nations, yet can never be regarded as accurate systems of the rules of natural justice.[59]

In view of all this it seems somewhat difficult to understand the suggestion that:

> When [Smith] contrasts laws that are in accordance with nature with those that depart from this 'norm' he simply means that the latter do not accord with the consensus of moral opinions in that type of society.[60]

Whole systems of law deviate from natural justice, and there is no reason to think that even 'the consensus of moral opinion' should not be capable of doing so on occasion. To identify natural justice with the consensus is to overlook, not only Smith's outline of the critical function of jurisprudence, but also much of what he had to say about the ideal, impartial spectator. Although the origin of a man's understanding of the spectator's standpoint is 'the consensus', this does not affect its validity.

VII

Smith never fulfilled the promise of a complete system of jurisprudence. 'In the *Enquiry Concerning the Nature and Causes of the Wealth of Nations,* I have partly executed this promise; at least so far as concerns police, revenue, and arms.'[61] But 'in what concerns justice', i.e. 'the theory of jurisprudence', or the natural jurisprudence, his work remained unfinished, or at least unpublished, and he ordered the manuscript for 'this great work' to be burnt before he died. At the end of *The Theory of Moral Sentiments* he did, however, state his intentions and they were clearly of the normative-critical kind outlined here. In the students' notes from his lectures we can further follow his plans in some detail, but the aspect of his thought which inevitably was neglected was the application of his natural law principles to the criticism of concrete, positive law. The lectures could not contain an agenda for systematic law reform. Their aim was to provide an introduction to the basic principles of law, and for reasons which should now be clear, this had to be an historical introduction. Nevertheless, scattered throughout the lectures and the *Wealth of Nations* we have a number of examples of how he would use the test of natural justice to criticise existing law. While we cannot go through all of these systematically,[62] it is of importance to look at some of the more important ones. This will not only give further strength to the claim made here, that Smith's intention was a genuine theory of natural law. It will also show the distinguishing structure of argument used by Smith. For while it is in the nature of any system of natural jurisprudence to be critical of positive law, this criticism can take various forms;

but, with the exception of Hume's anticipations, Smith's way of arguing was unique.

In general Smith followed traditional divisions of the system of justice,[63] and in all the main branches we find his critical principles applied in bigger or smaller issues. Here we will have to ignore the whole area of public law because its jurisprudential status is so complicated by its political relevance that it requires a more lengthy discussion than can be given in the present context.[64] Our main examples will be from private law which has the advantage that we can find support not only in the *Lectures on Jurisprudence,* but also in the *Wealth of Nations.*

The *Wealth of Nations* was an inquiry into 'Nature and Causes', and in so far as human actions were amongst the 'Causes' they were evaluated for their causal efficiency. All the way through the work it is, however, abundantly clear that it has a strong jurisprudential background according to which it is possible to evaluate human action in terms of natural justice. This composite structure of the critical side of Smith's argument is clearly represented by his strictures on two different sets of restrictions on manufacturers and farmers: 'Both laws were evident violations of natural liberty, and therefore unjust; and they were both too as impolitick as they were unjust.'[65] At the same time this passage indicates the main target of Smith's justice-criticism in the *Wealth of Nations;* namely infringements of one of the most basic rights within private law, that of individual liberty. This is no less the liberty of ordinary folk to work at what they want to and where they want to, than it is the freedom of merchants and manufacturers to do business as they want to. This is why he condemns oppressive apprenticeship laws; they are not only harmful but also 'a manifest encroachment upon the just liberty both of the workman, and of those who might be disposed to employ him'.[66] It is in the same spirit that he criticises the laws of settlement: 'To remove a man who has committed no misdemeanour from the parish where he chuses to reside, is an evident violation of natural liberty and justice.'[67] And much the same applies to the restrictions on 'artificers' who want to practise their trade overseas: 'It is unnecessary . . . to observe, how contrary such regulations are to the boasted liberty of the subject, of which we affect to be so very jealous; but which, in this case, is so plainly sacrificed to the futile interests of our merchants and manufacturers.'[68] Smith's parallel criticism of all the laws 'which the clamour of our merchants and manufacturers has extorted from the legislature, for the support of their own absurd and oppressive monopolies', is too well known to need much commentary: 'Like the laws of Draco, these laws may be said to be all written in blood.'[69] And the reason is plain: 'To hurt in any degree the interest of any one order of citizens, for no other purpose but to promote that of some other, is evidently contrary to that justice and equality of treatment which the sovereign owes to all the different orders of his subjects.'[70]

The other big issue over the natural right[71] to personal liberty was, of course, the problem of slavery. In Smith's view this problem was, however, so intricately tied up with the most basic problems of modern, as opposed to ancient, commercial society that it had to be attacked in a much more circuitous way than a straightforward justice-criticism — although that is what it comes to in the end — and we must therefore leave it here.[72]

While Smith's discussion of the natural right to personal liberty shows the depth of critical concern in his jurisprudence, the critical comments he makes about various parts of the law pertaining to 'estate rights' more clearly show us the type of spectator-reasoning which lies behind. In many ways no example is nicer than his discussion of the state of the law concerning all those things which 'must continue common by the rules of equity', such as 'wild beasts' and 'the fish of the sea and rivers', even when property has been 'extended to allmost every subject'.[73] 'The tyranny of the feudal government and the inclination men have to extort all they can from their inferiours', 'brought property in some measure into these subjects', and this has since been continued by various statutes from time to time.[74] But, says Smith, since *everyone* could hunt such animals without any *injury* being done, 'There can be no reason in equity given for this constitution'.[75] Furthermore, such statutes make nonsense of our property laws, for the ordinary criteria for property do not apply to such animals: 'they are not in our power, nor can they be considered as belonging to an estate as they are often changing their place, but ought to be common to all'.[76] So whatever reason might be given for these restrictions on 'the lower sort of people', 'the real reason is . . . the delight the great take in hunting and the great inclination they have to screw all they can out of their hands'.[77] Similar reasoning is then extended to the Franchises of Wafes and Treasure Trove, and it is used to support the freedom of the sea.[78]

Moving on to the property acquired by succession, we will see that Smith's criticism of the laws pertaining to the succession to land is on a very similar basis. The enforcement of primogeniture and entail became common in feudal times and had to a large extent stayed in the law since. Both in the *Lectures on Jurisprudence* and in the *Wealth of Nations* he identifies the 'circumstances, which first gave occasion to them, and which could alone render them reasonable'.[79] But whatever the political necessity at one time, there is never any doubt that these arrangements were and are 'contrary to nature, to reason, and to justice'.[80] Primogeniture rested on principles completely inconsistent with those of an impartial spectator, for 'the natural law of succession divides [land], like [moveables], among *all* the children of the family'.[81] And as far as entails were concerned,

> in the present state of Europe, when small as well as great estates derive their security from the laws of their country, nothing can be more completely absurd. They are founded upon the most absurd of all suppositions, the supposition that every successive generation of men have not an equal right to the earth, and to all that it possesses.[82]

Smith held that the principle of entail was simply inconsistent with the ordinary basis for our property law. Property law is based upon spectator approval as refined over generations into the laws of occupation, accession, and prescription; but the spectator works only amongst the living, so that the earth belongs to each generation of men 'altogether as well as it was their predecessors in their day'.[83] The only way in which the spectator goes beyond the living is when a person is newly dead and the memory of him is still fresh. Then,

> we enter as it were into his dead body, and conceive what our living souls would feel if they were joined with his body, and how much we would be distressed to see our last injunctions not performed. Such sentiments naturally enclined men to extend property a little farther than a man's lifetime.[84]

This piety for the dead is the foundation for testamentary succession, and it is by analogical extension of this that entail arises.[85] This extension was to a large extent due to the influence of the Christian belief in the continued existence of the soul of the deceased. But it is clearly a false analogy which renders the principle of entail inconsistent with the law of testamentary succession which was based on spectator sympathy with the will of the newly dead. Such sympathy cannot naturally be supposed to be concerned with anybody but 'those who are alive at the same time with him'.[86] To go beyond that is to introduce a complete arbitrariness into the law which makes nonsense of the principles which can otherwise guide our behaviour in this area.

Finally, from the real rights area of the law I should like to point to the way in which Smith deals with exclusive privileges. He points out that 'Some of them are founded upon natural reason', and gives a clear spectator account of these. But he then goes on to say that, 'The greatest part . . . of exclusive privileges are the creatures of the civil constitutions of the country.[87] The basis for these can only be public utility, and 'Some indeed are harmless enough', such as time-limited patents and copyrights. 'But there are few so harmless. All monopolies in particular are extremely detrimental.'[88] In other words, their supposed rationale is non-existent, and since they have no foundation in 'natural reason', they ought to be condemned.

Various of the laws protecting personal rights are dealt with in a similar vein, and particularly those regulating punishment — which protect the rights arising from delinquency — give rise to a number of critical discussions.[89] Outside private law it is worth noticing Smith's views on the law pertaining to divorce and polygamy. He argues at some length that easy access to divorce as well as the legalisation of polygamy would have various disastrous social consequences, exemplified by the corruption of manners in ancient Rome. In order to preserve the fabric of society, restrictive marriage legislation in these respects was necessary. But he stresses that this is purely a matter of necessary 'police' to prevent practices which would be 'productive of many bad consequences'.[90] For if we look at these practices with the eyes of natural justice we will see that,

> there is not any reall injustice either in voluntary divorce or in polygamy in those countries where they are allowed by the laws of the country . . . For with regard to voluntary divorce, there can not be said to be any injustice done to the person who is turned away in this manner . . . In the same manner where polygamy is allowed[91] . . . there can be no injustice in taking a wife in that manner. [When she knows the conditions] there can not be said to be any injury done her.[92]

Like Hume, he argued it would not be against the principles of natural justice to introduce voluntary divorce and polygamy into the law. Whether he was right that it was so impolitic that it — like an urgent problem of defence — nevertheless could set justice aside, is of course an entirely different problem.

VIII

These case studies indicate how Smith would realise the critical intentions of his natural jurisprudence. But at the same time they sharpen the edge of a question which the intentions alone would give rise to. If the natural jurisprudence, as suggested here, is the hard core of his overall system of jurisprudence, his 'science of a legislator',[93] to whom is this science addressed — who is the legislator? While the implication of the question is that a definite answer can be found, the fact is that Smith never gives such an answer, and these two circumstances might well tempt the interpreter to make his own informed guesses about the identity of the legislator. The argument to be pursued in conclusion here is that this would be a mistake, for Smith's apparent unwillingness to identify the addressee of his argument is in itself an important point in that argument. In order to show this I will argue negatively along three lines: the most important problems of justice which Smith's natural jurisprudence identifies in modern commercial society are not judicial in character; nor are they peculiarly British Parliamentary problems — and in that narrow sense 'political'; and finally, the natural jurisprudence which offers a solution for the problems is not meant as a general blueprint for modern society.

At the risk of over-exploiting the notion, we can take the 'legislator' as our clue. All the major problems of justice which Smith's natural jurisprudence pointed to were legislative rather than judicial in character; for irrespective of whether they arose out of common law or statute law, they could only be remedied by legislative activity. In this context the relevant impartial spectator was therefore not the judge, but the legislator. Take the restrictions in the personal liberty of tradesmen, manufacturers, merchants, etc., or the enforcement of primogeniture and entails in the succession to land, which we mentioned above. These are obviously 'laws of police' which can only be changed by legislative intervention.

At the same time these two examples serve to warn us against taking legislative problems to mean problems for a legislature and hence, for Smith, problems for Parliament. Although he naturally was particularly concerned with Britain, his general perspective was European, and the basic problems of justice were problems in the structure of modern commercial society as such. This in effect meant that they were problems for the 'civilized monarchies' of the Continent no less than they were for the 'mixed government' of Great Britain. Like Hume, Smith thought that the real novelty of the modern world was the attempt to live by rules of justice for the whole society and that this attempt and its problems were basically common European.[94] An attempt to identify the legislator in British parliamentary terms would not only parochialise Smith, it would also overlook the overwhelmingly important point that justice is not necessarily dependent upon political liberty and, consequently, that problems of justice may be coped with by 'despotical' as well as by 'free' governments.[95] Finally, an exclusively parliamentary perspective — whether British or otherwise — would run the danger of confusing the legislator with a mere 'politician', and Smith undoubtedly feared that in such hands his science would engender the despised 'spirit of system' — or be lost altogether.[96]

This brings us to our final theme. Smith's refusal to see the future of commercial society in any particular one of the available political systems is clearly underpinned by his scepticism towards complete systems of politics. While his jurisprudence could identify, explain, and offer remedies for specific — although wide-ranging — problems in modern society, it is completely against its spirit and against everything Smith had to say about political projectors and system builders[97] to see it as part of an overall blueprint for such a society. And although the system of natural justice nevertheless may appear as a utopian projection — as Smith himself was aware[98] — we should remember two things. As a system it was peculiar in that it aimed at the 'negative' rather than the 'positive' virtues. And exactly this circumstance should make it possible for the would-be statesman or legislator to strike the right balance between the two kinds of knowledge available to him: he will *act* from his knowledge of the context, but he will *understand* from a view of the system.[99] Smith's pride was that his science could encompass both.

NOTES

1. Smith, LJ(B), 1, and cf. LJ(A), i, 1. — I refer to the two sets of lecture notes in this volume by the standard abbreviation and pagination used in the Glasgow Edition of Smith's works.

2. See Section III below.

3. See especially Duncan Forbes, 'Sceptical Whiggism, Commerce and Liberty', in A. S. Skinner and T. Wilson (eds.), *Essays on Adam Smith* (Oxford, 1976); Donald Winch, *Adam Smith's Politics* (Cambridge, 1978), chs. 4 and 8, *passim,* and to some extent Hans Medick, *Naturzustand and Naturgeschichte der bürgerlichen Gesellschaft* (Göttingen, 1973).

4. My *The Science of a Legislator. The Natural Jurisprudence of David Hume and Adam Smith* (Cambridge, 1981) is a more considerable effort in this direction. Subsequently I refer to this as SoL.

5. Such arguments would have to be derived from considerations of the continued stability of the society, i.e. the most urgent 'public utility'. See Section II below, and SoL, ch. 4, sect. 4.

6. There is often an obvious connection between the principles of consistency and coherence in as much as inconsistent judgements about how to behave are likely to lead to incoherent patterns of behaviour. But as the example in the text indicates, this does not make the two principles identical. For more detailed discussion of these ideas of practical reasoning in Smith, see SoL, ch. 6, sect. 2.

7. It is forcefully formulated in TMS, II. ii. 3. 10. And cf. *ibid.*, II. ii. 1. 3 & 5; and *Lectures on Rhetoric and Belles Lettres,* ed. J. M. Lothian (Carbondale and Edwardsville, 1971) — henceforth LRBL — p. 181. For further discussion, see SoL, ch. 4, sect. 2.

8. See below, Section V.

9. For various reasons a system of the positive virtues, such as beneficence, would necessarily have a weaker normative character than a system of the negative virtue of justice, but not even philosophers — or maybe, especially not philosophers — had been aware of this. See TMS, VII. iv.

10. We return to this theme below, Section VI.

11. See SoL, ch. 8.

12. For the perspective suggested here, see especially WN, I. xi. p. 9, and V. i. f. 49-61: 'The more [the inferior ranks of people] are instructed, the less liable they are to the delusions of enthusiasm and superstition, which, among ignorant nations, frequently occasion the most dreadful disorders. An instructed and intelligent people besides are always more decent and orderly than an ignorant and stupid one. They feel themselves, each individually, more respectable, and more likely to obtain the respect of their lawful superiors, and they are therefore more disposed to respect those superiors. They are more disposed to examine, and more capable of seeing through, the interested complaints of faction and sedition, and they are, upon that account, less apt to be misled into any wanton or unnecessary opposition to the measures of government.' (WN, V.i.f. 61).

13. See quotation and references in the previous note.

14. This is sufficiently well testified in WN, V.i.f.

15. See TMS, VII. iv. 37. And see SoL, ch. 4, sect. 4, for further details on the distinction.

16. See Section VI below.

17. For these divisions, see LJ(A), i. 1-9; LJ(B). 5-6; and cf. LJ(A), vi. 1-7; LJ(B), 203-205.

18. For their distinct principles, see SoL, ch. 4, sect. 4.

19. Cf. LJ(A), iv. 35; LJ(B), 22-23. Also SoL, ch. 4, sect. 4, and ch. 6, sect. 5.

20. WN IV. ix. 51; and for details, WN, V. i. Parts 1-3.

21. Establishments such as customs which serve to protect trade in certain circumstances thus have as their only rationale the concern for national defence: WN, V. i. e.4. See also WN, IV. ii. 23ff. (the Navigation Act); IV. v. a. 27 (fishing bounty); IV. v. a. 36 (regulation of export of strategically important materials). Cf. SoL, ch. 4. sect. 4. Concerning Hume, see *Enquiries Concerning Human Understanding and Concerning the Principles of Morals,* ed. L. A. Selby-Bigge; 3rd, rev. ed., P. H. Nidditch (Oxford, 1975), p. 186; *A Treatise of Human Nature,* ed. L. A. Selby-Bigge (Oxford, 1965), pp. 567-69. Cf. SoL, ch. 2, sect. 11.

22. LJ(A), i. 7: 'Tho' the peace within doors be never so firmly established, yet if there be no security from injuries from without the property of individualls can not be secure. The danger to them on this head is no less to be feared than from those of their own society; and not only is the security of private persons in danger but the very being of the state. It is therefore requisite that an armed force should be maintained.' Cf. LJ(B), 6.

23. See references in note 20 above.

24. See WN, V. i. f. 60-61. Smith does not himself call it a moral duty, but that seems clearly to be the implication. Cf. also D. Winch, *Adam Smith's Politics,* ch. 5.

25. The former kind of evaluation may or may not include evaluation of the 'aim' or 'function' of the overall system.

26. The most central text concerning this mode of evaluation is TMS, IV. 1. And see SoL, ch. 3, sects. 7 & 10.

27. As opposed to cases of contemplation of non-human things and events: TMS, I. i. 4. 2-6, esp. 2. Cf. SoL, ch. 3, sect. 2.

28. For a fuller discussion of these central features of Smith's moral theory, see SoL, ch. 3, sect. 1-4.

29. See TMS, III. 3. 22ff., and V. 2. Cf. LJ(A), iii. 5; LJ(B), 102.

30. Concerning moral rule formation, see TMS III. 4. 7-12; concerning the sense of duty, see TMS, III. 5.

31. See WN, V. i. f.25.

32. Sections I and II of the Essay on the History of Astronomy provide the longest and most detailed discussion of the surprise and wonder function in human knowledge, but the theme recurs frequently in TMS and LRBL, and cf. WN, V. i. f. 24, and the Essay on the History of Ancient Physics, 2, in Adam Smith, *Essays on Philosophical Subjects* (eds. W. P. D. Wightman and J. C. Bryce, Oxford, 1980) [hereafter EPS]. Cf. J. R. Lindgren, *The Social Philosophy of Adam Smith* (The Hague, 1973), ch. 1; and SoL, ch. 3, sect. 10.

33. This contrast between the natural and the moral sciences is spelled out in a very important paragraph towards the end of the TMS VII. ii. 4. 14. And cf. WN V. i. f. 26. Smith's idea of the natural sciences as forms of system knowledge is expressed repeatedly in the essays referred to in the previous note; the two following ones also introduce his important machine-analogy: Essay on the History of Astronomy, EPS, IV.19; Essay on the History of Ancient Physics, EPS, 9.

34. For Smith's criticism of Hume in this respect, see TMS, IV. 2. 3ff. I have elsewhere tried to show that the concept of utility involved here has nothing to do with utilitarianism: SoL, ch. 2 sect. 11, and ch. 3, sect. 7.

35. TMS IV. 2. 2.

36. TMS IV. 2. 11.

37. For Smith's criticism of teleological explanations, see esp. TMS, II. ii. 3. 5; and for his accompanying idea of how to explain the unintended consequence phenomenon in social matters, see esp. TMS, II. i. 5. 10. Cf. SoL, ch. 3, sect. 9.

38. This is a frequently recurring theme in TMS II. ii. 3. 11-12; III. 2. 12. 33-35; III. 5. 7, 10, 12-13.

39. Concerning religion as a matter of contemplation, rather than action, see TMS, VI. ii. 3. 6; VII. ii. 1. 45-47. Concerning Smith's attitude to the morality which results from mistakes in this regard, see TMS III. 2. 34-35; and cf. WN, V. i. f. 30. Cf. Hume, *Inquiries Concerning Human Understanding and Concerning the Principles of Morals,* p. 270; and A Dialogue, *ibid.,* pp. 340-43. Cf. SoL, ch. 3, sec. 8.

40. 'The man of system . . . seems to imagine that he can arrange the different members of a great society with as much ease as the hand arranges the different pieces upon a chess-board. He does not consider that the pieces upon the chess-board have no other principle of motion besides that which the hand impresses upon them; but that, in the great chess-board of human society, every single piece has a principle of motion of its own, altogether different from that which the legislature might chuse to impress upon it. If those two principles coincide and act in the same direction, the game of human society will go on easily and harmoniously, and is very likely to be happy and successful. If they are opposite or different, the game will go on miserably, and the society must be at all times in the highest degree of disorder." TMS, VI. ii. 2. 17. The whole passage 15-18 is relevant.

41. TMS, VI. ii. 2. 15.

42. TMS, II. ii. 3. 1-4.

43. See TMS, II. ii. 3. 6-9; and Section IV above, text to notes 34-36.
44. TMS, I. iii. 1. 7-8.
45. TMS, I. iii. 1. 3. And cf. III. 2. 15: 'Pain . . . is, in almost all cases, a more pungent sensation than the opposite and correspondent pleasure. The one almost always depresses us much more below the ordinary, or what may be called the natural state of our happiness, than the other ever raises us above it.'
46. TMS, I. iii. 1. 2.
47. TMS, II. ii. 1. 3-5. The end of this quotation applies the principle of the moral primacy of the individual, mentioned in Section I above. Cf. also LJ(A), i, 9-11; LJ(B), 6ff.
48. Cf. LRBL, pp. 80-81.
49. TMS, II. ii. 1. 9.
50. TMS, III. 6. 10.
51. TMS, VI. ii. 2. 15.
52. Smith refers to Hutcheson and Pufendorf: LJ(A), i, 14. Cf. *ibid.,* 1 and 9.
53. Smith is here obviously talking of 'moralls' in a narrower sense than usual, and thus coming closer to the modern concept. See LJ(A), i. 14-15, and TMS, VII. ii. 1. 10. Cf. also Smith's whole discussion of casuistry *versus* jurisprudence in the final Section of TMS, 7-22 and 33-37.
54. For a detailed discussion of Smith's views on the development of government and law, see SoL, ch. 7.
55. R. L. Meek, 'Smith, Turgot, and the "Four Stages" Theory', *History of Political Economy,* Vol. III, (1971), p. 10. See my criticism of this line of interpretation in SoL, ch. 8.
56. See LJ(A), ii, 136-40; LJ(B), 192.
57. For the development of property in land, see esp. LJ(A), i, 47-53; LJ(B), 153.
58. See SoL, ch. 7, sects. 1 & 6, and ch. 8.
59. TMS, VII. iv.36.
60. T. D. Campbell, *Adam Smith's Science of Morals* (London, 1971), pp. 58-59.
61. TMS, Advertisement.
62. But see SoL, ch. 6.
63. He did not, however, always follow the same sequence in presenting the system to his students. LJ(A) thus follows Hutcheson in beginning with private law, then domestic law, and finally public law, before going on to laws of police, etc. But LJ(B) follows what Smith considered the 'civilian' system, where private and public law change places. See the editors' Introduction to LJ, p. 8.
64. But see SoL, ch. 5, sect. 6, and ch. 6, sect. 3 (text to notes 60-63).
65. WN, IV. v. b. 16.
66. WN, I. x. c. 12.
67. WN, I. x. c. 59. Cf. *ibid.,* 'There is scarce a poor man in England of forty years of age, I will venture to say, who has not in some part of his life felt himself most cruelly oppressed by this ill-contrived law of settlements.'
68. WN, IV. viii. 47.
69. WN, IV. viii. 17.
70. WN, IV. viii. 30.
71. For Smith's way of drawing the distinction between natural and acquired rights, see SoL, ch. 5, sect, 1.
72. See SoL, ch. 6, sect. 3 (text to notes 18-27).
73. LJ(A), i. 53, and 56. The argument concerning 'the common' stretches from i, 53-63.
74. *Ibid.,* 53-55.

75. *Ibid.*, 55.
76. *Ibid.*, 57.
77. *Ibid.*, 56.
78. *Ibid.*, 57-63.
79. WN, III. ii. 4. Cf. LJ(A), i. 131-40; LJ(B), 161-62.
80. LJ(A), i. 116.
81. WN, III. ii. 3. Italics added.
82. WN, III. ii. 6. Cf. LJ(A), i. 164; LJ(B), 168.
83. LJ(A), i. 164.
84. LJ(B), 165. Cf. LJ(A), i. 149ff., and TMS, I. i. 1. 13.
85. LJ(A), i. 154. 161-63, 164-66; LJ(B), 166, 168.
86. LJ(A), i. 165.
87. LJ(A), ii. 30. Cf. LJ(B), 174-75.
88. LJ(A), ii. 30-33. Cf. WN, V. i. e. 30.
89. See SoL, ch. 6, sect. 3.
90. LJ(B), 112, and LJ(A), iii. 25.
91. If they were practised in defiance of laws of police against them, the matter would be complicated by the civil disobedience involved; hence presumably Smith's caution here.
92. LJ(A), iii. 24-25; cf. LJ(B), 111-12. The polygamy issue had been alive in modern natural law since Christian Thomasius caused a scandal with his *Dissertatio de crimine bigamiae* (Leipzig, 1685).
93. WN, IV. ii. 39.
94. This is seen very clearly if we look at the main entries on the problem-side: slavery in the labour force, monopolies in manufacture and commerce, and primogeniture and entail on the land. While some countries, and especially England, had come further than others, those problems were still facing all of Europe in some degree and form. In historical terms slavery had only recently and by luck been abolished (LJ(A), iii. 117-22; LJ(B), 140-42; but contrast WN, III. ii. 12) and that only in a 'small corner of the world', namely a 'corner of Europe' (LJ(A), iii. 114 & 117; cf. *ibid.*, 101, and WN, III. ii. 8); and the countries of that corner were still practising slavery in their colonies (WN, IV. vii. b. 53-56). Although primogeniture and entail were of allodial and feudal origin, they were still being perfected in various parts of Europe as late the previous century (see e.g. LJ(B), 161 and 166; (LJ(A), i. 164), and they were still very wide-spread, even in England, although 'the common law of England . . . is said to abhor perpetuities' (WN, III. ii. 6; and cf. e.g. *ibid.*, 4). And finally, the European perspective in Smith's treatment of the restrictions in trade is sufficiently well known from Book IV of WN.
95. Concerning this theme, see D. Forbes, 'Sceptical Whiggism, Commerce and Liberty'.
96. See WN, IV. ii. 39, and LJ(B), 327, for Smith's opinion of politicians.
97. See Section IV above.
98. This is shown by his frank statement about the system of freedom for which he argued so strongly: 'To expect, indeed, that the freedom of trade should ever be entirely restored in Great Britain, is as absurd as to expect that an Oceana or Utopia should ever be established in it.' WN, IV. ii. 43.
99. See Section III above.

[10]

ADAM SMITH ON LAW

NEIL MACCORMICK*

PROLOGUE

So firm has been the grip of Bentham and Austin on the British juristic imagination that jurists have all too rarely considered their predecessors. From Bentham's and Austin's mixture of rigorous conceptual analysis and implausibly simplistic utilitarianism, we have sifted out the analytical element and our dominant jurisprudential tradition has concentrated on perfecting and re-arguing analytical schemes. That is not to be regretted in itself, since rigorous analysis is an essential groundwork for any worthwhile philosophical effort. It should, however, be deplored that we have failed to give adequate attention to what went before Bentham in eighteenth century legal theory. In particular, the writings of the Scottish enlightenment and the later seventeenth century—by jurists such as Stair, Erskine, Bankton, Kames, and John Millar and by philosophers such as Francis Hutcheson, David Hume, Adam Ferguson, Thomas Reid and Dugald Stewart—elaborate themes which should have been developed, not neglected.

The disputes over natural law and rationality in ethics among the Scottish moralists were carried on at a level to which Benthamite moralizing on the basis of a merely asserted principle of utility never aspired; and the attempts of the Scottish moralists to account for the historical development of legal orders within theories of economy and society has been altogether too much neglected since then—it has been left to sociologists such as William C. Lehmann to renew our interests in their theories.

It is within that general intellectual context that we must place Adam Smith as a theorist of law. Smith succeeded Francis Hutcheson as professor of moral philosophy at Glasgow in 1750 at the age of twenty-seven. He followed the contemporary understanding of the tasks of his office by giving a series of lectures on natural theology, ethics, jurisprudence, and political economy. His course on ethics was worked up for publication in 1759 under the title of *The Theory of Moral Sentiments*. The work on political economy led to the publication of *The Wealth of Nations* in 1776, thirteen years after his resignation from the Glasgow chair. He continued working on other

---

*Regius Professor of Public Law and the Law of Nature and Nations, University of Edinburgh, Scotland.

themes, but shortly before his death in 1790, he gave orders for the destruction of all of his manuscripts save a few essays entrusted to his executors for publication.

In 1896, however, Professor Edwin Cannan discovered and edited a remarkably full set of student's notes from Smith's "Lectures on Justice, Police, Revenue and Arms," being none other than the lectures on jurisprudence—of which presumably the more developed manuscript by Smith had been destroyed in 1790. Almost twenty years ago, Professor Lothian of Aberdeen discovered another more complete set of notes from the same course of lectures, apparently belonging to an earlier year. The recent publication of this version of Smith's *Lectures on Jurisprudence*, under the joint editorship of Professors R.L. Meek, D.D. Raphael and P.G. Stein, will doubtless occasion a revival of interest in this aspect of Smith's work—together, it may be hoped, with a revival of interest in the legal theories of the eighteenth century generally.

It was from the topics covered in those parts of the lectures dealing with police, revenue, and arms that the themes of *The Wealth of Nations* derived. The relevance of "revenue" is obvious, but it needs to be recalled that for Smith "police" had nothing much to do with the gentlemen in blue. "Police," Smith said, "is the second general division of jurisprudence. The name is French and is originally derived from the Greek *politeia*, which, though properly signifying the policy of civil government, came to mean only the regulation of the inferior parts of government, *viz.*, cleanliness, security, and cheapness or plenty. Smith dealt with cleanliness and security fairly summarily before proceeding to the theme of cheapness or plenty in Division II of Part II of the lectures. There we find much of the theorizing of *The Wealth of Nations* already present in embryo. "Arms" were dealt with in *The Wealth of Nations* under "Expenses of the Sovereign."[1]

In these days of interdisciplinary endeavour, it is pleasing to discover that the origins of economics were so firmly located by the inventor of the dismal science within the second general division of jurisprudence, namely, "police." It is time now for jurisprudents to inquire and discover what economics has now to offer for the understanding of law. Where would be a better place to start than by an inquiry into what Adam Smith himself had to offer?

---

1. A. Smith, An Inquiry into the Nature and Causes of the Wealth of Nations, bk. V. ch. I, pt. I (Glasgow ed. 1976) (1st ed. 1776).

In what follows I lay no claim to originality; I have been much influenced by works of colleagues such as Professor T.D. Campbell,[2] Professor Andrew Skinner,[3] Professor P.G. Stein,[4] and Mr. G.L. Davidson.[5] In particular, my account of what Smith has to say owes a great deal to Skinner's essay, *Adam Smith on Law and Government*. To some extent, one is faced with the task of reconstructing themes out of lectures which he had hoped would never be published. In that, I merely follow where others have led.

NATURAL RIGHTS AND POSITIVE LAW

One of the most fascinating things about Adam Smith is the way in which he combined, as the basic elements of the economy of different forms of human society, a theory of natural rights with a theory of the social development of laws and legal institutions. His lectures on justice begin with the confident assertion that "[t]he end of justice is to secure from injury."[6] Human beings may be injured in several respects; namely, as human beings simpliciter, as members of families, and as members of states. Taking the first of these categories as the principal one, which indeed it was for Smith, he tells us that a human being "may be injured in his body reputation or estate."[7] Smith draws an important distinction between injuries to body and reputation and injuries to estate. "These rights which a man has to the preservation of his body and reputation from injury are called natural, or as the civilians express them *iura hominum naturalia*."[8] Injuries to a person's estate are different, in the sense that "his rights to his estate are called acquired or *iura adventitia*, and are of two kinds, real and personal."[9]

---

2. T.D. CAMPBELL, ADAM'S SMITH'S SCIENCE OF MORALS (1971).

3. Skinner, *Adam Smith on Law and Government*, PERSPECTIVES IN JURISPRUDENCE (E. Attwooll ed. 1977).

4. P. Stein, *Law and Society in 18th Century Scottish Thought*, SCOTLAND AND THE AGE OF IMPROVEMENT (1970); P. Stein, *The General Notions of Contract and Property in 18th Century Scottish Thought*, 1963 JUR. REV. 1; P. Stein, *Legal Thought in 18th Century Scotland*, 1957 JUR. REV. 1; P. Stein, Rights and Relativism in Adam Smith (unpublished paper read to 1975 Conference for the Association for Legal and Social Philosophy).

5. G. Davidson, Adam Smith's Lecture on Justice (1974) (unpublished dissertation written for LL.B. at Cambridge University).

6. A. SMITH, LECTURES ON JURISPRUDENCE 397-99 (Glasgow ed. 1978) (also found in A. SMITH, LECTURES ON JUSTICE, POLICE, REVENUE AND ARMS 3-4 (E. Cannan ed. 1896)).

7. *Id.*

8. *Id.*

9. *Id.*

In drawing these distinctions, Smith was, of course, anything but original. As befitted a professor of moral philosophy giving lectures on justice, police, revenue and arms, he was simply expounding some distinctions common among civilian writers of the period. It was no doubt his good fortune to have been reared in the civilian tradition of the Scottish universities, a tradition which by contrast to that prevailing in contemporary English legal education secured a systematic and principled approach to tasks of legal description and analysis. But if the schema was unoriginal, the use to which Smith put it was far from unoriginal. Looking to his moral philosophy as expressed in the *Theory of Moral Sentiments*,[10] we find a particularly interesting account of what constitutes an injury; if we look to his political economy, which was already developing in the lectures on justice, police, revenue, and arms, we find one of the most interesting expositions anywhere of the correlations between conceptions of injury and forms of society.

First, I shall deal briefly with his general notion of injury. As is well known, Smith's general account of our moral perceptions advanced in the *Theory of Moral Sentiments* is based on the idea of the "impartial spectator."[11] Of the actions which human beings may take in relation to each other, some cause pain and distress. The person who suffers pain, distress or other harm from the action of another human being has a natural inclination to resent it, all the more so if he sees that the harmful act was intentional, and was intended to be harmful. Human beings have the capacity for sympathy (or as we might say, empathy) with each other. Someone who observes a harmful act intentionally being done by one person to another, can enter by sympathy into the feelings of the victim, and can in some degree, though not as acutely as the victim, share in the sense of resentment. But of course, this depends equally on being able to enter into and understand the motives of the attacker. If, for example, it should turn out that the attacker is retaliating against harm previously done, this may lead the spectator to share in the resentment of the attacker and to regard the attack as justified rather than to enter sympathetically into the resentment of the victim. Of course, if the spectator happens to be someone who is already "on the side of" either the attacker or the victim, this will

10. A. SMITH, THE THEORY OF MORAL SENTIMENTS (Glasgow ed. 1976) (1st ed. London and Edinburg 1759).

11. *Id.* at pt. II, § III, ch. 1; *see* T.D. CAMPBELL, *supra* note 2; Skinner, *supra* note 3.

render his approbation or disapprobation of the action no less partial than that of the party whose side he takes.

Since morality is based on a common sense of propriety and impropriety among human beings, the common position can be found only by reference to the position of an impartial spectator; that is, one who is not predisposed to take the side of either of the parties. What is more, the worth of an impartial spectator's judgment is dependent on the degree of his knowledge, and we can never have perfect knowledge of the actions, intentions, and motivations of other human beings. We can, however, have or acquire a relatively good understanding of our own intentions and motivations. The extent to which human beings possess a fully developed moral judgment depends on their, as it were, constructing within their breast an ideal impartial spectator who is genuinely impartial in relation to themselves and those with whom they deal, but who is fully informed of the intentions and motivations of the agent, because the impartial spectator shares them. So for each of us, our moral judgments are framed by a reference to this ideal impartial spectator, this "man within the breast" with whom we can enter into dialogue in moral matters.

Rough and crude as that explanation is, it enables one to understand Smith's idea of an injury. When a person suffers harm that he resents, as the result of the act of another person, and when the impartial spectator can enter into and fully share in the ensuing resentment in degree and kind, or rather, to the extent that the impartial spectator can enter into that resentment, we may say that the harm causing act was an injury. From the impartial spectator's point of view, an appropriate act of retaliation is then justified, and indeed constitutes a just punishment for the injury. Thence we derive our basic notion of injury, and our notion of justice as the punishment or other correction of injuries. We may observe that this leads to a theory of justice in which justice is necessarily conceived of as being corrective rather than distributive.

In turn, we can make sense of the idea that there are natural rights; there are natural rights to the extent that there are natural injuries. Natural injuries are those which people can suffer, inflict, and rightly resent in any social setting whatsoever. When one person hurts another in his body or his reputation, I do not need to know anything more about the social or economic background in order to know that a wrong or an injury has been done. Though different cultures may take different actions in repression of, retaliation for, or correction of the wrongdoing, we need postulate no substantial degree of cultural relativity in the recognition that a wrong has been done.

In some respects also, Smith is prepared to treat some basic elements of adventitious rights as being in the same sense natural. For example, if someone has taken possession of an ownerless thing, as by killing a wild animal, invasion by another of that possession would be resented, and the resentment would attract the sympathy of the impartial spectator.[12] The same is true for voluntary obligations. If someone knowingly puts another person in a position of relying on him for performance of some act, which for Smith is the essence of promising, then subsequent disappointment of the person who has that reasonable expectation is a wrong in the view of the impartial spectator.[13] Nevertheless, in general terms, although adventitious rights may have in such ways "natural" foundations, their protection and enforcement, and indeed in some measure their institution, are matters regulated by positive law. Further, they are matters that positive law regulates in various ways according to the circumstances, with the regulations being determined chiefly by the mode of economy of a society. This will sufficiently appear in due course. What presently has to be observed is the relationship between Smith's basic theory of positive law and his notion of injury.

So far as concerns the nature of positive law, Smith subscribes to the standard voluntarist notion, later adopted by Benthamite and Austinian "positivists," that the actual positive law of a state is to be identified with the command of the sovereign.[14] Positive law, as such, emanates from organized institutions of government. But as to its function, the aim of positive law is to secure justice, in the sense of the prevention and repression of injuries.[15] It is not a substitute for what is morally right, but a reinforcement of it. There are at least some circumstances in which people in society will exhibit a tendency to unjustly invade each other's rights, and in which there will not be proper security for the enjoyment of rights. In these circumstances there must be positive law, not to define, but to secure

12. *See* A. SMITH, *supra* note 6, at 459 (Cannan ed. at 107-09).

13. *Id.* at 472 (Cannan ed. at 130-31).

14. *See* A. SMITH, *supra* note 10, at pt. III, ch. 5, ¶ 6, p. 165. "All general rules are commonly denominated laws . . . [, for example,] laws of motion. But those general rules which our moral faculties observe . . . may more justly be denominated such. They have a much greater resemblance to what are properly called laws, those general rules which the sovereign lays down to direct the conduct of his subjects." *Id.*

15. *See* A. SMITH, *supra* note 10, at pt. II, § II, ch. 1, p. 78-82.

justice among people. It is when we consider what in Smith's view these circumstances are that require positive law, we hit upon the sociologically innovative aspect of his theorizing about law.

LAW AND ECONOMY IN GENERAL

At this point we must return to the theme of acquired rights. A person's estate is composed of the sum total of his acquired rights.[16] These Smith divides into the standard categories of real rights and personal rights. Real rights he subdivides into four kinds, of which the first three are standard: property, servitudes, pledges, and exclusive privileges. Property, Smith analyzes in terms of the right to exclusive possession of a thing, together with the power to recover the thing owned from any other possessor whatsoever. Servitudes and pledges (in which term Smith includes mortgages) he analyzes in a quite standard way. An exclusive privilege, says Smith, is like "that of a bookseller to vend a book for a certain number of years, and to hinder any other person from doing it during that period."[17] I do not know whether Smith's use of the concept of "exclusive privilege" in this context is original; certainly, it is a brilliant way of characterizing various forms of "incorporeal property" which have become much more common since Smith's time. Copyright obviously fits the category; as would patents and various forms of statutory monopoly, and even perhaps such things as equity shares. Smith also includes in "exclusive privilege" the right of an heir who has not yet entered on the inheritance, and suggests that there might be "natural" rights by way of exclusive privileges; for example where a hunter has started a hare and pursued her for some time and has thus, in Smith's view, a right against all comers to pursue her to the final kill.[18] The identification of this category of rights that are real but incorporeal is clearly of some importance; certainly for Smith, in light of his political economy, given his views on the undesirable quality of monopolies, the category was important.

Rights under contracts and the right to reparation of damage done by delinquency also belong to the category of acquired rights. Smith would certainly have been anxious to deny in both cases the fashionable contemporary thesis that such rights have no moral foundation; and it is submitted that he would be entirely correct. But he is surely right in also saying that even if the basic right to performance

16. *See* A. SMITH, *supra* note 6, at 399-401 (Cannan ed. at 6-8).
17. *Id.* at 400 (Cannon ed. at 7).
18. *Id.*

of a promise, or to be free from harm, are in a sense natural, nevertheless the remedial right to compensation for contracts broken or harm done is a creature of positive law.

"Acquired rights such as property require more explanation [than natural rights]. Property and civil government very much depend on one another. The preservation of property and the inequality of possession first formed it, and the state of property must always vary with the form of government."[19] It is this basic thesis of Smith's—that property and civil government, and therefore positive law (which is the creature of civil government), are closely intertwined—which is of the greatest interest to us. He put the same point another way: "Till there be property there can be no government, the very end of which is to secure wealth and to defend the rich from the poor."[20] These words, taken from the lectures, are echoed in the section of *The Wealth of Nations* dealing with "The Expense of Justice."[21] It was a fundamental tenet of Smith's, which nowadays most people wrongly ascribe to Karl Marx, that forms of government and property relations are mutually interdependent. Positive law is shaped, according to Smith, by the mode of economy of a society. People have not always lived in societies subjected to formal institutionalized magistracies or governments.

> Among nations of hunters, as there is scarce any property, or at least none that exceeds the value of two or three days' labour; so there is seldom any established magistrate, or any regular administration of justice. Men who have no property, can injure one another only in their persons or reputations. But when one man kills, wounds, beats or defames another, though he to whom the injury is done suffers, he who does it receives no benefit. It is otherwise with the injuries to property. The benefit of the person who does the injury is often equal to the loss of him who suffers it. Envy, malice, or resentment, are the only passions which can prompt one man to injure another in his person or reputation. But the greater part of men are not very frequently under the influence of these passions; and the very worst of men are so only occasionally.[22]

---

19. *Id.* at 401 (Cannan ed. at 8).
20. *Id.* at 404 (Cannan ed. at 15); *cf.* A. SMITH, *supra* note 1, bk. V, chap. I, pt. II.
21. A. SMITH, *supra* note 1, at bk. V, ch. I, pt. II.
22. *Id.*

Smith subscribed to and gave his own version of, though he did not invent, the theory of the "four stages" of human society.[23] That is, that in the evolution of human societies four main stages are discernible, in terms of the basic features of their economy. There are societies of hunters and fishermen, societies of shepherds, societies of agriculturalists and commercial societies. In the first of these stages people would own no permanent property; and for that reason, said Smith, they would not require institutionalized magistracies or positive laws. The corollary, which Smith regards as obvious, is that in societies that recognize private property and thus inequality of possessions, there are and must also be laws and regular systems of law enforcement. For once inequality of possession exists, there is the possibility of envy and resentment by the poor of the rich, who accordingly have to secure by some means their possessions against the depredations which are a permanent danger in such circumstances. Not merely does the establishment of property give rise to the risk of invasions of possessions, but it also gives rise to motives for interpersonal violence, assaults on reputation, and all those other wrongs which, as he assures us, would be relatively uncommon among nations of hunters. Governments and positive laws evolve as a means to secure the position of property owners and check the other modes of wrongdoing that are occasioned by the very existence of property regimes.

Thus it appears that in societies that have evolved beyond the stage of hunting and gathering, positive law is not so much a separate phenomenon brought into existence by the political economy as it is an intrinsic element of such economy. The development of a pastoral economy dependent for its subsistence on the produce of herds leads to an allocation of domesticated animals to individuals or families, and a protection of that allocation by means of enforced laws securing to "owners" possession of their beasts, their produce and their progeny. It would not be true to say that the development of a pastoral economy causes the existence of enforced laws of property; rather, the development of a pastoral economy is a development in which an intrinsic part is the recognition and protection of property rights in those things that to such a society represent the essentials of wealth; namely, herds.

A necessary feature of such a development is the existence of

23. *See* A. SMITH, *supra* note 6, at 14-15, 459-60 (Cannan ed. at 107). Mr. G.L. Davidson has pointed out to me a passage in Montesquieu's *Esprit des Lois* which is perhaps the original source of this idea, which was common among writers of the period. *See* MONTESQUIEU, ESPRIT DES LOIS bk. 18, ch. 8.

inequalities in the possession of the animals that increasingly represent exclusive necessities of life; the population grows beyond the point at which sustenance by hunting and fishing is a possibility, and the pasturage of herds in itself tends to diminish the numbers of wild animals available for hunting by those who would thus choose to subsist. Here we find an explanation of the origins of the subordination of one human being to another; the "origin of the distinction of ranks" as Smith[24] and his pupil John Millar[25] called it. Those who have not, become dependent on those who have; those who have, can do nothing with their excess produce other than maintain a train of dependents, over whom their power tends to the absolute, since they control the means of life of their dependents. The wealth of those who have gives them authority by giving others reason to accept that authority.

Pasturage itself may give way in turn, albeit extremely gradually, to the development of a settled agricultural system, which again is capable of sustaining a larger population on the same area of ground as a pastoral system. The development of settled agriculture replaces the nomadic system of pasturing when the agriculturists appropriate the pastures of the nomads. Again, the need for force to protect the land that is held is obvious; also obvious are the intrinsically necessary legal developments. Legal recognition must now be given to the possibility of the ownership of land as well as to the ownership of moveables, which hither to has constituted the only property.

In an agricultural economy as well as in a pastoral economy, control of the land, upon which all depend for their subsistence, confers power upon those who control it over those who do not, and places the latter in a condition of dependence on the former. The landlord is necessarily a lord over the people who depend on the land, as well as over the land itself. The establishment and maintenance of such lordship evidently depends on the organization of sufficient force to sustain the position of those at the top, as indeed the history of European feudalism indicates.

However, the very decentralization of power among great territorial magnates which earlier allodial and later feudal property involved created a permanent tension or rivalry between royal and baronial power. Kings in seeking to establish their position of pri-

24. *See* A. SMITH, *supra* note 10, at pt. I, § III, ch. 2, pp. 50-61.

25. J. MILLAR, Of the Origin of the Distinction of Ranks (4th ed. Edinburgh 1806), *reprinted in* W.C. LEHMAN, JOHN MILLAR OF GLASCOW (1960).

macy over the territorial lords, who (after the introduction to feudal tenure in place of allodial) were theoretically their vassals, naturally looked for allies in that struggle. In Europe, said Smith, kings found such allies in the cities.[26] By strengthening the independent rights of the cities, granting monopolies to their tradesmen's and merchants' guilds, kings secured a powerful source of support in the perennial struggles within feudalism. The burgesses, through taxation and other means, in return for their privileges, provided revenue for the King which increasingly enabled him to organize his own armed forces independently of the feudal host and so to transcend his original role as, essentially, *primus inter pares*.

At the same time, the growth of the cities erodes feudalism in another way. Cities must trade at least with their own hinterland in order to survive. But that process of trade creates, consolidates, and in due course increases a taste for the manufactures of the city. In the earliest stages of feudalism, the tenure of land is necessarily and essentially based on mutual personal services—protection and adjudication by the lord in return from services by the tenant, different in kind accordingly as the tenure is "free" or not; the landlord's interest is best served by maximizing the number of his dependents to the greatest productive capacity for the land. The growth of trade in manufactures gives to the landlord a new outlet for the excess production of his land, namely the purchase of luxury goods. As the taste for these grows, the more there is motivation for a commutation of personal services to money payments. The development of such commutation of services is of course well attested in history. Thus, land holding over time becomes a means of revenue rather than a basis for status relationships based (at least notionally) on mutuality of services. These developments, extended over a long period of time, and proceeding with local differences and at different paces according to local circumstances (the contrasts between lowland and highland Scotland, between Scotland and England, between Britain and the Netherlands were for Smith a source of obvious contemporary contrasts) constitute the gradual evolution of a commercial form of society out of the preceding feudal and agrarian order.[27]

Such a transformation again, and necessarily, involves or includes a transformation in legal relations. Most obviously, this is

26. A. SMITH, *supra* note 1, at bk. III.

27. I am entirely indebted for the account in this and the preceding five paragraphs to Andrew Skinner's essay, note 4, *supra* which drew to my attention the relevance for this purpose of Book III of THE WEALTH OF NATIONS, note 1 *supra*.

marked in a growth in the importance of contractual relations. People who work for their living do so not on the basis of a status relationship with a feudal superior who supplies land or access to the produce of land in return for personal, manorial, or military services. They do so by entering as free persons into contractual relations with those who have work for them to do, the contract being for service by the workman in return for payment by the master. The workman then takes his wages into the market in order to purchase the necessities of life. Labor and the produce of land are assimilated to the commodities produced by tradesmen and manufacturers, circulating in a market regulated by supply and demand. The alienability of property, rather than the right to its possession for use and enjoyment, becomes a key feature of the right of property. Increasingly land itself becomes subject to freedom of alienation, except where this is inhibited by legal means such as the Scots law on entails, which Smith and many of his associates strongly wanted to abolish.[28]

I am not a sufficient historian, economist, or sociologist to make an informed judgment on the general argument of Smith's which I have tried to outline here in an admittedly over-compressed form. Nevertheless, it does seem to me to have a certain intrinsic plausibility in broad terms, if not in details. It brings sharply to our attention the way in which laws and legal institutions are an inherent part of the economy of a society and must be understood and explained as such, if we wish to proceed beyond purely formal and structural analysis of legal systems considered in the abstract. In that respect, Smith's work has a clear lesson, even today, for any gathering of jurists and economists: neither group can regard the other's field of work as alien to its own interests and concerns. Economists ought not treat legal relationships either as indifferent to their questions or as mere background data assumed as invariant elements of the economic landscape. Jurists ought not regard economic relationships as existing apart from and indifferent to legal relations, for the latter are indeed an intrinsic part of the former.

RATIONALITY OR DETERMINATION

One question which should be considered is how far Smith's general theory is a deterministic one. In my view, it is not in any

28. Smith said of entails, "Upon the whole nothing can be more absurd than perpetual entails." A. SMITH, *supra* note 6, at 70, 468 (Cannan ed. at 124).

crude or simple sense an instance of economic determinism. As we saw in the quotation from *The Wealth of Nations*, with which the last section commenced, an important question for Smith is what rational motives people can have for various actions in given circumstances. "Where there is no property, or at least none that exceeds the value of two or three days' labor, civil government is not so necessary [as where there is 'valuable and extensive property']"[29] This is so because people in these circumstances lack any rational motive to envy or to do violence.

Human beings as rational choosers make choices in given circumstances, and the choices that seem to them rational are genuine choices based on reasons that are genuinely good. It does not follow, of course, that the outcome of individual rational choices, taken in the aggregate, was intended or foreseen by those who made the choices that cumulatively led to the net outcome. Kings may have had (genuinely) good reasons for favoring burgesses; burgesses individually and collectively undoubtedly had good reasons of self interest for accepting royal favors and making appropriate returns therefor. It does not follow that they chose jointly to transform feudal society into commercial. To say this is simply to repeat the old and obvious truth that human actions rationally chosen within a certain compass can have unintended outcomes well beyond that compass. Smith was well aware of that as a general tenet among enlightenment thinkers, and his own "Invisible Hand"[30] is, I take it, a particular exemplification of the general idea.

This has important implications for his own work. If Smith was an out-and-out determinist, there would be a more than paradoxical element about much of his own work in *The Wealth of Nations*. If forms of economy necessarily generate their own internal forces that sweep men along regardless of any illusory notions of rationality and choice, there would be little point in writing a book which is not merely descriptive, but is in an important measure prescriptive, advocating legislative and other policies (such as the abolition of statutory monopolies) that are aimed at improving the economic order and producing a more rational basis for a commercial economy.

---

29. A. SMITH, *supra* note 1, at bk. V, ch. I, pt. II.

30. *Id.* at bk. IV, ch. II, p. 456: "[Every individual in a market] intends only his own gain, and he is in this, as in many other cases, led by an invisible hand to promote an end which was no part of his intention." For a discussion of "invisible hand" explanations, see R. NOZICK, ANARCHY, STATE AND UTOPIA 18-22, 336-37 (1974).

Smith's overall position seems to be in principle a self-consistent one. The more we know and understand of our own circumstances, the more we can make genuinely rational choices guided by a well-founded view of individual or of collective interests. Therefore we ought to seek to understand our circumstances as well as possible, and ought to make those choices which seem most sensible given our necessarily imperfect, but always improvable, understanding of those circumstances. That Smith does not venture any predictions as to what will happen beyond commercial society is a strength rather than a weakness of his approach, since our capacity to foresee the unintended outsomes of what we now do is in practice and in principle bound to be imperfect. I would venture to suggest that it is a weakness and not a strength of Marx's that he observed no such modesty in his pretended capacity to foresee the future; we are still living with the unintended outcomes of that lack of theoretical modesty.

In any event, we have to take account of Smith's qualified rationalism in ethical as well as technical questions. He was by no means an advocate of the pursuit by each person of his own interest at all costs. He certainly held the view that human beings have natural rights, and that each person's pursuit of interests is legitimate only when subject to respect for those rights. At one point in *Theory of Moral Sentiments* he ascribes our knowledge of basic moral rights and duties to the moral norms implanted by God in man's nature.[31] To that extent he belongs within the natural law and not the utilitarian tradition. That each may pursue his own, and that governments ought to pursue the general utility, is not a single simple and overriding principle with Smith, but one which comes into operation only within the area of indifference of the basic moral code.

There is no doubt that Smith believed that the development and growth of commercial society represented "progress" and that progress was, on the whole, good. First of all, as we have seen, commercial relationships favor the liberty of individuals, and it is right that people be free from bondage. That people who are in bondage will not, in practice, be freed therefrom by their masters on the mere ground of their moral claim to freedom does, however, seem obvious to Smith. It is therefore a merit of the commercial system that it actually gives the slave owner a good motive (whether perceived by him or not) to grant his slaves their freedom. Free

31. A. SMITH, *supra* note 10, at pt. III, ch. 5, ¶ 6, p. 165.

wage laborers present a better deal overall to a capitalist than slaves, who never have any reason to produce more than guarantees their own subsistence. Free wage laborers have a motive to maximize production to increase their own income above subsistence level, which in turn also enhances the profits of their capitalist masters.[32] Secondly, and this point follows also from the first, a commercial economy is one which from generation to generation encourages the increase of wealth, and thus the general well-being. People in general are simply better off in commercial rather than in agrarian, pastoral, or hunting and fishing societies, even though there is a necessary inequality in the distribution of the resulting wealth.

Smith was, however, if less acutely than Adam Ferguson, well aware of the countervailing disadvantages of commercial society.[33] The division of labor produces among the lower classes a diminishing range of experience and of interests. The production line maximizes the production of pins at a severe human cost in terms of the restricted life the operatives enjoy. Children become employable at younger and younger ages, and lose the opportunities of education that rural children still enjoyed in the Scottish parish schools. In addition to depressing the education of the poor, this process weakened family structures and parental authority and contributed to drunkenness and disorder in the towns. The martial ardor of the nation and its capacity to defend itself in time of war was diminished by the same processes. A graphic illustration of this was supplied in Smith's own lifetime by the capacity of Charles Edward's Highland army to take practically the whole of Britain by storm until the return of the professional soldiery from the Continental wars.

It is difficult to acquit Smith, with hindsight, of a certain complacency in the blandness of his conclusion that despite all these evident defects, commercial society was on the whole genuinely progressive and good. Nevertheless he reached that conclusion, and advocated the rationalization of the laws and the economic practices of his time in order to promote what he took on the whole to be good. This clearly indicates that he did not pretend that the development of societies was the mere product of blind forces of nature independent of rational moral choices by human agents.

32. On this argument in general, A. SMITH, *supra* note 6, at 453-54 (Cannan ed. at 99-104).

33. *See id.* at 539-40 (Cannan ed. at 255-60); *cf.* A. FERGUSON, ESSAY ON THE HISTORY OF CIVIL SOCIETY (1966).

Two Particular Areas of Smith's Jurisprudence

So far this paper has dealt in relative generalities; in order to bring it to a close, it may be worthwhile to take up two particular points that illustrate how Smith's general account forms a setting for illuminating consideration of more particular matters. Since one purpose of such a collection as the present symposium is, I take it, to stimulate research in cross-disciplinary areas, this may in addition have the merit of suggesting the possible relevance of Smith's ability to draw attention to problems still worthy of consideration. I shall deal very briefly with aspects of contract and of the administration of justice.

Contract

I have already mentioned Smith's general theory of contractual and other voluntary obligations. "A promise is a declaration of your desire that the person for whom you promise should depend on you for the performance of it. Of consequence, the promise produces an obligation, and the breach of it, an injury."[34]

The foundation of contractual obligation thus explained is not culturally relative. However, according to Smith, the importance of contract as an institution certainly is. "Breach of contract is naturally the slightest of injuries" and in "rude ages" little regard is paid to it.[35] In the earliest periods of positive law, enforceable contracts would be those which related to matters of great substance, and which had been undertaken in circumstances of great formality—essential to indicate clearly to all parties, despite the "uncertainty of language," the character of the obligation being undertaken. By tracing the development of Roman law, Smith shows how we can perceive the steady evolution of a less and less formalistic approach to contracting. In contrasting Smith's own commercial society, and "the ancient state of contracts" Smith said, "At present almost anything will make a contract obligatory."[36]

34. A. SMITH, *supra* note 6, at 87, 472 (Cannan ed. at 131). This view is very similar to Lord Kames. H. Home, Lord Kames, ESSAYS ON THE PRINCIPLES OF MORALITY AND NATURAL RELIGION pt. I, essay II, ch. 6 ("The reliance upon us, produced by our own act, constitutes the obligation."). I have suggested elsewhere that this view can be elaborated so as to yield a better account of such obligations than that most commonly accepted among contemporary philosophers. MacCormick, *Voluntary Obligations and Normative Powers*, 46 ARISTOTELIAN SOC'Y SUPPLEMENTARY VOLUME 63-78 (1972).

35. A. SMITH, *supra* note 6, at 87, 472 (Cannan ed. at 131).

36. *Id.* at 473 (Cannan ed. at 132).

Why should all this be so? Not, says Smith, because of changes in the basic character of people; rather, it happens because of changes in their social and economic circumstances. In his discussion in the *Lectures* on the influence of commerce on manners he makes the very point that "probity and punctuality" in the keeping of undertakings is an effect rather than a cause of the development of commerce. He says that for fidelity to their word the Dutch are the most outstanding people in Europe, greatly superior to the English who are slightly superior to the Scots, among whom a distinction exists between the commercial and the "remote" parts of the country.

> This is not at all to be imputed to national character as some pretend. . . . It is far more reducible to self-interest, that general principle which regulates the actions of every man, and which leads men to act in a certain manner from views of advantage. . . . A dealer is afraid of losing his character and is scrupulous in observing every engagement. When a person makes perhaps twenty contracts in a day, he cannot gain so much by endeavouring to impose on his neighbour, as the very appearance of a cheat would make him lose. When people seldom deal with one another, we find that they are somewhat disposed to cheat, because they can gain more by a smart trick than they can lose by the injury which it does their character.[37]

As well as neatly and concretely illustrating the point made at the outset about Smith's ability to combine a theory of natural rights with a theory of the social development of laws and legal institutions, this statement points toward an area of interesting research. The trouble is that, at least for the United States, some of it has already been done. But it is surely a mark of Smith's acuteness that he should have so clearly anticipated such works as that of MacAulay[38] and Ross,[39] in broad outline at least.

The Administration of Justice

On this topic we must look to "Of the Expense of Justice" from the *The Wealth of Nations*.[40] It is in pastoral societies, says Smith,

37. *Id.* at 538-39 (Cannan ed. at 253).

38. *See, e.g.*, MacAulay, *Noncontractual Relations in Business: Preliminary Study*, 28 AM. SOC. REV. 55 (1963).

39. L. ROSS, SETTLED OUT OF COURT (1970). Of course, both Ross and MacAulay have covered enormous tracts of ground not contemplated by Smith, but he seems to me to be the "pointing in the same direction" as that which their much more elaborate studies pursue.

40. A. SMITH, *supra* note 1, at bk. V, ch. I, pt. II.

that we first find the beginnings of institutionalized adjudication, albeit in a rudimentary form in which lesser people look to great chieftains distinguished by wealth and power for determination and remedying of injuries. In addition to his position as a military leader, "his birth and fortune procure him some sort of judicial authority." So far from being a source of expense to him, however, this is in fact a source of revenue, for "those who applied to him for justice were always willing to pay for it."[41] Even in feudal and agrarian societies this persists. As late as the time of Henry II of England, Smith points out, the circuit judges were as much as anything else factors sent out to levy certain types of revenue, and the administration of justice—albeit now through delegates—was as much as anything else a means of procuring revenue. But so long as the giving of "presents" and the risk of amercements were essential adjuncts of litigation, the risk of corruption of justice was inevitably high, and was everywhere realized.[42]

What led to change in this? Smith's answer is that at some stage in feudal society the expenses of defense become so great that the King could no longer live off his own estates and feudal dues. Taxation becomes a necessity, but the *quid pro quo* generally demanded is that gifts and presents and fees should no longer be accepted or rendered in return for the adjudication of suits. Fixed salaries are appointed to the judges to compensate them for the loss of other income, the salaries being payable out of general revenue from taxation.

This in turn may procure its own mischiefs, for the judges may be unduly exposed to executive pressure. In addition, their income is no longer dependent on their industry and expeditiousness in the conduct of business—unlike the conditions of competition which formerly prevailed, to Smith's characteristic admiration, among the various different royal courts in England. Smith canvasses various ingenious schemes for remedying the former defect, suggesting, by analogy to the then still extant endowment of the Court of Session, that it might be apt to provide courts with certain land or funds, the income of which could sustain them independently of the executive. "The necessary instability of such a fund seems, however, to render it an improper one for the maintenance of an institution which ought to last forever."[43]

41. *Id.*
42. *Id.*
43. *Id.*

Smith's preferred solution, which he regards as a remedy for both mischiefs, is to find a system of charging fees for court business, which would be administered independently of the executive and of individual judges. The fees would be payable after the relevant work was done and would be apportioned among judges according to their diligence and expeditiousness in the discharge of business. The French *Parlements*, he points out, operate on a similar footing, and they are, if not convenient as courts of justice, neither suspected nor accused of corruption.

He has already anticipated the objection that this would be a retrogression from the position in which justice is administered gratis:

> Justice . . . never was in reality administered gratis in any country. Lawyers and attorneys, at least, must always be paid by the parties; and if they were not, they would perform their duty still worse than they actually perform it. The fees annually paid, to lawyers and attorneys, amount, in every court, to a much greater sum than the salaries of the judges. The circumstance of those salaries being paid by the crown, can nowhere much diminish the necessary expense of a law suit.[44]

The topicality of Smith's concerns can hardly be doubted in view of the considerable present concern about the quality and distribution of legal services in many jurisdictions. The more we are interested in trying to disseminate legal services—not just judicial services—through the community, the more acutely we face the problem of securing the genuine independence of such services and coupling it with proper efficiency—especially to the extent that lawyers' incomes cease to be dependent on client satisfaction.

Quite apart from that, Smith's penetrating observations about the real total expense of the administration of justice being far greater than the apparent Exchequer cost should prompt reflection. Much legislation is ostensibly cheap, and may indeed involve no immediate identified public expense at all. But ought we not inquire far more closely into its real cost in terms of burdens on court time, and its costs to those who have to employ lawyers to guide them through more and more complicated legal mazes, and all the rest of it? If reflection on Smith's work were to lead us to reflect more on the true overall cost of ostensibly beneficial laws, it would be well

44. *Id.*

worthwhile for that alone. There would be enough research projects concerning this to keep us all busy for a good long time—which seems in this context a good point on which to conclude this paper.

POSTSCRIPT

It is, no doubt, obvious that the writing of this article was prompted more by an interest in the history of legal and moral philosophy in the eighteenth century than by any pretension to economic expertise. At the time at which it was first written,[45] I was quite unfamiliar with the contemporary "Economic Analysis of Law" (E.A.L. for short) put forward by Richard Posner,[46] Ronald Coase,[47] Harold Demsetz[48] and others.

Having subsequently begun to scratch the surface of that theoretical approach,[49] I ought to add a brief comment about a significant contrast between Smith's approach and that of E.A.L. The contrast is to Smith's advantage. His theory of "natural rights" is a moral theory independent of and more fundamental than his analysis of the economic consequences of any legal ascription of rights to individuals. A particular example is his theory of promisees' rights, founded, he says, in the injustice of disappointing people in any matter upon which a promisor has intentionally induced them to rely. The enforcement of promissory or other "natural" rights is indeed subject to variation according to the degree of economic development of a society, and in any society it has economic consequences relevant to the desirability of given enforcement systems. But such consequences are not the justifying reason for recognizing or upholding the rights themselves.

By contrast, Posner's thesis holds that a given allocation or distribution of *any* rights whatsoever is justifiable only by the criterion of economic efficiency to the end of wealth-maximization.

45. It was originally written as a paper for a seminar organized in 1977 at the University of York by Professor C.K. Rowley on behalf of the (British) Social Science Research Council.

46. R. POSNER, ECONOMIC ANALYSIS OF LAW (1974).

47. Coase, *The Problem of Social Cost*, 3 J.L. AND ECON. 1 (1960).

48. Demsetz, *Wealth Distribution and the Ownership of Rights*, 1 J. LEGAL STUD. 223 (1972); Demsetz, WHEN DOES THE RULE OF LIABILITY MATTER?, 1 J. LEGAL STUD. 13 (1972).

49. My acquaintance was initially formed through Charles Fried's *Right and Wrong*, *see* C. FRIED, RIGHT AND WRONG 86-105 (1978), and an unpublished paper given by Dr. J.M. Finnis in Edinburgh. *See also* J.W. HARRIS, LEGAL PHILOSOPHIES 42-47 (1981) (and references therein).

Moreover, if I understand his and Coase's case correctly, such efficiency is established by reference to the optimal outcome of some ideal bargaining procedure.

In so far as such a supposed bargaining procedure is essential to the theory, it appears incoherent. The concept of a "bargain" requires at least two presuppositions: (a) that a promisee has a right to a promised performance (for otherwise there could be no idea of *binding* bargains, *i.e.*, mutual exchanges of binding promises); and (b) that persons have rights to security from physical and psychological assaults and acts of coercion, respect for which in any bargaining situation is a precondition of the validity of the bargain struck.

If E.A.L. does rest upon ideal bargains, it presupposes at least these "natural" rights. If E.A.L. then claims also to justify *these* rights it commits the fallacy of begging the question. If E.A.L. purports to be a complete theory of law, but fails to include in its explanation the rights which it presupposes, it commits the alternative fallacy of *ignoratio elenchi*. In either case, it is obliged to restrict its pretensions to its performance.[50]

A useful restriction might be a reformulation of E.A.L. as a theory of "adventitious" rights, including the forms of remedial right established by legal systems. This seems conformable to the observation that much of the most striking critical work of the economic analysts has been achieved in the area sketched somewhat amateurishly in the concluding section of my paper.

Be that as it may, Adam Smith's theory of law differs from E.A.L. in that it contains three distinct elements: (a) a theory of justice, that is, a moral theory of the rights the law ought to uphold; (b) an outline of an analytical theory of law, in the unsatisfactory "sovereign command" mode; and (c) a theory of the economic conditions and consequences of various kinds of legal order. Smith did not suppose, nor is there any reason to suppose, that the first of these can be subordinated to or derived from the third.

50. This argument is, in shortened form, essentially the same as Fried's. *See* C. FRIED, *supra* note 49, at 100-05.

[11]

New light on Adam Smith's Glasgow lectures on Jurisprudence

Ronald L. Meek

I

We now possess two separate sets of student's notes of Adam Smith's lectures on Jurisprudence at Glasgow University: the set published by Cannan in 1896[1] which, as now appears probable, relates to the course delivered in the 1763–64 session;[2] and the recently discovered set, soon to be published, which specifically relates to the course delivered in the 1762–63 session.[3] From these two sets of notes, taken together, we are now able to obtain a fairly accurate picture of what the Jurisprudence section of Smith's lectures to his Moral Philosophy class must have been like during his last two years at Glasgow.

But Smith's appointment as a professor at Glasgow dated from 1751—eleven years before the delivery of the earlier of the two courses in respect of which we possess student's notes. What were his Jurisprudence lectures like, then, in the first years of his teaching career at Glasgow? The information about this which has come down to us—most of it contained in Dugald Stewart's *Biographical Memoir* of Smith[4]—has so far been distressingly meagre and vague. We have the famous account of "Mr. Smith's lectures while a Professor at Glasgow" with which John Millar supplied Stewart in the early 1790's.[5] We have the intriguing extract quoted by Stewart from "a

RONALD MEEK is *Tyler Professor of Economics at the University of Leicester.*

1. Edwin Cannan (ed.), *Lectures on Justice, Police, Revenue and Arms, Delivered in the University of Glasgow by Adam Smith* (Oxford, 1896).

2. See R. L. Meek and A. S. Skinner, "The Development of Adam Smith's Ideas on the Division of Labour," *Economic Journal* 83 (1973): 1096–97.

3. The new notes are being edited by Professor D. Raphael, Professor P. Stein, and myself, for publication in Glasgow University's bicentennial edition of Smith's *Works and Correspondence*.

4. Dugald Stewart, *Biographical Memoir of Adam Smith*, Kelley reprint (New York, 1966). The original version of this *Memoir* was read by Stewart at the Royal Society of Edinburgh on 21 January and 18 March 1793.

5. Ibid., pp. 10–13.

short manuscript drawn up by Mr. Smith in the year 1755."[6] We have Stewart's statement about the "considerable change" which the plan of Smith's lectures underwent during his last four years at Glasgow, after the publication of *The Theory of Moral Sentiments* in 1759.[7] And that is just about all. The rest is virtually silence. This awkward gap in our knowledge about the early development of Smith's ideas has had to be filled by speculation and conjecture, and a number of crucial questions have remained unsolved. For example, to what extent did Smith, at the outset, base his Moral Philosophy course on Francis Hutcheson's? What role, in the early years, did "economics" play in his course, and at what point exactly was it brought in? Did he use the four-stages theory in his early lectures, or was this theory a later importation, derivative rather than original? We have all tried to make educated guesses about such questions as these, but only the boldest of us have dared to lay any claim to certainty.

The new document which it is the main purpose of this article to present does enable us, I think, to approach just a little closer to certainty on these issues than has hitherto been possible. The document consists of a set of notes, discovered in the Commonplace Book of a professorial colleague of Smith's, which appear to me to be selective extracts from a student's notes of a relatively early version of Smith's Jurisprudence lectures. When read together with the 1762–63 and Cannan notes, these extracts cast a certain amount of new light on the development of Smith's thought during his Glasgow period, and, in particular, on the three specific questions mentioned in the preceding paragraph.

The professorial colleague concerned was the celebrated John Anderson;[8] and the discovery of this set of notes in his Commonplace Book was made in July 1970 by Mr. A. H. Brown, now of St. Antony's College, Oxford. Mr. Brown was at that time working on Semyon Desnitsky, the noted Russian jurist and social thinker, who came to Glasgow University as a student in 1761 and who upon his return to Russia made good use of what he had learned at Glasgow

6. Ibid., pp. 67–68.

7. Ibid., p. 42. "After the publication of the *Theory of Moral Sentiments*," says Stewart, "Mr. Smith remained four years at Glasgow. . . . During that time, the plan of his lectures underwent a considerable change. His ethical doctrines, of which he had now published so valuable a part, occupied a much smaller portion of the course than formerly; and accordingly, his attention was naturally directed to a more complete illustration of the principles of Jurisprudence and of Political Economy."

8. On Anderson, see J. Muir, *John Anderson and the College He Founded* (Glasgow, 1950), and D. Murray, *Memories of the Old College of Glasgow* (Glasgow, 1927), pp. 113–19 and 379–93.

from Smith and Millar.[9] During his period of study at Glasgow Desnitsky had an altercation with John Anderson,[10] and Mr. Brown therefore spent some time going through the Anderson papers at Strathclyde University to see whether there was anything in them which might throw light on this incident. It was then that he found a set of notes in Anderson's Commonplace Book which seemed to him to bear an interesting resemblance to Adam Smith's lectures on Jurisprudence as reported in the 1762–63 and Cannan notes. My own initial reaction, when Mr. Brown told me of this discovery, was one of scepticism; and it was only some time later, after I had become rather more familiar with the 1762–63 notes and had studied the Anderson notes more carefully,[11] that I came round to the view that Mr. Brown's original intuition was well founded.

Anderson's Commonplace Book is bound in three octavo volumes. Each volume contains approximately 370 pages, numbered in pencil, the great majority of which are completely unused. The entries include (in addition to the set of notes with which we are mainly concerned here) a number of remarks on scientific subjects, comments on several recently published books, "*pensées*" on assorted topics, and (in Volume III) a number of observations on France written on the occasion of a visit to that country. The question of the dating of these entries will be considered in more detail below, in the second section of the present article: all that needs to be said at this juncture is that the last item in Volume III is specifically dated 1755, and that one's general impression is that the majority of the shorter comments, "*pensées*," etc. in Volumes I and II were probably written between 1753 and 1755. The set of notes in which we are interested appears at the back of Volume I on pp. 292–368, *starting on p. 368* (i.e., the notes are written, as it were, upside down).

The notes are reproduced in full at the end of this article, prefaced by an explanation of the conventions which I have adopted in editing them. There seems to be nothing in the form or presentation of the notes which is inconsistent with the hypothesis that they were selec-

9. On Desnitsky, see W. R. Scott, *Adam Smith as Student and Professor* (Glasgow, 1937), pp. 158 n. and 424 ff.; A. H. Brown, "S. E. Desnitsky, Adam Smith and the *Nakaz* of Catherine II," in *Oxford Slavonic Papers*, New Series, vol. 7, 1974; and A. H. Brown, "Adam Smith's First Russian Followers," in *Essays on Adam Smith*, ed. A. S. Skinner and T. Wilson (Clarendon Press, Oxford, 1975).

10. Mr. Brown tells the story in his article "Adam Smith's First Russian Followers," ibid.

11. I am extremely grateful to Mr. C. G. Wood, librarian of the Andersonian Library, University of Strathclyde, and to Mrs. E. Frame, sublibrarian, who gave me facilities for studying the notes and have been generous in providing me with other relevant material and information about Anderson.

tive extracts made by Anderson from a student's notes of *some* course of lectures (leaving aside for a moment the question of *which* course). There are indeed certain indications which could reasonably be regarded as positively suggesting this. The misspelling (p. 30)[12] "Colvin" for Kolben[13] and that of "course" for "courts" (p. 10), for example, look very much as if they may have had their origin in lecture-room mishearings. In a number of places the corrections made by Anderson (e.g., the deletion of repetitions on pp. 5, 11, 22, and 28) seem to suggest that he is copying from another document. In other places (more particularly in the first few pages) they seem to suggest that he is making an effort to improve the language and style of an imperfect original. Occasionally, it would appear, Anderson adds his own comments—as on p. 5 (where he makes this clear by his use of the words "My own"); on p. 12 (where the reference to "Mr. Hume's Essay" may possibly be his); and on p. 36 (where the reference to "Mr. Wallace" is very probably his).[14]

Let us now try to test the hypothesis that the notes had their origin in an early version of Smith's Jurisprudence lectures. For fairly obvious reasons this hypothesis is not at all an easy one to test. The basic comparison which it would seem most useful to make in this connection, at any rate in the first instance, is between the Anderson notes and the 1762–63 notes. Now the latter consist of a very long and reliable set of student's notes of the major part of Smith's Jurisprudence lectures in the 1762–63 session, based in all probability on shorthand notes taken down by the student in class and subsequently transcribed, whereas the former, if the hypothesis is correct, consist of a very short set of summarized extracts made by Anderson some time in the early or middle 1750's from notes of Smith's lectures taken down by a student about whose note-taking ability and methods very

12. This page reference and the similar ones which follow are to the pages of the Anderson manuscript, renumbered in accordance with a scheme described in the note which precedes the reproduction of the manuscript at the end of this article. The point where a new page of the manuscript (as so numbered) begins is indicated in the reproduction by an appropriate arabic italic numeral in square brackets.

13. The supposed "History of Africa" by "Colvin" mentioned on p. 30 of the notes would seem almost certainly to have been in fact a then very well-known book on the Cape of Good Hope by Peter Kolben (or Kolb), of which an English translation (*The Present State of the Cape of Good-Hope*) appeared in 1731. The peculiar custom which is referred to in the notes appears to be that described by Kolben on pp. 119–24 of Volume I of the translation. The beating (and/or abuse) of the mother by the son, it is true, occurs according to Kolben not after the father's death, as stated in the notes, but after the son's ceremonial induction into the society of men. The use by Kolben of the word "milk-sop" (p. 122), however, would seem to establish the connection pretty decisively.

14. Cf. pp. 455–56 of this article, below, and n.32.

little can be surmised. In view of this appreciable difference in the probable nature, origin, and date of the two documents, we could hardly expect to find—and in fact we do not find—a high degree of conformity between individual words and expressions, the construction of individual sentences, etc. We must therefore seek mainly for other types of conformity, asking ourselves, for example, whether the sequence of points in a significant number of chains of reasoning is more or less the same in both documents whether the same unusual or idiosyncratic arguments and illustrations are employed at key points in both; and whether the order of treatment of the different topics is more or less the same in both documents taken as a whole. And of these types of conformity, it is clear, we would have to be able to find a relatively large number before we could regard our hypothesis as confirmed. By a stroke of luck of a kind which is rarely vouchsafed to Smith scholars, this condition can in fact be fulfilled. For the hypothesis *not* to be correct, I believe, it would be necessary to postulate either the existence of some common literary source which has managed to escape the attention of all workers in this field, or the accumulation of a quite unbelievable number of coincidences.

As an example, let us take the long passage in the Anderson notes headed "Of Slaves," which begins halfway down p. 30 of the manuscript and ends at the foot of p. 35. A paragraph-by-paragraph comparison of this passage with the corresponding parts of the section on slavery in Volume III of the 1762–63 lecture notes[15] yields the following results:[16]

ANDERSON NOTES Of Slaves.	*1762–63 LECTURE NOTES* (Volume III)
Many causes of slavery—by way of punishment—in order to pay debt—but above all by war.—No humanity to prisoners of war, of old. If they did not kill them they thought them their property, and this the greatest origin of slavery.	I shall now observe the different methods in which slaves might be acquired in those countries where it has been in use.—The 1st, captives taken in war. . . . When the conqueror has got his enemy into his power there is then no one to pro-

15. In the Cannan notes, the relevant passages (with which a similar comparison may be made) appear on pp. 94–104 of the published version.

16. The extracts from the Anderson notes are printed exactly as they appear in the reproduction of the whole document at the end of this article, but with page numbers and textual notes omitted. The extracts from the 1762–63 lecture notes are printed more or less as they will appear in the published version, with page numbers inserted at appropriate intervals, but with textual and editorial notes omitted. In both cases the punctuation and capitalization have been cleaned up, but otherwise the reproductions are as close as possible to the original manuscripts. For an explanation of what the different kinds of brackets and braces mean, see the note of conventions which precedes the text of the Anderson notes, below.

—Slavery could not be introduced in a polished age, and all countries were at first rude.—In the heroick ages slaves were happy; in polished ages not so. In the first state, the slave eat and wrought with his master, and there subsisted an intimacy between them. In the last state, they were removed from the sight of their masters and therefore cruelly used. At present there is more sympathy between a farmer and his servant, than between a duke and his footman. And as the blacks seem not from their skin {to partake of the same nature with the whites, the imagination of a barbarous white supposes him not to be of the same nature with himself and therefore uses him ill with less scruple.} (Aristotle spends some ⟨?time⟩ in proving that a slave can have no virtue.) To be a slave in a despotic government is no worse than to be a freeman—see Montesquiou.

tect him; his life and all he has he owes to the mercy of his conqueror if he inclines to spare him. He is reckoned to belong intirely to the conqueror, in recompence for his delivery. . . . This seems to have been the originall introduction of slaves, and was universally received amongs⟨t⟩ all the early nations. . . . 3^{d} method is when criminalls are adjudged to slavery. Slavery is a punishment often inflicted on criminalls. . . . 4th is that by which insolvent debtors were adjudged or given over to their creditors (pp. 144–46). We may observe here that the state of slavery is a much more tollerable one in a [a] poor and barbarous people than in a rich and polished one. . . . In a poor country there can be no great difference betwixt the master and the slave in any respect. They will eat at the same table, work together, and be cloathed in the same manner, and will be alike in every other particular. In a rich country the disproportion betwixt them will be prodigious in all these respects. This dis⟨pro⟩portion will make the rich men much more sev⟨e⟩r⟨e⟩ to their slaves than the poorer ones. A man of great fortune, a nobleman, is much farther removed from the condition of his servant than a farmer. The farmer generally works along with his servant; they eat together, and are little different. The disproportion betwixt them, the condition of the nobleman and his servant, is so great that he will hardly look on him as being of the same kind; he thinks he has little title even to the ordinary enjoyments of life, and feels but little for his misfortunes. . . . The more arbitrary the government is in like manner the slaves are in the better condition, and the freer the people the more miserable are the slaves. . . . (pp. 105–10).

A slave in Rome had no religion, i.e., he did not share in the publick worship; he was considered in the same light with the cattle of his proprietor. Hence of old, see Tacitus, etc., it was common for the slaves to become Jews, as they held there was an universal deity, whereas in the heathen religion every deity had a particular province and there was no deity allotted for the slaves.

Slaves were admitted to no religious society and were reckond profane. . . . Each city had its peculiar deities. Minerva presided over Athens; Rome was under the protection of Mars and Jupiter who dwelt in the Capitoll. These were supposed to favour only their particular people. What had Jupiter who dwelt in the Capitoll to do with a slave who came from Syria or Cappadocia. . . . Their masters prayed for their thriving and multiplying in the same manner as for their cattle. . . . This it was which made all religions which taught the being of one supreme and universall god, who presided over all, be so greedily received by this order of men. Even the Jewish religion, which is of all others least adapted to make conquests, was greedily received by them. . . . Tacitus and [blank in MS] tell us that a great part hominum servilis et libertinae conditionis were greatly addicted to the Jewish religion (pp. 96–99).

We never hear of the insurrection of slaves in Persia, etc.

We see accordingly that no absolute monarch was ever in danger from the ⟨?slaves⟩, neither the Mogulls country, Persia modern or ancient, nor Turky, etc. ever were (pp. 104–5).

In Tyre, Carthage, and Lacedaemon the people lived well ⟨?compared⟩ to their slaves.—The Germans armed their slaves.

In the same manner Carthage, Tyre, Lacedemon, etc. were all in danger from their slaves (p. 104). Amongst the old Germans and others, as Tacitus tells, they were used with the greatest possible humanity (p. 106).

Corruptions bring on their own remedies.—The common law and not Christianity suppressed slavery—it was not abolished by humanity or the improvement of manners—but as the slaves were armed by their lords and so dangerous to the king, the king abolished

The circumstances which have made slavery be abolished in the corner of Europe in which it now is are peculiar to it, and which happening to concur at the same time have brought about that change. . . The clergy . . . promoted greatly the emancipation of the villains.

slavery.—Slavery subsisted under the emperours after Christianity was the popular religion.—The cannon law supposes slavery.—Slavery still subsists in Muscovy which is a Christian country.

The slaves . . . made the chief body of the soldier⟨s⟩ in these times, and in them the power of their superiors consisted. The kings interest also led him on this account to lessen the authority of the nobles and their vassalls over their villains (pp. 117–19). But we are not to imagine the temper of the Christian religion is necessarily contrary to slavery. The masters in our colonies are Christians, and yet slavery is allowed amongst them. The Constan⟨t⟩inopolitan emperors were very jealous Christians, and yet never thought of abolishing slavery. There are also many Christian countries where slavery is tollerated at this time (pp. 127–28). The Zars of Muscovy have very great power, yet slavery is still in use. . . (p. 122).

Our salters and colliers differ much from slaves. They can have property and consequently families; they can buy their liberty; the price of their labour is fixed by law; they are punished by law—that is, they are only confined to one trade and one master, the first of which was the state of the antient Egyptians.

The colliers in this manner have a great many of the priviledges of free men; their lives are under the protection of the laws as others; their property is also insured to them; and their liberty is not alltogether taken away. They have the benefit of marriage and the exercise of religion. So that they are no way restricted more than other men, excepting that they are bound to exercise a certain business and in a certain place. And this has been the case with many other persons who thought themselves free. . . . The old Aegyptians, who never thought themselves in any respect slaves, were after the time of Sesostris obliged in like manner to adhere to ⟨the⟩ exercise of their forefathers business (p. 128).

Were our salters and colliers put upon the same footing with other labourers, it would be much better for their masters.—When men are constrained to work for another they will not work so hard as if at

This immoderate price of labour in these works would soon fall if the masters of them would set their colliers and salters at liberty, and open the work to all free men. . . (p. 129). This work indeed, being

liberty—this is manifest in quarrying and other mines. In the Newcastle mines work is done cheaper than in this country. In this country a collier and salter can earn more than a quarrier or any other labourer who works as hard.—In the mines of Silesia, the miners go voluntary below ground and live there for years.

somewhat more dissagreable and more hazardous than others of the same sort, they might perhaps require wages somewhat higher, but this would not come above 8^{d} or 9^{d}; so that a collier has now about 4 times the wages he would have were the work open to all men. But notwithstanding of this high wages we see the colliers frequently run off from the works in this country to those about Newcastle, where they will not earn above 13^{d} or 14^{d} a day as the work is open; but we never saw any come from Newcastle here (p. 130).

Attempts to introduce agrarian laws, and the abolition of debts, were the sources of constant disorder in antient states, and are quite unknown in the modern.—The cause of this slavery—for as in every great town the inhabitants are either gentlemen or work hard, a man that has no land can get subsistence only by his labour; but of old the slaves were mechanicks and not freemen, and therefore the freemen who had no lands in Rome, Athens, etc. were entirely dependent on the great for their living—and the great were liberal, as the people had the disposal of all places.

We are told by Aristotle and Cicero that the two sources of all seditions at Athens and at Rome were the demands of the people for an agrarian law or an abolition of debts. This was no doubt a demand of the taking away so much of ones property and giving it to those to whom it did not belong. We never hear of any such demands as these at this time. . . . The poor people now who have neither a land estate nor any fortune in money, can gain a livelyhood by working as a servant to a farmer in the country, or by working to any tradesman whose business they understand. But at Rome the whole business was engrossed by the slaves, and the poor citizens who had neither an estate in land nor a fortune in money were in a very miserable condition; there was no business to which they could apply themselves with any hopes of success. The only means of support they had was either from the generall largesses which were made to them, or by the money they got for their votes at elections (pp. 141–42).

It will be seen that almost every point made in this relatively long section of the Anderson notes has its direct counterpart in the

1762–63 notes; that the language in which the points are expressed, although never exactly the same, is often much more similar than we might reasonably have expected; and that after the first paragraph of the Anderson notes the order of treatment of the different topics is more or less the same in both documents. Given the probability that Smith when delivering his lectures trusted at any rate to some extent to "extemporary elocution,"[17] and remembering that we are comparing a very full set of lecture notes with what is at the best a collection of summarized extracts from another (and probably much earlier) set of lecture notes, the degree of conformity revealed by this comparison must surely be regarded as very high indeed.

As another example, let us take the two references to Montesquieu on p. 26 of the Anderson notes. The first of these, which relates to Montesquieu's argument that since in hot climates women are married very young and are old at twenty it is natural that in such places polygamy should be introduced, reads as follows:

> See Montesquiou, B xvi, ch 2^{d}—et que la polygamie s'introduise. Suppose the fact true, it will only follow that he ought to take another but not that polygamy ought to be established.—But the fact is not true.—Intemperance in love indeed makes the easterns fond of very young women, as rapes are committed in London upon children five years old—but Cleopatra had a child at 40.—

The corresponding passage in the 1762–63 lecture notes is the following:

> It is ascerted also as an argument in favours of polygamy that in the warmer climates the women loose there beauty much sooner than they do in this country, and that at the time when their beauty [and] would render them fit to be the object of affection their weakness and youth render them all together unfit for being the objects of his confidence and proper to be put on an equall ⟨?footing⟩, as this time is past before the other comes. And on the other hand when their sense and experience would render ⟨them⟩ fit for this, their want of beauty and incapacity of bearing children counterballance it. They tell us that the women in those countries ripen much sooner than in the northern ones, that they are fit for marriage by 7 or 8 and leave bearing children in 20th or thereabouts. Now this fact is not better ascertained than the

17. John Millar reported to Dugald Stewart that Smith, in delivering his lectures, "trusted almost entirely to extemporary elocution" (Dugald Stewart, *Biographical Memoir of Adam Smith*, p. 13). Other accounts, however, are not entirely consistent with this.

former. We are told indeed that they have children by 11 or 12 years of age, and so would many women in this country as well as in the southern ones. It is said that Mahomet married his wife [blank in MS] at 5 and lived with her at 8. But this has probably been no more than the rape of an infant, which are but too common in more northern climates. On the other hand there is no certainty that they cease to bear children nearly as soon as is alledged. We find that Cleopatra, an Aegyptian, at the age of 36 when the women are past the prime of their beauty even in this country, had charms enough to retain Antony, a man generally very fickle, so as to bring on a separation with Octavia and his ruin; and about a year before this she had born a child. . . . But altho it was realy the case that the time in which a woman was capable of bearing children and being a proper companion for a man was limited to betwixt twelve and 20, this would not at all require the establishment of polygamy. It might indeed require voluntary divorce, that the husband, after the woman was incapable of being a proper companion for him, should have it in his power to put her away and take another, but it could never require that he should have more than one who were fit wives at the same time.[18]

It will be seen that in this passage all the arguments and illustrations that are briefly summarized in Anderson's extract duly appear and take their proper place. Remembering once again the very different nature of the two documents which we are comparing, the degree of conformity revealed in this comparison must be regarded as high.

The same is true in the case of the second reference to Montesquieu on p. 26, which relates to the latter's argument that if in a particular country there is a large surplus of women over men (as, allegedly, at Bantam in Java) this might be taken as justifying polygamy. Anderson's short summary reads as follows:

B. xvi, ch. 4. This opinion seems to be ill founded, for the births are not kept regularly in Asia.—Meaco is a capital.—It is filled with saraglios.—In Scotland if the people were numbered there wd be found more males in the kingdom than females.—

The corresponding passage in the 1762–63 lecture notes is the following:

It is advanced indeed in favours of polygamy by Montesquieu on the authority of [blank in MS] that at Bantam, the capitall of the

18. 1762–63 notes, Vol. III, pp. 37–40. Cf. the Cannan notes, published version, pp. 83–84.

island Java, there are 10 women born for one man; and a Dutch author tells us that on the coast of Guinea there are 50 women for one man. In Europe we are certain that the proportion is very different. It is generally thought that ⟨there⟩ are about 12 women to 13 men, and others say that there are about 16 to 17, and that proportion appears certainly to be hereabouts from the bills of mortality which are kept in different parts of Europe. . . . We are told that at Macao, the capitall of Japan, when the inhabitants were numbered there were found about 11 women to 9 men. . . . This fact we are indeed pretty well assured of, as it was found so on a publick numbering of the people. But then it does not even establish that there was so great a disproportion as it appears to do. For we are to consider that as this was the capitall of the country, in which the head man of their religion resided who alone had 500 or 600 wives, and many other rich men who would no doubt have considerable numbers, there would be collected here a number of women who might well be supposed to make this disproportion, altho in the other parts of the country they were born in the same proportion as in Europe, which is very probable. This is the only fact which is well attested, for we have never heard of any bills of mortality being kept in those countries of which this is related.[19]

Then again, take the account on pp. 19–20 of the Anderson notes of *fur manifestus* and *fur non manifestus* (manifest and nonmanifest thieves), which involves yet another reference to Montesquieu—this time to his statement that "Lycurgus, with a view of rendering the citizens dexterous and cunning, ordained that children should be practised in thieving, and that those who were caught in the act should be severely whipped."[20] Anderson's extract reads as follows:

Fur manifestus and non manifestus. Vide L'Esprit des Loix, an ingenious account but it seems not to be just.

For it does not appear that the Lacedaemonians were allowed to steal any thing but provisions from the publick table. Vide Plutarch.—And there was this distinction between the fur man. and non man. among all nations which is owing to this, that there is a greater hatred against the criminal if taken immediately than if afterwards or if his punishment is delayed—rubra manu among the Romans, taken in the fang among the Scotch.—

19. 1762–63 notes, Vol. II, pp. 34–37. Cf. the Cannan notes, pp. 81–83.
20. Montesquieu, *The Spirit of Laws*, Hafner ed. (New York, 1949), 2:163.

The corresponding passage in the 1762–63 lecture notes is the following:

> Amongst the Romans theft was punished with the restitution of double of the thing stolen, with this distinction, that if the thief was caught with the thing stolen about him he was to restore ⟨?four⟩ fo[u]ld, and two fold if he was not caught in the fact: in the fang or not in the fang (as it is expressed in the Scots law⟨)⟩ and in the Latin writers fur manifestus et nec manifestus. It will be proper to take the more notice of this, as the reason of it does not appear to be very evident, and that which is alledged by Montesquieu, tho very ingenious, does not appear to me to be the true one. He says that this law was borrowed from the Lacedemonians, who, as they traind their youth chiefly to the military art, encouraged them in theft, as it was imagined this might sharpen their wit and skill in the stratagems of war. Theft therefore was as they suppose not ⟨?at⟩ all discouraged amongst them, but rather honoured if it was not discovered before it was finished; but when the thief was discovered it was looked on as a disgrace, as being not cleverly performed. . . . But this does not appear probable in any part. For in the 1st place there is no good ground for imagining that the Lacedemonians encouraged theft. This is conjectured from some passages of [blank in MS], particularly one where he tells that there was a table kept at the publick charge for the old men of the city, but none for the younger men. They however were encouraged to pourloin for themselves what they could from the table, for the reason above assigned. This however is very different from what is properly denominated theft, which was not at all encouraged. . . . Punishment is always adapted originally to the resentment of the injured person; now the resentment of a person against the thief when he is caught in the fact ⟨?is greater⟩ than when he is only discovered afterwards and the theft must be proved against him, which gives the persons resentment time to cooll. The satisfaction he requires is much greater in the former than in the latter case. We see too that there was the same odds made in the punishment of other crimes. The murderer who was caught *rubro manu* was punished much more severely than he against whom the murder was afterwards proven.[21]

21. 1762–63 notes, Vol. II, p. 150. Cf. the Cannan notes, p. 147.

Once again there is the same kind of parallel between the two passages, and the degree of conformity seems much too close to be merely accidental.

And so one may go through the Anderson notes picking out many other passages of which there are close parallels in the 1762–63 notes[22]—and also of course in the Cannan notes,[23] and (occasionally) in the *Wealth of Nations*.[24] Naturally there are not only resemblances but also differences: and some of the latter (notably those discussed below) are of considerable interest and importance. But when one compares, for example, the sections in the Anderson notes on testaments, marriage and divorce, criminal law, and the origin of government with the corresponding sections in the 1762–63 and Cannan notes, the differences appear to be mainly in detail, ordering, and illustration rather than in fundamental approach. And even when the differences are major rather than minor—as, most notably, in the analysis of prices and money—a greater number of echoes of the Anderson version are in fact to be found in the 1762–63 and Cannan notes than might appear at first glance.[25]

For reasons of space, I shall not document any more of these parallels at this juncture, but proceed immediately to a comparison of the *order* in which the different individual subjects are treated in the Anderson notes (taking them as a whole) and in the 1762–63 notes. One preliminary point that has to be appreciated here is that the order of the main topics in the 1762–63 notes is radically different from their

22. Cf., e.g., the first paragraph on p. 4 of the Anderson notes with pp. 93–94 of Vol. I of the 1762–63 notes; the paragraph beginning "Of mankind . . ." on p. 36 of the Anderson notes with pp. 132–33 of Vol. III of the 1762–63 notes; and the last paragraph on p. 38 of the Anderson notes with pp. 36–38 of Vol. IV of the 1762–63 notes.

23. Cf., e.g., the first two sentences on p. 14 of the Anderson notes with the sentence beginning "In the same manner . . ." on p. 252 of the Cannan notes; the last paragraph on p. 23 of the Anderson notes with p. 75 of the Cannan notes; p. 25 of the Anderson notes with pp. 80–81 of the Cannan notes; and the comment on the exposure of children on p. 28 of the Anderson notes with the similar comment at the foot of p. 104 of the Cannan notes.

24. Cf., e.g., the statement on p. 12 of the Anderson notes that "Locke, Montesquiou, and Law think that the lowness of interest is owing to the plenty of money" with the statement in Book II, ch. IV of the *Wealth of Nations* that "Mr. Locke, Mr. Law, and Mr. Montesquieu . . . seem to have imagined that the increase of the quantity of gold and silver, in consequence of the discovery of the Spanish West Indies, was the real cause of the lowering of the rate of interest through the greater part of Europe."

25. Cf., e.g., pp. 7–8 of the Anderson notes with some of the comments on pp. 79–84 of Vol. II and pp. 71–75 and 119–24 of Vol. VI of the 1762–63 notes, and pp. 134, 176–77, and 188–89 of the Cannan notes.

order in the Cannan notes. Near the beginning of the latter, it will be remembered, the student reports Smith as saying:

> The civilians begin with considering government and then treat of property and other rights. Others who have written on this subject begin with the latter and then consider family and civil government. There are several advantages peculiar to each of these methods, though that of the civil law seems upon the whole preferable.[26]

In what follows in the Cannan notes—which, as I have already said, probably relate to the course delivered in the 1763–64 session—Smith duly adopts the method of "the civil law." In his 1762–63 course, however, it is clear from the recently discovered notes that he had adopted the alternative method, beginning with "property and other rights" and then going on to consider "family and civil government."

The sequence in which the different individual subjects are treated (within this broad framework) in the 1762–63 notes is set out in Table 1, side by side with a list of the pages on which the corresponding subjects are dealt with in the Anderson notes.

Table 1. Sequence of corresponding topics

Sequence of Topics in 1762–63 Lecture Notes	Pages in Anderson Notes on Which Corresponding Subjects are Dealt With
1. General	1
2. Property (including testaments)	1–6
3. Contract	7–14
4. Criminal law	15–22
5. Husband and wife	23–27
6. Parent and child	27–30
7. Master and servant	30–36
8. Government	37–39
9. Police	39

It will be seen that the sequence of the subjects in the two documents is almost exactly the same.[27] There are of course considerable differences in the relative amounts of space devoted to the different

26. Cannan notes, p. 8.

27. It will be observed that in the table I have juxtaposed pp. 7–14 of the Anderson notes (containing the main "economic" passages) with the "Contract" section of the 1762–63 notes. This procedure will be more fully justified in the third section of this article, below.

subjects in the two documents—notably in the case of "Police," where Anderson has extracted only two sentences from the student's notes. And there is another difference of much greater significance—namely, that in the Anderson notes the "economic" sections dealing with prices, money, interest, etc., are located round about the middle of the first half of the document, sandwiched between the sections dealing with testaments and those dealing with injuries, whereas in the 1762–63 notes almost all of the corresponding "economic" subjects are dealt with under the heading "Police" in the final part of the document.[28] This difference will be further discussed below: in the meantime, let us simply note that the close correspondence in the order in which the different subjects are treated in the two documents, when coupled with the high degree of conformity in the content of many passages, strongly suggests that the Anderson notes, like the 1762–63 notes, had their origin in lectures on Jurisprudence given by Adam Smith.

II

The next question to be discussed is that of the *dating* of the particular course of lectures to which the Anderson notes relate.

Smith was elected to the chair of Logic at Glasgow University on 9 January 1751 and admitted on 16 January, but he did not start teaching at the University until the beginning of the next academic session, in October 1751. In the 1751–52 session he not only lectured to his Logic class (mainly, it appears, on Rhetoric and Belles Lettres) but also gave some lectures on "natural jurisprudence and politics" to the Moral Philosophy class, the work of which (because of the illness of the then professor of Moral Philosophy, Thomas Craigie) was in that session shared out among "several masters." In November 1751 Craigie died, and a few months later Smith was translated from his chair of Logic to the now vacant chair of Moral Philosophy, being elected on 22 April 1752 and admitted on 29 April. His first *full* course of lectures to the Moral Philosophy class, therefore, was delivered in the 1752–53 session.[29]

28. It is probable, of course, that in the lectures from which the Anderson notes were derived various other "economic" matters were discussed under the heading "Police." But if we can assume that the order of the different subjects in the Anderson notes reflects their order in these lectures (which there seems no reason to doubt), it remains true—and very important—that prices, money, and interest were discussed *not* under the heading "Police" but under some other and earlier heading.

29. The facts in this paragraph have been derived from W. R. Scott, pp. 66–67 and 137–40; John Rae, *Life of Adam Smith* (London, 1895), pp. 42–46; and the minutes of University Meetings in the Glasgow University Archives. Special attention should be

For a number of reasons, most of which will become apparent below, it seems highly improbable that the Anderson notes relate to the courses which Smith gave in 1762–63 or 1763–64—the two sessions in respect of which we possess fairly full and reliable students' notes of his Jurisprudence lectures. Nor does it really seem at all likely that the Anderson notes relate to the lectures which Smith gave at Edinburgh before coming to Glasgow. It is at least possible, however, that they may relate to the lectures on "natural jurisprudence and politics" which he gave to Craigie's class in the 1751–52 session.[30] Thus the range of possible dates is quite a wide one: the relevant lectures *could* have been given in any one of the sessions during the period from 1751–52 to 1761–62. And when one tries to identify the particular session concerned, one soon comes face to face with a number of difficulties of an extraordinarily frustrating character.

Let us consider first the internal evidence in the Anderson notes themselves. These notes contain, as we have seen, a number of references to Montesquieu's *The Spirit of Laws*, which appeared in 1748. There is a mention of "Mr. Hume's Essay," in a context which suggests that it is the essay *Of Interest*—first published in 1752—which is being referred to.[31] There is also a mention of "Mr.

drawn to the minutes of the University Meeting held on 11 September 1751, which to my knowledge have not been previously noticed, and which cast a certain amount of additional light on the content of Smith's lectures to the Moral Philosophy class in the 1751–52 session. The Meeting decided that in Craigie's absence the teaching should be shared out as follows: "The Professor [of Divinity] undertakes to teach the Theologia Naturalis, and the first book of Mr. Hutchesons Ethicks, *and Mr. Smith the other two books de Jurisprudentia Naturali et Politicis*, and Mr. Rosse and Mr. Moor to teach the hour allotted for the private classe" (my italics).

30. Smith's lectures to Craigie's class (in which he no doubt used much of his Edinburgh material) did not include natural theology or ethics, whereas the full course which he began delivering in 1752–53 in his new capacity as professor of Moral Philosophy did include these subjects. The fact that the Anderson notes contain nothing on natural theology or ethics, therefore, may perhaps be regarded as a reason for considering the 1751–52 lectures as at least a *possible* source. But nothing can safely be deduced from the *absence* of anything in a set of notes like these; and there are other arguments, involving too many minutiae to be canvassed here, which tell in favor of a slightly later date than 1751–52.

31. The reference appears on p. 12 of the notes. Hume's essay *Of Interest* first appeared in a volume entitled *Political Discourses*, the publication date of which is given on the titlepage as 1752. If this volume did appear in 1752 it was probably very early in that year, and there is some evidence which suggests that it may in fact have appeared at the end of 1751. See on this question Jacob Viner, *Guide to John Rae's "Life of Adam Smith"* (New York, 1965), pp. 53–58. The comment in the notes which includes the reference to Hume's essay may well have been Anderson's own—in which case the only thing that necessarily follows is that *Anderson made his summary of the student's notes* after the appearance of Hume's essay.

Wallace," in a context which suggests that it is Robert Wallace's *Dissertation on the Numbers of Mankind in Antient and Modern Times*—first published in 1753—which is being referred to.[32] Rather more interesting, perhaps, is the fact that there are two specific page references in the notes,[33] which turn out to be to the first (English) edition of Francis Hutcheson's *Short Introduction to Moral Philosophy*, which appeared in 1747.[34] The interest arises because a second edition of this work, *in which the relevant pagination is different*, was published in 1753.[35] If this new edition had in fact been available at the time when the lectures were delivered, one might perhaps have expected Smith to have referred his students to it rather than to the earlier—and by then presumably rather scarce—edition. But this piece of evidence, although quite suggestive, is not of course by any means conclusive.

We must now go on to consider the other items in Anderson's Commonplace Book—at the back of Volume I of which, it will be recalled, the notes in which we are interested are to be found—to see whether dates can be attached to any of them. So far as Volume III is concerned there is no problem: all the entries consist of comments on France, evidently written during a period of residence in that country; and to a number of these entries Anderson himself has fixed specific

32. The reference appears on the left-hand page facing p. 36 of the notes, and the comment which includes it was very probably Anderson's own. At first glance it might seem rather unlikely that the "Mr. Wallace" referred to was Robert Wallace, since the statement in the text on p. 36 immediately opposite the comment refers to "the want of inhabitants in ancient nations, and where polygamy takes place," and Robert Wallace, as is well known, argues strongly in his *Dissertation* that there was not, in fact, any "want of inhabitants" in ancient nations. Wallace does recognize, however, that polygamy can have a deleterious effect on population; and he does endeavor to give reasons (including poverty and parental neglect, which are also mentioned on p. 36 of the Anderson notes) for what he regards as the relative scarcity of people in modern nations. Anderson's comment on the left-hand page, then, may plausibly be regarded as an attempt to put forward another reason, over and above those adduced by Wallace, for the lack of populousness in modern nations. It is perhaps worth noting that there is another reference to "Wallace" on p. 4 of Volume III of Anderson's Commonplace Book, where a note reads "See Wallace's Answer to L. Dun's Advices." This turns out to be a reference to a pamphlet by Robert Wallace entitled *The Doctrine of Passive Obedience and Non-resistance* which was published in Edinburgh in 1754. The only other point which needs to be added here is that there is no evidence to suggest that Smith himself, at this point in his lectures, made any reference to Wallace's *Dissertation*. Thus although Anderson could probably not have written his comment until after the appearance of the *Dissertation*, it is at least conceivable that Smith could have given the relevant lecture before its appearance.

33. They appear on pp. 3 and 5 of the notes.

34. The *Short Introduction* was an English translation of a work which Hutcheson originally published (in 1742) in Latin.

35. The passages quoted by Smith from pp. 156 and 172 of the first edition appear on pp. 147 and 162 respectively of the second edition.

dates, ranging from the middle of 1754[36] to December (*sic*) 1755.[37] In Volumes I and II, however, none of the entries is specifically dated, and it is rather difficult to ascribe even provisional dates to most of them. In Volume I there is a reference to Montesquieu in one of the entries,[38] which presumably shows that this entry could not have been written before 1748; and there are also some comments on Vernet's *Dialogues*, an English translation of which appeared in 1753.[39] The other items in Volume I—some miscellaneous comments on scientific subjects, and a note on the respective merits of different editions of Livy—do not seem to me to be datable with any degree of precision. Volume II begins with some observations on Anson's *A Voyage Round the World*, the edition concerned being described by Anderson as "2[d] Edit: London. 1748";[40] and the only other item in Volume II is a detailed scheme for the distribution of certain funds to Scottish ministers. One of the provisions of this scheme, however, is of some interest from the point of view of our present enquiry. After 1758, Anderson proposed, an individual who had not by then spent three years studying certain subjects at a university should not be eligible for a particular benefit. Read in its context, this statement would seem to indicate that the entry concerned was probably written round about 1753, or 1754 at the latest.

So far as these other items in the Commonplace Book are concerned, then, the three most important points which emerge are, first,

36. The earliest specific date—15 August 1754—appears on p. 13 of Volume III.

37. The date "December 1755" appears in the final entry in Volume III, which is written on the inside back cover. I am not quite sure, however, whether this entry was in fact written as late as December 1755, even though Anderson was very probably still in France at that time (see below, p. 459). It would seem at least possible from the context that the word "December," which is interpolated, was inserted at this point in error, and that the note was actually written (at Toulouse) at the beginning rather than the end of 1755. Since nothing hangs on this I shall not elaborate the point.

38. It appears on p. 15 of Volume I.

39. The comments appear on pp. 11–14 of Volume I. There is apparently some doubt about the date of publication of the first (French) edition of Jean Jacob Vernet's *Dialogues Socratiques*. One of the French biographical dictionaries which I have consulted states that the book was published in Paris in 1745, and with additions in 1755. Another, however, substitutes 1746 and 1756 for 1745 and 1755. The British Museum and the Bibliothèque Nationale hold only one edition, the titlepage of which states that it was published in Paris in 1754, but gives no indication of the number of the edition. However, the page references and actual quotations in Anderson's comment show clearly enough that he was in fact referring to an English translation of Vernet's book, entitled *Dialogues on Some Important Subjects*, which according to the titlepage was published in London in 1753.

40. The first edition of Anson's *A Voyage Round the World* was published in 1748. Copies of a second and third edition, both also dated 1748, are held by the British Museum.

that one of the entries in Volume I could not have been written before 1753; second, that one of the entries in Volume II was probably written not later than 1754; and third, that all the entries in Volume III were probably written between the middle of 1754 and some date in 1755. The general feeling one gets is that the period covered by these entries might well have been a relatively short one of not more than two or three years from, say, 1753 to 1755. But even if this were so it would not of course *necessarily* follow that the particular set of notes in Volume I in which we are interested belonged to the same period: there are very many blank pages in the Commonplace Book, and it would have been quite possible for this set of notes to have been inserted much later. All one can really say about this is that there are no other entries in the Commonplace Book which are definitely ascribable to a later date, and that the internal evidence in the notes themselves (such as it is) is at least *consistent* with their having been written between 1753 and 1755.

In view of all this, it seems worth while to ask some questions about the *motives* which might have impelled Anderson to make selective extracts from a student's notes of Smith's lectures, and about the *opportunities* which he might have had to do this. So far as his motives are concerned, I do not think that one need look much further than genuine interest.[41] When Smith came to Glasgow, his reputation had preceded him; and Anderson himself, in a letter of December 1750, told a correspondent that he was glad to hear that there were "two such able candidates for the Logic Chair in Glasgow, as Smith and Muirhead."[42] Later, of course, Anderson quarreled with Smith (and indeed with most of his other professorial colleagues), and this can perhaps be taken as another indication that the notes are more likely to be of an earlier than a later date.[43]

On the question of Anderson's opportunities, it can of course be said immediately that *after his arrival at Glasgow to take up his chair* (in October 1756, apparently) they would have been virtually unlimited. But in view of the fact that most of the evidence, uncertain

41. There is nothing at all in the notes to suggest that Anderson might have compiled them in order to catch Smith out in some way.

42. Letter of 27 December 1750 from Anderson to Gilbert Lang (original held by the Andersonian Library, University of Strathclyde).

43. It is interesting—and perhaps significant in the present context—that Anderson's antipathy towards Smith revealed itself rather earlier than is usually assumed. In a letter to Gilbert Lang dated 16 January 1755 (original held by the Andersonian Library, University of Strathclyde), Anderson tells his correspondent about his appointment to the chair of Oriental Languages at Glasgow. He had hoped, he says, to be appointed to the chair of Latin, but, as he puts it, "Doctor Cullen and Mr. Smith, in a manner that I need not relate, jockied me out of it."

though it is, would seem to point to the likelihood of a date for the notes rather earlier than this, we have to ask whether he might also have had an opportunity before 1756.

We know that in 1750 Anderson was appointed as tutor to Lord Doune, the son of the Earl of Moray, and that at that time his provisional plan was to "go to Scotland next summer, to Glasgow or St. Andrew's in winter, and abroad, after a stay of some years at one of these Universities."[44] This plan, however, was evidently altered: the accounts relating to Lord Doune's education, kept in the Moray Muniments, indicate that the boy remained at Harrow School for virtually the whole period of Anderson's tutorship—from August 1750 to August 1753, when Anderson took him back to the family seat at Donibristle.[45]

The next thing we know for certain about Anderson's movements at this period is that he went to France shortly after the middle of 1754 with a "Mr. Campbell" (presumably in some kind of tutorial capacity), apparently sailing from Dublin to Bordeaux.[46] While he was in France, on 17 December 1754, he was elected to the chair of Oriental Languages at Glasgow University. The Clerk was instructed to write to Anderson in France, telling him of his election and signifying to him "that the University desires in case of his acceptance, that he come hither against the sitting down of the College next session, that he may be ready to begin teaching the first of November."[47]

At a University Meeting on 13 February 1755, however, "a letter was read from the Primate of Ireland directed to the Principal by which he in a very civil but earnest manner makes application to the Principal and other members that they would allow Mr. Anderson to stay another winter with Mr. Campbell in France, providing his office can be supplied by one of the Masters during his absence."[48] The

44. Letter of 27 December 1750 to Gilbert Lang.

45. I have not myself inspected the relevant documents in the Moray Muniments. Mr. Wood, however, obtained photocopies of them some time ago, and according to information about them with which Mrs. Frame has kindly supplied me they show that Lord Doune remained at Harrow for the whole period of Anderson's tutorship—apart from vacations, when Anderson rented lodgings in London for the two of them and does not seem to have traveled very far from that city.

46. In Anderson's letter of 16 January 1755 to Gilbert Lang, which is written from Toulouse, Anderson speaks specifically of having arrived at Bordeaux from Dublin. "Mr. Campbell" is mentioned by name in the minutes of the University Meeting of 13 February 1755, to be quoted shortly in the text, and he is also mentioned in Volume III of Anderson's Commonplace Book.

47. Minutes of University Meeting of 17 December 1754 (Glasgow University Archives).

48. Minutes of University Meeting of 13 February 1755 (Glasgow University Archives). Leechman, Simson, and Smith were appointed as a committee "to draw

Meeting—not, it would appear, without some misgivings—resolved "to allow Mr. Anderson to be absent another winter." He returned to Scotland, however, in June 1755 and was formally admitted to his chair at a University Meeting on 25 June.[49] But this seems to have been only a relatively brief visit: his name appears among those present at a University Meeting on 26 June 1755, but not again until 25 October 1756. It seems very probable, therefore, that he took advantage of the privilege the University had afforded him and stayed another winter with "Mr. Campbell" in France.

This visit in June 1755 is the only one which we know for certain that Anderson paid to Glasgow University before he began teaching there in October 1756. But there is a gap of a whole year in our knowledge of Anderson's movements at this period—from August 1753, when he took Lord Doune back to Donibristle, to the middle of 1754, when he went to France with "Mr. Campbell." During that period he *could* quite possibly have been in Glasgow, either as the tutor of "Mr. Campbell" or in some other capacity. And whether this was so or not, *if* "Mr. Campbell" had been a student at Glasgow before he went to France with Anderson, and *if* he had attended Smith's lectures, our mystery might be well on the way to being solved: Anderson, out of interest, might very possibly have made selective extracts from the notes of Smith's lectures taken by "Mr. Campbell." Unfortunately luck deserts us at this crucial point: we are not sure who this "Mr. Campbell" actually was. Why, we may ask, did no less a personage than the Primate of Ireland intervene on his behalf in February 1755?[50] Rae, in his *Life of Adam Smith*, states in

up a civil letter to the Primate and acquaint him that the University has granted his desires, to be signed by the Clerk in name of the University, and sent off next post. . . ."

49. In a letter from Edinburgh dated 10 June 1755 (Glasgow University Archives, no. 26854), Anderson wrote to an unnamed person at Glasgow University informing him of his movements and asking "what day will be most convenient for my admission." At a University Meeting on 19 June 1755 Anderson "read the critical dissertation he had been appointed to make as his tryal," and it was agreed to admit him "upon Wednesday next at twelve of the clock, after he has signed the Confession of Faith." Andersen duly signed this at a Meeting on 25 June, and "thereafter he was solemnly received by all the members."

50. The letter from the Primate referred to in the minutes of the University Meeting of 13 February 1755 is extant (Glasgow University Archives, no. 26853). It does not throw very much more light on the identity of "Mr. Campbell," but it does at least clear up the doubt which existed in Scott's mind (Scott, p. 188 n.) as to which of the two possible holders of the office of "Primate of Ireland" was the one concerned: it was in fact George Stone, the Archbishop of Armagh. He states that he is making the request on behalf of "a gentleman of very great worth and fortune in this kingdom" who he seems to imply (but does not actually state) is the father of "Mr. Campbell." There is also extant in the Glasgow University Archives (no. 15626) a draft

passing that "Mr. Campbell" was in fact the Primate of Ireland's son, but I have been unable to find any evidence which would support this.[51] Nor have I been able to find any trace in the University of Glasgow Matriculation Albums, in the relevant period, of any student called "Campbell" with Irish connections—although this, of course, is not at all decisive on the point.

To sum up on the dating issue, then, the internal evidence in the notes themselves, together with that in the other entries in the Commonplace Book, is at the very least fully *consistent* with a date between 1753 and 1755 for the entry of the notes. Anderson's motive would possibly have been stronger then than later; and he could very well have had the necessary opportunity at some time during that period. One is obliged to admit, however, that the evidence is also *consistent* with a date after 1755. But the general feeling one gets, looking at the evidence as a whole—and looking, too, at the important *differences* between the Anderson notes and the 1762–63 notes, which we have still to consider—is that the balance of probability lies in favor of an earlier date rather than a later one. My own tentative guess would be that the relevant lectures were delivered in one of the three sessions 1751–52, 1752–53, or 1753–54.

III

The last question to be asked is the most interesting of all: what light, if any, do the Anderson notes throw on the development of Smith's thought during his Glasgow period? The best starting point here, I suggest, is a consideration of the question of the connection between Smith's work and that of his teacher Francis Hutcheson.

After the discovery of the Cannan lecture notes, a number of scholars—notably Cannan himself[52] and Scott[53]—drew attention to certain interesting parallels between the way in which Smith dealt

---

letter to the Primate prepared by Smith, in which it is stated (inter alia) that before the Primate's letter was received the University had already been solicited to the same effect by "several persons of the greatest distinction in this country particularly by the Earl of Glasgow the present Rector of the University." A letter from the Primate dated 8 March 1755 thanking the University for granting his request (Glasgow University Archives, no. 266339) does not add anything further. There is a distinct air of mystery about the whole affair: one detects throughout the presence of undercurrents which never come to the surface.

51. Rae, p. 85. Scott, p. 188 n., states that "Mr. Campbell" has not been identified. If he was in fact Archbishop Stone's son this might help to explain the mystery, since Stone was unmarried but was frequently accused of immorality by his political opponents. Not enough hangs on this, however, to make any further investigation—or speculation—profitable.

52. See, e.g., the "Editor's Introduction" to the Cannan notes, pp. xxiv–vi.

53. See in particular W. R. Scott, *Francis Hutcheson* (Cambridge, 1900), passim.

with Moral Philosophy in his lectures on the subject (as reported in the Cannan notes) and the way in which Hutcheson dealt with it in his *Short Introduction to Moral Philosophy* (1747) and *System of Moral Philosophy* (1755).[54] If we compare these works of Hutcheson's with the 1762–63 notes rather than with the Cannan notes, the parallels become more striking, since the order of treatment of the main subjects in the 1762–63 notes is much closer to Hutcheson's than the order of treatment in the Cannan notes. In the Cannan notes, as we have already seen,[55] Smith adopted the method of "the civilians," beginning with government and then treating of property and other rights. In the 1762–63 notes, however, Smith used a different method, beginning with property and other rights and then treating of family and civil government—and this, basically, was the method which Hutcheson had adopted.

If we now compare these works of Hutcheson's with the Anderson notes, the parallels become more striking still. It is not simply that—as we would expect from what has been said above—the order in which the main topics are treated is very close to Hutcheson's. There are also certain other indications which make the connection with Hutcheson much more manifest. For example, as I have already pointed out,[56] the notes contain two specific page references to Hutcheson's *Short Introduction*. The heading to the section on prices, "De Pretio Rerum" (p. 7), is a fairly clear echo of the title of the chapter on prices ("De Rerum Pretio") in the Latin work of Hutcheson's of which his *Short Introduction* was an English translation. The comments on oaths and vows on p. 22 of the Anderson notes, which appear to have no real counterpart in the 1762–63 or Cannan notes, probably owe their origin to a chapter on this subject in the *Short Introduction*.[57] And the comment on Plato on p. 23, of which once again there seems to be no counterpart in the 1762–63 or Cannan notes, may well have been derived from Hutcheson.[58] Most

54. The *Short Introduction*, as we have already seen, was an English translation of a work which Hutcheson originally published (in 1742) in Latin. The *System*, a much longer work, was a printed version of Hutcheson's lectures (presumably in their final form of the 1740's), published posthumously. From these two books, which are very similar in structure, we may readily reconstruct the elements of the Moral Philosophy course which Smith attended when he was a student at Glasgow. The references to the books in the text below are to the facsimile edition of Hutcheson's *Collected Works* published by Georg Olms Verlagsbuchhandlung, Hildesheim, in 1969.

55. See above, p. 453.

56. See above, p. 456.

57. Book II, ch. 11 (*Collected Works*, 4: 203–8). The corresponding chapter in the *System* will be found in the *Collected Works*, 6: 44–53.

58. See *Collected Works*, 6: 185.

important of all, however, is another consideration which will take a little more time to develop.

It relates to the location, in both the *Short Introduction* and the *System*, of the famous "economic" chapters in which prices, money, and interest are dealt with.[59] As is well known, Hutcheson in both books introduced these "economic" chapters in the course of a general discussion of *contract*. This procedure of his was by no means as arbitrary as has sometimes been suggested.[60] In Book II of both the *Short Introduction* and the *System* he embarks upon a study of what he calls "adventitious rights," which he classifies into "real" and "personal."[61] The principal real right is *property*, which is either "original" or "derived".[62] Derived property can be alienated or transferred in various ways—most notably by *contract* and by *testament* (or intestate succession).[63] In the *System*, at the beginning of his chapter on the transfer of property, he draws attention to "the necessity and use of frequent contracts and translations of property";[64] and at the end of this chapter, after discussing (inter alia) testamentary and intestate succession, he points out that personal rights too very often arise from contracts. A consideration of these rights, he says, "leads to the subject of contracts or covenants, the main engine of constituting either personal rights or real."[65] In the *Short Introduction* the reasons for the transition to a separate consideration of contracts are not quite so clearly spelt out: in this much shorter book, Hutcheson contents himself with saying at the beginning of the relevant chapter that property may be transferred "either *gratuitously* in donations; or for *valuable consideration* in commerce," and with promising to "treat of contracts and commerce hereafter."[66]

The next six chapters, then, in both the *Short Introduction* and the *System*, deal with contract and quasi-contract, in general and in particular. In this broad context, the famous chapter on prices and money takes its place quite naturally. It is related to what has gone before, since (as Hutcheson puts it in the *Short Introduction*) "to

59. Book II, chs. 12 and 13 of the *Short Introduction* (*Collected Works*, 4: 209–22); and Book II, chs. 12 and 13 of the *System* (*Collected Works*, 6: 53–77).

60. E.g., by W. L. Taylor, *Francis Hutcheson and David Hume as Predecessors of Adam Smith* (Durham, North Carolina, 1965), pp. 22–24.

61. *Collected Works*, 4: 147, and 5: 309.

62. Ibid., 4: 152, and 5: 324.

63. Ibid., 4: 171 ff. and 5: 340 ff.

64. Ibid., 5: 340.

65. Ibid., 5: 358.

66. Ibid., 4: 171.

maintain any commerce among men in interchanging of goods or services, the values of them must be some way estimated";[67] and it is also related to what comes after, since in the following chapter Hutcheson deals with (inter alia) "onerous contracts," in which "the parties profess to transfer mutually things of equal value."[68]

After the chapters on contract, Hutcheson proceeds directly to a discussion of "rights arising from injuries and damages done by others."[69] Thus the analysis of prices, money, and interest, in the embryo form in which it appears in Hutcheson, enters into the picture under the general heading of contract, which is dealt with immediately after the discussion of testaments and immediately before that of injuries. *And this, it would appear, is exactly how and where the analysis of prices, money, and interest entered into the course of Smith's lectures from which the Anderson notes were derived.* The *location* of the relevant sections in the Anderson notes is certainly the same: as we have already seen, they are sandwiched between the sections dealing with testaments and those dealing with injuries.[70] And the suggestion that Smith was at that time including his "economic" analysis under the general heading of contract is strengthened by the passage on p. 14 of the Anderson notes, which occurs immediately after the last of the "economic" sections and which clearly deals with an aspect of contracts in general.

It would seem very likely, then, that at the outset Smith's Moral Philosophy course (in certain respects at least) was rather closer to Hutcheson's than has generally been supposed; that in particular Smith's analysis of prices, money, and interest was at first presented under the general heading of contract, as it had been with Hutcheson; and that it was only later that this "economic" material, having no doubt been greatly expanded and developed, was transferred from "Contract" to "Police"—i.e., to the place in which it is found in the 1762–63 notes.[71]

But it is also clear from the Anderson notes that in certain other respects Smith had, at the time of the course to which these notes relate, already departed quite considerably from the lines laid down by Hutcheson. One obvious point here is that there was clearly much more straight *law* in Smith's course than there had been in

67. Ibid., 4: 209.
68. Ibid., 4: 214. Cf. 6: 64.
69. Ibid., 6: 86. Cf. 4: 228.
70. Cf. above, p. 454.
71. When one knows what one is looking for, one can see vestigial traces of its former inclusion under the "Contract" heading in the 1762–63 notes, Vol. II, pp. 79–84, and (correspondingly) in the Cannan notes, p. 134.

Hutcheson's. Another is that the content of the "De Pretio Rerum" section has been expanded appreciably beyond that of the corresponding sections in Hutcheson, so as to include a discussion of (for example) bills of exchange, paper money, and stocks, together with an updated analysis of interest apparently based on Hume's essay on the subject.[72] Finally, and perhaps most important of all, Smith has evidently in many places added a *historical* dimension to the argument, which in most contexts is much more pronounced than it ever was in Hutcheson. Perhaps we can surmise from the large number of direct and indirect references to Montesquieu in the Anderson notes[73] that the *Spirit of Laws* was one of the main literary influences leading Smith towards this historicization of the analysis.

In this connection, the use in the Anderson notes (on pp. 1–3 and 37) of a *stadial* theory (or theories) of socioeconomic development is of considerable interest. When we compare these passages with the corresponding ones in the 1762–63 and Cannan notes,[74] we can detect both resemblances and differences. The resemblances are sufficiently great to suggest that Smith had indeed, as some of us have recently ventured to conjecture,[75] developed the elements of at any rate *a* four-stages theory by the early or middle 1750's. The differences, however, seem to suggest that, at the time of the course to which the notes relate, he may still have had some little way to go before he arrived at the mature four-stages theory which is so clearly expounded and so ubiquitously applied in the 1762–63 and Cannan notes. In the Anderson notes, the first stage is characterized by "hunting and fishing"; the second stage appears to be characterized by the acquisition of "property in common" by a clan or a nation; and the third stage is characterized by the emergence of agriculture,

72. It *may*, of course, have included much more than this: Anderson's extracts are not necessarily all-inclusive, or even representative, and as I have said above, nothing can safely be deduced from the *absence* of anything in the Anderson notes.

73. There are direct references to Montesquieu on pp. 9, 12, 19, 26 (two references), 31, and 39 of the Anderson notes. There is also an indirect reference on p. 9: the opinion that the Jews were the inventors of bills of exchange, which Smith here refutes, was in fact Montesquieu's (*Spirit of Laws*, Book XXI, ch. 20). It is possible, of course, that Anderson, who thought highly of Montesquieu, paid special attention to the references to him in the lecture notes.

74. In the case of the 1762–63 notes, the comparison can most usefully be made with Vol. I, pp. 47–53 and 66–68, and Vol. IV, pp. 36–38; and in the case of the Cannan notes with pp. 108–10, and p. 20. These references, however, are by no means exhaustive.

75. Cf., e.g., R. L. Meek, "Smith, Turgot, and the 'Four Stages' Theory," *History of Political Economy* 3 (1971). I take this opportunity to state that in this article, as I now see it, I seriously underestimated the part played by Montesquieu in the development of the four-stages theory.

permanent settlements, and private property in land. In the 1762–63 and Cannan notes, all the stages are defined unambiguously in terms of different modes of subsistence—the first three being hunting, pasturage, and agriculture—and changes in the state of property are regarded as *consequences* of changes from one of these modes of subsistence to the next.

It is of course possible that at the time of the Anderson notes Smith was closer to the mature four-stages theory than these notes would at first sight seem to suggest. For example, in his discussion of the second stage he *may* in the relevant lecture have specifically associated "property in common" with pasturage (as he apparently did in the corresponding lecture in 1762–63),[76] but the student—or Anderson—may simply have failed to note this association. It seems rather more probable, however, that at the time of the Anderson notes Smith was still using his stadial theory more or less exclusively in connection with the problem of changes in the state of property, and had not yet fully succeeded in separating the mode-of-subsistence "basis" from the state-of-property "superstructure." As his ideas developed, we may perhaps surmise, this distinction was more clearly made, and the theory applied in a number of other spheres—and also, incidentally, emancipated from its connection with the two "principles" described at the beginning of the Anderson notes.

THE ANDERSON NOTES

The notes which follow appear at the back of Volume I of Anderson's Commonplace Book, on pp. 292–368, *starting on p. 368*. Anderson evidently turned the book upside down and commenced writing on p. 368, which was now (the book being upside down) the first right-hand facing page. When he had filled this page he turned it over and continued on the next right-hand page (p. 366), and so on for a total of 39 right-hand pages until the notes concluded on p. 292. On seven occasions he wrote additional notes on the left-hand facing page. In the reproduction of the notes which follows, I have renumbered the relevant right-hand facing pages from 1 to 39, indicating by an appropriate arabic italic numeral in square brackets [ ] the point at which each new right-hand page begins. Braces { } are used to indicate the additional notes which are written on left-hand facing pages. In most cases the appropriate place for the insertion of this material in the main text is not specifically indicated by Anderson and has had to be guessed at. In editing the text of the manuscript for publication, I have ignored Anderson's capitalization, and up to a point his punctuation, in the interests of readability. Common contractions for "the," "that," "which," "and," etc., are spelt out, together with words containing a raised letter; but most of the

76. 1762–63 notes, Vol. I, pp. 48–49.

other contractions are reproduced exactly as they appear in the manuscript. Most of the deletions, replacements, doubtful readings, etc., are listed in the textual notes set at the end of the text, referred to by letter superscripts. Straight interlineations which do not involve deletions, etc., are not specifically noted at all. Angle brackets ⟨ ⟩ are used to indicate words, letters, etc., which have been omitted from the text but which ought properly to be there; square brackets [ ] are used to indicate words, letters, etc., which are there but which ought properly to have been omitted. The spelling of the original has been retained, and so far as possible the dividing lines, dashes, etc., used by Anderson have been reproduced.

[1] Principle

To deprive a man of life or limbs or to give him pain is shocking to the rudest of our species when no enmity or grudge subsists, i.e., where no punishment is due or danger apprehended.

2 Principle

We acquire a liking for those creatures or[a] things[b] which we are much conversant with, and thus[c] to deprive us of them must give us pain.

Hunting and fishing are all the arts that[d] prevail in the first states of society. To deprive a man of the beast or fish he has caught, or of the fruit he has gathered, is depriving him of what cost him labour and so giving him pain, and is contrary to the laws of the rudest society.

By the second principle when a clan or nation hunt and fish [*2*] long (i.e., have lived long) in one tract of country they acquire an exclusive property and it is considered as theirs, i.e., they acquire property in common (vide the histories of America and Caesar and Tacitus), which is the second state of perfection in society.

When confined to one country their arable ground and crops are in common. {Tho contrary to[e] Act of Parliament, all unenclosed fields in this country, after the gathering in of the harvest, are in common. In such a state are the lands in Arabia and many parts of N. America all the year round, i.e., they have a common right to the fruits, and the land is considered as the property of no individual.} When their numbers encrease, when instruments of husbandry are invented (vide Hesiod[f]), and when they have built huts and towns, they will begin to labour little spots about their houses and[g] the *publick* fields [*3*] will be neglected, and hence will arise private property in lands founded both upon the first and second principle; which is[h] the third state of society advancing towards perfection. {By the Gothic holdings the prince was considered as the proprietor of the ground, and the land-holders had no right to accessions, etc. unless[i] expressly named in the charter.

Hence[j] in Scotland the land holder had originally[k] no right to fishing, lime stone, coal, gold and silver mines, etc.[l] But[m] as[n] these rights were very inconvenient to the land holders[o] they were all given away[p] in the charter except the right to gold and silver mines.}

P.156[q] one head of a family, by his first arriving in a vast island must not pretend to property in the whole, etc.

This will hold when the inhabitants are pushed for room and the common necessaries of life, as was the case in antient Greece. But where they fit out fleets in order to encrease their wealth, etc. they are deemed to have a property in[r] the whole no more than they can ever reasonably hope[s] to cultivate. Thus Brasil, Mexico, etc. are thought by all nations to be the property of the Spaniards.

[*4*] Children succeed to the goods of their *intestate* father, not on account of the *parental relation*, but on account of their connection with his[t] goods, etc., i.e., they succeed by the 2d[u] principle. For[v] in barbarous nations the children who had[w] left the family did not succeed at all, and the distant relations and servants who lived in the family succeeded equally to the children in it.—

Where there are no manufactures and where agriculture is little minded, the country must soon be overstocked with inhabitants; hence the Teutones, etc. made their invasions. Feu, the German word, signifies pay (as fee in English⟨)⟩. As the conquests were made by armies and by[x] generals who were not able to [*5*] maintain them, they were put in possession of the lands, instead of receiving pay, and were obliged to military service, etc.

P.172.[y] It is absurd that men, etc.

1. Whatever is said or done by a dying person makes the greatest impression on his surviving friends and acquaintances. {(My own) We remember triffling circumstances when[z] connected to an event that makes a strong impression upon us. And[a] when a dying person gives us his advice he is supposed to be perfectly disinterested, which is another cause of our regard.}

2. We have a sympathy to the dying person and place ourselves[s] in his stead.

3. It is for the interest of society that wills should be observed.

Among the antient Romans (vide Au. Gellius) and the patriarchs (vide the History of Abraham) the heir seemed to have[b] succeeded by the favour of the people and not by any established right.

Gap of three lines in MS

[*6*] As the feudal law had mil⟨i⟩tary service principally in view, and as a man at 16 was able to bear arms, 16 was the age of majority till the 12th century when such heavy armour came in fashion that a youth at that age could not bear it, and this produced the[c] change of the age of majority from 16 to one and twenty where it now continues.

Gap of half a page in MS

[*7*] De Pretio Rerum

The value of any commodity is equal to the sum of what[d] the majority of all the persons who want that commodity are willing to do or give for it.[e]

If all that the Europeans are willing to give for all the cinnamon imported this year is £50,00,[f] if double that quantity is imported next year, a pound of cin. which is sold this[g] year for 10 shs will next[h] year be sold for 5. Hence together with the additional expence the Dutch burn their spices.

Suppose 100 men want the same commodity, that[i] 99 are willing to give 10 shs for the pound, but that 1 is willing to give 20. The seller however will never think of asking more than 10 from that single person; and hence the value of the commodity must be regulated by the majority of the buyers. [*8*] Suppose a crown this year contains one oun. of silver and next year only half an oz.; it will then pass not for the half which it ought naturally to do but for[j] something more (perhaps 3 or 4 shs), and that on account of the ignorance of the people who receive it and of their debts. 1, on acct of their ignorance. As soldiers (etc.) are accustomed to receive 3 and 6^{d} and still receive the same number of pieces (for the coin is only supposed to be debased) they would be equally well pleased since they get as much drink, etc. for it as formerly. 2^{ly}, on acct of their debts. As to the person to whom they owe 10 shs this[k] year they will only pay 10 shs next year of a baser coin.

[*9*] Montesquieou's acct of money refuted—as to the aliquot parts of gold.—

The Jews not the inventors of bills of exchange.

1. There are letters equivalent to b. of ex. mentioned in Demosthenes orations.

2. The ordering[l] a distant[m] person by a letter to pay the debt he owes me, to the bearer of my letter must have been a very natural and

antient thing. But this does not come up to a bill of exchange. The great advantage attending a bill of ex. is that it is simple and admits of none of the delays attending prosecutions before common courts of justice. But, by an Act of the legislature in all commercial [*10*] states, the prosecutions for none acceptance, etc. are free from all the delays in the common course of justice.—The Jews therefore could not be the cause of this as they were so far from being a governing people that they[n] were persecuted in all countries.

About the end of the [the] 13th centy some of the trading towns saw the necessity of making quick dispatch in all prosecutions about bills of exchange; they established consuls, etc.[o] Other towns saw the necessity of the same laws in order to encourage commerce, and hence are all bills of exch.

Gap of four lines in MS

[*11*] {By law a man cannot be punished for coining medals, or pieces of silver and gold to his own arms, etc.—He is only punished for counterfeiting the coin and arms of the state.—}

I. Paper money by private banks.
II. Do by established banks, e.g. the banks of England and Amsterdam.
III. Do stocks such as the African Company.
IV. Credit upon governt security.

[p]The two first depend chiefly on their credit.—

The two last may be guilty of great frauds. The managers of the stocks may give out their dividend is doubly of what it is tho they expect more ships home that year. Upon the which many will buy very high and so may be greatly cheated. And

The[q] governt of any country may reduce the legal interest, or they may be obliged to stop payment by an invasion or civil war.—

[*12*] Locke, Montesquiou, and Law think that the lowness of interest is owing to the plenty of money. But, etc.— —as in Mr. Hume's Essay the[r] general[s] doctrine.—

No enclosures in England till the Reformation. The Spaniards were possessed of Peru, and thought that only miners were necessary to make them rich. The English knew they could reap no benefit from their mines but by selling them such goods as they wanted. Hence the flourishing of commerce in the reins[t] of Q El., K Jam., and the first 15 of K Ch the 1st—Corn can be easily exported; but hay or the feeding of cattle is unprofitable un[*13*]less the country is populous (or unless there is an easy export, e.g. Cork and Scotland). Hence tho[u] the country of England grew populous by large towns, villages, etc. of manufactures, there was no great demand for cattle, and as enclosures are necessary in grass farms hence England was unenclosed (as Scotland is at present) till the establishment of commerce.

Tho accumulated interest seems in itself to be very reasonable —yet it has been forbidden in all countries. 1. Because it may easily give room for the greatest oppressions. 2[ly], because it is the creditors fault if he wants his interest at the end of the[v] year as he may use diligence, etc.

[*14*] In general. Where there are penal laws against any action that very circumstance makes contracts in that case the better observed. Hence debts of honour are religiously kept by cheating gamesters.—And the smugglers in England when a boat comes off to them, they sell their goods and receive payment by the buyers throwing the money put up in bag into the smugglers ship. The⟨y⟩ have not time to count this money and can have no redress in case of a fraud.

[*15*] In order to judge of the reasonableness and origin of different punishments we must call to mind what[w] a private person feels when injured.

Our aversion to a murderer, etc. is principally fear and terror. Our aversion to a theif, contempt and disregard. Hence murderers have always suffered the last punishment. And theives have been fined, ducked, or punished with infamy.

It is true that in many countries theft is punished with death, but this is owing to its frequency, [*16*] and one may be tempted to mutilate or put to death by repeated provocations. It is true likewise that in this and most Gothic countries demembration and murder seemed to have been punished by fines, which was probably owing to these reasons. In the infancy of governments the magistrate commonly judges only in smaller differences. Two Indians, e.g., may wound or pursue the same deer and a difference about the property may easily arise. They appeal to a third person and if his judgement is thought right, his [*17*] neighbours make him their umpire likewise: vide Hesiod's account of the origin of government. But a person who had lost a limb or a brother by murder would not have patience to appeal to an arbitrator but would take vengeance at his own hand (among the Jews the relations of a murdered person could slay the murderer unless he fled to a city of refuge). Taking revenge in this way threw rude governments into convulsions, and was likewise attended with great danger to the avenger. Hence the magistrate and the avenger and the murder⟨er⟩ for the sake of mutual safety agreed to take money as a punishment.

[*18*] In all rude countries the laws cannot give sufficient protection to the innocent, for which reason the inhabitants are obliged to enter into small associations for their own safety. And as those of the same name and family are[x] connected together by blood, and by their situation (for in[y] countries where there is no commerce people seldom go far from home), hence the origin of clanship among[z] all unpolished[a] nations.

The Lex Talionis among all nations, vide the [*19*] Jewish laws, and the 12 Tables—at last abolished as too cruel a punishment, for if a man who had broke his neighbour's arm in a fit of passion were brought to the scaffold he must feel more than the injured person, who had no previous knowledge of what was to befall him.

Fur manifestus and non manifestus. Vide L'Esprit des Loix, an ingenious account but it seems not to be just.

For it does not appear that the Lacedaemonians were allowed to steal any [*20*] thing but provisions from the publick table. Vide Plutarch.—And there was this distinction between the fur man. and non man. among all nations which is owing to this, that there is a greater hatred against the criminal if taken immediately than if afterwards or if his punishment is delayed—rubra manu among the Romans, taken in the fang among the Scotch.—

Robberies punished with death because of their frequency. Forgery punished with, at present uni[*21*]versally, death. Because of the ease in forging, and the hurt it does to commerce. Among the antients not punished with death because few could write and many forms[b] were required.

There seems to have been no policy of insurance among the antients.

The civil law is in the right concerning its[c] determinations as to the advisers and employers of those who perpetrate crimes, and cannon law almost always in the wrong.

For such is the temper of mankind that they will [*22*] advise to crimes and propose things in a passion which they could not execute.[d]

The punishment of crimes committed 20 years before the criminal[e] was taken was not inflicted by the Roman[f] law, provided that sentence was not passed against him.

The force of oaths arises from the mind's attending, at that time, to all the motives which can induce the swearer to veracity.

A vow a promise to God, and[g] sometimes a promise to men or a man—i.e., there are two branches in a vow.—

[*23*] ___________________

In the most rude countries divorce is reckoned a hardship—or a thing extraordinary—and therefore a constant union between the husband and wife must be natural to men.

Plato is unjustly blamed for encouraging libidinous desires, since by his plan they would be under greater restraints than in the present state of society.

In barbarous ages the wife is not punished for infidelity, as in polished ages, because of her low state, she being considered as a slave (vid Homer's acct of Helen). For the same reason the infidelity of the husband is little minded in barbarous nations.—

[*24*] In polite ages adultery severely punished. 1st, because the intercourse between the sexes[h] is general. 2, marriage is a vow. Not so severely punished always in the man, because the dignity of the wife depends upon the dignity of the husband. And the men are the makers of the laws.—

Of Divorces

1. Liberty to divorce allowed to the husband and to him only, in the first ages of Rome and in all barbarous nations.—By the early Roman law the husband could judge his wife like his slave.

2. The second state of divorces is when the wife is allowed to divorce as well as the husband.

3. The 3 state is when the liberty of both is restrained within certain limits.

[*25*] Against Polygamy.

1. The inclinations,[i] in degree, of both sexes are proportioned to each other when uncorrupted.

Where polygamy takes place, many of the wives must be neglected—and there must be constant jealousies—for education cannot alter the natural effects of love entirely.

There is a melancholy among the women[j] of the east, and so the half of the species are miserable.

Unnatural lusts prevailed in antient Greece and Rome because there was a sort of polygamy by the multitude of female slaves, likewise at Algiers and likewise in Italy and London because whores are common in Italy and London.—

Where polygamy takes place there is such a multitude of children, that the estate cannot be divided among them.

[*26*] See Montesquiou, B xvi, ch 2^d—et que la polygamie s'introduise. Suppose the fact true, it will only follow that he ought to take another but not that polygamy ought to be established.—But the fact is not true.—Intemperance in love indeed makes the easterns fond of very young women, as rapes are committed in London upon children five years old—but Cleopatra had a child at 40.—

B. xvi, ch. 4. This opinion seems to be ill founded, for the births are not kept regularly in Asia.—[k]Meaco is a capital. It is filled with saraglios.—In Scotland if the people were numbered there wd be found more males in the kingdom than females.—

[*27*] The sentiment of love fixes upon one, and as polygamy is contrary to this sentiment it is contrary to nature.

The taking care of children natural in the highest degree.—

It arises too from the childs always being with, and being caressed by, its parent—where this does not take place the sentiment of the child goes along with the sentiments of all others, and he conforms to the general rule.

Exposing of Children

To do no good to our fellow creatures is not reckoned so criminal, as to do them direct hurt. And thus the exposition of children was considered as an imperfect [*28*] obligation.—It took place among the Greeks and Romans, but if the child lived several weeks the father had no right to expose it.—Miscarriage or abortion little minded in modern times, and the women who are guilty of the last think it less criminal to procure it in the first quarter of their pregnancy than in the last. Aristotle B.III recommends it. In rude societies, the government[l] was cautious of intermedling in private affairs and so of correcting this abuse.

Of Bastard

The mother is reckoned the proprietor of the bastard.

Mistresses much respected in barbarous ages, almost as much as the wife.—Teucer almost on a level with Ajax.—In this country bas[*29*]tards were highly respected.

Patria Potestas

This subsists among all barbarous nations—in full force in the times of the greatest liberty in Rome and little abused—taken away in the decline of the Empire when abused.—The helplesness of the child puts it in the power of the father.—Among the Romans, the son could be sold, scurged, or put to death by the father—the negroes sold by their fathers.

As in rude countries the wife is in a state of slavery, and the son inherits his father's absolute power, in all barbarous nations the mother is treated as a slave.—Telemachus is insolent to his mother thro' the [*30*] whole of the Odyssey.—Upon the death of his father, says Colvin in the History of Africa, the son goes home and beats his mother, and he is reckoned a milk-sop who does otherwise.

Of Slaves

Many causes of slavery—by way of punishment—in order to pay debt—but above all by war.—No humanity to prisoners of war, of old. If they did not kill them they thought them their property, and this the greatest origin of slavery.—Slavery could not be introduced in a polished age, and all countries were at first rude.—In [*31*] the heroick ages slaves were happy; in polished ages not so. In the first state, the slave eat and wrought with[m] his master, and there subsisted an intimacy between them. In the last state, they were removed from the sight of their masters and therefore cruelly used. At present there is more sympathy between a farmer and his servant, than between a duke and his footman. And as the blacks seem not from their skin {to partake of the same nature with the whites, the imagination of a barbarous white supposes him not to be of the same nature with himself, and therefore uses him ill with less scruple.} (Aristotle spends some ⟨?time⟩ in proving that a slave can have no virtue.) To be a slave in a despotic government is no worse than to be a freeman—see Montesquiou.

A slave in Rome had no religion, i.e., he did not share in the publick [*32*] worship; he was considered in the same light with the cattle of his proprietor. Hence of old, see Tacitus, etc., it was common for the slaves to become Jews, as they held there was an universal deity, whereas in the heathen religion every deity had a particular province and there was no deity allotted for the slaves.

We never hear of the insurrection of slaves in Persia, etc.

In Tyre, Carthage, and Lacedaemon the people lived well ⟨?compared⟩ to their slaves.—The Germans armed their slaves.

Corruptions bring on their own remedies.—The common law and not Christianity suppressed slavery—it was not abolished by humanity or the [*33*] improvement of manners—but as the slaves were armed by their lords and so dangerous to the king, the king abolished slavery.—Slavery subsisted under the emperours after Christianity was the popular religion.—The cannon law supposes slavery.—Slavery still subsists in Muscovy which is a Christian country.

Our salters and colliers differ much from slaves. They can have property and consequently families; they can buy their liberty; the price of their labour is fixed by law; they are punished by law—that is, they are only confined to one trade and one master,[n] the first of which [*34*] was the state of the antient Egyptians.

Were our salters and colliers put upon the same footing with other labourers, it would be much better for their masters.—When men are constrained to work for another they will not work so hard as if at liberty—this is manifest in quarrying and other mines. In the Newcastle mines work is done cheaper than in this country. In this country a collier and salter can earn more than a quarrier or any other labourer who works as hard.—In the mines of Silesia, the miners go voluntary below ground and live there for years.

[*35*] Attempts to introduce agrarian laws, and the abolition of debts, were the sources of constant disorder in antient states, and are quite unknown in the modern.—The cause of this slavery—for as in every great town the inhabitants are either gentlemen or work hard, a man that has no land can get subsistence only by his labour; but of old the slaves were mechanicks and not freemen, and therefore the freemen who had no lands in Rome, Athens, etc. were entirely dependent on the great for their living—and the great were liberal, as the people had the disposal of all places.

[*36*] (Plato and Aristotle—their great aim in their Republicks is to prevent disorders from agrarians and the abolition of debts—a modern legislator never thinks of this.)

Of mankind the half die under 7, and of these the children of the vulgar most commonly. It is not unusual in Wales, Ireland, and the Highlands to see women without a child who have born above a dozen, which is owing to their poverty which renders them unfit to bring up the most tender of all animals, viz infants.

This then must be one cause of the want of inhabitants in ancient nations, and where polygamy takes place. {There is a cause not mentioned by Mr. Wallace, viz the drinking of spiritous liquors.}

[*37*] Nothing has appeared more surprizing than the government of nations because the few govern the many.

In barbarous ages the 1st state of society is that of seperate families. The 2d the union of families for safety and the decis⟨i⟩on of differences; and familiarity and common interest unites them firmly together. 3ly. the wisdom and wealth of one procures him authority, and there is a common governour or chief but without any expressed prerogative.—In this state the older the wiser a good maxim in the choice of magistrates, because there are no means of acquiring knowledge by books, etc. Hence the governours or chiefs in Africa are old men [*38*]—Nestor celebrated for his age and wisdom.—Two chiefs may be often found in such a state, and as they have no power independent of wisdom, etc. it is not inconvenient, tho in polished nations, when each are supported by courts, attendants, etc. the most miserable of all institutions.

In this state governing often becomes hereditary in one family, because it is natural to transplant our love or dislike to the representative of the deceast person.

As in the first state families united for deciding differences and defending each other, so in the second villages, and so in the[o] third nations with their chiefs or kings {and in that state a king may become like Agammemnon in Homer, the king of kings.}

[*39*] Montesquiou's division of the powers in a state very just.

1. In the rude state of society, no laws passed unless every member is consulted, and a dissenter must leave that[p] society.

The laws of police are longer of being executed, and more difficult⟨l⟩y executed, in a free than in an absolute government. The laws of police are stricter and better executed in France than in England, and in Japan than in France.—

a. Replaces "of" *b*. "2 Principle" interlined above "things" and deleted *c*. Reading doubtful *d*. Replaces "which" *e*. Replaces "by" *f*. The words "Descrip of a plow" are interlined above "vide Hesiod" *g*. The words "(besides the fields which belong to the society)" are deleted at this point *h*. The last two words replace "and this will be" *i*. "na" deleted *j*. Replaces an illegible word *k*. The last four words replace "proprietor had" *l*. Several illegible words interlined and deleted *m*. Replaces "But as these were" *n*. "some" deleted *o*. "and" deleted *p*. Two or three illegible words deleted *q*. The words "in Hutcheson," followed by an illegible word, are interlined above "P.156" *r*. Replaces "to" *s*. "perhaps" deleted *t*. Replaces "the" *u*. Replaces "first" *v*. Reading doubtful; replaces an illegible word *w*. Replaces "have" *x*. Illegible word deleted *y*. "it" deleted *z*. Replaces "in" *a*. "at death" deleted. The word "on," written above "at," is also deleted *b*. Illegible word deleted *c*. The last five words replace four illegible words *d*. "all" deleted *e*. "Thus" deleted *f*. *Sic* *g*. Replaces "last" *h*. Replaces "this" *i*. Replaces "and" *j*. The last sixteen words replace "the value then would not be half but" *k*. Replaces "last" *l*. Reading doubtful *m*. The last two words replace "another" *n*. "are" deleted *o*. "and" deleted *p*. Illegible word deleted *q*. "the" deleted *r*. Reading doubtful *s*. The last two words replace "pretty much" *t*. Reading doubtful *u*. Reading doubtful *v*. Reading doubtful *w*. "we" deleted *x*. "more naturally" deleted *y*. Illegible word deleted *z*. Replaces "in" *a*. Replaces "uncivilised"; "countries" deleted *b*. Reading doubtful *c*. Replaces "that" *d*. "and they will propose things in a passion" deleted *e*. Replaces "prisoner" *f*. Replaces an illegible word *g*. Illegible word deleted *h*. The last three words replace "with women" *i*. "of" interlined and deleted *j*. Replaces an illegible word *k*. Illegible word deleted *l*. "(the government)" deleted *m*. Replaces an illegible word *n*. "which" deleted *o*. "second" deleted *p*. Reading doubtful

[12]

CORNELL
LAW REVIEW

Volume 64 April 1979 Number 4

ADAM SMITH'S JURISPRUDENCE—BETWEEN MORALITY AND ECONOMICS*

Peter Stein†

Adam Smith is best known as the father of political economy, the author of *The Wealth of Nations,*[1] published in 1776,[2] and the apostle of free enterprise. He died in 1790, although there are some who seem to believe that he is alive and well and living in retirement at the University of Chicago. By profession, however, he was a philosopher. He held the Chair of Moral Philosophy at the University of Glasgow from 1752 to 1763 and regarded as his most important work[3] *The Theory of Moral Sentiments,*[4] which first appeared in 1759.

---

* This Article was originally presented as the Frank Irvine Lecture at the Cornell Law School on February 15, 1979.

† M.A. 1951, LL.B. 1950, Cambridge; Ph.D. 1955, Aberdeen; F.B.A. (Fellow of the British Academy). Regius Professor of Civil Law in the University of Cambridge and Fellow of Queens' College, Cambridge since 1968. Professor Stein is the co-editor of Smith's LECTURES ON JURISPRUDENCE.

[1] A. SMITH, THE WEALTH OF NATIONS (R. Campbell, A. Skinner & W. Todd eds. 1976). All quotations from Adam Smith's writings are from the "Glasgow Edition" of his works, which include A. SMITH, THE THEORY OF MORAL SENTIMENTS (D. Raphael & A. Macfie eds. 1976) [hereinafter cited as THEORY OF MORAL SENTIMENTS]; A. SMITH, THE WEALTH OF NATIONS (R. Campbell, A. Skinner & W. Todd eds. 1976); and A. SMITH, LECTURES ON JURISPRUDENCE (R. Meek, D. Raphael & P. Stein eds. 1978) [hereinafter cited as LECTURES ON JURISPRUDENCE].

[2] The literature stimulated by the bicentenary of THE WEALTH OF NATIONS is enormous. *See* Recktenwold, *An Adam Smith Renaissance, anno 1976? The Bicentenary Output—A Reappraisal of His Scholarship,* 16 J. ECON. LIT. 56 (1978). For especially interesting contributions, see D. WINCH, ADAM SMITH'S POLITICS: AN ESSAY IN HISTORIOGRAPHIC REVISION (1978); ESSAYS ON ADAM SMITH (A. Skinner & T. Wilson eds. 1975).

[3] 1 MEMOIRS OF SIR SAMUEL ROMILLY 403 (1840) (quoted in J. RAE, LIFE OF ADAM SMITH 436 (1895)).

[4] THEORY OF MORAL SENTIMENTS, *supra* note 1.

At one time there was thought to be an "Adam Smith problem" in the sense of a basic incompatibility between the ethics of *The Theory of Moral Sentiments,* which was concerned with sympathy for one's fellows, and *The Wealth of Nations,* which stressed self-interest and rejected benevolence as a force in economic relations. More recently scholars have recognized that Smith's various studies were parts of a single whole, the study of man in society. Smith organized this study around the moral virtues of prudence, justice, and benevolence.[5] *The Wealth of Nations* dealt with prudence; *The Theory of Moral Sentiments* treated of benevolence. At Smith's death, the study remained incomplete, for he never published, as he intended to do, a third book exploring the virtue of justice. Today, I will attempt to sketch the main themes in Smith's view of justice, drawing on two reports, based on students' notes, of lectures on jurisprudence which he gave as part of the Moral Philosophy course at the University of Glasgow.[6]

I
Smith's Philosophical Framework

Smith recognized that a scientific understanding of man's relations with his fellows could only be developed by the experimental method used by Newton in the physical sciences. Such an understanding must be based on observation of how men actually behave in different situations. He also accepted that, although the conditions of society vary considerably in different places and different ages, human nature remains constant; man tends everywhere and at all times to have the same aspirations and feelings. But these aspirations and feelings are complex. In general, man wants to better his condition, to enjoy life, to seek pleasure and avoid pain; *i.e.,* his motives are self-regarding. However, in certain situations he has strong feelings of benevolence towards others and on occasion he will act against his own interests because he thinks it right to do so.

---

[5] *See* notes 10-17 and accompanying text *infra.*

[6] The first of the two reports to be discovered was originally published as Lectures on Justice, Police, Revenue, and Arms, Delivered in the University of Glasgow by Adam Smith (E. Cannan ed. 1896). Both this report and a longer version, which was discovered in 1958, appear in Lectures on Jurisprudence, *supra* note 1. For a more complete discussion, see *id., Introduction,* at 5-13. The present study is based on the fuller version, which is derived from his course in the academic year 1762-63.

A. *The Impartial Spectator*

In *The Theory of Moral Sentiments,* Smith discussed the basis for man's approval of certain acts as right and his disapproval of others as wrong. He rejected the idea that every man is endowed by nature with an innate moral sense. What then do we mean when we say that our conscience or "the man within the breast" tells us that this is what we ought to do or ought not to do? Smith sought the answer in the notion of sympathy, that there is in all men a desire to identify themselves with the joys and sorrows of others.

Hutcheson and Hume had referred to the approval and disapproval of spectators or observers in their analyses of moral judgment. Smith developed the notion of the impartial spectator to explain the judgment of conscience made by the agent about his own actions.[7] The approval and disapproval of oneself, which we call conscience, is an indirect effect of the judgments made by spectators. We all judge others as spectators and we all find others judging us; we then come to judge our own conduct by imagining whether an impartial spectator would approve or disapprove of it.

In seeking the good will of our fellows in society, we examine our feelings and actions and consider how they must appear to them. This is not easy. As Smith's account inspired his contemporary, Robert Burns, to put it:

> Oh, wad some Power the giftie gie us
> To see oursels as ithers see us!
> It wad frae mony a blunder free us
> An' foolish notion.[8]

Smith recognized that the actual spectator will usually not feel as strongly as the agent himself. The spectator's emotions will be apt to fall short of the violence of what is felt by the sufferer. Sympathy can never be exactly the same as the original feeling, so when he is judging himself, the sufferer must lower "his passion to that pitch, in which the spectators are capable of going along with him."[9]

---

[7] E. West, Adam Smith, The Man and His Works 95-127 (1976).

[8] *To A Louse,* in 1 *The Complete Works of Robert Burns* 257, 261 (J. Hunter ed. 1886). *Cf.* A. Macfie, The Individual in Society 66 (1967).

[9] Theory of Moral Sentiments, *supra* note 1, at 22.

B. *The Three Virtues*

The judgments of the impartial spectator thus provide the basis for a set of rules of conduct. Smith classified these rules under the three aforementioned virtues: prudence, justice, and beneficence (or benevolence).[10] "The man who acts according to the rules of perfect prudence, of strict justice, and of proper benevolence, may be said to be perfectly virtuous."[11]

Prudence is dictated by concern for our own interests, while justice and benevolence are dictated by concern for the interests of others. Prudence promotes the calculating behaviour by which a man preserves and increases his fortune. It is therefore the basis of saving and capital formation. By prudence a man puts himself in a position from which he can then help others. Smith observed that before we can feel much for others we must in some measure be at ease ourselves. But no one can be compelled to be prudent. It is up to the man himself; and prudence is not a very attractive virtue to others. "It commands a certain cold esteem," Smith says wistfully, "but seems not entitled to any very ardent love or admiration."[12]

Smith understood justice, in a narrow sense, as the observance of the legal rules which safeguard the citizen's life, liberty and property. Justice sets limits to the individual's pursuit of self-interest. It is on most occasions merely "a negative virtue, and only hinders us from hurting our neighbour. . . . We may often fulfil all the rules of justice by sitting still and doing nothing."[13] Unlike prudence, its exercise is not left to the individual's discretion; he is compelled by the law to keep within the limits. In short, justice is the necessary foundation of civil society.

Beneficence, on the other hand, improves society but is not a necessary condition; it is the "ornament which embellishes, not the foundation which supports the building."[14] Beneficence is the highest virtue: "[T]o feel much for others and little for ourselves, . . . to restrain our selfish, and indulge our benevolent affections, constitutes the perfection of human nature. . . ."[15] Although it is

---

[10] *See* Campbell, *Adam Smith's Theory of Justice, Prudence and Beneficence,* AM. ECON. REV., May, 1967, at 571.

[11] THEORY OF MORAL SENTIMENTS, *supra* note 1, at 237.

[12] *Id.* at 216.

[13] *Id.* at 82.

[14] *Id.* at 86.

[15] *Id.* at 25.

the most important social virtue, beneficence is merely an aspiration of man; it "is always free, it cannot be extorted by force, the mere want of it exposes to no punishment."[16] The impartial spectator inside us may reprove us for lack of beneficence, but he can do nothing more than reprove, "because the mere want of beneficence tends to do no real positive evil."[17]

II

Justice

Smith certainly intended to devote a third book to the virtue of justice. This idea, however, involved special problems. Until the middle of the eighteenth century, jurisprudence was dominated by the theorists of natural rights, exemplified by the Dutchman Hugo Grotius and the German Samuel Pufendorf.[18] They sought to establish the existence of universal principles of natural law binding on all men, without regard to time and place. These principles were axiomatic; they had the same certainty and universality as mathematical propositions. Of course, Grotius and Pufendorf recognized that much of a society's law was not natural but positive and varied from one sociey to another. Positive law should approximate to natural law as far as possible but since it depends on the will of the ruler, it was regarded as incapable of systematic treatment, and largely ignored by these theorists.

The publication of Montesquieu's *Spirit of the Laws* in 1748 changed the direction of legal thought.[19] Montesquieu showed for the first time that laws are connected with the circumstances of society. We take it so much for granted today that an adequate exposition of legal rules must take account of their social context that we have difficulty in grasping the tremendous originality of Montesquieu's work. He acknowledged that laws must be based on "the nature of things," but argued that the nature of things varies from one society to another and that among the factors affecting a society's laws are climate, manners, tradition of government and so on.

---

[16] *Id.* at 78.

[17] *Id.*.

[18] *See generally* H. Grotius, De Jure Belli ac Pacis (F. Kelsey trans. 1925) (1st ed. Paris 1625); S. Pufendorf, De Jure Naturae et Gentium Libri Octo (C. Oldfather & W. Oldfather trans. 1934) (1st ed. Lund 1672).

[19] For a more complete discussion of these developments, see generally P. Stein, Legal Evolution: The Story of an Idea, chs. 1-2 (1979).

Montesquieu largely contented himself with showing how factors such as these can account for differences in the laws of different societies; he did not concern himself much with the way in which a society's circumstances change or progress. Within a decade of the publication of his great work, however, the question of the process of legal change through the progress of society was a matter of considerable debate, both in France and in Scotland. So when, at the end of *The Theory of Moral Sentiments,* Smith announced a further study devoted to justice, he described it as an account of "the general principles of law and government, and of the different revolutions they have undergone in the different ages and periods of society."[20]

A. *Man's Rights*

Since the virtue of justice, for Smith, was the strict observance of the legal rules protecting the citizen and his property, the theory of justice formed the major part of jurisprudence, that is, "the theory of the rules by which civil governments ought to be directed."[21] More specifically, he defined justice in terms of property rights:

> The first and chief design of every system of government is to maintain justice; to prevent the members of a society from incroaching on one another's property . . . .[22]
>
> . . . .
>
> . . . Justice is violated whenever one is deprived of what he had a right to and could justly demand from others, or rather, when we do him any injury or hurt without a cause.[23]

In treating of rights, Smith took as his model the scheme adopted by Francis Hutcheson, his own teacher and a predecessor in the Glasgow Chair. At first sight his treatment seems squarely in the tradition of Grotius and Pufendorf. Rights are divided into three classes: those which a man enjoys as an individual, those he has as a member of a family and those which he has as a citizen of a state.[24] The injury which he suffers, and consequently the right

---

[20] THEORY OF MORAL SENTIMENTS, *supra* note 1, at 342.

[21] LECTURES ON JURISPRUDENCE, *supra* note 1, at 5. Other parts of jurisprudence were "police" (regulation of commerce), "revenue" and "arms" (including public international law).

[22] *Id.*

[23] *Id.* at 7.

[24] Man's rights as an individual and as a family member are discussed below. *See* notes

which he enjoys, is in each case peculiar to the role in which he is considered.[25] Throughout his discussion Smith confines himself to legal rights, enforceable by legal action.[26]

1. *Rights as an Individual*

The rights which a man enjoys as a man are natural in the sense that they arise independently of any human action. They are reducible to three: his rights to his person, to his reputation, and to his estate. Estate includes both rights to property and personal rights arising from contract or delinquency. So far, Smith adhered to the standard natural rights scheme. It was when he proceeded to consider the various ways in which property arises that he began to diverge from his predecessors. They had treated natural rights as applicable in any society. Smith observed that the rules concerning the acquisition of property were far from universally applicable. They varied considerably according to the state that the society in question had reached. He then introduced the four stages through which societies pass as they develop: hunters, shepherds, farmers, and manufacturers and traders.

The theory of the stages of society appeared almost simultaneously in Scotland and in France, and grew out of the debates which followed the publication of Montesquieu's *Spirit of the Laws.*[27] Montesquieu's followers developed his remarks in two ways. First, they concentrated on one of the many factors which he had identified as affecting the character of a society's laws, namely, the mode of subsistence of the inhabitants. Secondly, they seized on his reference to three such modes, farmers, huntsmen and shepherds, and converted it into a scheme of development applicable to societies generally—first a three- and then a four-stage theory.

In Scotland, the theory appeared in a group of thinkers who gathered around the genial figure of Henry Home, Lord

---

27-55 and accompanying text *infra*. It is not possible in a short article to deal adequately with Smith's analysis of man's rights as a citizen.

[25] LECTURES ON JURISPRUDENCE, *supra* note 1, at 7.

[26] Smith departed from tradition in distinguishing sharply between legal or "perfect" rights, on the one hand, and moral or "imperfect" rights, on the other. He was critical of the natural rights theorists for blurring this distinction and made it clear that he was only concerned with perfect rights, that is, legal rights relating to what we have a title to demand and to compel another to perform within the limits of the legal process. *Id.* at 9. Moral rights "correspond to those duties which ought to be performed to us by others but which we have no title to compel them to perform . . . ." *Id.* (footnote omitted).

[27] *See* R. MEEK, SOCIAL SCIENCE AND THE IGNOBLE SAVAGE 102-107 (1976).

Kames.[28] This group included David Hume (the philosopher), Adam Smith, John Millar, and John Dalrymple. It was Dalrymple's *An Essay Towards a General Theory of Feudal Property in Great Britain*, published in 1757, which first mentioned the four-stage theory in print. There is good reason to think, however, that Adam Smith first suggested it; certainly, the *Lectures on Jurisprudence* show that he first applied it consistently in his treatment of rights.

Smith was more interested than Montesquieu in primitive societies. He had a more critical understanding of the evidence provided by the literature of classical antiquity.[29] In addition he had studied the writings on the customs of the American Indians by two French Jesuits, Lafitau[30] and Charlevoix.[31] Lafitau's 1724 publication was notable for having drawn parallels between the style of life of the Iroquois and that of the ancient Greeks, and so "revealed to the world the simple truth that even the Greeks had once been savages."[32] Smith was probably also influenced by Machiavelli, whom he admired as an historian,[33] and his followers. They imposed a kind of cyclical pattern of rise and decay on the major periods of European history.

Smith never considered man in an isolated state. In the earliest type of society, that of hunters, a nation consists of a number of independent families; there is very little in the way of government or law, there is almost no private property, and theft is unimportant. Matters which concern only the members of a family are dealt with within the family.

> Disputes betwixt others can in this state but rarely occur, but if they do, and are of such a nature as would be apt to disturb the community, the whole community then interferes to make up the difference; which is ordinarily all the length they go, never

---

[28] *See generally* Stein, *Law and Society in Eighteenth Century Scottish Thought,* in SCOTLAND IN THE AGE OF IMPROVEMENT 148-68 (N. Phillipson & R. Mitchison eds. 1970).

[29] *See* Stein, *Adam Smith's Theory of Law and Society,* in CLASSICAL INFLUENCES ON WESTERN THOUGHT 1650-1870, 263-73 (R. Bolgar ed. 1979).

[30] J. LAFITAU, MOEURS DES SAUVAGES AMÉRIQUAINS, COMPARÉES AUX MOEURS DES PREMIERS TEMPS (W. Fenton & E. Moore eds. & trans. 1974).

[31] P. DE CHARLEVOIX, HISTOIRE ET DESCRIPTION GÉNERÁLE DE LA NOUVELLE FRANCE (Paris 1744).

[32] A. MOMIGLIANO, STUDIES IN HISTORIOGRAPHY 141 (1966).

[33] Smith commended Machiavelli as the only contemporary historian "who has contented himself with that which is the chief purpose of history, to relate events and connect them with their causes, without becoming a party on either side." A. SMITH, LECTURES ON RHETORIC AND BELLES LETTRES 110-11 (J. Lothian ed. 1963).

> daring to inflict what is properly called punishment. The design of their intermeddling is to preserve the public quiet, and the safety of the individuals; they therefore endeavour to bring about a reconcilement betwixt the parties at variance.[34]

The American Indians exemplified this state.

The second stage, that of shepherds, cannot co-exist with the first. "The appropriation of flocks and herds renders subsistence by hunting very uncertain and precarious."[35] The people are more numerous than at the hunting stage, and live a nomadic life, following the best grazing. Animals are now regarded as the property of particular individuals, with the result that "distinctions of rich and poor then arise."[36] Government proper begins at this stage, because when

> some have great wealth and others nothing, it is necessary that the arm of authority should be continually stretched forth, and permanent laws or regulations made which may ascertain [*i.e.*, secure] the property of the rich from the inroads of the poor . . . . Laws and government may be considered in this and indeed in every case as a combination of the rich to oppress the poor, and preserve to themselves the inequality of the goods which would otherwise be soon destroyed by the attacks of the poor, who if not hindered by the government would soon reduce the others to an equality with themselves by open violence. The government and laws hinder the poor from ever acquiring the wealth by violence which they would otherwise exert on the rich; they tell them they must either continue poor or acquire wealth in the same manner as they have done.[37]

At this stage, offences against the community are dealt with by expulsion. Smith likened society at this pastoral stage to a club: "The members of any club have it in their power to turn out any member, and so also have the members of such a community."[38] Laws are, of course, no more than conventions or settled practices. "The legislative is never met with amongst people in this state of society. [It is] the product of more refined manners and improved government. . . ."[39] Certain peoples described by Homer, whom Smith treats not as a poet but as a writer on social

---

[34] LECTURES ON JURISPRUDENCE, *supra* note 1, at 201.
[35] *Id.* at 202.
[36] *Id.*
[37] *Id.* at 208-09 (footnotes omitted).
[38] *Id.* at 204.
[39] *Id.* at 205.

anthropology, the Jews in the period of Genesis, the Germans described by Tacitus—all these exemplify the pastoral stage.

The third stage, that of agriculture, is marked by the appearance of private property in land. At first, property in land continued only so long as the land was actually being cultivated, and did not persist once the crop was out of the ground. Smith cited the practice of the country folk in Scotland of letting their cattle wander wherever they wanted as soon as the crop was harvested. This practice was in fact contrary to the Winter Herding Act of 1686, which ordered farmers to keep their cattle herded, in winter as well as in summer, under penalty of half a mark for each beast found on a neighbor's land. The ordinary people ignored the statute and its penalties, Smith said, for they were "so wedded to the notion that property in land continues no longer than the crop is on the ground that there is no possibility of getting them to observe it."[40] It is at this stage that regular courts are established and legislation begins.

The possibility of advancement beyond the agricultural stage depends on the ability of the society to produce a surplus of produce beyonds its own immediate needs and on the opportunity to export that surplus to other societies. A people who were

> settled in a country where they lived in pretty great ease and security and in a soil capable of yielding them good returns for cultivation, would not only improve the earth but also make considerable advances in the severall arts and sciences and manufactures, providing they had the opportunity of exporting their [surplus] produce and fruits of their labour.[41]

The Tartars and Arabs lacked these conditions, and so did not advance; the Greeks, on the other hand, possessed both and could enter the stage of commerce. A further extension and complication of laws is needed for this fourth stage.

In general, the principle of development is that "[t]he more improved any society is and the greater length the severall means of supporting the inhabitants are carried, the greater will be the number of their laws and regulations necessary to maintain justice, and prevent infringements of the right of property."[42] Locke

---

[40] *Id.* at 23 (footnote omitted).

[41] *Id.* at 223.

[42] *Id.* at 16.

had expressed something of this idea,[43] but Smith made it the basis of his whole treatment of rights. Moreover, changes in the concept of ownership of property and changes in the form of government go hand in hand. Smith envisaged a kind of cyclical evolution of types of government, each of which "seems to have a certain and fixed end which concludes it."[44]

Property means something quite different according to the state of progress a society has reached. It is no good talking in general terms about property; we must look to the nature of the society we are discussing and to its current ideas about private property. In defining injury to the property rights recognized by a given society. Smith turned again to the hard-worked impartial spectator. A man could be said to have suffered an injury only "when an impartial spectator would be of opinion he was injured, would join with him in his concern, and go along with him" if he defended his property against attack.[45] To find the views of the impartial spectator in any society it was thus necessary to look into the popular psychology of that society. For example, Homer was Smith's guide to the attitudes of the warrior society existing at the time of t[illegible]n war. Odysseus, when asked whether he was a merchant [illegible]ate, said he was a pirate.

> [T]his [illegible]ch more honourable character than that of a mercha[illegible] was allways looked on with great contempt by them. A[illegible] a military man who acquires his livelyhood by warlike [illegible] whereas a merchant is a peaceable one who has no [illegible]or military skill and would not be much esteemed i[illegible]n consisting of warriors chiefly.[46]

2. *Rights [illegible]ily Member*

After man as an individual comes man as a member of a family. Under this head, Smith considered three relationships: husband-wife, father-son, and master-servant. His treatment of marriage drew heavily on the history of the marriage laws of Rome.[47] In the earliest times, the wife was absolutely in the

---

[43] *See* J. Locke, *Essay Concerning the True Original, Extent and End of Civil Government,* in TWO TREATISES ON CIVIL GOVERNMENT ¶ 124, at 256 (1884).

[44] LECTURES ON JURISPRUDENCE, *supra* note 1, at 238.

[45] *Id.* at 17.

[46] *Id.* at 224.

[47] When tracing the development of particular legal institutions in detail, Smith was

power of her husband. The reason, Smith explains, was that at this period, the fortune a woman could bring to her husband on marriage was very small and insufficient to entitle her to bargain with him; her only option was to submit to his power. However, as the wealth of the society increased, rich heiresses became not uncommon and, in their favor, a new kind of marriage was introduced in which the wife remained independent of her husband's power. This sort of marriage was created by consent and could be dissolved by the will of either party. Yet "tho it had none of the old solemnities [it] was found by the lawyers to save the lady's honour and legitimate the children."[48] Since this form of marriage was found to be much more convenient and adapted to the licentiousness of the times, the old forms were abandoned.

After the fall of the Roman Empire, however, the barbarian successor societies were in an earlier stage of development than that of the Romans, and the wife was still under the subjection of her husband. Furthermore as a result of the influence of the Christian clergy, marriage came to be almost indissoluble.[49] In short, the relationship of husband and wife varied with the economic development of society and the degree of progress it had attained.

---

largely restricted to two systems for his illustrations: Roman law and English law. The Roman legal sources documented the development of the system for over a thousand years of antiquity—from the Twelve Tables in the fifth century B.C. to the legislation of the sixth century A.D., to say nothing of developments after the medieval revival of legal studies. Furthermore, nonlegal Latin literature provided the social background against which the law evolved. Only English law provided a similarly detailed set of written sources for tracing its development. It had borrowed less from Roman law than any other system, and for that reason, Smith felt it was closer to nature. It is "more deserving of the attention of a speculative man than any other, as being more formed on the naturall sentiments of mankind." LECTURES ON JURISPRUDENCE, *supra* note 1, at 98. The Scots lawyers of Kames' circle, with their interest in unification of law in Britain, were more conscious than their contemporaries in England of legal systems other than their own. Smith showed himself at home in both Roman law and English law, as well as Scots law, and could draw parallels from their respective histories.

[48] LECTURES ON JURISPRUDENCE, *supra* note 1, at 144.

[49] Smith took the opportunity in this context to make some curious comments on the change which he considers this indissolubility of marriage produced in the character of "the passion of love."

> This passion was formerly esteemed to be a very silly and ridiculous . . . one . . . . [T]here is no poems (sic) of a serious nature grounded on that subject either amongst the Greeks or Romans. There is no ancient tragedy, except Phaedra, the plot of which turns on a love story, tho there are many on all other passions, as anger, hatred, revenge, ambition, etc. . . . The reason why this passion made so little a figure then in comparison of what it now does is plainly this. The passion itself is as I said of nature rather ludicrous; the frequency and easieness of divorce made the gratification of it of no great mo-

The development of Roman law also provided a model for the second family relationship, that of father and son. Although the power of the father was at first altogether absolute, it gradually acquired limits. In the early Republic, the father had the legal power to sell his son to work for another man although, Smith argued, this power probably extended only to unmarried sons. It would be difficult for the father to sell a married son, since the son would have assumed obligations to his wife and children. In practice, moreover, the father's power would be curbed by pressure from other members of the family and by public opinion. When we observe the original concentration of all property in the father and the gradual recognition of the son's right to have property of his own, independently of his father, we see that "the power of the fathers, tho very considerable, does not appear to have been so unbounded as we are apt to imagine."[50]

In the case of the relationship of master and servant, Smith shows a deep understanding of how slavery operated in antiquity and draws important parallels with its working in his own time. He insisted that slavery was the norm in the world and that its abolition in one small corner of the world, namely western Europe, was exceptional. He showed in detail that slavery was inferior to free labour on economic grounds but he recognized that the condition of the slave, though legally the same in all societies which tolerate it, was "a much more tollerable one in a . . . poor and barbarous people than in a rich and polished one."[51]

In a poor country, where the number of slaves in relation to the number of freemen is small, slaves are a valuable asset and represent no threat. In a rich country, where their numbers are great, they considerably outnumber the freemen and so constitute a formidable body who must be repressed. Horace observed that no one who aspired to be a gentleman in the Rome of Augustus would have less than ten slaves,[52] and there are many illustrations

---

> ment . . . . [T]he union might be dissolved at any time. This was the case both amongst the Greeks and Romans. But when marriage became indissoluble, the matter was greatly altered. The choice of the object of this passion, which is commonly the forerunner of marriage, became a matter of the greatest importance. The union was perpetuall and consequently the choice of the person was a matter which would have a great influence on the future happiness of the parties. From that time therefore we find that love makes the subject of all our tragedies and romances . . . .

Id. at 149-50 (footnotes omitted). Smith himself never married.

[50] *Id.* at 175.

[51] *Id.* at 182.

[52] *See* Horace, *Satires* 1.2.3ff; 1.3.11ff.

of the barbarity with which Romans of that period treated their slaves. In contrast, Tacitus noted that the Germans of the same period treated their slaves with great humanity.[53]

Smith then drew a similar contrast between the contemporary treatment of slaves in the colonies of continental North American and that in the West Indian sugar islands. In the former their masters could not afford to keep a great number and they were "treated with great humanity and used in a very gentle manner."[54] On the other hand, in the sugar islands the planters could afford to keep a multitude of slaves. Faced with the constant threat of insurrection, the planters treated the slaves with "the greatest rigour and severity."[55]

B. *Legal Institutions*

The significance of Smith's evolutionary approach for jurisprudence is that it enabled him to explain the basis of legal institutions in a different way from that of the writers in the natural law tradition. They had stressed the will of the individuals involved in a transaction, and set it against the good of the community as a whole. Smith substituted an analysis of society's economic needs and popular psychology.

A vital institution in private law is contract, and Smith differed from Grotius and Pufendorf in explaining the nature of contractual obligation. The traditional explanation was that what made a contract binding was the promisor's declaration of his will which bound him to keep his word.[56] Smith argued that it was rather the expectation which the promisor's declaration created in the promisee. An impartial spectator would not always consider that every declaration of intent should be relied on by the promisee. Primitive societies make light of breaches of contract and do not always hold contracts binding. It is only with the advance of commerce that contracts become frequent. Only then is there a need for credit to be given and only then does an informal promise reasonably create in the promisee a ground of expectation, which would be disappointed if the promise were not fulfilled. The extent of the obligation is measured by the disappointment the breach of it would occasion.[57]

---

[53] *See* Tacitus, *Germania* 25.

[54] Lectures on Jurisprudence, *supra* note 1, at 183.

[55] *Id.* at 183.

[56] *See* 2 H. Grotius, *supra* note 18, at 2.11.2; 3 S. Pufendorf, *supra* note 18, at 3.5.5.

[57] *See* Lectures on Jurisprudence, *supra* note 1, at 86-102.

Again, when dealing with acquisition of property by succession on death, Smith differs from Grotius and Pufendorf. They explained intestate succession as based on the supposed will of the deceased.[58] The deceased normally expresses his intentions in his will, but if he fails to make a will, the law distributes his estate as he is presumed to have intended. This kind of explanation, argued Smith, is quite unhistorical because it implies that testamentary succession preceded intestate succession. In all societies, ancient and modern, the reverse is the case. The right to dispose of one's property after death by will "is one of the greatest extentions of property we can conceive, and consequently would not be early introduced into society."[59] In the age of hunters, there was no succession at all, a man's personal belongings, his weapons, being buried with him. In later stages, property was regarded as family property "which as it was maintained and procured by the labour of the whole family, was also the common support of the whole."[60] The head of the family alone could alienate family property in his lifetime, but not at his death. His descendants' claim to share in his property after his death was not based originally on his will, express or implied, but on the fact that they had themselves helped to procure and maintain the property.

Once more, Smith's historical approach led him to an explanation of the nature of criminal law different from that of the natural law writers. They had argued that the basis of punishment for crime was consideration of the public good.[61] The real source, said Smith, must be the resentment of the injured party. The measure of punishment is the degree of revenge the impartial spectator would find acceptable.[62] In early societies it was left to the victim to get his own satisfaction for crimes.

> In the description of the shield of Achilles, in one of the compartments the story represented is the friends of a slain man receiving presents from the slayer. The government did not then intermeddle in those affairs; and we find that the stranger who comes on board the ship of Telemachus tells us he fled from the friends of a man whom he had slain, and not from the officers of justice.[63]

---

[58] *See* 2 H. GROTIUS, *supra* note 18, at 2.7.3; 4 S. PUFENDORF, *supra* note 18, at 4.11.1.

[59] LECTURES ON JURISPRUDENCE, *supra* note 1, at 38.

[60] *Id.* at 39.

[61] *See* 2 H. GROTIUS, *supra* note 18, at 2.20.7; 8 S. PUFENDORF, *supra* note 18, at 8.3.9.

[62] LECTURES ON JURISPRUDENCE, *supra* note 1, at 104.

[63] *Id.* at 108.

Only later does the state concern itself with the prosecution of crimes.

If the injury is so great that the spectator can go along with the injured person in revenging himself by the death of the offender, that is the proper punishment, which is to be exacted by the victim or the magistrate acting the role of the impartial spectator. If the impartial spectator will only go along with a pecuniary penalty, then that is the punishment which ought to be inflicted. In support of this point, Smith cited a contemporary example. The British people conceived the "whimsical" notion that their prosperity depended on the woolen goods trade and therefore made the exportation of wool a felony punishable by death. But since, in natural equity, this exportation was no crime at all, it was found impossible to get informers or jurors who would convict. So the punishment had to be reduced to what was acceptable.[64]

Conclusion

Smith's jurisprudence is clearly of historical interest. Does it have lessons for us today? We may summarize its main aspects. First, unlike earlier writers who favoured armchair speculation, based on reason alone, about what law ought ideally to be, Smith thought that a legal theory should start from what is known about actual systems in different kinds of society. His account was based on a comprehensive knowledge of the available data from antiquity to his own times. He understood the complexity of these data and realized that sometimes the evidence of antiquity confirmed contemporary experience, as in the effects of slavery on society, and sometimes it illustrated a stage through which contemporary society had passed, as in the case of marriage.

Secondly, such a theory must account for legal change, and legal change is part of social change. Smith accepted that human society was progressing from barbarism to civilization; being a Deist, he believed that the general course of this progress was laid down by the invisible hand of an all-wise Author of Nature. Legal theory must therefore be historical in that it must view the development of law as part of the general progress of society.

Thirdly, and more particularly, Smith established the link between the form of the economy and the kind of law within a soci-

---

[64] *Id.* at 104-05.

ety. His contemporaries learned this lesson very quickly; as William Robertson, the leading orthodox historian of the period, put it: "In every enquiry concerning the operations of men who are united together in society, the first object of attention should be their mode of subsistence. According as that varies, their laws and policy must be different."[65]

Smith wanted to offer a systematic theory which would account for legal change in the light of the progress of society and the form of the economy. But he was well aware of the dangers of determinism in the social sciences. Human action could and did prevent societies from following the natural course of development. So, fourthly, Smith stressed also the psychological aspects of legal change. By constantly keeping in mind the views of the impartial spectator, he never lost sight of the need to take account of popular attitudes toward law. Some laws are enacted in the interest of particular groups or they are kept alive when the need for them has long passed. This may be irksome to the theorist but he cannot overlook the influence of factional interests or of popular prejudices.

> The man of system . . . is often so enamoured with the supposed beauty of his own ideal plan of government, that he cannot suffer the smallest deviation from any part of it. . . . He seems to imagine that he can arrange the different members of a great society with as much ease as the hand arranges the different pieces upon a chess-board. He does not consider that the pieces upon the chess-board have no other principle of motion besides that which the hand impresses upon them; but that, in the great chess-board of human society, every single piece has a principle of motion of its own, altogether different from that which the legislature might chuse to impress upon it. If these two principles coincide and act in the same direction, the game of human society will go on easily and harmoniously, and is very likely to be happy and successful. If they are opposite or different, the game will go on miserably, and the society must be at all times in the highest degree of disorder.[66]

Smith is saying that we must never overlook the fact that the individual members of society are free agents, responsible for their actions. The legislator must therefore "accommodate, as well as he

---

[65] 5 W. Robertson, Works 111, 128 (1808) (cited in Skinner, *Adam Smith: An Economic Interpretation of History,* in Essays on Adam Smith, *supra* note 2, at 175).

[66] Theory of Moral Sentiments, *supra* note 1, at 233-34 (footnotes omitted).

can, his public arrangements to the confirmed habits and prejudices of the people . . . . [H]e will endeavour to establish the best that the people can bear."[67]

Fifthly and finally, Smith was a realist and this realism led him to prefer down-to-earth explanations to subtle ones. He never lost the common sense approach characteristic of the Scottish philosophy of his time. For example, the rule found in many systems, which allows a husband to divorce his wife for adultery without granting her a corresponding right to divorce him, is not designed, as was usually claimed, to prevent spurious offspring being imposed on the husband. "The real reason is that it is men who make the laws with respect to this; they generally will be inclined to curb the women as much as possible and give themselves the more indulgence."[68]

Smith's jurisprudence is complex rather than simple, but so is the law that it seeks to explain. Starting from a desire to distinguish what a man can be compelled to do from what he ought to do, he was led to the position that what a man can be compelled to do depends on the economic state of the society in which he lives. Smith understood that the law of a society sits, a little uneasily perhaps, between its morality and its economics.

---

[67] *Id.* at 233.

[68] LECTURES ON JURISPRUDENCE, *supra* note 1, at 147 (footnote omitted).

Part IV
Politics

[13]

Liberalism, Civic Humanism, and the Case of Adam Smith

EDWARD J. HARPHAM
The University of Texas at Dallas

In this article, I examine critically Donald Winch's interpretation of the politics of Adam Smith. I explain how Winch wrests Smith's political thought out of the larger vision of commercial society that is found in his moral, political, and economic writings, and how Winch misreads Smith's understanding of particular political problems such as the dehumanized workforce and the standing army. I also show how Winch's civic humanist reading of Smith's political thought fails to appreciate Smith's liberal conceptualizations of corruption and public-mindedness in a modern commercial society. Finally, I suggest that our failure to understand the politics of Adam Smith does not lie in our liberal interpretation of his work, as Winch claims, but in our understanding of what constitutes liberal political discourse.

The concepts of virtue and corruption have played a major role in the history of political thought since the ancient Greeks. Traditionally, histories of political thought have associated the decline of these concepts with the rise of liberalism in the seventeenth, eighteenth, and nineteenth centuries, and Marxism in the nineteenth and twentieth centuries (Cropsey, 1957; Cumming, 1969; Sabine, 1961; Wolin, 1960). A growing interest in the economic forces underlying political change is seen to displace gradually classical attempts to view politics through moral categories, and to give rise to a modern mechanistic view of the political order.

Over the past 15 years, a number of important attempts have been made to reinterpret seventeenth-, eighteenth-, and nineteenth-century thought through a reading of the republican or civic humanist tradition (Bailyn, 1967; Kramnick, 1968; Pocock, 1973, 1975a, b; Robbins, 1959; Wood, 1972). Focusing upon the central role played by the concepts of virtue and corruption in the republican tradition, these studies have led to a striking revisionist understanding of an evolving Anglo-American tradition of political discourse. Among the most prominent of the revisionist interpretations has been the work of J. G. A. Pocock.

According to Pocock, there emerged in post-1688 England a purely secular form of social criticism that drew heavily upon the civic humanist tradition of renaissance Florence in order to understand the impact of an expanding commercial economy upon English political life. Rejecting or minimizing the role of the individual in the marketplace, or of the merchant class in the economy, this civic humanism was based upon a perception of changes in the role of the individual as citizen, and in the autonomous citizen's ability to perform certain political and military duties. The function of property in the civic humanist paradigm was to insure the autonomy of each individual citizen in the performance of one's duties. Property, particularly landed or real property, was perceived to be the foundation upon which an individual's civic personality and civic virtue rested.

Pocock's interpretation has culminated in a serious reevaluation of the importance of liberal modes of thought in the seventeenth and eighteenth centuries. For Pocock, civic humanist writers were "the first intellectuals on record to express an entirely secular awareness of social and economic changes going on in their society, and to say specifically that these changes affected both their values and their modes of perceiving reality" (1975b, p. 461). Civic humanists did not investigate the dynamics of the marketplace nor did they accept the assumptions of "possessive individualism." They analyzed the modes of property which left men unduly dependent upon others from the property-personality-civic autonomy matrix. To the degree to which emerging social types such as the monied interest could not conform to these

Received: October 17, 1983
Accepted for publication: December 21, 1983

I would like to thank Robert Cumming, Merle Levy, Michael Levy, and Alan Stone for their assistance in reading and discussing earlier drafts of the article. I also would like to thank the Institute for Humane Studies for its support. An earlier version of the article was presented at the 1983 meetings of the Southwestern Political Science Association.

criteria, civic humanists denounced them as undermining or corrupting the social and economic foundations upon which the polity rested. To the degree to which these social types could conform to these criteria, civic humanists championed them as forces promoting virtue and stabilizing the political order.[1]

In *Adam Smith's Politics,* Donald Winch has written "an essay in historical revision" that draws heavily upon the civic humanist interpretation of eighteenth-century thought. By placing Smith in the context of civic humanism, Winch seeks to show how Smith's political views were affected by attitudes that were not liberal-capitalist in orientation and to explain why Smith's politics were not simply an episode "that occurred some way along a road which runs from Locke to Marx" (1978, p. 180). Far from representing the cutting edge of a liberal vision of the world, the politics of Adam Smith were part of the evolving tradition of seventeenth- and eighteenth-century civic humanism.

In this article I examine critically the Winch interpretation of Adam Smith's political thought. I argue that Winch's civic humanist reading of Adam Smith's politics has led to a serious misunderstanding of Smith's thought. Winch wrests Smith's political thought out of the larger vision of commercial society that is found in his moral, political, and economic writings. As a result, Winch fails to appreciate the degree to which Smith's understanding of particular political problems, such as a dehumanized workforce or the standing army, exists not only outside the logic of civic humanist thought, but in direct opposition to it. I also explain why Winch's analysis fails to appreciate Smith's "liberal" conceptualizations of the problem of corruption and public-mindedness in a modern commercial society and how these, too, stand outside the orbit of seventeenth- and eighteenth-century civic humanism. Smith's vision of commercial society, his understanding of what holds it together, and his insight into what threatens to undermine it are a far cry from seventeenth- and eighteenth-century civic humanist thought. Our failure to understand the politics of Adam Smith does not lie, as Winch claims, in our liberal interpretation of his work, but in our understanding of what constitutes liberal political discourse.

[1]Kramnick (1982) recently has suggested that the civic humanist interpretation has gone too far in its attempt to read Lockean liberalism out of eighteenth-century Anglo-American political thought. Macpherson (1962), Meek (1967, 1977), and Hirschman (1977) also provide alternative interpretations of the development of political and economic ideas in eighteenth-century Anglo-American political thought.

Winch's Smith

At the heart of Winch's reading of Adam Smith's politics lies an attempt to recover a lost political dimension to Smith's thought. According to Winch (1978, p. 26), "Smith employs a consistent method or style of political analysis in his writings and lectures which cannot readily be encompassed within the categories of the liberal capitalist perspective." In order to understand this lost dimension "it is necessary to bear in mind that he is frequently employing a well-established public language for discussing such matters—a language, the resonances of which were already well known to the educated members of his immediate audience" (1978, p. 5). Surprisingly, Winch's explanation of exactly what this "well-established public language" encompasses is rather vague. Constant references to the work of J. G. A. Pocock and his ongoing attempt to read Smithian political ideas in light of the property-personality equation found in the civic humanist tradition leave little doubt that the "public language" Winch is referring to is civic humanism. Indeed, chapters 4-7 demonstrate a systematic attempt to read Smith's analysis of particular political questions of the day, such as the question of the relationship between commerce and liberty, the problem of a dehumanized workforce, the public debt issue, and the standing-army controversy, in terms of the ideas of contemporary civic humanist writers.

The problem with Winch's civic humanist reading of Smith's politics is that it ultimately fails to come to terms with the broader world view that structures Smith's analysis of particular political problems of the day. This world view does not work out of the assumptions or the logic of the traditional civic humanist language of discourse, nor does it reflect a suspicious outlook toward the modern commercial order as is found in the work of most civic humanists. Indeed, the Smithian world view both accepts and champions the modern commercial order. The difference between Smith's perception of commercial capitalism and that found in civic humanism can be best appreciated by looking briefly at two aspects of Smith's thought: his analysis of the rise of commercial societies in Book III of *The Wealth of Nations,* and his use of the "four-stage theory" in Book IV.

Of Commerce and Liberty

There is little doubt that Smith draws heavily upon the historical arguments developed by David

Hume in the essays "Of Commerce" and "Of Refinement in the Arts" as well as in *The History of England.* Smith himself credits Hume with being the first modern writer to understand the relationship between commerce and liberty (1965, p. 385). For Winch, the Humean connection puts Smith's thought solidly in the civic humanist tradition because "Hume's language and mode of conducting his argument . . . can also be described in terms of the civic humanist perspective" (1978, p. 74).

There are a number of problems with this interpretation. First, it fails to appreciate the larger political impetus behind Hume's political and philosophical writings. Hume did not develop his historical arguments about the relationship between commerce and liberty in the modern world in order to criticize modern commercial society from within a civic humanist perspective. As Forbes (1975) has shown, he developed it to move contemporary thinking about politics beyond the narrow court-country debate within which civic humanist arguments thrived. Ultimately, Hume sought to explain why commerce tended to promote, rather than to undercut, liberty in the modern world.

A second problem with this interpretation is that it fails to appreciate how antithetical the notion of liberty found in Hume's historical writings and in Smith's economic writings is to the civic humanist mind. Both Hume and Smith agree with their civic humanist contemporaries that feudalism had undercut liberty by fostering conditions of economic and social dependency. But the liberty that Hume and Smith believe accompany the "order and good government" introduced by commerce and manufactures is not that found in civic humanism. For the civic humanist, the idea of liberty is integrally connected to the idea of the independent citizen who is capable of engaging in politics and of acting in the public interest. Liberty thus is conceived in a highly positive manner along the lines of classical Greek thought. In contrast, the notion of liberty discussed by Hume and Smith is a mean, almost entirely negative liberty. Commerce and manufacture do not create the economic conditions that might enable citizens to engage in political activity. They only free individuals from the dependency found in the feudal system. Thus although the marketplace frees individuals from immediate personal servitude, it does not make them into autonomous, independent citizens.

The most disturbing problem with this interpretation is its failure to understand the role that this anti-civic humanist line of argument played in the larger line of argument developed in *The Wealth of Nations.* Smith's analysis of the relationship between commerce and liberty is not developed primarily to move beyond civic humanist thought, but to explain historically why, despite earlier successes, the mercantile system posed a serious threat to future economic growth. To appreciate the political import of the historical arguments developed by Smith in Book III of *The Wealth of Nations,* they must be read in light of his larger economic arguments and his critique of the mercantile system.

Book I of *The Wealth of Nations* centers around a discussion of the role played by the division of labor in promoting economic growth. Book II focuses on the role played by the accumulation and use of capital. Two ideas lie at the heart of Smith's capital theory. First, Smith asserts that the accumulation of capital is a necessary precondition to the division of labor. As the division of labor advances, an increasing amount of capital must be accumulated beforehand in order to provide workers with the equipment and materials necessary for production (1965, pp. 259-260). Second, he maintains that there is a distinction between productive and nonproductive labor. "The annual produce of the land and labour of any nation can be increased in its value by no other means, but by increasing either the number of its productive labourers, or the productive powers of those labourers who had before been employed" (1965, p. 326). In other words, capital expended on nonproductive activities is considered to be wasted capital, at least in terms of promoting economic growth and increasing the wealth of the nation.

Book II concludes with a discussion of why capital can be used more fruitfully in one sector of the economy than in another in light of these two ideas. Smith notes that capital employed in the retail trade can support those productive shopkeepers and tradesmen who sell directly to the consumer. In their profits "consists the whole value which its employment adds to the annual produce of the land and labour of the society" (1965, p. 343). Capital can also be used to promote the transportation of crude and manufactured products from where they abound to where they are needed. Employing capital in this manner not only directly supports the productive activities of wholesale merchants, but also indirectly puts into motion the labor of the farmer and the manufacturer. "Its operation in both these respects is a good deal superior to that of the capital of the retailer" (1965, p. 344). Capital also can be used in the manufacture and preparation of raw materials and produce for immediate use and consumption, which puts into motion an even greater quantity of productive labor than does an equal amount in the hands of a wholesale merchant. Finally, Smith notes that capital can be employed in obtaining the crude produce needed for the use and consumption of society. "The capital employed in agriculture, therefore, not only puts into motion a greater quantity of productive labour than any equal capital employed in manufactures, but in proportion too to the quantity of productive labour which it employs, it adds a much greater value to the annual produce of the land and labour of the country, to the real wealth and revenue of its inhabitants." Capital used in agriculture was considered to be "by far the most advantageous to the society" (1965, p. 345).

Smith's economic understanding of the place of agriculture in a commercial society clearly lies outside the civic humanist matrix of property-personality-virtue. Agriculture is important not because it is the foundation upon which civic virtue rests, but because it is the optimal sector for allocating capital. This point is reemphasized in chapter 1 of Book III of *The Wealth of Nations,* "Of the Natural Progress of Opulence," where Smith describes optimal capital allocation under conditions of natural liberty.

According to Smith, a man will naturally prefer to employ his capital in the improvement and cultivation of land, rather than in trade or manufacture, given equal or nearly equal profits. "The man who employs his capital in land, has it more under his view and command, and his fortune is much less liable to accidents, than that of the trader, who is obliged frequently to commit it, not only to the winds and the waves, but to the more uncertain elements of human folly and injustice, by giving great credits in distant countries to men, whose character and situation he can seldom be thoroughly acquainted" (1965, p. 358). Similarly, given equal or near equal profits, a man will naturally prefer to employ capital in domestic manufacturing than in foreign commerce. As Smith explains, "As the capital of the landlord or farmer is more secure than that of the manufacturer, so the capital of the manufacturer, being at all times more within his view and command, is more secure than that of the foreign merchant" (1965, p. 359). In other words, according to a "natural progress of opulence," capital is directed in a growing commercial society first to agriculture, then to manufacture, and finally to foreign commerce. "This order of things is so very natural, that in every society that had any territory, it has always, I believe, been in some degree observed" (1965, p. 360).

It is within the context of this discussion of the natural progress of the opulence that Smith takes up the historical arguments considered by Hume. Although Smith believes that economic growth must take place to some degree according to the natural progress of opulence, he observes that in all modern European states the "natural order of things" has become "in many respects, entirely inverted." Modern Europeans often find it more to their advantage to employ their capital in distant foreign commerce, even though much of the land in their own country remains underdeveloped or uncultivated. In addition, he points out that manufacture and commerce were responsible for giving birth to the major improvements in agriculture in Europe. In contrast to Hume, Smith thus is not interested primarily in explaining how commerce had promoted, rather than undermined, liberty in the modern world. Instead, he wants to explain what circumstances forced European states "necessarily . . . into this unnatural and retrograde order" (1965, p. 360). For Smith, this boils down to understanding how some political arrangements stifled natural economic growth, whereas others promoted a seemingly unnatural form.

The "economic" problematic that underlies Smith's historical arguments is clearly evident in three of the four chapters of Book III. In chapter 2 Smith explains how the feudal institutions of primogeniture and entails were responsible for undermining the natural progress of opulence from the fall of Rome to the modern commercial era. Because the great feudal landlords simply lacked the ability or the incentive to cultivate and improve the land, stimulus for economic growth in the countryside ultimately had to come from some sector of the economy that had escaped the restrictions of feudal laws and custom. In chapter 3 he describes how towns and cities gradually freed themselves from the political rule of the feudal landlords. Finally, in chapter 4 he discusses the impact that independent town life had upon European economic development.

For Smith, unlike Hume, the significance of the rise and development of commerce out of independent town life does not lie simply in the political fact that it introduced good government and liberty into the modern world; it lies in the economic fact that the modern mercantile order had developed contrary to the natural order of things. In the past, foreign commerce had been the leading sector of economic growth and had been responsible for stimulating growth in all other sectors of the economy. As Smith's capital theory shows, however, foreign commerce was also the least productive and most unstable sector of the economy. As long as the nation continued to rely upon foreign commerce as it had in the past, future economic prosperity would rest upon the most unstable of foundations.[2]

[2]Smith writes, "The capital, however, that is acquired to any country by commerce and manufactures, is all a very precarious and uncertain possession, till some part of it has been secured and realised in the cultivation and

In sum, Smith's discussion of the rise and development of commercial society out of the feudal system and his use of Humean historical arguments about the relationship between commerce and liberty lie outside the rhetoric of civic humanist critics of commercial society. Smith's arguments culminate not with a rejection of commercial society but with an appeal to throw off the mercantilist policies that continued to force the British economy into an "unnatural and retrograde order." Similarly, the call for a "system of natural liberty" is not a rejection of the modern commercial order and the economic growth that was an essential part of it; it is an affirmation of the commercial order and a call to place future economic growth on more secure foundations.

The Four-Stage Theory

Winch's misinterpretation of the politics of Adam Smith is not limited to his analysis of Smith's account of the rise of commercial societies in Book III of *The Wealth of Nations.* He also fails to appreciate fully how Smith's analyses of particular problems were shaped by the so-called four-stage theory, or how this theory set apart Smith's political ideas from the thought of other civic humanist writers. This failure is particularly evident in Winch's analysis of Smith's contribution to the standing army controversy (1978, chap. 5).

For most modern readers, Smith's inquiry into the nature and expense of military defense in the different stages of society seems rather inconsequential and parochial. In the context of eighteenth-century England, however, he was addressing one of the most sensitive political issues of the day—the question of the standing army. For civic humanist pamphleteers throughout the eighteenth century, the existence of the standing army was perceived to be a constant threat to civil liberty; it reflected the corruption introduced into the body politic by commerce. Only by maintaining a watchful citizen militia, they argued, was it possible to secure the nation from those forces that threatened it both from within and without (Pocock, 1973, chap. 4; Winch, 1978, chap. 5).

Like other contemporary civic humanist writers such as Adam Ferguson and John Millar, Smith was willing to concede that there were basically two methods by which a modern commercial society could protect itself from outside invasion. Either it could attempt to instill a martial spirit into the entire population "by means of a very rigorous police," an alternatiave supported by Ferguson, or it could "render the trade of a soldier a particular trade, separate and distinct from all the others" (1965, pp. 658-660). The first option, Smith notes, went against the interests as well as the natural inclinations of those who live in a commercial society. No matter how disciplined such a force might become, it would always be inferior to a well-disciplined and well-trained military force. His position in regard to the standing-army controversy thus pits him directly against contemporary civic humanists. Only by means of a professional standing army could a commercial society protect itself from the violence and injustice of other states.

Winch concedes that Smith's position on the standing-army controversy places him at odds with contemporary civic humanist thought, but he nevertheless maintains that the setting and the premises on which he poses the problem leave Smith in the civic humanist matrix. In particular, Winch notes that the discussion takes place in the context of a moral and social analysis of the consequences of the division of labor in modern societies and reflects a civic humanist concern over the preconditions for effective citizenship (1978, p. 113). Unfortunately, at least for Winch's argument, Smith himself does not use the republican notion of citizenship in his analysis of commercial society. Indeed, it will be argued below that such a concept, as well as the accompanying civic humanist notions of virtue and corruption, are foreign to his understanding of the modern commercial order. Moreover, his discussion of the social and moral consequences of the division of labor is actually part of a larger argument, the so-called four-stage theory, that places his analysis of the standing-army controversy firmly outside the civic humanist worldview.

Smith's four-stage theory originates with his contention in both the unpublished *Lectures on Justice, Police, Revenue and Arms* and Book V of *The Wealth of Nations* that there are four distinct stages to human society: hunting, pasturage, farming, and commerce. In categorizing each stage of human history by the mode of subsistence that predominates in it, Smith is not trying to make a Marxian-type argument that these are the actual stages of western European historical development. Instead, he is trying to formulate a

improvement of its lands. A merchant, it has been said very properly, is not necessarily the citizen of any particular country. It is in a great measure indifferent to him from what place he carries on his trade; and a very trifling disgust will make him remove his capital, and together with it all the industry which it supports, from one country to another. No part of it can be said to belong to any particular country, till it has been spread as it were over the face of that country, either in buildings, or in the lasting improvement of lands" (1965, p. 395). For a discussion of Smith's capital theory, see Bowley (1975) and Hollander (1973).

developmental perspective for understanding how and why different stages of economic development give rise to different sorts of political arrangements and what the proper role of political institutions should be in the modern commercial order (Höpfl, 1978; Skinner, 1967, 1975).

Significantly, this general line of argument bears little resemblance to the cyclical notions of time and economic change found in seventeenth- and eighteenth-century civic humanist thought.[3] On the contrary, it represents an extension of the natural histories of economic improvement and societal development found in the work of Locke, Mandeville, and Hume. Much like the natural histories of these earlier liberal writers, Smith's four-stage theory is used to explain why political institutions in a commercial society were necessarily different from those in earlier stages of society, and what the proper functions of these institutions were, given the social, political, and economic problems brought on by economic development.[4]

The way in which this liberal four-stage theory shapes Smith's perception of the standing-army controversy is delineated at the beginning of Book V of *The Wealth of Nations,* where he considers the duties that remain for a sovereign under the system of natural liberty. "The first duty of the sovereign," writes Smith, "that of protecting the society from the violence and invasion of other independent societies, can be performed only by means of a military force. But the expence both of preparing this military force in time of peace, and of employing it in time of war, is very different in the different stages of society, in the different periods of improvement" (1965, p. 653).

According to Smith, in a nation of hunters, every man is a warrior as well as a hunter. When a hunter goes to war, he maintains himself by his own labor, much as he would during times of peace. As a result, a hunter society "is at no sort of expence either to prepare him for the field, or to maintain him while he is in it" (1965, p. 653). The military situation in more advanced countries differs considerably from that found in the more primitive hunting societies. Shepherd societies have no fixed place of habitation, and thus, unlike hunter societies, are not completely limited by the bounty of nature. Although an army of hunters might be limited to 200 or 300 men because of their precarious mode of subsistence, an army of shepherds could potentially number in the thousands. A nation of shepherds thus is a much more formidable military opponent than a nation of hunters (1965, pp. 653-654).

The military situation found in more advanced farming societies is different still. In a farming society having little foreign commerce and no manufacture, every man remains a warrior or easily becomes one. The hardiness of ordinary life in a farming society prepares individuals physically and mentally for the rigors of war. As long as military expeditions begin after seed-time and end before harvest, an individual is able to participate in military affairs with little or no cost to himself. As in hunting and shepherd societies, the expense of war falls on the warriors themselves, not upon the sovereign (1965, p. 655). In terms of Smith's four-stage theory, the age of the husbandmen is effectively the age of the civic humanist citizen militia.

Three factors intervene in modern commercial societies to undermine the viability of citizen militias. First, the progress of manufactures makes it all but impossible for an individual who goes to war to maintain himself at his own expense. Whereas in an earlier stage of society a man could take to the field without seriously disturbing his source of income, in a commercial age a worker who is compelled to quit his place of work also loses his sole source of income. Similarly, farmers have little extra time for warfare, given the improvements that the progress of manufactures introduces into the countryside. As a result, "Military exercises come to be as much neglected by the inhabitants of the country as by those in the town, and the great body of the people becomes altogether unwarlike" (1965, p. 659). Second, improvements in the art of war make it one of the most intricate and complicated arts in a commercial society. In order to master this art it becomes necessary for the citizen to spend an increasing amount of time in military exercises. Third, the wealth that follows from the economic improvements found in commercial societies provokes the invasion of all their neighbors who desire their wealth. "An industrious, and upon that account a wealthy nation," Smith thus con-

[3]By noting that two important republican writers of the day, Adam Ferguson and John Millar, made arguments that paralleled those developed by Smith in his four-stage theory, Winch appears to argue that Smith therefore employs a civic humanist line of argument in his political thought. However, quite the contrary was the case. By grounding some of their arguments in a four-stage theory argument, both Ferguson and Millar were introducing tensions into their own thought that could not be easily reconciled with their republican values.

[4]It is important to recognize that the four-stage theory is not purely a product of the liberal tradition. The earliest modern versions of a stage-theory argument are found more frequently in continental rather than British writers. Moreover, Ronald Meek has argued that the four-stage theory is actually a pre-Marxist rather than a liberal theory. (See Cumming, 1969; Hőpfl, 1978; Meek, 1967, 1977; Skinner, 1967, 1975.)

cludes, "is of all nations the most likely to be attacked; and unless the state takes some new measures for the public defence, the natural habits of the people render them altogether incapable of defending themselves" (1965, p. 659).

By considering the question of the standing army in terms of the four-stage theory, Smith thus was able to account for the fact that at a certain age in societal development citizen militias could protect the nation from external threats. In addition, it enabled him to explain why in a commercial society such an option was no longer viable. In Smith's mind, a standing army had to be maintained by a commercial society if it were to "be perpetuated, or even preserved for any considerable time" (1965, p. 667). Far from revealing civic humanist leanings, the four-stage theory demonstrates how far out of touch with the problems of a modern commercial society Smith views civic humanist thought to be.

Corruption in Commercial Society

Two questions remain to be considered: What notions of corruption and public-mindedness does one find in Smith's work? How do these notions differ from those found in the civic humanist tradition? It is beyond the scope of this article to provide a comprehensive examination of the moral theory found in *A Theory of Moral Sentiments* (1976) or the way in which this moral theory complements and reinforces the economic arguments found in *The Wealth of Nations.* These issues have been dealt with at great length in other works on Smith (see Campbell, 1971; Cropsey, 1957; Lindgren, 1973; Morrow, 1969). However, we can briefly explain why Smith's notions of corruption and public-mindedness stand outside a civic humanist vision of the commercial order and what these show about a Smithian understanding of the problems confronting a modern commercial society.

One of the most striking differences between Smith's understanding of corruption and public-mindedness and that of contemporary civic humanist writers can be seen in the distinct underlying concerns. As noted earlier, civic humanists were concerned with the economic preconditions for independent action as a citizen. Landed property was perceived to be the foundation upon which an individual's civic personality was based because it enabled an individual to act autonomously and virtuously in public affairs. Significantly, Smith's discussion does not center around an analysis of the economic preconditions to effective citizenship, but around a discussion of the psychological ties that bind men together in all societies.

According to Smith, every independent state is divided into a number of different orders, each with its own particular privileges, powers, and immunities. The constitution of a particular state is determined by the orders found in a society and the distribution of powers, privileges, and immunities found among them (1976, pp. 376-377). Every individual is naturally, that is psychlogically, more attached to one's own particular order than to any other and seeks to expand and defend that order's privileges and immunities from the encroachments of other orders. This partiality is not necessarily bad, because it provides an important psychological check upon undesirable social changes. As Smith notes, "It tends to preserve whatever is the established balance among the different orders and societies into which the state is divided; and while it sometimes appears to obstruct some alterations of government which may be fashionable and popular at the time, it contributes in reality to the stability and permanency of the whole system" (1976, p. 377).

Along a similar line of argument, Smith maintains that the ties that ultimately bind these different orders together into a common political community, like those that tie individuals to their own order in society, are also derived from the moral sentiments. Indeed, Smith maintains that the distinction of ranks and the order of society are ultimately founded upon the disposition of mankind to go along with the passions of the rich and the powerful (1976, pp. 114-116). As Smith explains,

> That kings are the servants of the people, to be obeyed, resisted, deposed, or punished, as the public conveniency may require, is the doctrine of reason and philosophy; but it is not the doctrine of nature. Nature would teach us to submit to them for their own sake, to tremble and bow down before their exalted station, to regard their smile as a reward sufficient to compensate any services, and to dread their displeasure, though no other evil were to follow from it, as the severest of all mortifications. (1976, p. 116)

The political community found in a commercial society thus does not emerge out of the activities of economically independent citizens. It arises out of the natural disposition in individuals to defer to others in positions of authority.

A tone of uncertainty and anguish underlies Smith's discussion of the psychological phenomena found in all human societies that stands in contrast to the moderately upbeat and self-confident tone found in civic humanism. Smith's ideas reflect a world view that appears to be unsure of itself and of its future. His concern is not to create better citizens who can participate in the political life of the community, nor is it to reform the existing power structure. It is to maintain those conditions most highly conducive to the continuance of existing authority relations. The world of Adam Smith is not the civic humanist world analyzed by Pocock nor is it the world of nineteenth- and twentieth-century mass democracy. It is the troubled world of early liberalism sketched out by Wolin in *Politics and Vision* (1960, chap. 9). Nothing makes this more evident than Smith's conceptualization of the problems introduced into the commercial order by the division of labor.

Smith fully recognizes the devastating impact that the division of labor could have upon the work force. A man who spent his whole life performing a few simple operations naturally loses his ability to exercise his mind "and generally becomes as stupid and ignorant as it is possible for a human creature to become." As Smith explains,

> The torpor of his mind renders him, not only incapable of relishing or bearing a part in any rational conversation, but of conceiving any generous, noble, or tender sentiment, and consequently of forming any just judgment concerning many even of the ordinary duties of private life. Of the great and extensive interest of his country he is altogether incapable of judging; . . . The uniformity of his stationary life . . . corrupts even the activity of his body, and renders him incapable of exerting his strength with vigour and perseverance, in any other employment than that to which he has been bred. His dexterity at his own particular trade seems, in this manner, to be acquired at the expense of his intellectual, social, and martial virtues. But in every improved and civilized society this is the state into which the labouring poor, that is, the great body of the people, must necessarily fall, unless government takes some pains to prevent it." (1965, pp. 734-735)

In Winch's mind, this discussion of the mental mutilation of the work force brought on by the division of labor is further evidence of the humanistic side to Smith's politics. This reading simply fails to understand the concerns lying behind the discussion. Smith's concern is not with making workers into responsible citizens in the republican sense of the term. His four-stage theory had shown how foreign to a modern commercial society such a notion of citizenship was. In a commercial society, workers could not be expected to perform the military duties assumed by republican-minded citizens in farming societies (see Smith, 1965, pp. 658-659). Moreover, as the above quotation shows, Smith simply does not believe that a modern worker is capable of participating rationally in the political world. His concern is that the division of labor might dehumanize the worker to such a degree that the moral sentiments themselves might become corrupted and that the psychological bonds that tie the various orders in a society together might be torn asunder. Consequently, his solution to the problem of the division of labor, public education, is not aimed at creating independent citizens in the republican sense of the term; rather it is concerned with preventing "the almost entire corruption and degeneracy of the great body of the people" (1965, p. 734). This concern over the corruption of the moral sentiments of the people is shown clearly in a fascinating passage from Book V of *The Wealth of Nations.*

> Though the state was to derive no advantage from the instruction of the inferior ranks of people, it would still deserve its attention that they should not be altogether uninstructed. The state, however, derives no inconsiderable advantage from their instruction. The more they are instructed, the less liable they are to the delusions of enthusiasm and superstition, which, among ignorant nations, frequently occasion the most dreadful disorders. An instructed and intelligent people besides, are always more decent and orderly than an ignorant and stupid one. They feel themselves, each individually more respectable, and more likely to obtain the respect of their lawful superiors. . . . They are more disposed to examine, and more capable of seeing through the interested complaints of faction and sedition, and they are, upon that account, less apt to be misled into any wanton or unnecessary opposition to the measures of government. In free countries, where the safety of government depends very much upon the favorable judgment which the people may form of its conduct, it must surely be of the highest importance that they should not be disposed to judge rashly or capriciously concerning it. (1965, p. 740)

In short, the notion of corruption found in Smith's discussion is qualitatively different from that found in the civic humanist tradition. Rather than emerging out of a concern over the economic preconditions for the independent action on the part of the citizen, or centering around the property-personality-civic virtue paradigm traced out by Pocock, Smith's notion of corruption emerges out of his concern for the psychological attachments which tie men in different social orders together into a common political community and make authority relations possible.

Public-mindedness

Like his analysis of corruption in a commercial society, Smith's discussion of the problem of getting people to act in the public interest exists far outside the civic humanist world view. For the civic humanist, this problem was solved by creating "virtuous men" who had the economic independence to be able to transcend their private interests and to look upon the good of the community as a whole. Such a solution was unavailable to Smith. Smith recognizes that in a commercial society, individuals stood in constant need of the cooperation and assistance of others. One could not reasonably expect to gain this through either friendship or benevolence. Commercial society was simply too large and diverse for such bonds of affection to tie individuals together for any period of time. Indeed, Smith notes that an individual would be much more likely to gain the assistance of others by appealing to self-interest. "It is not from the benevolence of the butcher, the brewer, or the baker, that we expect our dinner, but from their regard to their own interest. We address ourselves, not to their humanity but to their self-love, and never talk to them of our own necessities but of their advantages" (1965, p. 14).[5]

For Smith, the problem of public-mindedness had to be dealt with in terms of the self-interest of individuals, not in spite of it. His concern was not to discuss how political actors could transcend their self-interest, but how this self-interest ultimately was tied to the public interest. When does the self-interest of an individual coincide with the public interest? When does it not? What factors might motivate political actors to seek out the public interest while acting in their own interest? These are the questions that propel his thought forward. His answers do not lie outside his economic theory, but are firmly embedded in it.

All too often, the underlying political objective of Smith's economic theory in *The Wealth of Nations* is forgotten by commentators. Smith was not writing an abstract treatise on economics that was to be read solely by academic scribes. He was addressing a particular order—the landlords in parliament—with a particular political objective in mind: to teach them what their economic interests were in a commercial society. Smith recognizes that of the three great orders in a commercial society, the landlords, the laborers, and the mercantile-manufacturers, only the latter had acquired a true understanding of what their specific interests were in matters of economic policy. Laborers had neither the time nor the necessary education or habits to think about public affairs in any systematic manner. The landlords, on the other hand, often suffered from an indolence "which is the natural effect of the ease and security of their situation" and which left them "not only ignorant but incapable of that application of mind which is necessary in order to foresee and understand the consequences of any public regulation" (1965, pp. 248-259).

The consequences of this state of affairs were devastating. By a superior knowledge of their own interest, the mercantile-manufacturer order had been able to impose its will upon the generosity of the "country gentleman" in parliament by convincing him that their interest, and not his or the laborers, was the interest of the public. As Smith warns, "The interests of the dealers, however, in any particular branch of trade or manufactures, is always in some respects different from, and even opposite to, that of the public" (1965, p. 250).

The economic theory developed in Book I of *The Wealth of Nations* is meant to provide the landlord order with an understanding of why the interest of the mercantile-manufacturer order differed from the general interest of society and why the interest of the landlord order was "strictly and inseparably" connected with it. In providing the members of the landlord order with an understanding of their own class-interest in economic affairs, Smith also was trying to teach them how to act in the long-run interest of the community as a whole. As Smith concludes at the end of Book I, "When the public deliberates concerning any regulation of commerce or police, the proprietors of land never can mislead it, with a view to promote the interest of their own particular order; at least, if they have any tolerable knowledge of that interest" (1965, p. 249). For Smith, economic theory thus held the key to getting people to act in the public interest. By teaching them what their own interest was in economic matters, those country gentlemen could also be pushed to act in the public interest.

Interestingly, Smith does not believe that economic theory rightly understood need appeal solely to policymakers' naked self-interest. It could also appeal to their love of system and their regard for the beauty of order, of art, and of con-

[5]Smith does note in *A Theory of Moral Sentiments,* "The wise and virtuous man is at all times willing that his own private interest should be sacrificed to the public interest of his own particular order or society. He is at all times willing, too, that the interest of this order or society should be sacrificed to the greater interest of the state or sovereignty of which it is only a subordinate part" (1976, p. 384). The notion of virtue discussed here, however, is a private-personal virtue, not a public one. In neither *The Wealth of Nations* nor in *A Theory of Moral Sentiments* does he argue that the solution to the problem of public-mindedness in a commercial society lies primarily in the creation of virtuous men. Kramnick argues that a new liberal notion of virtue emerged in eighteenth-century political thought that was tied into the idea of the self-centered individual who participated in the market (1982, pp. 663-664).

trivance; that is, to their moral sentiments. Smith writes,

> The perfection of police, the extension of trade and manufactures, are noble and magnificent objects. The contemplation of them pleases us, and we are interested in whatever can tend to advance them. They make part of the great system of government, and the wheels of the political machine seem to move with more harmony and ease by means of them. We take pleasure in beholding the perfection of so beautiful and so grand a system, and we are uneasy till we remove any obstruction that can in the least disturb or encumber the regularity of its motions. (1976, p. 305)

If a policymaker correctly understands the forces that move a modern commercial economy forward, he will be "animated to some degree of public spirit" and will feel some desire to remove those obstructions that prevent "so beautiful and so orderly a machine" from working properly. As Smith explains,

> Nothing tends so much to promote public spirit as the study of politics,—of the several systems of civil government, their advantages and disadvantages,—of the constitutions of our own country, its situation, and interest with regard to foreign nations, its commerce, its defense, the disadvantages it labours under, the dangers to which it may be exposed, how to remove the one and how to guard against the other. Upon this account political disquisitions, if just, and reasonable, and practicable, are of all the works of speculation, the most useful. Even the weakest and the worst of them are not altogether without their utility. They serve at least to animate the public passions of men, and rouse them to seek out the means of promoting the happiness of the society. (1976, p. 307)

In sum, for Smith the problem of instilling a concern over the public interest into the political order was not one that involved maintaining the economic preconditions for the independent action of an autonomous citizen. It was the establishment of the correct psychological disposition in the minds of policymakers to promote policies that served the public interest. The notion of public-mindedness found in Smith's work, like that of corruption, thus is quite different from that found in civic humanism. It is a liberal public-mindedness that accepts and, at times, champions, the self-interest that lies at the heart of modern commercial society. It is a liberal public-mindedness that is integrally related to liberal economic theory.

Conclusion

I have examined critically Donald Winch's civic humanist reading of Adam Smith's politics. My ongoing concern has been to explain why Smith's political thought should not be read apart from his economic thought or the larger conceptual framework within which his perception of commercial society operates. I do not mean to imply that conventional treatments of Smith's political thought fully appreciate the political dimension to Smith's thought. Winch is quite correct when he argues that far too little attention is paid to Smith's concern over the problems of corruption and public-mindedness in the modern commercial order. Unfortunately, Winch fails to see how closely connected to Smith's economic theory proper his understanding of these problems are. For Smith, economic theory is an important mode of political discourse that is integrally related to his political thought and his perception of the problems confronting the modern commercial order. Our failure to understand Smith as a political thinker does not reside simply in our failure to appreciate the "political" dimensions to his thought, but in our failure to understand how economic discourse itself shaped his perception of the modern commercial order.[6]

References

Bailyn, B. *The ideological origins of the American Revolution.* Cambridge, Mass.: Harvard University Press, 1967.

Bowley, M. *Studies in the history of economic theory before 1870.* London: Macmillan, 1973.

Campbell, T. D. *Adam Smith's science of morals.* London: George, Allen and Unwin, 1971.

Cropsey, J. *Polity and economy.* The Hague: Nijhoff, 1957.

Cumming, R. D. *Human nature and history: A study of the development of liberal political thought.* Chicago: University of Chicago Press, 1969.

Forbes, D. *Hume's philosophical politics.* Cambridge: Cambridge University Press, 1975.

Harpham, E. J. Natural law and early liberal economic thought: A reconsideration of Locke's theories of value. *Social Science Quarterly,* in press.

Hirschman, A. O. *The passions and the interests.* Princeton, N.J.: Princeton University Press, 1977.

[6]Political theorists' general failure to appreciate the political implications of liberal economic thought is not limited to the case of Adam Smith. For example, the actual economic writings of John Locke have all but been ignored by political theorists. For a discussion of the relationship between Lockean political and economic thought see Harpham (in press) and Vaughn (1980).

Hollander, S. *The economics of Adam Smith.* Toronto: University of Toronto Press, 1973.

Höpfl, H. M. From savage to Scotsman: Conjectural history in the Scottish enlightenment. *Journal of British Studies,* 1978, *17,* 19-40.

Kramnick, I. *Bolingbroke and his circle: The politics of nostalgia in the age of Walpole.* Cambridge, Mass.: Harvard University Press, 1968.

Kramnick, I. Republican revisionism revisited. *American Historical Review,* 1982, *87,* 629-664.

Lindgren, J. R. *The social philosophy of Adam Smith.* The Hague: Martinus Nijhoff, 1973.

Macpherson, C. B. *The political theory possessive individualism.* London: Oxford University Press, 1962.

Meek, R. *Economics and ideology.* London: Chapman and Hull, 1967.

Meek, R. *Smith, Marx, after: Ten essays on the development of economic thought.* London: Chapman and Hull, 1977.

Morrow, G. R. *The ethical and economic theories of Adam Smith.* New York: A. W. Kelley, 1969.

Pocock, J. G. A. Early modern capitalism—the Augustan perception. *Feudalism, capitalism and beyond.* E. Kamenka & R. S. Neale (Eds.). Canberra: Australian National University Press, 1975. (a)

Pocock, J. G. A. *The Machiavellian moment: Florentine political thought and the Atlantic republican tradition.* Princeton, N.J.: Princeton University Press, 1975. (b)

Pocock, J. G. A. *Politics, language and time: Essays on political thought and history.* New York: Atheneum, 1973.

Robbins, C. *The eighteenth century commonwealthman: Studies in the transmission, development and circumstances of English liberal thought from the restoration of Charles II until the war with the thirteen colonies.* Cambridge, Mass.: Harvard University Press, 1959.

Sabine, G. *A history of political theory* (3rd ed.). New York: Holt Rinehart and Winston, 1961.

Skinner, A. Adam Smith: An economic interpretation of history. *Essays on Adam Smith.* A. Smith & T. Wilson (Eds.). Oxford: Clarendon Press, 1975.

Skinner, A. Natural history in the age of Adam Smith. *Political Studies,* 1967, *15,* 32-48.

Smith, A. *An inquiry into the nature and the causes of the wealth of nations.* (E. Cannan & M. Lerner, Eds.). New York: Modern Library, 1965.

Smith, A. *Lectures on police, justice, revenue, and arms.* (E. Cannan, Ed.). New York: Kelley and Millman, 1956.

Smith, A. *A theory of moral sentiments.* Indianapolis: Liberty Classics, 1976.

Vaughn, K. I. *John Locke: Economist and social scientist.* Chicago: University of Chicago Press, 1980.

Winch, D. *Adam Smith's politics: An essay in historiographic revision.* Cambridge: Cambridge University Press, 1978.

Wolin, S. *Politics and vision: Continuity and innovation in western political thought.* Boston: Little, Brown, 1960.

Wood, G. *The creation of the American republic.* New York: W. W. Norton, 1972.

[14]

SCOTTISH POLITICAL ECONOMY BEYOND THE CIVIC TRADITION: GOVERNMENT AND ECONOMIC DEVELOPMENT IN THE *WEALTH OF NATIONS*[1]

John Robertson

'Considered as a branch of the science of a statesman or legislator', Adam Smith wrote in the *Wealth of Nations*, political economy proposes two distinct objects:

> first, to provide a plentiful revenue or subsistence for the people, or more properly to enable them to provide such a revenue or subsistence for themselves; and secondly, to supply the state or commonwealth with a revenue sufficient for the public services. It proposes to enrich both the people and the sovereign.[2]

Distinct as they are, however, the two objects of political economy as Smith here considers it are not necessarily in harmony: reading the *Wealth of Nations*, it emerges that the relation between economic development, 'the progress of opulence', and government, 'the state or commonwealth', presents a major problem.

The problem was not original to Smith: it faced him in his immediate social and intellectual context in eighteenth-century Scotland. Just such a problem lay at the heart of the recent experience of his native society. At the outset of the eighteenth century, the Scots had been required in the Treaty of Union with England to sacrifice their national political institutions to the quest for economic improvement; and the loss, however compensated, continued to cause them misgivings well into the second half of the century. Almost

[1] I wish to thank Lord Dacre of Glanton, Istvan Hont and Iain Hampsher-Monk for their helpful comments on earlier drafts.

[2] Adam Smith, *An Inquiry into the Nature and Causes of the Wealth of Nations* (1776), ed. R.H. Campbell, A.S. Skinner and W.B. Todd (2 vols., Oxford, 1976) (hereafter *Wealth of Nations*), Book IV, Introduction. Throughout this paper I shall use the reference system common to the Glasgow Edition of the Works and Correspondence of Adam Smith. The works in the Edition to be cited are: *The Theory of Moral Sentiments* (1759), ed. D.D. Raphael and A.L. Macfie (Oxford, 1976); *Lectures on Rhetoric and Belles Lettres* (Report of 1762–3), ed. J.C. Bryce (Oxford, 1983); *Lectures on Jurisprudence* (Reports of 1762–3 and 1766), ed. R.L. Meek, D.D. Raphael and P.G. Stein (Oxford, 1978); and *The Correspondence of Adam Smith*, ed. E.C. Mossner and I.S. Ross (Oxford, 1977).

HISTORY OF POLITICAL THOUGHT. Vol. IV. No. 3. Winter 1983.

certainly under the stimulus of this experience, moreover, Scottish thinkers had placed the problem of the relation between government and economic development at the centre of their historical and political writings. First in the years preceding the Union, when Andrew Fletcher of Saltoun led a remarkably sophisticated debate on the national predicament, and again in the period of the Enlightenment, at the instigation now of David Hume, the Scots had explored the demands which economic improvement makes of government institutions, and had sought to identify which form of government would be best adapted to the needs of a progressive, commercial society. It was this Scottish experience and debate which, I suggest, provided the starting-point for Smith's discussion of government and economic development in the *Wealth of Nations*.

The terms in which Smith's Scottish predecessors had come to grips with the problem were—as I have argued elsewhere, in a study to which this is the sequel—the terms of the civic tradition.[3] The civic I take to be that tradition of early modern political thought made familiar by the work of J.G.A. Pocock.[4] Of classical and more specifically Aristotelian genesis, the tradition's most authoritative exponents since the Renaissance had been the Florentine Machiavelli and the Englishman James Harrington. The tradition's concepts focused upon the institutional, moral and material conditions of free citizenship in a political community, viewed in a perspective secular and historical rather than theological and natural. These concepts defined a political community first and foremost by possession of a regular constitution, under which the institutions of civil government and a militia secured the freedom of all citizens to participate in the political life and defence of the community. Primary though the institutional framework was, however, it nonetheless depended on further moral and material conditions. If citizens were to take advantage of the freedom to participate given by the constitution they must be capable of moral virtue, of a commitment to the public good. In turn, fulfilment of this moral condition of citizenship depended on the possession of material independence or autonomy: only those—assumed to be few in number—in a position to satisfy their needs without making themselves dependent on others were capable of the requisite civic virtue. Conversely, failure to observe these material and moral conditions brought corruption. If a citizen lost his independence, or allowed himself to value private benefit

[3] John Robertson, 'The Scottish Enlightenment at the Limits of the Civic Tradition', in *Wealth and Virtue. The Shaping of Political Economy in the Scottish Enlightenment*, ed. I. Hont and M. Ignatieff (Cambridge, 1983), hereafter *Wealth and Virtue*. The following six paragraphs summarize the paper's argument.

[4] J.G.A. Pocock, *The Machiavellian Moment* (Princeton, N.J., 1975).

before public good, the consequent corruption would be fatal even to regular institutions. For the Scots, it was precisely this interdependence of the social and moral with the institutional dimensions of citizenship in a political community that made the concepts of the civic tradition so applicable when they sought to relate the demands of material improvement to the continuing institutional requirements of government.

Even so, it was a peculiarly Scottish development of the civic tradition that adapted its terms to the positive pursuit of wealth. Hitherto thinkers in the tradition had been hostile to wealth, preferring a social regime of Spartan austerity; at best wealth had been approved as a private pursuit, which citizens should keep strictly separate from their public, political activity. For the Scots of 1700, however, to escape from poverty was a national priority: and Andrew Fletcher took the initiative to adapt civic concepts to the pursuit of wealth as a public good. So to pursue wealth, Fletcher insisted, would not bring on corruption as long as Scottish society maintained a rigid hierarchy of ranks, clearly distinguishing the landowning citizen class from their inferiors, and imposing on the lowest orders a regime of domestic servitude. At the same time Fletcher urged a complementary political solution to Scotland's predicament. Scotland's independent parliament and militia should be rejuvenated, to act as regular institutions of self-government within the framework of a federal union of Great Britain (such a union in turn being conceived as part of a general European system of federated states). By such proposals, Fletcher would set the pursuit of economic improvement on a classically civic footing. Given a clear differentiation of citizens from the unfree, and the participatory institutions of a reformed parliament and a national militia, economic improvement could be seen as quite consistent with—indeed as the key to—Scotland's continuing survival as an independent political community.

Fletcher's particular vision of the Scottish political community may have been swept aside in the Treaty of Union; the problem he had confronted nevertheless continued to exercise the thinkers of the Scottish Enlightenment, David Hume first of all. Hume too deployed the concepts of the civic tradition to treat the problem: but where Fletcher's ingenious adaptation had preserved the concepts' traditional significance, this was radically altered by Hume. For Hume combined the fundamental civic concepts of citizenship and liberty with very different, individualist principles drawn from the jurisprudential traditions of political thought. Hume began from the proposition that wealth was created by the individual's free pursuit of his own interest. Beneficial as it was to the community, therefore, wealth was not in the first instance a public good: to the contrary, Hume argued, it was precisely in the attempt to make it so, by factious interests seeking to aggrandise the state at the expense of the individual, that the problem of government's relation to economic development was likely first to arise. To avoid such an outcome, Hume maintained that the priority for government in a commercial society must be to ensure the maximum possible security for the individual and his property, to safeguard his personal freedom from interference and oppression.

So far, this was to formulate the problem of government and economic development in terms other than the civic; only now did Hume graft civic concepts onto his individualist starting-point. As wealth increases and extends through society, so, Hume suggested, more and more of its members would tend to acquire the material independence and moral attributes that, in civic terms, equip men to be citizens. With the development of commerce, therefore, the role of government could not be limited to securing the personal liberty of the individual: government must also satisfy men's expectations as citizens, providing opportunities to participate in political life. The civic liberty 'to' participate must, in other words, be added to the juridical freedom of the individual 'from' interference. Such a combination of the concepts of liberty would only cohere, however, if the traditional civic concept of liberty underwent a radical extension. As the juridical liberty of the individual must be universal, so, Hume's analysis implied, the participatory liberty of the citizen would not remain the preserve of a few: it too must gradually be universalized.

The transformation of civic concepts wrought by Hume in formulating the problem of government and economic development is confirmed by the indications of his response. Nowhere in his writings, indeed, is a solution to the problem explicitly advanced; but one may be reconstructed by way of his observations on the history and influence of forms of government. These observations attached ever more importance to the adaptability of forms of government to economic progress. In Hume's view the republics of classical antiquity had been the first to achieve a regular form of government, ensuring the rule of law and regulating the power of magistrates: hence, he argued, those republics had been the first to foster the rise of commerce and the arts. Subsequently, Hume believed, the principles of regular government had also been assimilated by monarchies; and with the advantages of size, the absolute monarchies of modern Europe must now be supposed better adapted to economic development than the remaining republics. In the long term an absolute monarchy, such as the French, might even have the edge on Britain's uniquely free mixed form of government, of whose stability Hume was decidedly sceptical. Still, however, Hume admitted that the modern monarchic form of government was not perfect: its social conventions inhibited the full development of commerce and of political liberty alike.

Though themselves inconclusive, these historical observations on forms of government can in turn be seen to serve as the basis for Hume's own projected 'Idea of a perfect Commonwealth'. A republic in form, this perfect commonwealth was yet deliberately adapted to the circumstances of large states: it would thus achieve the combination of regular government with the advantages of scale required for economic development. At the same time, the principles on which Hume drew in order to frame the perfect commonwealth are readily identifiable. Presented as an improvement upon Harrington's *Oceana*, the 'Idea of a perfect Commonwealth', with its federal institutions and organization of defence by a militia, also bears a remarkable resemblance to Andrew Fletcher's constitutional scheme for Scotland and Britain: it thus demonstrates a continuing allegiance to the central institutional concepts of the civic tradition. Hume's allegiance was not given unconditionally, however. In line with his radical revision of the traditional account of the material and moral conditions of citizenship, his adaptation of the civic constitutional concepts substantially modified their traditional significance. In Hume's perfect commonwealth it is clear that priority will be given to securing the individual's freedom from interference in the pursuit of his own interest; the political liberty to participate in government will be extended only gradually. As Hume later made clear, moreover, the exercise of liberty in any government will depend on the government's possession of sufficient authority: even in the perfect commonwealth, the freedoms of the individual and the citizen alike presuppose the authority of the government to enforce them. Thus balancing the civic form of liberty against the juridical, and both against authority, Hume's constitutional model represented a compromise far removed from the strict civic vision of Andrew Fletcher. Hume's was a solution to the problem of government and economic development at the limits of the civic tradition.

Coming in this paper to a detailed account of Adam Smith's treatment of the same problem in the *Wealth of Nations*, I shall view it in the light of the preceding Scottish debate, and Hume's contribution in particular. There are two respects, I shall argue, in which Smith developed his analysis beyond Hume's. The first is conceptual. Even more sharply than Hume, Smith recognized the limitations of traditional civic concepts. In formulating the problem of government and economic development, Smith confirmed that the corollary of universal individual freedom would be the eventual universalizing of citizenship and its liberty; at the same time he showed a keener awareness of the obstacles to universal citizenship in the circumstances of commercial society. Smith's solution to the problem went further still, positively discarding the institutional principles of the civic tradition in favour of principles associated with the novel, indigenously British doctrine of parliamentary sovereignty. If Smith thus seems to move beyond the conceptual limits of the civic tradition, however, it is by way of a second, no less important development in the form of his analysis. Compared with Hume's, Smith's treatment of the problem of government and economic development in the *Wealth of Nations* is remarkable for its directness and coherence. Instead of considering the problem under the separate heads of commerce and government, Smith integrated the economic and the political in one systematic analysis. Both in formulation and in resolution the problem thus became explicitly and straightforwardly one of 'political economy'.

Emphasizing these two features of Smith's analysis, my interpretation runs counter to the prevailing historical approach to 'Adam Smith's politics'. In the view first taken by Duncan Forbes, and recently reinforced by Donald Winch and Knud Haakonssen, Smith's political arguments should be understood primarily in the framework of natural jurisprudence. It is, these scholars have argued, concepts derived from the jurisprudential tradition which shape the content of Smith's political thinking; while concepts of other provenances are not necessarily excluded, they are regarded as extraneous elements within the jurisprudential framework. It is also, the same scholars have claimed, the jurisprudential approach which alone can capture the nature of Smith's project as a whole–the characteristically eighteenth-century project of a 'science of politics'. This ambitious project was regrettably uncompleted on Smith's death; but the reports of his early Lectures on Jurisprudence can be taken as a basis for its reconstruction, thereby, it is suggested, supplying the framework in which the works he did publish—the *Theory of Moral Sentiments* (1759) and the *Wealth of Nations* (1776)—should be understood.[5]

This paper differs from the prevalent jurisprudential approach first of all in the importance it attaches to a distinct, civic dimension in Smith's political thought. Adherents of the jurisprudential approach have reacted variously to the presence of civic concepts in Smith's work. Forbes is notoriously dismissive, treating them as mere residues of 'vulgar whiggism'. Winch is less abrupt, acknowledging a civic flavour to several of Smith's political observations—on defence, public credit and the American Colonies: still, however, Winch appears to regard these as particular observations on individual political issues, outwith the systematic framework given by natural juris-

[5] Duncan Forbes, 'Sceptical Whiggism, Commerce and Liberty', in *Essays on Adam Smith*, ed. A.S. Skinner and T. Wilson (Oxford, 1976); Donald Winch, *Adam Smith's Politics. An Essay in Historiographic Revision* (Cambridge, 1978); Knud Haakonssen, *The Science of a Legislator. The Natural Jurisprudence of David Hume and Adam Smith* (Cambridge, 1981). Haakonssen's is the fullest attempt yet to reconstruct Smith's political science as a whole from the *Lectures on Jurisprudence*.

prudence.[6] A much more positive evaluation of a civic component in Smith's thought, it should be said, has been offered by Nicholas Phillipson. Giving historical substance to an approach also suggested by J.R. Lindgren, Phillipson has pointed to the 'civic moralist' themes prominent in the *Theory of Moral Sentiments*, and suggested ways in which these may be followed up in the *Wealth of Nations*.[7] Phillipson's emphasis, however, is upon Smith's use of the moral concepts associated with the civic tradition: insofar as the resulting interpretation allows Smith a politics at all, it appears to accept the jurisprudential framework. In the civic moralist as in the jurisprudential view of Smith the civic political concepts of citizenship and participatory liberty are discounted.

My contrary assertion of a civic dimension in Smith's political arguments is, as I have indicated, a strictly qualified one. It does not exclude but presupposes Smith's use of jurisprudential concepts.[8] It also presents Smith as far removed from the traditional civic perspective of Andrew Fletcher. Not only is it clear that Smith follows and extends Hume's revision of the traditional civic account of the material and moral conditions of citizenship; it is very much my argument that he looks outside the civic tradition for his constitutional principles. Nevertheless, Smith's treatment of the problem of government and economic development cannot be understood if jurisprudential concepts alone are taken to provide the determining framework of his thought. Smith may, like Hume, insist on the juridical freedom of the individual; but he also reiterates Hume's concern that government provide as well for the political liberty of citizens. Recognizably a civic concern in Hume, this is still so for Smith. However the extension of political liberty in commercial society may have to be balanced against the need to ensure the individual's juridical freedom, Smith continues to insist on its importance, and hence on the importance of citizenship. If, as indeed I argue, Smith moves beyond the civic tradition, it is only after having at once affirmed and transformed these, the tradition's fundamental concepts of liberty and citizenship.

[6] Forbes, 'Sceptical Whiggism', pp. 180–9; Winch, *Adam Smith's Politics*, Chs. 5–7, and now also, more definitely anti-civic, 'Adam Smith's "Enduring Particular Result": A Political and Cosmopolitan Perspective', in *Wealth and Virtue*.

[7] Nicholas Phillipson, 'Adam Smith as Civic Moralist', in *Wealth and Virtue*; J.R. Lindgren, *The Social Philosophy of Adam Smith* (The Hague, 1973).

[8] On the desirability of a convergence between the civic and the jurisprudential approaches in general see J.G.A. Pocock, 'Virtue, Rights and Manners: a Model for Historians of Political Thought', *Political Theory*, 9 (1981); and 'Cambridge Paradigms and Scotch Philosophers', in *Wealth and Virtue*,—although Pocock's view of the civic in these articles is perhaps closer to the 'civic moralist' than mine.

A second difference with the current jurisprudential approach to Smith's politics is implicit in this paper's suggestion that the relation between government and economic development is discussed in the *Wealth of Nations* by the integration of political with economic analysis within 'political economy'. Holding that the *Wealth of Nations* was, in Bagehot's phrase, but 'the enduring particular result' of 'a comprehensive and diffused ambition', exponents of the jurisprudential approach have been content to regard the political arguments of the work as more or less fragmentary and underdeveloped. Their coherence, it is supposed, is to be established not within the *Wealth of Nations*, but in the context of Smith's project as a whole.[9] In support of such an approach to the *Wealth of Nations*, moreover, there is Smith's own view of the work. It should be seen, Smith explained in 1790, at the very end of his life, as a partial fulfilment of the promise he had made in 1759 to follow the *Theory of Moral Sentiments* with 'an account of the general principles of law and government'. The *Wealth of Nations* covered the principles of revenue, police and arms; but Smith still intended to complete the account by writing 'the theory of jurisprudence'.[10] As for the particular problem of government and economic development, it was, as we saw in the opening words of this paper, treated in the *Wealth of Nations* as a problem of 'political economy' considered as 'a branch of the science of a statesman or legislator'.

Faced with Smith's own word on the relation of the *Wealth of Nations* and its 'political economy' to his greater design, my challenge to the jurisprudential approach again needs careful qualification. It is not my intention to deny that the political arguments of the *Wealth of Nations* may be profitably and consistently related to the arguments of Smith's other works. Still less is it to detract from the scope of Smith's intellectual ambition, the grandeur of his vision of his lifework. But that ambition was, after all, unfulfilled, that lifework never completed. The *Wealth of Nations* was the only major work Smith actually published after the *Theory of Moral Sentiments*; and once he had done so, he appears to have devoted the greater part of his remaining energy to revising those two works, not to writing the theory of juris-

[9] For recent, confident re-affirmations of this position see Duncan Forbes, 'Natural Law and the Scottish Enlightenment', in *The Origins and Nature of the Scottish Enlightenment*, ed. R.H. Campbell and A.S. Skinner (Edinburgh, 1982); and Winch, 'Adam Smith's "Enduring Particular Result"'—whence Bagehot's phrase—in *Wealth and Virtue*. I dissent from Winch's article in particular.

[10] *Theory of Moral Sentiments*, Advertisement (added in the sixth edition, 1790), and VII.iv.37 for the original promise. See also Smith's remarks on his uncompleted projects in a letter of 1785: *Correspondence of Adam Smith*, no. 248, to the Duc de la Rochefoucauld, 1 November 1785.

prudence.[11] However much Smith still cherished his 'comprehensive and diffused ambition', it was to the enduring of the particular results that he himself gave priority. In these circumstances, it does not seem to me necessary to give overriding weight to Smith's declarations of larger intent. It is not only permissible but preferable to begin with what he achieved and completed, and to work outwards from the *Wealth of Nations* to his larger enterprise, insofar as that can be reconstructed.

Such is the approach of this paper. It is simply my contention that when the political arguments of the *Wealth of Nations* are studied in relation to the same work's economic principles, they can together be understood independently of their place in any larger enterprise.[12] Far from being fragmentary and underdeveloped, those arguments have in the *Wealth of Nations* a coherence of their own within the analytical framework of 'political economy'. This political economy Smith might still introduce as 'a branch of the science of a statesman or legislator'. But the course of his subsequent analysis of the specific problem of government and economic development indicates that it is a branch which has become internally self-sufficient, and capable of direct application by the legislator. For all that Smith continued to subscribe to a more comprehensive idea of the science of a statesman or legislator, it is far from clear that such an idea was any longer necessary for the analytical and practical purposes of political economy in the *Wealth of Nations*.

* * *

Smith began his analysis of the relation between government and economic development from the same ground as Hume. His point of departure was the conviction that the individual's self-interested pursuit of wealth—the natural desire of 'bettering our condition', in the words of the *Wealth of Nations*—is

[11] Though it is not known how much of this projected work was included in the papers whose destruction Smith ordered just before his death, there is no evidence that it was anywhere near completion.

[12] In this paper I take the 'economic' principles of the *Wealth of Nations* to be simply the principles of the market economy. This is not of course to assume that the principles of the market economy were without historical antecedents of their own, or that such antecedents lay only in earlier economic writing. Both the civic (moral) and, still more, the jurisprudential traditions can be shown to have shaped Smith's economic as well as his political principles. Whatever those antecedents, however, the formal presentation of the principles of the market economy in the *Wealth of Nations* is in distinct and largely autonomous terms. On the relation between the economic argument of the *Wealth of Nations* and its antecedents see I. Hont and M. Ignatieff, 'Needs and Justice in the *Wealth of Nations*', Introductory Essay to *Wealth and Virtue*.

the motor of the progress of society as a whole.[13] At the same time Smith assumed that the cultivation of self-interest depended upon the security of property: and hence, again like Hume (and almost every other thinker in the jurisprudential tradition), he identified government's provision of that security through the institutions of justice and defence as the necessary condition of society's progress. Necessary though it thus is, however, the relation between government and economic development is also potentially problematic. In language rather more categorical than Hume's, Smith contended that 'the whole, or almost the whole public revenue, is in most countries employed in maintaining unproductive hands'. Should those 'unproductive' hands multiply unnecessarily, their demands may so encroach upon the funds necessary to maintain productive labour that economic development is checked and, before long, reversed.[14] Smith, it is true, immediately went on to proclaim his confidence that 'the uniform, constant, and uninterrupted effort of every man to better his condition' is frequently sufficient to sustain 'the natural progress of things towards improvement, in spite both of the extravagance of government, and of the greatest errors of administration'.[15] Nevertheless, it is a conviction that in the course of improvement there is an intensified pressure on those in govenment to frustrate the natural enterprise of society which provides the central polemical theme of the *Wealth of Nations* as a whole.

This conviction is rooted in an analysis of the deepening conflict of interests within commercial society. Here Smith broke ground untilled by Hume. Where his predecessor thought only broadly of factions based on interest, Smith analysed commercial society in specific economic terms, identifying the fundamental interests within it by their different sources of revenue or income. The 'three great, original and constituent orders of every civilized society, from whose revenue that of every other is ultimately derived,' are those who live by rent, those who live by wages, and those who live by profit—respectively the landowners, the labourers, and the employers of stock or capital.[16]

Smith explained that the interests of the first two of these orders, the landowners and the labourers, ought to be strictly connected with the general

[13] *Wealth of Nations*, II.iii.28; IV.vii.c.88;—even if as Smith also observed in the *Theory of Moral Sentiments*, material acquisition itself is largely delusory as a source of individual happiness: I.iii.2.1.

[14] *Wealth of Nations*, II.iii.30.

[15] *Ibid.*, II.iii.31.

[16] *Ibid.*, I.xi. p. 7.

interest of society, since the real level of both rent and wages will tend to increase with the growth of the real wealth of society. Only the employers of stock, whose profit can be increased without a simultaneous increase in the wealth of the nation, have an interest which can conflict with that of society at large. Unfortunately, however, landowners and labourers are presently no match for this third order in the knowledge and assertion of their own interests. The natural indolence of landowners, whose revenue costs them neither labour nor care, too often renders them ignorant of their interest and quite incapable of foreseeing the consequences of any public regulation. As for labourers, their condition and education commonly leave them incapable either of comprehending the interest of society, or of understanding its connection with their own. The capitalist merchants and master-manufacturers, by contrast, are well aware of their own interest, and fully prepared to impose it at the expense of society's. They have, Smith observed, 'generally an interest to deceive and even to oppress the publick.'[17]

The proof of Smith's charge against the third order lay in 'the mercantile system'. The better to maintain their profits, Smith demonstrated, merchants and manufacturers characteristically seek to persuade government to grant them an array of corporate privileges, fiscal concessions, preferential trading regulations and colonial monopolies, even though these distort the natural distribution of resources between the different sectors of the economy and encroach upon the freedom of other producing classes. In the event of such privileges and monopolies being challenged by foreign rivals or colonial subjects, moreover, the merchants and manufacturers also expect government to divert its own resources to the defence of their particular interest. Smith's prolonged assault on this system in Book IV of the *Wealth of Nations*, the undoubted rhetorical centrepiece of the entire work, is usually understood as the expression of a straightforward commitment to economic liberalism. When, however, the mercantile system is seen as the outcome of the manipulation of government by the trading interest, it is clear that simply ensuring men's natural economic liberty will not be enough. To prevent the improper regulation of economic activity and minimize the diversion of resources from all branches of productive enterprise, it will in addition be necessary to ensure that government itself cannot be subverted by the anti-social interest of the capitalist order.

Dismissive though Smith initially was of the capacity of the other two orders of commercial society to stand up to the merchants and manufacturers, there are passages elsewhere in the *Wealth of Nations* indicating that he did not altogether exclude the possibility. Both landowners and labourers have the

[17] *Ibid.*, I.xi. p. 8–10.

potential, at least, to play constructive parts in public life. In the case of the landowners, there is, as Nicholas Phillipson has pointed out, a suggestive distinction between great landowners of long-established family, and lesser country gentlemen and farmers.[18] The former Smith criticized sharply as inclined to cling to social privileges, such as the right of entail, for their political benefit, even though such privileges impede the fully economic development of the land.[19] Country gentlemen and farmers, on the other hand, Smith commended as 'of all people, the least subject to the wretched spirit of monopoly'. They generally seek neither to keep improvements to themselves, nor to combine against the public.[20] This section of the landowning class, therefore, might well be called upon to offset the subversive influence of the capitalist order on government.

It should be noted, however, that Smith did not think it wise to allow a landed any more than a mercantile interest actually to preponderate in government. The doctrine of Physiocracy, to which he turned his attention once he had finished with the mercantile system, shows that it is quite possible to overvalue the contribution of agriculture to economic development; and while he did not suggest that any government had yet been persuaded to adopt the doctrine, the consequences of one deluded into doing so could be still more damaging than even the effects of the mercantile system.[21] On its own, therefore, no section of the landowning order can be regarded as a completely reliable alternative to the capitalist.[22]

[18] Phillipson, 'Adam Smith as Civic Moralist'.

[19] *Wealth of Nations*, III.ii.4–7.

[20] *Ibid.*, IV.ii.21.

[21] *Ibid.*, IV.ix.

[22] It may be added that Smith did not elaborate on the identity of the 'country gentlemen and farmers' referred to at IV.ii.21, and the category of 'country gentlemen' in particular remains imprecise throughout the *Wealth of Nations*. In Book III, Smith insisted that a commitment to agricultural improvement could be relied on only in those whose holding was sufficiently small for them to farm it directly: the examples he cited were the yeoman and tenant farmers of England and, best of all, the independent small proprietors of North America. With the exception of those who had formerly been merchants, 'country gentlemen' were by contrast described as 'timid' undertakers: III.ii.20, III.iv.3, 19. Later, in Book V, Smith recommended that the tax system should specifically discourage improvement by landowners whose estates were of a size to require bailiffs if they were to be farmed directly: V.ii.c.15. To claim, as Phillipson does in 'Adam Smith as Civic Moralist', that Smith put his faith in a 'gentry' seems therefore to strain the evidence.

What then of the second great order of commercial society, the labouring? At first sight Smith's further remarks on the condition of labourers offer no hope at all. He was very far from sharing Hume's apparent confidence in the beneficent impact of commerce on the moral and political capacity of the common people. Instead Smith followed up his comment in Book I on the ignorance of the labourer with an ominous diagnosis in Book V of the degradation and 'mental mutilation' consequent upon the full development of the division of labour. His employment reduced to a few simple, monotonous operations, the labourer, Smith asserted, 'generally becomes as stupid and ignorant as it is possible for a human creature to become'. Incapable of just judgment in even the ordinary duties of private life, he is quite unable to judge the interests of his country, or to defend it in war. 'His dexterity at his own particular trade seems, in this manner, to be acquired at the expense of his intellectual, social, and martial virtues.'[23]

This damning judgment needs, however, to be set in the context of other observations on the material and juridical condition of the labouring class in commercial society. Right at the outset of the *Wealth of Nations*, Smith identified the object of economic development as the achievement of 'universal opulence'; and he insisted particularly on the benefit of this to the labourers themselves. Sharing in a 'general plenty', they enjoy not only the necessaries of life, but an unprecedentedly wide variety of household goods.[24] Later Smith observed that almost all the common people in modern commercial society also possess liberty in their own labour. It was, to be sure, by no means inevitable that the attainment of such freedom should accompany economic development; nevertheless it had done so in Western Europe.[25] To material self-sufficiency the labouring class had thus been able to add juridical independence: and for Smith—as for Hume—these were precisely the two conditions of a full participation in social life.

Such conditions are presupposed in the discussion of the social virtues of justice and benevolence in the *Theory of Moral Sentiments*. Accurate and precise sentiments of justice, Smith there observed, are not to be expected from a people living in conditions of rudeness and barbarism. It is the emergence of property and a system of ranks which fosters the sense of justice and the desire for order.[26] But given the limited, retributive character of

[23] *Wealth of Nations*, V.i.f.50.

[24] *Ibid.*, I.i.10–11.

[25] *Ibid.*, III.iii.5, III.iv.4.

[26] *Theory of Moral Sentiments*, VII.iv.36; II.ii.

Smith's concept of justice, still more significant is the virtue of benevolence, discussed in a passage added to the sixth edition of the work. In primitive, pastoral societies, Smith commented, benevolence is chiefly felt towards members of one's family or tribe, for this is the association most necessary for common defence. Once the authority of law is sufficient to give perfect security to every individual, however, the family tie soon narrows, and the range of benevolence extends to neighbours, colleagues, benefactors and social superiors.[27] It extends also, Smith went on, to the institutions of society, and, in general, to the 'love of our country'. As Smith then defined it, the love of our country

> seems, in ordinary cases, to involve in it two different principles; first, a certain respect and reverence for that constitution or form of government which is actually established; and secondly, an earnest desire to render the condition of our fellow-citizens as safe, respectable, and happy as we can. He is not a citizen who is not disposed to respect the laws and to obey the civil magistrate; and he is certainly not a good citizen who does not wish to promote, by every means in his power, the welfare of the whole society of his fellow citizens.[28]

Smith of course made no explicit connection between this analysis of the general conditions of moral sentiment and the analysis of the particular orders of commercial society, including the labouring, developed in the *Wealth of Nations*. But the *Theory of Moral Sentiments* gives no reason to suppose that a labouring class enjoying material self-sufficiency and juridical independence would be unable to cultivate the virtues of justice and benevolence. Could a remedy for the 'mental mutilation' of the division of labour be found, therefore, it would benefit not only the labourer himself, but society as a whole. Liberating the moral potential of the labouring class, it would yet enable it to play its part in public life—and so join the landowners in countering the anti-social designs of merchants and manufacturers.

The outcome of the *Wealth of Nations*' novel analysis of the conflict of interests in commercial society is thus, I suggest, a fresh formulation of the problem of government and economic development. At once restating and developing Hume's, Smith's formulation consolidates the revision which Hume had made of the traditional civic perspective. To Smith, as to Hume, wealth is first of all an individual, not a public, good: securing for the individual the greatest possible freedom from government interference is

[27] *Ibid.*, VI.ii.1.12–20.

[28] *Ibid.*, VI.ii.2.1–11.

accordingly the first condition of economic development.[29] At the same time, Smith followed Hume in supposing that the progress of commerce, bringing sufficiency and independence to all ranks, including the lowest, ought in the long run to universalize moral and political capacity. Far from accepting the traditional civic presumption that the producing section of society would be immutably excluded from citizenship, Smith re-affirmed Hume's conviction that in conditions of opulence all should ultimately be free to participate in public life. Still more clearly than Hume, furthermore, Smith insisted on the consequent interdependence of the forms of liberty in commercial society. It is the establishment of universal liberty under the law, the jurisprudential form of liberty, which makes possible the general cultivation of the virtues of justice and benevolence required for the ultimate universalization of the traditionally civic liberty to participate. In turn, liberty under the law will itself come to be fully secured only by the universal exercise of the freedom to participate: ensuring a balance of influences upon government, general participation will prevent the abuse of its power by particular interests. Specifically, the participation of the two orders whose interests coincide with society's, the orders of landowners and labourers, should then serve to check the anti-social interest of the order of stockholders.

At this point, however, Smith gave his reformulation of the problem of government and economic development a final original twist. Desirable as it is, the future participation of all in the public life of commercial society cannot be counted upon. Given the habitual indolence and ignorance of landowners, and the increasing degradation of labourers, there is on the contrary every likelihood that the freedom to participate will be monopolized by the very mercantile order whose influence it is supposed to forestall. Unless therefore the political alienation of the first two orders of society can be remedied, and landowners and labourers induced to act as citizens, the provision of civic, participatory liberty will simply facilitate the efforts of the third, capitalist order to encroach upon the individual freedom of everyone else. Without positive measures to release the liberty of all to participate, in short, it will not be possible to secure the maximum freedom for all under the law.

* * *

Smith's primary solution to the problem he had thus reformulated is developed in Book V of the *Wealth of Nations*. Cast in institutional terms, it is a solution, I shall argue, that differs from Hume's in being framed in line with

[29] This is as far as analysis of Smith's treatment of the problem is usually taken: see e.g. L. Billet, 'Political Order and Economic Development: Reflections on Adam Smith's *Wealth of Nations*', *Political Studies*, XXIII (1975), pp. 430–41.

explicitly economic principles, and in embodying constitutional principles foreign to the civic tradition.[30]

Formally, Book V is a discussion of the expenses and revenue of the 'Sovereign or Commonwealth', and Smith's first concern was simply with efficient government. As far as possible, he argued, the organization of defence, justice and the public revenue should be subject to economic standards of performance. In the case of defence, the relevant economic principle is that of the division of labour. A commercial society, Smith maintained, should rely on a standing army of professional soldiers rather than a part-time militia, because the former will cause less disruption of productive economic activity, while facilitating the acquisition of the complex skills of modern warfare.[31] In the administration of justice, the principles of self-interest and competition are applicable as well. Not only should the judiciary be a separate, specialist profession; judges should be rewarded on the basis of the number of suits decided; there ought to be competition between courts; and the cost ought to be met as far as possible by charging a fixed fee of plaintiffs.[32] Likewise, in the provision of public works as much scope as possible should be given to the self-interest of their undertakers, and wherever practicable a charge should be paid by those who benefit by their use.[33] Finally, Smith urged that public revenue should be raised by taxation rather than by borrowing, since in the long run a system of public credit removes the incentive to invest productively.[34] Taxation itself, he added,

[30] I do not deny that, as Phillipson argues in 'Adam Smith as Civic Moralist', Smith also struggled persistently to identify the terms of an ethical solution to the conflict of interests in commercial society. The success of the enterprise, however, appears doubtful. Smith might indeed ask in the *Theory of Moral Sentiments*

> What institution of government could tend so much to promote the happiness of mankind as the general prevalence of wisdom and virtue? All government is but an imperfect remedy for the deficiency of these. (IV.ii.1.)

But the prospect of the 'general prevalence' of wisdom and virtue is almost certainly utopian. Even in individuals, Smith acknowledged, the qualities of wisdom and virtue are exceptionally difficult to discern. *Ibid.*, VI.ii.1.20.

It seems to me therefore that the judgment of one of the first commentators to notice the problem of conflicting interests, Joseph Cropsey, still stands: failing the idea of a social or moral 'natural aristocracy', Smith fell back on a solution in institutional terms. *Polity and Economy. An Interpretation of the Principles of Adam Smith* (The Hague, 1957), pp. 67–70.

[31] *Wealth of Nations*, V.i.a.8–25.

[32] *Ibid.*, V.i.b.20–2.

[33] *Ibid.*, V.i.c–g.

[34] *Ibid.*, V.iii.47–56.

should be levied according to the four maxims of equity, certainty, convenience and administrative economy.[35]

If the prescription of efficient, economical government was Smith's first, it was not his only concern in Book V. Simultaneously, he was at pains to insist that the outcome of his recommendations would also be 'free government'. He made the point with particular emphasis in recommending a standing army. 'Men of republican principles' might be jealous of such an army as dangerous to liberty. But, Smith replied,

> where the sovereign is himself the general, and the principal nobility and gentry of the country the chief officers of the army; where the military force is placed under the command of those who have the greatest interest in the support of the civil authority, because they have themselves the greatest share of that authority, a standing army can never be dangerous to liberty.

On the contrary, a standing army may enable the sovereign to dispense with any discretionary power to check disorder, and tolerate a much larger degree of popular freedom.[36] The proposal of a separate, specialist judiciary had similarly positive implications for liberty. The judges' independence of the executive Smith held to be the essential condition of the impartial administration of justice, on which in turn depends '. . . the liberty of every individual, the sense which he has of his own security.'[37] By comparison Smith made little of the political advantages of taxation over public credit; but he did observe that reliance on taxation creates a healthy incentive to end a war as soon as there ceases to be 'a real or solid interest' to fight for.[38] Implicitly it is clear that taxation can only be levied equitably and economically if it has the consent of the payers.

Free government, however, also makes demands on the members of commercial society: specifically, in Smith's view, it requires them to be educated. Discussing education under the head of public works and institutions, Smith argued that it should be provided at public expense only for the common people, since these had not the means or inclination to obtain it for them-

[35] *Ibid.*, V.ii.b.2–7. Cf. for the above paragraph A.S. Skinner, *A System of Social Science. Papers relating to Adam Smith* (Oxford, 1979), Ch. 9, 'The Functions of Government', pp. 211–16.

[36] *Wealth of Nations*, V.i.a.41.

[37] *Ibid.*, V.i.b.25.

[38] *Ibid.*, V.iii.50.

selves.[39] Nevertheless, he was also insistent that the requirement of education be imposed upon all classes, upper and lower, since it formed an indispensable qualification for public life. For those of 'middling or more than middling rank and fortune' he recommended the introduction of some sort of probation, 'to be undergone by every person before he was permitted to exercise any liberal profession, or before he could be received as a candidate for any honourable office of trust or profit.'[40] At a lower level premiums and examinations should likewise be used to encourage the common people to take education; and to these inducements should be added compulsory military exercises, after the Greek and Roman example.[41]

Such military exercises, Smith acknowledged, might add little to a modern society's defence; but they had other advantages. Above all, by maintaining the martial spirit of the people they would take the first essential step towards remedying the 'mental mutilation' they suffered as a consequence of the division of labour. Broadening his argument, Smith went on to offer an explicitly political justification for educating the inferior ranks. The more instructed are the common people, he claimed, the less liable are they to the delusions of enthusiasm and superstition, and the more decent and orderly in their behaviour. Feeling themselves more respectable, they are more likely to obtain the respect of their lawful superiors, and to respect them in turn. They will be better able to see through 'the interested complaints of faction and sedition', and hence will be less apt to be misled into wanton opposition to government. And

> in free countries, where the safety of government depends very much upon the favourable judgement which the people may form of its conduct, it must surely be of the highest importance that they should not be disposed to judge rashly or capriciously concerning it.[42]

These successive arguments in Book V were a direct response to the problem of government and economic development. At the most obvious level, Smith's prescriptions for economical government confront head-on the 'unproductive' character of institutions: whenever possible, they suggest, the necessary diversion of resources should be regulated by subjecting government itself to the natural discipline of economic life. Yet simultaneously, Smith's conviction that his proposals would also result in 'free government' may be seen to meet the further, underlying, political dimension of the problem, created by the conflict of interests within commercial society. It is not enough, his arguments indicate, to contain the diversion of resources: the

[39] *Ibid.*, V.i.f.52–3.

[40] *Ibid.*, V.i.g.14.

[41] *Ibid.*, V.i.f.54–9.

[42] *Ibid.*, V.i.f.60–1.

institutions of government should be positively framed to secure the liberties of society.

To begin with, liberty under the law should be secured by ensuring a significant degree of autonomy to the essential institutions of justice and defence. An independent judiciary offers a first line of defence for individual freedom; a specialist standing army a second insofar as it enables government to do without a discretionary power to override the law. The autonomy of these institutions should be qualified, however, by provision for a certain freedom to participate, to ensure that they yet remain responsive to society at large. To prevent the army in particular being made an instrument of arbitrary rule, it should be commanded by 'the principal nobility and gentry in the country', those who have 'the greatest interest in the support of the civil authority'. And more generally, to prevent the squandering of the public revenue which supports the various branches of government, taxation should be subject to consent. But simply to provide the opportunity to participate is by itself insufficient: free government must further enjoin participation by means of education. Requiring that the middle and upper ranks be qualified before holding office, and imposing an elementary education and military exercises upon the lower, government should actively encourage the extension of the capacity for political liberty at every level of commercial society. In this way, it may be inferred, free government would rectify the indolence and ignorance which inhibit the landowning and labouring classes from asserting the identity of their interests with society's—and so release them to counter the influence of that third, mercantile order, which needs no encouragement to impose its particular, anti-social interest.

This solution to the problem of government and economic development was not arbitrarily advanced. As Smith made clear by the historical and comparative analyses which prefaced each of his major recommendations, it was framed within a comprehensive theory of social development, distinguishing the commercial stage from its predecessors. The general features of this historical or 'stadial' theory are by now well-known: but it is perhaps in the context of the present problem that its application to commercial society is clearest.[43] Specifically, the theory enabled Smith to isolate two critical

[43] The pioneering work on Smith's stadial theory was done by R.L. Meek, culminating in his *Social Science and the Ignoble Savage* (Cambridge, 1976); but Meek's focus on the theory's application to primitive societies may have encouraged an unnecessary scepticism over its relevance to commercial society, exemplified in Lindgren, *Social Philosophy of Adam Smith*, pp. xiii, 68. Andrew Skinner has made a series of attempts to provide a more balanced account of the theory, the latest of which is the most satisfactory: 'A Scottish Contribution to Marxist Sociology?', in *Classical and Marxian Political Economy. Essays in Honour of R.L. Meek*, ed. I. Bradley and M. Howard (London, 1982). See also the lengthy discussion of stadial theory in Haakonssen, *Science of a Legislator*, Chs. 7–8; but Haakonssen's concern is with the theory's place in the reconstruction of Smith's theory of jurisprudence, not with its actual significance in the *Wealth of Nations*.

features of the relation between government and economy at the commercial stage of development.

First, it showed that where in primitive societies the relation was but loosely articulated, in a commercial society it must be one of close interdependence. In both the hunting and the pastoral stages of development, every man is naturally a warrior, and defence costs the sovereign nothing. Even in the early agricultural stage men are free to serve in summer, and the cost of war, such as it is, can be paid out of hoards.[44] In a commercial society, by contrast, men are disinclined to leave productive employments for military service, and the expense of war is great, while the very wealth of society attracts acquisitive neighbours.[45] The means of defence, in short, become less readily available, just as the need for them increases. The same is true of justice, whose administration becomes more extensive and costly as the demand for its services grows.[46] If commerce thereby requires a much more precise balance between the needs of government and the economy than hitherto, it also, however, indicates the methods of attaining it. Simply by the application of the principle of the division of labour, commercial societies can provide for their defence at the least possible cost, and at the same time assure themselves of military superiority over their primitive neighbours.[47] Likewise, no more speedy, inexpensive and accountable system of justice can be envisaged than one which adopts commercial standards of specialization and competitiveness. The complexity of commercial society may give the problem of institutions an unprecedented urgency, but it also, on Smith's theory, makes possible its definitive solution.

What the stadial theory makes no less clear, secondly, however, is the dependence of that solution on human initiative. In primitive societies with crude and rudimentary institutions, economic, civil and military needs are combined as a matter of course.[48] In a complex commercial society, by comparison, the process of adaptation is by no means automatic. As Smith pointed out, the operation of the division of labour in the organization of defence does not occur in the natural course of economic development: it

[44] *Wealth of Nations*, V.i.a.2–7; V.ii.1–2.

[45] *Ibid.*, V.i.a.8–10, 15.

[46] *Ibid.*, V.i.b.24.

[47] *Ibid.*, V.i.a.39.

[48] *Ibid.*, V.i.a.2–7 and b.12.

must be introduced by 'the wisdom of the state'.[49] Far from being guaranteed by any 'invisible hand', the harmonization of government and economy in commercial society is, Smith believed, the task of the legislator.[50]

So direct and systematic a response to the problem of government and economic development marks a clear advance on Hume's treatment of the same subject. Hume's response, I indicated, was indirect, and has to be reconstructed by way of his observations on the history of forms of government and their success in encouraging commerce. These historical observations can then be seen as the basis for his projection of a model or perfect form of government whose institutions also matched the requirements of a fully commercial society. In the *Wealth of Nations*, by contrast, the problem is given an explicit solution, consistent with the main lines of the economic analysis already developed in the work. The institutions of commercial society should be framed in accordance with the economic principles appropriate to that stage of development, in a way which simultaneously furthers the ends of free government. Given these criteria, it is then the responsibility of the legislator to render theory into practice, and in due course to reform existing institutions. The problem, in short, is resolved within the framework in which Smith introduced it—that of political economy, with the legislator

[49] *Ibid.*, V.i.a.14. On Smith's theory, in other words, the economic 'base' does not straightforwardly and reductively determine the institutional 'superstructure'. To the contrary, the theory indicates that the rational, economic and free ordering of institutions will come about only as a result of conscious choice.

[50] Beyond distinguishing him from 'that insidious and crafty animal', the politician (IV.ii.39), Smith did not elaborate on the character of the legislator in the *Wealth of Nations*. Subsequently, revising the *Theory of Moral Sentiments* for its sixth edition in 1790, Smith incorporated there a discussion of the role and attributes of the 'statesman', treating him as a legislator. While the responsibility is described in appropriately lofty tones, it is nonetheless important to note that the statesman was to proceed gradually.

> Some general, and even systematical, idea of the perfection of policy and law, may no doubt be necessary for directing the views of the statesman. But to insist upon establishing, and upon establishing all at once, in spite of all opposition, everything which that idea may seem to require, must often be the highest degree of arrogance.

Smith went on to condemn in particular the arrogance of individual 'imperial and royal reformers'. *Theory of Moral Sentiments*, VI.ii.12–18. (This reference to 'imperial and royal reformers' indicates that Smith can hardly have been thinking of the French Revolution when he added this passage, as his editors Raphael and Macfie suggest: *ibid.*, p. 231, note 6.)

It seems clear that Smith's reference to the statesman or legislator in the singular was meant to be figurative: what he had in mind was not the founding law-giver of classical myth, but the institution of law-making or legislation as the means to reform the other institutions and practices of government.

being required to act directly upon political economy's prescriptions.[51] The very coherence and directness of Smith's solution does, however, leave one aspect of his response less clear than was the case with Hume: the constitutional principles informing the prescribed model of free government. To identify these principles, therefore, it is still necessary to examine Smith's historical commentary on particular forms of government. This will reveal that Smith's solution differed from Hume's not only in form, but also in conceptual content.

* * *

For the purposes of historical analysis in his Lectures on Jurisprudence, Smith had reduced the forms of government to two, the monarchical and the republican. In a monarchy the three parts of the sovereign power, the legislative, the judicial and the power of making peace and war, are vested in one person. In a republican government the several powers are committed to a greater number: if to 'the nobles or men of rank', it is an aristocracy; if to 'the whole body of the people conjunctly', it is a democracy.[52] This distinction recurs in the *Wealth of Nations*: but the assessment of different forms of government is there much more closely related to the economic performance of the societies for which they are responsible.

Smith acknowledged in his Lectures that the ancient world had produced the first examples of 'regular government' in the city States of Attica, formed to protect the infant trade and agriculture of the Greeks from the predatory nomads surrounding them.[53] There, and again in the *Wealth of Nations*, Smith also admitted a measure of subsequent economic development in antiquity, despite the harm done by the system of slavery.[54] Nevertheless, Smith was distinctly unwilling to allow that there had been a positive relation between ancient governments and their economies. Quite apart from the maintenance

[51] Both Winch, *Adam Smith's Politics*, pp. 130–3, and Haakonssen, *Science of a Legislator*, pp. 97–8, 188–9, emphasize the significance of the legislator in Smith's political thought. In line with their general approach, however, they view the legislator's role in relation to the application of the prescriptions of jurisprudence. Without denying this more ambitious role, what I emphasize here is the immediate practical responsibility given the legislator in the *Wealth of Nations* for carrying out the prescriptions of political economy.

[52] *Lectures on Jurisprudence* (A), iv.1–3, (B), 18–19.

[53] *Ibid.*, (A), iv.56–74.

[54] Even in his strongest criticism of ancient slavery, Smith still conceded the achievement of considerable prosperity: *Wealth of Nations*, IV.ix.47; cf. *Lectures on Jurisprudence* (A), iii.105–11, 139–47.

of slavery, ancient institutions of justice and defence were never properly adapted to economic needs. Smith was especially critical of the classical republics. They did not satisfactorily separate the judicial from other governmental powers;[55] and as they grew wealthy they were unable to reform their characteristic military organization, the city militia.[56] If anything, the later military monarchy of the Roman Empire had performed better than the republics, for it had at least secured regular civil justice. But the imperial armies had been commanded by men whose interest was not necessarily connected with the support of the constitution of the state; and there had been no countervailing civilian political institutions. The idea of representation being, as Smith observed, 'unknown in ancient times', the participatory assemblies of the republic had been unable to cope with the great increase in the numbers of Roman citizens: nothing, therefore, survived to limit the absolute power of the emperors in public affairs.[57]

Smith had no doubt of the superiority of modern over ancient governments. The separation of the judicial from the executive power was now widespread, and it could be taken for granted that all the great nations of Europe enjoyed the regular administration of justice.[58] Standing armies too were now kept by almost all the great powers, and the opulent and civilized nations were therefore secure against their poor and barbarous neighbours.[59] Only the proliferation of national debts gave cause for disquiet, the more so as they were usually accompanied by oppressive taxation.[60] These developments had affected both the republican and the monarchic forms of government; but Smith attached more significance to the achievement of the monarchies.

The republican form of government might seem to be 'the principal support of the present grandeur of Holland', since by according the merchant aris-

[55] Although the Roman republic registered a significant advance on its Greek predecessors in this respect, Smith still does not appear to have regarded the Roman Praetors as fully professional judges. Compare *Wealth of Nations*, V.i.b.24 and V.i.f.44 with the digression on the absence of legal argument from precedent in antiquity in Smith's *Lectures on Rhetoric and Belles Lettres*, ii.198–203. Haakonssen, *Science of a Legislator*, pp. 161–2 and 220 note 61, perhaps slightly exaggerates the Praetors' significance.

[56] *Wealth of Nations*, V.i.a.29; more fully, *Lectures on Jurisprudence* (A), iv.76–87.

[57] *Wealth of Nations*, V.i.a.41, IV.vii.c.77; also *Lectures on Jurisprudence* (A), iv.97–9.

[58] *Wealth of Nations*, V.i.b.24 and V.iii.7, 10 (which imply that the development of national debts presupposed the availability of regular justice).

[59] *Ibid.*, V.i.a.37–9.

[60] *Ibid.*, V.iii.57–8.

tocracy a share in government along with the nobility, it made them more willing to bear the heavy taxation needed to preserve the country from the sea as well as its enemies.[61] But Smith also remarked that while merchant aristocracies might be fitted to administer a mercantile project like the Bank of Amsterdam, they were not fitted to be sovereigns of great states. He evidently sensed Holland's relative economic and political decline as a great power.[62] There was in comparison no question of France's status as a great power; and Smith emphasized that its government was free insofar as its judicial institutions secured personal liberty under the law.[63] He was, however, sceptical of the possibility of reforming the wasteful and oppressive financial administration of the country;[64] and as a result his final assessment of the French monarchy was deliberately balanced. If France was 'certainly the great empire in Europe which, after that of Great Britain, enjoys the mildest and most indulgent government', its was a government which nevertheless still belonged to 'a gradation of despotism'.[65]

The British, it is clear, was one government with no part in this 'gradation'. Of no other existing government, indeed, was Smith so positive in his judgment: he seems to have believed that Britain's institutions came closer than any to satisfying the criteria of free government in a commercial society. The administration of justice, in England if not in Scotland, was competitive and efficient, and the separation of powers was secured by the appointment of professional judges for life.[66] Defence was entrusted to a standing army and navy, with the English militia and sizeable merchant and fishing fleets in reserve; and the peace-time military establishment was more moderate than that of any European state which could pretend to rival Britain in wealth and power.[67] The national debt was certainly a burden, and Smith warned that although at present it seemed to be supported with ease, it could not necessarily be supported for ever. But he also repeatedly acknowledged that the British system of taxation was more equitable and less oppressive than any

[61] *Ibid.*, V.ii.k.80.

[62] *Ibid.*, V.ii.a.4, 7; V.ii.k.79.

[63] *Ibid.*, V.i.b.20.

[64] *Ibid.*, V.ii.j.7 and k.77; V.iii.35–6.

[65] *Ibid.*, V.ii.k.78; V.i.g.19. Cf. this paragraph with Forbes, 'Sceptical Whiggism, Commerce and Liberty', pp. 188–97.

[66] *Wealth of Nations*, V.i.b.21; cf. *Lectures on Jurisprudence* (A), v.5.

[67] *Wealth of Nations*, V.i.a.20; IV.ii.24 and IV.v.a.27; V.iii.92.

other.[68] And this, he suggested, was largely due to the unique relation which had been established in Britain's constitution between taxation and consent through representation.[69]

Yet if the system of taxing by consent through representation was a unique constitutional asset, it was also at the heart of Britain's present crisis, the crisis which, even as Smith wrote the *Wealth of Nations*, seemed to throw into the balance the country's future as a commercial power—the conflict with the North American colonies. As Smith was well aware, taxation was at least as much an issue in the dispute with the colonies as the regulation of trade. Moreover, he believed that taxation, unlike trade, was an issue on which Britain was not altogether in the wrong. There was every justification for the colonies paying, not only for their own defence, but also their share in support of the general government of the empire. Equally however, there was every reason to doubt whether the colonies could be brought to raise the appropriate revenue. The colonial assemblies could not be managed so as to do so voluntarily, and would resist paying by requisition, even if it was clear that their contribution could be no more than their due proportion. Management was almost impossible because, although modelled on the House of Commons, the colonial assemblies were, as Smith put it, more 'republican' in form—more equally representative, and accordingly more open to the influence of their constituents. For their part members of the assemblies enjoyed a status as leaders of the colonial communities which would be lost if they were to submit to requisitions from Great Britain.[70] In the existing state of colonial and British representation, therefore, deadlock was inevitable.

[68] *Ibid.*, V.ii.k.66; V.iii.58.

[69] *Ibid.*, IV.vii.b.51. Further discussion of the system of securing consent by representation in Britain is to be found in the *Lectures on Jurisprudence*. To refute Locke's proposition that consent for taxation is a necessary condition of all allegiance, Smith had been careful to point out to his students how much the formal relation between taxation and consent was peculiar to Britain, and even then was still largely 'metaphorical'. *Lectures on Jurisprudence* (A), v.134–5, and (B), 94–5. Nevertheless, Smith made equally clear the extent to which Britain's 'rational system of liberty' depended on parliamentary control of government finance. Parliament had been able to establish this control at the end of the seventeenth century by exploiting the fortunate absence hitherto of a standing army and the dissipation of the crown's own ordinary revenues. In consequence Parliament, and the House of Commons in particular, now effectively regulated both the civil and the military expenditure of the crown; and Smith emphasized that the Commons owed its predominance, not only to its powers to initiate money bills and impeach ministers, but also to the authority which its members derived from the people they represented, and whom they had to satisfy at frequent elections. *Lectures on Jurisprudence* (A), iv. 168–79, v.1–2; (B), 61–3.

[70] *Wealth of Nations*, IV.vii.b.51 and c.67–74.

As early as 1776 Smith recognized that war would be no solution to this impasse, since the cost of the permanent subjection of the colonies would be prohibitive. But equally it was clear that Britain could not be expected to swallow a voluntary separation at once. Smith therefore offered a solution which tackled the problem of representation directly: he proposed a scheme for full imperial union with the colonies and the mother country represented in a single parliament. Taxation would be in proportion to representation, which would be determined by wealth and population. In such a parliament, Smith was confident, a proper degree of management could be achieved without undermining the colonial representatives' ultimate dependency on their constituents. At the same time the leading men of the colonies would gain a sufficiently large field for their ambition, thereby delivering the colonies from 'those rancorous and virulent factions which are inseparable from small democracies'. The colonies could also look forward to the removal of the seat of government to America, when, as could be expected in due course, their contribution to imperial revenue overtook that of Britain. As for the original British constitution, it would, Smith claimed, be 'completed' by such a union, and indeed seemed 'imperfect' without one.[71]

Smith self-deprecatingly described this proposal as 'a new Utopia'; and he concluded the *Wealth of Nations* with a hard-headed exhortation to Britain's rulers to give up the empire and accommodate their future designs to 'the real mediocrity of her circumstances'.[72] Yet even when defeat had forced Britain's rulers to do just that, and Smith himself came to revise the work for its third edition in 1784, the proposal remained.[73] Such adherence to a 'utopian' and by then clearly out-dated scheme appears puzzling—unless perhaps Smith regarded it as having rather more than a narrowly practical significance. That this may indeed have been the case is suggested by comparison with his treatment of the commercial issues raised by the American conflict. Andrew Skinner has argued that his purposes in devoting so much attention to those

[71] *Ibid.*, IV.vii.c.66, 75–9; V.iii.90. Cf. Winch, *Adam Smith's Politics*, Ch. 7, 'The Present Disturbances': but Winch takes Smith's central concern to be with management rather than representation.

[72] *Wealth of Nations*, V.iii.68, 92.

[73] At least one friend had urged its removal—in the most patronising tones:

> there are some pages about the middle of the second volume where you enter into a description about the measures we ought at present to take with respect to America, giving them a representation etc. which I wish had been omitted, because it is too much like a publication for the present moment. In subsequent editions when publick measures come to be settled, these pages will fall to be omitted or altered.

Correspondence of Adam Smith, No. 151: Letter of the Revd Hugh Blair, 3 April 1776.

issues were chiefly doctrinal. Smith, it can be seen, was little concerned with providing a comprehensive review of the commercial matters actually in dispute between Britain and the colonies, still less with influencing the immediate direction of policy. Rather he would marshall all the evidence of the folly of commercial regulations and monopolies which the American case provided in order to illustrate his theoretical critique of the mercantile system.[74] In much the same way, I would argue that a paradigmatic purpose may be detected in Smith's analysis of the constitutional dimension of the crisis. The question of America could be represented as an excellent example, not only of the danger of mercantile restrictions, but also, more generally, of the problem of institutions and economic development.

If Britain and America could be envisaged as one united, imperial society, it should be clear that they would together enjoy unequalled economic opportunities. Britain was already the most advanced nation in Europe, while America had a possibly unique chance to develop according to what Smith termed 'the natural progress of opulence'.[75] To realize such economic potential, of course, required that the empire be endowed with appropriate political institutions, and that the burden of maintaining them be equitably distributed. But these conditions could, at least in theory, be met. The requisite institutions of justice and defence now existed in Britain, and the principle of taxation by representative consent was established in the constitution. All that was needed to develop the economic potential of the two countries to the full, therefore, was the extension of those institutions to the colonies, and the translation of the principle of taxation by representative consent into a constitutional framework adapted to the colonies' growing resources and aspirations. Thus the purpose of the scheme of Atlantic empire. Effectively matching the criteria of Smith's model of efficient and free government in a commercial society, the proposal exemplified the solution to one of the central analytical problems of his political economy.

So resumed, what does Smith's commentary on particular forms of government—past, present and projected—reveal of his constitutional principles? It should at least be clear that they were not of the same historical derivation as Hume's. Smith may have described the ancient Greek republics as the earliest regular governments; but he did not there identify the first principles of free government. By contrast with Hume, who believed that the classical republican form of government, with all its flaws, had been responsible for the initial development of commerce and the arts, Smith denied that that form of

[74] Skinner, *A System of Social Science*, Ch. 8, 'Mercantilist Policy: the American Colonies'.

[75] *Wealth of Nations*, III.iv.19–20.

government had possessed any of the particular judicial, military and representative institutions appropriate to a commercial society. Instead, Smith suggested that it was in the modern world, and specifically in the civilized monarchies, that the requisite institutions had first emerged. If Smith thus ascribed a greater institutional originality to modern monarchy, however, he was also more insistent on its limitations. Where Hume supposed that the civilized monarchies of Europe had significantly improved upon the republican principles they inherited, raising regular government to a new level of perfection, Smith still considered them to belong to 'a gradation of despotism'. Their achievement in the spheres of justice and defence was offset, he believed, by their reliance on oppressive and wasteful systems of public finance.

Smith's divergence from Hume is yet clearer in relation to the existing government of Britain. Hume had accepted the conventional view of Britain's as a mixed government, combining monarchic with republican features. But far from sharing the common admiration for this unique mixture, Hume had been severely sceptical of its continued stability. In the long run, Hume judged mixed government to be less likely to cope with the pressures of economic development than civilized absolute monarchy, which compensated for its lack of political liberty by its capacity to ensure regular justice and to override the financiers. Little of this scepticism survives, however, in Smith's observations on British government. By-passing debate over the strengths and weaknesses of mixed government, Smith simply noted the extent to which Britain already possessed what he identified as the requisite institutions for a commercial society. Here alone had the independence of the judicial power been properly secured, and military organization adapted to the nation's needs; and in the system of taxation by representative consent, Britain enjoyed a constitutional asset not found in any of the continental monarchies. So well-formed, indeed, did Smith believe British government that he had but to project its perfection in an imperial parliamentary union with America to provide a paradigm of free government in a commercial society.

It is precisely this readiness to set aside Hume's reservations over the government of Britain, I now wish to suggest, that holds the key to Smith's constitutional principles. For his assessment of particular British institutions implies that Smith no longer found it necessary to think exclusively in terms of mixed government. In approving of an independent judiciary, it is true, Smith does not seem to have gone beyond the principle of the separation of powers, which was compatible with mixed government.[76] But his treatment of the two other institutions he singled out for commendation, the standing army and the system of representative, parliamentary consent for taxation, shows him to have moved onto ground whither one still subscribing to the doctrine of mixed government could not readily follow.

This is clearest in the case of the standing army. In the perspective of mixed government, as Hume had had to acknowledge, to entrust defence to professional soldiers was necessarily to give the monarch a preponderant weight in the constitution. Smith, however, saw no such danger. Brushing aside the objections of men of 'republican principles', he would argue that an army subordinate to the sovereign and commanded by the leading classes in society is a strength rather than a threat to liberty. Less obvious, but, it can be argued, not less critical, was Smith's departure from the mixed government view of parliamentary representation. According to that view, parliament should be considered the republican element in the constitution; and thence, as Hume recognized, it was but a short step to regarding members of parliament as but delegates, bound by the instructions of their constituents.[77] Smith, however, can be seen to have rejected this interpretation of the representative relation in his discussion of Britain's imperial crisis. It was, he observed, just because of the 'republican' influence of electors over the members of the American colonial assemblies that these were so unmanageable: and to diminish such influence was the object of his scheme of imperial parliamentary union. What was needed to secure the principle of parliamentary consent on an imperial basis, he argued, was a directly proportional relation between representation and taxation; but this should not be confused, as it was liable to be in the doctrine of mixed government, by a view of representation as delegation.

In renouncing the mixed government view of the British constitution in these two respects, Smith may be seen to have taken advantage of distinct, alternative constitutional principles. Since the beginning of the century, political commentators of 'Court' or 'Whig' persuasion had sought both to defend the standing army on the self-same grounds of subordination to civil authority and integration into the social hierarchy, and to distinguish repre-

[76] On occasion, moreover, he could still describe the British constitution in general terms as a mixed government: *ibid.*, IV.vii.c.78.

[77] Hume appreciated that British MPs were not delegates, obliged to receive instructions from their constituents; but he does not seem to have regarded the distinction between delegation and representation as a critical one. A balance between the two was part of the mixture of British government; and in a passage included in his *Essays* between 1742 and 1760, he dismissed the controversy over instructions as 'very frivolous': 'Of the First Principles of Government', *Philosophical Works*, III, pp. 112–13.

sentation from delegation, denying the legitimacy of instructions. When Hume wrote, in the mid-century, such arguments were not yet in the ascendant; but by 1776, the outbreak of the American rebellion and the publication of the *Wealth of Nations*, they had won general acceptance among the parliamentary classes. By adopting them, it is important to note, Smith did not commit himself exclusively to the Court or Whig viewpoint, with its uncompromising hostility to the claims of the colonists. Nor did he commit himself to an alternative general theory of the constitution. Both the standing army and the distinction between representation and delegation were in principle closely tied to the concept of parliamentary sovereignty;[78] but as it was of the essence of parliamentary sovereignty that it evolved piecemeal, adoption of its subordinate principles did not necessitate explicit reference to the concept itself. It was enough that alternative principles on which to assess the British constitution were available, permitting Smith to break free of the doctrine of mixed government to which Hume reluctantly still felt bound.

And not only the doctrine of mixed government. Smith was also free to dispense with the more general body of constitutional principle of which that doctrine had been a particular, local variant: the civic tradition. Once again comparison with Hume is telling. Diagnosing the precariousness of mixed government, and yet acknowledging the lack of political liberty under continental absolute monarchy, Hume had fallen back on fundamental constitutional principles of the civic tradition to frame an 'Idea of a perfect Commonwealth'. However radically Hume can also be seen to have modified the traditional significance of civic principles to accommodate the social consequences of economic development, the principles themselves remained. In the *Wealth of Nations*, by contrast, those civic principles are conspicuous by their absence. Evidently they were no longer needed. Viewing British government in terms more appropriate to parliamentary sovereignty than to mixed government, there was no reason to doubt its superiority over any other existing form. It had improved upon the strengths of the monarchies in justice and defence; it had evolved a unique system of representative parliamentary consent for taxation: as a result its institutions were better adapted than all others to economic development. True, it was not yet flawless. In the long term it would require radical reform to ensure that representation was properly proportional to taxation; (and to support the consequent extension of the electorate, the provision of public education for the lower ranks would have to be generalized). But such reform could occur within the present constitutional framework. Smith, therefore, had no occasion to invoke civic principles, no occasion to write an 'Idea of a perfect Commonwealth'. To

[78] As indeed was the independence of the judiciary, in that judges were removeable only by parliamentary impeachment.

exemplify his idea of free government, he had only to project the perfection of British government.[79]

* * *

From that final vantage-point, Smith may be thought to have moved quite beyond the limits of the civic tradition, previously reached by Hume. It has already been argued that by his formulation of the problem of government and economic development Smith confirmed and extended his predecessor's revision of the traditional social and moral premises of political community. But the implication of his response to the problem went still further, questioning whether it was worth even attempting a corresponding revision of civic constitutional principles. To enable the legislator in a commercial society to meet the institutional demands of economic development, it appeared to Smith simpler to begin to define the concept of free government anew, on principles displayed in the British constitution.

To regard Smith's constitutional arguments as a straightforward progression beyond Hume's would of course be misleading. Contingent historical

[79] Oddly, it is just in this comparison of Smith's project of imperial parliamentary union with Hume's 'Idea of a perfect Commonwealth' that Winch, and now also Phillipson, have identified a resemblance between the institutional principles of the two thinkers: *Adam Smith's Politics*, pp. 172, 178–80; 'Adam Smith as Civic Moralist', *Wealth and Virtue*, pp. 194–7. It would seem, however, that the only argument with which Winch can support such a resemblance rather confirms the contrast between the two models. For in referring to the 'American' application of both models, Winch forgets that Hume appealed to those who sought to elaborate a sophisticated republican alternative to parliamentary sovereignty; Smith, by contrast, offered the perfection of parliamentary sovereignty.

Forbes too has aligned Smith's constitutional thinking with Hume's, on the different grounds that Smith subscribed to 'the commonplace Blackstonian view' of the British constitution as a mixed government: 'Sceptical Whiggism, Commerce and Liberty', p. 186. But this is also misleading. Not only can Smith himself be seen to have adopted specific principles associated with the doctrine of parliamentary sovereignty; but Blackstone's *Commentaries* contain resounding general affirmations of the same doctrine. Even if Blackstone throughout (and Smith occasionally, in the *Wealth of Nations*) continued to think of the British constitution in terms of mixed government as well as parliamentary sovereignty, the resulting constitutional doctrine was still markedly different from Hume's more strictly civic view, which had no place for the concept of sovereignty.

Haakonssen offers an interesting analysis of the way in which Smith combined the concepts of sovereignty and the division of powers in his Lectures—and also points to Smith's reported description of the constitution as 'a happy mixture of all the different forms of government properly restrained': *Science of a Legislator*, pp. 130–3, 169–70; *Lectures on Jurisprudence* (B), 63. Through reliance on the Lectures, however, Haakonssen misses the diminished importance of the classical account of forms of government in the *Wealth of Nations*, and the bringing to the forefront of the principles of parliamentary sovereignty.

circumstances—the later maturing of Smith's political thought, the changing context of British constitutional debate—were what made possible Smith's break with the doctrine of mixed government, and thence with civic constitutional principles. It would indeed be an insular, Whiggish view that saw the rejection of civic principles in favour of those of parliamentary sovereignty as 'progress'. At the same time, it is important to emphasize once more that it was not Smith's purpose in the *Wealth of Nations* to elaborate a complete constitutional doctrine. Given the critical importance he attached to the relation between government and economic development, he could not avoid a reckoning with political and constitutional theory. But in the solution as in the formulation of the problem, that reckoning is conducted in integral relation with the economic analysis of the *Wealth of Nations*. Whatever the status of political economy as 'a branch of the science of a statesman or legislator', within the *Wealth of Nations* itself it is political and constitutional principles which are rendered a branch of political economy. To keep Smith's adoption of the principles of parliamentary sovereignty in proper perspective, therefore, it should be recognized that those constitutional principles have themselves been assimilated into political economy.

Even when these cautions have been entered, however, the *Wealth of Nations* may still be thought to mark a new departure. The assimilation of the indigenous British constitutional principles of parliamentary sovereignty into political economy was itself an original achievement, and one whose significance outlasted the work's immediate eighteenth-century context. The legislators of nineteenth-century Britain who held the sovereignty of parliament and the laws of the market to be the touchstones of government and economy may have been indifferent to Adam Smith's own grander political vision; theirs may not be the appropriate vantage-point for a historian wishing to understand Smith's enterprise as a whole.[80] But those legislators' oft-avowed gratitude to the author of the *Wealth of Nations* in particular was not misplaced. The constitutional and economic principles which they acted on are already present in the political economy of the *Wealth of Nations*. That enduring work is, after all, rather more Gladstonian in character than it has lately been fashionable to admit.

John Robertson ST HUGH'S COLLEGE, OXFORD

[80] Winch, *Adam Smith's Politics*; Winch, 'Adam Smith's "Enduring Particular Result" '.

[15]

ADAM SMITH'S SECOND THOUGHTS:

ECONOMIC LIBERALISM AND ITS UNINTENDED CONSEQUENCES

By Jeremy Shearmur

ECONOMIC LIBERALISM AND MORAL TRADITIONS

Those who favour 'economic liberalism' - that approach to the problems of human social and economic organization that gives pride of place to the operations of the free market - seldom take the view that markets are <u>all</u> we need. They often also accord a positive role in society to tradition, to shared moral codes, or perhaps to shared religious practices. In part, these are invoked, within a market system, to deal with such issues as social cohesion and a sense of community, the relief of distress through charitable works, and to allow for the cultivation, by the individual, of moral virtue or a well-developed personality. In part, however, they are also invoked, at least by some writers, as having a role in sustaining the institutions of economic liberalism itself. It has often been argued that a 'free market' requires an appropriate institutional framework if it is to function adequately.[1] And one interpretation of economic liberalism - that which stretches from Hume, through Adam Smith, to F.A. von Hayek - takes the view that the institutions and codes of conduct required for the operation of liberalism must rest on a non-rational acceptance, on the part of the members of the society in question, of those forms of behaviour that come 'naturally' to them, or upon their falling in, largely uncritically, with the traditions of their society as they are handed down.[2] (A view of this kind, while at odds with the more radical 'rationalism' that has sometimes been taken to characterize economic liberalism, does offer a picture of social organization which seems to complement economic liberalism, in that it also obviates the need for the centralized control of society.)

It is one thing, however, for such a combination of views to be found attractive; it is quite another for it to be viable.[3] And it might surely be further questioned whether the continued existence of such traditions and social practices is really compatible with economic liberalism. Let me immediately mention one possible difficulty here. Social customs, and moral and religious traditions, are clearly bound up with certain 'ways of life'. But 'ways of life' have an economic component and, under economic liberalism, this economic component is not sacrosanct. It is open to anyone who thinks that he can better provide any given good or service to have a go at doing so. But there is no particular reason to suppose that some new - and let us suppose successful - operation will necessarily form a suitable basis for the continued practice of those old traditions, or that there will arise new social and moral traditions that adequately perform the same function, in their place.

Now, should there be anything in such ideas, the advice of such thinkers as Hayek - and certain American neo-conservatives - that we should espouse both economic freedom and the products of tradition may prove paradoxical. Economic freedom may prove an awkward bedfellow, with a strong tendency to hog all the bedclothes, and, indeed, to kick its partner out of bed.

AUTHORITY, CIVIL SOCIETY, AND THE CONSEQUENCES OF LIBERTY

It was certain vague and ill-formed ideas of this character that were concerning me at around the time when I was asked if I woulc like to deliver a paper to the Adam Smith Club. And as Adam Smith himself is - despite the huge bicentennial output - still one of my interests, I was challenged to think of these issues in relation to his work. It seemed to me, on reflection, that not only do issues such as these arise in the work of Adam Smith, but that they do so in such a way as to pose a serious problem for economic liberalism itself.

The issue with which I will be particularly concerned arises in connection with Smith's discussion of civil society in his Lectures on Jurisprudence. Smith there tells us:[4]

> There are two principles which induce men to enter into a civil society, which we shall call the principles of authority and utility.

Now, of these, the second is pretty straightforward - Adam Smith tells us:[5]

> The second principle which induces men to obey the civil magistrate is utility. Every one is sensible of the necessity ... of this principle to preserve justice and peace in ... society. By civil institutions, the poorest may get redress of injuries from the wealthiest and most powerful ...

But it is Smith's discussion of the other principle that, I think, is of particular interest. Smith's discussion in the Lectures on Jurisprudence is brief, but we are also referred to his Theory of Moral Sentiments, from which I will shortly take my account. First, however, a little must be said. As those who know the Lectures on Jurisprudence will recollect, Smith there puts forward a sketch of the development of society through four stages; the stages are distinguished by their mode of subsistence and Smith gives an account of the way in which the mode of subsistence characterizes the form of government, the legal institutions, the typical moral ideas, the extent of the division of labour, and, indeed, the ability to wage war of the societies in question. Smith gives a sort of historical treatment of these things, but it was what Dugald Stewart was later to call a 'conjectural or theoretical history', in which the history is told, or better, reconstructed, from a theoretical point of view. Now the role that Smith gives to the mode of subsistence and to wealth in this story has led to one interesting consequence - that Smith has, in this account, been regarded by some as a sort of precursor of Historical Materialism; something which, while perhaps understandable, seems to me ultimately misleading.[6] Indeed, Smith himself makes clear that while:[7]

> ...superior wealth...contributes to confer authority

he explains at once that:

> This proceeds not from any dependence that the poor have upon the rich, for in general the poor are independent, and support themselves by their labour, yet though they expect no benefit from the rich, they have a strong propensity to pay them respect.

This disposition, indeed, is that first principle, authority, which, on Smith's account, induces men into civil society, and it is to Smith's discussion of this that we will now turn.

Smith tells us, in the Theory of Moral Sentiments, that:[8]

> The man of rank and distinction...is observed by all the world. Every body is eager to look at him, and to conceive, at least by sympathy, that joy and exultation with which his circumstances naturally inspire him. His actions are the objects of...public care. Scarce a word, scarce a gesture, can fall from him that is

> altogether neglected. In a great assembly he is the person upon whom all direct their eyes; it is upon him that their passions seem all to wait with expectation, in order to receive that movement and direction which he shall impress upon them; and if his behaviour is not altogether absurd, he has, every moment, an opportunity of interesting mankind, and of rendering himself the object of the observation and fellow-feeling of everybody about him.

Smith then tells us something of the mechanism behind this:[9]

> When we consider the condition of the great, in those delusive colours in which the imagination is apt to paint it, it seems to be almost the abstract idea of a perfect and happy state. It is the very state which, in all our waking dreams and idle reveries, we had sketched out to ourselves as the final object of all our desires. We feel, therefore, a peculiar sympathy with the satisfaction of those who are in it. We favour all their inclinations, and forward all their wishes. What pity, we think, that any thing should spoil and corrupt so agreeable a situation! We could even wish them immortal; and it seems hard to us, that death should at last put an end to such perfect enjoyment. It is cruel, we think, in Nature to compel them from their exalted stations to that humble, but hospitable home, which she has provided for all her children. Great King live for ever! is the compliment, which, after the manner of eastern adulation, we should readily make them, if experience did not teach us its absurdity.

Now, while Smith is somewhat ambivalent about this impulse (witness the reference to 'those delusive colours in which the imagination is apt to paint it'), he gives it a major role not only in bringing about civil society, but also in the shaping of the conduct and characters of that society's ordinary members. This impulse, together with the various other psychological mechanisms invoked in Smith's Theory of Moral Sentiments, operating in the various different circumstances in which individuals find themselves, go to produce Smith's account of the social formation of the individual's character, and of how he internalises the moral codes and social customs of his society.

I have emphasised all this because, while one may or may not agree with the precise details of Smith's discussion, the kind of phenomenon to which he points in his remarks about 'authority' does, surely, exist. But look for a moment at one important fact: Smith's assumption that the person who will be the recipient of such attention will be 'the man of rank and distinction' in what is, effectively, a face-to-face society, and that the consequences of the influence of the people in respect of whom this mechanism operates will be to bring people into civil society, and to induce in them patterns of conduct that have a positive function for the operation of such a society. It would seem to me that it is precisely this connection that may be - and, indeed, has been - affected by the consequences of economic liberalism. For economic liberalism loosens the connections between the possession of wealth or the ability to exercise social influence along the lines that Smith had suggested and what could be called the conservative assumption that the people who exercise this influence will do so in a way that plays a positive role in the functioning of a liberal society.

For, on the liberal view of things, the appropriate institutional arrangements having been made, the abilities of man are liberated in such a way that individuals, by the pursuit of economic self-interest in the market, are able to benefit both themselves and others. One consequence of these developments is a gain in disposable wealth by the average member of the community, and a shaping of developments in industry and society by his preferences as expressed through his expenditure.

But it is just this fact which leads to the separation, to which I have alluded above, between the man of rank and distinction and the man of superior wealth - and, indeed, the object of Smith's mechanism, more generally. For, with the general increase in wealth that comes from the operation (under suitable conditions) of economic freedom, and the spread of disposable income which goes with it, individuals can become wealthy, and achieve a 'fortunate' position, by the satisfaction of mass tastes. Moreover, as Smith himself might well have appreciated, as is evidenced by his reference to 'those delusive colours in which the imagination is apt to paint it', and the doubts that he elsewhere raises as to whether the rich are as fortunate as we are inclined to believe, there is room for a fairly radical separation between the fact of wealth and those who are the objects of the mechanism about which Smith talked: it is more by an image than by the reality of wealth that we are influenced.

As a result, it is not surprising to find that those in respect of whom Smith's mechanism might today be seen as operating are the products of image-building industries, designed to catch mass disposable income. For I would suggest that the sort of mechanisms to which Smith referred still do operate, but that today they operate particularly with respect to popular musicians, film and television stars, footballers, and so forth. And while, to be sure, there is still interest in the Royal Family, in the aristocracy, and in the doings of those of 'higher social rank', this has now, at the very least, to be shared with the interest shown in these other groups, and ordinary members of society are not under the day-to-day influence of these latter figures in the way that they were in the society about which Smith was writing.

Now if we turn back to the use that Smith made of this mechanism, there is a problem. For while, say, a great interest in the fortunes, habits, etc. of the local landowner, and of those in higher social ranks than oneself in a stable, hierarchical society would act as a form of social cement, and as one of the things that draws people into civil society, we can see that the operation of economic liberty itself has led us to different results. Smith's mechanism itself is still more or less recognisable, but that which serves as its starting-point is different; the man of rank and distinction has been supplanted. In his place, we have something rather different - people whose behaviour and habits are by no means things which, if taken as a model, will continue to sustain civil society. Rather than examplars of the traditional standards of decent behaviour so favoured by conservatives, one has offered up for emulation people of little taste, with no tradition of how to behave in a position of wealth or influence behind them; people whose behaviour, or the objects of whose sympathy, are incapable of acting as a model for any sort of society. Though, lest I mislead you, my point here is not that I happen to dislike the behaviour of the idols of mass culture so much as that the way they behave, and the behaviour they inspire, can hardly form a general model for ordinary people in their day-to-day lives. Furthermore, it is difficult to see such influences as helping to sustain civil society or as playing a functional role within it.

Now, interestingly enough, it would seem as if Smith, in his later years, expressed certain qualms about these matters himself. For, in his last major piece of work, the revision of his Theory of Moral Sentiments for its sixth edition, Smith added a new chapter:[10] 'Of the corruption of our moral sentiments, which is occasioned by this disposition to admire the rich and the great, and to despise or neglect persons of poor and mean condition.'

This new chapter of Smith's commences:[11]

> This disposition to admire, and almost to worship, the rich and the powerful, and to despise, or, at least, to neglect persons of poor and mean condition, though necessary both to establish and to maintain the distinction of ranks and the order of society, is, at the same time, the great and most universal cause of the corruption of our moral sentiments.

And while, in it, Smith is concerned largely with:[12] 'the complaint of moralists in all ages' that 'wealth and greatness are often regarded with the respect and admiration which are due only to wisdom and virtue; and [that] the contempt, of which vice and folly are the only proper objects, is often most unjustly bestowed upon poverty and weakness', he includes an attack on the 'man of fashion', and on the way in which the style of life followed by such people serves as a disastrous model for the 'poor man'.

What Smith does not offer us, however, is any suggestion about what could or should be done in the face of such problems - problems which indicate that there may be a difference between the actual consequences of the operation of 'natural' social mechanisms, and the consequences that Smith was looking on these mechanisms to produce.

Thus, when I was considering the paper that I should deliver to the Adam Smith Club, it was thoughts about these issues that were very much on my mind. Above all, I was concerned with the problem: How might Smith himself have reacted to these consequences of the operation of economic freedom as they have emerged in our own society, and how, in general terms, might he have suggested that we try to solve the problems to which these developments have led?

OF MICE AND MENIPPUS

Indeed, a few months ago, I was, one night, thinking over these things just before going to bed. I had been reading again some passages from the Lectures on Jurisprudence and the Wealth of Nations, and thinking hard. The evening was drawing on, and I realised that, somewhat exceptionally, I had omitted to get myself anything to eat. I went out into the kitchen, and cobbled together a sort of curry - and in it, I remember now, I used some fennel seed I had bought at a little Greek shop near where I live. I had my meal, and then went to bed. I am an inveterate reader in bed and, on this occasion, having finished my usual light reading, I turned to my copy of Lucian. I don't know if you know his writings, but if you don't, I would strongly recommend them.[13] He was a second century literary satirist; and while, it appears, most of his work consists of playing with existing ideas and literary conventions, he is very entertaining, and has much that is humorous to say about fanaticism of all kinds, and especially about religious and philosophical humbug. In particular, he tells some very nice stories about a visit that his hero, Menippus, makes to the moon, and also about some trips that he made to Hades.

At any rate, after reading for a bit, the effect of my evening's work and my heavy meal began to tell, and I turned over, switched out the light, and went to sleep.

Some hours later, I was woken up by a scratching sound. As I suffer sometimes from mice, I simply snuggled down further in bed, and tried to return to sleep. But the scratching sound became more persistent, and so, eventually, I sat up. I was amazed to see a ghostly figure, tapping on the end of my bed. He was about five feet six inches tall, quite plump, and with a somewhat florrid face. He looked not unlike a butler in P.G. Wodehouse but he was wearing a sort of toga. As you can imagine, I was a bit taken aback. But this was nothing to my reaction when he addressed me by name;

'Shearmur', he said, 'don't worry - it's Menippus; you know, you have been reading about me in Lucian. Now, I've been dead quite a few years, but, as you know, there is the institution of the Refrigerium[14] - the dead have occasional holidays - and I was so taken with your problem that I decided to use one of mine in order to give you a hand. For, or so it would seem to me, the obvious way to resolve your problem is to go and have a word with Smith himself.'

I hardly knew how to react or what to say. But Menippus did not pause; rather, he took my arm, and started to hurry me off towards the window. I tried to say something about its being high up, but did not get the chance, as he was nattering away about Hades, and how to get me in there. He said that these things had changed a bit, and so I would not have to put on flour to make me look dead, or to try to dress up like Hercules as he had had to do...he thought that he could fix things without much trouble. By this time, I found that I had been bustled out of the window, and somehow, down to the ground. He walked along Finsbury Park Road, but when we got to Riversdale Road, instead of the terraced houses that I knew as being there, there was an actual stream, which we followed along, as far as Green Lanes, where, on the site of what I knew as the reservoir, there was a huge lake or sea - I could not make out the far side as it was misty. And across it there came, slowly, a boat, propelled by a strange figure, who, my guide told me, was Charon.

While we were waiting for the boat, I started to think a bit, and it struck me that, in the stories that I had heard about Hades, it was necessary to bring the dead back to life by giving them blood - by killing a sheep, and so forth.[15] As I had not got one with me, I asked Menippus about it. He agreed that it was usual, but then, after some thought, considered that claret might now be more acceptable, and suggested that I run back home for some bottles. While I was there, I also picked up a few coins, as I remembered something about having to pay Charon for the crossing.

It was there, I think, that I made my mistake, as, when I got back to the lake, and Menippus had sorted everything out about my passage, I obviously did something wrong as far as Charon was concerned. I offered him a couple of ten pence pieces. His reaction was, to say the least, heated; he nearly pushed me off the boat, and, while I was not able to catch all that he said, it included some disparaging remarks about government monopoly money, and a demand for payment in real money - for gold, silver, or at least some sort of a commodity reserve unit. Happily, Menippus stepped in, and, from a purse concealed about his person, he produced a small gold coin, which pacified Charon.

As we struck out across the 'lake', which I decided must be the Styx, the mist, which had been hanging around us from the start, gradually closed in, and soon we were in a thick, cold fog. Gradually the water seemed to get more choppy, and the whole climate grew colder. A cold breeze then sprang up, which started to sweep away the fog. I was surprised to catch glimpses of a coastline ahead of us - and, indeed, before that, of an island; surprised, I say, because they looked in a way familiar. Suddenly I realised - the island was Inchkeith, that little island in the Firth of Forth which Hume had talked about in a letter to Smith as a possible meeting place between him in Edinburgh and Smith in Kirkcaldy.[16] And the coastline was that of Leith, the port of Edinburgh. The boat was beached, and I made my way up towards Edinburgh. It was a bit difficult, as there was not a soul about, and I had then only the dimmest memories of the hinterland of Leith; but the rough ideas that I had did suffice, and I managed to make my way up to Canongate, and to Smith's old residence, Panmure House.

Once again, no-one was about, and I pushed the door open, and made my way inside. And there, in a large room, on the right hand side of the house, was Smith himself, together with a few friends. By this point, I felt that I could not be taken aback any more than I was, but the sight of them there, like a lot of wizened corpses, was a bit dismaying. In fact, they all looked like old Bentham in his glass case at University College. However, Menippus, who had been walking along behind me, came forward, and told me that it was now that I should bring out the claret. It all came back to me - the stuff in Homer, about Odysseus making a ditch, and pouring sheep's blood into it, so that the souls in Hades could drink, and gain some semblance of life. I was looking around, wondering exactly what I should do, when Menippus came up with some glasses - which, of course, was the answer; and, sure enough, as the liquid was poured out, and its bouquet spread around the room, there were stirrings of life among Smith and his companions; they twitched, stirred, and came over for a glass.

Some little time later, when a few glasses had been consumed, we got down to talking.

I must confess that I hogged the discussion a bit. I started off with a list of all my old speculations about Smith's writings with a request for comments - you know, all the sort of things that may have occurred to you, too, if you have read Smith's works: to what extent can one reconstruct the promised[17] 'sort of theory and history of Law and Government' from his Lectures on Jurisprudence and the Wealth of Nations, and, similarly, his 'Philosophical history of all the different branches of literature, of Philosophy, Poetry and Eloquence' from the Lectures on Rhetoric and the Essays. Also, there were some problems of my own. To what extent can one reconstruct Smith's philosophical psychology form the Lectures on Rhetoric. Also, the problem of the interpretation of his ideas about history; and the question of the nature of his epistemology - particularly in view of his use of biological counter-examples to the theory of association, and his fascinating conventionalist suggestions about the philosophy of science; to say nothing of all those problems in the Wealth of Nations... But I am doing just the same here as I did there, coming out, non-stop, with everything. I finished, as you might imagine, with a statement of the problem that was so concerning me. That is to say, the conflict that could be said to exist between the mechanism of 'authority' that he had pointed out as operating in social life (what one might today call the 'film-star effect') and to which he had given a role as social cement, and the consequences upon the operation of this mechanism of the social transformation effected by the economic liberalism that he so favoured. The problem, in short, that Smith's conservative assumption, that those to whom this mechanism would extend our feelings of sympathy would be people whose behaviour and preferences would reinforce social conventions and smooth the operation of civil society, had been sabotaged by the consequences of economic freedom itself.

After all this had been said, and the shocking news about the state of our own society had been given, I prepared to listen to what Smith had to say. Indeed, in order to take full note of the judgement that he would give, I moved to the desk, on which his clerk used to take dictation, where there was a pen and ink to hand. I then turned round to face Smith, full of expectation.

However, what I got was a brief lecture to the effect that, while it was my privilege to come to see him, he considered that it would not be appropriate for me to take back with me a transcription - or, indeed, a memory! - of what he would have to say. For, after all, he said, knowledge must be publicly accessible, and while, of course, my evidence would be authentic, if I were allowed to return with it, there would be nothing to stop people making all sorts of tomfool claims, saying that they had got their information from Smith himself.

As a result, while I have a dim memory of a lot of animated conversation, I fear that I cannot report to you anything of Smith's contribution to our discussion at all. Smith, however, did sympathise with my disappointment - and also, indeed, with the situation of Menippus, who, quite understandably, felt a bit put out - and he called to my mind some passages in his work which bear on the issue. In consequence, while I cannot offer you Smith's second thoughts on this particular problem we do have something which might be called Smith's second thoughts on a similar problem in which he saw undesirable consequences following from the operation of economic liberty.

INCONVENIENCES ARISING FROM A COMMERCIAL SPIRIT

There is, in the Lectures on Jurisprudence, a particularly interesting section which discusses the influence of commerce upon manners.[18] Here, Smith discusses various consequences of the operation of economic freedom and economic development upon society. He first notes the way in which what are often taken as 'national characteristics' may be properly seen as the result of the moulding of individual character by the situations that individuals are in, and the expectations that others have about their behaviour (together with the operation of certain fixed motives), so that the punctiliousness of the commercial Dutch about keeping their word in matters of commerce, as compared with the behaviour of the English, and, above all, the Scots, is explained in terms of the operation of 'self interest, that general principle which regulates the actions of every man'.[19] As, for a Dutch trader, making many contracts a day, a reputation for honesty is important, whereas, for a highland Scot, who is little involved in trade, it is of little importance at all.

From this, Smith moves to discuss some 'inconveniences....arising from a commercial spirit'.[20] After saying something about the stultifying effect on the individual of the extreme division of labour (he refers to being occupied in making the 'seventeenth part of a pin or the eightieth part of a button' - which represents the other side of the gain in wealth through the operation of the division of labour in just such cases), and commenting that, as a result, 'in every commercial nation, the low people are exceedingly stupid', he moves to the question of education. Here he points out that one undesirable consequence of the advance of commerce is that education is neglected. His point is that the division of labour has led to the simplifying of various tasks involved in production, so that a child's parents will have the opportunity to put him to work, rather than educating him:[21]

> In rich and commercial nations the division of labour, having reduced all trades to very simple operations, affords an opportunity of employing children very young. In this country [Scotland]..... where the division of labour is not far advanced, even the meanest porter can read and write, because the price of education is cheap, and a parent can employ his child no other way at six or seven years of age. This, however, is not the case in the commercial parts of England. A boy of six or seven years of age at Birmingham can gain his threepence or sixpence a day, and parents find it to be their interest to set them soon to work. Thus their education is neglected. The education which low people's children receive is not indeed at any rate considerable; however, it does them an immense deal of service, and the want of it is certainly one of their greatest misfortunes. By it they learn to read, and this gives them the benefit of religion, which is a great advantage, not only considered in a pious sense, but as it affords them a subject for thought and speculation. From this we may observe the benefit of country schools,

> and, however much neglected, must acknowledge them to be an excellent institution. But, besides this want of education, there is another great loss which attends the putting boys too soon to work. The boy begins to find that his father is obliged to him, and therefore throws off his authority. When he is grown up he has no ideas with which he can amuse himself. When he is away from his work he must therefore betake himself to drunkenness and riot. Accordingly, we find that in the commercial parts of England, the tradesmen are for the most part in this despicable condition: their work through half the week is sufficient to maintain them, and through want of education they have no amusement for the other but riot and debauchery. So it may very justly be said that the people who clothe the whole world are in rags themselves.

After this discussion, Smith goes on to speak of another effect of the commercial spirit - the weakening of the military qualities of a people through commerce, and the way in which this can leave them prey to less commercially developed nations. He ends with a brief summary of his points, concluding:[22]

> To remedy these defects would be an object worthy of serious attention.

Now, what is not without interest is that, as some of you may know, there is a parallel discussion, later, in the Wealth of Nations. But what is striking is that Smith does, there, propose a remedy:[23]

> For a very small expense the *publick* can facilitate, can encourage, and can even *impose* upon almost the whole body of the people, the necessity of acquiring those most essential parts of education. The publick can facilitate this acquisition by establishing in every parish or district a little school, where children may be taught for a reward so moderate, that even a common labourer may afford it; the master being partly, but not wholly, paid by the publick...
> (italics mine)

Smith also adds that:[24]

> The publick can encourage the acquisition of those most essential parts of education by giving small premiums, and little badges of distinction, to the children of the common people who excel in them.

And, further,

> The *publick* can *impose* upon almost the whole body of the people the necessity of acquiring those most essential parts of education, by obliging every man to undergo an examination or probation in them before he can obtain the freedom in any corporation, or be allowed to set up any trade either in a village or town corporate.
> (italics mine).

There is also, in The Wealth of Nations, another discussion of the theme of undesirable consequences of the growth of commerce which is particularly pertinent. If, again, I may quote:[25]

> A man of rank and fortune is by his station the distinguished member of a great society, who attend to every part of his conduct, and who thereby oblige him to attend to every part of it himself. His authority and consideration depend very much upon the respect which this society bears to him. He dare not do any thing which would disgrace or discredit him in it, and he is obliged to a very strict observation of that species of morals, whether liberal or austere, which the general consent of this society proscribes to persons of his rank and fortune. A man of low condition, on the contrary, is far from being a distinguished member of any great society. While he remains in a country village his conduct may be attended to, and he may be obliged to attend to it himself. In this situation, and in this situation only, he may have what is called a character to lose. But as soon as he comes to a great city, he is sunk in obscurity and darkness. His conduct is observed and attended to by nobody, and he is therefore very likely to neglect it himself, and to abandon himself to every sort of low profligacy and vice.

At this point, Smith discusses the way in which a solution to this problem emerges spontaneously, through the formation of religious sects:[26]

> A man of low condition never emerges so effectually from this obscurity, his conduct never excites so much the attention of any respectable society, as by his becoming the member of a small religious sect. He from that moment acquires a degree of consideration which he never had before. All his brother sectaries are, for the credit of the sect, interested to observe his conduct...

But, somewhat surprisingly, Smith then comments that 'The morals of these little sects, indeed, have frequently been rather disagreeably rigorous and unsocial' and he moves to discuss 'easy and effectual remedies' by means of which '*the state* might...correct whatever was unsocial or disagreeably rigorous in the morals of the little sects into which the country was divided' (italics mine)!

In fact, however, Smith had earlier announced a principle in connection with the whole subject of education, which would seem to apply in all these cases:[27]

> Ought the publick...to give no attention...to the education of the people? Or if it ought to give any, what are the different parts of education which it ought to attend to in the different orders of the people? and in what manner ought it to attend to them?
> In some cases, the state of society necessarily places the greater part of individuals in such situations as naturally form in them, without any attention of government, almost all the abilities and virtues which that state requires, or perhaps can admit of. In other cases the state of...society does not place the greater part of individuals in such situations, and some attention of government is necessary in order to prevent the almost entire corruption and degeneracy of the great body of the people.

Now, I appreciate that one may well say that these are not exactly *second* thoughts on Smith's part. But they are, certainly, *later* thoughts. While, in the *Lectures on Jurisprudence*, we have discussed the *problems* with which we have dealt here, in book five of *The Wealth of Nations* we actually have *remedies* proposed; the challenge that Smith put out at the end of his discussion in the *Lectures on Jurisprudence* is taken up - but the answers that are given are not those that would give joy to the economic liberal. For Smith here is quite clearly suggesting that there should be an interventionist answer to some of the problems raised by the operation of economic freedom itself. And I now feel pretty sure that the answer that Smith gave me, that night, was along similar lines.

That, at least, was my impression as I woke up, the next morning, in bed, with a splitting headache, and some empty claret bottles by my side.

I feel that it is a great shame that I was not allowed to take a record of what Smith had to say,[28] for there is obviously a problem here. A liberal may well say that in cases where things do not 'naturally' happen in a desirable fashion the government should intervene. (Smith's concern in the examples that we have discussed was both with things which he considered to be intrinsically undesirable and with things which were dysfunctional for the state of the society in which they were occurring.) But how should this be done, and what will be the consequences of the fact that it is done; what are the principles which should govern such intervention, and how do these relate to other principles that operate in the society in question; and how do we make sure that an authority that has the power to intervene in this way only does what the liberal theorist intends it to do?

Such issues, I think, pose difficult problems for the 'Hume/Smith/Hayek' tradition of conservative liberalism. But they also pose problems for other forms of liberalism too. A more 'rationalistic' liberal may not look at shared social customs, at moral or religious traditions, or at those forms of conduct that come 'naturally' to man, as playing a positive role in the operation of his ideal society. But he may nonetheless face similar problems if any of these things develop in such a way that they pose a threat to the institutions of a liberal society, or to the values that sustain it - and it would surely be absurdly optimistic to suppose that such problems will never occur.

If I may conclude by quoting from Smith yet once more:

To remedy these defects would be an object worthy of serious attention.

Notes

1. Cp., for example, N. Rosenberg, 'Institutional Aspects of the Wealth of Nations', Journal of Political Economy, 68, 1960.
2. A view which has its rationale in what could be called the abstract, diffuse and systematic character of the institutions of a liberal society. Cp. my 'Abstract Institutions in an Open Society', in Wittgenstein, The Vienna Circle and Critical Rationalism, H.P.T. Vienna and Reidel, Holland, 1979, pp. 349-54.
3. Cp., for example, the issue that can be raised in relation to Hayek's work, as to whether whatever is delivered to us by tradition, or by the supposed selective mechanisms of social evolution, in fact corresponds to an instantiation of the principles of that Rechtsstaat liberalism that Hayek favours. See, on this, R. Hamowy, 'Freedom and the Rule of Law in F.A. Hayek', Il Politico, 2, 1971, pp. 349-71; J. Gray, 'F.A. Hayek on Liberty and Tradition', Journal of Libertarian Studies, IV, No.2, 1980, pp. 119-37; and 'Hayek on Liberty, Rights and Justice', Ethics, 92, Oct. 1981, pp. 73-84; and my 'The Austrian Connection: F.A. von Hayek and the Thought of Carl Menger', in B. Smith and W. Grassl, eds., Austrian Philosophy and Austrian Politics, Philosophia Verlag, Munich, forthcoming.
4. See Adam Smith, Lectures on Jurisprudence, Clarendon Press, Oxford, 1978, p. 401.
5. Ibid., p. 402
6. I have discussed this issue in an unpublished paper 'Smith's Individualism'; there is a brief report on the case against this interpretation of Smith in Knud Haakonssen, Natural Justice, Edinburgh PhD thesis, 1978. The nub of the matter is that economic developments in Europe did not, in Smith's view, follow their natural course, after the fall of Rome. The fall of Rome, in its turn, seems, in Smith's view, to have been the consequence of people behaving in a manner that came 'naturally' to them, but which was disastrous in its consequences - a disaster that Smith seems to have regarded as similar in character to the debacle of 1745, and to have been the product of a situation that stood in need of remedy by governmental action, to be taken on the basis of a theoretical overview of the course of social development. This would seem to me most plausibly understandable as an echo of the 'civic humanist' tradition and of that theme, going back to Polybius, of there being a natural cycle of constitutional forms, 'naturally' ending in disaster, but which, however, might be halted by the intervention of a statesman, equipped with the knowledge of these developments that was given to him by the theorist/philosopher. Cp. Lectures on Jurisprudence, p. 414: 'We now come to show how this military monarchy came to share that fated dissolution that awaits every state and constitution whatever.'
7. Adam Smith, Lectures on Jurisprudence, p. 401.
8. Adam Smith, Theory of Moral Sentiments, Clarendon Press, Oxford, 1976, part I, Section 3, Chapter 2, p. 51.
9. Ibid., pp. 51-2.
10. Adam Smith, Theory of Moral Sentiments, part I, Section 3, Chapter 3, pp. 61-6. My attention was drawn to this material, and to its significance in the context of my present paper, by George Davie. See also his review of the Glasgow edition of The Theory of Moral Sentiments, in British Society for Eighteenth Century Studies, Newsletter 12, June 1977, pp. 28-30.
11. Ibid., p.61.
12. Ibid., p.62.

13. I would especially recommend, for their entertainment value, Lucian, Satirical Sketches, tr. Paul Turner, Penguin, Harmondsworth, 1961.
14. See C.S. Lewis, The Great Divorce, Collins/Fontana, London, 1972, p.60. I should add, however, that Lewis is in no way to blame for my conflation, in the text, of ideas relating to Greek and Christian conceptions of the afterlife.
15. See Lucian, op.cit., p. 120; and also the passage in the Odyssey in which Odysseus meets the shade of his mother.
16. See J.Y.T. Greig, ed, The Letters of David Hume, volume ii, Clarendon Press, Oxford, 1932, letter 432.
17. See Smith's letter to Le duc de la Rochefoucauld, 1st Nov., 1785, No. 286, in E.C. Mossner and I.S. Ross, eds, The Correspondence of Adam Smith, Clarendon Press, Oxford, 1977, pp. 286-7.
18. See Lectures on Jurisprudence, pp. 538-41.
19. Ibid., p. 538.
20. Ibid., p. 539.
21. Ibid., pp. 539-40.
22. Ibid., p. 541.
23. Wealth of Nations, 1976, volume 2, Part 5, Section 1, p. 785.
24. Ibid., p. 786.
25. Ibid., p. 795.
26. Ibid., pp. 795-6.
27. Ibid., p. 781.
28. The historical situation is actually much more complicated than I have indicated in this paper. For some suggestions as to what was at issue, see D. Winch, Adam Smith's Politics, Cambridge University Press, 1981; C. Robbins, The Eighteenth Century Commonwealthman, Harvard University Press, 1959; J.G.A. Pocock, The Machiavellian Moment, Princeton University Press, 1975; G. Davie, The Scottish Enlightenment, Historical Association, 1981; and I. Hont and M. Ignatieff eds., Virtue and Commerce, Cambridge University Press, 1983. See also Knud Haakonssen's most interesting study of the 'natural jurisprudence' of Hume and Smith, The Science of a Legislator, Cambridge University Press, 1981.

The Author: Jeremy Shearmur was formerly assistant to Karl Popper at the London School of Economics. He has taught philosophy at Edinburgh University, and is currently teaching political theory at Manchester University. He has contributed to a wide range of academic journals, scholarly symposia and conferences.

This publication is a revised version of a paper delivered to the Adam Smith Club.

[16]

Adam Ferguson, Adam Smith, and the Problem of National Defense*

Richard B. Sher
New Jersey Institute of Technology

I

It has long been recognized that eighteenth-century Scotland gave birth to political economy as a sophisticated scholarly discipline. Hailing from a relatively impoverished nation that had joined its larger southern neighbor in 1707 to form a new "British" state, Adam Smith and other Scottish political economists were concerned not only with observing, describing, and explaining the realities of economic life as they saw them but also with leading Scotland toward material progress and wealth. It has also been recognized, however, that in Scotland political economy was a branch of a remarkably comprehensive academic discipline known as moral philosophy, and that Scottish moralists were acutely sensitive to the ambiguities and paradoxes inherent in economic growth. At times this sensitivity was expressed through the language of the civic humanist or classical republican tradition, which emphasized public virtue, a unified civic personality that joined the private individual with the public citizen, and economic independence based on land ownership, as opposed to the blatantly self-interested attitudes and activities associated with the accumulation of commercial wealth. This tension between modernization and morality, wealth and virtue, accounts for much of the recent interest in the social thought of the Scottish Enlightenment.[1]

* I wish to thank the National Endowment for the Humanities and the Institute for Advanced Studies in the Humanities, University of Edinburgh, for funding the research on which this article is based. Thanks also to Hiroshi Mizuta, David Raynor, and John Robertson for valuable criticisms; to Michael Barfoot and Yasuo Amoh for assistance with transcriptions of Ferguson's lecture notes; to John Pocock and the members of his Folger Institute Seminar on the History of British Political Thought for fruitful discussion of an earlier draft in February 1987; and to the helpful special collections staff at Edinburgh University Library, whose trustees kindly permitted me to publish excerpts from Ferguson's moral philosophy lecture notes.

[1] J. G. A. Pocock, *The Machiavellian Moment: Florentine Political Thought and the Atlantic Republican Tradition* (Princeton, N.J., 1975), chap. 14; Istvan Hont and Michael Ignatieff, eds., *Wealth and Virtue: The Shaping of Political Economy in the Scottish Enlightenment* (Cambridge, 1983); Herbert F. Thomson, "The Scottish Enlightenment and Political Economy," and Salim Rashid's "Commentary," both in

[*Journal of Modern History* 61 (June 1989): 240–268]

The problem of the division of labor illustrates this tension. Norbert Waszek has identified three features of the eighteenth-century Scottish approach to this subject that set it apart from analyses by other thinkers from Plato to Mandeville, Möser, Rousseau, and the authors of the *Encyclopédie*. First, the Scots gave the division of labor a more prominent role in political economy, often as the primary cause of economic growth. Second, they discussed the concept in a modern context, embracing both the latest technology and the new trading conditions of a developing world economy. Third, their appreciation for the positive effects of the division of labor was tempered by their awareness of its ''far-reaching drawbacks,'' particularly in the form of short-term economic disruptions, social inequality, and dehumanization of the work force.[2]

It is hardly surprising that Waszek draws most heavily upon the two ''Adams'' of the Scottish Enlightenment, for the contrast between Adam Smith and Adam Ferguson is revealing. Born in the same year (1723), and members of the same wider circle of literati that clustered around David Hume and the Moderate party in the Church of Scotland, both Smith and Ferguson emerged from the didactic tradition of Whig-Presbyterian moral philosophy that had been shaped above all by Smith's teacher Francis Hutcheson, and both became professors of moral philosophy in their own right (Smith at Glasgow from 1752 to 1764, Ferguson at Edinburgh from 1764 to 1785). They shared many of the same concerns about the stadial development of societies and the pros and cons of modernization. Both viewed the division of labor[3] as a—if not *the*—critical factor in the modernization process. As Ferguson wrote in his *Essay on the History of Civil Society* (1767), ''a people can make no great progress in cultivating the arts of life, until they have separated, and committed to different persons, the several tasks, which require a peculiar skill and attention.''[4] Smith, of course, took the analysis farther in the famous opening chapters of the *Wealth of Nations* (1776), where he argued that the division of labor was the driving force behind economic

---

Pre-Classical Economic Thought: From the Greeks to the Scottish Enlightenment, ed. S. Todd Lowry (Boston, 1987), pp. 221–63.

[2] Norbert Waszek, ''The Division of Labor: From the Scottish Enlightenment to Hegel,'' *Owl of Minerva* 15 (1983): 51–75, esp. 54–57; see also Waszek, *The Scottish Enlightenment and Hegel's Account of ''Civil Society''* (Dordrecht, 1988), chap. 6.

[3] This term was one of several used by Scottish authors, with no apparent concern for nuances of meaning. Ferguson, e.g., used at least the following terms interchangeably with it: ''separation of arts and professions,'' ''subdivision of arts and professions,'' ''separation of labour,'' ''separation of tasks,'' ''subdivision of labour,'' ''subdivision of tasks,'' ''separation of employments,'' ''separation of departments, professions and tasks,'' and ''separation of tasks and professions.''

[4] Adam Ferguson, *An Essay on the History of Civil Society*, ed. Duncan Forbes (Edinburgh, 1966), p. 180. These words appear in the first paragraph of pt. 4, sec. 1: ''Of the Separation of Arts and Professions.''

growth.[5] Yet, as Waszek and others have shown, both men were well aware of the limitations and unfavorable consequences of the division of labor, particularly when viewed from a social perspective. The contrast appears in their priorities and emphases: whereas Smith's thrust was on the positive aspects of the division of labor and economic growth generally, Ferguson's was on the dangers they posed. And whereas Smith was willing to treat nations and individuals from an economic point of view, Ferguson spurned this "modern" approach and insisted on the priority of Stoic and civic humanist moral ideals.[6]

Nowhere do these differences appear more clearly than in the debate over national defense. As filtered through the neo-Harringtonian, commonwealthman writers of late seventeenth-century England, the civic humanist tradition demanded militias rather than standing armies, not necessarily because militias were considered more effective from a military point of view but because militias were considered necessary for reinforcing and protecting liberty.[7] This perspective was transferred to eighteenth-century Scotland chiefly through the writings of Andrew Fletcher of Saltoun.[8] But once again the debate acquired a distinctive Scottish character during the age of Smith and Ferguson. For one thing, advocates of militias during the mature Scottish Enlightenment subtly moved the focus of the debate from constitutional

[5] Adam Smith, *An Enquiry into the Nature and Causes of the Wealth of Nations,* ed. R. H. Campbell, A. S. Skinner, and W. B. Todd, 2 vols. (Oxford, 1979), I.i–iii; hereafter cited as *WN*. Citations to *WN* are to book, chapter, section, and paragraph rather than page number.

[6] Works that have specifically compared and contrasted Smith and Ferguson include Hiroshi Mizuta, "Two Adams in the Scottish Enlightenment: Adam Smith and Adam Ferguson on Progress," *Studies on Voltaire and the Eighteenth Century* 191 (1981): 812–19; Hermann Huth, *Soziale und individualistische Auffassung im 18. Jahrhundert, vornehmlich bei Adam Smith und Adam Ferguson* (Leipzig, 1907); Ronald Hamowy, "Adam Smith, Adam Ferguson, and the Division of Labour," *Economica* 35 (1968): 249–59; and August Oncken, "Adam Smith und Adam Ferguson," *Zeitschrift für Sozialwissenschaft* 12 (1909): 129–37, 206–16. Hamowy and Oncken's articles argue that a rift between Smith and Ferguson during the 1780s had its roots in Smith's charge that Ferguson plagiarized his ideas on the division of labor, but the evidence to support this thesis is slight.

[7] Lois G. Schwoerer, *"No Standing Armies!" The Anti-Army Ideology in Seventeenth-Century England* (Baltimore, 1974); Lawrence Delbert Cress, *Citizens in Arms: The Army and Militia in American Society to the War of 1812* (Chapel Hill, N.C., 1982), chap. 2, and "Radical Whiggery on the Role of the Military: Ideological Roots of the American Revolutionary Militia," *Journal of the History of Ideas* 40 (1979): 43–60.

[8] John Robertson, *The Scottish Enlightenment and the Militia Issue* (Edinburgh, 1985), chap. 2.

liberty to civic virtue.[9] That is, their primary concern was no longer the danger of a standing army tipping the constitutional balance in favor of monarchy; it was the danger that a people defended by a standing army alone would become "effeminate," materialistic, selfish—in short, corrupt—and that such a people would be both incapable and unworthy of defense. Their political liberty would be lost because of deficiencies in their national character.

One effect of this moral approach to the problem of national defense was to shift emphasis from an antiarmy to a promilitia position—a shift that was at least partly a reflection of the fact that by the middle of the eighteenth century no one in Britain could seriously argue that militias should entirely replace standing armies. Another effect was to bring to the forefront the tension between modernization and morality. Standing armies were associated with modernity not only because they were literally the products of the modern European nation-state but also because they appeared to embody modern principles of efficiency and economic rationality. Above all, they embodied the principal of the division of labor and its corollary, specialization of function, which made for a more efficient army while at the same time threatening to disqualify untrained civilians for effective military service. One contribution of the Scottish Enlightenment, then, was to situate the problem of national defense within the wider framework of political economy and moral philosophy.

Nationalism was another distinctive feature of the debate over military defense in the Scottish Enlightenment. The militia act of 1757 had deliberately excluded Scotland, largely because of English fears about arming a nation that had given considerable support to the Jacobite rebellion of 1745–46. Throughout the duration of the Seven Years' War Scottish militia supporters schemed to extend the provisions of the English bill to the North, and serious, though ultimately unsuccessful, campaigns to enact such a Scots militia bill in Parliament were mounted in 1759–60 and 1762.[10] Scotland's proud tradition of military glory and supposed mistreatment at the hands of England formed prominent themes in those campaigns. Among the cause's most active and zealous spokesmen was Adam Ferguson, who had already published one anonymous pamphlet on behalf of a British militia before Scotland's exclusion from the provisions of the militia act.[11] Besides writing promilitia pamphlets and letters, Ferguson was instrumental in establishing,

[9] Richard B. Sher, *Church and University in the Scottish Enlightenment: The Moderate Literati of Edinburgh* (Princeton, N.J., and Edinburgh, 1985), pp. 219–20.

[10] Ibid., chap. 6; Robertson, *Scottish Enlightenment*, chap. 4.

[11] Adam Ferguson, *Reflections Previous to the Establishment of a Militia* (London, 1756).

early in 1762, the Poker Club, which met weekly at an Edinburgh tavern to stir up zeal for a Scots militia in a convivial setting. Adam Smith's role in the Scots militia campaigns of the Seven Years' War was more subdued than Ferguson's, but Smith was a member of the Poker Club and was supportive enough of the 1760 Scots militia bill to complain to William Strahan that Nathaniel Hooke's Jacobite memoirs "are published at an unlucky time, and may throw a damp upon our militia."[12]

Ferguson's *Essay on the History of Civil Society,* published a few years after the Seven Years' War and the Scots militia campaigns had ended, discussed the question of national defense on a higher theoretical plane. There was no mention of Scotland's quest for a militia—no mention, in fact, of the word "militia" at all. Yet in the two sections of the fifth part of the book ("Of the Decline of Nations") that were devoted to the topic "Of Relaxations in the National Spirit incident to Polished Nations," Ferguson asserted that

> the separation of professions, while it seems to promise improvement of skill, and is actually the cause why the productions of every art become more perfect as commerce advances; yet in its termination, and ultimate effects, serves, in some measure, to break the bands of society. . . . Under the *distinction* of callings, by which the members of polished society are separated from each other, every individual is supposed to possess his species of talent, or his peculiar skill, in which the others are confessedly ignorant; and society is made to consist of parts, of which none is animated with the spirit of society itself. [P. 218]

This civic humanist lament on the dangerous consequences of the division of labor was then applied to the problem of national defense. To put the entire responsibility for national defense in the hands of a specialized force, "whether these be foreigners or natives," is dangerous because it weakens a people's capacity for fortitude and self-defense (p. 227). This is a particularly serious problem for "polished and mercantile" states, which could benefit from "a lesson, which it has cost civilized nations many ages to unlearn, That the fortune of a man is entire while he remains possessed of himself" (p. 228). Thus, the division of labor not only weakens national defense but dismembers "the human character": "The subdivision of arts and professions, in certain examples, tends to improve the practice of them, and to promote their ends. By having separated the arts of the clothier and the tanner,

[12] Smith to Strahan, April 4, 1760, in *The Correspondence of Adam Smith,* 2d ed., ed. Ernest Campbell Mossner and Ian Simpson Ross (Oxford, 1987), 68; hereafter cited as *Smith Correspondence*. At the time of this letter the militia bill had been debated once in the House of Commons and was awaiting its second reading on April 15, when it was soundly defeated.

we are the better supplied with shoes and with cloth. But to separate the arts which form the citizen and the statesman, the arts of policy and war, is an attempt to dismember the human character, and to destroy those very arts we mean to improve'' (p. 230). In this way, Ferguson made it clear that national defense was for him an economic and moral problem as well as a military and political one.

The American crisis brought the issue of national defense to the foreground once again,[13] and in the mid-1770s the Poker Club was revived by Ferguson and his friends. In November 1775 Lord Mountstuart—whom Ferguson had served as private tutor early in the Seven Years' War—introduced a new Scots militia bill that earned him unanimous election to the Poker two months later. At that time Ferguson wrote enthusiastically to a friend that ''the sense of this Country where it has been taken is every where favourable to the Militia.''[14] On March 5 Mountstuart's bill became the first of its kind to survive a second reading in the House of Commons. Four days later—and five days before the bill was tabled and effectively defeated in Parliament—the *Wealth of Nations* was published at London.

Considering Smith's apparent support for the Scots militia bill of 1760, membership in the Poker Club, and friendship with many of the leading Scots militia proponents, one might have expected some sympathy for militias in Smith's treatment of military questions. In the part of the *Wealth of Nations* titled ''Of the Expence of Defence,'' however, Smith painted a dismal picture of militias as vastly inferior to standing armies in all periods and places.[15] The foundation of his argument was the division of labor, which dictated a preference for a specialized fighting force. The discussion had an almost polemical tone, as if the author were campaigning for standing armies and against militias. Smith made three slightly different declaratory statements in the space of just a few pages to hammer home his point. First, after discussing different ways of disciplining and exercising a militia, Smith wrote: ''A militia, however, in whatever manner it may be either disciplined or exercised, must always be much inferior to a well-disciplined and well-exercised standing army.'' Several paragraphs later he asserted that ''the history of all ages . . . bears testimony to the irresistible superiority which a

[13] Sher, *Church and University,* chap. 6; Robertson, *Scottish Enlightenment,* chap. 5.

[14] Ferguson to John Home, January 27, 1776, National Library of Scotland, Edinburgh, MS 124, fols. 76–77.

[15] For further discussion of Smith's views on national defense and the opposition they provoked in Scotland and America, see Sher, *Church and University,* chap. 6; Robertson, *Scottish Enlightenment,* chap. 7; Donald Winch, *Adam Smith's Politics: A Study in Historiographic Revision* (Cambridge, 1978), chap. 5; Cress, *Citizens in Arms,* pp. 28–33.

well-regulated standing army has over a militia.'' And toward the end of the section he declared that ''a well-regulated standing army is superior to every militia'' (*WN*, V.i.a.23, 28, 39). It is true that later in the book Smith stressed the importance of cultivating a ''martial spirit'' among the people (*WN*, V.i.f.59–60), but that discussion did little to soften the blow struck by his earlier comparison of militias and standing armies as alternative systems of military organization.

Scots militia supporters were upset by Smith's treatment of the national defense issue in the *Wealth of Nations*. The timing of the book's appearance could hardly have been worse from their point of view—or more ironic from ours, in light of the concern Smith had expressed to Strahan (publisher of the *Wealth of Nations*) upon publication of Nathaniel Hooke's memoirs while the Scots militia bill of 1760 was under consideration by Parliament. Was not Smith himself doing the same thing Hooke's book had done sixteen years earlier? His very manner of formulating the question—militia *versus* standing army—seemed to play into the hands of the opponents of the Scots militia bill. It is impossible to know the extent to which Smith's discussion of national defense actually helped to bring about the bill's defeat in Parliament, but it is not difficult to see why supporters of the Scots militia would have been deeply troubled by its untimely appearance.

As a leader of that cause among the Edinburgh literati, Adam Ferguson was one of those known to be dismayed by his friend's treatment of the national defense issue. ''You have provoked, it is true, the church, the universities, and the merchants, against all of whom I am willing to take your part,'' Ferguson wrote to Smith on April 18; ''but you have likewise provoked the militia, and there I must be against you.'' Believing that Smith's writings on the militia were not only wrong but socially irresponsible as well, Ferguson commented sharply: ''The gentlemen and peasants of this country do not need the authority of philosophers to make them supine and negligent of every resource they might have in themselves, in the case of certain extremities, of which the pressure, God knows, may be at no great distance.''[16] Ferguson, however, did not elaborate on precisely how he would ''be against'' Smith. His discussion of the militia question ended with a seemingly innocuous remark that suggested continuation of their debate in the convivial atmosphere of a club such as the Poker: ''But of this more at Philippi.''

Yet the matter was quite serious. Early in 1778 another Scots militia supporter—evidently Ferguson's close friend Alexander Carlyle—published at London *A Letter to His Grace the Duke of Buccleugh, on National Defence; With Some Remarks on Dr Smith's Chapter on that Subject, in his Book*

[16] Ferguson to Smith, April 18, 1776, in *Smith Correspondence*, pp. 193–94.

entitled An Inquiry into the Nature and Causes of the Wealth of Nations.[17] There the section on the "expence of defence" was sharply criticized, and the tension between the demands of commerce and martial virtue was noted in civic humanist terms reminiscent of Ferguson:

> But if there should be some small interference [between commerce and a militia], it is surely better to be a little less rich and commercial, than by ceasing to be men, to endanger our existence as a nation. Let us attend to the examples that are pointed out to us in the downfall of other nations; let us guard with jealous vigilance the constitution of our country; lest, like the greatest empire that ever was, that of the Romans in their decadency, we become so luxurious or effeminate, as to leave the use of arms to strangers and mercenaries. [P. 47]

Smith's response to this pamphlet was peculiar. In a letter to Andreas Holt of October 1780, he declared himself "a little surprized" at having been attacked in this manner and charged that the author of that work "had not read mine to the end. He fancies that because I insist that a Militia is in all cases inferior to a well regulated and well disciplined standing Army, that I disaprove of Militias altogether. With regard to that subject, he and I happened to be precisely of the same opinion."[18] It was, in fact, Smith who had not read his critic's work to the end,[19] for in the *Letter on National Defence* Carlyle not only cited but also praised (pp. 50–51) Smith's call for nurturing a martial spirit among the people, and he quite correctly observed that his opponent's discussion of the expense of defense earlier in the *Wealth of Nations* was antimilitia "however contrary it may seem to other parts of his book" (p. 30). It was naive of Smith to think that a Scots militia supporter who read the *Wealth of Nations* through to the end would have reason to forgive his antimilitia sins. Whatever sympathies Smith may have entertained

[17] Later in 1778 this pamphlet was reprinted at Edinburgh, with a different subtitle that did not allude specifically to Smith or the *Wealth of Nations*. Though Smith himself believed the pamphlet was by an acquaintance of his named Douglas (*Smith Correspondence*, p. 251)—possibly Rev. Robert Douglas of Galashiels—modern bibliographers have commonly ascribed it to Carlyle. The newly accessible Carlyle manuscripts in the National Library of Scotland contain a document that seems to support the latter attribution: it is an early draft of part of the pamphlet, corresponding to pp. 19–52 of the London edition, and apparently written in Carlyle's own hand (MS 23,920, fols. 30–37; this reference courtesy of T. I. Rae). Smith must have felt the irony in this pamphlet's use of the duke of Buccleuch as the model of martial virtue and foil to Smith, for after giving up his professorship at Glasgow University Smith had been employed as the young duke's tutor on the Continent during the mid-1760s.

[18] Ibid., p. 251.

[19] Winch, *Smith's Politics*, p. 112.

for the Scots militia cause were rendered insignificant by the logic of his argument. His commitment to the division of labor and modernization was primary and applied to the military as well as the commercial sphere. Moreover, Smith never attempted to clarify his position in later editions of the *Wealth of Nations*. Though the second edition of that work was already in the press when the *Letter on National Defence* appeared, the substantially revised third edition of 1784 provided an excellent opportunity for clarification that Smith deliberately passed up.

If the first edition of the *Wealth of Nations* contained Smith's last word on the militia, what response did it call forth from Ferguson? He could hardly have failed to realize that the sections of the *Wealth of Nations* covering national defense and martial spirit were, inter alia, a reply to the sections of his *Essay on Civil Society* dealing with ''Relaxations in the National Spirit.'' Yet John Robertson has pointed out that Ferguson's later works—including his textbook *Institutes of Moral Philosophy* (1769; rev. ed. 1773 and 1785) and his comprehensive ''retrospect'' of his moral philosophy course, *Principles of Moral and Political Science* (1792)—have almost nothing to say about the militia issue, national defense, or martial virtue.[20] What, then, did Ferguson mean when he vowed to ''be against'' Smith on this issue? The remainder of this article will show that, for at least thirty years after publication of the *Wealth of Nations*, Ferguson continued to grapple with the issue of national defense and to express his ideas on that subject through academic lectures, private correspondence, and various unpublished writings that have received little or no scholarly attention. One aspect of these activities was to continue a lifelong debate with Adam Smith that centered on the concepts of wealth, division of labor, militias, standing armies, and civic virtue.

II

Buried deep within Ferguson's moral philosophy lecture notes in Edinburgh University Library are previously neglected notes of lectures on national defense. There are two extant versions of these lectures, the first consisting of two continuous (though not contiguous) lectures dated April 8, 1776 (hereafter called 76A) and April 9, 1776 (hereafter called 76B), and the second of a lecture dated April 3, 1777 (hereafter called 77A) that is situated between 76A and 76B.[21] The lecture of April 9, 1776 is also marked April 6, 1780 and

[20] Robertson, *Scottish Enlightenment*, p. 209.

[21] Edinburgh University Library, Dc.1.85. 76A occupies fols. 438–42, 76B fols. 458–61, and 77A fols. 448–52. Dc.1.84 and Dc.1.85 constitute a set of two bound volumes of lecture notes that move from the beginning to the end of Ferguson's course. They do so, however, in a confusing manner, with overlapping lectures interleaved by topic in most—but not all—cases. Usually Ferguson revised existing lectures, but from

April 7, 1784, which are presumably the dates on which Ferguson made further revisions. It should be emphasized that these are Ferguson's own lecture notes, not those of a student. They therefore constitute a more authoritative, and potentially more useful, document than student lecture notes such as those of Adam Smith on rhetoric and jurisprudence, though on the other hand they may be less accurate and less complete in conveying what was actually said in the classroom at any particular time.[22] That these lecture notes have never been published and have attracted no scholarly attention should not lead us to minimize their possible influence. Between 1776 and 1785, more young people in Scotland may have heard these lectures on national defense by Ferguson (a popular teacher whose audience sometimes numbered a hundred or more) than read about that subject in the *Wealth of Nations*. The timing of the 1776 lectures is once again important: they were delivered exactly one month after the *Wealth of Nations* was published, three and a half weeks after the Scots militia bill was defeated in the House of Commons, and less than two weeks before Ferguson's letter to Smith pledging to "be against" him on the militia question.

Moreover, the Mizuta lecture notes cited in note 22 provide additional circumstantial evidence that Ferguson's lectures on national defense of April 1776 were prepared in response to the publication of the *Wealth of Nations* and the defeat of the Scots militia bill. Dating the Mizuta lecture notes is difficult, but a brief report on them, prepared for the owner by the late historian of political economy Ronald Meek, concludes on the basis of internal evidence that they "must be before W[ealth] of N[ations]" and after the publication of Sir James Steuart's *Inquiry into the Principles of Political Oeconomy* in 1767. This dating is significant because the Mizuta lecture notes contain no discussion of national defense in the modern world such as one finds in the Edinburgh University Library notes of April 1776 and April 1777 that were

time to time he would entirely rewrite a set of notes. The placement of lectures covering the same or similar topics is roughly chronological, from 1775 through 1785, though some of the lectures are out of place or undated. Crossed out words and sentences, insertions in the text and margin, careless spelling and grammar, and missing pages add to the confusion. In short, these are in every sense a teacher's own working notes.

[22] The Beinecke Library at Yale University recently acquired a much smaller collection of Ferguson's own lecture notes (currently uncataloged), which on examination turned out to be of no use for the purposes of this article. I have also examined the two known sets of student notes of Ferguson's moral philosophy lectures: (1) a slim bound volume of notes by John Lockhart from the 1779–80 session, in Edinburgh Public Library, MS YB1413M/81311A, and (2) a 525-page set of notes covering an apparently complete course of eighty-seven lectures. I am grateful to the owner of the latter set of notes, Professor Hiroshi Mizuta of Meijo University in Negoya, Japan, for providing me with a copy just weeks before this article was to go to press.

prepared by Ferguson after the *Wealth of Nations*. Military matters figure prominently only in a discussion of warfare among barbarous states toward the beginning of the course (lectures 15–16), where it is briefly observed in conclusion that "with regard to war barbarous nations are greatly inferior to those which are more polished. For regular discipline is more than a match for the superior strength of uncivilized nations" (fol. 62). It is just possible, of course, that Ferguson added his lectures on modern national defense during the early 1770s, before the appearance of the *Wealth of Nations*, but it is far more likely that he did so in direct response to the intellectual and political crisis of national defense in March 1776.

To understand what Ferguson was getting at in his lectures on national defense, it is helpful to know something about their place in his moral philosophy course. From the *Institutes* we know that course was divided into seven major parts: the natural history of man, the theory of mind, the knowledge of God (natural religion), moral laws, jurisprudence, casuistry, and politics. National defense was treated under politics. In Ferguson's view any subject could be studied either from the point of view of its existing arrangements or from the point of view of the improvements of which it is capable. These two approaches Ferguson called "physical science" and "moral philosophy" ("or moral science"), respectively. To ascertain the facts of politics in the manner of a physical scientist was important, Ferguson believed, but it was still more important to establish normative standards on the basis of those facts, in the manner of the moral philosopher. For only the moral philosopher could discern which political arrangements were best for a particular society, given its national character and specific circumstances.[23]

Politics as a subject of moral philosophy was divided by Ferguson into the study of institutions (political law) and the study of national resources (political economy). Political economy was defined as the study of three particular national resources: wealth, revenue, and people. It was the last of these types of resources that led Ferguson to the subject of national defense.[24]

[23] For more on this aspect of Ferguson's thought, see Sher, *Church and University* (n. 9 above), chap. 5. Fuller treatment of the didactic element in the teaching of Ferguson and other Edinburgh moral philosophy professors may be found in Richard B. Sher, "Professors of Virtue: The Social History of the Edinburgh Moral Philosophy Chair in the Eighteenth Century," in *Studies in the Philosophy of the Scottish Enlightenment,* Oxford Studies in the History of Philosophy, vol. 1, ed. M. A. Stewart (Oxford, 1989).

[24] In the Mizuta notes, interestingly, national resources are limited to wealth and revenue, with "people" reduced to a subcategory of wealth and discussed almost exclusively in terms of population. This difference suggests that in 1776 Ferguson altered his definition of political economy in order to give national defense and national character a more prominent place within it.

Regarded as a national resource, people could be considered in terms of ''their numbers, their union, and Character'' (76B). Their character, in turn, could be viewed either in relation to the constitution or form of the state (e.g., a virtuous character is suited to democracy) or in relation to the two primary needs or ''objects'' of the state. One of these objects is ''subsistence'' and beyond that ''riches or wealth.'' For this purpose an ''industrious & skillful'' character is vital. The second object of the state is national defense and safety. Here what is required is ''a People Courageous & Obedient[,] inured to Discipline & to Arms'' (76A). By means of this chain of argument, Ferguson set the stage for the critical question to be treated in his discussion of national defense—namely, how can a society best determine to whom to give arms and in whom to nurture a courageous character in order to employ its human resources most effectively?

Implicit in the problem of national defense as Ferguson articulated it was the tension between wealth and virtue, industry and courage. In one version of his lectures he praised ''personal courage'' in civic humanist terms as

> the foundation of ease of Generosity & greatness of mind. Of personal consideration & authority.
>
> This is the tenure by which men Ultimately hold their rights and are Secured from becoming the Property of any one who has the presumption to Usurp Dominion.
>
> And this Quality is in a great degree the measure of the Citizens Value to himself as well as to his country. [77A]

Ideally, every citizen should possess this quality, and ''the whole people'' may ''be Assembled & employed on every Alarm'' (77A). But in practice only ''nations of small extent and consisting of small numbers'' (76A) can employ the whole population for purposes of defense; ''in states of a greater extent this is neither necessary nor Possible'' (77A).

Although Ferguson does not tell his students exactly why this is so, the answer is obvious from his formulation of the problem. The nation's two primary objects—wealth and safety—must be delicately balanced. A people wholly industrious but lacking martial virtue would fall prey to its enemies,[25] just as a thoroughly courageous people lacking industrious attributes would remain hopelessly impoverished. The tiny—and presumably poor and unstratified—nation in which this tension between wealth and safety, industry and virtue, does not arise is an anomaly that can be quickly dismissed. Ferguson's real concern is with larger and more ''polished'' societies in which

[25] As Smith put it in the *Wealth of Nations,* V.i.a.15: ''An industrious, and upon that account a wealthy nation, is of all nations the most likely to be attacked'' and, unless effective measures are taken by it, the least able to defend itself.

this tension is very real. If every individual in such societies cannot be trained in the ways of war, how then do such societies defend themselves? If only a part can bear arms and practice martial virtue, how is that part to be chosen?

There are, says Ferguson, three ways in which this problem can be solved: (1) "fair rotation" among all citizens; (2) limitation of arms and martial virtue to the "superior ranks"; and (3) institution of a professional standing army composed of men from home or abroad. The first of these alternatives was the one used by "all the antient republics" when they are considered "as constituted by the Free men alone" (76A). The second alternative was the one practiced both by the ancient republics "if the servile as well as the Free" are taken into consideration and by "all the Feudal States of Modern Europe etc." ("The military leader & his followers. Others were despised") (76A). The third system is apparently unique to modern, polished nations, in which individuals are "selected at home or brought from abroad & consist of persons who embrace the Profession of Soldiers & submit to its hardships and dangers, on account of the appointments & establishments made for them in this Capacity" (76A).

Ferguson's preferences are clear: "1st best. 2d next & third worst" (76A). Since courage and the right to bear arms are good for the state and for the individual, it follows that "where circumstances allow of this advantage,[26] every Citizen ought to have the advantage & the security which the spirit and capacity of self defence tends to give" (76A). Fair rotation is the next best thing to an army of the whole community, but in practice it turns out to be equally impractical except as a supplementary device unless all the citizens are "nearly upon a footing of equality" (76A).[27] In a modern, populous, polished, and diversified nation like Great Britain, then, the main competition falls between the second and third alternatives. The main point that Ferguson tries to impress upon his young pupils in these lectures is the inferiority—indeed, the danger—of a defense system based solely on the institution of a professional army.

Ferguson has several things to say in favor of utilizing men of high rank in the military. First,

> Power Naturally follows the use of the sword. And the sword therefore shoud be committed to those who are most worthy of power.
>
> When the sword is committed to the hands of the unworthy, Power soon follows likewise into the same hands.

[26] The word "it" was later added in place of the words "this advantage," which have been crossed out.

[27] These words were later revised to read "of a certain consideration."

When the West India planters gave their arms to be carried by their slaves they found that they had at the same time exchanged their conditions. [76A][28]

Unless arms are borne by the higher classes, then, those classes are not safe from revolution and rebellion. A second, equally conservative, argument is that men of high rank are "best Educated" and "have the greatest interest in [the state's] Preservation" (76B).[29]

The third argument is the most distinctly Fergusonian and the most interesting. Men of high rank must dominate the military, Ferguson states, "because the abilitys of the Statesman & those of the Warrior are intimately connected. When they are separated the statesman becomes a Clerk & a Baubler and the soldier a mere Gladiator or executioner" (76B). In both the 1776 and 1777 versions of this argument, Ferguson contrasted this point with the advantages of the division of labor in the commercial world: "While the separation of mechanical Trades is an improvement in the arts of commerce, That of the higher Political functions is a corruption & a defect" (76A); and "The Separation of professions that is so useful in Mechanical productions is ruinous here. Whoever is to act with men shoud have a competent knowledge of human affairs" (77A). "To prepare the Statesman for all occasions he shoud be acquainted with War & qualifyed to act with men on the most arduous occasions" (76B). This way of stating his case suggests that Ferguson was composing his lectures with the *Wealth of Nations* in mind, for in that book Smith not only praised the division of labor in the economic sphere but also insisted, in his chapter on national defense, that the same principle held sway in regard to the military: "the division of labour is as necessary for the improvement of this, as of every other art" (*WN*, V.i.a.14).

Of course, Ferguson did not deny that professional armies had a role to play in the modern world, but his approach to this subject was decidedly different from Smith's. The two Adams were at one in seeing the problem as unique to civilized, economically advanced nations in which every citizen could not be a warrior and in which incentives for military service were lacking among the upper classes. At this stage of social development some kind of state-supported military force became necessary, but how was that force to be constituted? Smith's preference for standing armies rested wholly on their

[28] In a later revision the last sentence was crossed out.

[29] Smith made similar points more than once, as when he observed that where "the military force is placed under the command of those who have the greatest interest in the support of the civil authority, because they have themselves the greatest share of that authority, a standing army can never be dangerous to liberty" (*WN*, V.i.a.41); cf. Adam Smith, *Lectures on Jurisprudence*, ed. R. L. Meek, D. D. Raphael, and P. G. Stein (Oxford, 1978), pp. 543–44.

military superiority, as demonstrated by historical examples and by the growing complexity of modern warfare that made the principle of the division of labor decisive (*WN*, V.i.a.8–11). Specifically, Smith believed a standing army had greater proficiency with weapons than any militia ever could. Far more important, it could maintain "regularity, order, and prompt obedience to command," which in Smith's opinion constituted the primary problem of modern military organization (*WN*, V.i.a.22).[30]

Ferguson's formulation of the problem was very different:

> In the advanced state of arts, commerce, and National Enlargement, There arises a species of military service for which the labourer & the trader wants leisure and in which persons of Rank have not sufficient Inducements of honour.
>
> There are fortresses to be garrisoned,[31] Distant settlements to be maintained & distant wars to be supported. For neither of these the Tradesman can without public loss be taken from his Workshop.
>
> The statesman cannot be taken from his Department, & in ordinary times of Peace there is no honour to be won for the man of Rank.
>
> In these instances a Military Professiõn or standing army must be formed. [76B]

Note that in this passage Ferguson justified the existence of standing armies in polished nations not because of their superior discipline or fighting ability (though this was reluctantly admitted in a passage cited below) but because of their ability to perform three functions that were either too demeaning or too "distant" to be performed by citizen-soliders: defending "fortresses to be garrisoned," manning "Distant settlements," and fighting "distant wars." For Ferguson, as for Smith, standing armies were called forth by the special conditions found in modern, commercial societies, but the particular conditions cited by the two philosophers differed. Smith viewed the genesis of standing armies as basic to the general problem of maintaining a viable military force anywhere in the modern, civilized world, whereas Ferguson

[30] In the *Wealth of Nations* Smith argued this point on grounds of changes in military technology: the invention of firearms made discipline more important than individual skill with arms, and this change in turn made the standing army supreme in the modern world. In both extant versions of his lectures on jurisprudence, however, Smith based his argument on broader historical changes of an economic and social nature. He believed that in ancient Rome as in modern Europe the progress of "arts and manufactures" had transformed the military from the province of "the rich and better sort of people" to "the lower ranks," thereby introducing the problem of discipline that was chiefly responsible for stimulating the growth of standing armies; *Lectures on Jurisprudence*, p. 233, and esp. pp. 542–43.

[31] The words "is an ordinary garrison duty" were added in a later revision, replacing "are fortresses to be garrisoned."

saw it as a response to specific problems that had little or nothing to do with "national defense" in the traditional sense of that term as the defense of the homeland itself.

Central to Smith's account of "the irresistible superiority which a well-regulated standing army has over a militia" was the belief that the militia of a civilized or commercial society must be "altogether incapable of resisting the attack of such an army" (*WN*, V.i.a.37). As noted above, Smith's later attempts to justify the inculcation of "martial spirit" in the people of such a society seem feeble in light of his earlier attacks on the military viability of militias. He suggested that a martial spirit among the people could reduce the size of a nation's standing army and "very much facilitate the operations of that army against a foreign invader" (*WN*, V.i.f.59), but he never specified how these benefits would be obtained. It is not at all clear from this discussion that Smith meant to recommend the formation of an actual militia, even though this is what he implied he meant in his letter to Andreas Holt cited earlier. Indeed, the logic of Smith's argument in the chapter on the expense of defense did not allow for a militia that could fight effectively against a foreign standing army.[32] In the end Smith's advocacy of "martial spirit" had far more to do with educating the people and preventing "mental mutilation, deformity and wretchedness" (*WN*, V.i.f.60) among them than with defending the nation. That is why Smith placed his discussion of the need for martial spirit in a section of his book devoted to the expense of education rather than of defense. And perhaps that is why he introduced his famous "mental mutilation" passage with a revealing conditional clause: "Even though the martial spirit of the people were of no use towards the defence of the society" (*WN*, V.i.f.60).

It is difficult to imagine Adam Ferguson ever writing such a clause, even if only for the sake of argument. On the contrary, Ferguson set out to demonstrate in no uncertain terms that, despite the importance of standing armies, a martial character was also necessary among the people for specifically military reasons: "Where this order[33] is admitted and necessary, It does not follow that the remainder of the people ought to have no military character.[34] The labourer tho he cannot garrison a distant Frontier nor make

[32] Though according to one report Smith used to tell his students that "a militia commanded by landed gentlemen in possession of the public offices of the nation . . . would no doubt be the best security against the standing army of another nation" (*Lectures on Jurisprudence*, p. 543), it is difficult to square this statement with what he had to say in the section on the expense of defense in the *Wealth of Nations*.

[33] The word "order" was later replaced by "military profession."

[34] The words "have no military character" were later (1784?) crossed out and replaced by the words "drop every idea of defending themselves." At the same time

war at a Distance without giving up his Trade, may nevertheless be ready to defend himself and his family, may take Part in the defence of his Town & his Country, if an Ennemy shoud come to assail them'' (76B). These words read like a reply to Smith's assertions about economic development causing the great body of the people to become ''altogether unwarlike'' and ''altogether incapable of defending themselves'' (*WN*, V.i.f.60). Continuing this line of argument, Ferguson expands on the military advantages enjoyed by nonprofessionals defending their homeland:

> The Husbandman, the Labourer, and the Country Gentleman may in the use of arms and discipline be inferior to the Professional Soldier. But there is no reason why he shoud be inferior to what a Citizen may be made. He has the advantage of Affection and Principle over the Mercenary Soldier.
>
> This body of men are stationed at their own home[,] the place they shoud defend without any expence. They are more numerous than the Ennemy that is likely to attack them. And if inferior at first, the Rudiments of Discipline & order may on any real occasion be improved & the distinction between the Citizen & the soldier by profession disappear. [76B]

Thus, Ferguson counters arguments for the absolute superiority of standing armies over militias with the view that nonprofessionals enjoy three major advantages over a standing army: (1) they care about the land they are defending because it is theirs; (2) they defend their home region free of charge; (3) they are more numerous than the enemy. Moreover, in a real crisis they can quickly learn the ''rudiments of discipline and order'' and become the equals of professionals.[35]

The closest Ferguson comes to a direct reference to the national defense controversies of his own day is in his lecture of April 3, 1777 (77A). There he unleashes an attack against ''a mean & a dangerous Corruption'' found in nations ''in the advanced periods of Art & in the tranquillity of Large & Polished States.'' The corruption is that such nations begin to ''consider the Military as a Subordinate Character in the state.'' ''It is an Error that in process of time must correct itself,'' Ferguson warns, if the social hierarchy is to be preserved. This observation leads to further warnings about where his students will find the real danger that military establishments may pose to contemporary societies:

---

the original wording was added as a marginal note: ''It does not follow that the remainder of the people ought to have no military character.''

[35] Smith, too, believed that a militia could evolve into a standing army, but only after serving ''several successive campaigns in the field'' (*WN*, V.i.a.27). He would never have accepted Ferguson's rather naive claim that a popular militia could acquire professional military discipline at the moment of confrontation with an enemy.

> The great hazard to which the Nations of Europe are exposed is that which arises not from the occasional formation of Armys under Military Law to defend their Countrey & by which the use of Arms may in Rotation be diffused to the whole people or proper ranks of the People. But from the Establishment of a separate Military Profession & from [the] unwarlike Character & defenceless state of all the other orders of the People.
>
> In this happy Kingdom the State has already shown some sense of this danger & in the pursuit of its Plan it is hoped may be able to diminish or remove this danger.

This last sentence referred either to the English militia that Ferguson hoped to extend to Scotland or to the plan to establish Scottish "fencible" regiments, raised by Scottish peers such as the duke of Buccleuch to provide local defense.[36] Either way, it reveals the sense of partisan involvement in this issue that Ferguson brought to the classroom. For him, national defense was no abstract philosophical question but a matter of pressing concern, and the role of a moral philosophy professor was to instill the right principles of active citizenship and public virtue into his young students.

The conclusion of the discussion of national defense in Ferguson's 1777 lecture draws out the civic humanist implications of his approach. After conceding the superiority of, and the need for, standing armies in "actual service" of a military nature, Ferguson qualifies this point by emphasizing the necessity of supplementing such an army with a domestic defensive force:

> But this in no way affects the question relating to what is proper in free Nations to preserve the Martial Spirit of the People.
>
> A People having Propertys and honours for which they can do nothing themselves when every other defence may have failed are in an Awkward & a Precarious Situation in which they cannot long Remain.
>
> And we may return to our conclusion that the capacity of the people to defend themselves and their country is a principal measure of their political value.

In equating a people's ability to defend their "propertys and honours" with their "political value" and, in a sense, their civic personality, Ferguson went a good deal further down the civic humanist path than Smith was prepared to do.[37]

It appears, then, that Smith's discussion of national defense in the *Wealth of Nations* raised serious problems for Ferguson, and that one of the things Ferguson was trying to accomplish in his moral philosophy lectures on that

[36] Buccleuch's regiment and three others from different parts of Scotland were approved in 1778, but the precedent for raising Scottish "fencibles" had been set by the duke of Argyll during the Seven Years' War.

[37] For an excellent discussion of Smith's movement away from civic or civic humanist principles, see John Robertson, "Scottish Political Economy beyond the Civic Tradition: Government and Economic Development in the *Wealth of Nations*," *History of Political Thought* 4 (1983): 451–82.

subject was to dispute some of Smith's main principles. There is no doubt that Ferguson greatly admired the rest of Smith's book. Besides the fact that he said as much to Smith in his letter of April 18, 1776,[38] there is an interesting piece of evidence elsewhere in Ferguson's lecture notes. Ferguson was in the habit of concluding his course with a list of authors recommended for further reading: Xenophon, Plato, Aristotle, Cicero, Seneca, Epictetus, and Marcus Aurelius among the ancients, and Shaftesbury, Hutcheson, and Montesquieu among the moderns. In his final lecture of the 1775–76 session—delivered six days after his letter to Smith and fifteen days after he finished lecturing on national defense—Ferguson appended the following sentence: "And I will add Dr Smith in what relates to the Causes of National Wealth[,] the resources of Nation[s] & the important science of Political Oeconomy" (fol. 551).[39]

But Ferguson's high regard for Smith's abilities as a political economist served to highlight the differences between the two Adams in regard to military matters. Smith wanted a standing army to defend the nation with the highest level of professionalism and the least possible disruption of the economic order. His support for militias was secondary, if not downright inconsistent. Ferguson, by contrast, gave the highest priority to the civic ideal of virtuous citizen-soldiers, led by men of rank and substance, who would defend the homeland while a professional army manned distant outposts and engaged enemies on foreign soil.

Why, then, did Ferguson not include his ideas on national defense in either his textbook or his retrospect of his moral philosophy lectures? One can, for example, identify the place where a full discussion of national defense such as one finds in the lecture notes was purged from the manuscript of Ferguson's last published version of his moral philosophy course.[40] Given the circumstances of his day, his reticence is understandable. The militia issue was highly controversial during the second half of the eighteenth century, and Ferguson always took care to shield himself. The convivial militia club he helped to found in 1762 was deliberately secretive in almost every respect,

[38] *Smith Correspondence*, p. 193: "You may believe, that on further acquaintance with your work my esteem is not a little increased. You are surely to reign alone on these subjects, to form the opinions, and I hope to govern at least the coming generations."

[39] Similarly, John Lockhart's notes from Ferguson's class in 1779–80 (n. 22 above) conclude with an identical list of classical and modern authors whose works were recommended for further reading, including "Dr Smith's causes of national wealth." There is no mention of Smith, however, in the discussion of recommended authors in Ferguson's own lecture notes for April 21, 1785 (fol. 538).

[40] Adam Ferguson, *Principles of Moral and Political Science; being chiefly a retrospect of lectures delivered in the College of Edinburgh*, 2 vols. (London, 1792), 2:409–19.

from the cryptic name "Poker" that Ferguson chose for it to the clandestine political activities that the club may or may not have performed.[41] His two known militia pamphlets were both published anonymously, and Ferguson never publicly acknowledged authorship.[42] Moreover, insofar as the militia became a national Scottish issue, it may have seemed too parochial to merit discussion in philosophical and historical works of a general nature. When Ferguson published under his own name he either avoided the subject of national defense entirely or dealt with it in an abstract or theoretical manner, as in his celebrated *Essay.* In the classroom he was somewhat less guarded on this subject than in his avowed publications, but the quasi-public nature of his lecture course evidently obliged him to observe certain restraints.

III

It was in his personal correspondence more than anywhere else that Ferguson bared his soul on the issue of national defense. An example from the era of the American War is the long, important letter that he wrote to the politically

[41] Only in its last years did the Poker begin to work for a militia openly, as John Robertson shows in *Scottish Enlightenment* (n. 8 above), p. 149. But Robertson's argument that, whatever the intentions of its founders, the Poker was in fact *merely* a convivial club is not borne out by the evidence, including his own discovery of the Poker's direct involvement in the militia agitation of 1782 (which he dismisses as "a partial exception" that "proves the rule"), and Alexander Carlyle's statement (which Robertson does not mention) that "the Great Object of [the Poker Club's] meetings was National, *of which they never lost sight*" amidst all their conviviality (Carlyle, *Anecdotes and Characters of the Times,* ed. James Kinsley [London, 1973], p. 282, emphasis added; cf. Ferguson's description of the Poker in Sher, *Church and University* [n. 9 above], p. 232). Robertson's reluctance to take the Poker Club seriously reflects a more general reluctance to take literally the promilitia pronouncements and activities of Ferguson, Carlyle, and their Moderate friends, who, he argues on highly speculative grounds, wanted merely "the image rather than the institution of a militia" (*Scottish Enlightenment,* pp. 185–86).

[42] Both *Reflections Previous to the Establishment of a Militia* and *The History of the Proceedings in the Case of Margaret, Commonly called Peg, only lawful Sister of John Bull, Esq.* (London, 1761) are attributed to Ferguson in *The Autobiography of Dr. Alexander Carlyle of Inveresk, 1722–1805,* ed. John Hill Burton, new ed. (Edinburgh and London, 1910). The first of these pamphlets is presumably the one that David Hume had in mind when he referred, in a letter of April 30, 1757, to "Ferguson's Pamphlet with regard to the Militia" (Ernest Campbell Mossner, "New Hume Letters to Lord Elibank, 1748–1776," *Texas Studies in Literature and Language* 4 [1962]: 441). Authorship of the second pamphlet was such a closely guarded secret that David R. Raynor has recently claimed it for David Hume—see his *Sister Peg: A Pamphlet Hitherto Unknown by David Hume* (Cambridge, 1982) and my review disputing his attribution in *Philosophical Books* 24 (1983): 85–91.

influential William Eden, later Baron Auckland, on January 2, 1780.[43] As the sections of this letter dealing with national defense have never been published, it will be useful to reproduce them here, beginning with a lengthy passage extolling the Swiss militia:[44]

I think that our first concern is at Home. To have this Island in a Military Posture far above Insult. A numerous Army well appointed in the Field and Arms every where in the Hands of the People. Many are averse to the last Circumstance from a Notion that it will make the People Idle and endanger the Peace, and I have been so long upon that Hobby Horse that I am perhaps blind to his Defects: But the only People in Europe who are regularly [armed] are the most Industrious and the most Peaceable Citizens, and I believe that there is no Power in Europe that can Invade their Countrey without exposing himself to Disgrace and Ridicule. There are many Differences between them and us, I own: but none, to make me suppose that a Landholder and Father of a Family will become Idle and Riotous upon having a Stand of Arms in his House, here any more than there. . . . A people with Arms in their Hands contain many Armies and gall an Ennemy with Hostilitys wherever he goes. This Aid would be usefull upon every Supposition and may be absolutely necessary if to act offensively we Detach much of our Army and Fleet to a Distance. To effect this I apprehend that little more would be necessary besides some little Honorary Prize to be annually shot for, by Persons of a certain condition, who have Arms of their own.

This passage contains several of the same ideas that Ferguson expressed somewhat more politely in his moral philosophy lecture notes: that a citizen army would be necessary to protect the homeland against foreign invasion while the standing army was engaged in combat overseas; that a properly disciplined armed populace would pose no danger to social order; and that only "Persons of a certain condition," who could afford to buy "Arms of their own," would participate in the business of defense.

After asserting his preference for military advancement on the basis of merit rather than seniority, Ferguson returned to another of the central themes of his lecture notes on national defense:

My other wish is that some Arrangement were thought of to make our Statesmen Warriours, and conversely. . . . I am far from any Hopes that we shall see, as in the

[43] Ferguson to William Eden, January 2, 1780, Auckland Papers, British Library, MS 34,417, fols. 3–12. At this time Eden was a member of Parliament and lord of trade, as well as author of a recent book that treated colonial affairs, *Four Letters to the Earl of Carlisle* (London, 1779). In 1778 he had served in America, along with Ferguson, on the unsuccessful Carlisle peace commission.

[44] Compare Ferguson's passionate account of his firsthand observation of the Swiss militia in a letter to Alexander Carlyle of April 29, 1775, in John Small, "Biographical Sketch of Adam Ferguson," *Transactions of the Royal Society of Edinburgh* 23 (1864): 620.

best Times of the Roman Republic, a Head or Heads on the same shoulders equally qualified for the Council, or Senate, the Popular Assembly, the Bar, the Judgment Seat, the Camp and the Head of the Army, and indeed admirably well qualified for all of them: but I am satisfied it would be a very easy Matter to make Military as well as Political Consideration a necessary recommendation to the Council, the Cabinet or higher Departments of State, and every man who is to perceive with his own Senses the weight of every Circumstance he is to admit in the Scale.

Here, as elsewhere in his treatment of national defense, Ferguson begins with concessions to the "modern" principles that Smith had articulated. There is no returning to the perfect union of statesmen and warriors found in the heyday of the Roman Republic, he realizes. But if the Roman model can never be restored in its purest form, it is at least possible to salvage enough of that ancient ideal to prevent (as he put it in his lecture notes) the statesman from becoming a mere clerk or babbler and the soldier from becoming a mere gladiator or executioner. Statesmen must be chosen for their military as well as their political knowledge and ability. To say this was to risk violating Smith's sacred principle, the division of labor. It was also to announce that the growth of "modern" notions of economic and political progress was not an entirely good thing, and that classical ideals of civic virtue must have their place in a healthy polity not only for moral or educational reasons but also for practical military ones.

After publishing the *Wealth of Nations* Adam Smith continued to attend the Poker Club fairly regularly until its demise in 1784.[45] What could Ferguson and the other members have thought of his presence there? From his active membership in the Poker and his previously cited letter to Andreas Holt, it is known that Smith continued to support the Scots militia, which he apparently viewed as a useful supplement to a standing army primarily for the moral and educational reasons previously noted. Yet he never indicated how a militia could possibly be effective as a military institution and, as noted earlier, in later editions of the *Wealth of Nations* he never attempted to lessen the damage done by his devastating critique of militias in the section on the "expence of defence," despite all the furor it had engendered among the friends of the Scots militia cause.

Adam Smith died in 1790, seven years before a Scottish militia act became a reality, but Adam Ferguson was very much alive during that age of almost continual warfare with revolutionary France. Although it had been twelve

[45] According to Poker Club attendance records compiled by Jeremy Cater (Edinburgh University Library, Dc.5.126*), Smith attended no Poker Club meetings in 1775 but three in 1776, two in 1777, and twelve more before the club disbanded. These numbers contradict Donald Winch's statement that Smith left the Poker in 1774 (*Adam Smith's Politics*, p. 104).

years since he had last lectured to Edinburgh University moral philosophy students on the importance of maintaining a strong domestic military force for national defense, Ferguson remained intensely interested in this question. In common with his old fellow militia agitator Alexander Carlyle he judged the Scottish militia act of 1797 to be "a sort of Press Act" that conscripted unwilling young men for undetermined periods of service.[46] The problem was not merely theoretical, for Ferguson's son James was at this time subject to the provisions of the act. From his farm near Peebles in the Borders the elderly philosopher pondered the conflict between parental responsibility and public virtue: "My son, now about 20, had some pretence to exemption, his name being inrolled in some one of the artillery companies, but I thought the best I could do was to set an example to my neighbour Farmers in cheerfully giving up his name to the Ballot. And if college call him away I trust that money will procure a substitute."[47] James did put his name to the ballot, and under the influence of his patriotic father he prepared to serve his country with Stoic resignation: "James tells me there was a full attendance of all the militia men now under Ballot. But such is the effect of the Law that not one proposed to serve otherwise than by substitute; and the Poorest Shepherd Boy proposes to spend the earnings of a whole life to procure a substitute rather than enlist for an indefinite time for a Militia man. James and I are agreed if substitutes are not to be found he is to serve and is the only one who will do so quasi willingly. But in these times every man must be military whatever else he may be."[48] However much he disliked the specific provisions of the Scottish militia act or dreaded losing his son to it, Ferguson remained a militia man at heart.

Ferguson's vision of militia recruitment was thoroughly idealistic, and for this reason he was more partial to the Volunteer Corps than to the compulsory militia established by the act of 1797. When he was nearly eighty years old Ferguson elaborated on his vision in three long letters to his former student, the powerful Scottish political manager Henry Dundas, first Viscount Melville.[49] In these letters Ferguson painted a noble picture of a militia of honor and virtue. "The less that the Iron hand of necessity is felt, the Better," he noted. He envisioned a "Legion of Honour" for which members would be selected rather than solicited; service in it would be a badge of distinction for

[46] On the repressive nature of the militia act of 1797 and the riots it touched off, see Kenneth J. Logue, *Popular Disturbances in Scotland, 1780–1815* (Edinburgh, 1979), chap. 3.

[47] Ferguson to Carlyle, October 2, 1797, Edinburgh University Library, La.II.243, no. 57.

[48] Ferguson to Carlyle, December 25, 1798, ibid., no. 58.

[49] Ferguson to Dundas, January 18, January 28, and August 2, 1802, Melville Papers, William L. Clements Library, University of Michigan.

which men would compete. "Patrimonial or pecuniary qualifications" would be established, and a mechanism would be devised for having parish ministers testify that a prospective Volunteer "is without reproach, and in his condition of Life orderly independent and frugal." Ferguson's fear was that a militia established by "compulsory statute" might "leave an impression of servitude and consequently some degree of repugnance" among the recruits. "In the Volunteers," on the other hand, "there can be no repugnance; for they consist of the willing, and as such are likely to be a selection of the most worthy. The honours they bear will be alluring to numbers, & take like a fashion; infect the mass of the People & to make free with a familiar allusion like ye[a]st propagate a kind of military Ferment or Verve through the whole."

This vision of a martial "Legion of Honour" was nothing new for Ferguson: he had advocated something similar in a militia pamphlet published nearly half a century earlier.[50] In the same way, the Dundas letters echoed two related concerns that were initially raised by Ferguson in that early militia pamphlet and were subsequently developed in his university lectures and letter to Eden on national defense. The first is the critical importance of the "upper ranks" in setting the example for others to follow.[51] "As Fashions . . . for the most part descend from the High to the Low," Ferguson observed to Dundas, "it is surely not too much presumption to hope, that there are many well informed liberal & high minded in the upper Ranks who will be pleased to set an Example, of so much advantage to their Country." The sovereign himself should join the corps for ceremonial purposes, for "the gracious Regard of the King & the Example of those about him will have a Powerfull Charm." It is particularly among political rulers that Ferguson most regrets the loss of martial virtue. To counter this tendency he proposes a plan for restoring, on British soil, the Roman ideals he cherished: "If I had my wish, every member in either house of Parliament under fifty years of age, should enroll his name in some Volunteer Corps and give due attention to its forms. . . . If I durst talk of Enactment: looking forward to a future period, suppose twenty one years after the present date; might it not be enacted, That after the year 1823 no one should be qualified for a seat in either House of Parliament untill after sixteen years of age his name had stood enrolled five years in a Volunteer Corps and his attendance on its duties been regular." Ferguson's "wish" appears all the more archaic for having been expressed in the form of a piece of practical legislation. The aged philosopher was fighting a rearguard action for classical

[50] Ferguson, *Reflections*, pp. 38–48; Sher, *Church and University* (n. 9 above), pp. 220–21.

[51] Compare Ferguson, *Reflections*, pp. 34–35: "Upon recollecting what we know of the History of all Nations, it will appear, that none ever possest a permanent military Force lodged in the Nerves and Sinews of a People, where they, who carried the Arms of the Public, were not the most respectable Part of the Nation."

civic values at a time when those values were reaching the brink of extinction in Britain. This he well knew. "We are perhaps too apt to slight such [military] feats as unworthy at least of Gentlemen," he warned, "but in this we differ from the wisest nations of antiquity, who sought for vigour of mind and the Emulation of glory in the excercises and display of a Vigorous body."

The theme of military virtue among the "upper Ranks" was closely connected with another, more general topic: the danger of the division of labor where military matters are concerned.[52] "While every Individual is opening a Separate Career for himself: it is surely a supreme Object of state, that none should be lost to the Community in any of its essential Departments whether of order Resource or defence," Ferguson wrote to Dundas in 1802. "I agree with The Persians of old who are said to have taught all their Children to shoot the Bow as well as to speak Truth. In these indeed there was no matter for separate Professions, any more than, in our case, there is reason to withhold the Powers of Defence from any one who has a Country to defend." And in a discussion of education he suggested to Dundas that "Military & Practical schools" be annexed to every university so that "letters might accompany practice & the Library Student be kept in mind of his Manhood & the common cause of His King and his Country which may at some interesting time require his exertions."

IV

Late in life Ferguson also expressed his views on national defense in miscellaneous writings that have survived in manuscript form. One such manuscript, apparently an early draft of volume 2 of the *Principles of Moral and Political Science,* contains some interesting passages on this subject.[53] There Ferguson makes a case for "the partial distribution of arms and the unequal possession of the military character" as the primary cause of the

[52] Compare Ferguson, *Reflections,* p. 12: "It may be allowed that the Perfection now attained in every Art, and the Attention required to furnish what is demanded in every Branch of Business, have led away from the military Profession great Numbers of our People; and that Applications are become frequent, which seem to disqualify Men in a great Degree for the Use of Arms. But Self-defence is the Business of all: and we have already gone too far, in the Opinion that Trade and Manufacture are the only Requisites in our Country. In Pursuit of such an Idea, we labour to acquire Wealth; but neglect the Means of defending it. We would turn this Nation into a Company of Manufacturers, where each is confined to a particular Branch, and sunk into the Habits and Peculiarities of his Trade. In this we consult the Success of Manufacture; but slight the Honours of the human Nature."

[53] Edinburgh University Library, Dc.1.86. This manuscript consists of neatly written formal prose, in a form suggesting preparation for the press, and quite unlike the two volumes of lecture notes discussed in Sec. II above. The structure of the work closely parallels that of the *Principles.*

subjugation of the many by the few in societies throughout the world. He admits that "the unequal distribution of wealth" is another, partial explanation for this phenomenon, but the military dimension is given more weight. "Hence it is that so many governments are established in which the safety of the people is so little consulted, and in which the many are treated as the property of one or a few." The same imbalance is considered the chief cause of the ability of "a few soldiers of fortune" to control "entire pacific provinces" as well as of the enslavement of even the freest nations "when they themselves drop the use of arms and trust their protection to any other hands than their own." The discussion breaks off in the middle of a sentence that begins: "The people in general, who owe their freedom to the use of arms which they once possessed, suffer" (fols. 977–81). Though we do not know exactly where Ferguson was headed in this unfinished, undated manuscript, it is clear that he was developing in a slightly different form the familiar theme of broad-based military participation.

Other familiar martial themes were voiced in Ferguson's unpublished essays, especially "Of Statesmen & Warriours" and "Of the Separation of Departments Profesions and Tasks resulting from The Progress of Arts in Society."[54] In both essays Ferguson tried to show the limitations of the division of labor in the military sphere. "Of Statesmen & Warriours" stressed the importance of "a certain Vigour of mind" (pp. 36, 42) among soldiers from ancient Sparta and Rome through Napoleon's victories in Europe. "The Valour of Freemen armed in defence of their Country is akin to that of the Parent in defence of her Young the Effect of an Ardent Affection Approaching to Enthousiasm which Stifles the sense of Difficulty or Danger," Ferguson argued (p. 39). This essay did not deal specifically with the militia question, for its focus was on the need for new, Napoleonic criteria for advancement of army officers; but the spirit of the essay was characteristically Fergusonian in its constant emphasis on "vigour" and "ardour" as fundamental traits of a successful fighting force.

When he turned to the issue of statesmen, Ferguson emphasized once again the need to avoid excessive separation of military knowledge and statesmanship. The statesman who does not know warfare "is no more than a Clerk in Office and a Bable[r] in council," he writes, in a variation on one of his

[54] No. 4 and no. 15, respectively, in the manuscript collection of thirty-two essays in Edinburgh University Library, Dc.1.42. These essays cannot be dated with certainty, but some of the paper on which they were written bears an 1806 watermark. References to essay no. 4 are drawn from *Adam Ferguson's Unpublished Essays*, ed. W. M. Philip, 3 vols. (n.p., 1986), 3:34–52, though this edition is far from satisfactory. References to essay no. 15 are from the excellent edition edited by Yasuo Amoh in "Adam Ferguson and the Division of Labour: An Unpublished Essay by Adam Ferguson," *Kochi University Review of Social Science* (Kochi, Japan), no. 29 (1987), pp. 71–85.

favorite themes, just as a Roman warrior without statesmanship was considered "a mere prize fighter & Bully whose only form of proceeding is mere Violence or Force" (pp. 47–48). Yet this separation of warriors and statesmen is exactly what he finds in the nations of "Modern Europe." Perhaps the most interesting passage in the essay traces this problem to scientific specialization in the modern world: "We sometimes boast the superiority of modern to antient times in science[.] But all we are entitled to say is that we have applied to different Branches of Study. The Greeks & Romans appl[i]ed to that Branch which concerned them most Men Manners the Forms of State and the Conduct of Men whether in Peace or in War. We have ransacked Nature The Earth & the Heavens for Geographical Physical and Astronomical Science[.] Man himself is forgotten or considered only as a party in Trade and a Dealer in Manufactures & Money" (p. 48). The last line in this passage struck specifically at the science of political economy, whose greatest exponent was Adam Smith. Ferguson was not bemoaning a perceived shift toward materialistic, acquisitive values among people in modern, polished nations; he was criticizing the tendency of political economists to study, and in a sense foster, only that side of human nature. If in Ferguson's eyes the great crime of modern science is to forsake the study of humanity for the study of the physical world, the crime of political economy is to study humanity from a perspective so narrow that man's capacity for moral behavior and for development of a unified civic personality is obscured.

The essay "Of the Separation of Departments Profesions and Tasks" contains Ferguson's fullest critique of the division of labor. The first half treats general social and economic limitations of this principle, sometimes with apparent reference to the *Wealth of Nations*.[55] The second half of the essay is devoted specifically to the limitations of the division of labor in regard to "the Bussiness of State and of War" (p. 80). As one would expect, Ferguson reformulates his old arguments about the need for emulating, as far as possible, the Roman model of a strict alliance between these two departments. This leads him to consider the need for including "Military Tactics and Manual Exercise . . . amidst the Rudiments of Education in early Life" (p. 83), one subject on which Ferguson and Smith agreed:

> No age can with advantage Legislate unalterably for the Ages that follow.
> On this account a late writer of Eminence on the Wealth and other concerns of Nations places Education on the same foot with Trade and other concerns most safely

[55] Early in the essay, e.g., Ferguson noted that "we are told" (alluding, no doubt, to the famous first chapter of the *Wealth of Nations*, though perhaps also to the *Encyclopédie* of 1755) that the efficiency of pinmaking can be greatly improved by means of the division of labor, "yet there are limits to this Separation of Labour" (p. 75). His point was to show that certain tasks, such as the pointing of a pin, could not be profitably subdivided.

entrusted to the Per[son] concerned & reprobates fixed Institutions or Intervention of Government. From this general Rule however he excepts every Case in which Defence or publick safety is at stake and of Course should except Education so far as the publick safety is concerned. [P. 84]

Having gone this far with Smith, Ferguson concluded the essay with a flourish that was his alone:

He who cannot defend himself is not a Man & he who cannot take part in the defence of his Country is not a Citizen nor worthy of the Protection which the Laws of Country bestow. Other cares may be delegated & become matter of separate Profession to a part of the People: but to set Valour apart as the Characteristic of a few were to [s]hare [?] Virtue & Happiness itself as a matter of Profession & study peculiar to a devision of the Community. To furnish shoes or erect Palaces may be the object of separate Professions but to be [a] man is the equal concern of all and the want of Courage degrades him no less than the want of Understanding or Truth.

Men are wise to avail themselves of every advantage which the subdivision of arts and the separation of Employments can give: but where this Expedient is noxious to the Genius & Character of Man it is Wisdom to check or restrain it.

Let the Statesman be asha[med] to own he is no Warriour and the warriour to own he is no statesman. Under these confessions the one is a mere Clerk in office The other a mere prize fighter & a Bully. [P. 85]

In this passage, as in others cited in these pages, Ferguson carried on his debate with Adam Smith on the question of national defense. From the time the *Wealth of Nations* made its appearance Ferguson had candidly pledged to "be against" his friend in this matter. I have tried to show that although Ferguson is not known to have published anything against Smith on the militia question, his moral philosophy lectures, letters to influential politicians such as Eden and Dundas, and miscellaneous unpublished writings attempted to refute or redefine some of Smith's ideas for more than a quarter of a century after 1776. He could not accept the idea that the division of labor, important as it was in the economic sphere, was necessarily a good thing where military and political matters were concerned; or the idea that a militia as such could not be effective against a standing army; or the idea that a martial spirit was not essential for the actual defense of a modern, commercial society; or the idea that the "upper ranks" in such a society could no longer seek to emulate the Roman republican ideal of expertise and leadership in both the political and military arenas; or the idea that man might be fruitfully studied "only as a Party in Trade and a Dealer in Manufactures & Money."

My contention that Ferguson's thinking about national defense developed in opposition to Smith's requires qualification. Though circumstantial evidence strongly suggests that Ferguson's lectures on this subject were written or revised in response to the *Wealth of Nations* and the Scots militia crisis of March 1776, we cannot, at present, be certain of this. Ferguson's ideas reveal a basic continuity from the time of his earliest known militia pamphlet, published twenty years before the *Wealth of Nations*, to the end of his life. There were others besides Smith touting the advantages of the division of labor, economic development, and standing armies in the eighteenth century, and Smith himself stressed the importance of military training and a martial spirit for the character of a people. Like Ferguson, Smith was a moral philosopher who treated political economy as but one part in a comprehensive system that included ethics, jurisprudence, and much else. He even claimed to be a supporter of the militia cause in Scotland.

Nevertheless, when the complete records of the two Adams are compared on this issue, it becomes clear that they disagreed fundamentally in their priorities and emphases, and that their writings may be seen as constituting a debate on national defense. As Smith stressed the usefulness of the modern science of political economy, the efficiency of the division of labor, and the advantages of a standing army over a militia, Ferguson distinguished himself as the Scottish Enlightenment's leading spokesman for martial virtue, the institution of a militia, the cultivation of a unified civic personality, and other values associated with the concept of civic humanism in its eighteenth-century manifestation. With an occasional wistful glance backward, Smith took his stand on the side of the moderns, whereas Ferguson, for all his respect for the new prosperity of the eighteenth century, yearned for the classical ideal of the independent citizen who demonstrates his patriotism and civic virtue by bearing arms.

[17]

Adam Smith and the Liberal Tradition

Donald Winch

I. INTRODUCTION

Sussex to Sydney may seem a long way to come in order to report on a case of mistaken identity, but that, in part at least, is what the editor of this volume must have anticipated when he invited me to write this paper. In a book published nearly a decade ago, I suggested that the writings of Adam Smith — one of which especially, the *Wealth of Nations*, has always occupied a prominent place in almost everybody's idea of the liberal canon — were not best understood within those orthodox liberal-capitalist perspectives that have dominated both liberal and Marxist interpretations of the significance of his work since the 19th century (see Winch, 1978). Surrounded by some leading interpreters and exponents of liberalism in one or other of its potent modern forms, this volume might seem as good an opportunity as any to renounce these earlier heresies. Yet while I readily confess to some exaggeration through ignorance and omission, as well as to a failure to grasp the full implications of what I was contending, I am unwilling to go much further. It also occurred to me that giving reasons for not being able to retract, despite recognising the cogency of some of the criticisms of my case, could provide the best, certainly the most honest, basis for my contribution to this book.

One further introductory remark seems in order. Despite the self-referential form of much of what I have to say, I hope that this approach will give access to some of the larger issues connected with liberalism as a political philosophy or ideology. In saying this I am simply presuming that an understanding of whether an actual historical figure called Adam Smith was successful in combining the economic, moral and political dimensions of his position, and if so, how this was achieved, has considerable significance to the doctrines we associate with liberalism, not least because so many of its exponents and critics have invoked Smith's name in support of their diagnoses of its dilemmas, possibilities and limits. With a last apology for taking a scoundrel's refuge in autobiography, therefore, I begin with some remarks on my essay on *Adam Smith's Politics* and its critics.

II. *ADAM SMITH'S POLITICS* IN CONTEXT

Apart from wishing to illustrate the virtues of a particular mode of historical interpretation, I was advancing a number of substantive claims that can be summarised as follows. The first set of claims was negative: it consisted in showing how the imposition of anachronistic 19th- and 20th-century categories onto the work of an 18th-century author — for whom, after all, the term 'liberal' could only have broad adjectival significance — had resulted in systematic distortion and loss of meaning. Second, and still in a sceptical or negative vein, I was arguing against what for brevity if not beauty I shall describe as the predominantly apolitical, economistic, even deterministic viewpoints on Smith, making use of the evidence, some of it new, provided by the *Lectures on Jurisprudence* to suggest what the 'theory and history of law and government' that he projected but failed to finish might have looked like. This also entailed an attempt to place the *Wealth of Nations* within the wider context of Smith's 'science of a statesman or legislator' — a context that was undoubtedly 'political' in one or two of the significant senses of the term, where this includes questions of a moral, constitutional, and juristic nature. Third, in dealing with Smith's analysis of a number of contemporary political issues — with what might be termed the 'art' corresponding to his 'science' of politics — I was able to make use of Duncan Forbes's fruitful insights into what he calls the 'sceptical' or 'scientific' Whiggism of Hume and Smith, as well as the large body of revisionist literature centring on the work of J.G.A. Pocock and others, which has revealed the strength of 'classical republican' or 'civic humanist' ideas within Anglo-American political culture during the 18th century (see Forbes, 1975; Pocock, 1975). Apart from showing that Smith adopted and recommended a characteristic style or stance to the philosopher faced with contemporary political problems, a stance that could be variously described as sceptical, realistic, moderate, contemplative, cynical, or conservative, I wished to maintain that his politics recognised the existence of a dimension to political life and action that, again in shorthand terms, I will call 'republican' or 'civic' — a dimension that could neither be reduced to, nor reproduced by, models of political and economic behaviour based solely on assumptions about the rational pursuit of self-interest by individuals.

Winch: Adam Smith and the Liberal Tradition

As I shall presently maintain, however, far from wishing to advance a 'civic humanist' alternative to the usual 'liberal' interpretations of Smith's politics, I went to some trouble to show just why and where such an interpretation was likely to fail when applied to Smith's more complex political vision. Though far from indifferent to how economic circumstances affected the capacity of men to perform their duties and protect their rights as citizens — as shown in particular by his diagnosis and remedies for the moral, political and military drawbacks associated with the extension of the division of labour in commercial society — when compared with the stress placed on citizenly virtue and corruption by both ancient and modern exponents of classical republican values, Smith's politics is far more readily seen as a politics of constitutional and other machinery designed to curb those activities by individuals and groups that ran counter to the public interest. While many would characterise this as a 'liberal' position, it should be noticed that the affinities are with Hume, Montesquieu and, say, Madison, rather than with Locke — whether Locke is seen, unhelpfully, as the evil genius of 'possessive' or 'bourgeois' individualism, or as the founder of a liberal defence of limited government constructed along contractarian lines. In so far as Locke enters the picture at all, it is for a number of qualities he has in common with such other 17th-century natural law theorists as Grotius and Pufendorf.

The forward linkages between Smith and the Benthamites in any notion of an unbroken tradition of liberal thinking have often been recognised as problematic, perhaps even libellous — notably by Hayek and his followers (the original statement of this view, much developed in later writings, can be found in Hayek, 1948). But if Hume and Smith could not be readily located on a spectrum that stretched from Hobbes and Locke at one end to Bentham and John Stuart Mill at the other, then perhaps the whole idea of a liberal tradition, true or false, owed more to the teleological presumptions of Whig historiography than to anything that could be demonstrated by means of genuine historical continuities or imputed philosophical similarities. Hence the agnostic tone of one of my conclusions, namely that Smith's politics were pre-industrial, pre-capitalist and pre-democratic.

III. CRITICS AND OTHERS

In retrospect, I have reason to be grateful for the tolerance and generosity of my reviewers, particularly those who were political theorists and historians of political thought. Several members of the guild in which I had served my apprenticeship, that of the economists and historians of economic thought, were either bemused or far more resistant (the most dismissive review was by Sowell, 1979; a longer and more appreciative one by Hollander, 1979, made use of what I took to be one of my main conclusions to criticise the book — a sure sign that I had failed to get my message across). They seemed less willing to come to terms with an argument that had little relevance to the way they read the *Wealth of Nations* (or rather perhaps, their favourite parts of this protean work), chiefly for premonitions of modern, mostly economic-theoretical, concerns. Indeed, faced with the kind of evidence necessary to establish the nature of Smith's science of the legislator, that is, with the material on 18th-century political conventions and language, I suspect that many of those who are strongly wedded to the traditional view of Smith's writings feel a good deal of impatience. After all, while the familiar view has a clear line of development reaching to the present, one that has been the subject of a good deal of loving attention over the past 200 years or so, this does not appear to be the case with Smith's science of the legislator. Is there not a risk of losing sight of Smith's originality in all this attention to the 18th-century contextual wallpaper? How much light could the parochial language of 18th-century political discourse really shed on Smith's trans-historical qualities? Surely his politics, in any significant sense, is fully described by his criticism of the mercantile system and state; by his espousal of the system of natural liberty; by the importance he attached, both as historian and moral philosopher, to the rule of law; and by his apparent sympathy for constitutional forms of government?

Before dealing with such questions let me mention one major criticism of my book that I had no difficulty in accepting. Some critics who were willing to be convinced that Smith's 'science of the legislator' went beyond and could not be reduced to the standard issues summarised in the literature on laissez-faire and state intervention in economic life felt that I had not dealt adequately with the ethical underpinnings and philosophical foundations of Smith's natural jurisprudence and his conception of what constituted legislative wisdom or prudence (see Forbes, 1978; Kettler, 1979). This was plainly true, and it was with considerable admiration and some relief that I later read Knud Haakonssen's (1981) study of *The Science of a Legislator; the Natural Jurisprudence of David Hume and Adam Smith.* This deals with both the moral and the natural jurisprudential foundations of Smith's approach to knowledge in this sphere, and gives a more satisfying account of just how theory and history are brought together in Smith's treatment of law and government to comprise a consistent body of critical and historical jurisprudence with links encompassing most of Smith's main works, including the new *Lectures on Jurisprudence.* It also provides a less tendentious account of the differences between Smithian and Benthamite jurisprudence than can be found elsewhere.

While I could not have matched Knud Haakonssen over this territory, I felt better equipped, in principle at least, to deal with another

Winch: Adam Smith and the Liberal Tradition

partially justifiable criticism, namely that in the attempt to recover a lost or missing political dimension, I had bypassed Smith's economics and consequently failed to establish the relationship between the two spheres (Dunn, 1978 made this point, as did Hamowy, 1979). Thus while there are plenty of references to the system of natural liberty in the book, I was more interested in the use of the invisible hand metaphor as it appears in the *Theory of Moral Sentiments*, and was not keen to rehearse the familiar issues surrounding laissez-faire and all that, upon which I had little to say that differed from the work of, say, Jacob Viner (1958), Nathan Rosenberg (1960), and Andrew Skinner (1979). As I have subsequently discovered, however, the task of expressing the relationship between Smith's politics and his economics is not as easy as I anticipated, and it could provide the crucial point of access to the problems of modern liberalism mentioned earlier.

IV. CIVIC HUMANISM AND LIBERALISM

It is a common criticism of those who subscribe to the historiographic position adopted in my book, a position that is strongly wedded to authorial intention and the study of texts within contemporary linguistic and historical contexts, that it replaces forward-looking studies of historical figures with less recognisable backward or sideways-looking portraits, thereby severing the connections that must exist between any influential author and his progeny (this point was made in an otherwise very generous review by Cropsey, 1979, and in a more elaborate way by Cumming, 1981). My book was, indeed, rather puritanically historicist, and I accept that those who ply the historical trade in this way have a kind of obligation to pursue what the Germans call *Wirkungsgeschichte* — the study of how seminal works make their way in the world and are transformed in the process. Again in common with Knud Haakonssen, this is something I have attempted to do in later work (see Haakonssen, 1984a, 1984b, 1985; Winch, 1983a; and essays 1-3 in Collini et al., 1983). But there is, of course, a great deal of difference between a genuine *Wirkungsgeschichte* and the manufactured genealogies that appear in so many accounts of the liberal tradition, where most of the work is being performed by definitions.

For example, I doubt if there is much more to be said, by way of historical argument at least, to those for whom liberalism as an ideology is intimately bound up with the concept and career of 'possessive individualism' as originally defined by the late C. B. Macpherson. Along with many others, I have taken issue with this position, and have yet to see any signs of a response that goes beyond repetition of the original claims (for his review of my book, see Macpherson, 1979; see also Winch, 1985a, 1985b). However, another interpretation of liberalism, one that is primarily associated with the work of Sheldon Wolin and sees it as a form of anxiety and pessimism about the human fate, poses less well-rehearsed issues which I should like to examine by considering the criticisms of my book put forward by Edward J. Harpham. He clearly feels that I have upset or failed to grasp the centrality of Smith's liberalism, which he treats as one of the natural categories of political discourse; and that I have consequently wrested 'Smith's political thought out of the larger vision of commercial society that is found in his moral, political and economic writings' (Harpham, 1984:764).

If true, these would be destructive criticisms; but since they largely derive from a blatant misreading of my position, I am forced to conclude that something else must be at stake. Harpham's mistaken basic premise — that I was advancing a civic humanist alternative to the liberal reading of Adam Smith's politics — has clearly led him to believe that if he can show how a civic humanist reading fails to fit much that was characteristic of Smith's position, he has thereby established that Smith can continue to stand as a monument to everything that constitutes liberal political discourse. As already mentioned, however, far from putting forward such a reading, I thought I had shown how Smith, in common with his friend David Hume, was largely engaged in an enterprise that was in many respects **antipathetic** to that tradition. There is nothing in Harpham's rehearsal of the now familiar evidence concerning Smith's views on commerce, liberty, economic growth, the mercantile system, and what has become known as the four-stages theory, that conflicts with what I and many others have written. A goodly part of my concluding chapter, for example, was devoted to examining the ways in which Smith and Hume share a political perspective that differs from such contemporaries as Adam Ferguson, who can more properly be described as an exponent of 'Machiavellian moralism', the 'Country' stance, 'republican principles', and other synonyms for features that have been assembled under the term 'civic humanism' or 'civic moralism' (for a rehearsal of further doubts about the capacity of civic moralist interpretations to deal with the more important features of Smith's thinking, see Winch, 1983b).

What then seems to have gone wrong? Part of the problem lies in Harpham's rigid dichotomy between civic humanism and liberalism. Both of these are terms of interpretative art that have been applied retrospectively, and any study purporting to have a historical basis might wish to signify this fact by placing quotation marks around them at the outset. For what might appear to be a minor question of historiographic taste conceals, I suspect, a more important difference of opinion that can be brought to the surface by asking a simple question: why should 'civic humanism' and 'liberalism' be considered not only as mutually exclusive, but as the only viable alternatives, such that if Smith can be

Winch: Adam Smith and the Liberal Tradition

shown to occupy one position he cannot possibly be having any truck with the other?

My own answer would begin by rejecting the simple binary choice on offer. Taking for granted (as most students of 18th-century political thought, including Harpham, manifestly do) the continuing reality of a style of political thinking that is usefully captured by some such term as civic humanism, why should we expect everything Smith or Hume wrote to be a flat contradiction of this mode of thought? They are frequently to be found opposing its conclusions and methods of reasoning; but it is part of the evidence for the continuing strength of these ideas that they should have found it both necessary and useful to engage in debate with them. Nor should we be surprised if in the course of debate they adopted the categories and sometimes endorsed republican values, even when doubting or ultimately rejecting their widespread applicability to modern monarchies and commercial societies. We might also become aware, as Harpham does not appear to be, of interesting differences between Hume and Smith on these matters. For example, we might note their differences over public debt or the militia question, where Hume occupied a position closer to that of 'Country' writers.

Harpham attaches great significance to the four-stages theory as a delineating, if not originating, feature of the modern liberal position. He maintains that by subscribing to this theory Ferguson and Millar 'were introducing tensions into their own thought that could not be easily reconciled with their republican values' (Harpham, 1984:769). Since he gives no reasons for this judgment it can only be taken as further evidence that he regards the liberal and civic categories as mutually exclusive. This could explain why he does not consider it necessary to address himself to the more intriguing question of why the four-stages theory does not feature in Hume's writings — a matter of some substance if he wishes to keep his 'liberals' and 'republicans' in sealed compartments. Presumably Millar was introducing another 'tension' into his thought by subscribing to the Hume-Smith idea of deference to authority as an explanation for political obligation. Holding republican values, he should have been more interested, in a way that Smith was somehow obliged not to be, in 'the economic preconditions to effective citizenship'.

I also wonder how many students of Smith's writings will join Harpham in recognising the 'tone of uncertainty and anguish' that underlies Smith's discussion of sympathy and deference in civil society, comparing it with the 'moderately upbeat and self-confident tone found in civic humanism' (Harpham, 1984:770). Ferguson has surely not been alone in reversing this charge by maintaining that Smith took far too cool and contemplative a view of contemporary political anxieties (Kettler, 1977). If Smith was chiefly concerned, as Harpham claims, 'to maintain those conditions most highly conducive to the continuance of existing authority relations', how can we explain, for example, his attack on primogeniture and entail, those twin supports of the landed aristocracy in Britain? Why must we subscribe dogmatically to the view that certain positions were 'unavailable' to him? I would agree, as I put it in the book in question, that 'Smith does not share the passionate concern for the decline of citizenship that can be found, for example, in Ferguson' (Winch, 1978:175), but that does not mean we have to cast aside the civic features of Smith's diagnosis of the effects on the mass of society of the division of labour, and overlook entirely the civic provenance of his educational and other remedies for the problem — a subject to which I shall return later.

V. THE LEGISLATOR, THE STATE AND POLITICS

A politics of machinery designed to curb and harness the forces of self-interest may have less need for virtuous men, and may adopt a decidedly sceptical view, as Smith often does, towards those who present themselves to the world as possessing special virtue. But this does not imply that public-spiritedness, in common with beneficence in private relationships, does not exist, cannot be encouraged, and has to be shunned or denied when it is present. At no point does Harpham consider the evidence adduced by Haakonssen and myself concerning Smith's conception of the 'legislator' — the man whose deliberations, when compared with 'that insidious and crafty animal', the politician, were 'governed by general principles which are always the same' (Smith, 1976a:468; see also Winch, 1978:12-13, 159-60, 170-73; Winch, 1983a; and Haakonssen, 1981:97, 135, 164, 180, 188). What this evidence shows is that Smith does not belong to the deterministic end of the spectrum at which materialistic forces are held to dominate historical outcomes and 'natural' economic processes leave the legislator with little to do beyond issuing pious warnings about 'artificial' impediments. Nor does he belong with those other 18th-century advocates of the science of the legislator who, in the words of J. H. Burns, saw the legislator as 'a continuously active figure, modifying, regulating, and sustaining the dynamic structure of political life' (Burns, 1967:6). This vision of the legislator as moulder or *machiniste* fits Bentham and his French and Italian predecessors far closer than it does Smith. Like Montesquieu and Hume, Smith conforms more with what Burns describes as an alternative Enlightenment style of 'circumstantial empiricism — a cautious and in the end an essentially conservative approach to social institutions' (1967:12). This certainly fits the famous passages in the *Theory of Moral Sentiments* (1976b) in which Smith contrasts the virtues of the man of 'public spirit' with the 'man of system', and where he speaks of the wise legislator accommodating 'his public arrangements to the confirmed habits and prejudices of the people', emulating Solon in establishing, if not the best system of laws, then 'the best that the people can bear' (1976b:VI.ii.2.16-17 [233-8]).

Once these matters are brought into play, it becomes possible to ask such questions as: to whom was Smith's 'science of the legislator' addressed? Does the science not presuppose the existence of persons or groups who might, however occasionally, base their conduct on general principles that are always the same, and otherwise embody qualities of public-spiritedness? Legislators might be hard to find in a world dominated by politicians, but there had to be possibilities for encouraging the legislator's point of view, if only by animating 'the public passions of men', and leading them 'to seek out the means of promoting the happiness of the society' (1976b:iv.i.11. [186-7]). Smith tried his hand as legislative expert operating behind the scenes, but he probably expected to have his greatest influence through the slow and irregular process of altering the state of that powerful if nebulous entity called 'opinion', upon which, as Hume argued, all government depended.

To this I would now add something that is clearer than it was to me ten years ago, namely that by serving as an ideal location to which contributions to knowledge or science could be addressed, the concept of the legislator provided a flexible way of speaking about another major abstraction, the state. In Smith's formulation it was more flexible than the later Hegelian and post-Hegelian alternative because it allowed for non-coercive forms of mutual interaction between state and civil society. It did not require rigid assumptions of autonomy, primacy, or parasitism — complete freedom of action by an impartial agency possessing exclusive powers of coercion, a state-centred view of the world on the one hand, or a derivative and conspiratorial view of the state as the agent of the dominant economic forces in society on the other. Smith depicts state and civil society as being almost interchangeable; and his definition of the 'constitution' of a state is sociological rather than legal, more corporatist than individualist.

> Upon the manner in which any state is divided into the different orders and societies which compose it, and upon the particular distribution which has been made of their respective powers, privileges, and immunities, depends, what is called, the constitution of that particular state. Upon the ability of each particular order of society to maintain its own powers, privileges, and immunities, against the encroachment of every other, depends the stability of that particular constitution ... That particular constitution is necessarily more or less altered, whenever any of its subordinate parts is either raised above or depressed below whatever had been its former rank and condition. (1976b:VI.ii.2.8-9 [230-31])

Traditions of Liberalism

This passage suggests that reciprocal interaction between government and society which should be expected of someone whose lectures on jurisprudence were designed to show how law and government not only 'grew up with society' but represented 'the highest effort of wisdom and prudence'. Smith's rejection of rationalistic accounts of political obligation and the origins of government enabled him to forge links between political institutions and such broader social and psychological phenomena as deference within a society of ranks and the 'powers, priveleges, and immunities' of the 'different orders and societies' that comprise any state. It also made regard for questions connected with the climate of 'opinion', normal or pathological, and whether expressed through representative institutions or not, an important aspect of the life of legislators (see, however, Robertson, 1983, for an interpretation that places greater stress on representation). Such an approach licensed inquiry into a range of institutions capable of mediating between state and civil society, operating in the large space separating the private and public spheres — the realm in which, as Nathan Rosenberg was one of the first to make plain, Smith proved so fertile in advancing institutional expedients.

None of this plays any part in Harpham's defence of Smith's exclusively liberal credentials, and it is equally absent in the Wolinian interpretation of liberalism that Harpham wishes to reinstate. Public-spiritedness, being a quality that is valued only by civic humanists, cannot be part of Smith's understanding. In its place there is something called 'liberal public-mindedness', which Harpham first describes as 'the correct psychological disposition in the minds of policy-makers', later defining it as follows: 'It is a liberal public-mindedness that accepts and, at times, champions, the self-interest that lies at the heart of modern commercial society. It is a liberal public-mindedness that is integrally related to liberal economic theory' (Harpham, 1984:772).

The triple invocation here of the unexplained term 'liberal' amounts to no more than an assertion of what needs to be proved, namely that this term covers everything of importance that is going on in Smith's politics. But the defensive thrust of the argument is clear, and the message is a comforting one to all those who wish to retain the view that Smith's politics and science of the legislator do not encompass his political economy as a special case, but are themselves encompassed by it. In simpler terms, it confirms the idea that whatever political message there is in Smith can be found **within** his economics and is still best described as liberalism, with or without an initial capital. Thus while I believe that Harpham misrepresents my case and proves his own by failing to confront the full range of evidence that is relevant, his position has the virtue of bringing certain issues into sharper focus.

Winch: Adam Smith and the Liberal Tradition

The Wolinian interpretation requires us to believe that Smith's significance to the history of political thought lies in his decisive deflection of things political towards things economic by giving primacy to unintended consequences and the self-regulating processes of civil society (Wolin, 1960:ch. 9; for a more recent and in some respects less qualified statement of this position in relation to Smith, see Wolin, 1981). According to this interpretation, Smith adumbrated a profoundly 'antipolitical' or 'depoliticised' position within which political notions of the common good were replaced by economic goals that could be achieved via mechanisms that made the minimum call either on altruism or on our capacity to construct a political order. At best, this style of thought can be credited with an instrumentalist view of knowledge that excludes *paideia*. It is a mechanistic form of constitutional expertise based on a reductive view of human behaviour — a negative philosophy of checks and balances that is antagonistic to higher and more positive notions of the ends of political life.

I am more concerned with the characterising as opposed to the evaluative aspects of this position, and my first attempt to bring the difference of opinion to a point would run as follows. For someone writing when Smith did, it is possible to attach meaning to a term such as 'economic liberal', but additional evidence is needed to convince me that being an 18th-century **economic** liberal necessarily entails being a **political** liberal in the sense that I take to be implied by the 19th-century term, liberalism. In other words, I lack Harpham's confidence in asserting that Smith's economic theory is 'integrally related to his political thought' in such a way that only liberalism can capture the nature of that relationship. This accounts, of course, for his feeling that I have divorced Smith's economic and political thinking; and I readily confess that any simple one-to-one relationship between Smith's economic and political theory, where the latter includes his jurisprudence, his constitutionalist ideas, as well as his moral philosophy, eludes me. For my part, I am puzzled by the complete absence in Harpham's discussion of the one historical category that, more than any other, helps to describe Smith's philosophical position, namely that associated with a modernised form of natural jurisprudence. And if we have to apply more obviously political labels, I cannot see how or why we should do without a term that served a valuable descriptive/evaluative purpose for well over a century, namely Whig. There is surely a strong case for describing Smith's politics as a variety of the Whig genus — 'Court', Rockinghamite, or 'sceptical'. Indeed, I debated whether a better title for this offering would be: 'Why Smith is a Whig but not necessarily a Liberal'.

Traditions of Liberalism

VI. SMITH AND PUBLIC CHOICE

To dispel any notion that I am engaged in purely semantic games, I should like to turn to some areas in which the historical Smith seems to diverge from what some of his modern admirers would like to believe is the case, where my object will be to implant the idea that we do not necessarily gain by translating Smith into the most readily available, or favoured, 20th-century vocabulary.

The 'constitutionalist' character of Smith's politics has been recognised in recent years by those who are keen to stress the fundamental affinities between his work and that of modern public choice theory. From my point of view, there seems to be more room initially for closer debate with this position than with that of, say, George Stigler and some other Chicago theorists who would foster onto Smith a fairly crude self-interest model of legal or political behaviour by a deductive process that takes no account whatsoever of the evidence provided by the *Theory of Moral Sentiments* and the *Lectures on Jurisprudence* (for my criticisms of Stigler see Winch, 1978:165-8, 171). Smith is accorded a prominent place in the genealogy of public choice theory advanced by James Buchanan, who maintains that this theory is little more than 'a rediscovery and elaboration of a part of the conventional wisdom of the eighteenth and nineteenth centuries, and notably the conventional wisdom that informed classical political economy. Adam Smith, David Hume, and the American Founding Fathers would have considered the central principles of public choice theory to be so elementary as scarcely to warrant attention' (Buchanan, 1978:18). Buchanan also adds a Hobbesian and Lockean 'contractualist' dimension to this genealogy that will have to be considered in a moment, but I should first like to mention the more detailed historical work undertaken from the same perspective by Edwin G. West (1976) under the heading of what he calls Smith's 'economics of politics' — work with which I find it possible to agree on a number of important points (an 'evaluative survey' of recent work on Smith appears in Thweatt, 1988, together with a commentary by myself — parts of which feature in the next few paragraphs).

For example, West and I agree on the 'constitutionalist' emphasis of Smith's politics, though in addition to the concern with constitutional balance and stability I would draw attention to a matching interest in possible fragility or 'seeds of decay' — an interest in the dangers attending the **loss** of constitutional stability and legitimacy that is prominent in Smith's reactions to the American and French Revolutions and could account for a feature of Smith's politics that is disturbing to 20th-century civil libertarians, namely his interest in **strong** government. West and I also agree that to Smith one of the main threats to stability lay in the undue influence exerted by extra-parliamentary interest groups in their efforts to secure exclusive privileges. Such privileges could not be justified in terms of a concept of public interest that combines consideration of expediency and justice, but does not imply anything so hard-edged and single-minded as, say, the Benthamite maximand. We also agree on the 'accommodative' (and hence conservative) features of Smith's view of the legislator's duties, and on the far smaller part played by notions of representative democracy in Smith's work when compared with that of his more *dirigiste* Benthamite successors. Where West and I differ is on whether the categories of public choice theory adequately capture and characterise Smith's overall position. I remain unconvinced that his science of the legislator can usefully be rendered into the language of the Friedmanite 'second invisible hand', 'minimum vote requirements', 'rent-seeking activities', 'contractarianism', and 'the search for Pareto optimal moves' — at least not without significant loss in the process.

Although Buchanan seems prepared to concede (to Hayek?) that the legal or constitutional background against which the pursuit of self-interest does or should take place may be 'morally derived', 'externally imposed', or 'evolved as custom', he appears to have a decided preference for the normative or constructivist attractions of the 'economic' or 'contractarian' approach (Buchanan, 1986:32). The assumptions behind this preference are the well-known ones, namely that the term 'economic' implies that the starting point and building blocks of any model of politics must be individuals (rather than corporate entities) whose prime characteristic is that they possess 'separate and potentially differing interests and values', but need to 'interact for the purposes of securing individually valued benefits of cooperative effort'. According to Buchanan, once these presuppositions are accepted 'the ultimate model of politics is contractarian. *There is simply no feasible alternative*' (1986:240). As he also explains, 'the constitutionalist-contractarian interprets the political process as a *generalization of the market*' (1986:65; original emphasis).

We appear to have returned then via a roundabout route to the conclusion that Smith's credentials can best be established by treating his politics simply as the other side of the coin on which his economics of free markets is embossed. Yet what was said earlier about the 'sociological' and corporatist features of Smith's view of state/civil society relations, especially when taken in conjunction with his flat rejection of contractarian accounts of political obligation and the origins of government in favour of a more naturalistic approach, makes his incorporation within the preferred genealogy of public choice theorists highly problematic.[1] The difficult balance Smith's legislator was

1 Buchanan recognises Smith's anti-contractarian position on the origin of government, and his failure to employ 'conceptualised contract as a

supposed to aim for and embody under the novel conditions created by commercial society is not, in my opinion, translatable into a calculus centring on the optimum size of the public sector judged from a 20th-century economists' viewpoint.

Another indicative source of disagreement with West can be found in what he was one of the first to discuss as 'alienation' — the problem raised by Smith's discussion of the drawbacks associated with the division of labour (West, 1969). In common with Harpham on this, West is unwilling to recognise the civic or Aristotelian implications of Smith's diagnosis and remedy for the problem. This can be detected in his dismissive remarks on Smith's educational remedies ('the tamest of conclusions'). A different verdict would surely be required if West was prepared to accept that one of the duties of Smith's legislator was the preservation of the 'character' of his people, and once it is recognised that Smith spoke of enforcing 'imperfect rights' (mutual obligations), while at the same time recognising the dangers of action under this rubric (1976b:II.ii.1.8 [81]). Smith's legislator is expected to know and to do less than his Benthamite (or Paretian) equivalent in one sense, yet, paradoxically, to know and to do more in another. Education is only part of the remedy for 'corruption' or loss of 'character' — a case, let it be noted, where an unintended consequence dictates some form of enabling intervention at the local government level — but the participatory dimension to this remedy gets lost when the whole question is reduced to one of deciding, public-choice fashion, how elementary education should be financed.

West has accused me of downgrading the status of laissez-faire in Smith's thinking to that of a 'myth'. I do not think this is so. Within the context of anti-mercantilism, as part of the rejection of Hobbesian or Mandevillian assumptions of non-sociability, and as an antidote to the arrogance of the 'man of system', the slogan may still have its uses — always provided that distinctions between Smith's world and that envisaged by the 19th- and 20th-century debate on the state's responsibilities are observed. Viner may have been wrong, as he later admitted, to see conflict between the *Theory of Moral Sentiments* and the *Wealth of Nations*, but he was surely right to notice that the duties of the legislator under the heading of justice in the latter work open up a potentially wider field of intervention to prevent 'oppression' than one might expect on the basis of the treatment given to commutative justice in the former work (Viner, 1958:237-8). I would also claim that

benchmark or criterion with which to evaluate alternative political structures'. Nevertheless, he maintains, in a way that is obscure to me, that Smith's 'device of the "impartial spectator" serves this function'; see Buchanan, 1979:121.

recognition of the full scope of Smith's science of the legislator adds interest to a rather tired body of literature by drawing attention to the fact that, for Smith, government in civilised communities had to be strong, adaptable, and probably expanding, even if he hoped its operations would not be extensive and detailed in the economic field.

VII. LIBERTY AND UTILITY

Terence Hutchison (1981) has drawn attention to another important lacuna in Smith's position that would make it difficult to include him wholeheartedly within any modern public choice genealogy. Hutchison has noted that Turgot clearly recognised the irredeemably **subjective** nature of utility, and hence foresaw some of the connections between exchange value and utility later codified by post-marginalist economists, thereby foreshadowing an integral part of the microeconomics that is so important to the modern libertarian understanding of market behaviour. In contrast, Smith's concept of utility was an **objective** one (biological or moralistic), and therefore does not have the kind of proleptic qualities required for membership of the libertarian lineage. Indeed, Hutchison believes that in this respect at least Smith may have given rise to that unfortunate tendency among his later English 'classical' followers of cultivating labour and absolute theories of value. But Hutchison's main charge is one of logical contradiction. Smith's views on utility are, he maintains, 'quite incompatible with [his] libertarian values and the whole ethical and political message of *The Wealth of Nations*. For such a concept of objective utility permits the implication that values, choices, and priorities are not to be decided by the purely subjective tastes and desires of individuals, but by objective qualities of 'usefulness' which experts or officials can more accurately assess and decide for us' (Hutchison, 1981:39).

It would not be the first time that Smith was convicted of having left a confused will and testament: Marxists have been pointing to the divided legacy on the labour theory of value for many years (see, e.g., Meek, 1977). Hutchison has undoubtedly posed an interesting counter-factual problem, but the answer should not, in my opinion, lead to the conclusion that we are faced with 'an unfortunate aberration, quite inconsistent with [Smith's] fundamental politico-economic philosophy' (1981:44). Hutchison assumes that since Smith is a libertarian of a particular stamp, this dictates the combination of ideas that **ought** to be found in his writings. What makes this an interesting counter-factual problem, of course, rather than one derived from a failure to register what positions were genuinely available to a past author, is that Smith, quite as much as Turgot, defended the system of natural liberty by emphasising the 'impertinence' of politicians and the limits to the knowledge possessed by those who professed to act in the service of the public good. With regard to what was undoubtedly the most sensitive free-market question of the day — the effects, beneficial or otherwise, of the network of controls exerted over the domestic and international grain trade in countries such as France and Britain — there are further ironies in the situation. Thus after the failure of Turgot's attempt as Louis XVIth's Minister of Finances to create free trade in grain in 1774, Smith's strong support for the same policy in 1776 has earned him the reputation for being its 'only standard-bearer' (Hont and Ignatieff, 1983:18). More ironically still, the economist whom Hutchison credits with having the greatest influence over Turgot on the matter of subjective utility, the Abbé Galiani, was also the leading opponent of free trade in grain during periods of scarcity. It begins to seem as though empirical and political assessments of the impact of different policies were at least as important as theoretical rigour to the contemporary participants. It also seems worth noting the risks of slippage in understanding when perception of the 'correct' logical and ideological connections seems to require a process of doctrinal development that reached fruition only some hundred years or so after an author's death.

For this reason too, I would prefer to approach Hutchison's counter-factual proposition by examining more closely the undoubted objectivist features of Smith's position. A good deal can and has been said about those respects in which Smith is, or rather is not, a utilitarian in morals and politics. Here I should simply like to mention a related and equally problematic feature of his position, namely that as a moral philosopher he frequently adopts an objectivist position towards the satisfaction of individual material wants which leads him to condemn 'frivolous utility' and take an ascetic view of the happiness associated with wealth attainment generally (see, e.g., Hirschman, 1982:ch.3). Here the relevant context and contrast is provided not by Galiani, Turgot, and later economic exponents of utility theory inhabiting an intellectual world dominated by given resources and wants, but by Rousseau, Mandeville, and an 18th-century debate on the way in which wants are endlessly generated as a result of the social processes of envy and emulation — a world far removed from Robinsonades and atomistic bargaining exercises. And once this is recognised as the more relevant context for what Smith is arguing, the role in which he cast himself in the debate is perhaps better described not as that of an objectivist in Hutchison's sense so much as that of an anti-utopian or moral and sociological realist.

Rousseau's discourse on inequality was not merely the subject of one of Smith's earliest published writings, but it can be plausibly argued that Smith was responding to Rousseau in the *Theory of Moral Sentiments* when dealing with economic ambition and the beneficial role of the invisible hand in distributing its unequal results (see Raphael, 1985:71-2, 79-80; Ignatieff, 1984:ch.4; and Winch, 1985a:241-2). In common with Mandeville, whom Smith recognised as the source of the position Rousseau was inverting in his discourse on inequality, Smith accepts the deceptive basis of individual ambition, while commending, on the whole, its social consequences. Although the pursuit of wealth and inequality are inseparable, this need not have the dire consequences predicted by Rousseau. The individual benefits associated with material goods were generally exaggerated, but economic growth was capable of generating rising absolute living standards for the mass of society and of producing 'a gradual descent of fortunes', with less 'servile dependency' in social relationships as another of its beneficial byproducts.

It follows that Smith had no more reason to accept the 'violence' of Rousseau's 'republican' solutions to the problem of containing emulation and inequality than he had to accept the need for mercantile restrictions as a means of increasing national wealth. Constitutional machinery and the rule of law were capable of restraining some of the worst excesses of economic and other striving in a world in which economic progress and inequality went hand in hand, but there could be no guarantee in such matters. A society based solely on rules of commutative justice was less attractive than one based on benevolence and public spirit as well; but it would be a viable form of society. This is what I have called Smith's realism, though Michael Ignatieff, in a perceptive discussion of the Rousseau-Smith contrast, may well be correct in suggesting that Smith relies on a 'stoic hope' that some men at least will always be capable of distinguishing between wants and needs. I certainly share Ignatieff's further conclusion that: 'Smith's vision of progress contained no myth of future deliverance, no fantasy of human self-transcendance through the mastery of the means of production. Progress delivered only one ambiguous good: increasing the freedom of individuals to choose between need and desire. It could not promise a future in which men would be relieved of the burden of stoic choice' (Ignatieff, 1984:127).

VIII. RECOVERY OR RECRUITMENT

The distinction between needs and desires has no place, I take it, in a world where subjective concepts of utility rule; and if Smith's objectivism is to be counted as 'an unfortunate aberration' that could lead to temporary suspension or even exclusion from the preferred liberal lineage, then a historian such as myself must say so be it. All the closed doctrines out of which the grand '-isms' and 'traditions' in the history of political thought are constructed require some such rules of membership based on an uncertain mixture of theoretical purity and moral evaluation. But if the writing of intellectual history is undertaken more with a view to recovery than recruitment, the '-isms' become a hindrance and an embarrassment, especially when one does not have the testimony of the authors themselves on the categories into which they are being recruited. This is the root of my continuing objection to the inclusion of Smith within a liberal tradition and my preference for a version of something Smith would have readily grasped, namely varieties of the Whig genus.

This would be a weak personal preference, accompanied by no desire to legislate for others, were it not for the tendency among those who wish to debate the nature of liberalism to enforce doctrinal closure by ignoring or denying important or even merely interesting features of Smith's thinking — as I have tried to illustrate above with regard to 'republican' values, the concept of a legislator, 'contractualism', and objective notions of utility. Moreover, if the liberal label requires me to believe that everything that is of interest about Smith's politics can be derived from his economics, the label no longer describes, even in simplistic terms, what the bottle contains. For it is one of the prime features of Smith's outlook, as I understand it, that stoic choices have to be made in a world that does not permit extensive foresight; that neither historical nor competitive economic processes are likely to solve, once and for all, the problems of sustaining a just political order; that while systems of economic reproduction cannot be ignored when discussing the nature of polities, there is no one-to-one relationship between forms of government and economic success, no **necessary** relationship between commercial prosperity and liberty (this is most clearly spelled out in Forbes, 1975:194-201).

It is precisely the absence of such simple relationships between polity, economy, and society in Smith that makes him of continuing interest to later generations operating with the benefit of hindsight. For example, it enables us to consider the circumstances in which Smith's political and economic vision might be placed at odds with one another. Thus we we can ask, as Albert Hirschman (1977:117-35) has invited us to do, whether Smith's apparent belief in the compatibility of economic striving with social and political stability has proved to be unduly complacent. Or, in similar vein, we can ask with John Dunn (1985:66) whether the very dynamic forces released by commercial society could undermine one of Smith's assumptions about political stability, namely that deference within a system of social classes or ranks would persist. Smith seemed to feel that America provided the most propitious circumstances for economic and political liberty to thrive together, free from feudal remnants and an oppressive aristocracy — a belief shared by many contemporary Americans and by some modern historians of Jeffersonian republicanism (see, e.g., Appleby, 1984). Why then were Smith's hopes for America unfulfilled, particularly so far as acceptance of laissez-faire in economic matters was concerned?

Winch: Adam Smith and the Liberal Tradition

Am I wrong in detecting that similar questions are a prominent feature of debates between modern liberals and libertarians? Most liberals accept what Smith upheld, namely that competitive markets require an appropriate legal and institutional framework within which to work properly; and some have argued that, ideally, this framework ought to be one that commands customary or non-rational acceptance. In my opinion, though it cannot be argued here, Smith is less of a 'Burkean' (or Hayekian?) in these matters than is sometimes thought (see Haakonssen, 1981:132). But those who question whether Hayek's economic liberalism can live side by side with his more conservative (Whig?) theory of traditional institutions and the anti-constructivist elements in his thinking; and those who ask whether there is a conflict between the projective and retrospective sides of human nature that are being appealed to in support of the conservative and libertarian theories — surely they are pursuing the same issues? This question, I take it, is the one that most separates public choice theorists such as James Buchanan from anti-constructivists such as Hayek (see, e.g., Buchanan, 1986).

Traditions of Liberalism

References

Appleby, J.O. (1984), *Capitalism and a New Social Order; The Republican Vision of the 1790s*, New York, Columbia University Press.

Buchanan, J.M. (1978), 'From private preferences to public philosophy: Notes on the development of public choice', pp. 1-20 in A. Seldon (ed.), *The Economics of Politics*, London, Institute of Economic Affairs.

——— (1979), 'The justice of natural liberty', pp. 117-31 in G.P. O'Driscoll (ed.), *Adam Smith and Modern Political Economy*, Ames, Iowa, Iowa State University Press.

——— (1986), *Liberty, Market and State*, Brighton, Harvester Press.

Burns, J.H. (1967), *The Fabric of Felicity: The Legislator and the Human Condition*, Inaugural Lecture, University College, London.

Collini, S., D. Winch and J. Burrow (1983), *That Noble Science of Politics*, Cambridge, Cambridge University Press.

Cropsey, J. (1979), Book Review, *Political Theory* 7:424-8.

Cumming, R.D. (1981), 'Giving back words; Things, money, persons', *Social Research* 48:227-59.

Dunn, J. (1978), Book Review, *Times Literary Supplement* 3 November.

——— (1985), *Rethinking Modern Political Theory*, Cambridge, Cambridge University Press.

Forbes, D. (1975), 'Sceptical Whiggism, commerce and liberty', pp.179-201 in A.S. Skinner and T.G. Wilson (eds), *Essays on Adam Smith*, Oxford, Oxford University Press.

——— (1978), Book Review, *Times Higher Educational Supplement* July 7.

Haakonssen, K. (1981), *The Science of a Legislator; The Natural Jurisprudence of David Hume and Adam Smith*, Cambridge, Cambridge University Press.

———(1984a), 'From moral philosophy to political economy: The contribution of Dugald Stewart', pp. 211-32 in V. Hope (ed.), *Philosophers of the Scottish Enlightenment*, Edinburgh, Edinburgh University Press.

——— (1984b), 'The science of a legislator in James Mackintosh's moral philosophy', *Juridical Review* June:41-68.

——— (1985), 'John Millar and the science of a legislator', *Juridical Review* June, 41-68.

Hamowy, R. (1979), Book Review, *American Historical Review* April:418-9.

Winch: Adam Smith and the Liberal Tradition

Harpham, E. (1984), 'Liberalism, civic humanism and the case of Adam Smith', *American Political Science Review* 78:764-74.

Hayek, F.A. (1948), *Individualism and the Economic Order*, Chicago, Chicago University Press.

Hirschman, A.O. (1977), *The Passions and the Interests*, Princeton, Princeton University Press.

——(1982), *Shifting Involvements*, Princeton, Princeton University Press.

Hollander, S. (1979), Book Review, *Journal of Economic Literature* 17:542-5.

Hont, I. and M. Ignatieff (1983), 'Needs and justice in the *Wealth of Nations*', pp. 1-44 in *Wealth and Virtue; The Shaping of Political Economy in the Scottish Enlightenment*, Cambridge, Cambridge University Press.

Hutchison, T. (1981), 'Turgot and Smith', pp. 33-45 in C. Bordes and J. Morange (eds), *Turgot, Economiste et Administrateur*, Paris, Presses Universitaires de France.

Ignatieff, M. (1984), *The Needs of Strangers*, London, Chatto and Windus.

Kettler, D. (1977), 'History and theory in Ferguson's *Essay on the History of Civil Society;* A reconsideration', *Political Theory* 5:437-60.

—— (1979), Book Review, *American Political Science Review* 73:868-9.

Macpherson, C.B. (1979), Book Review, *History of Political Economy* 11:450-4.

Meek, R. (1977), 'Value in the history of economic thought', pp. 149-164 in *Smith, Marx and After*, London, Chapman & Hall.

Pocock, J.G.A. (1975), *The Machiavellian Moment*, Princeton, Princeton University Press.

Raphael, D.D. (1985), *Adam Smith*, Oxford, Oxford University Press.

Robertson, J. (1983), 'Scottish political economy beyond the civic tradition: Government and economic development in the *Wealth of Nations*', *History of Political Thought* 4:451-82.

Rosenberg, N. (1960), 'Some institutional aspects of the *Wealth of Nations*', *Journal of Political Economy* 68:557-70.

Skinner, A.S. (1979), *A System of Social Science*, Oxford, Oxford University Press.

Smith, A. (1976a), *An Inquiry into the Nature and Causes of the Wealth of Nations*, R.H. Campbell and A.S. Skinner (eds), Oxford, Clarendon Press.

—— (1976b), *The Theory of Moral Sentiments*, D.D. Raphael and A.L. Macfic (eds), Oxford, Clarendon Press.

—— (1978), *Lectures on Jurisprudence*, R.L. Meek, D.D. Raphael and P.G. Stein (eds), Oxford, Clarendon Press.

Sowell, T. (1979), Book Review, *Journal of Economic History* 39:604-5.

Thweatt, W.O. (ed.) (1988), *Classical Political Economy; A Survey of Recent Literature*, Boston, Kluwer-Nijhoff.

Viner, J. (1958), 'Adam Smith and laissez-faire', pp. 213-45 in *Long View and the Short*, Glencoe, Illinois, The Free Press.

West, E.G. (1969), 'The political economy of alienation: Karl Marx and Adam Smith', *Oxford Economic Papers* 21:1-23.

——— (1976), 'Adam Smith's economics of politics', *History of Political Economy* 8:515-39.

Winch, D. (1978), *Adam Smith's Politics. An Essay in Historiographic Revision*, Cambridge, Cambridge University Press.

——— (1983a), 'Science and the legislator: Adam Smith and after', *Economic Journal* 93:501-20.

——— (1983b), 'Adam Smith's "enduring particular result"; A political and cosmopolitan perspective', pp. 253-69 in I. Hont and M. Ignatieff (eds.), *Wealth and Virtue; The Shaping of Political Economy in the Scottish Enlightenment*, Cambridge, Cambridge University Press.

——— (1985a), 'The Burke-Smith problem and late eighteenth-century political and economic thought', *Historical Journal* 28:231-47.

——— (1985b), 'Economic liberalism as ideology: The Appleby version', *Economic History Review* 38:287-97.

Wolin, S. (1960), *Politics and Vision*, Boston, Little Brown and Company.

——— (1981), 'The new public philosophy', *Democracy* 23-36.

Part V
Civil Society

[18]

Women and Humanity in Scottish Enlightenment Social Thought: The Case of Adam Smith

Henry C. Clark

Introduction

The so-called Adam Smith Problem has percolated through scholarship for the better part of a century. It has hinged on whether the argument of Smith's *Theory of Moral Sentiments* (1759), based on a natural and universal capacity for sympathy, could be reconciled with the *Wealth of Nations* (1776), with its suggestion of an equally universal pursuit of self-interest.[1] But if, as some have said, nineteenth-century scholarship invented this problem by ignoring Smith's treatment of political economy as one of the moral sciences, then twentieth-century scholarship has more often than not solved the problem by simply ignoring the moral side of the equation altogether.

One result of this narrowing of contexts has been to link Smith's reputation with the fortunes of the economic system of which he has

1. For a convenient summary see Richard F. Teichgraeber III, "Rethinking Das Adam Smith Problem," in *New Perspectives on the Politics and Culture of Early Modern Scotland*, ed. John Dwyer, Roger A. Mason and Alexander Murdoch (Edinburgh, 1982), esp. 249-254. Throughout this essay I use the 1976 Oxford University Press editions of *The Theory of Moral Sentiments*, ed. D.D. Raphael and A.L. Macfie (repr., 1982) and *An Inquiry into the Nature and Causes of the Wealth of Nations*, ed. W.B. Todd (repr., 1981), 2 vols., and I follow the numbering system of the editors. Hereafter, the works will be abbreviated in the text as *TMS* and *WN*, respectively.

Henry C. Clark is an Associate Professor of History at Canisius College.

become the symbol. In the first half of this century the ascendancy of socialism and its variants led to a virtual disappearance of scholarly interest in Adam Smith's economic theory. Since the midcentury, as the high tide of socialism has more or less steadily receded in the Western world, a considerable revival of interest in the Scottish polymath has occurred, crystallizing around the bicentennial of the *Wealth of Nations* in 1976 and the publication of the Glasgow edition of his works.[2]

Although Smith's admirers have increased in number in recent years, his detractors remain abundant. And ironically, proponents of the classical and neoclassical economics inspired by him have done much to engender this current hostility. By emphasizing those aspects of Smith's thought that appear to envision a mechanistic system of material growth founded solely on the rational pursuit of self-interest, they have opened the way to the moral critique of capitalism that has dominated the twentieth century, and that has proven remarkably strong apart from the practical fate of the dominant socialist alternative.

Thus, to take one example, a long-established body of Marxist criticism has now begun to pass the baton to a new tradition of scholarship inspired directly or indirectly by feminist theory. Whether this state of affairs reflects the continuing deficiencies of market-based social orders, or the self-defeating tendency of capitalism to generate an intelligentsia instinctively hostile to it, is a large and intriguing question, though one beyond the scope of this essay.[3] The governing assumption here in this essay is that at least some of the antagonism toward Smith's thought arises from a residual misunderstanding of the historical context of his enterprise, and particularly of the crucial role of his moral theory in articulating a modified affirmation of modern society. It is further argued that Marxism and feminism are in some ways equally well placed for such a misunderstanding.

To begin, the two traditions share more than a hostility to liberal individualism:[4] they are also affiliated by a strong affirmation of egalitarianism and by a propensity to take the putative inegalitarian experience of the nineteenth century as a standard of evaluation for the

2. Edwin G. West, "Developments in the Literature on Adam Smith: An Evaluative Survey," in *Classical Political Economy*, ed. William Thwcatt (Boston, 1988), p. 14.

3. One early discussion of this largely overlooked problem is Joseph Schumpeter, "The Sociology of the Intellectual," in *Capitalism, Socialism, and Democracy*, 3rd. ed. (New York, 1950; orig. pub. 1942), pp. 145-156.

4. For one of the very few recent exceptions to this statement, see Joan Kennedy Taylor, *Reclaiming the Mainstream: Individualist Feminism Rediscovered* (Washington, 1992).

founding theories of the eighteenth.[5] Marxists, for example, have argued that industrial capitalism polarized rich and poor, propertied and propertyless, and that it narrowed the range of opportunities for the skilled, artisanal workers of Old Europe, replacing them with an alienated factory proletariat. They have also seen capitalism as replacing a "moral economy" with the harsh, pragmatic realism of the "dismal science." Smith's ideas are thought to have prepared the way for this alienation by expressing an implicit hostility to workers in particular, and the masses in general and by writing a warrant for an amoral "system" of political economy.[6]

Feminism, for its part, has seen a comparable atrophy of female autonomy in the development of an ideology of public-and-private domains---the so-called "two-spheres" thesis---that came to fruition in the Victorian age. While often depicting the previous century as a promising period whose opportunities were snuffed out by the male-dominated tendencies of the French Revolution, feminists have also found Enlightenment roots for the domestication of women.[7] In this context feminists have generally adapted their interpretations of Adam Smith to fit the larger framework of this "two-spheres" thesis.[8]

5. This 'anticipatory' tendency is common to both Marxist and feminist analysis. For a critique of the former, see Roger Emerson, "Conjectural History and the Scottish Philosophers," in Canadian Historical Association *Historical Papers* (1984): 63-90.

6. Thus, according to one of the most prominent Marxist critics of Smith, there were "no worries [in *WN*] that a more or less unfettered capitalism might generate chronic unemployment." See Ronald L. Meek, *Smith, Marx, and After* (London, 1977), p. 4. See also the body of literature initiated by the late E.P. Thompson, "The Moral Economy of the English Crowd in the Eighteenth Century," in *Past and Present* 50 (1971):76-136. For a critique of the longer tradition of moral attacks on capitalism, see H.B. Acton, *The Morals of Markets and Related Essays*, ed. David Gordon and Jeremy Shearmur (Indianapolis, 1993).

7. The "two-spheres" thesis is the subject of a vast literature. One recent work that is well-respected by feminists is Joan Landes, *Women and the Public Sphere in the Age of the French Revolution* (Ithaca, 1988).

8. Among the works to be discussed below are Carol Kay, "Canon, Ideology, and Gender: Mary Wollstonecraft's Critique of Adam Smith," *New Political Science* 15 (1986):63-76; Deidre Dawson, "Is Sympathy so Surprising? Adam Smith and French Fictions of Sympathy," *Eighteenth-Century Life* 15 (1991): 147-162; David Marshall, *The Figure of Theater: Shaftesbury, Defoe, Adam Smith and George Eliot* (New York, 1986), pp. 167-192; Jane Rendall, "Virtue and Commerce: Women in the Making of Adam Smith's Political Economy," in *Women in Western Political Philosophy*, ed. Ellen Kennedy and Susan Mendus (New York, 1987); G.J. Barker-Benfield, *The Culture of Sensibility* (Chicago, 1992), esp. pp. 134-144; John Dwyer, *Virtuous Discourse* (Edinburg, 1987); Dwyer, *The Age of the Passions: Interpretations of Adam Smith and Enlightened Scottish Culture*, forthcoming; I am grateful to Professor Dwyer for the opportunity to consult this stimulating manuscript before publication. Probably the most hard-edged, openly ideological essay in the above tradition is Lucinda

Although generally as critical of Smith's intellectual enterprise as their Marxist colleagues and predecessors, feminist scholars have exhibited significant differences in the sources and objects of their analyses. Whereas Marxists have tended either to ignore or to underplay the importance of Smith's moral theory, feminists have taken the importance of that theory for granted; indeed, they have used it as their principal avenue of attack. Almost all who have written on the subject believe that the eighteenth-century preoccupation with sensibility---whether in its fictional literature (such as in the novels of Richardson, Stern, Henry MacKenzie, or others) or its moral thought (such as that of the Scottish Enlightenment)---is "gendered" in specific and important ways. The culture of sensibility, in this view, contains substantive distinctions between the affective or moral lives of men and of women. In this regard, some have seen Smith himself as hostile to female moral agency.[9] Others, while granting the premium Smith's doctrine of sympathy placed upon a female sensibility, nonetheless are quick to view him as relegating that positive capacity to inferior status.[10] Either way, the conclusion has been that Smith is no more a friend to women than to the artisanal working class. And indeed, the two traditions of Marxism and feminism are sometimes combined to make precisely this point.[11]

Jane Rendall uses recent work in the Cambridge school to attempt a reworking of the "two spheres" argument for Adam Smith's moral theory. By Rendall's account Smith resolved the tension between virtue and rights inherited from the natural jurisprudence tradition of Pufendorf and his followers at the University of Glasgow, and he did so

Cole, "(Anti)-feminist Sympathies: The Politics of Relationship in Smith, Wollstonecraft, and More," *English Literary History* 58 (1991):107-140. Cole agonizes at one point (132) over how "the demands of historical analysis conflict with the exigencies of feminist politics."

9. See Marshall, *The Figure of Theater*, p. 184 and *passim*.

10. See Kay, "Canon, Ideology, and Gender," p. 71.

11. Dwyer makes the connection explicit when he argues that the Scottish discourse of sensibility typified by Smith's *Theory of Moral Sentiments* contributed to a state of affairs in which "working people, the young, and an entire sex came under the increased supervision of elite adult males." See his "Postscript," *The Age of the Passions*. Cole explains that her interpretation is "based on the idea that Smith is somehow related to what we would now call the tradition of possessive individualism" and describes Smith as hardhearted toward the poor; see her "(Anti)feminist Sympathies," pp. 134-135, n. 9, and p. 113. For a more nuanced, closely reasoned treatment of this question, see Istvan Hont and Michael Ignatieff, "Needs and Justice in the *Wealth of Nations*: An Introductory Essay," in Hont and Ignatieff, eds., *Wealth and Virtue: The Shaping of Political Economy in the Scottish Enlightenment* (Cambridge, 1983), pp. 1-44.

by retiring the traditional notion of male virtue as the precondition for citizenship. At the same time he relegated a redefined virtue to the "private" domain of home and family, where women would act as guardians, and made rights central to the new "public" domain of the marketplace, which would perforce be as male-centered as the civic arena of classicism.[12]

In *Virtuous Discourse* John Dwyer in a sense makes the opposite argument. While many of Smith's countrymen responded to the era's increasing selfishness by urging their readers to rebuild a community made problematic by the spread of commerce, Dwyer writes, Smith retreated behind the walls of Stoic fortitude against the "whining moralists" of the new sensibility. These modernists cleared the way for a validation of female moral agency by softening the older conceptions of virtue and replacing them with a species of "virtuous discourse" amenable to men and women alike. Their protofeminist egalitarianism, however, became the object of Smith's scorn. "Humanity is the virtue of a woman," he wrote provocatively, "generosity of a man," (*TMS*, IV.2.10) prompting Dwyer to comment that Smith "dismissed [the virtue of] humanity in terms that can only be described as sexist."[13] Indeed, in Dwyer's view Smith turned his back on Scottish communitarianism and ultimately endorsed "someone resembling a Nietzschean übermensch."[14]

In the present essay, I propose to show that Smith's conception of women in modern society can only be understood in the context of his moral theory as a whole. In particular I wish to make the following arguments: the language of "humanity" in particular and of the virtues in general is not nearly as "gendered" as has been made out; indeed, humanity itself is in many ways a defining virtue for the very commercial society that Smith tried to conceptualize, and it transcends both the male-female and the public-private boundaries. A proper appreciation of this discourse makes clear that women are not excluded from moral agency, nor do their characteristic virtues hold an inferior place on a hierarchy of moral excellences. On the other hand, Smith was not a utopian; the modern notion of autonomy, so crucial to

12. Rendall, "Virtue and Commerce," esp. pp. 70-72.

13. Dwyer, "From Sympathy to Self-Interest: The Ethical Foundation of Smithian Economics," chapter one of *The Age of the Passions*.

14. Dwyer, *Virtuous Discourse*, pp. 169, 183. See also Dwyer's "Introduction--A 'Peculiar Blessing': Social Converse in Scotland from Hutcheson to Burns," in *Sociability and Society in Eighteenth-Century Scotland*, ed. John Dwyer and Richard B. Sher, a special number of *Eighteenth-Century Life*, n.s., 1 & 2 (1991): 16.

contemporary feminism, was alien to him. All historical progress, for men and women alike, was in his view partial, provisional, and costly, more than likely paid for by some corresponding loss. Close attention to the functioning of natural-law theory and the neoclassical morality of character in Smith's thought can help both to avoid the temptation to anachronism and to understand in a more nuanced way the significance that Smith, and the Scottish Enlightenment, attributed to the condition of women in commercial society.

I

Smith did not choose to address in a sustained fashion the relative moral or social possibilities of men and women. In the face of this obstacle, feminist scholars have tended to burden a small number of Smith's isolated and quotable comments with the heavy weight of distinctly modern theoretical inferences. They have also frequently looked forward in time and lamented the residual limits on female autonomy found in Enlightenment social thought. The alternative proposed here is to begin with a fuller appreciation of the general purposes with which Smith began, "funneling down" to specific inferences about gender clearly justified by his writings. Such modest inferences are the most that we can hope for under the circumstances.

Perhaps the fundamental divide between Smith and his recent interpreters concerns the place of the moral imagination. Feminism, like Marxism, tends to share the postmodern conviction about the inescapable partiality of perspectives.[15] But for Smith, the capacity for at least some transcendence of one's interests was not only possible, it was an innate capacity in all human beings and the indispensable starting point for moral education.

Feminists have argued, in contrast, that the "impartial spectator" that anchors Smith's moral theory is really a man.[16] If this were true, it would indeed lend credence to the suggestion that Smith intends to

15. As one typical articulation of this view would have it, "[T]he consensus of most of the dominant theories is that all thought does, indeed, develop from particular standpoints, perspectives, interests." George Levine, Peter Brooks, Jonathan Culler, Marjorie Garber, E. Ann Kaplan, and Catharine R. Stimpson, *Speaking for the Humanities*, American Council of Learned Societies Occasional Paper, No. 7 (ISSN 1041-536X), 10. For a critique of the "emotivism" that is the moral-philosophical variant of this perspectivism, see Alasdair MacIntyre's *After Virtue* (Notre Dame, 1981), ch. 2-3. My broader indebtedness to this work will be clear enough in the pages that follow.

16. Barker-Benfield, *The Culture of Sensibility*, p. 140, cites *TMS*, p. 25 for this claim, but no such statement appears there.

exclude women from his moral community, because, as we shall see below (part V), Smith was well aware of men's capacity to judge partially with regard to women. But in fact, by describing it as a tribunal, as a "demigod" within the breast, Smith was expressing confidence in the imagination to transcend one's own perspective--whatever be the principle of its partiality. When the demigod, who is part mortal and part immortal, achieves the requisite impartiality within us, we are to follow it; when not, we are to appeal to "a still higher tribunal,...the all-seeing Judge of the world." (*TMS*, III.2.31-33 and *passim*)[17]

It is through the language of the virtues that Smith differentiates and more closely defines the operation of this moral imagination in social life. Feminist interpreters of Smith, like students of the eighteenth century as a whole, have tended to translate Smith's virtues-discourse into an idiom more agreeable to the concerns of twentieth-century theory.[18] And yet, the virtues are central to Smith's enterprise in *TMS* and are discussed with care and subtlety. Although he distinguishes himself at various points in the treatise from the Stoics, the Epicureans, Christian ascetics, the philosophers of benevolence and of prudence, he fundamentally locates his theory relative to others in his rejection of what he called the "licentious systems." These latter theories based themselves on self-love by rejecting the possibility of virtue or disinterested action, and they found expression in the works of the Duke of La Rochefoucauld (1613-80), Hobbes (1588-1679), and especially Bernard Mandeville (1670-1733).

Whereas Mandeville's *The Fable of the Bees* (1714, 1723) was widely perceived in its time as a reductionist enterprise, tracing the claim or appearance of any virtue back to its roots in self-interest, Smith attempted what might be called an expository enterprise; he attempted to explain and account for the *feelings* that people in common life have that a difference exists between self-interested and disinterested action. The impartial spectator that anchors this analysis, and the formation of conscience that is its ultimate product, depends for its functioning upon the existence of virtues and virtuous characters, and not merely the appearance of such.

But not only does Smith share the traditional aim of painting vivid "characters" of virtue that his (all-male) students might find worthy of

17. See Knud Haakonssen, *The Science of a Legislator: The Natural Jurisprudence of David Hume and Adam Smith* (Cambridge, 1981), pp. 55-62.

18. For a critique of this tendency, see Carol Blum, *Rousseau and the Republic of Virtue: The Language of Politics in the French Revolution* (Ithaca, 1986), pp. 14-15, 28-30.

emulation, he also wishes to sketch a social psychology of moral life, a modern and scientific analysis of the roots and nature of morality. Like many eighteenth-century thinkers, Smith wished to apply a certain Newtonian systematicity to the study of the human condition,[19] one of whose elements was a new and dynamic system of the virtues not dissimilar to his "natural system of liberty." Whereas most of his predecessors had described a relatively static, even hierarchical order in which the virtues were arranged in "tables" or other schemas, Smith's doctrine of sympathy generated a conception of society that was "systematic" in the Newtonian sense; the principles of an individual's conduct--i.e., not only the feelings and actions, but the developed virtues--interact with and modify those of another in analyzable, albeit not rigidly determined ways.[20]

We can, therefore, make a couple of preliminary observations. The first concerns the scope of Smith's moral universe. Just as Mandeville was an equal opportunity excluder from the community of virtue, so too did Smith regard the capacity for disinterestedness as a fundamentally human one. To take a concrete example: Modesty, often seen as a distinctively female virtue, Mandeville unmasks as a "Reflexion on our own Unworthiness, proceeding from an Apprehension that others either do, or might, if they knew all, deservedly despise us."[21] But since Smith does not unmask "modesty," or "humanity," or any other supposedly female virtues, his rejection of one of the most pervasive tendencies in late seventeenth- and eighteenth-century thought had the effect of including women in the community of moral agents in a fundamental way. Humanity is the *virtue* of a woman, after all, as well as the virtue of a *woman*.

Secondly, his praise of generosity, which he describes as a masculine virtue, should likewise be seen in context. Although in a sense the defining virtue for that broad Stoic-aristocratic paradigm so popular throughout the seventeenth century, generosity receives little treatment from Smith. While he cites admiringly the traditional example of the soldier willing to sacrifice his life for the public good, Smith does not make these heroic virtues an important part of his theory, citing

19. For an introductory discussion of Smith's view of the Newtonian method, see D.D. Raphael and A.S. Skinner, "General Introduction," in *Essays on Philosophical Subjects*, ed. W.P.D. Wightman (Oxford, 1980; repr. 1982), 1, pp. 11-15

20. For the standard argument, see T.D. Campbell, *Adam Smith's Science of Morals* (London, 1971).

21. Bernard Mandeville, *The Fable of the Bees*, 2 vols., ed. and intro. F.B. Kaye (Oxford, repr. 1988), 1:64-65.

generosity with any prominence only this once in the entire treatise. He was not of course indifferent to the models of heroism found in classical literature, but he hoped to define a spectrum of the virtues that could take account of the more mundane realities of a commercial society. For Smith, the days of the "übermensch," Nietzschean or otherwise, were over, if they had ever existed.

This is made clear by the central place Smith allots to "humanity" in his natural system of the virtues, which appears early in the first book of *TMS*. After describing in elementary terms the social-psychological process by which moral concepts are first acquired, he writes as follows:

> Upon...two different efforts, upon that of the spectator to enter into the sentiments of the person principally concerned, and upon that of the person principally concerned, to bring down his emotions to what the spectator can go along with, are founded two different sets of virtues. The soft, the gentle, the amiable virtues, the virtues of candid condescension and indulgent humanity, are founded upon the one: the great, the awful and respectable, the virtues of self-denial, of self-government, of that command of the passions which subjects all the movements of our nature to what our own dignity and honour, and the propriety of our own conduct require, take their origin from the other. (*TMS*, I.i.5.1)[22]

Throughout the treatise Smith makes clear that this description is no mere taxonomy of two parallel tables of the virtues, but rather the parameters of a dynamic framework meant to indicate how individual and society can each approximate a certain equilibrium. The impulses that all humans, regardless of sex, have both to sympathize with others' sufferings and to soften the expression of their own out of consideration for others' probable responses, provide a general framework for understanding the casual and occasional "genderings" of these phenomena that appear in the treatise. Both humanity and self-command are generic attributes before they take shape in any specific way for one sex or the other. Men also need humanity; women also

22. For an earlier discussion of the relation between humanity and self-command, see A.S. Skinner, "Moral Philosophy and Civil Society," *A System of Social Science: Papers Relating to Adam Smith* (Oxford, 1979), pp. 42-67, esp. 43-45.

need self-command; and they need these skills pervasively, throughout the whole quiet, unheralded course of daily life.[23]

II

Not only does humanity hold a place fully equal to self-command in Smith's moral philosophy, but the two virtues are complementary and mutually dependent both within the individual and in civil society as a whole. This complementarity exemplifies the dynamic quality of Smith's conception of moral life. Self-command is admirable not only because it contributes to Stoic tranquillity or bespeaks strength of character, but also, paradoxically, because of its advantages in the economy of sympathetic relations--the "free communication of sentiments" that is the ideal form of our relations with others. (*TMS*, VII.iv.28)

One person's self-command diminishes the demands that need to be made upon another's humanity. Conversely, to the degree that our own humanity enables us to reach out to meet the sufferings of another, it has the effect of diminishing the demand that we make upon that person's self-command. As if in anticipation of a "masculinist" objection to the premium he has thus placed upon the "softer" virtues of humanity, Smith writes: "Our sensibility to the feelings of others, so far from being inconsistent with the manhood of self-command, is the very principle upon which that manhood is founded. The very same principle or instinct which, in the misfortune of our neighbour, prompts us to compassionate his sorrow; in our own misfortune, prompts us to restrain the abject and miserable lamentations of our own." (*TMS*, III.3.34) Thus, a balance between humanity and self-command is better than the overweening status of one or the other virtue. In Smith's reworking of these traditional Stoic concepts, they are bound together in a kind of double helix of reciprocity.

In his historical-sociological voice, Smith sheds further light on the place that he assigns to humanity and self-command in his moral philosophy.[24] He articulates a distinction between the moral universes of primitive and civilized society that combines the insights of the Scottish four-stages theory of history (which he had done much to

23. Carol Kay is therefore anachronistic when she writes that Smith "seems to divide up the whole moral psychology by a suggested sex difference [between humanity and self-command] that is not acknowledged." "Canon, Ideology, and Gender," p. 72.

24. His failure always to distinguish between these two kinds of discourse has led to confusion in Smith scholarship. See Campbell's *Adam Smith's Science of Morals*, pp. 19-21.

develop) with the simpler dualism of contemporary natural-law theory.[25] It was not that the civilized were capable of virtue and the uncivilized were not (as had been the case with some early modern colonialists in the Aristotelian tradition),[26] but rather that the effective range of capacities differed in the two cases.

Self-command represented the defining virtue of primitive society because the "natural" impulses of pity and sympathy--the bedrock of any real moral community--could not flourish in its physically precarious conditions. It was not possible to interest in one's own daily aggravations those who were themselves preoccupied with survival. Accordingly, the "magnanimity and self-command [of the inhabitants of primitive society]...are almost beyond the conception of Europeans." (*TMS*, V.2.9)

Smith attributed to commercial society a kind of moderate virtue, less dazzling than that of the saint, the sage or the state-builder, but more useful, because more frequently activated. This situation made moral agency more accessible to women as well as men. "Among civilized nations," we read, "the virtues which are founded upon humanity, are more cultivated than those which are founded upon self-denial and the command of the passions." (*TMS*, V.2.8) The generalized leisure of a social order that has largely assured subsistence offers the latitude necessary for indulging the impulses of pity and sympathy. Humanity is not impossible in primitive society, nor self-command in civilized society, but different circumstances suggest different priorities in the respective ages.

The role of "humanity" in Smith's historical theory transcends gender in important ways. First, he explicitly argues that the prevalence of humanity in civilized society makes for more honest and forthcoming behavior. "A polished people," he writes, "being accustomed to give way, in some measure, to the movements of nature, become frank, open, and sincere. Barbarians, on the contrary, being obliged to smother and conceal the appearance of every passion, necessarily acquire the habits of falsehood and dissimulation." (*TMS*, V.2.11) Elsewhere in the treatise, Smith severely limits his praise for the man of prudence (a

25. On the connection between these two traditions, see Istvan Hont, "The Language of Sociability and Commerce: Samuel Pufendorf and the Theoretical Foundations of the 'Four-Stages Theory,'" in *The Languages of Political Theory in Early Modern Europe*, ed. Anthony Pagden (Cambridge, 1987), pp. 255, 260.

26. On this, see Anthony Pagden, *The Fall of Natural Man: The American Indian and the Origins of Modern Ethnography* (Cambridge, 1983).

figure sometimes seen as the centerpiece of his system)[27] precisely because such a character, though sincere and capable of friendship, is not always frank and open. (*TMS*, VI.1.8-9) Whereas Rousseau sees natural pity being gradually eroded and replaced by the self-regarding "reason" of modern individualism,[28] Smith takes the view that compassion and sympathy, though natural impulses, need the conquest of the problem of subsistence in order to flourish into real virtues capable of approximating his desired social equilibrium.

Secondly, the man of excessive prudence also lacks a certain "general sociality," which prevents him from enjoying another of the assets of modernity, namely its conversation and sociability.(*TMS*, V.2.10) Commercial society is a society of strangers that, as Michael Ignatieff notes, ministers to desires as well as to needs.[29] Its peculiar mode of animated civility is at least as available to women as to men. Indeed, for Smith the sociable conversation of friends and acquaintances is not merely a prevalent activity, but also a medium of moral education. The status of "humanity" as a governing modern virtue thus becomes, among other things, a function of the formative influence of daily conversation in that society.[30]

Thirdly, love is a more socially acceptable sentiment in civilized society, a development that Smith appears to regard as beneficial to lovers of both sexes. (*TMS*, V.2.9) The dynamics of modernization as a whole, on his view, have a tendency to refine sexual attraction no less than other passions. The indulgence of these passions is more in keeping with the standards of propriety prevalent in civilized societies precisely because the "essential parts of [one's] character" are not seen to be disturbed by them. "As long as they do not allow themselves to be transported to do any thing contrary to justice or humanity, they lose but little reputation, though the serenity of their countenance, or the

27. See Laurence Dickey, "Historicizing the 'Adam Smith Problem': Conceptual, Historiographical, and Textual Issues," in *Journal of Modern History* 58 (1986): 579-609. For a recent critique of Dickey's interpretation, see D.D. Raphael, "Adam Smith 1790: The Man Recalled; the Philosopher Revived," in Peter Jones and Andrew S. Skinner, eds., *Adam Smith Reviewed* (Edinburgh, 1992), pp. 93-118, esp. 104-108.

28. See Jean-Jacques Rousseau, "Discourse on the Origins of Inequality," in *The First and Second Discourses*, ed. Roger D. Masters, trans. Roger D. and Judith R. Masters (New York, 1964), pp. 130-133.

29. Michael Ignatieff, *The Needs of Strangers* (London, 1984), pp. 107-131, esp. 122-123.

30. See my "Conversation and Moderate Virtue in Adam Smith's *Theory of Moral Sentiments*," in *Review of Politics* 54 (1992): 185-210, for an elaboration of this argument.

composure of their discourse and behaviour, should be somewhat ruffled and disturbed." (*TMS*, V.2.9-10)[31]

This is the general context in which the claim that Smith recoiled against current effeminacy by attacking the "whining and melancholy moralists" should, in my view, be considered.[32] A close look at the passage from which that quotation is taken indicates that Smith distinguished himself not only from these sentimentalists but also from their polar opposites, the Stoics. Far from indulging a splenetic misogyny, Smith was engaging in his characteristic activity of mediation--seeking a proper balance between two equally valid but incomplete conceptions of the moral life. For Smith, propriety consists in a modulation of our emotive responses to the sufferings of self and other, and an effective resistance to our natural inclination to express too much emotion toward the former and not enough toward the latter. "One set [the sentimentalists] have laboured to increase our sensibility to the interests of others; another [the Stoics], to diminish that to our own." (*TMS*, III.3.8)

Thus, after attacking the sentimentalists for exaggerating our ability to empathize with others, he makes an equally searching critique of the Stoics' answer to the same problem. His argument here is important enough to merit citation at length:

> The sense of propriety, so far from requiring us to eradicate altogether that extraordinary sensibility, which we naturally feel for the misfortunes of our nearest connections, is always much more offended by the defect, than it ever is by the excess of that sensibility. The stoical apathy is, in such cases, never agreeable, and all the metaphysical sophisms by which it is supported can seldom serve any other purpose than to blow up the hard insensibility of a coxcomb to ten times its native impertinence. The poets and romance writers, who best paint the refinements and delicacies of love and friendship, and of all other private and domestic affections, Racine and Voltaire; Richardson, Maurivaux

31. Dwyer has recently argued the opposite, namely that Smith "was much more inclined to sympathize with those 'savages' who regarded it [love] as an 'unpardonable effeminacy.'" See his "Smith, Millar and the Natural History of Love," in *The Age of the Passions*.

32. *TMS*, III.3.9, from Dwyer, *Virtuous Discourse*, p. 169.

> [sic], and Riccoboni; are, in such cases, much better instructors than Zeno, Chrysippus, or Epictetus. (*TMS*, III.3.14)[33]

For Smith, therefore, too much sensibility is preferable to too little, although the ideal moral agent avoids the pitfalls of Stoicism and sentimentalism alike. Indeed, at the outset of his treatise, in establishing his general framework, Smith makes the point more forcefully. Not only is the capacity to feel and express sorrow at the afflictions of our companions an essential element of propriety, but the failure to do so is a violation precisely of the requirements of humanity (it "is real and gross inhumanity"). (*TMS*, I.i.2.4)[34]

Although indulgence of humanity carried to an excess is dangerous, Smith also asserts the need to preserve its spontaneity against the temptation of an exaggerated self-command to reduce moral life to mere rule-following. In opposition to the Christian claim that good actions ought always to be motivated by a desire to do one's duty by fulfilling divine commandments, he writes that actions "to which the benevolent affections would prompt us, ought to proceed as much from the passions themselves, as from any regard to the general rules of conduct." (*TMS*, III.6.4) The proper education of the passions is therefore the very definition of the moral life.

III

The foregoing will help explain why the "two-spheres" thesis provides an inappropriate framework for understanding Smith's moral theory. Just as Marxists have tended to reduce Smith's social thought to factors of production or class analysis, so too have feminists often reduced Smith's moral theory to his (notoriously elusive) politics. For Cole, Smith's sympathy-discourse is embedded in considerations of

33. Dawson has taken note of the same passage ("Is Sympathy so Surprising?," p. 151), but has not noticed that it forms part of a lengthy argument for the preferability of excessive to defective sensibility.

34. Cole argues that whereas women tend on Smith's analysis to share the sufferings of others, Smith felt it necessary to delegitimize such commiseration and replace it with a more positive mode of sympathy--a sharing of the joys of others--that would both validate the inequalities in the existing social hierarchy and provide scope for the positive ambitions of "(upwardly mobile) men." See "(Anti)feminist Sympathies," pp. 112-117; the quote is at p. 117. But the passages just cited, and others that could be added, are useful reminders that the ability to share joys and sorrows are equally essential elements of sympathy, and that they transcend group boundaries such as those of gender.

"party politics" and of "identification...with power," and is "political" in its reflection of a current consensus. For Kay, "Smith makes morality depend on social opinion." For Dawson, "Smith's ethics supports the status quo," in contrast to the 1798 commentary on it by his admirer Sophie de Grouchy, the marquise de Condorcet, who harbored the worthier aspiration of exploring "how sympathy can be...used to build a better world."[35]

But the author of the *Wealth of Nations* can scarcely be accused of complacency about the status quo. He did believe, however, that political or social reform could only keep pace with moral development. The late Friedrich Hayek once remarked that "the rules of conduct evolved by individuals are the source from which collective political action derives what moral standards it possesses,"[36] a statement with which Smith would probably have agreed. "What institution of government," he asked, "could tend so much to promote the happiness of mankind as the general prevalence of wisdom and virtue? All government is but an imperfect remedy for the deficiency of these." (*TMS*, IV.2.1) Indeed, Smith's theory of civilizational development suggests that the capacity of a state to construct fair and impartial institutions depends ultimately upon the ability of its people to achieve a moral order that embodies the transcendent potential of the impartial spectator.

More specifically, Smith's language of the virtues, far from wedding him to the status quo, provided a means whereby the "impartial observer" of social reality could begin to transcend any status quo. Virtues such as humanity and self-command, which contain their own complex array of duties and possibilities, intimate standards of judgment for any given social practice. Moreover the virtue of humanity, though it begins in the domestic sphere, only reaches its potential when it includes in its embrace the state of which we are a member, and indeed the human race as a whole. (*TMS*, VI.ii.1-2) As such, it cuts across the "public-private" divide, as indeed does self-command.

But there is one virtue for which a rigid public-private distinction is maintained, and that is justice. Because justice can be extorted by the full coercive power of the state, it needs to be scrupulously defined and circumscribed. (*TMS*, II.ii) Failure to appreciate this on the part of feminist commentators arises partly from their predilection for what the

35. Cole, "(Anti)feminist Sympathies," pp. 111, 130-131; Kay, "Canon, Ideology, and Gender," p. 74; Dawson, "Is Sympathy so Surprising?", p. 159. See also Marshall, *The Figure of Theatre*, p. 184.

36. Friedrich A. Hayek, *The Road to Serfdom* (Chicago, 1944), p. 213.

late Michael Oakeshott in another context called the "rationalist fallacy" --namely, the tendency to exaggerate the importance of conscious, deliberate activity in shaping any social order.[37] But of all traditions, the Scottish Enlightenment, with its well-documented interest in the "invisible hand" and the "unintended consequences" of largely unreflective action, is least vulnerable to such an error. Like his confreres, Smith inclined to explain historical evolution by hidden moral and material sinews rather than by Whiggish reference to the purposive domains of law, constitution-building and politics in general.[38] Civil society, with its slow, undramatic development, has done more to bring about deep and meaningful change, in Smith's view, than the heroic and visible efforts of state-founders, legislators, and reformers.[39]

Whether the virtue of "humanity," for example, turns out to be politically conservative or reformist cannot be determined in any general way in advance, but depends upon circumstance.[40] In some contexts, that virtue serves as a necessary check against the coldly calculating "spirit of system" which Smith detected at work toward the end of his life in the French Revolution. (*TMS*, VI.ii.2.15-18) Here, since humanity ties one affectively to actual people with their actual interests, and against the abstract tendency to treat people as pieces on a chessboard, it plays a broadly conservative role. On the other hand, the *Wealth of Nations* evokes "common humanity" in its discussion of appropriate wage levels for the working class.[41] More telling is Smith's remark on slavery in *Theory of Moral Sentiments*. There, he appeals to the presumed humanity of his readers in contrasting the magnanimity of the slave

37. Michael Oakeshott, "Rationalism in Politics," in *Rationalism in Politics and Other Essays*, foreword Timothy Fuller (Indianapolis, 1991; orig. pub. 1962), p. 25 and *passim*.

38. Smith's ironic account of the rise of medieval towns is a famous example. "Having sold their birth-right, not like Esau for a mess of pottage in time of hunger and necessity, but in the wantonness of plenty, for trinkets and baubles, fitter to be the playthings of children than the serious pursuits of men, they [the great landowners of feudal Europe] became as insignificant as any substantial burgher or tradesman in a city." *WN*, III.iv.15.

39. Cole writes of the "political or 'civilizing' impulses" (109) as if the two are synonymous; but on Smith's view, they are not. For two alternative accounts justly stressing the primacy of civil society in Smith's moral vision, see Joseph Cropsey, "Adam Smith and Political Philosophy," in Andrew S. Skinner and Thomas Wilson, eds., *Essays on Adam Smith* (Oxford, 1975), p. 136, and Ronald Hamowy, *The Scottish Enlightenment and the Theory of Spontaneous Order*, foreword Ian Ross (Carbondale, IL, 1987).

40. See *TMS*, IV.ii.2.11, for Smith's classic statement on the need for balance between conservation and reform.

41. *WN*, I.viii.16.

with the baseness of the master. "Fortune never exerted more cruelly her empire over mankind, than when she subjected those nations of heroes to the refuse of the jails of Europe," he writes in a scathing passage, "to wretches who possess the virtues neither of the countries which they come from, nor of those which they go to, and whose levity, brutality, and baseness, so justly expose them to the contempt of the vanquished." (*TMS*, V.2.9) Here, in Smith's typically dynamic fashion, the self-command of the slave draws forth the humanity of the impartial observer, and both virtues together militate toward reform rather than conservation.

IV

The practical implications of the "impartial spectator" for the condition of women are at least marginally clearer in Smith's *Lectures on Jurisprudence* than in *TMS*. The notes to these lectures indicate Smith's awareness of the possibility of male partiality in judging cases involving women. Although their subject matter dictated that the *Lectures on Jurisprudence* would be governed by a discourse of rights rather than the discourse of virtues treated above, the question of sympathy was never far from the surface.[42] Property itself was defined largely in psychological terms as possessions whose claimants commanded the sympathy of the impartial spectator. Thus, after writing that "the only case where the origin of natural rights is not altogether plain, is in that of property," (*LJ*, i.24) Smith evokes *TMS* for an elucidation: "we may conceive an injury was done one when an impartial spectator would be of opinion he was injured, would join with him in his concern and go along with him when he defend[ed] the subject in his possession against any violent attack, or used force to recover what had been thus wrongfully wrested out of his hands." (*LJ*, i.36; see also i.37-43, i.77-78, i.93-94, i.150-151) In stark contrast to the familiar Lockean model, the relational development of moral concepts in Smith's scheme provides property with an essentially relational foundation.[43]

42. The fullest recent treatment of the Scottish school as a whole is Maria Elosegui, "Mujer, Propriedad y Matrimonio en los Ilustrados Escoceses," *Anuario de Filosofía del Derecho* Madrid IX (1991):17-51, esp. 19-34. A useful starting point for Smith's *Lectures on Jurisprudence* is John W. Cairns, "The Influence of Smith's Jurisprudence on Legal Education in Scotland," in *Adam Smith Reviewed*, pp. 168-189, and its bibliography at pp. 186-189.

43. For a fuller discussion, see Haakonssen's *The Science of a Legislator*, pp. 104-111.

In his discussion of marriage customs Smith makes explicit some of the sexual implications of such an impartial-spectator analysis.[44] He criticizes the Romans for having legislated on adultery in such a way as to advance the interests of the men--fathers and husbands--who wrote the laws. The medieval clergy, he remarks with uncharacteristic approbation, were more impartial, and their innovations in the laws of adultery--by which women as well as men could bring charges against an unfaithful spouse--were accordingly more equitable.

Moving from property to sexual relations, the impartial spectator is no less taken by the spectacle of a wife's jealousy and sense of betrayal than by that of a husband. Although convention has given men a condition of economic and social superiority over women, a superiority which accounts for society's tendency to sympathize more with aggrieved husbands, nature--which is more evident in the moral-psychological microcosm of experience than in the socio-economic macrocosm--draws us in the opposite direction. (*LJ*, iii.13-16)[45]

Parenthood is another area where sympathy appears to militate toward a moral equality in the status of the sexes. The chief task of parents is to instruct their children in the proper modulation of their sentiments. Each parent has an equally important share in the teaching of this process. "[T]he child being dependent on the parents is obliged... to yield its will to theirs, to bring down its passions and curb its desires to such a pitch as they can go along with." (*LJ*, 142) This lesson in self-command, taught by both parents to children of both sexes as an indispensable feature of social propriety, belongs in that realm of the universally human that transcends gender.

Smith applies the same principles to his extended treatment of polygamy and monogamy.[46] Although most of the arguments in this

44. *Ibid.*, pp. 123-127.

45. See also William Robertson, *The Progress of Society in Europe*, ed. and intro. Felix Gilbert (Chicago, 1972), pp. 52-54, although Robertson does not single out adultery law as one of his examples of the beneficent, if unintended, effects of ecclesiastical jurisprudence.

46. Polygamy had attracted the attention of natural jurisprudence at least since the great natural-law theorists of the seventeenth century. With his usual thoroughness Pufendorf enumerated the arguments for and against regarding the practice as a violation of natural law, ultimately "leaving the decision to the reader." See Samuel Pufendorf, *De jure naturæ et gentium, libri octo*, trans. C.H. and W.A. Oldfather (Oxford, 1934; from the ed. of 1688), Vol. 2, bk. vi, ch. 1, sect. 16-19. While ostensibly neutral on the question, Pufendorf concludes by stressing the natural disadvantages of polygamy by comparison with monogamy. This would set the pattern for much eighteenth-century reflection on the subject, especially in the natural-law tradition. Whereas Mandeville drew on skeptical

connection are traditional, what is distinctive is the way he again appeals to the psycho-social theory in *TMS* to make his case. The first criterion by which he assesses these customs concerns their effects upon the sympathy-structures, so to speak, prevailing in their respective societies. In this regard, jealousy is more intrinsic to polygamy than to monogamy. Because the affection and sympathy a man has for any one of his wives cannot be as unstinting as that of any of the latter toward him, the inequity in the system of sympathy leads naturally to female jealousy. (*LJ* [A], iii.25) Conversely, even the man who seems favored in such an arrangement must be afflicted with jealousy, namely in his relations with other men. The "free communication and society" (*LJ* [A], iii.32) essential both to the pleasure of civilized life and ultimately to political liberty can only be assured by guaranteeing the equality of men. But human nature assures that this equality can only be achieved by preserving a moral equality between men and women.[47] Thus, his naturalistic justification for Western monogamy rests on an inclusion of women within the moral community.

V

Far from being on the Stoic or masculinist edge of contemporary thought on the condition of women, Smith's discourse of "humanity" should be seen as part of a remarkably consistent tendency across the Scottish Enlightenment to connect the spread of commercial culture to the diffusion of sympathy, and to relate both in broadly positive ways to the changing condition of women. His use of the virtues as an idiom for articulating a modernist, non-Rousseauian social analysis was a prevalent one. Hume, for example, in an essay directed (ironically) at his female readers, cites one of the purposes of the study of history: "To remark the rise, progress, declension, and final extinction of the most flourishing empires: The virtues, which contributed to their greatness,

assumptions to suggest that polygamy was regarded as wrong only in those societies where custom so teaches ("A Search into the Nature of Society," in *Fable of the Bees*, I, 330), both Hume and Montesquieu took the opposite view.

47. This same tension between human nature and history—and between sexual equality in the one case and sexual subordination in the other—appears in Smith's discussion of chastity in *TMS*, VII.iv.21.

and the vices, which drew on their ruin."[48] John Millar of Glasgow, Smith's student, described his own intellectual purpose as an historian in nearly identical terms: "to compare the predominant virtues and vices of the different periods of society."[49] William Robertson, who was thought by some contemporaries, though not necessarily by Smith, to have plagiarized from the latter's lectures on jurisprudence, argued that medieval Europeans had slipped into barbarism by abandoning the virtues of self-command and generosity associated with the "simple state" of "uncivilized nations" without yet having acquired that "degree of refinement" produced by commercial society.[50]

The Scottish treatment of progress, however, was far from teleological. There was a tendency to regard change as involving a mixture of gain and loss. In his second *Inquiry* Hume captures this spirit when he contrasts the style of virtue available to ancients and moderns. The "grandeur and force of sentiment" of ancient virtue, he writes, "astonishes our narrow souls," while they in turn would find "incredible" the "humanity, clemency...and other social virtues" characteristic of modern times. "Such is the compensation," he blandly concludes, "which nature, or rather education, has made in the distribution of excellencies and virtues, in those different ages."[51] On balance, though, women are as much as men the beneficiaries of whatever positive changes modernity has brought.

One of the implications of this contrast between modern and premodern concerns the place of women in an expanding moral community. In his essay in defense of luxury Hume evokes "the spirit of the age" to depict a general process of "refinement" as the thread connecting improvements in science and technology, the arts, social relations, and politics. In such improving times, he writes,

48. David Hume, "On the Study of History," in *Essays Moral, Political, and Literary*, ed. Eugene F. Miller (Indianapolis, 1987), p. 566. The essay was withdrawn after the 1760 edition.

49. John Millar of Glasgow, *Historical View of English Government*, 4 vols. (London, 1818), v. 4, p. 175.

50. See *The Progress of Society in Europe*, p. 21. For the plagiarism question, see *Correspondence of Adam Smith*, ed. E.C. Mossner and I.S. Ross (Oxford, 1977; repr. 1987), n. 2, p. 192.

51. David Hume, "An Enquiry Concerning the Principles of Morals," in *Enquiries*, 3rd ed., intro. L.A. Selby-Rigge, rev. P.H. Nidditch (Oxford, 1975; repr. from the 1777 ed.), sect. vii, pp. 256-257. It is particularly interesting, in light of the discussion above, to note that Hume finds these modern virtues "in the administration of government."

> Both sexes meet in an easy and sociable manner; and the tempers of men, as well as their behaviour, refine apace. So that, beside the improvements which they receive from knowledge and the liberal arts, it is impossible but they must feel an encrease of humanity, from the very habit of conversing together, and contributing to each other's pleasure and entertainment. Thus, *industry, knowledge,* and *humanity,* are linked together by an indissoluble chain, and are found...to be peculiar to the more polished, and...luxurious ages.[52]

The Scot who most systematically thought about the changing condition of women was John Millar. Politically more engaged than Smith but theoretically not unsophisticated, Millar provides a revealing variation on themes learned from his teacher.[53] By his own well-known account, Millar "had the benefit of hearing his [Smith's] lectures on the History of Civil Society and of enjoying his unreserved conversation on the subject."[54]

In a series of essays published posthumously by his executors as part of his *Historical View of English Government,* Millar offered an unusually explicit application of virtues-discourse to historical analysis. He began by decrying Rousseau's "paradoxical" preference for primitive over modern society. To achieve a posture of impartiality, he proposed judging the respective strengths and weaknesses of primitive and civilized societies according to their nurturing of, on his own analysis, three sets of virtues: courage and fortitude, sobriety and temperance, justice and generosity. Thus, like his teacher, Millar regarded the virtues as furnishing at least part of an objective standard by which to evaluate the norms and customs of any society.

52. Hume, "Of Refinement in the Arts," in *Essays,* p. 271. The work was originally entitled "Of Luxury." (Emphasis in original) Hume's view of sexual equality is of course considerably more complicated than this brief summary indicates. A recent treatment is Annette C. Baier, "Hume on Women's Complexion," in *The Science of Man in the Scottish Enlightenment,* ed. Peter Jones (Edinburgh, 1990), pp. 33-53. See also "The Mirror," in *The British Essayists,* ed. James Ferguson Esq., 2nd ed. (London, 1823), 40 vols., v. 29, no. 58.

53. A starting point for this important but enigmatic figure is Michael Ignatieff, "John Millar and Individualism," in Hont and Ignatieff, *Wealth and Virtue,* pp. 317-345, which contains a useful summary of the range of recent interpretations. Ignatieff makes some acute criticisms of what he calls "anticipatory" readings of Millar in the light of nineteenth-century developments, esp. pp. 317-324.

54. Millar, *Historical View of English Government,* II, pp. 429-430, note. Millar is referring here to the lectures on jurisprudence.

Whether the condition of a group of people--as judged by their capacity for exercising these or other virtues--is improved or worsened by something so all-encompassing as the "rise of commercial society" cannot, on Millar's account, be stated in simple terms. Although the argument has recently been made that Millar was optimistic about the public sphere under capitalism, reserving his doubts for the effects of commercialism on the private sphere,[55] it might be truer to say that Millar optimistically assessed commercial society relative to its predecessor stages while drawing upon an eclectic language of the virtues to assess its dangers and shortcomings in all areas, private and public alike.

To take one example: even though he admired the virtue of generosity, Millar saw it as more appropriate for another age. He wrote that conditions of commercial society are "unfavourable to generosity," because that virtue is "the fruit of a violent impulse" contrary to the "tone of moderation" called for in a civilized country.[56] Courage, however, held a complex position in modern society. This virtue, by which Millar means bravery and which he carefully distinguishes from fortitude or self-command, is on the one hand more likely in modern than in primitive society; it is a public virtue that requires the sympathy and approbation of one's fellows, a sympathy prevalent in modern society. But on the other hand, as commerce implicates an ever wider sector of the population in the "arts of peace," the social demand for courage declines, and with it the capacity for the virtue itself.[57]

The *plebs* in the public sphere are affected by similarly conflicting pressures. A heightened sensitivity to rights increases their demand for justice; indeed the virtue of justice becomes better developed in the commercial age. But the atrophy of courage makes commoners reluctant to push their claims to the limit, so that a timely show of force by a prudent government can usually keep them under control, since "[t]he wealth of each individual is a pledge for his quiet and orderly behaviour." Unlike Tocqueville two generations later, Millar concludes that such a docile people will nonetheless mount "a vigorous opposition

55. Ignatieff, "John Millar and Individualism," p. 342 and *passim*.

56. *Historical View of the English Government*, IV, p. 246.

57. *Historical View of English Government*, IV, pp. 178-180, 185-187. In the course of this analysis Millar unravels Hume's confident "spirit of the age" notion of "industry, knowledge and humanity" all rising together as part of a single process of "refinement."

to such acts of tyranny as are manifestly subversive of the fundamental rights of mankind."[58]

The gender implications of this analysis are equally complex and nuanced. While courage is more common among men, subject to the qualification just mentioned, fortitude or self-command is actually more likely to be found among women. This is because fortitude, which as Smith had argued is less prevalent in modern society, becomes necessary by the "want of humanity" on the part of one's intimates, a deficiency women are less apt to experience than men. Far from being a contradiction of Smith's notion of the "manhood of self-command"--a figure of speech well tailored for the teenage boys in Smith's philosophy classes--what Millar offers is an example of its complex relationship with "humanity."[59]

But to understand the framework in which Millar situates his view of the history of women, it is necessary to return to the earlier *Origin of Ranks*.[60] In that work Millar uses the four-stages theory learned from Smith's lectures. The evolution toward a commercial order, he argues, fosters conditions conducive to a regime of liberty such as had developed in Britain since 1688. He traces the evolution of several phenomena to illustrate this argument--chief among them being the condition of women (treated first), the forms of paternal and tribal authority, and the institutions of domestic servitude and slavery. The practical orientation of his enterprise is well expressed toward the conclusion: "[A]ccording as men have made greater progress in commerce and the arts, the establishment of domestic freedom is of greater importance;...in opulent and polished nations, its influence extends to the great body of the people,...whose comfortable situation ought never to be overlooked in the provisions that are made for national happiness."[61]

The rise of commerce, Millar makes clear, is as broadly beneficial to the condition of women as it is, say, to the poor. On his Whiggish

58. *Historical View of English Government*, IV, pp. 200-201. The reasons for Millar's optimism on this point remain unclear.

59. *Historical View of English Government*, IV, pp. 178-181, 185-186.

60. "On the Origin of the Distinction of Ranks," in *John Millar of Glasgow, 1735-1801: His Life and Thought and His Contributions to Sociological Analysis*, ed. William C. Lehmann (Cambridge, 1960); hereafter cited as *Origin of Ranks*. Originally published in 1771, it is the third edition of 1779 that Lehmann reprints. For a different approach to this subject, see Paul Bowles, "John Millar, the Four-Stages Theory, and Women's Position in Society," *History of Political Economy* 16 (1984): 619-638.

61. *Origin of Ranks*, p. 316.

account of this topic,[62] the patriarchal authority inherited from previous eras is weakened by the natural tendencies of commercial society in at least three different but related ways: First, as the spread of prosperity brings the "pleasurable arts" close to the merely "useful arts" in status, a "free communication between the sexes" is approximated and a "taste for refined and elegant amusement" develops, bringing disproportionate benefit to women.[63] Second, the diversification of economic opportunities makes children less dependent upon the father; it therefore tends to "raise the members of his family to a state of freedom and independence." Third, within the family itself as general prosperity widens the circle of sociability, the father learns the rules of daily civility that characterize a complex society and which limit his occasions to invoke paternal authority. "Being often engaged in the business and conversation of the world, and finding, in many cases, the necessity of conforming to the humours of those with whom he converses, he becomes less impatient of contradiction, and less apt to give way to the irregular sallies of passion."[64] Male self-command, then, is a quiet and unintended by-product of a commercial order.

The dangers to moral order posed by an overly "opulent and luxurious" country such as imperial Rome or modern Britain--the loss of marital fidelity brought on by license, the reduction of marriage to monetary considerations, and the like--which are the subject of polemic warnings in Millar's later work, should be seen in this context.[65] They qualify without erasing the historical improvements chronicled in his earlier writing. If these posthumously published essays fail to carry the conviction of his earlier work, perhaps it was because Millar replaced the broad canvas of the four-stages theory for the cramped space of the bully pulpit.[66] Even at his moralistic worst, however, Millar never

62. For a discussion of the "skeptical" and "scientific" dimensions of Millar's Whiggism, see Ignatieff, "John Millar and Individualism," pp. 326-332. J.G.A. Pocock views him as a typical example of "Scottish scientific Whiggism" in his "The Varieties of Whiggism from Exclusion to Reform: A History of Ideology and Discourse," in *Virtue, Commerce, and History* (Cambridge, 1985), p. 298.

63. *Origin of Ranks*, p. 239. This "free communication" restores the condition of the earliest societies, only now with the substantial additions of friendship and settled property. See also "The Advancement of Manufactures, Commerce, and the Arts, since the Reign of William III; and the Tendency of this Advancement to Diffuse a Spirit of Liberty and Independency," in *Historical View* IV, pp. 102-137.

64. *Origin of Ranks*, pp. 238-239.

65. *Ibid.*, p. 225.

66. Ignatieff also points out (342-343) that the *Edinburgh Reviewers* found them lacking in the depth of historical scholarship displayed in Millar's earlier work.

passed into the sort of sexual nostalgia that beguiled so many during his time, at home and on the Continent, where the French Revolution waged war against many of the trends he had so deftly charted.[67]

Conclusion

No more than his "moderate" Scottish contemporaries did Adam Smith craft a moral theory designed to relegate virtue in general or the "female" virtue of "humanity" in particular to the shadows of domesticity.[68] Nor did the arena of public ambition--where the participants were observably more likely to be men than women in his time--hold the stark superiority for him that it possessed for the classical theorists by whom he was most influenced.[69] His theory of historical development committed him to the view that the life choices ordinary people make in private are as important to the happiness of the species as its public decisions. It was precisely this fact, in conjunction with his belief in the ability of the moral imagination to transcend immediate interests, that gave larger social and even political significance to his moral theory.

The core of this theory was an attempt, not uncommon in the Scottish Enlightenment, to reconcile a system of virtues drawn in deliberately eclectic fashion from classical philosophy, on the one hand, with the peculiar demands of modern commercial society, on the other. As Millar's case reminds us, this language of the virtues is full of pitfalls for the modern interpreter. For example, generosity, by Smith's definition a masculine virtue, is not to be confused with self-command in the way that feminists have sometimes done. Although generosity is more in demand in archaic, warrior-based societies than in commercial ones where humanity is more at home, the case with self-command is more complex. Traditionally, self-command functioned to control the selfish passions, (*TMS*, I.i.5.5) and Smith was enough of an historian to

67. See Ignatieff, "John Millar and Individualism," pp. 332-335.

68. The standard account of the values of this milieu is Richard B. Sher, *Church and University in the Scottish Enlightenment* (Princeton, 1985).

69. Cole ("[Anti]feminist sympathies," p. 114) would have Smith relegating commiseration to women and privileging a more positive sympathy for socially ambitious men. But as Rendall points out ("Virtue and Commerce," p. 61), "women were by no means exempt" from such social ambition on Smith's account.

know which of the two sexes had done more damage to social order by indulging these in the past. But as commercial society increasingly validated the indulgence of self-interest, the pursuit of individual happiness, and the sharing of one's sentiments with others, it stood to reason that the duties of self-command would soften and diversify in turn.[70]

If on occasion Smith seems to tilt more toward self-command, this was not because he thought it more useful or agreeable than humanity. It was rather because he regarded humanity as the naturally dominant partner in modern society. Like Burke he searched for (moral) equipoise. Perhaps he was afraid of a public life in which people competed in expressing their discontents or in bemoaning alien miseries they could do little about. In a global society of strangers, in which the claims of one's fellows on our sympathy are in principle limitless, in which the sufferings even of faraway Chinamen might be brought to one's attention at any moment,[71] he does seem to have envisioned a certain regulation of compassion, a certain principle of propriety, as necessary to sound individual and social health and as a therapy for the Rousseauian neurosis of aimless and undiscriminating affect. In the face of such a politics of sensibility, perhaps he feared that moral self-government would erode, bringing down its corollary capacity for political self-government.[72]

But setting such speculation aside, Smith clearly exhibited particular concern about the coldly calculating utopians he saw appear in the era of the French Revolution. Their "spirit of system," their willingness to treat their fellows as abstract pieces on a chessboard, were not in the interests of either conservation or reform. The danger they posed to the achievements of civilized society could best be checked, he thought, by appealing precisely to his readers' sense of humanity. He did not live quite long enough to encounter Burke's assertion that revolutionary politics "harden the breast" against normal feelings of humanity, but he thought in similar categories because he helped develop them.[73]

70. See the suggestive discussion of the modernity of Smithian self-command in Jerry Z. Muller, *Designing the Decent Society* (New York, 1993).

71. *TMS*, III.3.4-5 for the famous case of the Chinese earthquake. For some stimulating reflections on the moral implications of eighteenth-century commercialism, see Thomas Haskell, "Capitalism and the Humanitarian Sensibility," *American Historical Review* 90 (1985): 339-361.

72. I hope to address this problem in more detail in an essay on "Compassion and Liberty in Adam Smith's Moral Theory" in the near future.

73. Edmund Burke, *Reflections on the Revolution in France* (New York, 1973), p. 77.

Whether his particular "balance of the affections" (*TMS*, VII.ii.4.2) measured up to the real needs of eighteenth-century modernity--and whether his assessment of that modernity has anything to say to us today--is of course another question; but the historian should at least see that some such balance was his goal.

[19]

Smith, Turgot, and the "Four Stages" Theory

Ronald L. Meek

I

In the good old days, when I was a fierce young Marxist instead of a benign middle-aged Meeksist, I became very interested in the work of the members of the so-called Scottish historical school, which Roy Pascal rescued from oblivion in his famous article of 1938.[1] I was impressed in particular by John Millar, whose work was pervaded by a theory of history and society which seemed to me to be a kind of preview of the materialist conception of history upon which I had been brought up. I was interested also, of course, in the work of the other members of the school—notably that of Adam Ferguson, William Robertson, and Adam Smith; but these three seemed to be rather shadowy and peripheral figures in the face of the gigantic presence of the great John Millar.

The basic ideas which I detected, or thought I detected, in the work of Millar and his associates taken as a whole were roughly as follows, to proceed from the more to the less general:

1. Everything in society and in history was bound together by a succession of causes and effects. Thus the task of the historian was to seek for reasons and causes, with the aid of the new scientific methodology which had already proved so fruitful in other spheres of enquiry.
2. Society developed blindly, but not arbitrarily. As Ferguson put it: "Every step and every movement of the multitude, even in what are termed enlightened ages, are made with equal blindness to the future; and nations stumble upon establishments, which are indeed the result of human action, but not

Dr. Meek *is Professor of Economics at the University of Leicester.*

1. Roy Pascal, "Property and Society: The Scottish Historical School of the Eighteenth Century," *Modern Quarterly*, March 1938.

the execution of any human design.''[2] But social changes did occur, and in the process of change certain uniformities and regularities were observable. The great task was to explain these, in terms of the *laws* which lay behind social development.

3. In the process of development the key factor was the ''mode of subsistence.'' As Robertson said: ''In every inquiry concerning the operations of men when united in society, the first object of attention should be their mode of subsistence. According as that varies, their laws and policy must be different.''[3]
4. In tracing out the process of development, particular emphasis should be placed on the reciprocal interconnection between property and government. Smith put the point magistrally: ''Property and civil government very much depend on one another. The preservation of property and the inequality of possession first formed it, and the state of property must always vary with the form of government.''[4]
5. Emphasis should also be placed on the emergence and growth of a social surplus, upon which depended the rise of towns, the arts, manufactures, new social classes, etc.
6. Development should be regarded as proceeding through four normally consecutive stages, each based on a particular ''mode of subsistence''—viz., hunting, pasturage, agriculture, and commerce. To each stage there corresponded different ideas and institutions relating to property; to each there corresponded different ideas and institutions relating to government; and in relation to each, general statements could be made about the state of manners and morals, the social surplus, the legal system, the division of labor, etc.

All these ideas were tied up together with a sensationalist psychology or theory of knowledge, derived in one way or another from Locke; and even making allowances for my youthful ardor, I do not think I was all that wrong in describing this theoretical system as *a,* if not *the,* materialist conception of history.

2. Adam Ferguson, *Essay on the History of Civil Society,* 6th ed. (London, 1793), p. 205.

3. William Robertson, *The History of America* (Edinburgh, 1777), 1:324.

4. Adam Smith, *Lectures on Justice, Police, Revenue and Arms,* ed. Edwin Cannan (Oxford, 1896), p. 8.

At this stage of my life I misguidedly regarded myself as a kind of naturalized Scot, and it was thus with a glow of patriotic pride that I proclaimed the emergence of this theoretical system as an exclusively Scottish phenomenon, explaining its origin in terms of the rather special social and economic situation of Scotland at the time.[5] When I started working on the French Physiocrats, however, I soon realized that this was too insular a view. For Quesnay and Mirabeau, as well, had put forward *a* materialist conception of history. When you knew what you were looking for, it was there as clear as crystal, not only in Quesnay's marginal notes on Mirabeau's early economic manuscripts but also in cold print, particularly in chapter 8 of *Rural Philosophy* (1763) and in *Natural Right* (1765).[6] And when Skinner revealed the existence of a rather similar set of ideas in the work of Sir James Steuart—who had had, so to speak, a foot on either side of the English Channel—this seemed finally to confirm that the phenomenon in question was in fact a joint Scottish and French one.

A little later I embarked upon two editorial jobs, upon which I am still engaged. The first of these relates to the new set of student's notes of Adam Smith's Glasgow lectures on jurisprudence which was discovered a few years ago in Aberdeen.[7] The second relates to certain early "sociological" works written by the young Turgot during his period at the Sorbonne.[8] Carrying out these two editorial jobs more or less simultaneously, I naturally looked at the Scottish and French material concerned to see if there were any traces in it of

5. See my *Economics and Ideology and Other Essays* (London, 1967), pp. 47–8.

6. See my *Economics of Physiocracy* (London, 1962), pp. 43–71.

7. I am editing these notes jointly with Professor D. Raphael, of Reading University, and Professor P. Stein, of Cambridge University, for the forthcoming bicentenary edition of Smith's *Works and Correspondence.* The views expressed in the present article, however, are mine alone, and neither of my two collaborators should be held responsible for them.

8. I hasten to say that the present article is not meant as a contribution to the so-called Turgot-Smith controversy, which is now just about as stale as bimetallism. It is true that I shall be impliedly claiming that the Turgot-Smith controversialists have overlooked one of the most important of the new ideas developed and held in common by Turgot and Smith. But the idea in question was more "sociological" than "economic" in character, and in any event the two men almost certainly developed it quite independently of one another—two facts which take what I have to say right outside the orbit of the traditional controversy. (I reserve the right, however, to prove incontrovertibly in a subsequent article that Smith was the author of the famous translation of Turgot's Six Edicts into Sanskrit.)

the view of history and society in which I was interested. It was not necessary, I soon found, to look very far. Almost immediately it became evident that two further reorientations of my notions were going to be required.

First, it was clear from the new set of notes of Smith's jurisprudence lectures that those of us who had put Smith down as a more or less peripheral member of the Scottish historical school were simply wrong. Although our editorial work on the new notes is not yet completed, it can at least be said that the set of basic ideas outlined above appears more clearly, extensively, and sharply in the new notes than it does in the Cannan notes.[9] In particular, the "four stages" theory is given considerable prominence; it is perhaps not too much to say that it is revealed as the basic conceptual framework within which the major part of Smith's argument is set.

It was with new eyes, therefore, that I went back to Dugald Stewart's biographical memoir of Smith to reread the contemporary descriptions of his Glasgow lectures which it contains. In the account of the lectures supplied to Stewart by Millar, the following passage relating to the section on justice occurs:

> Upon this subject he followed the plan that seems to be suggested by Montesquieu; endeavouring to trace the gradual progress of jurisprudence, both public and private, from the rudest to the most refined ages, and to point out the effects of those arts which contribute to subsistence, and to the accumulation of property, in producing correspondent improvements or alterations in law and government.[10]

I must confess that I had always thought that in this passage Millar was exaggerating a little, perhaps describing more what he would have liked to see in Smith's lectures than what was actually there. With the new notes in front of one, however, the accuracy of Millar's

9. The new notes do not extend as far as the Cannan notes—they stop short in the middle of the economics section—but most of the material up to there is found in the new notes in greatly expanded form. My provisional hypothesis is that the new notes are a student's transcription of *shorthand* notes taken down by him in class during the 1762–63 session.

10. Dugald Stewart, *Biographical Memoir of Adam Smith* (Kelley reprint; New York, 1966), p. 12.

description is rather spectacularly confirmed. And one can also better appreciate the significance of that remarkable section of the memoir[11] in which Stewart talks for several pages about Smith's great interest in "Theoretical or Conjectural History," which is claimed to have pervaded most of his writings, his conversation, and in particular his lectures on jurisprudence.

This line of inquiry, says Stewart, began with Montesquieu, who "attempted to account, from the changes in the condition of mankind, which take place in the different stages of their progress, for the corresponding alterations which their institutions undergo."[12] As a description of Montesquieu's approach this is a little inept: very few traces of a stadial view of this type can in fact be found in *L'esprit des lois.* As a description of Smith's approach, however, it is very accurate indeed; and the passage as a whole enables us to understand better Millar's famous statement that if Montesquieu was the Lord Bacon in this field of enquiry, Adam Smith was the Newton.[13] The moral of all this, surely, is that it would be unwise to underestimate the seminal character of Smith's own contribution in this field and the extent to which he influenced the other members of the school, including Millar himself.

The second reorientation of my notions which was required became clear when I passed from a reading of the new lecture notes to a reading of those early writings of Turgot which I had undertaken to edit. What suddenly became obvious to me was the crucial role which the "four stages" theory must have played in the emergence of the new Franco-Scottish view of sociohistorical development.

My starting point here was the two lectures which the young Turgot gave at the Sorbonne in 1750, the second of which is quite well known because of the doctrine of perfectibility which is clearly stated in it. Much more important, however, is another document, dating apparently from the same period, entitled "Plan of Two Discourses on Universal History."[14] Here we find many of the ingredients of the new view, including most notably a quite advanced

11. Ibid., pp. 32–37.

12. Ibid., p. 35.

13. John Millar, *An Historical View of the English Government* (London, 1787), p. 528.

14. *Œuvres de Turgot,* ed. Schelle, 1 (Paris, 1913): 275 ff.

statement of the "four stages" theory—or at any rate of a "three stages" theory, with a distinct hint of the fourth stage. Hunting, pasturage, and agriculture are very clearly defined and distinguished, and Turgot describes the way in which population, property, slavery, the social surplus, the system of government, etc., change as mankind proceeds from one stage to the next. The development of this idea in Turgot's mind during the two or three years immediately prior to its mature expression in this document can up to a point be traced, but this is not the place for such an exercise. Suffice it to say that in the "Plan" (and in one or two other documents composed by Turgot at this time), the stadial view of social development is beginning to become a kind of general conceptual framework, in much the same way as it did in Smith's lectures on jurisprudence.

This rather startling fact led me to realize that I had hitherto tended to underestimate the role of the "four stages" idea in the emergence of the eighteenth-century version of the materialist conception. This idea was not, it now appeared, a kind of end product, a particular proposition which emerged after a more general proposition had been developed and applied. Rather, after Montesquieu's very vague hints about the possibility and necessity of a new science of society, it was the idea whose emergence made the further development of such a science feasible.[15]

II

On the assumption, then, that the "four stages" theory was in fact much more important than has generally been appreciated, let us try to construct a kind of calendar of its development. The great problem here is where we should put Smith. Let us therefore proceed as if Smith had not existed, leaving until later the question of where he should be fitted in.

The first date on our calendar is 1750/51, when Turgot's contributions appear to have been written.[16] I have tried fairly diligently

15. I would have got on to this a lot earlier if I had treated with the respect they deserved a number of inspired hints in the early pages of Duncan Forbes's article "'Scientific' Whiggism: Adam Smith and John Millar," *Cambridge Journal* 7, no. 11 (1954):643–70.

16. Turgot's first specific reference to the idea would appear to be in some

to find earlier expressions of the "four stages" theory or of ideas closely akin to it, but much to my own surprise have failed. I can find nothing, for example, in the Greeks, Cantillon, Mandeville, Bolingbroke, Hume, Hutcheson, Voltaire, Priestley, or Montesquieu which could really be said to rank as a definite anticipation. All I have been able to discover are certain fairly general lines of thought which could conceivably have led, either directly or indirectly, to the emergence of the theory round about 1750. (These lines of thought are discussed at the end of the present article.) But the theory as such would seem to have no ancestors.

If we are prepared to skip over Rousseau—which I feel we are obliged to do by our terms of reference—the second date on our calendar must surely be 1757, when the celebrated interview took place between Quesnay and Mirabeau at Versailles. Mirabeau's account of this meeting[17] is no doubt highly suspect, but from what he says it seems at least probable that the idea of a more or less orderly progression through the hunting, pasturage, and agricultural stages had by this time come to occupy an important place in Quesnay's theoretical system.

The third date on our calendar, marked by what appears to be the first expression *in print* of the new idea, is 1758, the year in which Lord Kames's *Historical Law-Tracts* was published.[18] The "four stages" theory appears suddenly in the form of a lengthy footnote in the first essay in the book, that on the history of the criminal law.[19] It comes in again at the beginning of the second essay, on the history of promises and covenants,[20] and in the third essay, on the history of property, it becomes all-pervasive. In the earlier works of Kames, so far as I can see, there were no more than the vaguest hints of the idea, even in contexts where one would most have expected to find it (e.g., in discussions of property).

---

remarks on a book by Maupertuis dated 9 March 1750. *Œuvres,* 1:172. The "Plan of Two Discourses on Universal History," according to Schelle, dates from "vers 1751."

17. In a letter to Rousseau written about ten years afterwards. See my *Economics of Physiocracy,* pp. 16–18.

18. Although not published until 1758, it seems probable that Kames's book was started, and parts finished, several years earlier. Cf. Alexander F. Tytler, *Memoirs of Kames,* 2d ed. (Edinburgh, 1814), 1:299.

19. Kames, pp. 77–80.

20. Kames, pp. 92–93.

The fourth date is 1763, the year in which Quesnay and Mirabeau published their *Rural Philosophy.* In chapter 8 of this book there is a very explicit statement of the hunting-pasturage-agriculture idea, which is linked up clearly with the more general notion that everything is subordinate to the means of subsistence.[21]

After this our calendar becomes very crowded. In the late 1760s and early 1770s the mature works of the Scottish historical school began to appear—Ferguson's *Essay on the History of Civil Society* in 1767, Robertson's *History of the Reign of the Emperor Charles V* in 1769,[22] and Millar's *Observations Concerning the Distinction of Ranks in Society* in 1771; and other important works by authors associated with the school soon followed—notably, in 1774, Kames's *Sketches of the History of Man.* In most of these works the "four stages" theory was used as an important frame of reference and linked up with some or all of the other ideas listed in the first part of this essay to form one or another variant of the "materialist conception of history" of the eighteenth century.

III

The missing piece in this jigsaw puzzle is obviously Smith. Whereabouts ought his contribution to be fitted in? All that we really know for certain is that in the lectures on jurisprudence which he gave at Glasgow University *in 1762–63* (the session to which the newly found notes specifically refer) he made extensive use of the "four stages" theory. But, of course, he had begun lecturing to the moral philosophy class at Glasgow as early as October 1751; and for three years before that he had given his famous public lectures in Edinburgh. From which period, then, does Smith's use of the "four stages" theory in fact date? It is unlikely that we shall ever find an absolutely certain answer to this question, but I think it is possible to move some distance towards one by the use of a little "Theoretical or Conjectural History" of our own. What I hope to suggest, with its aid, is that

21. See my *Economics of Physiocracy,* pp. 57–64. The first part of the chapter bears a striking resemblance to a passage in Smith's lectures (cf. Cannan ed., pp. 159–61).

22. Robertson's *History of Scotland* had already appeared in 1759.

Smith's use of the "four stages" theory *probably* dates from the latter part of his Edinburgh period.

Our starting point here is Millar's description of the "Justice" section of Smith's moral philosophy lectures at Glasgow, which I have already quoted above (cf. note 10). From the context, and from certain other considerations, it seems very probable that Millar's description related to the lectures as Smith delivered them during his earliest years as a professor at Glasgow, which was when Millar himself attended them;[23] and all things considered, it seems likely that the form and content of this particular part of the course were not essentially different in those early years from what they were in 1762–63. It is very probable, then, that Smith was putting forward the "four stages" theory in his moral philosophy lectures at Glasgow at any rate by 1755—a date which, as we shall see immediately, is quite crucial.

In 1755, Stewart tells us, Smith drew up, and "presented . . . to a society of which he was then a member," a "short manuscript" giving "a pretty long enumeration . . . of certain leading principles, both political and literary, to which he was anxious to establish his exclusive right." The context in which Stewart's account of this paper appears is a discussion of the originality or otherwise of the doctrines of the *Wealth of Nations,* with particular reference to the question of whether the Physiocrats anticipated Smith's views on the freedom of trade and industry. Stewart reminds his listeners that "Mr. Smith's Political Lectures, comprehending the fundamental principles of his *Inquiry,* were delivered at Glasgow as early as the year 1752 or 1753; at a period, surely, when there existed no French performance on the subject, that could be of much use to him in guiding his researches."[24] Shortly afterwards there follows the ac-

23. The most important piece of evidence on these points is John Craig's account of Millar's early contacts with Smith at Glasgow. See the "Account of the Life and Writings of John Millar, Esq." prefixed to the 4th ed. of Millar's book, *The Origin of the Distinction of Ranks* (Edinburgh, 1806), pp. iv–v. If one reads this in conjunction with the description of Smith's lectures given by Millar to Stewart, and with the acknowledgment of his obligation to Smith made by Millar in his *Historical View of the English Government* (see above, n. 13), it is difficult not to reach the conclusions stated in the text.

24. Stewart, *Memoir of Adam Smith,* p. 66. In a long note to this section written in 1810 (pp. 88–95) Stewart states that when his memoir was first written he "was not fully aware to what an extent the French Economists had been

count of the "short manuscript," which is so important that it must be reproduced in full:

> I am aware that the evidence I have hitherto produced of Mr. Smith's originality may be objected to as not perfectly decisive, as it rests entirely on the recollection of those students who attended his first courses of Moral Philosophy at Glasgow; a recollection which, at the distance of forty years, cannot be supposed to be very accurate. There exists, however, fortunately, a short manuscript drawn up by Mr. Smith in the year 1755, and presented by him to a society of which he was then a member; in which paper, a pretty long enumeration is given of certain leading principles, both political and literary, to which he was anxious to establish his exclusive right, in order to prevent the possibility of some rival claims which he thought he had reason to apprehend, and to which his situation as a Professor, added to his unreserved communications in private companies, rendered him peculiarly liable. This paper is at present in my possession. It is expressed with a good deal of that honest and indignant warmth, which is perhaps unavoidable by a man who is conscious of the purity of his own intentions, when he suspects that advantages have been taken of the frankness of his temper. On such occasions, due allowances are not always made for those plagiarisms, which, however cruel in their effects, do not necessarily imply bad faith in those who are guilty of them; for the bulk of mankind, incapable themselves of original thought, are perfectly unable to form a conception of the nature of the injury done to a man of inventive genius, by encroaching on a favourite speculation. For reasons known to some members of this Society, it would be improper by the publication of this manuscript, to revive the memory of private differences; and I should not have even alluded to it, if I did not think it a valuable document of the

anticipated in some of their most important conclusions, by writers (chiefly British) of a much earlier date." He still defends Smith's originality, however; and it is perhaps significant that at the very end of the note the following sentence appears: "Mr. Smith's Lectures, it must be remembered, (to the fame of which he owed his appointment at Glasgow,) were read at Edinburgh as early as 1748."

progress of Mr. Smith's political ideas at a very early period. Many of the most important opinions in *The Wealth of Nations* are there detailed; but I shall quote only the following sentences:—"Man is generally considered by statesmen and projectors as the materials of a sort of political mechanics. Projectors disturb nature in the course of her operations in human affairs; and it requires no more than to let her alone, and give her fair play in the pursuit of her ends, that she may establish her own designs."—And in another passage:—"Little else is requisite to carry a State to the highest degree of opulence from the lowest barbarism, but peace, easy taxes, and a tolerable administration of justice; all the rest being brought about by the natural course of things. All governments which thwart this natural course, which force things into another channel, or which endeavour to arrest the progress of society at a particular point, are unnatural, and to support themselves are obliged to be oppressive and tyrannical. . . . A great part of the opinions," he observes, "enumerated in this paper, is treated of at length in some lectures which I have still by me, and which were written in the hand of a clerk who left my service six years ago. They have all of them been the constant subjects of my lectures since I first taught Mr. Craigie's class, the first winter I spent in Glasgow, down to this day, without any considerable variation. They had all of them been the subjects of lectures which I read at Edinburgh the winter before I left it, and I can adduce innumerable witnesses, both from that place and from this, who will ascertain them sufficiently to be mine."[25]

The last three sentences of this account, purporting to be a direct quotation of Smith's own words in his paper, are of primary importance in the present connection. One notes, first, the careful reference to "Mr. Craigie's class," which Smith would not have singled out in this way if it had been his "literary" rather than his "political" principles to which he wished to draw particular attention. One notes, second, Smith's insistence on the fact that *all* the opinions enumerated in the paper had not only been the "constant subjects" of his

25. Stewart, *Memoir of Adam Smith,* pp. 67–68.

lectures at Glasgow but had also been the subjects of lectures given at Edinburgh the winter before he left it (1750–51). And one notes, third, that "a great part" (not "all") of these opinions had been treated of at length in some lectures "written in the hand of a clerk who left my service six years ago"—i.e., presumably in 1749. The implication of the latter statement is ambiguous: in the context, it could be taken to imply either that Smith gave lectures on "political" subjects at Edinburgh *before* the winter of 1750–51 in which a great part, but not all, of the opinions concerned were put forward, or simply that the documentary evidence he was able to produce in 1755 concerning what he said in the winter of 1750–51 was incomplete. But the central point is not ambiguous: all the "political" opinions enumerated in the paper, Smith is claiming, date from the Edinburgh period.

The only real question at issue, therefore, is whether this list of opinions included the "four stages" theory. I would myself think it most unlikely that it did not do so. It is true that Stewart's account concentrates attention on "economic" rather than "sociological" principles. It must be remembered, however, that Stewart was mainly concerned at this point in his *Biographical Memoir* with the question of the originality of the doctrines of the *Wealth of Nations*; and it is noteworthy that even with this constraint the second of the two "opinions" of Smith's which Stewart quotes should perhaps be construed as being basically "sociological" rather than "economic."[26] The point is, surely, that in 1755 the *Wealth of Nations* was still almost a quarter of a century away, and the danger of plagiarization of such "economic" ideas as Smith might have arrived at by 1755 could hardly have been very serious. But if Smith had by 1755 arrived at the main "sociological" ideas which we know he was putting forward in his lectures only seven years later—and this at least seems virtually certain—then he might very reasonably have feared plagiarization of these. Studies in the general field of the "history of civil society" were being given a considerable impetus in France at this time by the work of Rousseau, as Smith himself

26. There is an interesting—and possibly deliberate—link between this "opinion" and the one ascribed to Smith earlier in Stewart's narrative (p. 36) in the course of his discussion of Smith's excursions into the field of "Theoretical or Conjectural History."

pointed out in the *Edinburgh Review* in the same crucial year 1755; and nearer home, men like Robertson and Kames were also showing signs of a developing interest in "the first beginnings and gradual progress of society." Even to one without Smith's rather suspicious and volatile temperament, it might have seemed advisable at this time to stake a claim to originality in respect of "sociological" ideas as novel and important as the "four stages" theory.

There is another reason, of a more intriguing if at the same time more conjectural kind, why Stewart may have felt it advisable to disguise or soft-pedal the predominantly "sociological" character of the leading principles in respect of which Smith had apprehended "rival claims" in 1755. It may well be that the mysterious "private differences," the memory of which Stewart was so anxious not to revive, had in fact been with Robertson—who was in the final stages of his last illness at the very time when Stewart delivered his memoir of Smith to the Select Society,[27] and who was of course the principal of Stewart's university. We know that Smith accused Robertson of borrowing the "first vol." of his *History of the Reign of the Emperor Charles V* from his lectures;[28] and although this particular book of Robertson's did not appear until 1769 there are a number of reasons why Smith, even as early as 1755, might have feared that Robertson was about to make some "rival claims." Robertson had quite probably attended the lectures which Smith gave at Edinburgh;[29] in January 1755 he preached his famous sermon, "The Situation of the

27. See Stewart's "Memoir of Robertson," reprinted in the Kelley edition of *Biographical Memoirs of Adam Smith*, pp. 198–99.

28. The reference here is to the account given (at second hand) by John Callander of Craigforth (Edinburgh University MSS, La. II, 451(2)). The "first vol." referred to is clearly the long introductory section entitled A View of the Progess of Society in Europe, from the Subversion of the Roman Empire, to the Beginning of the Sixteenth Century, together with the even longer set of notes appended to it under the title Proofs and Illustrations. The sixth note is of particular importance, and will be referred to again below.

29. It seems probable on a whole number of grounds that Robertson attended, but I know of no definite evidence to this effect. Scott, it is true, includes him in the list of definite attenders. William R. Scott, *Adam Smith as Student and Professor* (Glasgow, 1937) p. 63. But this seems to be based on a gross misquotation of the Callander document (ibid., pp. 54–5), in which it is made to appear that the word "here" in the phrase "which he here gave" must necessarily refer to Edinburgh. (When read in the full context it seems much more likely to refer to Glasgow.) The Callander document cannot in fact be used as evidence either for or against Robertson's attendance at the Edinburgh lectures.

World at the Time of Christ's Appearance,'' with its strong socio-historical overtones; in 1755 he published a review of a book about America which showed him already making ''sociological'' generalizations about early society on the basis of an account of the Indian nations;[30] and in 1754–55, too, he was playing a prominent part, along with Smith, in the activities of the Select Society, which was then debating such questions as ''Whether the difference of national characters be chiefly owing to the nature of different climates, or to moral and political causes?''[31]

Further evidence concerning the probable backdating of the ''four stages'' theory to the Edinburgh period is provided by two of the four documents allegedly representing ''very early work'' which Scott discovered ''amongst letters kept by Adam Smith'' and reproduced in facsimile under the titles respectively of ''Division of Labour'' and ''Land and Water Carriage.''[32] The particular reason adduced by Scott for ascribing the four documents to the Edinburgh period[33] is fatuous; and it is almost certain that the other two—the ''Justice'' manuscript and the ''paper on prices''—are in fact of later date.[34] But the ''Division of Labour'' and ''Land and Water Carriage'' documents can indeed, in my opinion, be at least pro-

30. *The Edinburgh Review for the Year 1775*, 2d ed. (1818), pp. 103–5.

31. See the first note to Stewart's ''Memoir of Robertson,'' pp. 203–5. Another possibility, of an equally conjectural kind, is that one of the people from whom Smith in 1755 apprehended ''rival claims'' was none other than Lord Kames—who, as we have already seen, was to produce the ''four stages'' theory out of the blue in his *Historical Law-Tracts* in 1758. It is true that Smith later referred to Kames (in a letter to him) as ''so old and so good a friend''; and it is *possibly* true that Smith on another occasion said, ''We must every one of us acknowledge Kames for our master'' (Tytler, *Memoirs of Kames*, 1:271, 218). It is also true, however—at any rate if we are to believe Boswell—that Smith on yet another occasion wholeheartedly endorsed Hume's description of Kames as ''the most arrogant Man in the world.'' *The Private Papers of James Boswell*, ed. Scott and Pottle, vol. 15 (1934), p. 12.

32. Scott, *Adam Smith as Student and Professor*, pp. 379–85.

33. ''The many avocations of Adam Smith during the first eight years at Glasgow make it highly improbable, if not impossible, that they could have been written then, and thus they may be assigned to the Edinburgh period'' (ibid., pp. 57–8).

34. On the ''Justice'' manuscript, see D. D. Raphael, ''Adam Smith and the 'Infection of David Hume's Society,' '' *Journal of the History of Ideas* 30, no. 2 (April-June 1969). The ''paper on prices'' seems to me to be almost certainly the copy referred to in Smith's letter of 23 May 1769 to Lord Hailes. See *Adam Smith as Student and Professor*, pp. 265–6.

visionally ascribed to the Edinburgh period, although full confirmation of this may never be obtained.[35] The interesting feature of both these documents is that such "economic" propositions as they contain are still firmly embedded in a "sociological" context. The "Land and Water Carriage" piece, fairly clearly, is part of an essay or lecture, of a basically "materialist" character, designed to show how the relative cheapness and convenience of water carriage helps to dictate the particular regions where, in the general process of socioeconomic development, the "first improvements" in arts and industry take place. And the "Division of Labour" document—which is the more important of the two in the present connection—is just as clearly part of a similarly oriented piece designed to show the way in which the division of labor originates and is extended and altered as society proceeds from one socioeconomic stage of development to another. In the last two pages of this document we are introduced successively to "a savage tribe of North Americans, who are generally hunters"; to "a tribe of Tartars, or wild Arabs, who are generally shepherds"; and to a society after "the invention . . . of agriculture." Three of the four stages in the "four stages" theory are thus clearly delineated, and the type of use made of the stadial concept is very much the same in kind as that made of it in the Glasgow lectures. It would seem at least possible that these two documents were among those mentioned by Smith in his 1755 paper as being still by him and "written in the hand of a clerk who left my service six years ago." But whether this is so or not, the second of the two documents—assuming that it can indeed be properly ascribed to the Edinburgh period—provides clear evidence for the backdating of the "four stages" theory to that period.

IV

If Smith's version of the "four stages" theory can in fact be dated back to the winter of 1750–51 or earlier, we are clearly in

35. My provisional opinion on this matter is based on a comparison—which I hope to develop in a subsequent article—between the treatment of the division of labor in the two documents concerned and its treatment in (*a*) the so-called "Early Draft of the *Wealth of Nations*," (*b*) the 1762–63 lecture notes, (*c*) the Cannan lecture notes, and (*d*) the *Wealth of Nations* itself.

the presence of one of the most remarkable coincidences in the whole history of social and economic thought, since it was precisely at this time that the young Turgot was writing down his own version of the same theory. There was no possibility at this stage of either of the two men having influenced the other, and there was no common source—or at any rate none that I have been able to find—upon which they might have drawn, at least for direct inspiration. We would seem to be face to face with the genuinely original and independent discovery by two young men in their twenties, in two different countries and at exactly the same time, of an extremely important conceptual principle.

What could have caused this? There are always two types of influence which operate in such cases—first, the great global or environmental causes which in some way encourage or engender the general attitudes lying behind the new view; and second, the more specific "literary" sources from which the actual building blocks are derived. So far as the first of these sets of causes is concerned, I do not feel that I have much to add to or take away from what I have already written in various places on this question, although I would now wish to place more emphasis on the important connection between the "four stages" theory and the concepts of progress and the perfectibility of mankind—a connection which was of course particularly evident in the work of Turgot.[36] But on the second set of causes there are a few brief remarks which I think I can usefully make in conclusion. As I now see it, there are three streams of thought in particular which may well have had an important influence.

The first stream of thought was provided by a long line of lawyers writing about the historical origin of property in what may be called the Pufendorf-Locke tradition. The seminal idea here was Pufendorf's notion that "not all things passed into proprietorship at one time, but successively,"[37] and his hints that the successive stages were related to different modes of subsistence. This idea was filled out a little by Locke in his famous chapter on property in the second

36. Sidney Pollard has recently emphasized this in a very interesting way in his book *The Idea of Progress* (New York, 1969).

37. Samuel Pufendorf, *De jure naturae et gentium libri octo,* trans. C. H. and W. A. Oldfather (Oxford, 1934), p. 551. The whole of chapter 4, "Of the Origin of Dominion," is interesting in this connection, in particular pp. 539–40, 550–51, and 554.

Treatise, with some interesting biblical illustrations which were later to become widely used, and also some illustrations from America which were destined to become of even greater importance. The tradition was carried on in the eighteenth century by writers like Hume, Hutcheson and Kames when they were dealing with the question of the origin of property, and it may well be that the young Smith was influenced by it. Certainly, at any rate, it was in connection with the problem of the origin and development of property that the "four stages" theory was most extensively illustrated and applied by Smith in his lectures.

The second stream of thought was provided by a succession of studies of the Indian tribes of North America, in particular the well-known books by Charlevoix and Lafitau, which were very frequently quoted by almost all the historians of civil society in the latter half of the eighteenth century. The works concerned comprised a heterogeneous mixture of travelers' tales, genuine anthropological research, and argument and speculation about the origins of the Indians. They were important for three reasons:

(i) The contrast between the primitive, static society of the Indian tribes and the advanced, relatively dynamic societies of western Europe which they revealed was so striking that it stimulated an interest in the causes of these differences, and through this a more general interest in the causes of development as such.

(ii) A number of the works concerned made it clear that there were very strong resemblances between the Indians and certain ancient peoples—for example, the early Greeks. Thus the view arose that in America one could see, re-created as in a laboratory and laid out conveniently for study, the true infancy of the world.

(iii) The early controversies about the origin of the Indians were almost all based on the assumption that if it could be proved that the Indians had the same basic habits and characteristics as, say, the early Greeks, then it followed that they must in fact have descended from the early Greeks. This must surely have provoked, by way of reaction, the idea that any similarities were in fact due to similarities of situation—that, as Robertson put it, "the character and occupations of the hunter in America must be little different from those, say, of an Asiatic, who depends for subsistence on the chase."[38]

38. The quotation is from a passage near the beginning of book 4 of Robert-

It seems very likely that Smith and Turgot—and also, perhaps, Quesnay—reacted in much the same way, although at an earlier date than Robertson.[39]

The third stream of thought was provided by those writing in the tradition of the so-called providential view of history, which up to the middle of the eighteenth century was more or less orthodox in France and of which the best-known example was Bossuet's *Histoire universelle.* The influence of this tradition may have been particularly important in the case of Turgot, not because he accepted it but precisely because he tried to substitute something else for it—and, like most people in such a situation, was influenced by the doctrine he was rejecting. Bossuet had claimed that although God makes history, He very seldom does this by intervening directly: He works through "chains of particular causes" and, as Bossuet put it, "prepares the effects in the most distant causes." Now the "chains of particular causes" which Bossuet and other writers in the same tradition postulated were up to a point "materialist" in character, which meant that a historian like Turgot could push God out of the picture as a historical agent, concentrate on the analysis of the "chains of particular causes," and still have something interesting and important

son's *History of America,* in which the view concerned is spelt out very explicitly. Cf. also the sixth note in the "Proofs and Illustrations" appended to his *History of the Reign of the Emperor Charles V.*

39. So far as Smith is concerned, we know at any rate that he approved of a work on the philosophy of history in which this reaction was strongly expressed. I refer to John Logan's *Elements of the Philosophy of History* (Edinburgh, 1781), which is a kind of short sketch or analysis of a course of lectures given by Logan in Edinburgh in 1779–81 under the patronage of Robertson, Blair, and others. "Similar situations produce similar appearances," wrote Logan, "and, where the state of society is the same, nations will resemble one another. The want of attention to this hath filled the world with infinite volumes. The most remote resemblances in language, customs, or manners, has suggested the idea of deriving one nation from another" (pp. 16–17). Smith's favorable opinion of Logan's historical work is contained in a letter dated 29 September 1783, which John Rae published on pp. 396–97 of his *Life of Adam Smith.* Logan's *Elements of the Philosophy of History* contains quite a number of other interesting "materialist" statements—as also does his later book *A View of Antient History,* vol. 1 (London, 1788) and vol. 2 (London, 1791), which he published under the curious pseudonym of William Rutherford, D.D., and for which he solicited Smith's contribution (see *Adam Smith as Student and Professor,* p. 304). The question of Logan's connection with Smith—and with the Scottish enlightenment in general—has not been sufficiently explored. It is a subject which would make a good Ph.D. thesis, and possibly something rather more.

to say. Bossuet had talked in terms of a succession of religious "epochs"; Turgot could talk in terms of a succession of socio-economic "stages." Bossuet had emphasized the way in which law-givers and conquerors were subject to a major force outside them-selves: they made history, but since God worked *through* them they did not make it as they wished. Turgot, similarly, could emphasize the way in which certain historical laws and necessities worked *through* individuals to produce a regular, law-governed developmental process.

All in all, then, I think that these three streams of thought may have been more important than any others in forming the new approach. Their influence was certainly much more concrete than that of Montesquieu, whose *Esprit des lois* probably acted mainly as a kind of green light, an *ex cathedra* "go ahead" to the new view.[40] To paraphrase Millar, Montesquieu may in a general sense have pointed out the road, but it was Turgot and Smith, building their new theory out of these earlier materials—and out of their own genius—who were the real Newtons.[41]

40. I sometimes wonder, however, whether the attention of Turgot (and perhaps of Smith) was caught by a little-noticed sentence near the end of bk. 1 sec. 3 of *L'esprit des lois* in which Montesquieu says that laws ought to be related "au genre de vie des peuples, laboureurs, chasseurs ou pasteurs."

41. The article above is a revised version of a lecture given at a History of Economic Thought Conference at Sheffield University on 3 January 1970. In the process of revision I have extended some of the arguments and added a number of references, but I have made no real attempt to transform what was essentially an informal talk into a formal paper.

ADAM SMITH ON FEUDALISM, COMMERCE AND SLAVERY

*John Salter**

I
Introduction

The influence of the materialist interpretation of Adam Smith's treatment of history, associated with Roy Pascal, Ronald Meek and Andrew Skinner,[1] has been weakened, if not entirely eclipsed, by writers such as Donald Winch and Knud Haakonssen who have objected strongly to the narrowing of the scope for an independent political and jurisprudential sphere which, they argue, materialist readings of Smith imply. Thus Donald Winch writes:

> if we take the 'science of the legislator' seriously, materialist interpretations of Smith's use of the four stages, with their more or less mono-causal overtones, have unfortunate implications: they place severe limitations on any genuinely *political* vision of society. Political and legal institutions are treated as epiphenomenal to underlying economic forces, leaving little or no scope for a science of the legislator designed to show what active steps should be taken to remove injustices and adapt institutions to changing circumstances.[2]

Knud Haakonssen has taken a similar position. He emphasizes Smith's stated purpose of providing a normative theory of justice, and details the basis which Smith provided for such a theory in the *Theory of Moral Sentiments*. As Haakonssen points out, such a project would have little point if Smith believed that politics and law were merely reflections of some other underlying forces.[3]

* For their helpful comments and criticisms, I thank Alistair Edwards, Michael Evans, Hillel Steiner, Ursula Vogel, Robert Wokler and two anonymous referees.

[1] R. Pascal, 'Property and Society: the Scottish Contribution of the Eighteenth Century', *Modern Quarterly*, 1 (1938), pp. 167–79. R.L. Meek, 'The Scottish Contribution to Marxist Sociology', in *Democracy and the Labour Movement*, ed. J. Saville (London, 1954). Reprinted with amendments in R.L. Meek, *Economics and Ideology and Other Essays: Studies in the Development of Economic Thought* (London, 1967). R.L. Meek, *The Economics of Physiocracy: Essays and Translations*, (London, 1962). R.L. Meek, 'Smith, Turgot and the "Four Stages" Theory', *History of Political Economy*, 3 (1971), pp. 9–27. R.L. Meek, *Social Science and the Ignoble Savage* (Cambridge,1976). R.L. Meek, 'The Great Whole Man', *The Times Literary Supplement* (3 December 1976). A.S. Skinner, 'Economics and History — the Scottish Enlightenment', *Scottish Journal of Political Economy*, 12 (1965). A.S Skinner, Adam Smith: 'An Economic Interpretation of History', in *Essays on Adam Smith*, ed. A.S. Skinner and T. Wilson (Oxford, 1975). A.S. Skinner, 'A Scottish Contribution to Marxist Sociology?', in *Classical and Marxian Political Economy*, ed. I. Bradley and M. Howard (London, 1982).

[2] D. Winch, 'Adam Smith's "Enduring Particular Result": A Political and Cosmopolitan Perspective', in *Wealth and Virtue*, ed. I. Hont and M. Ignatieff (Cambridge, 1983), p. 258.

[3] K. Haakonssen, *The Science of a Legislator* (Cambridge, 1989).

Few authors would deny the importance of the contribution of Pascal, Meek and Skinner in drawing attention to the four stages theory and to the fact that it provided a point of reference for Smith's discussion of property and government. For its critics, the fundamental flaw in the materialist interpretation is the determinism that materialism is said to imply. Haakonssen for example, writes: 'let us face squarely the central issue at stake in a discussion of a materialist conception of history, that of determinism'.[4] His discussion of determinism suggests that he is using the term in the sense of economic reductionism, a view which denies causal significance to all levels other than the economic.[5] Haakonssen's principal concern is to show how Smith allowed for human agency, especially through law and political and legal institutions; for morals and intellectual and religious beliefs; and also for chance and the influence of exceptional individuals. The force of this line of criticism will have been felt strongly by anyone who believes that Smith held to an extreme form of economic reductionism in which economic forces, somehow transcendentally produce political and legal outcomes without the involvement of individuals acting as politicians, legislators, soldiers etc., or that individuals acting in these capacities are mere cyphers or 'places' in a structure, which do no more than reflect underlying material forces.

That the materialist reading of Smith in question encouraged such a simplistic interpretation is undeniable, less so because it identified a form of materialism connected with the relationship between property, power and dependence, than because this relationship was transposed to the plane of an over-arching historical theory, by linking it with Smith's use of the four stages. The significance of the four stages for Meek was that it provided an explanation of how wealth distribution depended upon the stage of society. It was thus possible to identify an economic 'base' which developed independently of the 'superstructure' and which acted upon it through its characteristic patterns of distribution. In this form, the materialist thesis was open to numerous qualifications and objections. For example, the distribution of wealth in Smith depends upon a range of factors, from the consequences of the upheaval following the collapse of the Roman empire to the contingent fact that Elizabeth I had no heirs and sold off the royal demesnes, and does not appear to be related in any systematic way to the stage of society. The agricultural stage and the commercial stage are both consistent with a variety of institutional forms; for example England, France, Germany and Spain are all examples of societies which have arrived at the commercial stage but which have different political characteristics.

[4] *Ibid.*, p. 185. See also H.M. Hopfl, 'From Savage to Scotsman: Conjectural History in the Scottish Enlightenment', *Journal of British Studies*, Vol. XVII, no. 2 (1978), who criticizes materialistic interpretations of Smith for their supposed determinism on similar grounds to Haakonssen.

[5] Haakonssen is not, I think, opposed to describing Smith as a determinist where determinism means that events can be described as a chain of cause and effect — his 'antidotes' to determinism do not imply that Smith was not a determinist in this sense. See *ibid.*, pp. 185–6.

Skinner himself came to doubt many aspects of the materialist interpretation and subjected it to criticism along the same lines as Winch and Haakonssen. However, Skinner continued to insist on 'the importance of broadly economic forces in the interpretation of actual historical events — a proposition which is nowhere more obvious than in Smith's analysis of the breakdown of the feudal state and the role ascribed therein to the development of trade and manufactures'.[6] It is this aspect of the materialist interpretation with which I will be principally concerned in this paper.

A theme which was introduced by Pascal, and developed in detail by Skinner, was that Smith's account of the destruction of feudalism by the rise of commerce and manufacturing could be read as an account of the transition from the third to the fourth economic stages. Moreover, the central institutional change in this transition, according to Pascal and Skinner, was the abolition of serfdom and its replacement by a system of agrarian capitalism based on free tenancies. This interpretation of Smith has had a significant impact outside the immediate area of Smith scholarship. It has provided substantial scholarly textual support for the view that Smith was interested in the question of the transition from feudalism to capitalism prior to Marx. It also appears to establish the Smithian roots of the particular theory of transition which was advanced by Paul Sweezy in the context of the post war debates on the transition from feudalism to capitalism.[7] As Skinner noted: 'It is particularly interesting to observe . . . that Smith would appear to side with Paul Sweezy, and against Maurice Dobb, in suggesting that the feudal state had failed as a result of exogenous rather than endogenous pressures.'[8]

Independently of the work of Pascal and Skinner, Robert Brenner has argued that 'the *method* of an entire line of writers in the Marxist tradition'[9] can be traced to Smith. The characteristics and deficiencies of this method, according to Brenner, derive from the fact that it accepts Smith's 'individualistic-mechanist presuppositions' which lead to the view that 'the development of trade and the division of labour unfailingly bring about economic development',[10] and fails to appreciate that growth and the extension of the division of labour require the prior transformation of productive relations. Sweezy's theory, according to Brenner, is an 'extension' of Smith's model which retains its inadequacies:

[6] Skinner, 'A Scottish Contribution', p. 100.

[7] See *The Transition from Feudalism to Capitalism*, ed. R. Hilton (London, 1976). That Smith conceived of the transition from feudalism to capitalism prior to Marx is argued by Eric Hobsbawm against William Letwin's claim that it was a Marxist invention. See *Times Literary Supplement* (25 March and 1 April 1977).

[8] Skinner, 'A Scottish Contribution', p. 100.

[9] R. Brenner, 'The Origins of Capitalist Development: a Critique of Neo-Smithian Marxism', in *New Left Review*, 104 (1977), p. 27.

[10] *Ibid.*

> the fact is that such flowerings of commercial relations cum divisions of labour have been a more or less regular feature of human history for thousands of years. Because the occurrence of such 'commercial revolutions' has been relatively so common, the key question which must be answered by Sweezy and Wallerstein is why the rise of trade/division of labour should have set off the transition to capitalism in the case of feudal Europe?[11]

But while Brenner traced the *method* of this Marxist tradition to Smith, and regarded Sweezy's theory as an extension, the interpretation of Smith proposed by Pascal and Skinner finds Sweezy's theory already present in the pages of the *Wealth of Nations*. Other writers have built upon this discovery and Smith has been cited, along with the other members of the Scottish school, as being one of the founders of productive force determinism.[12]

In Book III of the *Wealth of Nations* Smith was concerned to argue that the decline of feudal power, brought about by the progress of commerce and opulence, resulted in the introduction of 'order and good government, and with them the liberty and security of individuals'. Duncan Forbes has described this as 'the great theme of European history, embracing the absolute as well as the free governments'.[13] If Skinner's interpretation of Smith is correct and the demise of feudalism means for Smith, as for Marx, the demise of an economic system which is replaced by capitalism, then liberty and justice, which are dependent on the introduction of order and good government, are inextricably bound up with the institutions of capitalism.

This view of liberty and justice contrasts sharply with the anti-materialist view of Winch and Haakonssen and it detracts from what Haakonssen regarded as one of Smith's primary purposes, that of drawing up the 'parallels and contrasts between mankind's three great attempts to live by the laws of justice in a commercial society'.[14] Haakonssen is surely correct in suggesting that liberty and justice are not exclusively modern and not dependent upon capitalism. Smith does refer to a modern meaning of freedom in the *Wealth of Nations* in discussing the removal of the attributes of slavery and villeinage from the town dwellers who, as a consequence Smith says, 'became really free in our present sense of the word Freedom'.[15] But this is a particular usage of the word freedom which is not, as I will argue below, implied by 'the liberty and security of individuals' dependent upon 'order and good government' which was the

[11] *Ibid.*, p. 40.

[12] See S. Rigby, *Marxism and History* (Manchester, 1987), Ch. 5.

[13] D. Forbes, 'Sceptical Whiggism: Commerce and Liberty', in *Essays on Adam Smith*, ed. Skinner and Wilson, p. 193.

[14] Haakonssen, *The Science of a Legislator*, p. 188.

[15] A. Smith, *An Inquiry into the Nature and Causes of the Wealth of Nations*, ed. R.H. Campbell, A.S. Skinner and W.B. Todd (Oxford, 1976), III. iii. 5.

theme of Smith's account of the destruction of feudal power by the progress of commerce and opulence.

I will argue in what follows that the reading of Smith which attributes to him a theory of the transition from feudalism to capitalism, and the implications which follow from it, are unfounded. There are three key aspects of the interpretation which I will challenge. First, that Smith's account of the destruction of feudal power by the progress of commerce is related to an explanation of the transition to the commercial stage; second, that the decline in baronial power incorporates Smith's account of the ending of serfdom and a change in relations of production in the Marxian sense; and third, that the rise of international commerce — the 'prime-mover' in the whole process, is a force which is external to European feudalism.

While the purpose of Smith's discussion of the effects of commercial progress in modern Europe was not, then, to explain the origins of agrarian capitalism, it was clearly designed to explain how the destruction of feudal power constituted a major *political* revolution. The nature of this revolution and its significance for the relationship between commerce and liberty has been the object of considerable dispute amongst Smith scholars. The contributions of Winch and Haakonssen, by insisting on the centrality of Smith's political and jurisprudential interests and on the role of his advocacy, guard against simplistic, deterministic interpretations. However, I will argue that their reluctance to concede any ground at all to a materialist interpretation has led them to a position in which the significance of this revolution is severely restricted. This is because they both deny that for Smith political power was based on the economic dependence of the poor on the rich. They argue that the power which the rich have over the poor is a matter of sympathy and admiration and not of economic dependence. This position, as I will argue, denies them the basis for *any* coherent interpretation of Smith's account of the decline in the power of the barons.

Pascal and Skinner, in focusing attention on the relationship between property, economic dependence and political power, and in showing how commercial progress, by reducing economic dependence, led to the demise of feudal power, made a lasting contribution which survives the criticisms which Winch, Haakonssen and others have made of materialist interpretations of Smith. I will argue, moreover, that materialism, when stripped of its premonitions of the Marxist theory of the transition from feudalism to capitalism, and of its associations with determinism, is an appropriate term to describe an important dimension of Smith's treatment of the relationship between commerce and liberty. I will take materialism to mean that for certain actions, laws, policies and political and legal institutions to be possible, certain material conditions have to be present and that these material conditions, while usually the result of human actions are not the result of design, of purposeful human action. Materialism in this sense accurately describes Smith's discussion of the way in which, on a number of occasions, but in its most fully developed form in his account of the demise of feudalism, the progress of commerce and opulence have the effect of creating strong central government, which he believed was a precondition for liberty and justice.

Materialism in this sense does not, of course, imply determinism or economic reductionism. If materialism and the kind of economic reductionism which has been the target of criticism were synonymous, the question of whether Smith was a materialist would be superseded by the question of whether materialism was a defensible position to adopt in any circumstances. Materialism, in the sense being suggested, does not imply that there is a necessary and automatic connection between commerce and liberty. Neither does it limit the scope for advocacy. Smith's advocacy was directed towards the implementation of the system of perfect liberty, which he regarded as the system most favourable to commercial progress. But Smith also spoke of liberty in the more general sense which had been attained in most of the modern European states where a tolerable degree of security had been introduced by the appearance of strong central governments and this was the unintended result of economic progress. It is therefore the contention of this paper that it is possible to give due recognition to the normative dimension of Smith's treatment of liberty and justice while, at the same time, acknowledging Smith's materialism.

The argument of this paper can be summarized as follows. The materialist interpretation, and particularly the contributions of Pascal and Skinner, justifiably stressed the importance of the way in which political power was based on wealth and how economic progress acted to destroy arbitrary centres of power. However, by embedding Smith's account of the demise of feudalism in the four stages theory, and by interpreting it as part of a theory of the transition from feudalism to agrarian capitalism, the materialist interpretation deflected attention away from Smith's primary purpose of explaining how commercial progress created a more favourable climate for justice and liberty by causing changes in the structure of sovereignty. The contributions of Winch and Haakonssen have provided a valuable antidote to some of the deterministic implications of the materialist interpretation. In particular, they have succeeded in recapturing the ground on which Smith discussed liberty and justice as questions for the legislator and have countered the view that they are automatic outcomes of material processes. However, by equating materialism with determinism and by directly challenging the centrality of Smith's treatment of the relationship between property, dependence and political power, they place undue weight on the normative dimension of Smith's treatment of liberty and justice and obscure what can appropriately be described as a materialist dimension.

II
The Marxian Interpretation

Roy Pascal's 1938 article 'Property and Society', which deals with the Scottish Historical School, is taken to be the first statement of this so-called Marxian interpretation of Smith. Pascal points out that Smith regarded history as a material process: 'The process of social development is not governed by a supernatural (religious) or a moral principle; nor by man's foresight and reason . . . Smith sees social development . . . as a completely secular, material process.'[16] Pascal draws attention, without providing a detailed treatment, to Smith's use of four distinct economic stages of society. He simply notes that according to Smith government begins with property in land and herds, that is with the shepherding and agricultural stages, and that the basis of government is the defence of the property of the rich against the poor. 'Smith applies these general principles in contrasting the social institutions of the various stages of society, showing the evolution of civil government (monarchy, aristocracy, republic)'.[17]

According to Pascal, Smith's account of the destruction of feudalism by the rise of commerce and manufacturing, the fullest account of which appears in the *Wealth of Nations* Book III, is an account of 'the development of commerce and manufacture out of an agricultural society'.[18] Central to this stadial transformation is the abolition of serfdom:

> When exchange and industry were developed, it became possible for the barons to acquire *things*. In the feudal system, their only use for their property was the gaining of power; their relation to their serfs was one of a military leader to his retainers. Now, however, they become obsessed with the desire of turning their serfs into wealth producers. They therefore do everything to encourage production, introduce permanent and hereditary lease-holding, free the serfs, etc. Acting with a view to their own interest, the barons destroy their own power, and create the possibility of regular government.[19]

Ronald Meek's contributions to this subject were principally concerned with the presence of a materialistic explanation of government, organized around the four stages theory which he found in the Glasgow *Lectures on Jurisprudence*. In comparison with Meek, however, Andrew Skinner's discussion of the so-called historical materialism in Smith focused attention on the more sociological concerns of the *Wealth of Nations*.[20] While Skinner's account of the relationship between the four stages and forms of government was broadly similar to Meek's, there was another dimension to Skinner's interpretation which appeared in his 1965 article and which played a greater role in his later contributions. In addition to the relationship between the substructure or mode

[16] Pascal, 'Property and Society', pp. 170–1.

[17] *Ibid.*, pp. 171–2.

[18] *Ibid.*, p. 172.

[19] *Ibid.*

[20] This has the advantage of focusing on one of Smith's published works. As R.D. Cummings has pointed out, Smith chose to consign his unpublished notes to the flames. See R.D. Cummings, 'The Four Stages', in *Political Theory and Political Economy*, ed. C.B. Macpherson, mimeo, Conference for the Study of Political Thought (Toronto, 1974).

of subsistence and the nature of property and government, Skinner claimed that it is also part of the Scottish argument that changes in the mode of subsistence are brought about by 'quantitative' developments in the 'productive forces'. Thus, while Meek had identified two levels of analysis in the Scottish 'materialism' — the mode of subsistence and the forms of property and government, Skinner identified three interrelated levels: the productive forces, the type of economic organization and the pattern of dependence and authority.[21]

The major illustration of the relationship between the forces of production and the type of economic organization given by Skinner is the emergence of the 'exchange economy' from the agrarian economy. The growth of manufacturing and trade, which are characterized by Skinner as the forces of production, dissolved the ties of dependence that characterized the agrarian economy and eventually caused the break up of the agrarian economy and its replacement by the exchange economy: 'Smith argues in effect that the *quantitative* development of manufactures based on the cities eventually produced a qualitative change in creating the institutions of the exchange economy, that is of the fourth economic stage.'[22]

Skinner has described these qualitative changes in the following way:

> since the object was now to maximize the disposable surplus, it was in the proprietor's interest to change the forms of leasehold in order to encourage output and increase returns. In this way, Smith traced the gradual change from the use of slave labour on the land, to the origin of the 'metayer' system where the tenant had limited property rights, until the whole process finally resulted in the appearance of 'farmers properly so called who cultivated the land with their own stock, paying a rent certain to the landlord' (WN III.ii.14).[23]

In 'A Scottish Contribution to Marxist Sociology?' (1982) Skinner made explicit what was implicit in his 1965 contribution, namely the distinction between the statement of the four stages and their relationship to government, and the process of transition between the stages. As the question mark in the title of the 1982 article suggests, Skinner came to question the materialist interpretation: 'Smith gave due weight to the importance of economic factors, but also to the role played by political considerations, quirks of character, physical elements and pure accident'.[24] However, Skinner came to see Smith's account of the emergence of the exchange economy as the most robust and clear-cut example of 'historical materialism' in Smith's works.

[21] Skinner, 'Economics and History', p. 21.

[22] Skinner, 'Adam Smith: an Economic Interpretation of History', p. 167.

[23] *Ibid.*, p. 166.

[24] Skinner, 'A Scottish Contribution', p. 102.

III
A Critique

The Four Economic Stages

It is clear from the way Smith first introduces the stages in the *Lectures on Jurisprudence*, and from the way he subsequently discusses them, that they are not totally distinct and mutually exclusive. In particular, the age of commerce is not a post-agricultural society. All that Smith has to say about the age of commerce at this point is that it arrives when exchange between societies follows on from the development of exchange within societies. From the examples he gives it is clear that agriculture has not been superseded but that commerce is a development of the agricultural economy.[25] Ronald Meek, however, claimed that by the commercial stage Smith meant 'the use of capitalist methods of production, the accumulation of capital, the improvement of the useful arts, the extension of the division of labour, and commerce'.[26] Meek's definition has to be seen in relation to his view that 'Smith propounds the four stages theory in his Glasgow lectures on Jurisprudence and later analyses a "commercial society" in detail in his *Wealth of Nations*'.[27] It is clear that the society analysed in the *Wealth of Nations* is a commercial society; Smith does not say, however, that all commercial societies have all the characteristics which are to be found in the contemporary society he analyses in the *Wealth of Nations*. The fact that the sequence of stages up to and including commercial society was attained prior to the downfall of Rome emphasizes this point. While the full development of commerce may not have been reached until much later, it clearly existed in the ancient period and the only distinction that Smith makes is that in Rome commerce was not 'particularly studied and a theory laid down'.[28]

Andrew Skinner's introduction of the term 'exchange economy' distinguishes the '*modern,* as distinct from *classical*, form'[29] of the fourth economic stage. Skinner claims the analysis of the *Wealth of Nations* is concerned with the transition to the fourth economic phase in its modern form. What is significant in Skinner's treatment is that the Exchange Economy is defined in terms of the productive relations of agrarian capitalism. The transition is thus the substitution of one set of productive relations (agrarian capitalism) for another (serfdom or feudalism defined in the Marxist sense). Thus while the third and the fourth economic stages, as they are discussed by Smith, are not

[25] See A. Smith, *Lectures on Jurisprudence [A]* (1762), ed. R.L. Meek, D.D. Raphael and P.G. Stein (Oxford, 1978), i. 31.

[26] R.L. Meek, 'Political Theory and Political Economy, 1750–1800', in C.B. Macpherson, *Political Theory and Political Economy*, p. 7.

[27] *Ibid.*, p. 8.

[28] Smith, *Lectures on Jurisprudence [A]*, iv. 93.

[29] Skinner, 'A System of Social Science', p. 88.

mutually exclusive, the agrarian/feudal stage as defined by Skinner and Skinner's exchange economy are.

It is thus possible to see the significance of Skinner's distinction between the quantitative development of commerce and manufacture, for which he uses the term productive forces, and the commercial stage defined as an economic system. Such a distinction is clearly necessary if 'commerce' is to stand for both cause and effect: for the instrument which brings about the new economic system and the new economic system itself. This, however, is an unnecessary elaboration of Smith's views and amounts to redefining Smith's categories in terms of Marxian ones.

While Smith identified four ages of society which are referred to in this literature as modes of subsistence, he does not make use of a concept which corresponds to what Marx meant by mode of production. This is illustrated most clearly by Smith's treatment of slavery. Slavery does not correspond to any of the four ages but can exist in any of them, and in Smith's opinion would probably exist in all of them because of man's natural desire to dominate others.[30] Slavery has only been abolished in a small corner of Europe for special reasons. Since Smith did not believe that commercial society was restricted to the same small corner of Europe, we must conclude that the commercial age of society does not preclude the existence of slavery. Furthermore, Smith's treatment of feudalism was quite unlike that of Marx and Marxist historians. For Smith serfdom was not the same as, and bore no special relationship to, feudalism. Feudalism was for Smith a particular form of *government* which is to be distinguished from the other forms of government with which Smith deals, namely democratic, republic, military, allodial and absolute monarchy.

The claim, therefore, that Smith provided an account of the transition from feudalism to the fourth economic stage (whether this is defined as the commercial stage as in Smith or the exchange economy as in Skinner) simply does not make sense in terms of the categories employed by Smith. One may expect to find in Smith a discussion of transitions between different forms of government, for example from allodial to feudal to absolutism, or of transitions between economic stages, for example the transition from agriculture to commerce, but identifying feudalism with the agrarian stage and identifying a transition from feudalism to the commercial stage as Skinner does involves a confusion of the categories employed by Smith.

In view of this, it can be doubted whether, as Skinner claims, Smith's account of the development of modern Europe from the collapse of the Roman empire complements the account of the progress of the four stages by providing a mechanism of how the transition took place between the third and the fourth stage.[31] To the extent that Smith provided an explanation for the process of transition between stages, it was the pressure of population.[32] The account of

[30] Smith, *Lectures on Jurisprudence [A]*, iii. 114–16.

[31] Skinner, 'A Scottish Contribution', p. 99.

[32] Smith, *Lectures on Jurisprudence [A]*, i. 27–32.

the emergence of modern Europe deals with a series of political changes and the corresponding developments in the progress of opulence.

The Prime Mover

The original debate on the transition from feudalism to capitalism between Dobb and Sweezy in the early 1950s focused on whether the prime mover in the process of transition was internal or external to European feudalism.[33] In arguing that the prime mover was an externally located foreign trade, Sweezy was drawing heavily on the work of Henri Pirenne who had argued that commerce, located in the Middle-Eastern–Mediterranean area, was the external force which revived the Western European economy.[34] The similarities between Smith's and Pirenne's accounts of the origins of European towns and the role played by foreign trade has been noted by Louis Dow and Gene Mumy.[35] In view of these similarities and of Smith's description of the way in which the political and institutional features of the allodial and feudal periods impedes the progress of commercial activity,[36] it is not surprising that some readers have concluded that an external stimulus was required and found the evidence for this in the role Smith ascribes to foreign trade. That political interventions played an important role in the establishment and growth of towns as centres of commerce is generally acknowledged.[37] But Smith's discussion shows how this development reached a point, because of the backward nature of agriculture, beyond which further development was impossible. It is ultimately only because an external market appears that continued progress is possible and it is for this reason that some interpreters of Smith have found the 'prime mover' in the events to be foreign commerce originating outside European feudalism.

It follows from this reading that the process of European development which Smith is describing is dependent upon non-European development, opening him to the charge which was made against Sweezy by Kohachiro Takahashi:

> If we say that historical development takes place according to external forces, the question remains, however, how those external forces arose, and where they came from. In the last analysis these forces which manifest themselves externally must be explained internally to history.[38]

[33] See Hilton, *The Transition from Feudalism to Capitalism.*

[34] H. Pirenne, *Economic and Social History of Medieval Europe* (London, 1936).

[35] G.E. Mumy, 'Town and Country in Adam Smith's The Wealth of Nations', in *Science and Society*, XLII, 4 (Winter 1978–9); and L.A. Dow, 'The Rise of the City: Adam Smith Versus Henri Pirenne', *Review of Social Economy*, 32 (October 1974), pp. 170–85.

[36] Smith, *Wealth of Nations*, III. ii.

[37] For example, D. Winch, *Adam Smith's Politics* (Cambridge, 1978); Skinner, 'A Scottish Contribution', and Mumy, 'Town and Country'.

[38] K. Takahashi, 'A Contribution to the Discussion', in Hilton, *The Transition from Feudalism to Capitalism.*

However, this interpretation is in need of substantial qualification for two reasons. First, Smith's view that bad laws and institutions can interrupt the progress of commerce[39] is mitigated somewhat by the following comment, suggesting that human intervention slowed down commercial progress considerably but did not halt it altogether:

> frugality and good conduct, however, is upon most occasions, it appears from experience, sufficient to compensate, not only the private prodigality and misconduct of individuals, but the publick extravagance of government. The uniform, constant, and uninterrupted effort of every man to better his condition, the principle from which publick and national, as well as private opulence is originally derived, is frequently powerful enough to maintain the natural progress of things towards improvement, in spite both of the extravagance of government, and of the greatest errors of administration.[40]

The second qualification to the view that Smith treated commerce as an external prime mover is that, while commerce can be regarded as external to a particular region or country, it is not external to European feudalism as a whole. In Europe, the commercial towns did not develop on the basis of the agricultural sector in the same regions, but these towns acted as focal points at which the limited surpluses of a number of regions could be concentrated:

> Each of those countries, perhaps, taken singly, could not afford it [a city JS] but a small part, either of its subsistence, or of its employment; but all of them taken together could afford it but a great subsistence and a great employment.[41]

When Smith says:

> The inhabitants of trading cities, by importing the improved manufactures and expensive luxuries of richer countries, afforded some food to the vanity of the great proprietors, who eagerly purchased them with great quantities of the rude produce of their own lands

and:

> The commerce of a great part of Europe in those times consisted of their own rude, for the manufactured products of more civilized nations[42]

he gives examples of intra-European trade to illustrate his point.[43] The fact that Smith says that finer manufactures in Europe were originally introduced by

[39] For example, Smith, *Wealth of Nations*, II. iii. 36 and IV. v. b. 43.

[40] *Ibid.*, II. iii. 31.

[41] *Ibid.*, III. iii. 13.

[42] *Ibid.*, III. iii. 15.

[43] *Ibid.*

imitation, and that in some cases that meant imitation of the manufactures of non-European countries, does not detract from the fact that the logic of his argument does not require that foreign commerce be other than exclusively European.

The Abolition of Slavery

The crucial feature of Skinner's interpretation, however, is that Smith's account of the abolition of slavery is incorporated into the sequence of events in which the progress of commerce leads to the destruction of the power of the feudal barons. In discussing the effects of the progress of commerce on agricultural tenancy in the *Wealth of Nations* III. iv., however, Smith does *not* say, as Skinner claims he does, that the progress of commerce leads to the ending of slavery. Nor is such a view consistent with the explanations Smith does give for the ending of slavery.

Smith's account of the transition from the use of slavery to the metayer and steel bow systems, and then to the system of farmers properly so-called, appears in the *Wealth of Nations* III. ii. and is not related to the progress of commerce and manufacturing towns which is discussed in the *Wealth of Nations* III. iv. In spite of the economic disadvantages of slavery, Smith argued that 'it is not likely that slavery should be ever abolished, and it was owing to some peculiar circumstances that it has been abolished in the small corner of the world in which it now is'.[44] He goes on to say that in a democratic government it is highly unlikely that slavery would ever be abolished, because of the vested interest of the legislators who would themselves own slaves: 'the love of domination and authority and the pleasure that men take in having everything done by their express orders . . . will make it impossible for the slaves in a free country ever to recover their liberty'.[45]

In the *Lectures*, Smith accounts for the abolition of slavery in the following way. First, the effect of the clergy who 'saw then or thought they did that it would tend greatly to aggrandize the power of [th]e church, that these people over whom they had the greatest influence were set at liberty and rendered independent of their masters'.[46] Second, it was also in the interest of the kings to abolish slavery 'to lessen the authority of the nobles and their vassals over their villains'.[47] Smith adds that it was also in the economic interest of the clergy to encourage the abolition of slavery as they 'saw too perhaps that their lands were but very ill cultivated when under the management of these villains'.[48]

44 Smith, *Lectures on Jurisprudence [A]*, iii. 114.

45 *Ibid.*

46 *Ibid.*, iii. 118.

47 *Ibid.*, iii. 119.

48 *Ibid.*, iii. 121.

The account given in the *Wealth of Nations* is somewhat different. After discussing the inefficiency of slavery in Book III. ii., Smith says:

> It is probable that it was partly on account of this advantage, and partly on account of the encroachments which the sovereign, always jealous of the great lords, gradually encouraged their villains to make upon their authority, and which seem at last to have been such as rendered this species of servitude altogether inconvenient, that tenure in villanage gradually wore out through the greater part of Europe. *The time and manner, however, in which so important a revolution was brought about, is one of the most obscure points in history.*[49]

Thus, while Smith, in the *Wealth of Nations*, gives more weight to economic factors, his statement that the time and manner of the ending of slavery was obscure suggests that he did not intend it to be the subject of the very prominent theme of Book III.iv. about the effects of the progress of commerce.

The principal effect of the improvements in commerce and manufacturing, as Smith makes clear in Book III. iv., is the recovery of agriculture following from changes in government and in the form of leases. In this famous story, Smith identifies three ways in which the towns improved the countryside: as a market for agricultural produce; as a result of wealthy townspeople purchasing and improving land; and last and most important, 'commerce and manufactures gradually introduced order and good government, and with them, the liberty and security of individuals, among the inhabitants of the country'.[50] The great landlords dismissed their retainers in order to dispose of their surpluses on new forms of consumption and thereby forfeited their power.

Changes in tenancy also resulted. Tenants, Smith explains, were at this time all tenants at will and '[a] tenant at will, who possesses land sufficient to maintain his family for little more than a quit rent, is as dependent as any servant or retainer whatever, and must obey him with as little reserve'.[51] As a result of the economic changes, the number of tenants was reduced, and the landlords increased the rents of the remaining ones to an economic level which the tenants would only agree to in return for security of tenure.

The reading of Smith which ascribes to him the theory that the progress of commerce led to the abolition of serfdom seems to arise from the belief that 'tenants at will' refers to serfs or slaves. However, in the *Lectures on Jurisprudence* Smith describes tenants at will as friends or relations of the proprietor who had very advantageous leases.[52] Also, in the *Wealth of Nations* Smith says that the authority of the lord over his retainers and tenants stems from the fact that they are 'fed entirely by his bounty'. It is thus by sharing his surpluses, in

[49] Smith, *Wealth of Nations*, III. ii. 12 (emphasis added).

[50] *Ibid.*, III. iv. 4.

[51] *Ibid.*, III. iv. 6.

[52] Smith, *Lectures on Jurisprudence [A]*, iv. 155.

the form of lenient rents in the case of the tenants, that the lord gains loyalty in politics and war. This does not describe either the economic or the political relationship between the lord and his serfs. Serfs can hardly be said to share the surpluses of the landlords. Coercion, not bribery, is the basis of the landlord's authority over the serf. Furthermore, since the serf does not play any role in politics or war he is not the object of the landlord's largesse. In the *Lectures on Jurisprudence* Smith makes it clear that his argument about economic dependence being the basis of authority does not apply to servile labour: 'in Rome, where all the luxury was supported by slaves who had no weight in the state, the luxury of the nobility destroyed all their power'.[53] Smith contrasted this with a situation without slavery where tradesmen, who would be dependent for their custom on the rich, would thus have to support the rich in elections.[54]

The important development in agricultural relations which Smith is describing in Book III of the *Wealth of Nations*, therefore, is the origin of long term and secure leases and not the demise of serfdom. The effect of long term leases in addition to productivity gains, was that landlords no longer exercised the influence over their tenants which lenient rents gave them:

> Even a tenant at will, who pays the full value of the land, is not altogether dependent upon the landlord. The pecuniary advantages which they receive from one another, are mutual and equal, and such a tenant will expose neither his life or his fortune in the service of the proprietor. But if he has a lease for a long term of years, he is altogether independent; . . .[55]

Landlords thus lose political influence over their tenants as they do over their retainers.

IV
Commerce and Liberty

The result of the decline in the power of the feudal barons throughout a large part of Europe, brought about by the progress of commerce, was absolutist government. This was a development which was favourable to liberty because regular government was no longer interrupted by the barons. In the above-quoted passage where Smith says 'commerce and manufactures gradually introduced order and good government, and with them, the liberty and security of individuals, among the inhabitants of the country',[56] he is referring to the common developments in a large part of Europe, and liberty and security, in the sense that he is using the terms here, do not depend upon particular, national

[53] *Ibid.*, iv. 73.

[54] See also A. Smith, *Lectures on Jurisprudence [B]* (1766), ed. R.L. Meek, D.D. Raphael and P.G. Stein (Oxford, 1978), p. 410.

[55] Smith, *Wealth of Nations*, III. iv. 14.

[56] *Ibid.*, III. iv. 4.

institutional developments. The separation of the judiciary from the executive, which a number of writers have seen as a theme central to the question of liberty, is also a European phenomenon and, on this question at least, Winch does not see any conflict between a development which has definite causes and which is also an object of Smith's advocacy: 'Smith is clearly engaging in direct advocacy, even though he attributes the origin of the separation of powers to the impersonal processes of progress and historical accident'.[57] Absolute governments could become despotic and this was true to some extent in France. Duncan Forbes has argued, however, that Smith agreed with Hume who 'insisted that the purpose of government was for practical purposes realized in all the civilized states, free or absolute . . . They had a high degree of liberty, as well as all the other marks of a civilized society: an established order of ranks, a highly developed division of labour, opulence and so on'.[58] Commerce is thus favourable to liberty because it resulted in the establishment of governments 'which afforded to industry, the only encouragement it requires, some tolerable security that it shall enjoy the fruits of its own labour'.[59] and this was the consequence of the political revolution which was 'brought about by two different orders of people who had not the least intention to serve the publick . . . Neither of them had either the knowledge or foresight of that great revolution which the folly of the one, and the industry of the other, was gradually bringing about'.[60]

But while liberty in this sense, which provides a minimum degree of security under the rule of law, is the unintended outcome of economic progress and does not depend upon knowledge or foresight, the same is not, of course, true of the system of laws and police which, in Smith's view, is the most favourable to commercial progress. It is in this context that Smith's advocacy in favour of certain kinds of laws and regulations have received a great deal of attention from Winch and Haakonssen. Smith's attention to the tasks of the legislator shows that commercial societies are not perfect, that oppression and injustices remain and that the effects of commerce, particularly in relation to the corruption of morals, can threaten the safety of governments. Haakonssen has shown how the progress of commerce can mitigate many of these problems, but not without the legislator providing the legal framework for commerce to flourish.[61]

However, in the course of criticizing materialist readings of Smith in order to draw attention to Smith's normative purposes, Haakonssen has restricted the significance of the relationship between property and political power to the point where Smith's account of the unintended revolution brought about by the progress of commerce becomes incomprehensible. The ability of the feudal

[57] Winch, *Adam Smith's Politics*, p. 96. See also Haakonssen, *The Science of a Legislator*, p. 270.

[58] Forbes, 'Sceptical Whiggism', p. 192.

[59] Smith, *Wealth of Nations*, I. xi. n. 1.

[60] *Ibid.*, III. iv. 17.

[61] Haakonssen, *The Science of a Legislator*, pp. 179–81.

barons to interrupt regular government was based upon the political and military support which their wealth gave them. The connection between wealth and political power hinges, at least partly, on the economic dependence of the poor on the rich. When those without property depend for their livelihood on the generosity of the rich, political authority is created and the poor must obey the wishes of the rich to secure their livelihood. Haakonssen, however, has questioned the economic connection between property and power. He argues that for Smith it is taste and vanity, rather than the procurement of the necessities of subsistence, which are the principal motivation of mankind, and that economic motivation is rarely the basis for the important relationship between dependence and authority. It is rather 'men's aestheticizing participation in the lives of the rich through sympathy, whereas hopes of personal gain play little or no role'.[62] For Haakonssen, the strength of government is less a question of wealth than of opinion[63] and the sequence in which the progress of commerce leads to the decline in the powers of the feudal barons would not appear to illustrate a process of any great general significance. In fact, if the psychological basis for the relationship between property and power is all that matters, there is no reason why commercial progress should alter the structure of sovereignty at all: the barons do not lose their wealth, they use it for different purposes. Why therefore do they not continue to command the obedience of those who admire and respect them for their riches?

Winch's approach, which recognizes that there is both a psychological and an economic basis for the connection between property and power[64] leads him to distinguish between commercial and pre-commercial societies:

> One of the benefits which modern societies derived from the decline of feudalism was that power and property were no longer connected. This was true of all forms of government but it was especially true of 'free countries' where, as Smith said 'the safety of governments depends very much upon the favourable judgement which the people may form of its conduct'.[65]

[62] *Ibid.*, p. 184.

[63] *Ibid.*, p. 131.

[64] In support of his case Haakonssen quotes Smith in *Lectures on Jurisprudence [B]*: 'in general the poor are independent, and support themselves by their labour, yet tho' they expect no benefit from them [the rich] they have a strong propensity to pay them respect.' (Smith, *Lectures on Jurisprudence [B]*, 12.) However, this has to be seen against Smith's account of the progress of government where, for example, he says in relation to the age of shepherds: 'This inequality of fortune, making a distinction between the rich and the poor, gave the former much influence over the latter, for they who had no flocks or herds must have depended on those who had them, because they could not now gain a subsistence from hunting as the rich had made the game, now become tame, their own property.' (*Ibid.*, 20.) See also Smith, *Lectures on Jurisprudence [A]*, iv. 7–8.

[65] Winch, *Adam Smith's Politics*, p. 169.

The problem with this formulation is that if property and power are unconnected in all societies, in what sense are commercial societies different from non-commercial societies? What does it mean to say that property and power are 'especially' unconnected in commercial societies? Political power is not the result of property but of property which yields a surplus in excess of the consumption and investment requirements of the owners. In this respect, commercial societies are no different from any others. The distinction is that in commercial societies the number of property holders who posses such a degree of wealth is reduced, not because of the reduction of wealth holdings but because of the increase in consumption and investment opportunities.[66] This allowed Smith to distinguish between different modern European states: in the case of Germany, for example, where wealth holdings tended to be larger than elsewhere, the progress of commerce failed to restrict the number of power bases sufficiently for strong central government to emerge.[67] In other places the monarch was the only property holder whose wealth was not entirely consumed by personal expenditure. But in all cases, political power resided in those who possessed the superior wealth.

It is only by recognizing the connection between property and power in all societies that the full implications of the political revolution can be grasped. Moreover, this is more than an isolated event. It illustrates a theme of general significance. As Winch has noted: 'commerce is more than a stage of society; it is a constant cause producing the same effects at all stages';[68] the effects being to reduce the number of power bases thereby altering the structure of sovereignty in a way that is generally favourable to liberty and justice. The problem with the four stages interpretation was that liberty and justice were associated with particular institutional forms and patterns of wealth distribution, which in turn depended upon the transition from feudalism to the stage of commerce. Skinner, for instance, writes: 'Smith observed that the new sources of wealth, arising from commerce, manufacturing, agriculture, etc., were likely to be more equally distributed',[69] leading to a more equal distribution of political power. In support of this argument, however, it is John Millar and not Smith whom Skinner quotes. Millar did indeed believe that commercial activity would lead to the redistribution of wealth, and that the monarchy and the feudal lords would thereby lose some of their political power.[70] Millar also believed that the opposite tendency was at work since the progress of opulence would create standing armies, thus increasing the power of the sovereign.[71] Smith's

[66] Smith, *Lectures on Jurisprudence [A]*, iv. 161–2.

[67] *Ibid.*, iv. 162–3.

[68] Winch, *Adam Smith's Politics*, p. 64.

[69] Skinner, 'A Scottish Contribution', p. 90.

[70] J. Millar, *The Origin and Distinction of Ranks* (1779), in W.C. Lehman, *John Millar of Glasgow 1735–1801* (Cambridge, 1960), p. 292.

[71] *Ibid.*, p. 284.

argument, however, is not that inequalities would diminish, but that they would cease to create dependence between the nobility and the populace. Whether the monarchy or the populace, or indeed the great nobility and princes, would be the beneficiaries depended upon the existing distribution of wealth. If liberty and justice are exclusively modern, as Skinner's reading implies, not least because the revolution involves the ending of slavery, then '[t]he obvious parallels between the three great attempts by mankind to live in commercial societies, in Greece, in Rome, and in modern Europe,'[72] recede, and the relationship between commerce and liberty is restricted to the context of a single European political revolution.

The interconnections between patterns of distribution and the degree of commerce are thus closely related to the strength and autonomy of governments, and it is in this sense that Smith can be described as a materialist. The presence or absence of slavery is also a factor. In the *Lectures on Jurisprudence* Smith argues that without the institution of slavery the economic power of the rich can sometimes continue to be translated into political power, even with the progress of commerce and luxury.[73] Without slavery, Smith argues, the rich can still exert considerable influence over tradesmen who want their custom. It is also possible to see, in connection with Haakonsen's principal objections to a materialist interpretation, that there is no conflict between a materialist account of sovereignty in this restricted sense and Smith's normative theory of justice founded upon the principles of sympathy and the impartial spectator. As Haakonssen emphasizes, advocacy on the basis of Smith's theory of justice is unlikely to be very effective unless governments have attained the requisite degree of autonomy for justice to be a possibility.

Liberty and Slavery

A final issue concerns the relationship between liberty and slavery which arises because of a highly influential contribution by Duncan Forbes.[74] Forbes has argued that in view of Smith's discussion of slavery in relation to man's love of domination and authority, which he regards as natural to man, and because Smith concluded from this that slavery would be more or less universal, its abolition in Europe must be viewed as a special case. Since slavery would appear to be inconsistent with freedom, in the sense of liberty and security under the law, liberty also must be viewed as an exception which appears only in a small part of modern Europe. Forbes makes this observation in the context of a discussion of the relationship between commerce and liberty, in the sense of freedom under the rule of law. He says that the abolition of slavery 'in Europe was a unique event, due to the very special and exceptional circumstances, . . .

[72] Haakonssen, *The Science of a Legislator*, p. 178.

[73] Smith, *Lectures on Jurisprudence [A]*, iv. 73.

[74] D. Forbes, 'Sceptical Whiggism'.

And this famous story of the destruction of baronial and ecclesiastical power needs to be looked at more closely before one generalizes about it'.[75] He concludes:

> Surely no 'law' of commerce giving rise to liberty could be drawn from such peculiar conditions? . . . One cannot have freedom without commerce and manufactures, but opulence without freedom is the norm rather than the exception.[76]

However, if what I have said above about the ending of slavery in Europe is correct, then Forbes's argument would appear to be even more forceful. The destruction of baronial and ecclesiastical power was not coincident with the abolition of slavery or serfdom, but continued as long as the relationship between landlords and the direct producers was not based on clearly defined economic contracts. Liberty, as defined by Forbes, is not the product of commerce even in the restricted context of European history.

However, if we are prepared to regard liberty, even in the sense of security under the law, as a matter of degree rather than a perfected state, the force of Forbes's argument can be mitigated somewhat. As Haakonssen has pointed out, Smith's treatment of slavery is not incorporated into his discussion of natural law.[77] Smith's discussion of justice in relation to slavery focused on the rights and treatment of slaves rather than its abolition, and he argued that slaves were worse off in free and prosperous countries.[78] Smith could still talk of freedom in situations where slavery existed, and emphasized that what mattered for the rights and treatment of slaves was strong government — although even strong governments could not be expected to abolish slavery.[79] Moreover, Forbes provides an excellent discussion of the different senses in which Smith used the words 'freedom' and 'liberty' and, as argued above, when Smith does refer to freedom 'in our present sense of the word' in relation to the removal of the attributes of villeinage and slavery from the inhabitants of the towns, he is using the term in a different way from the freedom which comes from the ending of feudal dependence which was brought about by the progress of commerce.

If, on the other hand, slavery is to be regarded as incompatible with any degree of liberty and, as a consequence, liberty is to be regarded as an exceptional condition for mankind, then it is not just the connection between commerce and liberty which is called into question. We are once again confronted by the question posed by Haakonsen, for entirely different reasons: what was the practical significance of Smith's extended consideration of liberty and justice

[75] *Ibid.*, p. 200.

[76] *Ibid.*, pp. 200–1.

[77] Haakonssen, *The Science of a Legislator*, p. 72.

[78] Smith, *Lectures on Jurisprudence [B]*, 136–7.

[79] *Ibid.*, 135; also Smith, *Lectures on Jurisprudence [A]*, iii. 104; and *ibid.*, 89–101, where Smith discusses the treatment and rights of slaves.

as normative questions for the legislator if liberty is a virtually unattainable state? By viewing liberty as a matter of degree, both Smith's normative interests in liberty and justice and the materialistic dimension to his treatment of commerce and liberty, defended in this paper, become comprehensible. This certainly does not lead to anything as deterministic as a 'law' of commerce giving rise to liberty, but it would expand the significance of the destruction of baronial and ecclesiastical power beyond the events in modern Europe by allowing it to be seen in parallel with the other occasions when Smith explained the decline in aristocratic power by the progress of opulence.

V
Conclusion

The materialist interpretation of Smith, from its beginnings in the contribution of Pascal, interpreted the account of the destruction of feudal power in the context of the transition from the third to the fourth economic stage, a transition which incorporated the demise of slavery and serfdom. This has had two unfortunate implications. The relationship between commerce and liberty and justice is restricted to the developments in modern Europe. The progress of commerce is favourable to liberty and justice, on this reading, because it ushers in a new economic system — the exchange economy — in which servile labour has been replaced by commercial rents and wage labour. This has exaggerated the extent to which Smith regarded liberty and justice as modern, dependent on the institutions and wealth distribution of the commercial society of his own day, and has detracted from the normative dimensions of Smith's interest in liberty and justice which Winch and Haakonssen have brought to the fore. However, the recognition of Smith's normative purposes should not preclude the recognition that he was also concerned to demonstrate that the progress of commerce and opulence tended to produce strong central government, which he saw as a precondition of liberty and justice, a theme which can justifiably be called materialistic.

The second consequence is that it has led to exaggerated claims regarding the similarity between Smith's account of the decline of feudalism and certain Marxist explanations of the transition from feudalism to capitalism. Anticipatory readings of Smith have been the subject of a great deal of critical comment in the literature.[80] Such an approach is particularly inappropriate in the present context since, as is well known, Marx read Smith and was influenced by him. A more promising approach might have been to have traced these influences with the same care and rigour with which Meek discussed the origins of the four stages theory.[81] This is not, of course, the place to undertake such a task; but I will conclude by noting that Marx provided an accurate summary of

[80] For example see Winch, *Adam Smith's Politics*.

[81] See Meek, *Social Science and the Ignoble Savage*.

Smith's discussion of the effects of commerce on feudalism, and certainly did not take him to be saying that the result was capitalist relations of production:

> Monetary wealth — as merchant wealth — had admittedly helped to speed up and to dissolve the old relations of production, and made it possible for the proprietor of land for example, as A. Smith already nicely develops, to exchange his grain and cattle etc. for use values brought from afar, instead of squandering the use values he himself produced, along with his retainers, and to locate his wealth in great part in the mass of his co-consuming retainers. It gave the *exchange value* of his revenue a higher significance for him. The same thing took place in regard to his tenants, *who were already semi-capitalists, but very hemmed-in ones.*[82]

Marx's general point is that merchant wealth cannot by itself lead to capitalism: 'Or else ancient Rome, Byzantium etc. would have ended their history with free labour and capital'.[83] But this is not an implied criticism of Smith: Marx does not take Smith to be offering an explanation of the demise of serfdom, as his reference to Smith's tenants as 'semi-capitalists' shows. Smith's argument that commerce helped to dissolve the power of the feudal barons is one of which Marx approves and which is repeated in Volume I of Capital, where he explains the dissolution of the bands of feudal retainers and the evictions of the peasants from their lands by the rapid rise of the Flemish wool manufactures.[84] For Marx, however, the nobility by this time were already commercially minded, and the progress of commerce does not involve the fundamental change in their behaviour which is described with such scepticism by Smith. Marx says: 'The old nobility had been devoured by the great feudal wars. The new nobility was the child of its time, for which money was the power of all powers.'[85] As Smith describes the process, however, it is the introduction of commerce which transforms the nobility from warriors into merchants.[86]

The main point to emphasize, however, is that the significance of the dissolution of feudalism for Smith and Marx differed according to their different definitions of feudalism and to the different processes they were attempting to illustrate. Marx gave the central place in his analysis of different societies to their relations of production and, in particular, to the way in which the economic surplus was generated from the labourer: the progress of commerce contributed to the transformation of relations of production in that '[a] mass of free

[82] K. Marx, *Grundrisse* (Harmondsworth, 1973), p. 508 (emphasis added).

[83] *Ibid.*, p. 506.

[84] K. Marx, *Capital* (London, 1974), Vol. 1, p. 672.

[85] *Ibid.*

[86] Smith's argument is open to serious criticism which arises because the condition for the prolonged existence of allodial and feudal violence is the absence of outlets for the surplus other than expenditure on retainers. This leads to an unconvincing explanation of the way in which feudal power is ultimately destroyed as G.E. Mumy has argued. See Mumy, 'Town and Country'.

proletarians was hurled on the labour market'.[87] Smith by contrast, focused his attention not on the way the economic surplus was generated but on the way in which the surplus was consumed. By sharing his surplus the landlord gained authority by the dependence thus created. It was this form of authority that was swept away by the progress of commerce.

John Salter UNIVERSITY OF MANCHESTER

[87] Marx, *Capital*, Vol. 1, p. 672.

Part VI
The Nature of Smith's Theory

[21]

Historicizing the "Adam Smith Problem": Conceptual, Historiographical, and Textual Issues*

Laurence Dickey
Columbia University

In 1965, in his "Guide to John Rae's *Life of Adam Smith*," Jacob Viner felt compelled to explain to his readers why a "guide" had to be added to Rae's very old (1895) and conventional biography of Smith.[1] The problem, Viner told his audience, was that many of the errors in Rae's work had gone undetected and uncorrected for years, with the result that they had become "institutionalized" in Smith scholarship.[2] These errors of omission and commission, Viner argued, should have been tended to long ago. As he saw it, though, the sad fact was that Smith scholars had been remiss in their scholarly duties for years.[3] They had failed not only to provide a modern biography of Smith but also to prepare a scholarly edition of Smith's works and correspondence.[4] Hence, the need for a guide to Rae's work; hence, Viner's criticism of the complacency of Smith scholarship during his lifetime.

Since Viner's reprimand, much has changed in Smith scholarship. There are several reasons for this. First, in 1969 John Dunn published a book on John Locke that signaled the beginning of a reexamination of Locke that is still going on today.[5] And since Locke and Smith have been traditionally associated with each other within the idea complex of English liberalism, some of the splash of Lockean revisionism has spilled over onto Smith.[6] In 1969, another publication—*Revisions in Mercan-*

* I wish to dedicate this essay to Albert O. Hirschman, who has recently retired as professor of social science at the Institute for Advanced Study at Princeton. Were it not for his work and encouragement this essay would not have been written. I would also like to thank the Institute for Advanced Study for financial support during the period this essay was written.

[1] J. Viner, "Guide to John Rae's *Life of Adam Smith*," in *Life of Adam Smith*, by John Rae (New York, 1965), pp. 5–16.

[2] Ibid., pp. 14, 16.

[3] Ibid., pp. 9–10. Viner cites W. R. Scott's *Adam Smith as Student and Professor* (London, 1937) as an exception.

[4] Ibid. Viner notes the beginning of preparation for what would become the Glasgow edition of Smith's complete works.

[5] John Dunn, *The Political Thought of John Locke* (Cambridge, 1969).

[6] Dunn himself has recently ventured into the area of Smith scholarship. See his "From Applied Theology to Social Analysis: The Break between John Locke

[*Journal of Modern History* 58 (September 1986): 579–609]

tilism, a collection of essays on eighteenth-century economic thought—marked the beginning of a reevaluation of the role mercantilism played in eighteenth-century thought.[7] Again, aspects of this revisionism touched Smith, who, as J. Schumpeter noted, was mainly responsible for the short shrift mercantilists have received at the hands of modern scholars.[8] By the mid-seventies, moreover, scholars of various sorts—many of whom are associated with the so-called Cambridge School of social and political theory—were rediscovering the "Scottish Enlightenment."[9] In 1975, John Pocock's *Machiavellian Moment* drew attention to the interplay between "commerce and virtue" in Scottish thought.[10] In 1977, Albert Hirschman's *Passions and Interests* stressed the importance the idea of *doux-commerce* had for the social and political thought of the eighteenth century in general and for James Steuart, a Scot, in particular.[11] At about the same time, Fred Hirsch presented us with *Social Limits to Growth*.[12] And that book, among other things, raised many interesting questions about the relationship between the economic and noneconomic aspects of eighteenth-century liberal thought and particularly about Smith's thought. Finally, in 1976, the Glasgow edition of Smith's collected works and correspondence began to appear.[13] And since many of today's finest Smith scholars were associated with the edition, the publication helped spark interest in Smith as a thinker.[14]

As a result, Smith has become the focus of much new scholarly interest. And one of the early fruits of this interest was Donald Winch's *Adam*

---

and the Scottish Enlightenment," in *Wealth and Virtue: Political Economy in the Scottish Enlightenment*, ed. I. Hont and M. Ignatieff (Cambridge, 1983), pp. 119–35. Henceforth, this fine collection of essays will be cited as *WV*.

[7] D. C. Coleman, ed., *Revisions in Mercantilism* (London, 1969). Aspects of this revisionism may be seen in I. Hont and M. Ignatieff, "Needs and Justice in the *Wealth of Nations:* An Introductory Essay," in *WV*, pp. 14–20. The revision was foreshadowed in A. W. Coats, "Adam Smith: The Modern Reappraisal," *Renaissance and Modern Studies* 6 (1962): 25–48.

[8] J. Schumpeter, *History of Economic Analysis*, ed. E. Schumpeter (New York, 1954), p. 361.

[9] For an assessment of the school's impact on Scottish Enlightenment scholarship, see J. G. A. Pocock, "Cambridge Paradigms and Scotch Philosophers," in *WV*, pp. 235–52.

[10] J. G. A. Pocock, *The Machiavellian Moment* (Princeton, N.J., 1975).

[11] A. Hirschman, *The Passions and the Interests* (Princeton, N.J., 1977).

[12] F. Hirsch, *Social Limits to Growth* (Cambridge, Mass., 1976).

[13] See *The Glasgow Edition of the Works and Correspondence of Adam Smith*, 6 vols. (Oxford, 1976). Throughout this essay the first and second volumes of this edition, *The Theory of Moral Sentiments*, ed. A. Macfie and D. Raphael, and *An Inquiry into the Nature and Causes of the Wealth of Nations*, ed. R. Campbell and A. Skinner, will be referred to as *TMS* and *WN*, respectively.

[14] I am thinking here of the essays collected in *Essays on Adam Smith*, ed. A. Skinner and T. Wilson (Oxford, 1976).

Smith's Politics, whose subtitle, *An Essay in Historiographic Revision*, expresses quite well what I shall try to do in this essay myself.[15]

Very briefly, what I propose to do is approach Adam Smith from the perspective of the so-called Adam Smith problem (ASP). In that context, the essay will focus on three different but related aspects of that problem. First, I shall offer an overview of the Adam Smith problem as it exists as a conceptual concern among Smith scholars today. Here, I shall discuss the problem as it has appeared in some of the most recent and best Smith scholarship. Second, I shall try to explain why the conventional approach to the ASP is *historically* inadequate. And finally, in the process of doing that, I shall propose a historicized version of the ASP that I think raises rather different conceptual questions about the problem's meaning for Smith scholarship today. The structure of the essay, then, is as follows: by turns it will be conceptual, then historical, then conceptual again.

The Adam Smith Problem Today

Given all the work that has been done on Smith in the last twenty years, it is somewhat surprising that the basic contours of the ASP have not really changed since August Oncken gave rather full expression to them in 1898.[16] Take, for example, four recent formulations of the problem: (1) Garry Wills—The Adam Smith problem involves "the difficulty of reconciling the 1759 *TMS* . . . with the 1776 *Wealth of Nations*."[17] (2) Fred Hirsch—The ASP is concerned with whether or not "Smith's economic analysis in *Wealth of Nations* . . . rested . . . on his social analysis in the *Theory of Moral Sentiment*."[18] (3) Donald Winch—"The poles" of the Adam Smith problem are "marked out by the *Theory of Moral Sentiment* on the one side, and the *Wealth of Nations* on the other."[19] (4) Robert Heilbroner—The "once heated, now largely quiescent [ASP] raises the question of the relationship between the intensely moral focus of . . . the *Theory of Moral Sentiment* and the moral indifference of the *Wealth of Nations*."[20]

In this form, the ASP seems to turn on two issues: that of the relation between *TMS* (1759) and *WN* (1776), and that of continuity and change

[15] D. Winch, *Adam Smith's Politics* (Cambridge, 1978).

[16] A. Oncken, "Das Adam Smith-Problem," in *Zeitschrift für Sozialwissenschaft*, ed. J. Wolf (Berlin, 1898), 1:25–33, 101–8, 276–87; a shorter version of this essay appeared as "The Consistency of Adam Smith," *Economic Journal* 7 (1897): 443–50.

[17] G. Wills, "Benevolent Adam Smith," *New York Review of Books* 25 (February 1978): 40.

[18] Hirsch, p. 137.

[19] Winch, p. 2; cf. pp. 9–10, 92–93, 167–68.

[20] R. Heilbroner, "The Socialization of the Individual in Adam Smith," in *History of Political Economy* 14, no. 3 (1982): 427.

in Smith's thought as it developed between the two books. If one looks at the recent Glasgow edition of the *TMS*, it becomes most obvious that the editors have framed the ASP this way.[21] There, they tell us three things about the problem. First, they tell us that the problem is a creation (or fetish) of late nineteenth-century German scholarship.[22] Second, they tell us that the core of the ASP rests on "the hypothesis that the moral philosopher who made sympathy the basis of social behavior in *TMS* did an about-turn from altruistic to egoistic theory in the *WN*."[23] Finally, they tell us that the main evidence for this hypothesis is the assertion that Smith's contact with the Physiocrats in France between 1764 and 1766 turned him into a materialist. Hence, his abandonment of the altruism of *TMS* as a framework for his thought.[24]

Having identified the ASP this way, the editors of the Glasgow edition are quick to dismiss it as a problem because there is much evidence to suggest that Smith had already formulated the argument of the *WN* long before his trip to France. For this reason, the editors happily report, the ASP must be seen as "a pseudo-problem based on ignorance and misunderstanding [of the relation between the *TMS* and *WN*]."[25]

Now, there is nothing wrong with what the Glasgow editors have written about that form of the ASP, a form that Oncken had given expression to almost ninety years ago.[26] But the editors, I think, have done a disservice to Smith scholarship by formulating the problem this way. They have, I would argue, taken the "low road" with regard to the conceptual questions the ASP really raises. For they have clearly and deliberately ignored some of the more difficult aspects of the problem. Suffice it to say, the ASP is not just a late nineteenth-century creation. And by claiming that the ASP is a "pseudo-problem," the editors have deflected interest away from it, and that, I think, is an egregious scholarly error.[27]

[21] See A. Macfie and D. Raphael's "Introduction" to Smith, *TMS* (n. 13 above).

[22] Ibid., p. 20.

[23] Ibid.

[24] Ibid.

[25] Ibid.

[26] See Oncken (n. 16 above), pp. 28–31. As others have pointed out, though, there are other dimensions to the ASP. Two that immediately come to mind are the relation between interventionism and laissez-faire in *WN* and the relation between the different conceptions of the division of labor in the same book.

[27] Winch (n. 15 above), p. 10, concurs with the editors. Also see T. Campbell, *Adam Smith's Science of Morals* (London, 1971), p. 19, where the ASP is characterized as an "unnecessary controversy." At a deeper level, this view of the ASP, which treats the problem as passé, is part of a recent effort to see Smith's work as an "integrated whole." The connection has been appreciated by H. Recktenwald, "An Adam Smith Renaissance Anno 1976? The Bicentenary Out-

To explain why this is so, I would like to identify some of the deeper issues involved in the ASP. What I propose to do is demonstrate that the ASP is what Weber would have called a composite conceptual problem—which is to say, it has different *conceptual layers* that need to be identified and sorted out before any sense can be made of the problem as a whole.[28] To this end, Smith scholarship may be divided into three groups of studies, each of which addresses the ASP from a different perspective. For the sake of convenience, I shall refer to the first group as the argument for continuity; the second, as the argument for change; and the third group as the argument for continuity and change.

The editors' introduction to the Glasgow edition of *TMS* is a fine example of the continuity argument. There the editors insist for several reasons on a basic similarity between *TMS* and the *WN*.[29] First of all, they claim that the ASP has been informed by the mistaken "assumption that sympathy [the theme of *TMS*] and selfishness [the theme of *WN*] can be set side by side as motives" for action and distinguished from one another on that basis.[30] As the editors proceed to point out, sympathy was not, as self-love was, a motive for action in *TMS*.[31] Conversely, in the *WN*, Smith's concern was with "self-love," not "selfishness."[32] In both books, the editors argue, Smith equated self-love with interested behavior that had moderation and a sense of "fair play" built into it.[33] They conclude, therefore, that "it is . . . impossible to accept the view that there is any difference of substance between *TMS* and *WN* on self-interest as a motive."[34]

Earlier in their introduction the editors had made the case for continuity another way. Having declared that "*TMS* and *WN* are [essentially] at

---

put—A Reappraisal of His Scholarship," in *Journal of Economic Literature* 16 (1978): 56, 66. For a more critical perspective on the connection, see R. Teichgraeber III, "Rethinking *Das Adam Smith Problem*," in *Journal of British Studies* 20, no. 2 (1981): 109–10.

[28] For a discussion of Weber's idea, see R. Bendix, "Concepts and Generalizations in Comparative Sociological Studies," *American Sociological Review* 28, no. 4 (1963): esp. 533.

[29] Macfie and Raphael, esp. pp. 9, 18, 20–22.

[30] Ibid., p. 21.

[31] Ibid.

[32] Ibid., p. 22.

[33] The famous "fair play" passage may be found in Smith, *TMS* (n. 13 above), p. 83. It runs: "In the race for wealth, and honours, and preferments, he may run as hard as he can, and strain every nerve and muscle, in order to outstrip all his competitors. But if he should justle, or throw down any of them, the indulgence of the spectators is entirely at an end. It is a violation of fair play, which they cannot admit of."

[34] Macfie and Raphael (n. 21 above), p. 22.

one,"[35] they cite the "bettering our condition" passage in *TMS* as an anticipation of the use Smith makes of the phrase in *WN*.[36] Their judgment: since "both books treat the desire to better our condition as natural and proper," there is continuity between the two books.[37]

To substantiate their argument further, the editors point to another telling continuity between *TMS* and *WN*. In 1759, the editors note, Smith had written about "that eminent esteem with which all men naturally regard a steady perseverance in the practice of frugality, industry and application, though directed to no other purpose than the acquisition of fortune."[38] This, the editors continue, anticipates a key chapter in *WN* in which Smith praises "industry and frugality."[39] Again, continuity between the two books.

The result of these kinds of arguments may be summarized by quoting from two authorities who have used this argument for continuity to make general points about the ASP. First, from Alec Macfie, one of the Glasgow editors. Writing elsewhere, he claimed that "it would appear that the *WN* is simply a special case—the economic case—of the philosophy implicit in the *TMS*. It works out the economic side of that 'self-love' which is given *its appropriate place* in the developed ethical system of the *earlier* book."[40] The second quote comes from Winch. He writes: "The *TMS* contains Smith's general theory of morality . . . ; it consistently operates on a higher level of theoretical generality . . . than the *WN*. The latter work can, therefore, be regarded as a specialized application to the detailed field of economic action of the general social . . . behavior contained in the earlier work."[41]

There are four key points to remember about the continuity argument. First, note that this argument maintains that the ethical system of *TMS* "contains" the economic argument of *WN*.[42] Second, note that, in saying this, the *WN* is conceptually assimilated back *into* the *TMS*. And there it is possible to deny that an ASP exists because it is clear from the "fair play" statement that Smith never meant to abide a dog-eat-dog laissez-faire.[43] Third, note that, in *TMS*, containment takes a nonpolitical

[35] Ibid., p. 9.
[36] Ibid., cited on p. 9; discussed by Heilbroner (n. 20 above), pp. 431–32.
[37] Macfie and Raphael, p. 9.
[38] Ibid., p. 9; the citation is from *TMS*, pp. 189–90.
[39] Ibid., p. 9.
[40] A. Macfie, *The Individual in Society* (London, 1967), pp. 75–76; my emphasis.
[41] Winch (n. 15 above), p. 10. Also see T. Campbell (n. 27 above), pp. 16, 18.
[42] K. Polanyi, *The Great Transformation* (Boston, 1944), p. 62, notes how the word "contain" must be construed in this context.
[43] See n. 33 above for the "fair play" reference.

form.[44] And, finally, remember that the argument for continuity conceptually insists that *TMS* is the single ''motivating center'' of Smith's thought.[45] Everything that Smith writes after that is an elaboration of themes developed in that book—which is to say that this treatment of the ASP refuses to allow Smith fundamentally to change his mind about things.[46] And that is what I was referring to earlier when I said that this was an unhistorical view of Smith as a thinker.

A second approach to the ASP emphasizes the lack of continuity between *TMS* and *WN*. One of the key spokesmen for this view is Viner.[47] In his classic essay ''Adam Smith and Laissez-faire,'' Viner points out that *TMS* aimed at developing a ''system of ethics on the basis of a doctrine of a harmonious order in nature.''[48] In this system, which in the 1750s Smith had called a ''system of natural liberty,'' Viner detects an attempt to attribute ''beneficient'' ends to the ''matter-of-fact processes of nature.''[49] He cites numerous passages from *TMS*, including the famous one on the ''invisible hand,'' as evidence for this view.[50]

The decisive point in Viner's argument is reached when he goes on to claim ''that on the points at which [*TMS* and *WN*] come into contact'' they are irreconcilably ''divergent.''[51] That, Viner enthuses, was a positive development, because, whereas in *TMS* economic containment was presented in the form of wishful thinking about ''a system of natural liberty,'' in *WN* Smith posited specific institutional agencies for correcting ''flaws''

[44] Polanyi, esp. chap. 10, is illuminating on the eighteenth-century attempt to designate ''society'' as a nonpolitical institutional mechanism of police.

[45] I borrow the idea of ''motivating'' centers from Eric Voegelin, *Order and History* (London, 1956) 1:137–38, 162. He develops the idea in the context of discussing the differing historical layers of the Old Testament. On a less grand scale, this is what I am doing with the different editions of *TMS*.

[46] As Recktenwald (n. 27 above) has observed, the attempt to view Smith's work as an ''integrated whole'' entails designating *TMS* (1759) as the key to Smith's system. For an example of this strategy, see Campbell (n. 27 above), esp. pp. 16, 21, 46.

[47] J. Viner's essay, ''Adam Smith and Laissez-faire,'' may be found in his *The Long View and the Short* (Glencoe, Ill., 1958). Though Viner's essay is old, its basic thrust is consistent with the recent effort to explain Smith's interventionism in terms of his commitment to an overall economic strategy of growth. See, e.g., Hont and Ignatieff (n. 7 above), esp. p. 21. R. Black, ''Smith's Contribution in Historical Perspective,'' in *The Market and the State*, ed. A. Skinner and T. Wilson (Oxford, 1976), esp. p. 60, notes the recent interest in Smith as a ''growth'' strategist. For a current restatement of much that Viner said, see A. Skinner, *Adam Smith and the Role of the State* (Glasgow, 1974).

[48] Viner, ''Adam Smith and Laissez-faire,'' p. 215. Cf. p. 220.

[49] Ibid., pp. 216–17.

[50] Ibid., p. 217.

[51] Ibid., p. 221. Cf. pp. 216, 228.

that developed within that ''system.''[52] After presenting a long list of ''interventions'' Smith allowed government to make in *WN*,[53] Viner concludes that there is ''a wide divergence between the perfectly harmonious, completely beneficent natural order of *TMS* and the partial and limited harmony in the economic order of *WN*.''[54]

Now there is clearly a change here in how the ASP has been conceptualized. For whereas the Glasgow editors ''solve'' the problem by assimilating the economic argument of *WN* back into the context of *TMS*, Viner absorbs the natural harmony of interest doctrine of *TMS* into *WN* and then allows it to be superseded there as the interventionism of the mature Smith develops. In this context, three crucial changes need to be noted. First, Viner establishes the *WN*, not *TMS*, as the ''motivating center'' of Smith's thought. Second, the strategy of economic containment has changed also—it is no longer nonpolitical but is quite specifically political in an interventionist sense. Finally, the ASP in this framework takes the form of the argument of laissez-faire versus interventionism that has figured so prominently among Smith scholars over the years.[55] Hence, the notable absence of discussion of this dimension of the ASP in the work of the Glasgow editors.

The third and final way of treating the ASP tries to reconcile these two modes of historiographical discourse. It starts by accepting the *TMS* and *WN* as ''rival centers of meaning'' in Smith's thought.[56] It then explains the relationship between the two books in terms of a continuity *and* change argument rather than in terms of a continuity *versus* change argument. Hirsch's recent work, *Social Limits to Growth,* is my example. According to Hirsch, the *TMS* and *WN* may be treated as complementary texts because they were written at a time when ''special conditions associated with a transition phase'' of historical development made it possible to hold to the arguments of both books at once.[57] By that Hirsch means to draw attention to the existence in the late eighteenth century of a collective, ''pre-market social ethos'' that Smith could assume would act as a check on individual excesses within a market economy.[58] As Hirsch succinctly put it, this premarket ethos ''provided the neces-

[52] Ibid., pp. 216, 228–31.

[53] Ibid., pp. 228–44. Hence, Viner's conclusion (p. 244): ''Adam Smith was not a doctrinaire advocate of laissez faire.''

[54] Ibid., p. 228.

[55] Oncken (n. 16 above), pp. 26–27, identified the interventionism and laissez-faire issue as central to the ASP.

[56] The phrase is Voegelin's (n. 45 above).

[57] Hirsch (n. 12 above), p. 11.

[58] Ibid., p. 12.

sary social binding for an individualistic, nonaltruistic market economy."[59]

Two points about the continuity with change argument. First, the *TMS* and the *WN* are taken as complementary for *historical* rather than *logical* reasons. And, second, Hirsch's formulation of the ASP leaves us with two "motivating centers" for Smith's thought. In this respect, Hirsch has historicized the ASP for us, but he has not tried to solve it as a conceptual problem. He has allowed, or appealed to, history to do that for him.

At this point, I think, the conceptual contours of the ASP should be fairly clear—the issue invariably seems to turn on one's estimation of which book, *TMS* or *WN*, deserves priority as a "motivating center" in Smith's thought as it developed from 1759 to 1776.

In the remainder of this essay, I would like to explain why these renderings of the ASP are inadequate. And in the process of doing that, I shall propose an alternative, more historically based mode of conceptualization, one that has three rather than one or two motivating centers.

The *TMS*: The 1759 and 1790 Editions

Let me begin by focusing on a problem of scholarship that raises a troubling question about how the ASP is currently conceptualized. In his stimulating study of Adam Smith, Joseph Cropsey makes the following argument.[60] In the context of explaining Smith's intentions in *TMS*, Cropsey notes a tension in Smith's thought. On the one hand, Cropsey points out, Smith dismissed "moral education" as a realistic way of influencing behavior in the modern world.[61] It was interest, not benevolence, that governed human action. On the other hand, Cropsey remarks, Smith continued "to affirm the fundamentally 'practical' character of moral philosophy . . . as a means to make people 'good.'"[62] To prove all of this, Cropsey cites several passages from *TMS* which make this point.[63] And with this evidence at hand he concludes that in *TMS* Smith was ambivalent about the power of moral education in the modern world.

[59] Ibid., p. 142; cf. pp. 137–38, where Smith is the subject.

[60] J. Cropsey, *Polity and Economy: An Interpretation of the Principles of Adam Smith* (The Hague, 1957).

[61] Ibid., p. 24.

[62] Ibid., p. 25.

[63] Cropsey cites Smith, *TMS* (n. 13 above), pp. 76–78n., 307 in the first case and pp. 259, 293 in the second case (the citations are to the Glasgow ed.). The passage (p. 259) runs: "The great secret of education is to direct vanity to proper objects." The first set of quotes comes from the 1759 edition of *TMS*; the second set from the 1790 one.

What Cropsey fails to comment on here is that the passages he quotes to establish Smith's ambivalence come from the first and sixth editions of *TMS*. Now there is about a thirty-years' difference between the two editions. When I realized this, it occurred to me that instead of being ambivalent about moral eduction in 1759, as Cropsey would have us believe, perhaps Smith had changed his mind about its value by 1790. With that in mind, I began to investigate the 1790 edition of the *TMS*. It is on the basis of my work on that text that I propose to proceed. Suffice to say here that if the 1790 edition is allowed to present itself as another ''motivating center'' of Smith's thought, then the conceptual dimensions of the ASP will change enormously.[64]

The Glasgow edition of *TMS* has quite a bit to say about the 1790 edition. There the editors tell us the following about it: that it ''contains very extensive additions and other significant changes'';[65] that the inclusion in the 1790 of an ''entirely new Part VI'' was ''a major change'';[66] that in the 1790 edition there was a ''change of emphasis'' in the material that reflected ''the thought of the more mature man who had written *WN*.''[67] Having said all this, the editors then curiously insist that the 1790 edition ''rounds out and clarifies, rather than changes, Smith's ethical theory'' and that ''the new material in edition six is simply a development of Smith's earlier position and at the same time reflects some of the interests of *WN*.''[68] As a result, the editors arrive at the following conclusion: ''Smith's account of ethics and human behavior *is basically the same* in edition six of 1790 as in edition one of 1759. There is development but no alteration.''[69] Coming from two fine Smith scholars, this conclusion would seem to be decisive. If, however, one looks closely at the text, it will become apparent that this is clearly not the case.

To explain what I am driving at here, I would like to proceed according to the following agenda. First, I shall examine the Glasgow editors' argument for continuity of development between the 1759 and 1790 editions. Next, I shall show why that argument is quite misleading. Then, I shall try to explain how the changes Smith made in the 1790 edition can be *systematically* related to each other in a way that allows us to constitute the 1790 edition as a third motivating center of Smith's thought. Finally, I shall offer some suggestions about what the ASP adds

[64] One of the few scholars to sense this was A. O. Lovejoy. See his *Reflections on Human Nature* (Baltimore, 1961), esp. pp. 190–91, 213–15, 263–64.

[65] Macfie and Raphael (n. 21 above), p. 1.

[66] Ibid., p. 18.

[67] Ibid., pp. 8–9.

[68] Ibid., pp. 18, 24, respectively.

[69] Ibid., p. 20; my emphasis.

up to if it is stretched out historically from a one- and/or two-term sequence to a three-term one—which is to say, I shall be asking questions about the meaning of Smith's thought as a developmental sequence as it runs from 1759 through 1776 to 1790.

As I have already indicated, the editors of the Glasgow edition insist on the fundamental "sameness" of the 1759 and 1790 versions of the *TMS*. At the core of their argument is the claim that the prudent man of 1759 is the frugal man of 1776 (the year *WN* appeared) who then becomes a prudent man once again in 1790.[70] To substantiate this claim, the editors cite a key passage from the 1790 edition: "In the steadiness of his industry and frugality, in his steadily sacrificing the ease and enjoyment of the present moment for the probable expectation of the still greater ease and enjoyment of a more distant but more lasting period of time, the prudent man is always both supported and rewarded by the entire approbation of the impartial spectator, and of the representative of the impartial spectator, the man within the breast."[71] On the basis of this passage they argue that "the prudent man of *TMS* [1790] is the frugal man of *WN* [of 1776]."[72] And since the editors have already declared that the frugal man of *WN* differs hardly at all from the prudent man of *TMS* (1759),[73] it follows for the editors that the 1759 and 1790 versions are "basically the same."[74]

One crucial point about this argument is pertinent here: namely, its basic thrust is wholly consistent with the editors' wish to designate 1759 as the sole motivating center of Smith's thought. Thus, their effort to pull the prudent man of 1790 back into the frugal man of 1776, who is then himself pulled back to 1759. The consequence of this, of course, is that instead of having to contend with three motivating centers in Smith's intellectual life, the editors need deal with one within which the other two *must find their place*.[75]

With all due respect to the Glasgow editors, this argument simply will not do.[76] For as I read the text of 1790, it tells a very different story

[70] For the editors' argument, see ibid., pp. 9, 18. For examples of the influence of this line of interpretation, see Heilbroner (n. 20 above), p. 427 and Winch (n. 15 above), p. 93n.

[71] Cited in Macfie and Raphael, p. 9; they are referring to *TMS*, p. 215.

[72] Ibid., p. 18.

[73] Ibid., p. 9.

[74] Ibid., p. 20.

[75] In Clifford Geertz's terms (*The Interpretation of Cultures* [New York, 1973], p. 97), the editors are offering an assessment of Smith's "mood," not an explanation of the direction of his "motivations" taken over time.

[76] A clear indication of why the argument will not do can be seen in Macfie and Raphael (n. 21 above), p. 20. There the editors offer three poor arguments for why *TMS* and *WN* should be treated as one. The first is because "the same

indeed. Take, for example, the passage just cited from the 1790 edition.[77] If that citation is read in the context of what is said in the next few paragraphs (12–15), its meaning changes markedly.

12. The man who lives within his income, is naturally contented with his situation, which, by continual, though small accumulations, is growing better and better every day. He . . . has no anxiety to change so comfortable a situation, and does not go in quest of new enterprises and adventures, which might endanger, but could not well increase, the secure tranquility which he actually enjoys.

13. The prudent man is not willing to subject himself to any responsibility which his duty does not impose upon him. He is not a bustler in business where he has no concern; is not a meddler in other people's affairs; is not a professed counsellor or adviser, who obtrudes his advice where nobody is asking it. He confines himself, as much as his duty will permit, to his own affairs, and has no taste for that foolish importance which many people wish to derive from appearing to have some influence in the management of those of other people. He is averse to enter into any party disputes, hates faction, and is not always very forward to listen to the voice even of noble and great ambition. When distinctly called upon, he will not decline the service of his country, but he will not cabal in order to force himself into it, and would be much better pleased that the public business were well managed by some other person, than that he himself should have the trouble, and incur the responsibility, of managing it. In the bottom of his heart he would prefer the undisturbed enjoyment of secure tranquility, not only to all the vain splendour of successful ambition, *but to the real and solid glory of performing the greatest and most magnanimous actions.*

14. *Prudence,* in short, when directed merely to the care of the health, of the fortune, and of the rank and reputation of the individual, *though it is regarded as a most respectable and even, in some degree, as an amiable and agreeable quality, yet it never is considered as one, either of the most endearing, or of the most ennobling of the virtues. It commands a certain cold esteem,* but seems not entitled to any very ardent love or admiration.

15. Wise and judicious conduct, when directed to greater and nobler purposes than the care of the health, the fortune, the rank and reputation of the individual, is frequently and very properly called prudence. We talk of the prudence of the great general, of the great statesman, of the great legislator. Prudence is, in all these cases, combined with many greater and more splendid virtues, with valour, with extensive and strong benevolence, with a sacred regard to the rules of justice, and all these supported by a proper degree of self-command. *This superior prudence,* when carried to the highest degree of perfection, necessarily supposes the art, the talent, and the habit or disposition of acting with the most perfect propriety in every possible circumstance and situation. It necessarily supposes the utmost perfection of all the intellectual and of all the moral virtues. It is the best head joined to the best heart. It is the most perfect wisdom combined with

---

man'' wrote both books; the second is because ''the new material added to edition 6 of *TMS* clearly comes from the author of *WN*''; and the third is because the writer of edition 1 of *TMS* was ''the potential author of *WN*.''

[77] See n. 71 above.

the most perfect virtue. It constitutes very nearly the character of the Academical or Peripatetic sage, as *the inferior prudence* does that of the Epicurean.[78]

In paragraphs 12 and 13, Smith is clearly fleshing out the character of the prudent/frugal man of the earlier works. Here, he identifies security, tranquility, and privacy as watchwords of this type of man. But notice how the last sentence of paragraph 13 cues the reader to a shift in Smith's evaluation of that type of man. For in paragraphs 14 and 15 Smith makes it quite clear that there is something wrong with the type of man he has been describing. That man "commands" only our "cold esteem" because he lives a life of "inferior" rather than "superior" prudence.[79]

If we insert the prudent man of 1759 into this framework, it becomes obvious that, while on one level, there certainly is a linguistic continuity between the two editions, on another level there is not. And that is because in 1790 Smith had come to regard the prudent/frugal man of 1759 and 1776 in what I would call "minimalist" terms.[80] As he put it a few pages later, the minimalist man is a "citizen" insofar as he obeys the law; but he only becomes a truly "good citizen" when he wishes "to promote, by every means in his power, the welfare of the whole society of his fellow-citizens."[81]

Clearly, Smith has deliberately altered the framework of values in which he treats the prudent/frugal man. Granted, the prudent/frugal man is still a feature in the 1790 edition; but Smith has raised a question about his values, especially about his "public spiritedness," and that was not a concern in Smith's earlier work.[82]

If this were an isolated instance of concern, we might very well overlook it. But the fact is that Smith's reservations about the values of the prudent/

[78] Smith, *TMS* (n. 13 above), pp. 215–16; my emphasis.

[79] As a conclusion to this all new part 6 (ibid., pp. 262–64), Smith reiterated the point, referring to certain forms of prudential behavior as "vulgar," worthy only of our "cold esteem."

[80] Among recent Smith scholars, this view of justice is regarded as part of the jurisprudential school of natural law thought. See, e.g., Hont and Ignatieff (n. 7 above), pp. 38–39; and K. Haakonssen, *The Science of the Legislator* (Cambridge, 1981), pp. 86–98.

[81] Smith, *TMS*, p. 231.

[82] It should be noted here that Smith's new appreciation of public spiritedness has little in common with the civic humanist, civil liberal, and natural jurisprudential traditions of thought that have received recent attention in *WV* (see, esp. chaps. 1 and 9). For by 1790 Smith's views on a wide range of issues prevented him from identifying with any of these traditions. He was groping, I would argue, for a conception of the public that would provide an answer to what I would call the dilemma of either a "commercial culture" or a "liberal civilization." Consult n. 114 below for another formulation of this dilemma.

frugal man inform many of the other themes Smith chose to elaborate in the 1790 edition. Obviously, I cannot go into great detail here; but I believe you can get some sense of the scope of the changes in the 1790 edition from the following considerations. First, Smith spent a good deal of time revising the sixth edition of the *TMS*. In a letter to a friend during the late 1780s, he remarked that he had been "laboring very hard" on these revisions for almost four years.[83] These were not cosmetic changes for him. Second, a rough page count of the edition reveals that about one-third of the book was newly written. Again, the magnitude of the change suggests a firm commitment on the part of Smith to what he was doing. Finally, it is clear to me that in the 1790 edition Smith made *a systematic effort* to raise questions about the values of the kind of prudent/frugal/law-abiding man he had previously written about. I have already suggested that this was the point behind Smith's discussion of "inferior" and "superior" prudence. The same purpose can be detected in several other themes newly discussed in the 1790 edition.

Consider the following examples. First, the Glasgow editors single out "self-command" as a thematic constant between the first and sixth editions of *TMS*.[84] For as they see it, "the moral quality of prudence depends on its association with the stoic virtue of self-command."[85] What the editors do not discuss is the great change that the idea of self-command undergoes in Smith's mind between 1759 and 1790. In 1759, self-command was associated with (1) those who have a capacity to "abstain from present pleasure, in order to secure greater pleasure to come" and (2) those who exhibit "a steady perseverance in the practice of frugality, industry, and application, though directed to no other purpose than the acquisition of fortune."[86] This man, Smith states without qualification in 1759, "commands our approbation."[87]

Compare this with what Smith says about self-command in 1790. I offer a set of three examples. First, Smith introduces us in 1790 to "different shades and gradations of . . . self-command."[88] Then he links these "gradations" with three kinds of men. There is a "weak" man whose capacity for self-command "is not of long continuance"; a "man

[83] Smith, quoted in Macfie and Raphael, p. 42.

[84] Ibid., p. 9.

[85] Ibid. According to the editors (pp. 5–10, 18), Smith's work from 1759 to 1790 was consistently oriented by stoic principles. In the section titled, "Smith's Concept of Human Nature," I take exception to this view.

[86] Cited in Macfie and Raphael (n. 21 above), p. 9; the references in *TMS* are to pages 189 and 189–90, respectively.

[87] Smith, *TMS*, p. 190.

[88] Ibid., p. 145.

of a little more firmness''; and a ''man of real constancy and firmness.''[89] Smith identifies the third man in this group as ''the wise and just man who has been thoroughly bred in the great school of self-command.''[90] This man, Smith goes on to tell us, is a man of conscience, a man who has learned how to ''conquer'' his ''natural sensibility.''[91] We see what results from this in the following quotation:

> In such paroxysms of distress, if I may be allowed to call them so, the wisest and firmest man, in order to preserve his equanimity, is obliged, I imagine, to make a considerable, and even a painful exertion. *His own natural feeling of his own distress, his own natural view of his own situation, presses hard upon him,* and he cannot, without a very great effort, *fix his attention upon that of the impartial spectator.* Both views present themselves to him at the same time. His sense of honour, his regard to his own dignity, directs him to fix his whole attention upon the one view. His natural, his untaught and undisciplined feelings, are continually calling it off to the other. He does not, in this case, perfectly identify himself with the ideal man within the breast, he does not become himself the impartial spectator of his own conduct. The different views of both characters exist in his mind separate and distinct from one another, and each directing him to a behavior different from that to which the other directs him. When he follows that view which honour and dignity point out to him, Nature does not, indeed, leave him without a recompense. He enjoys his own complete self-approbation, and the applause of every candid and impartial spectator. By her unalterable laws, however, he still suffers; and the recompense which she bestows, though very considerable, is not sufficient completely to compensate the sufferings which those laws inflict. Neither is it fit that it should. If it did completely compensate them, he could, from self-interest, have no motive for avoiding an accident which must necessarily diminish his utility both to himself and to society; and Nature, from her parental care of both, meant that he should anxiously avoid all such accidents. He suffers, therefore, and though, in the agony of the paroxysm, he maintains, not only the manhood of his countenance, but the sedateness and sobriety of his judgement, it requires his utmost and most fatiguing exertions, to do so.[92]

Thus, in 1790, Smith presents us with a vision of this third man in a state of tension, a state in which an ideal self and natural self struggle for hegemony over his *character*.

A second example that makes the same point comes from a later section newly added to the 1790 edition. There Smith presents us with a man struggling with different standards of self-evaluation. Smith writes:

> In estimating our own merit, in judging of our character and conduct, there are two different standards to which *we naturally compare* them. The one is the idea

[89] Ibid., developed on pp. 145–47.
[90] Ibid., p. 146.
[91] Ibid., p. 147.
[92] Ibid., p. 148; my emphasis.

of *exact propriety and perfection*, so far as we are each of us capable of comprehending that idea. The other is that degree of *approximation* to this idea *which is commonly attained in the world*, and which the greater part of our friends and companions, of our rivals and competitors, may have actually arrived at. We very seldom (I am disposed to think, we never) attempt to judge of ourselves without giving more or less attention to both these different standards. But the attention of different men, and even of the same man at different times, is often very unequally divided between them; and is sometimes principally directed towards the one, and sometimes towards the other.

So far as our attention is directed towards the first standard, the wisest and best of us all, can, in his own character and conduct, see nothing but weakness and imperfection; can discover no ground for arrogance and presumption, but a great deal for humility, regret and repentance. So far as our attention is directed towards the second, we may be affected either in the one way or in the other, and feel ourselves, either really above, or really below, the standard to which we compare ourselves. *The wise and virtuous man directs his principal* attention to the first standard; the idea of exact propriety and perfection.[93]

And, as Smith goes on to note, this means that the wise man, the man who was truly schooled in self-command, "endeavors as well as he can, to assimilate his own character to [the] archetype of perfection."[94]

A final example of this line of argument is just as instructive. Here Smith distinguishes, again, between two types of man. He writes:

But this desire of the approbation, and this aversion to the disapprobation of his brethren, would not alone have rendered him fit for that society for which he was made. Nature, accordingly, has endowed him, not only with a desire of being approved of, but with a desire of being what ought to be approved of; or of being what he himself approves of in other men. The first desire could only have made him wish *to appear to be fit for society*. The second was necessary in order to render him anxious *to be really fit*. The first could only have prompted him to *the affectation of virtue*, and to the concealment of vice. The second was necessary in order to inspire him with *the real love of virtue*, and with the real abhorrence of vice. In every well-formed mind this second desire seems to be the strongest of the two. It is only the weakest and most superficial of mankind who can be much delighted with that praise which they themselves know to be altogether unmerited. *A weak man* may sometimes be pleased with it, but a *wise man* rejects it upon all occasions. But, though a wise man feels little pleasure from praise where he knows there is no *praise-worthiness*, he *often feels* the *highest in doing what he knows to be praise-worthy, though he knows equally well that no praise is ever to be bestowed upon it*. To obtain the approbation of mankind, where no approbation is due, can never be an object of any importance to him. To obtain that approbation where it is really due, may sometimes be an object of no great importance to him. But to be that thing which deserves approbation, must always be an object of the highest.[95]

[93] Ibid., p. 247; my emphasis.
[94] Ibid.
[95] Ibid., p. 117; my emphasis.

There is, then, a man who appears "to be fit for society" and a man who is "really fit" for society. According to Smith, the first man "affects" virtue, for the sake of others; the second man truly loves virtue for its own sake, for its "praiseworthiness."[96] He concludes here by calling the first man "weak," the second man "wise."

What is the point of these three textual additions to the 1790 edition of *TMS?* Simply this—in each case an idea that had been discussed in 1759 was greatly expanded upon in 1790.[97] In the process of expansion, however, Smith placed these ideas in a new hierarchy of value which, I think, created tensions between the 1759 and 1790 editions of *TMS*. This explains, I think, the "dramatic action" within the 1790 text.[98] For in each example I have cited, Smith presents the reader with a clear value choice between different modes of symbolic *action*. And it is clear from Smith's moral tone which mode he is urging upon his reader.

Another addition to the 1790 edition further confirms the view that the 1759 and 1790 editions of *TMS* are very different books indeed. In 1759, Smith had written some very interesting pages on vanity and ambition as they affect human behavior.[99] Smith argued that rich men—the context indicates he has aristocrats in mind—enjoy being rich because of the attention they receive from others for being rich.[100] So admired, Smith continued, the rich aristocrat becomes a role model for others.[101] Smith then asserted that the "reputation" of the rich is undeserved.[102] For they lack merit; they lack, that is, "talent," "knowledge," "industry," and so on.[103] In this context, Smith introduces us to someone whom he calls "a private man." He writes:

> The most perfect modesty and plainness, joined to as much negligence as is consistent with the respect due to the company, ought to be the chief characteristics

[96] For contrasting interpretations of the importance of Smith's conception of praiseworthiness see Lovejoy (n. 64 above), pp. 263–64; and L. Stephen, *History of English Thought in the Eighteenth Century*, 3d ed. (New York, 1949), 2:70–77. I have more to say about the conception in the section titled "Smith's Concept of Human Nature."

[97] Macfie and Raphael (n. 21 above), p. 18, admit that self-command was given "more extensive treatment" in 1790 and that prudence received "increased attention" in edition 6. Their explanation for this: Smith's warmer regard for Stoicism.

[98] I develop the idea below, in the section titled "Smith's Concept of Human Nature."

[99] See Smith, *TMS* (n. 13 above), pp. 50–61.

[100] Ibid., pp. 50–51.

[101] Ibid., pp. 51–52.

[102] Ibid., pp. 52–54.

[103] Ibid., p. 54.

of the behaviour of a private man. If ever he hopes to distinguish himself, it must be by more important virtues. He must acquire dependants to balance the dependants of the great, and he has no other fund to pay them from, but the labour of his body, and the activity of his mind. He must cultivate these therefore: he must acquire superior knowledge in his profession, and superior industry in the exercise of it. He must be patient in labour, resolute in danger, and firm in distress. These talents he must bring into public view, by the difficulty, importance, and, at the same time, good judgement of his undertakings, and by the severe and unrelenting application with which he pursues them. Probity and prudence, generosity, and frankness, must characterize his behaviour upon all ordinary occasions, and he must, at the same time, be forward to engage in all those situations, in which it requires the greatest talents and virtues to act with propriety, but in which the greatest applause is to be acquired by those who can acquit themselves with honour.[104]

This, obviously, is the prudent man of the 1759 edition of *TMS*. He possesses all those character traits that are lacking in the rich man of the preceding paragraphs.

The point of this juxtaposition becomes clear a page later when Smith warns the private-prudent man, ''Never come within the circle of ambition; nor ever bring yourself into comparison with [the rich].''[105] So, in 1759 we have two types of men—one who is aristocratic, rich, and vain; another who is private, prudent, and industrious.

How different this typology is in 1790. For it was then that Smith added five pages to the end of the 1759 section on ambition.[106] The addition tells an interesting story. It begins with the following claim: ''This disposition to admire, and almost to worship, the rich and the powerful, and to despise, or, at least, to neglect persons of poor and mean condition, though necessary both to establish and to maintain the distinction of ranks and the order of society, is, at the same time, the great and most universal cause of the corruption of our moral sentiments.''[107] Smith's point is clear—admiration of the rich is the main cause of the corruption of our moral sentiments.

But notice what Smith says next. He writes:

We desire both to be respectable and to be respected. We dread both to be contemptible and to be contemned. But, upon coming into the world, we soon find that wisdom and virtue are by no means the sole objects of respect; nor vice and folly, of contempt. We frequently see the respectful attentions of the world more strongly directed *towards the rich and the great, than towards the wise*

[104] Ibid., p. 55.
[105] Ibid., p. 57.
[106] Ibid., pp. 61–66.
[107] Ibid., p. 61.

and the virtuous. We see frequently the vices and follies of the powerful much less despised than the poverty and weakness of the innocent. To deserve, to acquire, and to enjoy the respect and admiration of mankind, are the great objects of ambition and emulation. *Two different roads are presented to us,* equally leading to the attainment of this so much desired object; the *one, by the study of wisdom and the practice of virtue;* the other, *by the acquisition of wealth and greatness. Two different characters* are presented to our emulation; the one, of proud ambition and ostentatious avidity; the other, of humble modesty and equitable justice. *Two different models, two different pictures, are held out to us,* according to which we may fashion our own character and behaviour; the one more gaudy and glittering in its colouring; the other more correct and more exquisitely beautiful in its outline: the one forcing itself upon the notice of every wandering eye; the other, attracting the attention of scarce any body but the most studious and careful observer. *They are the wise and the virtuous chiefly, a select,* though, I am afraid, but *a small party,* who are the real and steady admirers of wisdom and virtue. *The great mob of mankind* are the admirers and worshippers, and, what may seem more extraordinary, most frequently the disinterested admirers and worshippers, *of wealth and greatness.*[108]

Here, obviously, the typology of characters in 1790 has changed relative to the 1759 edition. Yes, we still have two types of men juxtaposed. But notice how they have changed! No longer is it a typology of aristocratic/rich *versus* prudent/private. Rather, it is a typology of "rich and great" *versus* "wise and virtuous." Notice, moreover, what Smith says toward the end of that paragraph. He says "wise and virtuous" men are a "select" and "small party." They do not admire wealth. The "great mob of mankind," however, does admire and worship wealth. Clearly, the content of the juxtaposition has changed between 1759 and 1790. The question is, Why? I think Smith provides an answer a page later. There he writes the following:

It is from our disposition to admire, and consequently to imitate, the rich and the great, that they are enabled to set, or to lead what is called the fashion. Their dress is the fashionable dress; the language of their conversation, the fashionable style; their air and deportment, the fashionable behavior. Even their vices and follies are fashionable; and the greater part of men are proud to imitate and resemble them in the very qualities which dishonour and degrade them. *Vain men* often give themselves airs of a fashionable profligacy, which, in their hearts, they do not approve of, and of which, perhaps, they are really not guilty. They desire to be praised for what they themselves do not think praise-worthy, and are *ashamed of unfashionable virtues* which they sometimes practise in secret, and for which they have secretly some degree of real veneration. There are hypocrites of wealth and greatness, as well as of religion and virtue; and a vain man is as apt to pretend to be what he is not, in the one way, as a cunning man is in the other. He assumes the equipage and splendid way of living of his

[108] Ibid., p. 62; my emphasis.

superiors, without considering that whatever may be praise-worthy in any of these, derives its whole merit and propriety from its suitableness to that situation and fortune which both require and can easily support the expence. Many a poor man places his glory in being thought rich, without considering that the duties (if one may call such follies by so very venerable a name) which that reputation imposes upon him, must soon reduce him to beggary, and render his situation still more unlike that of those whom he admires and imitates, than it had been originally.

To attain to this envied situation, *the candidates for fortune* too frequently abandon the paths of virtue; for unhappily, the road which leads to the one, and that which leads to the other, lie sometimes in very opposite directions.[109]

The point? Despite his 1759 warning about emulating the rich, "the greater part of men" had chosen to do so by 1790. He calls this group "vain men," "candidates for fortune," "ambitious men," and men of "fashion."[110]

Given the scope and thrust of these changes, we must ask why Smith made these additions to the 1790 edition of *TMS*. My answer would be that he had changed his mind about the social, political, and cultural consequences of the behavior of the prudent man of 1759. Consider the following. In 1759, prudence and industry were set against vanity and frivolousness. Smith clearly identified with the former.[111] In 1790, however, the prudent man seems to have been both assimilated into the category of vanity and replaced in the typology by the wise and virtuous man who refuses to worship wealth. To put it another way, whereas in 1759 Smith *assumed* the prudent man would be the "carrier" of values with which he identified, in 1790 that man had become unreliable, for he was fast succumbing to vanity and to the lure of luxury. Hence, Smith's creation of, and identification with, the wise man whose task it now was to direct the vanity of others to more appropriate objects of admiration.[112]

We have in 1790, in other words, a competition going on between systems of value in which Smith has himself assumed the role of the Impartial Spectator—the conscience of a people as it were. The object

[109] Ibid., p. 64; my emphasis.

[110] Recent work on consumerism in late eighteenth-century England offers much evidence that Smith's concerns were not untypical. See, e.g., N. McKendrick, J. Brewer, and J. Plumb, *The Birth of a Consumer Society* (Bloomington, Ind., 1982), esp. pp. 9–33.

[111] Which is to say that in 1759 Smith had problems with aristocratic materialism but not necessarily with the materialism of more prudent "middling" groups.

[112] As was observed in n. 63 above, Cropsey cites Smith's statement to this effect as evidence of ambivalence. Given the circumstances of the remark, and given the overall thrust of the 1790 revisions, it is hard to see just why it should be construed as such.

of that competition, I think, was what the eighteenth century would have called men of "middling virtue."[113] Once this is realized, it becomes clear that Smith's concerns of 1790 addressed the problem of this "middling" group's tendency to opt for selfish "bourgeois" rather than "liberal" high-minded values.[114]

In any event, it should be obvious that Smith's thinking about the prudent man of 1759 had changed considerably by 1790. True, the Glasgow editors could counter by claiming that what I have described is simply Smith's "enlargement" of prudence.[115] But I could counter, in turn, by saying that the "meaning" of this change in the sixth edition marked a "retreat from" rather than an "enlargement of" his earlier position.

Indeed, the 1790 text suggests that the assumptions upon which Smith had based his strategy of economic containment in 1759 were now very much in doubt. Thus, a new system of restraints had to be devised in order to insure that the pursuit of economic self-interest would remain "innocent" and not become "vicious." The problem was that, by 1790 society itself, the "great mob of mankind," as Smith had put it, had been enlisted as a sanctioning agent of this pursuit.[116] For that reason, Smith had to invoke the figure of the "wise man," a metaphor for a moral and/or cultural elite, to provide new arguments and moral incentives for containment. When he did that, he was talking as Kant, Schiller, and Hegel would talk in the 1790s and as Coleridge would talk somewhat later.[117]

[113] For a summary of recent scholarship on this group, see L. Stone, "The New Eighteenth Century," *New York Review of Books* 31, no. 5 (1984): 42–48.

[114] R. D. Cumming, "Giving Back Words: Things, Money, Persons," *Social Research* 48 (1981): esp. 258, raises the issue in general and in terms of Smith scholarship in particular.

[115] A good deal of what R. Williams says about J. S. Mill's attempt to "enlarge" utilitarianism would seem, *conceptually*, to apply to Smith here. For Williams's argument, see *Culture and Society* (New York, 1958), chap. 3. As Williams sees it, the issue is: when does an "enlargement" of an idea become an "alternative" to it? Or, to put it another way, when does a liberal critique of what passes for liberalism become antiliberal?

[116] One of the many merits of Hirschman (n. 11 above; pp. 109–10) is that he has appreciated this point. Polanyi (n. 42 above), too, has understood this well. Hence, Polanyi's concern to develop a definition of the "social" that would challenge the economized sense of the social that prevailed among late eighteenth- and nineteenth-century English liberals.

[117] Aspects of the parallels to which I am alluding here can be seen in B. Knights's *The Idea of the Clerisy in the Nineteenth Century* (Cambridge, 1978). Much of what Knights says about Coleridge (chap. 2) would serve to characterize key aspects of Smith's position in 1790.

Smith's Concept of Human Nature: "Dramatic Action" in *TMS*[118]

There is a final way to bring the argument of this essay into sharper focus. Let me begin by recalling something Carl Becker told us long ago: that the word "nature" was one of the "magic words" in the vocabulary of eighteenth-century enlightened thought.[119] Now, we know from A. O. Lovejoy's work on the subject that the "fashion of appealing to something called 'nature' for norms" of conduct began in antiquity and that there had always been a "multiplicity of meanings latent in the term" when it was used in a normative way.[120] And yet, even though Lovejoy knew that "the sacred word 'nature'" was "probably the most equivocal in the vocabulary of the European peoples," he insisted that a "knowledge of the range of its meanings, *and of the processes of thought . . . by which one sense of it gives rise to, or easily passes over into, others* is an indispensible prerequisite for any discriminating reading" of the western intellectual tradition.[121] I think that Lovejoy's advice can be applied with profit to the conception of nature Adam Smith employs in the different editions of *TMS*.

Eighteenth-century thinkers had been aware of the different normative connotations of the word "nature" at least since Pascal. For Pascal had asked, "But what is nature? Why is custom not natural?"[122] We know, for example, that in 1759 one English writer, who eventually became a translator of Rousseau's work, specifically questioned the antisocial meaning the "ingenious" Genevan had attached to the word "nature" in his *Second Discourse*.[123] For it was quite obvious to this writer, at least,

[118] For a concise statement of the "dramatic action" perspective, see Kenneth Burke, *A Grammar of Motives* (Berkeley, 1969), p. 243.

[119] C. Becker, *The Heavenly City of the Eighteenth Century Philosophers* (New Haven, Conn., 1932), p. 47; also noted by P. Hazard, *European Thought in the Eighteenth Century*, trans. J. May (New York, 1963), p. 113; and by A. O. Lovejoy, *The Great Chain of Being* (London, 1964), p. 184.

[120] See Lovejoy and G. Boas's monumental *Primitivism and Related Ideas in Antiquity* (New York, 1980), p. 12. Compare pp. 13, 111.

[121] Ibid., p. 12; my emphasis.

[122] Pascal, quoted in Becker, p. 54. For similar statements see Voltaire and Jacques Bernard, quoted in Hazard, pp. 286, 310, respectively; and Friedrich Grimm, quoted in R. Palmer, *Catholics and Unbelievers in Eighteenth Century France* (Princeton, N.J., 1947), p. 211. Above all, see A. Ferguson's treatment of "nature" in *An Essay on the History of Civil Society*, ed. L. Schneider (New Brunswick, N.J., 1980), esp. pp. 8–10.

[123] See R. Sewall, "Rousseau's *Second Discourse* in England from 1755 to 1762," in *Philological Quarterly* 17, no. 2 (1938): 101. The translator is one W. Kenrick.

that "by nature" man was "a social animal," not at all like the man whom Rousseau had described for us.[124]

In this context, I think, Smith's use of the word "nature" in the 1759 and 1790 editions of *TMS* is most revealing. Here, of course, I cannot offer anything like a comprehensive treatment of the subject, but I can provide a basic sense of how Smith's usage fits into the arguments previously made in this essay.

Take, for example, what Smith did with the word "nature" in part 3 of *TMS* between 1759 and 1790. In 1759, Smith had written the following about how one should go about evaluating one's own conduct: "A Great part, perhaps the greatest part of human happiness and misery arises . . . from the degree of approbation or disapprobation which we feel from the consideration of it."[125] Two pages later in the same edition, Smith made the same point another way:

> A moral being is an accountable being. An accountable being, as the word expresses, is a being that must give an account of its actions to some other, and that consequently must regulate them according to the good-liking of this other. Man is accountable to God and his fellow creatures. But tho' he is, no doubt, principally accountable to God, in the order of time, he must necessarily conceive himself as accountable to his fellow creatures, before he can form any idea of the Deity, or of the rules by which that Divine Being will judge of his conduct.[126]

And in at least three other instances in the opening pages to part 3 of the 1759 edition, Smith used the "society as a mirror" image to express the idea that the best way for us "to scrutinize the propriety of our own conduct" was through "the eyes of other people."[127] Smith's point here is clear: society was the "natural" source of "those measures and rules" to which man is "accountable" for his conduct.[128]

What is most interesting about this line of argument is that most of the references to it were dropped in the 1790 edition of *TMS*. Smith's decision to do this is even more striking when we juxtapose the deletions

[124] Ibid.

[125] See Smith, *TMS* (n. 13 above), p. 109, ed. n.

[126] Ibid., p. 111, ed. n.

[127] See, e.g., *TMS*, pp. 110, 112, 112n. The image had been used by Nicolas de Malebranche and Hume. For a comment on the image, see G. Morrow, "The Significance of the Doctrine of Sympathy in Hume and Adam Smith," in *Philosophical Review* 32, no. 1 (1923): 61, 70.

[128] Smith, *TMS*, p. 109, ed. n., uses the term "naturally" to describe the process whereby these rules are established. J. Dunn, "From Applied Theology to Social Analysis" (n. 6 above), p. 131, is quite right to characterize this as "essentially" a "naturalistic theory of . . . human moral sentiments."

with the references that replaced them in the 1790 edition. Three crucial additions to chapter 2, part 3, reveal a good deal about the new direction Smith's thinking was taking around 1790.

First, there is the new opening passage to chapter 2. It runs as follows: "Man naturally desires, not only to be loved, but to be lovely; or to be that thing which is the natural and proper object of love. He naturally dreads, not only to be hated, but to be hateful. He desires, not only praise, but praiseworthiness; or to be that thing which, though it should be praised by nobody, is, however, the natural and proper object of praise. He dreads, not only blame, but blame-worthiness; or to be that thing which, though it should be blamed by nobody, is, however, the natural and proper object of blame."[129] Note how Smith uses the word "natural" here. On the one hand, Smith says man "naturally" desires "praise." On the other hand, man "naturally" desires "praiseworthiness." But then Smith introduces a distinction between praise and praiseworthiness, for he tells us that "praiseworthiness" is "that thing which, though it should be praised by nobody, is, however, the natural and proper object of praise."[130] From this he draws the following conclusion: "The love of praise-worthiness is by no means derived altogether from the love of praise. Those two principles, though they resemble one another, though they are connected, and often blended with one another, are yet, in many respects, distinct and independent of one another."[131]

What Smith has done here should be obvious: he has used the distinction between praise and praiseworthiness deliberately to build "ambiguity" into his conception of what is natural to man.[132] And by doing this he presented his reader with a very different view of just how "accountable" man should be to society for the "rules" that govern his conduct.

We know, moreover, that this was Smith's intention because two pages later he elaborates the point with reference to the word "nature" itself. He writes:

> But this desire of the approbation, and this aversion to the disapprobation of his brethren, would not alone have rendered him fit for that society for which he was made. *Nature, accordingly, has endowed him, not only with a desire of*

[129] Smith, *TMS*, pp. 113–14.

[130] Compare Lovejoy; and Stephen (both n. 96 above).

[131] Smith, *TMS*, p. 114.

[132] Ambiguity, especially in the meaning of words, is central to K. Burke's idea of "dramatic action" (n. 118 above). He discusses this most clearly in *A Grammar of Motives*, pp. xviii–xix. His point is that we should refrain from disposing of ambiguities and instead focus on clarifying "the resources of ambiguity." With regard to specific exploitations of the ambiguity of the word "nature," see Lovejoy and Boas, p. 111.

being approved of, but with a desire of being what ought to be approved of; or of being what he himself approves of in other men. The first desire could only have made him wish to appear to be fit for society. The second was necessary in order to render him anxious to be really fit. The first could only have prompted him to the affectation of virtue, and to the concealment of vice. The second was necessary in order to inspire him with the real love of virtue, and with the real abhorrence of vice. In every well-formed mind this second desire seems to be the strongest of the two. It is only the weakest and most superficial of mankind who can be much delighted with that praise which they themselves know to be altogether unmerited. A weak man may sometimes be pleased with it, but a wise man rejects it upon all occasions. But, though a wise man feels little pleasure from praise where he knows there is no praise-worthiness, he often feels the highest in doing what he knows to be praise-worthy, though he knows equally well that no praise is ever to be bestowed upon it. To obtain the approbation of mankind, where no approbation is due, can never be an object of any importance to him. To obtain that approbation where it is really due, may sometimes be an object of no great importance to him. But to be that thing which deserves approbation, must always be an object of the highest.

To desire, or even to accept of praise, where no praise is due, can be the effect only of the most contemptible vanity. To desire it where it is really due, is to desire no more than that a most essential act of justice should be done to us. The love of just fame, of true glory, even for its own sake, and independent of any advantage which he can derive from it, is not unworthy even of a wise man. He sometimes, however, neglects, and even despises it; and he is never more apt to do so than when he has the most perfect assurance of the perfect propriety of every part of his own conduct. His self-approbation, in this case, stands in need of no confirmation from the approbation of other men. It is alone sufficient, and he is contented with it. This self-approbation, if not the only, is at least the principal object, about which he can or ought to be anxious. The love of it, is the love of virtue.[133]

Clearly, Smith is now operating, quite self-consciously, with two different conceptions of nature.[134] One of these conceptions focuses on "being approved of" and offers itself as a principle of socialization. The other conception concerns itself with "what ought to be approved of" and is presented as an ethico-teleological principle—the "real love of virtue."[135]

[133] Smith, *TMS*, pp. 116–17; my emphasis.

[134] Heilbroner (n. 20 above), p. 429, n. 6, sensed this without pursuing it when he remarked that *TMS* was "written in two voices." Had he followed up on the point, he might very well have answered, along the lines attempted here, his own question about "the sociology of Smith's rhetoric."

[135] Lovejoy, *Reflections on Human Nature* (n. 64 above), p. 264, notes the religious character of the latter conception. J. Viner, in *The Role of Providence in the Social Order* (Princeton, N.J., 1972), pp. 81–82, explains why this religio-teleological conception has been either ignored by Smith scholars or treated as of only "nuisance value" by them. For a good example of the latter, see Campbell (n. 27 above), p. 70. I say more about the teleological aspect of Smith's thought in the text below.

A few pages later Smith skillfully exploits this ambiguity and, by so doing, seems to express a dissatisfaction with the principles of socialization that governed behavior in his day.[136] He writes, "Praise and blame express what actually are; praise-worthiness and blameworthiness, *what naturally ought to be* the sentiments of other people with regard to our character and conduct."[137] Again, the "naturally ought to be" phrase cues the reader that Smith has shifted the discussion of the question of what is natural to man from a context of duty in a minimalist social sense to a context of duty in a teleological or moral sense.[138]

What, I ask, are we to make of this shift? What is Smith trying to do here? A good way to answer these questions, I think, is to understand, à la Kenneth Burke, that, whereas nature had been a "scene" word for Smith in 1759, it was an "agent" word for him in 1790.[139] That is to say, in 1759 Smith equated what was "natural" to man with what was "social" about him; and, by implication, he understood the social as "containing" the actions of individual agents.[140] Hence the strong correlation between duty and social accountability in 1759.

In 1790, though, the "ought to be" and "real love of virtue" phrases alert the reader to the fact that Smith is uneasy about the socialization principles of his own day. It is not that these principles were not working effectively; on the contrary, they were working all too well. But they were working to draw men in the direction of "vain" rather than "virtuous" pursuits; and this Smith regarded as a threat to the integrity of man's moral personality.[141] Hence, the new concern to use education "to direct vanity to proper objects."[142] Hence, the decision to present what is natural to man in terms of an ethico-teleological argument that encouraged man for moral reasons to distance himself, somewhat, from conventional norms of social behavior.[143]

[136] That is, nature is transformed from an all inclusive expression of man's social being to something man must transcend for ethical reasons.

[137] Smith, *TMS* (n. 13 above), p. 126; my emphasis.

[138] Haakonssen (n. 80 above), chap. 4, esp. pp. 87–98, insists that Smith should be understood as espousing only the former. Haakonssen refuses, moreover, to acknowledge the latter as a Smithian position. As he sees it, we must choose between Smith as a proponent of a minimalist conception of justice, in which case justice is a negative virtue, or Smith as a utopian perfectionist with a politics to match. Since he rejects the latter as in any way relevant to Smith, we are left only with the former. Again, Smith is forced into an unhistorical straitjacket.

[139] Burke uses the distinction while discussing Rousseau, p. 152.

[140] As Burke notes, p. 3, scene words "contain" agents and their acts—which is precisely what Smith wished the idea of "society" to do.

[141] See Smith, *TMS*, p. 117.

[142] Ibid., p. 259.

[143] Most scholars recognize this aspect of Smith's argument. But they read it as if it were written in 1759 rather than in 1790. As a result, they interpret the

If Kenneth Burke's distinction between nature as a scene and as an agent concept helps explain what Smith was doing with the word between 1759 and 1790, Burke's more general remarks about why thinkers tend to shift the emphasis from the one to the other is equally as important.[144] For according to Burke, when a thinker exploits the ambiguity of the word ''nature'' the way Smith did in 1790, he is being "tenderminded"[145]—tenderminded in that he is ''desynonymizing'' two terms, nature and society, that previously he had treated as synonymous.[146] In this context, Burke would say, Smith was reading a teleological purpose into the word "nature" in order to motivate his readers to pursue more high-minded moral values than prudence, society, or the law required them to.[147] And if this were the case, as I think it is, we might speak with Burke and characterize Smith's moment of ''strategic'' desynonymization as a manifestation of ''coy theology.''[148]

To claim that Smith in 1790 was operating with a quasi-religious conception of nature is, of course, to fly in the face of conventional wisdom about Smith as a thinker.[149] But that wisdom has always been premised conceptually on the belief that the *WN* articulated Smith's final word on

---

argument in terms of simultaneity and ambivalence rather than in terms of succession and change. That, I think, is a *historical* mistake.

[144] K. Burke develops the point in *Language as Symbolic Action* (Berkeley, 1966), p. 46. Compare Lovejoy and Boas (n. 120 above), p. 13.

[145] Burke, *Language as Symbolic Action,* p. 46.

[146] Burke, *A Grammar of Motives* (n. 118 above), p. 192, to wit: ''The great departures of human thought can be eventually reduced to a moment where the thinker treats as opposite, key terms formerly considered apposite, or v.v. So we are admonished to be on the look-out for those moments when strategic synonymizings or desynonymizings occur.'' Compare Lovejoy and Boas, pp. 188–89, for a conceptual parallel in Aristotle.

[147] This distinction, I think, lies behind Smith's differentiation (*TMS* [n. 13 above], p. 231) of the ''citizen'' and the ''good citizen.'' Smith scholars who resist this line of interpretation nevertheless are invariably forced to concede that Smith operated with two different standards of virtue. They try (see, e.g., Campbell [n. 27 above], p. 168) to finesse the problem by regarding both standards as ''social.'' That, of course, is to miss Smith's point entirely. For an attempt to use John Rawls to make the two ''socials'' point, see K. Arrow, ''The Division of Labor in the Economy, the Polity, and Society,'' in *Adam Smith and Modern Political Economy,* ed. G. O'Driscoll (Ames, Iowa, 1979), p. 157. For a brilliant and much earlier formulation of the two ''socials'' thesis, see G. Morrow, *The Ethical and Economic Theories of Adam Smith* (New York, 1923), esp. p. 15, 36–38, 54–58. Also interesting in this regard is D. Raphael's distinction between social recognition as an abstract ideal and social praxis as its specific expression.

[148] Burke uses the phrase to characterize the purpose behind ''tenderminded'' conceptions of ''nature.'' See Burke, *Language as Symbolic Action,* p. 46.

[149] See, e.g., Dunn, ''From Applied Theology to Social Analysis'' (n. 6 above), pp. 119–20, 128.

human nature. If, however, we accept, as I think we must, the 1790 edition as a new motivating center in Smith's thought, then the plausibility of our overall argument becomes not only possible but also quite probable.[150] Why quite probable? Because, in addition to the scope of the textual changes Smith actually made in the 1790 edition of *TMS*, many other important thinkers were making similar adjustments in their conceptions of human nature at about this time.

We know, for example, that there was a neo-Puritan revival in England at the end of the eighteenth century.[151] And we know that much of the force of this revival derived from opposition to the conspicuous consumption "contagion" that had "infected" England since the 1750s.[152] Beyond that, we know that key German thinkers—Lessing, Kant, Schiller, and Hegel—were using teleologically based arguments to make the case for a continuous reformation of morality that obliged man to go beyond mere prudence and law-abidingness in his everyday conduct.[153]

Among the Germans, though, the inclination toward "coy theology" took a more obvious religious form. It expressed itself in a theology of history in which providential religious and progressive secular aspects of eighteenth-century thought converged to form a view of "civil society" that was at once commercially and morally minded. Even more revealing for our purposes here is that this theology of history had its roots in a Christian, not a Stoic, tradition, a Christian tradition that ran from some of the early church fathers through seventeenth-century Calvinist covenant theology into eighteenth-century Protestant thought.[154] In fact, this tradition—I call it the theology of the divine economy—originally developed in opposition to Stoic materialism—which explains why it so often used teleological conceptions of a purposeful Christian life to make its case against the Stoics.[155]

For many scholars, of course, this all adds up to typical eighteenth-century German metaphysical fare. But as R. S. Crane and Ernest Tuveson

[150] In fairness to Dunn (ibid.), he cites the 1790 edition of *TMS* as an important development in Smith's thought. But he badly skews his argument (e.g., p. 128) by quoting from the 1790 edition as if it were the 1759 edition and vice versa.

[151] Discussed by S. Wade, Jr., "The Idea of Luxury in Eighteenth Century England" (Ph.D. diss., Harvard University, 1968). I am grateful to Albert Hirschman for the reference and for allowing me to use his personal copy.

[152] On some of the aspects of the consumption-contagion-luxury syndrome, see McKendrick et al. (n. 110 above), pp. 10–11.

[153] See my *Hegel: Religion, Economics and Politics, 1770–1806* (Cambridge, in press), esp. pt. 2.

[154] I have traced the tradition from Clement of Alexandria to Lessing in ibid., pt. 1.

[155] See the relevant sections of J. Dillon, *The Middle Platonists* (London, 1977), and S. Lilla, *Clement of Alexandria* (Oxford, 1971).

have shown, this theology of history figured quite prominently in eighteenth-century Protestant thought in England.[156] Thus, it should not be surprising that there is evidence of this theological tradition in the new additions to the 1790 edition of *TMS*. In the all new chapter 6, Smith wrote the following:

The wise and virtuous man directs his principal attention to the first standard; the idea of exact propriety and perfection. There exists in the mind of every man, an idea of this kind, gradually formed from his observations upon the character and conduct both of himself and of other people. *It is the slow, gradual, and progressive work of the great demigod within the breast,* the great judge and arbiter of conduct. This idea is in every man more or less accurately drawn, its colouring is more or less just, its outlines are more or less exactly designed, according to the delicacy and acuteness of that sensibility, with which those observations were made, and according to the care and attention employed in making them. In the wise and virtuous man they have been made with the most acute and delicate sensibility, and the utmost care and attention have been employed in making them. Every day some feature is improved; every day some blemish is corrected. He has studied this idea more than other people, he comprehends it more distinctly, he has formed a much more correct image of it, and is much more deeply enamoured of its exquisite and divine beauty. *He endeavors as well as he can, to assimilate his own character to this archetype of perfection.* But he imitates the work of *a divine artist,* which can never be equalled. He feels the imperfect success of all his best endeavours, and sees, with grief and affliction, in how many different features the mortal copy falls short of the immortal original. He remembers, with concern and humiliation, how often, from want of attention, from want of judgement, from want of temper, he has, both in words and actions, both in conduct and conversation, violated the exact rules of perfect propriety; and has so far departed from that model, according to which he wished to fashion his own character and conduct. When he directs his attention towards the second standard, indeed, that degree of excellence which his friends and acquaintances have commonly arrived at, he may be sensible of his own superiority. But, as his principal attention is always directed towards the first standard, he is necessarily much more humbled by the one comparison, than he ever can be elevated by the other. He is never so elated as to look down with insolence even upon those who are really below him. He feels so well his own imperfection, he knows so well the difficulty with which he *attained his own distant approximation to rectitude,* that he cannot regard with contempt the still greater imperfection of other people. Far from insulting over their inferiority, he views it with the most indulgent commiseration, and, by his advice as well as example, is at all times willing to promote their further advancement. If, in any particular qualification, they happen

[156] R. S. Crane, ''Anglican Apologetics and the Idea of Progress, 1699–1745,'' *Modern Philology* 31, nos. 3 and 4 (1933–34): 273–306, 349–82; and E. Tuveson, *Millennium and Utopia* (Berkeley, 1949), esp. chap. 5. Of equal value is Lovejoy's *The Great Chain of Being* (n. 119 above), chaps. 6–7, 9. There, esp. pp. 242–65, Lovejoy identifies some of the key ideas of what he calls (pp. 246, 250) a ''new eschatology.'' That eschatology was one of progressive revelation in history and had a quite obvious teleological dimension to it.

to be superior to him (for who is so perfect as not to have many superiors in many different qualifications?), far from envying their superiority, he, who knows how difficult it is to excel, esteems and honours their excellence, and never fails to bestow upon it the full measure of applause which it deserves. His whole mind, in short, is deeply impressed, his whole behaviour and deportment are distinctly stamped with the character of real modesty; with that of a very moderate estimation of his own merit, and, at the same time, of a full sense of the merit of other people.[157]

The language here—the concern with assimilationism, with differentiating the pursuit of perfectibility from that of perfection, with approximationism and with humility—is mainline Protestant theology shaped in the image of the theology of the divine economy.[158] And anyone who has read in that tradition will be struck by the similarity between that tradition's and Smith's overall position relative to the proper relation between wealth and virtue in a Christian life.[159]

If I am right about this, about the meaning of the shift in Smith's conception of nature and about its quasi-religious character, then it would appear that, toward the end of the 1780s, Smith was becoming increasingly alarmed by what Hirsch has called "the depleting moral legacy" of commercial society.[160] Smith's new concern, I think, derived from the perception that for a commercial society to function properly—in a ''civilized'' way—it would have to maintain a high degree of collective vigilance and ''propriety'' with regard to its morality. The problem, of course, was that the *actual* interplay between commercial and moral values in society was tilting the balance between the two toward the pursuit of the

[157] Smith, *TMS* (n. 13 above), pp. 247–48; my emphasis.

[158] The language Smith uses in *TMS*, pp. 247–48, is extremely revealing. Quite obviously there is a good deal of Plato in it. But several of the specific formulations are typical, Christian adaptations of Plato's idea of *homoiosis* (assimilationism) to Christian eschatological purposes. For a strikingly similar use of language to the same purpose, see J. Addison, quoted in Lovejoy, *The Great Chain of Being*, p. 247. Lovejoy regards Addison as a proponent of a ''new eschatology'' (n. 156 above) that, in the history of ideas, is really a ''revival of an old one.'' Given the language parallel, the Addison-Smith connection is, perhaps, important.

[159] My previous work on this subject has not focused on the tradition's line of development in English thought. I have reason to believe, though, that the English line might well begin with the Cambridge Platonists, running from there through Crane's Anglican apologists to the end of the century.

[160] See Hirsch (n. 12 above), esp. pt. 3. For an interesting historical rendering of Hirsch's argument, see J. Pocock, ''The Political Economy of Burke's Analysis of the French Revolution,'' *Historical Journal* 25 (1982): esp. pp. 336–47. As I read Pocock, he is claiming that in 1790 Burke tried to reverse the *doux-commerce* thesis that hitherto had been so prominent in Scottish thought. Smith, I am suggesting, was moving in a similar direction at about the same time.

former *at the expense* of the latter. In the face of that development, Smith realized that the virtuousness of prudent and frugal men could no longer be taken for granted. Hence, the kind of changes we have noted in the meaning of Smith's language in the 1790 edition of *TMS*.

The Adam Smith Problem Historicized

Needless to say, this shift in the focus and meaning of Smith's terminology raises questions not only about conventional interpretations of Smith as a thinker but also about Smith's position in the history of British liberalism. For example, much of what S. Wolin has to say about Smith would seem to apply more to the Smith of 1759 than to the man who revised the *TMS* in 1790.[161] By the same token, a good deal of what Dunn says about the ''caesura'' that developed in the history of liberalism between Locke and Smith needs to be reformulated,[162] for Dunn, by his own selection of quotations, has made the Smith of 1790 a Lockean figure in the very ''theocentric'' sense that Dunn wishes to deny him.[163] There is, at any rate, good reason to rethink some of the claims that have been made about the Locke-Smith-liberalism connection.

All this, I think, follows from constituting the 1790 edition of *TMS* as a third motivating center of Smith's thought. At the same time, our refusal to read the 1759 and 1790 editions of *TMS* as if they constituted one book that was written, however ambivalently, at a single point in time, obliges us to historicize the ASP. That is, it requires us to stretch the ASP out in time so that it constitutes a developmental sequence that begins in 1759, runs through 1776, and culminates in 1790. What that sequence adds up to as a pattern of development is, to my mind, anything but obvious—which is to say, the ASP is still very much alive today.

Clearly, I have not addressed the developmental aspect of the ASP in this essay. But I believe it is safe to say that Smith's pattern of development does not unfold according to an internal logic that was systematically set in Smith's mind by 1759. On the contrary, there is solid evidence that a great change took place in Smith's thinking in the early 1760s, at the time when he discovered the idea of the division of labor and began to use that idea as an alternative to sympathy as an explanation for social cohesiveness. In this paper I have suggested that another such break in the pattern of his thought occurred in the 1780s. Much work, therefore, needs to be done before we can truly lay the ASP to rest.

161 S. Wolin, *Politics and Vision* (Boston, 1960), chap. 9, esp. pp. 330–45.

162 Dunn, ''From Applied Theology to Social Analysis'' (n. 6 above), pp. 119–21.

163 Ibid., p. 128. Why Dunn, who knows there are differences between the earlier and later editions of *TMS*, misquoted the text is a puzzle.

[22]

Rethinking *Das Adam Smith Problem*

RICHARD TEICHGRAEBER III

During the last decade, there has been a steady growth in scholarship concerning the moral and philosophical dimensions of Adam Smith's economic theory. The reasons are various: a determination to take Smith out of the dark shadow cast on him by Karl Marx, the perceived intellectual impoverishment of socialism, and an historical concern for tracing the peculiarly Scottish dimensions of the *Wealth of Nations* (1776). This renewed interest in Smith appears to be more than a sudden intellectual fashion.[1] The now completed publication of the "Glasgow Edition of the Works and Correspondence of Adam Smith" provides the basis for the work of systematically reconstructing Smith's intellectual career. Most students of Smith would agree that at the moment this work of reconstruction has just begun.

One of the curious features of recent Adam Smith scholarship has been its perfunctory treatment of "*das Adam Smith Problem*," a problem that once seemed at the very center of understanding the moral and philosophical dimensions of Smith's work. In the last decades of the nineteenth century a group of German scholars coined that phrase to describe what they saw as a possibly fundamental break between the assumptions that guided Smith's first work, *The Theory of Moral Sentiments* (1759), and those that supported the economic theory of his later work, the *Wealth of Nations.* On the one hand, Smith's explanation of moral judgment was based upon the psychological principle of "sympathy," a capacity inherent in every individual which allows a person to "enter into" the situation of another and thereby bring his own "sentiments" into accord with those of his fellow. But on the other hand, in the *Wealth of Nations* Smith asserted that every individual was essentially self-interested:

An earlier version of this essay was presented at the tenth annual meeting of the American Society for Eighteenth-Century Studies, Atlanta, April 18-21, 1979. My thanks to Nan Keohane, John Pocock, Roger Emerson, Donald Winch, Nicholas Phillipson, Daniel Singal, John Dwyer, and Roger Mason for comments that aided in my revision of that essay.

[1]Among recent English-language studies, the following are worthy of mention: Thomas D. Campbell, *Adam Smith's Science of Morals* (London, 1941); Ronald L. Meek, *Smith, Marx, and After* (London, 1977); A.L. Macfie, *The Individual and Society* (London, 1967); Vernard Foley, *The Social Physics of Adam Smith* (West Lafayette, 1976); Ralph Anspach, "The Implications of the Theory of Moral Sentiments for Adam Smith's Economic Thought," *History of Political Economy,* Spring 1972, 9(1), pp. 176-206. Smith's place in the Scottish Enlightenment is currently the topic of a lively controversy. For the present state of the debate, see the separate essays of Nicholas Phillipson, Donald Winch, and J.G.A. Pocock in *Wealth and Virtue: Political Economy and the Scottish Englightenment,* eds. I. Hunt and M. Ignatieff (Cambridge, 1981).

> It is not from the benevolence of the butcher, the brewer, or the baker, that we expect our dinner, but from their regard to their own interest. We address ourselves, not to their humanity, but to their self-love, and never talk to them of our own necessities but of their own advantages.[2]

The principals in the discussion of *das Adam Smith Problem* offered at least three separate explanations for this apparent divergence in Smith's philosophical standpoint.[3] August Oncken compared Smith with Immanuel Kant and found in Smith's work a proto-Kantian dualism. A division between the sensible *Güterwelt,* where men are mechanically moved by physical desires, and the *ethische Welt* of freedom marked both the *Theory of Moral Sentiments* and the *Wealth of Nations,* Oncken argued. And the presence of such a division dispelled the notion that there was a fundamental difference between the two books. A different explanation was offered by Wilhelm Paszkowski, who described the *Wealth of Nations* as a purely technical and specialized inquiry and the *Theory of Moral Sentiments* as a traditional humanistic work of moral theory that dealt with man as he ought to be. Finally, Richard Zeyss argued that *das Adam Smith Problem* had been misconceived in some important respects. In the first place, Smith's notion of moral judgment could not be reduced to the doctrine of sympathy alone. Zeyss correctly pointed out that for Smith man's "virtue" consisted of at least three major elements: prudence, justice, and benevolence. Prudence was a characteristic of self-interested conduct—and also one particularly helpful in economic pursuits. Justice described a "negative virtue," conduct in accord with those public laws meant to restrain excessive self-interest. Finally, benevolence, while the highest form of virtue, for Smith was primarily a feature of private relationships. In brief, Zeyss's argument concluded that there had never been a fundamental opposition between the moral and the economic theories of Adam Smith.

Zeyss did not put *das Adam Smith Problem* to rest, however. The question of Smith's philosophical intentions arose again in 1896 when Edwin Cannan published a manuscript copy of notes taken down by one of Smith's students at the University of Glasgow in 1763.[4] The Glasgow *Lectures* showed that many of the main principles of Smith's economic

[2]Adam Smith, *An Inquiry into the Nature and Causes of the Wealth of Nations,* 2 volumes, eds., R.H. Campbell and A.S. Skinner (Oxford, 1976), I, 26-27. All references are from this edition, hereafter: WN.

[3]See August Oncken, "Das Adam Smith-Problem," *Zeitschrift für Socialwissenschaft,* ed. Julius Wolf, I Jahrgang (Berlin, 1898), 25-33, 101-8, 276-87; Richard Zeyss, *Adam Smith und der Eigennutz* (Tübingen, 1889). For Paszkowski and the broad course of the debate about *das Adam Smith Problem,* I rely primarily on Glenn R. Morrow, *The Ethical and Economic Theories of Adam Smith* (New York, 1923), pp. 1-12.

[4]Edwin Cannan (ed.), *Lectures on Justice, Police, Revenue and Arms* (Oxford, 1896).

quences of the division of labor (in the *Wealth of Nations)* and his account of the psychological motivation for moral choice and social harmony (in the *Theory*) should be seen as composing two social systems that must be analyzed separately. And in conclusion, Cumming would also have us see the *Wealth of Nations* as a work that represents a fundamental disruption of a long-standing tradition of Western moral and political thought in which economic concerns had been viewed as instrumental, rather than as primary ends in themselves.[11]

In the bicentennial-related scholarship on Smith only Andrew Skinner has attempted to disprove this argument. His attempt to show that Smith's thought can be read as a coherent "system of social science," however, has not been pursued with enough rigor to render it especially persuasive.[12] Most of the bicentennial scholarship chooses not to engage in a serious examination of the question of the consistency of Smith's intentions. By and large, treatments of *das Adam Smith Problem* have ignored the provocative reformulations of that problem by Cropsey and Cumming. Again drawing on arguments first put forward by Zeyss, Morrow, or Viner, the popular wisdom now is that the problem can in fact be stated and solved without much difficulty.[13] In the end, perhaps the only novel position to come out of the work connected with the *Wealth of Nations* bicentennial is the surprisingly extreme position taken by D.D. Raphael and A.L. Macfie, the editors of the otherwise admirable new Glasgow edition of the *Theory*. They appear to suggest that *das Adam Smith Problem* should be entombed once and for all:

> The so-called "Adam Smith problem" was a pseudo-problem based on ignorance and misunderstanding. Anybody who reads TMS, first in one of the earlier editions and then in edition 6, will not have the slightest inclination to be puzzled that the same man wrote this book and WN, or to suppose that he underwent any radical change of view about human conduct.[14]

I

Should we want to save *das Adam Smith Problem* from the cemetery of historiographical curiosities? If one conceives of that problem in its orig-

[11]*Ibid.*, pp. 174-78, 213-20.

[12]Andrew S. Skinner, *A System of Social Science: Papers Relating to Adam Smith* Oxford, 1979). Skinner himself describes his work as "a modest commentary;" see p. 3.

[13]This is a position implied or stated in the following works that have appeared in bicentennial publications: Thomas Wilson, "Sympathy and Self-Interest," in *The Market and the State*, ed. Thomas Wilson and Andrew S. Skinner (Oxford, 1976), pp. 73-99; Thomas Sowell, "Adam Smith in Theory and Practice," in *Adam Smith and Modern Political Economy*, ed. Gerald D. O'Driscoll, Jr. (Ames, 1979), pp. 3-18; D.D. Raphael, "The Impartial Spectator," in *Essays on Adam Smith*, ed. Andrew S. Skinner and Thomas Wilson (Oxford, 1975), pp. 83-99.

[14]TMS, p. 20.

inal and somewhat oversimplified form, and also chooses to ignore its fascination for at least two serious and able scholars, certainly not. But if one uses it, as Cropsey and Cumming have done, in a revamped form to describe the very complex task of establishing Smith's intentions as a moral and social theorist, it would appear that the puzzle of Adam Smith still remains very much alive and subject to further study.

How would one go about solving the puzzle? It is a task that can be approached in at least two ways, the second of which this paper will attempt to suggest. The first would be to see if Cannan's Glasgow *Lectures* (now supplemented by additional student notes, discovered in 1958, on the same topics)[15] bridge what Smith himself acknowledged was the considerable philosophical gap between the *Theory of Moral Sentiments* and the *Wealth of Nations*. Establishing Smith's intentions here involves the long overdue recovery of Smith's politics. Much of this work has been done recently by Donald Winch and Duncan Forbes. Although in somewhat different ways, both Winch and Forbes show that Smith held a view of politics that was neither "trivial nor vestigial." In *Adam Smith's Politics,* Winch is especially convincing in his suggestion that one of the main difficulties in establishing Smith's intentions has been the neglect of that great variety of eighteenth-century political themes that appeared in Smith's work. Indeed, the center of Winch's account is his demonstration of the great extent to which the famous "invisible hand" did not work for the public good. Winch urges us to see Smith as a very politically-minded economist who specified a number of areas in which statesmen or legislators would have to intervene.[16]

Forbes takes a slightly different approach in his attempt to recover the eighteenth-century context of Smith's thought. For Forbes, Smith's political views are best understood as "in essence Humean." By this he means that Smith too was a "sceptical Whig," determined to establish a naturalistic "science of politics" that dispensed with the "cherished idols" of "vulgar Whiggism." Especially significant here was Smith's attempt (following after those of Hume and Montesquieu) to put forward a notion of liberty that "was not Anglocentric but which applied to all civilized Europe. . . ." Forbes specifically takes issue here with Cropsey's view that the freedom that would come with laizzez-faire commercial capitalism also represented the freedom necessary to the creation of democratic political institutions. In the context of eighteenth-century European politics, Forbes argues, Smith's "system of natural liberty" cannot be read as a call for free government. It was rather a call for more economically enlightened governments, which by promoting "free" commercial capitalism generated a stable, prosperous, yet still politically heterogeneous "civilization."[17]

---

[15]In the "Glasgow Edition" these are now printed with Cannan's material as *Lectures on Jurisprudence,* ed. R.L. Meek *et al.* Oxford, 1978).

[16]Donald Winch, *Adam Smith's Politics* (Cambridge, 1978). See esp. chaps. 5-8.

[17]Duncan Forbes, "Sceptical Whiggism, Commerce, and Liberty," in *Essays on Adam Smith,* pp. 179-201.

Adam Smith's Politics is the first wide-ranging and rigorously historical reading of Smith's work. As such it represents a major contribution to the project of establishing Smith's intentions, that is, to resolving *das Adam Smith Problem* in its revamped form. But the book is marked by a curious, and ultimately unresolved, tension between what might be called the "weak" and the "strong" versions of its main argument. The "weak" version is the observation that in recovering the historical Smith we find that his politics was neither "trivial nor vestigial." This point seems unarguable. The "strong" version is the often implied claim that since it is misleading to regard politics as occupying an unimportant role in Smith's thought, it then follows that for Smith politics also represented an important and autonomous realm of value in human affairs. That point may or may not be right, but Winch simply does not make a strong enough case for it.

The major weakness in Winch's argument also marks Forbes's account: the treatment of the *Theory of Moral Sentiments* in both cases is very sketchy. It is important to note that Smith took clear positions on eighteenth-century political problems and ideologies. But is it not equally important to understand the moral assumptions that underpinned those positions? Winch describes Smith as "the master of the art of equipoise."[18] Forbes calls him a "sceptical Whig." One wonders why these able eighteenth-century intellectual historians tell us so little of Smith as moral philosopher.

II

The lacuna may be explained in part by the fact that the *Theory of the Moral Sentiments* cannot be fully understood if read primarily within the context of concerns peculiar to the eighteenth century. There can be no question here of giving even a truncated résumé of all the themes Smith drew together in the *Theory*. What can be done briefly is to suggest elements of what is offered here as a new, and not unreasonably proleptic, reading of the *Theory*. This reading asks that the book be set against the background of certain long-standing and basic normative assumptions that guided a tradition of humanistic moral philosophy dating back to the Renaissance.[19] A few of these normative assumptions merit special attention; the commentary that follows is meant to suggest how Smith's formulations of these assumptions represent another, and hitherto neglected, part of the problem of establishing his intentions.

[18] *Adam Smith's Politics*, p. 144; also see pp. 164-87.

[19] I should note that scholars have frequently emphasized the significant continuities between the Renaissance and the eighteenth century. Some literary critics still speak of the eighteenth century as the "Silver Age" of the Renaissance. However, in tracing the changing meaning of those words that held particular significance for Renaissance humanists and for one of their eighteenth-century admirers in Scotland, my concern here will be to show that the continuities are not everywhere as deep as we may think.

(1) *"Virtue."* The *Theory of Moral Sentiments* is a work that defines the meaning of the word "virtue." The book is not tightly knit, but there are two questions at its center. The first is: what are the qualities of a virtuous man? The second: what is it in man's nature that prompts him to make judgements about the presence or absence of "virtue" in the conduct of others?

In his attempt to define the meaning of the word "virtue," Smith joined in an ancient intellectual project that had been given new life during the Renaissance. Renaissance humanist thinkers (beginning with Petrarch) had revived the Ciceronian ideal of *virtus* in their attack on the dark Augustinian strain of Christianity that had prevailed in medieval thought and culture.[20] Augustine and his followers claimed that the classical ideal of pursuing "virtue," a term that best described an all-encompassing human excellence, had been foreclosed by original sin and man's innate corruption. Renaissance humanists refused to embrace this view. They claimed instead that man in fact was capable of attaining such excellence and the main aim of one's life ought to be the pursuit of "virtue."

When Renaissance thinkers spoke of "virtue," they focussed primarily on two broad points. First, a man of true virtue should display all the leading Christian virtues and, second, he should also pursue those central cardinal virtues argued by classical moralists. Most Renaissance humanists were determined always to couch their discussions of "virtue" in a Christian framework. Nonetheless, the novelty of their arguments in the end rested in their successful restoration of classical ideals. There were at least four of recurring significance, all of which are to be found in the *Theory of Moral Sentiments.* First was the virtue of prudence. This included reason, intelligence, circumspection, and foresight. Next was temperance, which was broken down in terms such as modesty, abstinence, honesty, and moderation. Fortitude was a third central virtue; the least complicated of the group, it was to be seen in the conduct of all heroic men. Finally, there was justice. This virtue might be discussed in its "divine," "natural," or "civil" aspects. But in general it was considered the overarching virtue that, as Plato had emphasized, was the very greatest good of all.

It has recently become something of a commonplace in intellectual history to say that the notion of "virtue" put forward by Renaissance humanists (and taken up by their disciples in the seventeenth and eighteenth centuries) found that economic activity, particularly the individual's pursuit of wealth, unless strictly controlled, represented a very dangerous threat to the virtuous life. As Thomas Horne has put it in his recent study of Bernard Mandeville, virtue depended on one's willingness to adopt a publicly minded stance, while "commercial activity tended to

[20]See Quentin Skinner, *The Foundations of Modern Political Thought: Volume One, The Renaissance* (Cambridge, 1978). I have borrowed extensively from Skinner's account of "virtue" (esp. pp. 88-100) in what follows.

change legitimate concerns for the self into selfishness, to enlarge private concerns and diminish the awareness of public needs."[21]

Like most commonplaces, however, this one should be subject to careful scrutiny. For example, Quentin Skinner's recent volume on Renaissance political thought shows that the supposedly irresolvable confrontation of "virtue" and "commerce" was in fact amicably resolved in the minds of some humanists.[22] In the first half of the fifteenth century, Leonardi Bruni and Bracciolini Poggio argued that as long as each individual pursued his own business affairs with industriousness and intelligence, we might safely assume that the result of enlightened self-interest in "commerce" would be beneficial to "virtue" in the community as a whole.

As a general rule, most Renaissance and early modern humanists did find the pursuit of wealth a threat to individual "virtue" and to the moral integrity of society as a whole. Skinner's account of two thinkers who found "virtue" and "commerce" compatible does suggest, however, that recent scholarship emphasizing the confrontation of "commerce" and "virtue" in the field of eighteenth-century British thought, the age in which Smith plays such a crucial role, may be somewhat misleading. Indeed, given the central place of "virtue" in Smith's moral philosophy, it is clear that what we need in Smith's case is an explanation of how his theory of "virtue" allowed for the pursuit of "commerce."

The great difficulty in explaining this connection in Smith's thought—and thus also the reason for being clear at the outset about the traditional humanistic notion of "virtue"—is that he made no elaborate, direct argument linking the terms "virtue" and "commerce." At one point in the *Theory of Moral Sentiments,* Smith does write that "In the middling and inferiour stations of life, the road to virtue and that to fortune . . . are, happily, in most cases very nearly the same." But this remark appears after Smith had admitted that in the end "virtue" appeared to be of abiding interest only to a select few and that "the great mob of mankind are admirers and worshippers . . . of wealth and greatness" for their own sake.[23]

How then would one trace the connection between "virtue" and "commerce" in Smith's thought? If "virtue" remained a central normative term for Smith, it would seem that we would have to search for this connection in Smith's broader conceptualization of what "virtue" entailed. The content of "virtue" in the *Theory* was usually discussed under the two broad headings of "humanity" and "self-command." Smith's notion of a moral personality, not unlike that of many humanists before him, was a hybrid of Christian benevolence and classical stoical self-discipline. The first qual-

[21]Thomas A. Horne, *The Social Thought of Bernard Mandeville: Virtue and Commerce in Eighteenth-Century England* (London, 1978), p. ix. Also see J.G.A. Pocock, *The Machiavellian Moment: Florentine Thought and the Atlantic Republican Tradition,* esp. pp. 423-505.

[22]*Foundations of Modern Political Thought,* I, 73-74, 108-9.

[23]TMS, p. 63.

ity was man's "gentle virtue," the second, his "austere virtue."[24] Successfully balancing the two to meet the particular contingencies of one's life was the essence of moral conduct.

But why was the conduct of such a virtuous personality bound to meet with our approval? Smith argued that if man were governed by the laws of nature, he was by instinct concerned with the "propagation of the species." But at the same time he was equally interested in his own "self-preservation."[25] How were his altruistic and his self-interested motives to be reconciled? Smith contended that this was not a task that nature had "entrusted to human reason." Its determinations were "too slow and uncertain." The reconciliation was accomplished instead by "sympathy," yet another of man's "original and immediate" instincts.[26] Our ability to make moral judgments was founded on the fact that the passions of individuals simply correspond with one another in the face of certain events, of particular instances of human happiness or suffering.

Only in theory, then, was it possible that our rational pursuit of self-interest might set us in conflict with one another. In practice a "correspondence of sentiments" invariably prevents our differences from becoming divisive. A society of virtuous men was one in which individuals were allowed to attend to their own self-interest, broadly defined. But it was also a realm wherein each man was bound to attend to the "passions" and "sentiments" of others. In making judgments about those passions and sentiments, an activity we engage in by instinct, Smith suggested that we are thereby involved in the work of making moral decisions.

(2) *"Sympathy."* Smith conceded that there was nothing original in his definition of the content of "virtue." He contended that his special contribution to the discussion of "virtue" came in the realm of what today we call moral psychology. "Sympathy," Smith argued, provided a more appropriate explanation of our feelings of moral approval or disapproval than did Francis Hutcheson's then popular notion of a separate "moral sense." Hutcheson had founded moral judgment upon "a sentiment of a peculiar nature, distinct from every other." But in reality Smith wrote, nature always works

> with the strictest economy, and produces a multitude of effects from one and the same course . . . sympathy, a power which has always been taken notice of, and with which the mind is manifestly endowed, is . . . sufficient to account for all the effects ascribed to this peculiar faculty.[27]

The novelty of Smith's theory, then, was its apparently successful simplification of the principles of moral psychology.

[24]TMS, p. 153.
[25]TMS, p. 77.
[26]TMS, pp. 76-77.
[27]TMS, p. 321.

Although entirely justified in their concern to explain the moral dimensions of the *Wealth of Nations,* the originators of *das Adam Smith Problem* (as we have seen already) misconceived an important part of this problem when they equated Smith's account of sympathy with benevolence alone and then tried to explain the disavowal of benevolence in the famous passage from Book I of the *Wealth of Nations.* Zeyss and other scholars rightly have pointed out that Smith's notion of virtue involved more than sympathy; it also entailed prudence. And prudence has been seen (most recently by Raphael and Macfie) to contribute a moral dimension—perhaps best described as "frugality"—to self-interested economic activity.[28]

But a careful reading of the relevant passages in the *Wealth of Nations* and the *Theory of Moral Sentiments* shows that Smith never made such an argument. "Prudence" in the *Wealth of Nations* is a principle guiding improvement in the narrow, and at best morally neutral, economic sense: "An augmentation of fortune is the means by which the greater part of men propose or wish to better their condition. It is the means most vulgar and obvious . . ."[29] There is nothing about the augmentation of fortune, however, in the discussion of prudence in the *Theory of Moral Sentiments.* The virtue of the "prudent man" is seen as caution rather than enterprise; there is a reverence here toward "the ordinary decorums of life and conversation." The prudent man is sociable and capable of friendship, but his particular virtues have no bearing on the "public business." His aim is to maintain a polite, comfortable, private life.[30]

Where, then, does Adam Smith assign a positive moral role to self-interest in human affairs? Perhaps strangely, it in fact appeared in his account of sympathy. Every individual, Smith observed, lives in a world where he must observe the actions and feelings of others. When confronted with the particular misfortune of another, each person, simply because he is witness to distress, instinctively tries "to put himself into the situation of the other and to bring home to himself every little circumstance of distress which can possibly occur to the sufferer." This initial, almost complete "correspondence of sentiments between spectator and the person principally concerned," however, cannot hold for very long. In the end, it is in fact impossible for the spectator to surrender that final modicum of self-interest that must separate him from his neighbor.[31]

It must be the case, then, that two efforts are involved in social relationships where "sympathy" comes into play. First, the individual who is the "spectator" tries to enter into the "sentiments" of the person directly affected by a particular event. Yet, secondly, the inevitable self-restraint of the sympathetic spectator must eventually have some influence on the

[28] TMS, p. 18.

[29] WNI, 341-42.

[30] TMS, p. 339.

[31] TMS, pp. 9-10 and pp. 20-21. My account of sympathy here takes issue with Robert Boyden Lamb, "Adam Smith's System: Sympathy not Self-Interest," *Journal of the History of Ideas,* XXXV, no. 4, (Oct.-Dec., 1974), 671-82.

perception of that person who is the object of his limited sympathy. Smith suggested that someone in distress longs for "the relief which nothing can afford him but the entire concord of the affections of the spectator with his own."[32] But Smith also explicitly denied that the primary purpose of sympathy was either "relief" or "consolation." Sympathy was not meant to encourage or legitimize emotions involved in distress or happiness. Its purpose was to temper them. In the end, the only means by which a troubled individual might hope to find consolation was by "lowering his passions to that pitch in which spectators are capable of going along with him." The victim of bad fortune after all must continue to live in his given society, and that necessity forces him to temper the demands he might make for himself. Because he lives in a society where there is "sympathy," but never an absolute "correspondence of sentiments," he must always "flatten" his impulsive passions in order to reduce them "to harmony and concord with the emotions of those who are about him."[33]

It is this morally constructive interplay between Smith's essentially stoic notion of "sympathy" and self-interest that perhaps proved to be the philosophical starting point for what in the *Wealth of Nations* would become a more thoroughgoing ethos of economic individualism. For to put it very simply, what we find here is Adam Smith as a moral advocate of what he called a "society of strangers."[34] Excessive sympathy, according to Smith, encouraged men to ignore the necessary self-restraints that should order social encounters among individuals. Our familiarity with others, in other words, breeds moral laxness. Smith argued that "sympathy" would most dependably support a social order in which man had no reason for the excessive indulgence of his sympathy. When confronted with our misfortune, our friends give us too much sympathy. Hence, we will naturally

> expect . . . less sympathy from an assembly of strangers, and we assume, therefore, still more tranquility before them . . . if we are not at all masters of ourselves, the presence of a mere acquaintance will really compose us, still more than that of a friend; and that of an assembly of strangers still more than that of an acquaintance.[35]

---

[32]TMS, pp. 21-22.

[33]TMS, p. 22.

[34]Also see TMS, pp. 85-86: ". . . though among different members of society here should be no love and affection, the society, though less happy and agreeable, will not necessarily be dissolved." In the famous "invisible hand" passage in the *Wealth of Nations,* Smith asserted that in a free market economy every individual would seek his own personal gain above all else. Here there would be no consciously altruistic or benevolent motives governing man's conduct. The activity of manufacturing and trade certainly creates social relationships. But if every man "intends only his own securtiy," can we not say that he thereby remains a stranger to his fellow men? See WN, p. 456.

[35]TMS, p. 22.

The same argument appeared again later on in the *Theory*, and here it was made even more pointedly: "Are you in adversity? . . . Live with strangers . . . do not regulate your sorrow according to the indulgent sympathy of your intimate friends."[36]

It is important that this reading of "sympathy" in the *Theory of Moral Sentiments* not appear to claim too much for itself. It cannot be said that Smith's moral "society of strangers" provides a fully causal explanation of the intellectual transition from the *Theory* to the *Wealth of Nations*. What should be emphasized perhaps is that we misconceive the nature of Smith's intentions if we understand free and self-interested "commerce," as Joseph Cropsey has argued, as a "substitute for virtue."[37] What we should want to discover is why Smith's theory of "virtue" happened to prove so accommodating to "commerce." Smith's stoic notion of sympathy provides a partial, but also plausible, answer to that question.

(3) *"Justice, the negative virtue."* Another way to understand the ascendancy of economic self-interest in Smith's thought is to be clear about the place of politics in his theory of virtue. In Part VII of the *Theory*, a brief history of moral philosophy added to the sixth edition of the work published in 1790, Smith emphasized that all serious moral theorists should be concerned to provide a series of practical "rules" relevant to both private and public life. He also pointed out that historically there had been three different types of thinking about moral rules: ethics, casuistry, and jurisprudence. The main source of difference among the three was the extent of the precision in the practical rules each tried to provide.[38]

In making this distinction, Smith presented a typology of "virtue," a conceptualization of the different realms of moral philosophy, that was a central element of his thought. First, there was a categorical distinction between ethics and casuistry, those two ways of considering rules of "virtue" apart from justice. In Western thought, ethics had been best exemplified for Smith in the thinking of the stoic Roman moral theorists, whose powerful influence on Smith we have already seen in the preceding account of "sympathy." The stoic philosophers had

> contented themselves with describing in a general manner the different vices and virtues, and with pointing out the deformity and misery of the one disposition as well as the propriety and happiness of the other, but have not affected to lay down many precise rules that are to hold good unexceptionably in all particular cases.[39]

An "ethical" philosopher did not prescribe definite rules, but he could

[36]TMS, p. 154.

[37]*Polity and Economy*, p. 100.

[38]For more on this point, see Robert D. Cumming, *Human Nature and History*, II, 216-18. Smith's account of moral rules is in TMS pp. 327-40.

[39]TMS, pp. 328-29.

specify various kinds of virtuous conduct and the "sentiments" of the heart upon which particular virtues are founded. An "ethical" philosopher, in other words, was what Smith had attempted to be in the *Theory:* a moral psychologist And on the basis of this moral psychology, the ethical philosopher could then hope to describe the conduct "to which each virtue would prompt us."[40]

Smith's definition of the "ethical" philosopher, then, was a combination of the moral psychologist and the rhetorician. He looked at the "casuist" as a thinker who tried to fulfill an impossible task: specifying a set of rules to govern every aspect of human life. To gain this end, medieval Christian theology had been forced to deny the inescapable "common sentiments of mankind." This denial in turn had reduced morality to an exclusively punitive concern for "breaches" of moral duty. Casuistry in its various ancient, medieval, and "modern," (or rationalist) forms, represented a harsh and unneeded intellectualization of the problem of "virtue." Casuists always attempted "to no purpose, to direct by precise rules what it belongs to feelings and sentiments only to judge of."[41]

The upshot of all this is not surprising: "The two useful parts of moral philosophy," Smith concluded, were "Ethics and Jurisprudence, casuistry ought to be rejected altogether. . . ."[42] But why, then, did justice represent "the only virtue with regard to which . . . exact rules can properly be given?" Smith's answer was that while they resembled casuists in their pursuit of "exact and precise rules," theorists of justice did not share the casuists' pretensions of comprehensiveness. They correctly understood the problem of "rules," because they saw that rules concerning justice could have reference only to a specific and narrow range of concerns. Theories of justice examined what it is that may be "exacted by force," what it is that the individual "ought to think himself bound to perform . . . from the most conscientious dread, either of wronging his neighbour, or of violating the integrity of his own character." Theories of justice were meant to prescribe rules for "the decisions of judges and arbiters," not "rules for the conduct of good men." The observance of such rules therefore gained us nothing but our freedom from arbitrary external punishment.[43]

Justice, then, was a "negative virtue" that had nothing to do with benevolence and thus nothing to do with the "ethics" of the individual. On the one hand, Smith argued that men usually "fulfilled the rules of justice by sitting still and doing nothing." On the other, he claimed that individual ethics were founded on an active "beneficent tendency" in man. The altruistic actions prompted by "sympathy" could have no place in the realm of "law and government," because they were not of the sort that Smith thought could be compelled into being by an external authority. We might disapprove of another's actions on "ethical" grounds. But as long as

[40]TMS, p. 328.
[41]TMS, p. 339.
[42]TMS, p. 340.
[43]TMS, p. 330.

that action causes no tangible harm to another, it ought not to be dealt with as a problem of law and politics. An ethical agent arrived at his decisions freely and independently. To oblige a man "to perform what in gratitude he ought to perform, and what every impartial spectator would approve him performing, would . . . be still more improper than his neglecting to perform it."[44]

What human "sentiment" was it that underpinned the "negative virtue"? To answer this question Smith in part borrowed from Hobbes and Mandeville. Although he thought they had exaggerated the point, Smith acknowledged that their accounts of man's fears about the reliability of the ethical bearings of his fellows were reasonable.[45] Because of the primacy of "feelings and sentiments" in human conduct, however, Smith argued against Hobbes and Mandeville that man's fears here could be dealt with only in terms of some other countervailing psychological principle. For Smith, that principle was "resentment," and his description of how it worked was at the center of his psychological conception of justice.[46]

Man's distress over the ethical failures of others often, and naturally enough, provoked "resentment." But Smith insisted that in a society governed by laws "resentment" would not play a significant role in one's personal social life. Instead, it would find its place in the realm of "law and government." "Resentment seems to have been given us by nature for defense and for defense only. It is the safeguard of justice and the security of innocence."[47] "Resentment," then, was the political analogue of "sympathy." But the analogy is an inverted one, and thereby also the basis for distinguishing between ethics as the "positive virtue" of private and social life and justice as the "negative virtue" of the political realm. Sympathy is a feature of human nature that should be allowed to come into play freely. Resentment is a feeling that both justified and invited control by an external authority. The approbation we feel for the punishment of a crime, for example, is not founded primarily on our conscious "regard to public utility which is commonly taken to be the foundation of it. It is our sympathy with the resentment of the sufferer which is the real principle. . . ."[48]

The psychological distinction between sympathy and resentment also helps to explain why justice must take such a relatively inferior position in Smith's hierarchy of virtue. In the *Theory,* and later in the Glasgow *Lectures* and the *Wealth of Nations,* Smith argued that observance of the rules of justice—and it was this observance that he thought man's primary

[44]TMS, pp. 78-79.
[45]TMS, pp. 308-10.
[46]TMS, p. 79.
[47]TMS, p. 79.
[48]TMS, p. 79. I do not mean here to hint at the old equation of "sympathy" and "benevolence." Like sympathy, resentment is a non-rational or "natural" sentiment in human relationships. In this respect there may be no categorical distinction between the two. It is clear, however, that Smith explained the psychology of our desire for justice as retributive. In doing so, he wants to show that it is sustained by "negative" motives that should find no place in the realm of personal morality.

political responsibility—did not speak for the individual as one with a positive interest in consciously shaping the public life he shared with others. (This of course was the notion of "virtue" at the heart of classical and Renaissance civic humanism.) A breach of the rules of justice exposed the individual to punishment, but it did not follow that one's adherence to such rules deserved public reward or recognition.

> There is, no doubt, a propriety in the practice of justice, and it merits, upon that account, all the approbation which is due to moral propriety. But as it does no real positive good, it is entitled to very little gratitude. *Mere justice is, upon most occasions, but a negative virtue* and only hinders us from hurting our neighbour. The man who barely abstains from violating either the person or the estate or the reputation of his neighbours has surely very little positive merit. He fulfills, however, all the rules of what is peculiarly called justice, and does everything which his equals can, with propriety, force him to do, or which they can punish him for not doing.[49]

As an actor in Smith's narrowly conceived realm of public "virtue," then, the just, law-abiding individual would not be concerned with joining in efforts of collective self-assertion and self-definition. His primary task was to avoid encroaching on "the person or the estate or the reputation" of his neighbor. In brief, we are concerned about justice for one main reason: we wish to have "security from injury."[50]

Smith borrowed from Hume's theory of justice in making some of the above arguments; Hume described justice as the "cautious, jealous virtue."[51] The significant point about the *Theory,* however, is that it demon-

[49]TMS, p. 82, my emphasis.

[50]*Lectures,* ed. Cannan, p. 3.

[51]L.A. Selby-Bigge (ed.), *Enquiries concerning Human Understanding and concerning the Principles of Morals* rev. P.H. Nidditch (3rd ed., Oxford, 1975), p. 184.

A full account of Adam Smith's "negative" view of justice would begin with the natural law jurisprudence of Hugo Grotius (1583-1645). The key work is *De jure belli ac pacis* (1625), where we find that Grotius was of two minds about justice. In some instances, he talked of justice in its generic sense: it was the inclusive "virtue" that stood for every moral virtue. It was that "sovereign virtue" that expressed our concern to achieve equity for every virtuous man. In other places, however, Grotius defined justice of a more constricted nature. It was simply that special virtue that rendered to another that which was his due. Justice was an exclusive, rather than an inclusive, virtue. And this was essentially the notion of justice whose psychological underpinnings Adam Smith explained in the *Theory of Moral Sentiments.* On Grotius, see two recent very important studies: Richard Tuck, *Natural Rights Theories: Their Origin and Development* (Cambridge, 1979) esp. pp. 58-81, and James Tully, *A Discourse on Property: John Locke and his Adversaries* (Cambridge, 1980), esp. pp. 81-85. The same ambivalently two-sided definition of justice is to be found in Francis Hutcheson, perhaps the foremost disciple of Grotius in Scotland, as well as Smith's teacher at the University of Glasgow, 1731-40. See e.g., his discussions of justice as both a "sovereign" and an exclusive virtue in *A Short Introduction to Moral Philosophy* (1747), pp. 67-68 and 103-4.

strated in more detail the range of practical implications that followed from the separation of private morality and justice that had first been explored in Hume's *Treatise*. Where Hume distinguished between "natural" and "artificial" virtue in his discussion of ethics and justice, Smith created a hierarchical typology of "virtue" in which justice was a secondary concern. In Smith's case, this perhaps also explains why the formulation of a final more comprehensive theory of justice was postponed: comparatively speaking, it was not a pressing intellectual problem for him. The primary concern for an "ethical" thinker, for an empirical moralist, was not politics, but the realms of human psychology and of society—issues that dominated most of the argument in the *Theory*.

III

To summarize, the broad issue the *Theory of Moral Sentiments* raises for the project of establishing Smith's intentions can be put as follows. It is less a question of understanding the book's particular arguments (although these of course remain open to dispute), than it is a problem of deciding which is the appropriate intellectual-historical framework within which those arguments ought to be viewed. When seen as a document in the history of early modern humanist thought, which is the approach taken in this essay, the *Theory* presents the curious and fascinating case of a work that retained the vocabulary of Western humanist thought (that is, crucial normative terms such as "prudence," "temperance," "fortitude," "justice" and "virtue") and yet at the same time altered the practical import of that vocabulary.

The argument of this paper has been that there were at least three alterations that deserve special attention. First is Smith's general conceptualization of the meaning of "virtue." In traditional humanistic thought, the possession of "virtue" was taken as the pursuit of a single ideal that encompassed all its manifestations. In the *Theory*, this notion of "virtue" as defining a comprehensive unity of ends was absent.

Second, this is not to say that Smith simply abandoned the humanistic concern for "virtue" and later replaced it with a straightforward endorsement of economic self-interest, as Albert Hirschman has recently suggested.[52] It was rather that Smith gave an account of "virtue" in the plural. And the crucial distinction here was that between ethics and justice. Both were realms of "virtue" but of categorically different kinds. By and large, the *Theory* was an example of ethics, of personal moral rules. It was, moreover, an account of types of personal "virtue" that included at least one positive and fairly elaborate psychological account of how man's moral "sentiments" come into play in a society of individuals invited to be primarily concerned with their own self-interests. Smith's argument was that in a "society of strangers" "sympathy" in practice translated into the

[52] Albert O. Hirschman, *The Passions and the Interests: Political Arguments for Capitalism Before its Triumph* (Princeton, 1977), p. 100.

virtues of self-restraint and self-discipline. If one accepts Smith's argument, where else would this ethic of self-command be more practicable than in a society fully based on self-interest?

Third, the ascendancy of economic life in Smith's thought must also be explained in terms of the sharp limitation of the moral weight traditional humanism had given to politics. In his accounts of justice and "public spirit" in the *Theory,* we find Smith devalued politics as a realm of man's "virtue." Both the classical humanist ideal of citizenship and the notion of justice as the overarching "virtue" in human life were ignored. Smith found that the conduct of law-abiding, moderately public-spirited men was necessary to maintain a social order. But it did not represent a "real positive good." Here we have not only a case of "virtue" in the plural, but also of "virtue" as a hierarchy of human concerns in which politics is at best of secondary importance. We find in the *Theory* that individual morality was depoliticized and politics demoralized.

In brief, the *Theory of Moral Sentiments* is a book that in its often labyrinthine discussions of the problem of "virtue" both encouraged and partook of a major transformation of the traditional assumptions of Western humanist thought. Rousseau once complained, in the same decade that Smith wrote the *Theory,* that "The ancient politicians spoke incessantly of morals and virtue, ours speak only of commerce and money."[53] But if eighteenth-century politicians were reading the *Theory,* Rousseau was wrong in at least one very important respect. The displacement of the broad ideals of classical and Christian humanism by the more narrow yet practicable goals of economic growth was certainly a central theme in Western eighteenth-century thought. But an awareness of what the humanist tradition had asked of man did not suddenly die out. Indeed, what is suggested in Smith's work taken in its entirety is that the notion of a society defined primarily in terms of the free pursuit of economic self-interest was part of a conscious and complex effort to restrict the range of man's self-conceptions, especially in the realm of politics. The humanist concern for "virtue" remained in Smith. It is the classical assumption that the term "virtue" can be used to describe an ideal of all-encompassing human excellence that has been abandoned. This point is at the center of a "*das Adam Smith Problem*" that should still perplex us.

NEWCOMB COLLEGE, TULANE UNIVERSITY

[53]"Les anciens politiques parloient sans cesse de moeurs et de vertu: les nôtres ne parlent que de commerce et d'argent." The translation here is from *The Social Contract and Discourses,* trans. and intro. G.D.H. Cole (New York, 1950), p. 161.

[23]

The Historical Journal, 35, 1 (1992), pp. 91–113
Printed in Great Britain

ADAM SMITH: SCOTTISH MORAL PHILOSOPHER AS POLITICAL ECONOMIST*

DONALD WINCH
University of Sussex

ABSTRACT. *By contrast with those for whom the* Wealth of nations *marks the origin of economics as an autonomous science, this article argues that Smith's significance lies in his attempt to repossess political economy by restoring its links with the sciences of morals and natural jurisprudence – those concerns which are characteristic of his writings as a moral philosopher. The case proceeds by re-examining two topics derived from these sciences. The first begins with Smith's ungenerous treatment of his mercantile predecessors as a clue to what he believed was distinctive about his own system. Smith was antagonistic to precisely those rationalist, utilitarian and reductive models of behaviour based on self-interest that he is held to have in common with mercantile writers; he was answering rather than joining those who felt it necessary to isolate and legitimate rational economic self-seeking. The second topic turns on Smith's natural jurisprudence: his application of the criteria of natural justice when criticizing mercantile policies and institutions, where the emphasis falls on the negative injunctions of commutative justice rather than the positive ones of distributive justice. The separation of the ethics of the* Theory of moral sentiments *from the* Wealth of nations, *therefore, tells us more about Smith's successors than Smith himself.*

I

The [Glasgow] College was torn by parties, and Dr S[mith] embraced that side which was most popular among the people of condition; that is, the rich merchants of the town, among whom he was well received, and from whose conversation, particularlv that of Mr. Glasford, he learned many facts necessary for improving his Lectures; *for living in a great commercial town, he had converted the chair of Moral Philosophy into a professorship of trade and finance.*[1]

The above statement appeared in *The Times* a few weeks after Adam Smith's death in 1790, along with other items of biographical gossip. The anonymous author of the piece was clearly not an admirer; he adopted a supercilious English manner towards his Scottish subject throughout. Smith's well-known

* This paper was originally written as a contribution to an international symposium to commemorate the bicentenary of the death of Adam Smith held in Nagoya, Japan, in April, 1990. I am grateful to the Fellows of St Catharine's College, Cambridge for their hospitality while writing the paper, and for the helpful comments of Donald Coleman, David Raphael, and Quentin Skinner.

[1] 'Biographical anecdotes of the late Dr. Smith', *The Times*, 16 Aug. 1790.

antagonism towards merchant and manufacturing pressure groups lends interest to the opening part of this statement; but I have chosen instead to stress the final, almost throw-away line. Bearing in mind the malicious tone of the rest of the piece, it can be confidently described as a sneer. Faced with the published outcome of Smith's alleged conversion of his chair into a 'professorship of trade and finance', however, those historians who are chiefly interested in the emergence of economics as an autonomous discipline, with its own priorities and style of reasoning, would presumably substitute a cheer. Although they would not be alone in this, it is still worth considering whether the event late twentieth-century economists and increasing numbers of other, more ideologically inclined, admirers celebrate bears any relationship to what Smith would like to have been remembered for.[2]

Several influential schools of thought converge in the belief that the advancement of economics as a science – a science capable of delineating 'economy' as a self-regulating realm – required the separation of its subject matter from the extraneous considerations embodied in *moral* philosophy. This did not rule out, indeed it may have required, a close relationship with the ruling forms of *natural* philosophy considered as models (Cartesian, Baconian, or Newtonian) for constructing explanations of human behaviour, but the laws underlying the creation and maintenance of the economic order had to be separated from ethics and politics, where the act of separation could either be treated as an intellectual innovation deriving, say, from the application of Newtonian perspectives to economic behaviour, or seen as a response, more or less mediated, to the growing contemporary significance of a distinctive constellation of economic forces and relationships – where the constellation can variously be described as the rise of capitalism, the spread of the market economy, the victory of political economy over 'moral economy', or the diffusion of (to use Smith's term) commercial society.[3]

To this body of literature can be added another, mostly by political

[2] This question was tentatively raised at the Glasgow celebrations in 1976 in my comment on R. D. C. Black's 'Adam Smith in historical perspective', in T. Wilson and A. S. Skinner (eds.), *The market and the state* (Oxford, 1976), pp. 67–72; and at greater length in *Adam Smith's politics; an essay in historiographic revision* (Cambridge, 1978).

[3] Joseph Schumpeter's belief that 'the garb of philosophy is removable' from economics, and that 'economic analysis has not been shaped at any time by the philosophical opinions that economists happened to have', provides the rationale for his *History of economic analysis* (New York, 1954), p. 31. See also W. L. Letwin, *The origins of scientific economics; English economic thought, 1660–1776* (London, 1963): 'A subject is not opened to scientific enquiry until its technical aspect has been sundered from its moral aspect... there can be no doubt that economic theory owes its present development to the fact that some men, in thinking of economic phenomena, forcefully suspended all judgements of theology, morality, and justice, were willing to consider the economy as nothing more than an intricate mechanism, refraining for the while from asking whether the mechanism worked for good or evil' (pp. 147–8). Although Joyce Oldham Appleby is more interested in ideology than science, she adopts a similar position in her *Economic thought and ideology in seventeenth-century England* (Princeton, 1978). Whether seen as science or ideology, this perspective has, of course, a much longer pedigree, featuring as it does in explanations for the rise of capitalism or the emancipation of a liberal economic ideology from its moral and political integument in the

theorists, which finds in Smith the decisive moment when economy eclipsed polity, when the language of political economy assumed dominance over the branch of moral philosophy devoted to politics – to man's duties and rights as citizen under the various forms of government available.[4] This too can be expressed in varying tones of regret or congratulation, where the latter is best epitomized by those who see the *Wealth of nations* as the successful culmination of a long-standing attempt by philosophers to domesticate modern self-interested man – the ravenous creature revealed by Hobbes – by transforming him into modern economic man behaving in a manner that was capable of producing public benefit under the right circumstances.[5] While some political theorists concentrate on the deflecting and impoverishing effect of the move Smith is supposed to have accomplished, therefore, others take the more orthodox route of defending the resulting contribution to the political tradition we know as liberalism, with or without an initial capital.[6]

Those who are concerned with a more historical Smith will not feel obliged to follow these routes – most of which appear to be preoccupied with anxieties and outcomes that have tenuous connection with Smith. As far as the economists' literature is concerned, it is entirely possible to maintain that what is important about the *Wealth of nations* does not lie so much in its undoubted contribution to what later became known as economic analysis, in its post-Newtonian attempt to expose the equilibrating mechanisms at work in commercial society, but in the manner in which Smith repossessed and

---

work of Karl Marx and his followers, as well as that by Max Weber, Richard Tawney, Karl Polanyi, C. B. Macpherson, Louis Dumont and many others. E. P. Thompson's version turns on the replacement of 'moral economy' by political economy, where the latter is 'disinfested of intrusive moral categories'; see 'The moral economy of the English crowd in the eighteenth century', *Past and Present*, L (1971), 89–90. All such schema depend on a view of precisely when and how 'modern' or 'capitalist' society actually emerged; for an account which shows that in England at least economic individualism can be traced back to at least 1250, well before any period assumed in the above literature, see Alan Macfarlane, *The origins of English individualism; the family, property and social Transition* (Oxford, 1978).

[4] The arguments that underpin this position are considered in my *Adam Smith's politics*, chapters I and VIII. For recent restatements of the view that Smith cannot be considered as a political theorist see Shannon C. Stimson, 'Republicanism and the recovery of the political in Adam Smith', *Critical issues in social thought* (London, 1989), pp. 91–112, where the conclusion turns on her belief that Smith's theory of history overwhelms his theory of politics by refusing 'to lend a genuine efficacy to political action'. See also Nicholas Xenos, 'Classical political economy: the apolitical discourse of civil society', *Humanities in Society*, III (1980), 229–42, for whom 'the end of government has become encapsulated within the system of political economy itself', leaving politics 'totally subordinate to political economy' (pp. 236–7).

[5] See, e.g. Milton L. Meyers, *The soul of modern economic man; ideas of self-interest, Thomas Hobbes to Adam Smith* (Chicago, 1983), p. 120. Meyer's conclusion, if not style of argument, has some similarities with that of Albert Hirschman, for whom also Smith provides the end of a story of how the passions might be deployed to control interests; see *The passions and the interests* (Princeton, 1977), pp. 100–13.

[6] For my own encounter with this viewpoint see 'Adam Smith and the liberal tradition', in K. Haakonssen (ed.), *Traditions of liberalism; essays on John Locke, Adam Smith and John Stuart Mill* (Sydney, 1988), pp. 83–104.

repositioned existing forms of economic discourse by placing them within an intellectual context that derives from some of the central concerns of Scottish moral philosophy, particularly as it had emerged from the hands of Frances Hutcheson and David Hume. Thus while the existence of a work such as the *Wealth of nations* may have aided the process by which political economy was separated from moral philosophy, absorption seems a more accurate brief description of what Smith was actually doing when he embarked on his ambitious attempt to provide the anatomy and physiology of commercial society, together with related excursions into its history and pathology.

The particular philosophical perspective Smith brought to bear on political economy – what made his espousal of the 'perfect system of natural liberty and justice' differ from other systems – depended on a combination of the sciences of natural jurisprudence and ethics, where both elements had lately undergone considerable revision in the hands of Hutcheson, Hume, and Smith himself. Smith's main published contribution to this enterprise was contained in his *Theory of moral sentiments*, though we can also discern the outlines of the jurisprudential side of his unfinished project to produce 'an account of the general principles of law and government' in his lectures on jurisprudence – the lectures from which the *Wealth of nations* emerged as an expanded treatment of the sections dealing with 'police, revenue, and arms'. Smith was not seeking *economic* laws in the manner of his successors and some of his predecessors; he was not simply constructing a mechanical model of how a freely competitive market economy might work under ideal conditions. Nor was he employing economic theory in collaboration with some ad hoc and largely subjective ethical and political judgements as the basis for the proposals with regard to economic policy he was making. If we wish to understand the strategy of science and persuasion employed by Smith when addressing legislators, and the rationale for the anti-utopian approach to policy that he adopted, we have to turn to his work as a moral philosopher, especially to the criticisms of the 'man of system' and the 'spirit of system' in the *Theory of moral sentiments* (VI. ii. 2. 15–18).[7] An educated eighteenth-century reader of the *Wealth of nations* might be able to divine this without having read any of Smith's contributions to moral philosophy, but twentieth-century economists who attempt to do so usually land in difficulties. Herein lies the first of many reasons for maintaining that an understanding of Smith's political economy requires knowledge of his work as a moral philosopher.[8]

[7] This, and all subsequent citations, refers to the *Glasgow edition of the works and correspondence of Adam Smith*, using the conventional abbreviations.

[8] In part at least, reconstructing Smith's 'science of a legislator' was the object of my *Adam Smith's politics*, but the politics loomed larger than the natural jurisprudence. I have also argued this case with special reference to Smith's views on the corn trade in 'Science and the legislator; Adam Smith and after', *Economic Journal*, XCIII (1983), 501–20. For a fuller account that covers the whole field of the regulations of 'police' in its relationship to Smith's jurisprudence see K. Haakonssen, *The science of a legislator; the natural jurisprudence of David Hume and Adam Smith* (Cambridge, 1981).

Before exploring this argument further, however, it may be helpful to clear another simple source of misunderstanding out of the way. When speaking of the separation of economics from ethics, or, indeed, its absorption within it, I am not referring to the kinds of issue made familiar by methodological debate over the distinction between positive and normative propositions. Interest in, and application of this distinction within economics has a history of its own that differs from the one considered here.[9] Thus while Smith, following in Hume's footsteps, can certainly be described as endorsing the application of Newtonian methods to moral subjects; and while he was equally sympathetic towards attempts to give non-partisan explanations for historical and political events, in which moral appraisal was suspended in order to concentrate on causal relationships, this was not the only purpose of history.[10] He would certainly not have considered an inquiry into the wealth of nations that confined itself to positive propositions as being worth pursuing, whatever some of his more tidy-minded nineteenth-century successors may have come to believe.[11] As is well known, eighteenth-century usage did not distinguish between 'science' and 'philosophy', and Smith made little effort to avoid the ambiguities present in natural law terminology; he was content to allow empirical fact and ideal to live cheek by jowl, and thereby encompassed both what could be explained as normally the case and what could be justified or criticized from a moral and jurisprudential standpoint at the same time.

It is equally well known that in the *Theory of moral sentiments* Smith was primarily interested in constructing a *science* of morals.[12] As in the case of the *Wealth of nations*, the reliability and persuasiveness of any normative judgements and recommendations depended on the truth of the theory or system being propounded, where truth had to meet the Newtonian criteria of conforming with experiment and observation. In these matters Smith took the view – one that was perhaps peculiar to the eighteenth century – that it was

[9] It is dealt with in T. W. Hutchison, '*Positive*' *economics and policy objectives* (London, 1964), especially chapter 1.

[10] In his *Lectures on rhetoric and belles lettres* Smith praised Machiavelli as 'of all Modern Historians the only one who has contented himself with that which is the chief purpose of History, to relate Events and connect them with their causes without becoming a party on either side'; but see also his treatment of 'internal' causes in history, namely the influence of motives and the effect of events 'on the minds of the chief actors'. With regard to the moral role of history Smith emphasised that 'the facts must be real, otherwise they will not assist us in our future conduct', a statement that ought to be noted by those who stress the *conjectural* status of Smith's use of history: see LRBL, pp. 91, 93, 114.

[11] The distinction between the 'science' and 'art' of political economy belongs to the 1830s and 1840s, and was often associated with criticism of Smith for confusing the two; see 'Higher Maxims: happiness versus wealth in Malthus and Ricardo', in S. Collini, D. Winch, and J. Burrow, *That noble science of politics; a study in nineteenth-century intellectual history* (Cambridge, 1983), pp. 65–89.

[12] As is most fully argued by T. D. Campbell, *Adam Smith's science of morals* (London, 1971); see also D. D. Raphael, 'Adam Smith: philosophy, science, and social science', in S. C. Brown (ed.), *Philosophers of the Enlightenment* (Brighton, 1979), pp. 77–93. This is not to deny the hortatory content of TMS, though it seems significant that Smith's final advice to students was to regulate their conduct by any one of the available non-licentious moral codes; see TMS, VII.ii.4.5.

more difficult for those constructing systems of moral philosophy to impose false notions on their readers, the subjects of their science, than it was in natural philosophy (TMS, VII.ii.4.14).

Having now brought both of Smith's major works into play (from now on in the inelegant abbreviated form of TMS and WN), the relationship between them must be considered. What has been said so far implies that they not only *can* legitimately be considered together, but, for some purposes at least, *must* be so considered. But the question of how far Smith might be said to have taken it for granted that readers of WN were familiar with TMS also needs to be brought into the open, where, as is often the case with Smith, there are few overt autobiographical clues as to his own hopes and aspirations. On this two polar positions can be discerned, the first of which holds that since the two books were being revised at much the same time, the presumption should be that, barring any internal contradictions overlooked by Smith, they form a seamless web that allows the interpreter to pass between the two works in either direction. At the other extreme, there is the view, most popular perhaps among economists and those historians who write with economists in mind, that WN can legitimately be read as a self-standing work in the light of the subsequent, largely autonomous, development of economic discourse.[13]

No amount of argument will settle this kind of dispute, which derives from legitimate differences in the questions it is possible to ask of past writings. Intermediate positions can, however, be fruitfully compared and debated. Thus we can follow the example of those scholars who have traced in detail how and where the concerns of TMS and WN interpenetrate one another.[14] As an extension of this pursuit we can make use of Smith's essays on philosophical subjects, his lectures on rhetoric, and, above all, as far as WN is concerned, his lectures on jurisprudence, to form a picture of his intellectual project taken as a whole. But it is also worth bearing in mind two valid points made by those sceptics who question the need to consider TMS when interpreting WN. Regardless of the pattern of Smith's teaching and his programmatic statements about the connections between his various works, finished and unfinished, the sceptics argue that we should remember two obvious facts. First, that the work whose publication Smith sanctioned personally must be given priority; and, secondly, that there are no *specific* cross-references to TMS in WN, or, for that matter, to WN in the body of TMS.[15] From these facts one could either infer that we have the author's

[13] See, however, J. Robertson, 'The legacy of Adam Smith; government and economic development in the *Wealth of nations*, in R. Bellamy (ed.), *Victorian liberalism; nineteenth-century political thought and practice* (London, 1990), pp. 15–41 for a more sophisticated argument in favour of relying on WN alone.

[14] As good examples published over a lengthy period see Glenn R. Morrow, *The ethical and economic theories of Adam Smith* (New York, 1923); A. L. Macfie, *The individual in society* (London, 1967); and A. S. Skinner, *A system of social science* (Oxford, 1979). As a result of the diligence of the editors of the Glasgow edition, of course, we have a large number of suggested parallels between WN and TMS.

[15] When giving his lectures Smith did refer students to TMS; see LJB, p. 401. But in his published work the only cross-reference occurs in the 'Advertisement' to TMS, where WN is

blessing for taking WN solely on its own terms, or that we should be parsimonious in our appeals to TMS as a means of interpreting WN. Having been accused of making too much of Smith's programmatic statements and unpublished lectures in previous work, I shall adopt a more parsimonious approach here. Thus I shall take WN as an initial starting point and only move to TMS when it is clear that on a particular subject he gives a fuller treatment there of the precise matter in hand.

My question then becomes: how did the author of TMS repossess and reposition what passed for political economy before he wrote WN? Since the question is too large to consider fully in a single paper, I shall deal with two topics, the first involving his science of ethics, the second arising from his science of jurisprudence: Smith's treatment of his mercantile predecessors in the light of the common assumption that self-interest ruled in economic dealings; and the role played by considerations of natural justice in WN.

II

An obvious starting point is provided by the account Smith gives in Book IV of the two existing systems of political economy, mercantile and agricultural. Of these two, the mercantile system, Smith's own negative polemical construction, was more important, largely because it represented, according to Smith, the combination of doctrine and practice that prevailed in Britain and other commercial societies. Smith paid tribute to the work of Quesnay and the French *économistes* as 'the nearest approximation to the truth that has yet been published upon the subject of political economy' (WN, IV. ix. 38); but their agricultural system had never been tried in practice and could be treated as an heroic utopian speculation, marred by its doctrinal error on the unique productiveness of agriculture and by its belief, common to all utopias, that 'only under a certain precise regimen' of perfect liberty and perfect justice could any society prosper (WN, IV. ix. 28). Smith's debts to physiocratic literature when building his own system may have been larger than he conceded; but there can be little doubt that in dealing with the mercantile system he was constructing an anti-type that serves as a valuable inverted mirror-image of his own system.

The merits and demerits of Smith's treatment of what, as a result of conflict during the nineteenth century between orthodox classical political economy and the categories favoured by German historical writers, has become known as mercantilism continue to exercise economic historians and historians of economic thought and policy during the pre-Smithian period.[16] Among the

mentioned as the realized part of his original plan to publish 'an account of the general principles of law and government'.

[16] A useful compendium can be found in D. C. Coleman (ed.), *Revisions in mercantilism* (London, 1969). Coleman has returned to the subject in recent years in two articles which criticize Smith's interpretation of mercantilism: see 'Mercantilism revisited', *Historical Journal*, XXIII (1980),

many charges brought against Smith on this subject have been those of simple historical inaccuracy; failure to discriminate between disparate authors, thereby creating a posited unity of doctrine where little or none existed; and a wilful disregard of the distinction between doctrine and the 'unplanned miscellany' of official practice, with the consequence that he was unable to give an adequate explanation for the actual measures adopted by mercantile states.[17] To such charges can be added a culpable niggardliness in acknowledging intellectual debts to all those who wrote on economic subjects before him.

Lack of generosity clearly does not describe Smith's attitude to Hume, many of whose essays, like WN itself, though in shorter compass, subject the ruling political and economic maxims of the day to critical scrutiny. Even so, Smith spoke more loudly and frequently in praise of Hume as philosopher and historian – not least when he was about to controvert him – than he did of Hume as an economic writer.[18] Whether one takes this as a sign of congenital mean-spiritedness or as evidence of a keen and justifiable sense of his own originality depends on the attitude one adopts to Smith's system. The protagonists of pre-Smithian political economy in its various guises have understandably been less willing than Smith's Scottish friends to accept the originality of Smith's achievement on his own (implicit) reckoning.[19] Indeed, even on philosophical and historical matters, with the exception of Hume, the 'never-to-be-forgotten' Hutcheson, and to a lesser extent, Lord Kames, Smith did not refer to other Scots in his published work, even those contemporaries and pupils, such as Adam Ferguson, William Robertson and John Millar, who had already published work embodying approaches that have been seen as sufficiently close in spirit to justify use of *the* Scottish Enlightenment as a collective term. In the notorious case of Sir James Steuart's *Inquiry into the principles of political oeconomy* (1767), the only work in English with claims to being a complete system of political economy that was neither mercantile in Smith's sense, nor agricultural in the French sense, Smith was silently dismissive.[20] Steuart's work, it can be conjectured, suffered in Smith's eyes, not as is still sometimes claimed, as a result of its mercantile tendencies, so much

773–91; and 'Adam Smith, businessmen, and the mercantile system in England', *History of European Ideas*, IX (1988), 161–70.

[17] The phrase 'unplanned miscellany' can be found in Coleman's 1988 article, p. 164.

[18] The only explicit references to Hume's economic opinions in WN are a neutral reference to Hume on paper money (II.ii.96) and a positive endorsement of Hume on the rate of interest (II.iv.9). The lectures on jurisprudence contain a fuller reference to Hume's economic essays; see LJA, p. 507 and implicitly elsewhere, though also register a doubt as to whether Hume, when writing on paper money, has not fallen into mercantile error.

[19] See the letters 150, 151, 152, 153 and 154 from Hume, Hugh Blair, Joseph Black, William Robertson, and Adam Ferguson in Corr., pp. 186–94.

[20] See his statement to Sir William Pulteney that: 'I have the same opinion of Sir James Stewart's Book that you have. Without once mentioning it, I flatter myself that every false principle in it, will meet with a clear and distinct confrontation in mine.' Corr., p. 164.

as for having been developed outside the philosophical framework that had come to inform discussions of political economy in Scotland during the second half of the eighteenth century – a framework that did not assume the existence, as Steuart did, of an omnipotent and all-knowing statesman or legislator.[21]

But the crucial case concerns those whom Smith scorned as the 'pretended doctors' of the mercantile system. Although he did not follow the extreme line adopted with Steuart, his references to particular authors are sparse, with a tendency to suggest that after Thomas Mun most writers, including 'some of the best English writers on commerce', were held in thrall by their confusion of wealth with specie, and hence by an erroneous obsession with a favourable balance of trade as the best means of ensuring the supply of specie. Apart from this pervasive doctrinal error, Smith's aggregative treatment of his English predecessors provides few additional clues as to what led him to be so dismissive.[22] This applies even to those, like Locke, whose philosophical reputation might have entitled his economic writings to greater consideration.[23] It is well known that Smith had 'little faith in Political Arithmetic' (WN, IV.v.b.30); and to this can be added the observation that he did not make use of the entry into general matters of political economy provided by the eighteenth-century debate on 'populousness' – a route explored by several of his predecessors, including Montesquieu, Hume and Wallace, as well as Cantillon and Steuart, and one that was later to be pursued by Malthus.[24] Yet, as many commentators have shown, some of the writers who were either overlooked or comprehensively dismissed had advanced interesting examples of economic analysis of the kind that has subsequently been recognized as

[21] As summed up by Steuart's statement that: 'In treating every question of political oeconomy I constantly suppose a statesman at the head of government, systematically conducting every part of it.' See *Inquiry into the principles of political oeconomy*, edited by A. S. Skinner in 2 volumes (Edinburgh, 1966), I, 122. In denying the usefulness of 'mercantilist' as a description of Steuart's position I am taking issue with Gary M. Anderson and Robert D. Tollison, 'Sir James Steuart as the apotheosis of mercantilism and his relation to Adam Smith', *Southern Economic Journal*, LX (1984), 456–68; and following the interpretation of A. S. Skinner in 'Sir James Steuart: author of a system', *Scottish Journal of Political Economy*, XXVIII (1981), 20–1.

[22] Those mentioned in WN are as follows: John Locke, Thomas Mun, and Bernard de Mandeville. From the earlier draft and LJ it is possible to add references to Joshua Gee and Jonathan Swift (see LJA, pp. 392–4) together with the judgement that 'allmost all authors after Mun [1664]' (up to Hume?) have defined wealth as specie (LJA, p. 300). In WN (IV.i.35) there is a reference to 'some of the best English writers on commerce', but it prefaces a remark about how they allow their recognition that goods constitute wealth 'to slip out of their memory.' But Smith's library contained a fair sample of the works of the 'best English writers', and he makes use of their findings on specific matters: e.g. Josiah Child (WN, V.i.e.9.11–12), Mathew Decker ('an excellent authority', WN, IV.v.a.20), Charles Smith ('ingenious and well-informed', WN, IV.ii.20; IV.v.a.4). Joseph Harris has been suggested by the editors of the Glasgow edition as a pervasive source on money and other matters.

[23] In LJA Smith says that Locke gave the system 'somewhat more of a philosophicall air and the appearance of probability by some amendments'; see LJA, p. 381 and repeated in LJB, p. 508.

[24] See R. D. C. Black, 'Le theorie della popolazione prima di Malthus in Inghilterra e in Irlanda', *Le teorie della popolazione prima di Malthus*, a cura di Gabriella Gioli (Milan, 1987), pp. 47–69.

promisingly 'scientific', anticipating and even being more acute on specific doctrines than later writings by Smith and his followers.[25] Why then did Smith repay his supposed debts to this literature in such a grudging way?

The simplest answer could be that, rightly or wrongly, Smith recognized no debts, and that he found something else in the mercantile literature that overshadowed whatever economic acumen was to be found there. Politically, we know the source of Smith's distaste: it lay in the harm to the public interest perpetrated by those powerful merchant and manufacturing interest groups that had taken up mercantile doctrines for self-interested purposes and had exerted a malign influence on the 'policy of Europe' in general and the British legislature in particular. He stressed the errors of mercantile logic with respect to the balance of trade and the importance attached to specie; but his main target lay in the use made of such doctrines by mercantile pressure groups attempting to pass off what was in their collective interest as being in the interest of the nation at large. He believed that the policies and practices embodying the system were impolitic and self-contradictory; and he made a special point of demonstrating how the welfare of consumers (especially those in the lower income groups), wage-earners, and land-owners had consistently been sacrificed to that of an importunate pressure group that was unfit to advise legislators on matters affecting the wealth of nations.

All this is well known, but what is more relevant to my argument, especially in the next section of this paper, is that the gains and losses entailed in mercantile legislation were not reckoned solely according to some quasi-utilitarian calculus measured in terms of income transferred or pecuniary benefits foregone. Criticisms of economic inexpediency are consistently fortified by reference to cases where 'the ordinary laws of justice' were being sacrificed 'to an idea of public utility, to a sort of reasons of state' (WN, IV.v.b.39); where natural rights were being infringed; and where a pervasive kind of disorder had been introduced into the body politic. Justice is not given an overriding status, but it is one of the considerations that ought to be constantly borne in mind by those appraising policies and institutions.

What Smith accurately characterized then as a 'very violent attack ... upon the whole commercial system of Great Britain' (Corr., p. 251) had distinct moral and political bearings of a kind that cannot be dismissed as personal prejudice or as an attempt to achieve public fame. The charge has been raised against Smith that he courted his public's prejudices by attacking monopoly – a doubly dubious charge in view of its circularity (a successful work, by definition, must be popular) and inaccuracy (WN did not achieve immediate

[25] The locus classicus of the opinion that Smith merely synthesized and rarely surpassed the best work of his predecessors can be found in Schumpeter's *History of economic analysis*, pp. 183–94, 557–8; see also p. 361 where Smith's treatment of mercantile writings is described as 'unintelligent criticism', and the judgement on p. 376: 'If Smith and his followers had refined and developed the "mercantilist" propositions instead of throwing them away, a much truer and much richer theory of international economic relations could have been developed.' For a recent and extensive attempt to document a similar view, though without Schumpeter's condescension, see T. W. Hutchison, *Before Adam Smith; the emergence of political economy, 1662–1776* (Oxford, 1988).

success).[26] Once more, it is worth noting, with due allowance for flattery, what Smith's friends commended him for doing in their early letters of congratulation. Thus Hugh Blair wrote that: 'You have done great Service to the World by overturning all that interested Sophistry of Merchants, with which they had Confounded the whole Subject of Commerce.' Joseph Black spoke of the time that would be needed 'before others who are not so quick sighted and whose minds are warped by Prejudice or Interest can understand and relish such a comprehensive System composed with such just and liberal Sentiments.' Ferguson believed that Smith would 'reign alone on these subjects' and 'form the opinions, and I hope to govern at least the coming generations', though he predicted that the merchants, as well as the church and the universities, would be provoked by the attacks Smith had made upon them. At somewhat greater length, but with an interesting characterization of the nature of the enemy (emphasis supplied), William Robertson said that: 'You have formed into a regular and consistent system one of the most intricate and important parts of political science, and if the English be capable of extending their ideas beyond *the narrow and illiberal arrangements introduced by the mercantile supporters of Revolution principles, and countenanced by Locke and some of their favourite writers*, I should think your Book will occasion a total change in several important articles both in police and finance.'[27]

III

At this point, another reason can be given for distancing Smith qua moral philosopher-cum-political-economist from many of his mercantile predecessors. It concerns what might loosely be described as their Hobbism, or, perhaps more appropriately, their Mandevillism. Self-confessed Hobbists and Mandevillians are, of course, hard to find. I am employing the terms loosely to cover the a-moral, a-religious utilitarianism that has been discerned in mercantile writings and was widely associated with the names of Hobbes and Mandeville at the time.[28] More precisely, I mean the use of rational economic man assumptions and the adherence to reductive systems in which the pursuit of self-interest was treated as the sole motive required to understand human behaviour, whether in social, political or economic settings. In some influential accounts of the career of liberal individualism, Hobbes and Locke still serve as the founding fathers of a tradition that culminates in Smith; and the leading characteristics of this tradition have been summarized as being 'instrumental,

[26] Schumpeter, once more, is the main source of the charge: see *History of economic analysis*, pp. 184–6. For evidence of the slowness with which WN actually made its way in the world see K. Willis, 'The role in parliament of the economic ideas of Adam Smith, 1776–1800', *History of Political Economy*, XIV (1979), 505–44; S. Rashid, 'Adam Smith's rise to fame; a re-examination of the evidence', *The Eighteenth Century*, XXIII (1982), 64–85; and R. F. Teichgraeber, '"Less abused than I had reason to expect": the reception of the *Wealth of nations* in Britain, 1776–90', *Historical Journal*, XXX (1987), 337–66.

[27] See Corr., pp. 187, 190, 192, 193.

[28] See e.g. E. Heckscher, *Mercantilism* (London, 1935), I, 286–315; and R. H. Tawney's introduction to the reprint of T. Wilson, *Discourse upon usury* (London, 1925).

utilitarian, individualistic, egalitarian, abstract, and rational'.[29] Those who have praised the anticipatory qualities of mercantile writings for displaying these qualities, believing that in this respect a foundation was being laid for Smith, could have inadvertently put their finger on exactly what Smith wished to reject.[30] Just as it would not be difficult to show that Smith was unsympathetic to both William Petty's Baconian emphasis on 'number, weight, and measure' and Dudley North's Cartesian method, to mention two figures sometimes cited as having paved the way towards the 'scientific attitude' in economics, so is it with these other reductive features of mercantile thinking. Those economists who have only read WN, or rather some of the most-quoted parts of this work, especially those dealing with the pervasiveness of the urge to self-improvement and the irrelevance of benevolence when dealing with butchers and bakers, may find this puzzling. But if we have regard to TMS as well, the puzzle dissolves into something more interesting that could provide an important clue to Smith's desire to separate himself from his predecessors.

In setting the stage for the two central concepts in Smith's moral philosophy, sympathy and the impartial spectator, the opening books of TMS argue that man's need for society cannot be derived from 'certain refinements of self-love' (I.i.2.1). The pleasures and pains of society are felt instantaneously, and while a sense of utility may appear to underly our capacity to approve or disapprove of the behaviour of others, and hence of ourselves, this is merely an 'after-thought' rather than its origin (I.i.4.4). These two views based on self-interest and utility respectively, the second of which Smith associates with Hume, are what Smith wishes to oppose; he contends with them throughout the whole work, returning to deal with them more fully as systems of moral philosophy in the final book.

In this book one finds Smith's attack on Mandeville as the author of a 'licentious system' that was at one end of the spectrum – or rather, in view of Mandeville's unwillingness to distinguish between virtue and vice, just off it (TMS, VII.ii.4). Unlike Hutcheson, who had mounted two separate critiques of Mandeville, Smith was less concerned with the *actual* licentiousness of Mandeville's conclusions. Smith believed that the propagation of moral systems had *some* influence for good or ill on conduct, but his main interest lay

[29] By Joyce Oldham Appleby in *Capitalism and a new social order* (New York, 1984), pp. 19–23.

[30] The best example of this position can be found in Joyce Oldham Appleby's *Economic thought and ideology in seventeenth-century England*; see pp. 183–93, 258, 272–3 where she speaks of the 'inexorability of human beings acting out of self-interest', of the use of 'mechanical and impersonal' models, of the concern with the 'lawfullness of necessity', Locke's 'utilitarian conception of honour', and the daring use of Hobbesian assumptions and 'predictable laws of human behaviour' as features of mercantile thinking that Smith adopted, though apparently in depleted form. Appleby relies to a large extent on the work of C. B. Macpherson on 'possessive individualism.' For some incidental comments on Macpherson's view of Smith see my review article on 'The Burke–Smith problem and late eighteenth-century political and economic thought', *Historical Journal*, XXVIII (1985), 232–9; and for some criticisms of Appleby's misunderstanding of Smith from the same standpoint, 'Economic liberalism as ideology: the Appleby version', *Economic History Review*, XXXVIII (1985), 287–97.

in the intellectual error committed by Mandeville and those who had been seduced by his sophistry – namely the failure to take account, as an empirical fact, of certain human capacities and the social practices built upon them, chiefly those involved in distinguishing between desiring praise and being praiseworthy.

Nevertheless, Smith recognized the element of truth that lay behind Mandeville's scandalous attempts to prove that private vice and public benefit were indissolubly connected (TMS, VII.4.14); and in WN especially he matched Mandeville's cynicism when describing unintended social or historical outcomes, and when ridiculing the claims of merchants to be acting virtuously by serving the public good. We also know that the account of ambition in TMS (I.iii.2), like that of Mandeville (and, incidentally, Hobbes), relies heavily on vanity and competition for social status, psychological assumptions that were carried over into WN. Smith's relation to Mandeville, therefore, is by no means a simple one based on outright antagonism.[31] And the situation is made more complex, and interesting, by virtue of another connection, namely that between Mandeville and Rousseau, where the latter figures in TMS without ever being mentioned openly.

In his first published work, the letter to the editors of the *Edinburgh review* in 1755–6, Smith had pointed out that Mandeville's *Fable of the bees* 'has given occasion to the system of Mr. Rousseau' in his *Discourse on inequality*, despite the apparent opposition between their conclusions with regard to the 'primitive state of mankind'. They were united in supposing 'that there is in man no powerful instinct which necessarily determines him to seek society for its own sake'; and they both maintained that justice and inequality 'were originally the inventions of the cunning and the powerful, in order to maintain or to acquire an unnatural and unjust superiority over the rest of their fellow-creatures'.[32] When arguing against these views in TMS, therefore, Smith is engaged with Rousseau as much as with Mandeville.

Translating Rousseau's distinction between an acceptable, 'natural', self-preserving *amour de soi* and an unacceptable, 'artificial', emulative *amour propre* into Smith's English, one can point first to Smith's positive assessment of self-love and prudence. This was a case where he differed from Hutcheson as well as Mandeville in believing that prudential regard for personal affairs could be a virtue and that it was possible for this virtue to be distinguished from mere selfishness and vice. The second divergence from Rousseau's critique of *amour propre* turns on Smith's refusal to deny the social benefits associated with the desire to better one's condition by pursuing the objects of vanity. Thus while the same basic assumption of man's unsocial proclivities was present in both Mandeville and Rousseau, in erecting his own moral philosophy on the *opposite* foundation, Smith had built closer to Mandeville by accepting the realism and

[31] As several recent commentators have noted: see especially T. A. Horne, 'Envy and commercial society; Mandeville and Smith on "private vices, public benefits"', *Political Theory*, IX (1981), 551–69; and D. Castiglione, 'Mandeville moralized', *Annali della Fondazione Luigi Einaudi*, XVII (1983), 239–90.

[32] See *Essays on philosophical subjects*, pp. 250–1.

higher explanatory content of Mandeville's cynical observations. And yet in his evaluation of the actual benefits to the individual of the pursuit of the objects of vanity, Smith, while rejecting both Mandeville's equation of vanity with vice and Rousseau's utopianism, often seems to share the latter's stoicism. These objects do not confer greater happiness; they are not worthy of the effort involved to acquire them, though their pursuit is attended by genuine, if unintended social benefits. Such witholding of moral approval, while appreciating the benefits to society, is one of the additional freedoms enjoyed by Smith as a naturalistic observer and moralist, employing the doctrine of unintended consequences for purposes of explanation.[33] But Smith's continuing concern with the underlying issue can be gauged from his additions to the 1790 edition of TMS, especially those parts which stress 'the corruption of our moral sentiments' involved in the propensity to admire the rich and powerful, and the expanded account he gives of the qualities of the prudent or frugal man who is capable of exercising self-command and therefore of resisting the temptations of short-sighted avarice and vanity (TMS, I. iii. 3 and VI. i).[34]

Smith also attacked Hobbes (as well as Pufendorf and Mandeville) for constructing a system in which self-interest was the primary human motive. Again, he acknowledged that when self-interest was connected with regard for public utility in judging social and political institutions, such systems possessed an 'appearance of probability' (TMS, VII. iii. 1. 2). But Smith had earlier criticized a version of this doctrine (attributed to Hume) when expounding his own, as he saw it, more comprehensive theory based on sympathy. On the related issue of the role of reason, though this time fully in line with Hutcheson and Hume, Smith believed that while inductive reason enabled us to construct rules of justice and general codes of morality, reason was not the original basis on which notions of right and wrong were based. As with Hume, this was a matter of the passions or, as Smith put it, of 'immediate sense and feeling'.

But if this was Smith's position with regard to both licentious and non-licentious systems of morals that gave primacy to self-interest, utility, and reason, how can we explain his willingness to make the individual's desire to improve his condition the moving force in WN, and his famous statement concerning the irrelevance of benevolence in economic dealings, when tackling the preeminently economic side of life that took place within anonymous markets, the central institution of commercial society? The answer with regard to utility and reason has already been given: Smith consistently maintained that while public utility might be the outcome of any

[33] See J. W. Burrow, *Whigs and liberals; continuity and change in English political thought* (Oxford, 1988), chapter III.

[34] I have benefited from Michael Ignatieff's highly perceptive comparison of Rousseau and Smith in *The needs of strangers*, (London, 1984), chapter IV, and the related article he has written on 'Smith, Rousseau and the republic of needs', in T. C. Smout (ed.), *Scotland and Europe, 1200–1850* (Edinburgh, 1986), pp. 187–206. See also L. Dickey, 'Historicizing the "Adam Smith problem": conceptual, historiographical and textual issues', *Journal of Modern History*, LVIII (1986), 579–609 which stresses the 1790 changes, though evaluates them differently.

well-functioning moral or economic system, and that possessing such qualities it provided the kind of aesthetic pleasures that all successful systems require to satisfy the imagination, it was still not an adequate explanation of how that outcome was produced. It was also the source of a 'spirit of system' that had done harm when acted upon by statesmen or politicians who were unheedful of anti-utopian wisdom in such matters: 'When [the man of public spirit] cannot establish the right, he will not disdain to ameliorate the wrong; but like Solon, when he cannot establish the best system of laws, he will endeavour to establish the best that the people can bear' (TMS, VI.ii.2.15–18). This judgement is certainly of relevance to his remarks on the agricultural system and his modest hopes for implementing his own alternative to the mercantile system in WN.

In understanding the role of self-interest in WN we have still perhaps to bear in mind the fallacy that underlay so much of the older literature on the Adam Smith Problem, namely the view that treats sympathy as being *opposed* by self-interest, a confusion between benevolence and sympathy and a failure to appreciate that the 'prudent man' described in TMS is essentially the same person assumed to be at work in commercial society.[35] We may have no need of the benevolence of the butcher when we appeal to his self-interest in selling us meat, but that does not mean we have no imaginative sympathy, no capacity to understand and approve or disapprove of his behaviour.[36] Another prevalent source of misunderstanding seems to arise from confusing the 'sub-rational' instincts that Smith uses to explain the propensity to truck and barter as well as the desire for self-improvement with the posited behaviour of the creature called rational economic man.[37] The emergence and legitimacy of this creature has troubled so many generations of social theorists from the mid-nineteenth-century onwards that we tend to assume Smith invented or borrowed him, and that the whole idea of economic self-interest was especially problematic to Smith. Yet he was clearly not the first moral philosopher to take up the question of the compatibility of private interest with public good; and he did not feel the need to take upon himself, as Mandeville and Rousseau did for their own reasons, the whole burden of explaining something quite peculiar, something that was in urgent need of justification, namely how the economic realm had emerged and whether it could be legitimated in terms of those categories which were traditional to ancient or Christian notions of virtue. It may say a good deal about nineteenth- and twentieth-century social theory that we have constantly sought to explain and legitimize the peculiarities of economic striving and competition, but this, I would maintain, was not Smith's central problem.

According to TMS, acting on the basis of self-interest is one of the few

[35] See e.g. L. Dumont, *From Mandeville to Marx: the genesis and triumph of economic ideology* (London, 1977), p. 61.

[36] See D. D. Raphael, *Adam Smith* (Oxford, 1985), chapters III and V.

[37] The term 'sub-rational' is that of Jacob Viner; see *The role of providence in the social order* (Princeton, 1972), p. 79.

passions that could be taken for granted: 'We are not ready to suspect any person of being defective in selfishness, this is by no means the weak side of human nature, or the failing of which we are apt to be suspicious' (VII.ii.3.16). The instinct to barter, like the 'the desire of bettering our condition' is 'a desire which, though generally calm and dispassionate, comes with us from the womb, and never leaves us till we go into the grave' (WN, II.iii.28). This is as true of the history of the human race as it is of individuals. The opportunity to exercise the instinct was the only factor differentiating the beginning from the most recent practices: 'Our ancestors were idle for want of a sufficient encouragement to industry' (WN, II.iii.12). But being an instinct, it cannot be conceived as the *rational* pursuit of self-interest without denying the substance of Smith's moral philosophy, according to which reason is usually an inferior guide to conduct.

Smith is interested in pointing out that our perceptions of our interests are frequently faulty; that we suffer from over-weaning conceit; that our behaviour, even in economic settings, is capable of being blown off course by other motives such as love of dominance and love of ease. Honour, or public approbation, accounts for the fact that some professions 'in point of pecuniary gain... are generally under-recompensed' (WN, I.x.b.2 and 24). The neglect of insurance in shipping is the result of 'mere thoughtless rashness and presumptuous contempt of the risk' – an explanation that also accounts for the willingness of soldiers to endure hardship and discount danger in their search for fame and excitement: 'These romantick hopes make the whole price of their blood' (WN, I.x.b.28–30). An uneconomic institution such as slavery can only be explained by the love to domineer, wherever the law allows scope for its exercise (WN, III.ii.10). Love of ease accounts for the indolence of large landowners and recipients of high and easily earned profits, meaning that institutional expedients, beyond the market, have to be resorted to in order to match performance with self-interest.[38]

In these respects, self-interest is bound up with and overlaid by other psychological propensities. Yet its consistency and strength makes it different from the other motives or instincts that underly social interaction. When directed at our most basic needs – hunger, thirst and sex – almost every expression of the propensity 'excites contempt', showing that 'these principles of the human mind which are most beneficial to society are by no means marked by nature as the most honourable' (LJB, p.527; TMS, I.ii.1.1–2). Even when directed towards more respectable ends – 'the care of the health, of the fortune, and of the rank and reputation of the individual' – it is only worthy of 'a certain cold esteem' (TMS, VI.i.14). With regard to benevolence and other forms of propriety, we have to learn what behaviour earns the approbation of friends and strangers. Even in the sphere of justice, where the negative virtue of simply refraining from injuring others is the main object, a learning process is required. Hence what we can either call the providentialist

[38] See the compendium of such cases assembled by N. Rosenberg. 'Some institutional aspects of the *Wealth of nations*', *Journal of Political Economy*, LXVIII (1960), 557–70.

or evolutionary basis for Smith's treatment of morals: economic transactions based on mutual need are 'so strongly implanted by nature that they have no occasion for that additional force which the weaker principles need' (LJB, p. 527). Similarly with the division of labour: it could be traced to a universal human propensity to engage in truck and barter, to persuade others to supply our needs. It was not based on differences in natural talents, and it required no elaborate historical hypotheses such as those put forward by Mandeville and Rousseau. What Smith had to explain was how the progress of opulence had been retarded or distorted, rather than how it ever got started.

In an earlier stage of society, the allodial and feudal period, a story Smith tells in both the lectures on jurisprudence and in Book III of WN, retardation and inversion of the natural progress of opulence was due to the discouragement of agricultural improvement, to the laws of primogeniture and entail, to the contempt in which merchants and mercantile activities were held, and to the unproductive use by feudal landowners of the social surplus arising in agriculture. At this stage of the story then, a short-sighted landowners' conspiracy was the distorting force at work, and it was not until the power of the feudal barons was undermined by the growth of commerce and manufacturing in the towns, operating with royal encouragement, that order and good government could be extended from the towns to the countryside. Far from being public enemies, merchants, simply by following 'their own pedlar principle', became the unconscious agents of 'a revolution of the greatest importance to the publick happiness' (WN, III.iv.17): 'The habits, besides, of order, oeconomy and attention, to which mercantile business naturally forms a merchant, render him much fitter to execute, with profit and success, any project of improvement' (WN, III.iv.3). Considered individually and as a character type, therefore, merchants are unwitting public benefactors. Why then does this change when commerical society becomes established? Indeed, given the beneficent operation of the invisible hand in turning private interest to public good, is Smith not guilty of self-contradiction when he treats businessmen, as Donald Coleman has tellingly put it, as though they were 'conscious demon kings but unconscious social benefactors'?[39]

One of the reasons for believing Smith to be guilty of contradiction on this matter derives from a failure to observe the distinction between *individual* pursuit of self-interest under competitive conditions, when all the rules of fair play and strict justice are being observed, and *collective* pursuit of self-interest through combination, monopoly, and extra-parliamentary pressure group activity. Employing these concerted tactics, merchants, who come closest to

[39] See Coleman, 'Adam Smith, businessmen, and the mercantile system', p. 167. George J. Stigler makes similar criticisms of Smith's failure to follow through with the self-interest principle in his 'Smith's travels on the ship of state', in A. S. Skinner and T. Wilson (eds.), *Essays on Adam Smith* (Oxford, 1975), pp. 237–46. For an attempt to show, however, that Smith was a full-blooded 'public choice' theorist see Gary M. Anderson, 'The butcher, the baker, and the policy-maker: Adam Smith on public choice, with a reply by Stigler', *History of Political Economy*, XXI (1989), 641–60. Neither Stigler nor Anderson find it necessary to refer to TMS when interpreting WN.

possessing a rational perception of their interests, were to be suspected precisely because this perception was accompanied by the capacity to conspire against the public good. In commercial societies, such practices had perpetuated the earlier inversion of the natural progress of opulence, destroyed the 'natural balance of industry', and given rise to widespread infringements of natural liberty and justice.

As an antidote to this state of affairs Smith advocated the system of natural liberty, and in this sense only can it be said that he exalted economic individualism over political collectivism. As Book V of WN makes clear, the inescapable duties of the sovereign lay in the fields of defence, justice, and certain public works which included education. In TMS another category for collective action is mentioned, namely in the sphere of 'imperfect rights', where political agency might be called upon to do more than provide an orderly and just setting within which individuals make their moral and economic choices. Smith recognized that in all civilized nations the magistrate was entrusted with the power 'of promoting the prosperity of the commonwealth by establishing good discipline, and by discouraging every sort of vice and impropriety; he may prescribe rules, therefore, which not only prohibit mutual injuries among fellow-citizens, but command mutual good offices to a certain degree'. But it is also characteristic of Smith's position that he adds immediately that: 'Of all the duties of a law-giver, however, this, perhaps, is that which requires the greatest delicacy and reserve to execute with propriety and judgment. To neglect it altogether exposes the commonwealth to many gross disorders and shocking enormities, and to push it too far is destructive of all liberty, security and justice' (TMS, II. ii. i. 8). Could this too be an oblique response to the 'violence' of Rousseau's republican solutions to the problems raised in his discourse on inequality?

IV

The reference to a well-intentioned law enjoining 'mutual good offices' that could undermine liberty, security and justice is echoed in at least one place in WN, when Smith speaks of the conspiratorial gatherings of businessmen. His conclusion is that: 'It is impossible indeed to prevent such meetings, by any law which either could be executed, or would be consistent with liberty and justice.' The remedy conforms with what has insightfully been described as 'the primacy of the negative' in Smith's jurisprudence,[40] as illustrated by the continuation of the quotation: 'But though the law cannot hinder people of the same trade from sometimes assembling together, it ought to do nothing to facilitate such assemblies; much less to render them necessary' (WN, I. x. c. 27). This is not a confession of inability to act, a collapse into world-weariness in the face of a corrupt world: the negative measures designed to curb the spirit of combination that follow are specific and practical. Intervention to establish

[40] See K. Haakonssen, *Science of a legislator*, pp. 85, 89, 97.

the principles of non-intervention, to correct the malign influence of existing forms of intervention, underly the entire reformist programme of WN.

Only a very unobservant reader of WN could fail to notice the frequency with which Smith invokes natural justice when praising or condemning policies and institutions. But Smith's inability or unwillingness to complete his projected work on the science of jurisprudence has left readers in some doubt as to the content of the science, and what weight ought to be attached to its findings in WN. The idea that it is some kind of removable option or modish conversational rhetoric has, for many commentators, filled the resulting gap. Even so, the final remarks in TMS on the science are clear enough: it was to be 'a theory of the principles which ought to run through and be the foundation of the laws of all nations' (TMS, VII. 4. 37); and the observation that immediately precedes this provides the rationale for his criticisms of the mercantile system in WN: 'Sometimes what is called the constitution of the state, that is the interest of the government; sometimes the interest of particular orders of men who tyrannize the government, warp the positive laws of the country from what natural justice would prescribe.'

The account of the psychological basis of justice given in TMS shows what instincts lie behind our resentment of injury and how the resulting rules come to form the foundation for social existence. Smith is at one with Hume on the centrality of justice, though Smith's theory goes beyond Hume in dealing with personal as well as acquired rights such as those typified by property. Conducting a thought-experiment by asking on what minimum basis society could exist, justice becomes the pillar, benevolence merely 'the ornament which embellishes' (TMS, II. ii. 3. 4) – which does not mean, of course, that a society based solely on justice would be preferable. There is a clear connection between what Smith says on this subject in TMS and the minimalist definition of commercial society in WN, where the division of labour is so thoroughly established that 'every man... lives by exchanging, or becomes in some measure a merchant', relying on appeals to self-love to meet his wants (WN, I. iv. 1): 'Society may subsist among different men, as among different merchants, from a sense of utility, without any mutual love of affection; and though no man in it should owe any obligation, or be bound in gratitude to any other, it may still be upheld by a mercenary exchange of good offices according to an agreed valuation' (TMS, II. ii. 3. 2). Without suggesting some form of anti-trade snobbery on Smith's part, the memory of the 'cold esteem' commanded by mere prudence lingers on. Like any other sensible person, Smith would prefer a society in which benevolence and public spirit were present, but not if they had to be purchased at the expense of liberty, security and justice.

While the rules of justice might embody negative virtues, by contrast with the positive virtues contained within codes of benevolence, they were capable of strict definition and enforcement: hence Smith's caution on the subject of 'imperfect rights' and any *legal* requirement of 'mutual good offices'. A negative definition of justice, which means that in our ordinary behaviour we can act justly by doing nothing, does not imply unimportance, or that what is true for individuals applies to the sovereign, whose most important active duty (after defence) was to uphold and administer the rules of justice. Smith defines this duty in WN as 'protecting, as far as possible, every member of the society from the injustice or oppression of every other member of it' (WN, IV. ix. 51) – a definition which underlines his restriction of its content in TMS to commutative as opposed to distributive justice (TMS, VII. ii. 1. 10). Smith shares this restriction with Hume, and one is entitled to infer that Hume's reasons for not treating our notions of relative desert as between individuals and groups – however natural and 'agreeable' such notions might be – as capable of being enforced, as applying to Smith as well.[41] This accords with Smith's defence of a society of ranks based on visible distinctions of wealth, and his statement that the man of public spirit 'will respect the established powers and privileges even of individuals, and still more those of the great orders and societies, into which the state is divided', even when he considers them 'as in some measure abusive' (TMS, VI. ii. 2. 16).[42] Redistribution of income and wealth through positive intervention is another case where beneficent laws could infringe liberty and justice.

But having said this, the persistent emphasis in WN on what is unjust and oppressive may seem to belie or weaken the restriction to commutative justice. There is certainly more emphasis on such matters than one finds in Hume, though equality of treatment before the law is paramount for both men. Again, the stress falls on the negative: 'To hurt in any degree the interest of any one order of citizens, for no other purpose but to promote that of some other, is evidently contrary to that justice and equality of treatment which the sovereign owes to all the different orders of his subjects' (WN, viii. 30). Are we not back with a quietist interpretation of the famous passage in TMS on the invisible hand, telling us how, despite the 'natural selfishness and rapacity' of the rich, they are led by their desire for 'baubles and trinkets' to redistribute their income among the other ranks of society (TMS, IV. 1. 10)? In WN, and with more rhetorical force in the early draft of this work, Smith tells us something similar when he says that despite oppressive inequality and the unfair distribution of rewards and burdens in society, the division of labour provides a higher standard of living to the poor than that enjoyed by an African king (WN, I. i. 11). But the main thrust of the work is in the opposite direction: it can be found in the statements on how the benefits of economic activity should be distributed to those who do most of the work in society (WN, I. viii. 36), in the defence of high wages (WN, I. viii), in the attacks on the effect of mercantile restrictions on consumers, and so on. While all this can be cited as evidence of Smith's concern with 'welfare' – as we now rather feebly

[41] See D. D. Raphael, 'Hume and Smith on justice and utility', *Proceedings of the Aristotelian Society*, LXXII (1972–3), 101–3. On the 'agreeable' notion of desert and its inadmissability within any desirable or workable system of justice see D. Hume, *Enquiries concerning the human understanding and concerning the principles of morals*, ed. by L. A. Selby-Bigge (Oxford, 2nd edn, 1902), pp. 193–5.

[42] Support for this interpretation can also be derived from Smith's favourable comments on 'the gradual descent of fortunes' in England in LJA, p. 196.

put it – even of his interest in a form of economic democracy, the limits placed on this by a commutative view of justice and the primacy of the negative should not be overlooked. The system of natural liberty, should it ever come into existence, will produce a fairer distribution of income and fewer injustices in the form of infringements of natural liberties or rights, such as those affecting choice of occupation, place of residence, and modes of employing capital and other types of property. But Smith only seeks to remove existing forms of intervention: he does not espouse any positive programme of redistribution, unless the decision to tax luxury goods rather than those consumed by the bulk of society falls into this category.

With regard to wealth as opposed to income redistribution, Smith has more to say. The system of natural liberty would enable more people, one could say, to be 'enfranchised' – in an economic sense. By allowing the natural progress of opulence fuller scope, a larger number of independent producers, both in agriculture and in manufacturing, would emerge. Maintenance of the progressive state that accompanies more rapid capital accumulation, and the more efficient allocation of capital between competing employments, will certainly benefit wage-earners. Independence achieved through capital accumulation would also be placed within reach of more people.

In commerce and manufacturing, informal combination and the exclusive trading company stood in the way of this process of enfranchisement. Although it was more difficult to monopolize agriculture, other serious barriers to the diffusion of independent ownership existed in the form of the laws of primogeniture and entail. Such feudal relics were designed to concentrate wealth and power, and continued to perform that function, despite the effect of commercial prosperity in allowing merchants to become landowners and farmers. On this subject Smith sometimes employs a language of natural rights that is as strong as his use of the same terminology when discussing the effect of apprenticeship laws in depriving labour to its right to a fair share of produce (cf. WN, I.x.c. 12 and III.ii). What negative measures Smith espoused in order to weaken these barriers is not clear (to me at least), though he may have hoped that commerce would undermine primogeniture by means of the process which his pupil, John Millar, described as the 'fluctuation of fortunes'.[43] We can be more sure that the absence of such feudal relics was one of Smith's reasons for believing that America provided a setting in which commerce and liberty would thrive together. In fact, it is one of the peculiarities of Smith's position that since the 'policy of Europe' had inverted the natural progress of opulence at its very outset, only America, where non-feudal types of agricultural production had become established *before* commerce and manufacturing, could still follow the natural course.

Finally, there is that other category which prevents the rules of natural justice from being established, 'the constitution of the state', or 'the interest of the government.' With regard to the latter, the simplest equivalent

[43] See John Millar, *Historical view of the English government* (London, 1812), IV, 136.

treatment in WN seems to be that given to prodigality and unproductive expenditure (WN, II. iii. 30–36), to which the dangers inherent in public debt can be added (WN, V. iii). The definition of 'constitution' in TMS follows natural law usage and applies to the constellation of 'powers, privileges and immunities' of the respective 'orders and societies' that comprise any state (TMS, VI. ii. 2. 8–9).[44] The stability of this 'constitution' depends on a kind of dynamic equilibrium, as each order seeks to protect its powers from the encroachment of others. When Smith uses 'constitution of the state' in WN, it is when describing the 'real disorder' introduced by any regulation that favours one order at the expense of others (WN, IV. ii. 44). Although we are back with the attack on the mercantile state, prevention of this kind of disorder goes beyond avoidance of what is impolitic or unjust to indicate a broader political role for the statesman or legislator – to whom, after all, WN is addressed.

V

By way of concluding comment, and at the risk of placing too much weight on a journalistic comment, one could take the opening quotation from *The Times* as an early sign that TMS was not to be an equal partner with WN in sustaining Smith's posthumous reputation. The complementary parts of his ambitious plan were to live separate lives, with ethics and economics no longer coexisting under the same philosophical roof. Occasional attempts by political economists to reunite them, such as that made by John Stuart Mill in his *Principles of political economy* in 1848, did so by making use of a concept of rational economic man that was alien to Smith's enterprise, and by abandoning what has been treated here as one form taken by Scottish moral philosophy in the eighteenth century. Canonization as the saint of free enterprise economics, a process which began in Britain with the 1876 centenary celebrations presided over by Gladstone, has reached its apotheosis in the 1990s. Not only is WN being treated in some circles as the work of a living prophet, at the expense of mere historical figures such as Marx, but the whole of eastern Europe is now being claimed as part of his empire. Some gestures are made towards TMS, chiefly towards the 'man of system' remarks, interpreted anachronistically as an attack on socialist planners and totalitarian regimes – the existence of which, unless what the eighteenth century called 'oriental despotism' is made to serve the purpose, could not be known to Smith. Alternatively, TMS is thought of as being vaguely about 'benevolence', rather than 'sympathy', where benevolence takes on nineteenth-century connotations of 'charity' on the part of the rich and fortunate towards those less so. Smith's remarks about the futility (or was it fragility) of relying on the humanity or regard for justice of the rich and powerful (TMS, IV. 1. 10) would presumably, therefore, be regarded as highly cynical by some of his present-

[44] Compare this with Emmerich de Vattel's definition in *Le droit des gens* (Paris, 1863), III, 153: 'Le règlement fondamental qui determine la manière dont l'autorité publique doit être exercée est ce qui forme la constitution de l'Etat.'

day admirers. Smith may even have played an accidental part in creating these misunderstandings by destroying those unpublished parts of his project that would have linked WN and TMS more closely. The ultimate irony is the fact that he devoted so much of the last year of life to revising TMS, in the clear hope that it would be at least as important as WN.

[24]

ADAM SMITH'S *CONSIDERATIONS* ON LANGUAGE

BY CHRISTOPHER J. BERRY*

Adam Smith's *Considerations concerning the First Formation of Languages* was first published as an appendix to the third edition (1767) of the *Theory of Moral Sentiments* but has not been viewed in its own right at any length. This is so even though Smith himself, according to Dugald Stewart, "set a high value" upon it:[1] an estimation that is borne out with the discovery of the student notes of Smith's lectures on rhetoric and *belles-lettres*, delivered at Glasgow, 1762–63 (though these themselves were an expansion of some lectures given some ten years previously at Edinburgh[2]) since, alone, it seems, of these lectures, the one on the origin of language was the only one Smith thought it worthwhile both to expand and publish.[3]

The fact that Smith should have lectured on this particular topic is not surprising. There are two very general reasons why this is the case; first, because of a distinctive feature of the Scottish Enlightenment, namely, its preoccupation with "style," rhetoric, and a general concern with language both written and spoken. The great fear of the Scots was that they would appear provincial alongside the more fashionable centers of London and Paris. There are numerous manifestations of this fear. It can be seen to be one of the motivations behind the establishment of the innumerable clubs that existed in eighteenth-century Scotland; indeed, one of the best known of these clubs, the Select (whose members included Kames, Hume, Blair, and Smith himself[4]) established the Select Society for Promoting the Reading and Speaking of the English Language in Scotland.[5] There was further the curious incident of the importation (from Ireland) of Thomas Sheridan, in 1761, to give lectures in Edinburgh on Elocution and the English Tongue.[6] Finally, we can note what is, perhaps, the most characteristic feature of this preoccupation, the desire to eradicate "Scotticisms." For example, James Beattie published in 1787 (after the original pamphlet had proved so popular that all copies were accounted for) a little book, the title of which is

*I should like to thank Mr. A. S. Skinner, University of Glasgow, for his comments and suggestions on an earlier draft of this paper.

[1]"Accounts of the Life and Writings of Adam Smith LL.D." prefixed to *Theory of Moral Sentiments* (Bohn Library edit.; London, 1871), xxxiv. Cf. Stewart, *Works*, ed. W. Hamilton (Edinburgh, 1854), IV, 23.

[2]J. M. Lothian, *Adam Smith's Lectures on Rhetoric & Belles-Lettres* (London, 1963), xvi.

[3]See W. R. Scott, *Adam Smith as Student and Professor* (Glasgow, 1927), 52 who conjectures Smith finally published the *Considerations* because he became aware that the work for the *Wealth of Nations* would absorb much of his time and hence make it difficult to expand the theme fully.

[4]List in W. Robertson, *Works*, ed. D. Stewart (London, 1840) xxxii–iii.

[5]D. D. McElroy, *Scotland's Age of Improvement* (Washington, 1969), 58.

[6]Lothian, *op. cit.*, xxxii–iv; McElroy, *op. cit.*, 56–57; and for a full analysis: W. S. Howell, *Eighteenth Century British Logic and Rhetoric* (Princeton, 1971), 214–43. For a contemporary comment: T. Somerville, *My Own Life and Times* (Edinburgh, 1861), 56.

instructive, *Scotticisms; arranged in Alphabetical Order designed to correct Improprieties of Speech and Writing*, and the aim of which was "to put young writers and speakers on their guard against some of those Scotch idioms, which, in this country, are liable to be mistaken for English."[7]

It is against this particular background and preoccupation that we are to understand the great popularity not only of Smith's lectures on rhetoric[8] but also those of Stevenson (Professor of Logic, Edinburgh) and, preeminently, Hugh Blair, the first Regius Professor of Rhetoric and *Belles-Lettres* at Edinburgh.[9] Not only were Smith's lectures popular but also they were influential, especially on Blair, who not only was one of Smith's audience in the early Edinburgh lectures but who did later borrow part of Smith's manuscript for his own use.[10]

In addition to this contemporary concern there is in Smith also a pedagogic element. John Millar, in his account of Smith's Logic class at Glasgow, notes that after a general review of ancient logic Smith "dedicated all the rest of his time to the delivery of a system of rhetoric and belles-lettres" because he believed, apart from this being more suited to the youthfulness of his class, that "The best method of explaining and illustrating the various powers of the human mind, the most useful part of metaphysics, arises from an examination of the several ways of communicating our thoughts by speech, and from an attention to the principles of those literary compositions which contribute to persuasion or entertainment."[11]

Yet, even allowing for this pedagogic factor, Smith's interest in language is of wider significance and this constitutes the second broad reason, mentioned above, for his treatment of this topic. Language was a genuine and legitimate concern for Smith qua philosopher. In this he was not exceptional, since the whole question of the origin of language was one that exercised many of the leading (and lesser) minds of the eighteenth century. Smith certainly was aware of this general debate, though the only source that he in fact cites, in the *Considerations*, is Rousseau's *Essay on Inequality* (a book which Smith reviewed in a letter to the editors of the abortive *Edinburgh Review* of 1755/56, though on that occasion he neither commented upon nor translated the passages pertaining to language), though, of course, Rousseau himself refers to the work of Condillac. However, in a letter to George Baird, Smith remarks, *a propos* of an abstract of William Ward's *Essay on Grammar*, that it was Girard's *Les Vrais Principes de la Langue Françoise* "which first set me thinking upon these subjects. I have received more instruction from it than from any other I have yet seen upon them [nouns Substantive]." He also goes on to note that he received "a good deal of entertainment" from the grammatical articles in the *Encyclopédie*.[12] Regardless of

[7]Introduction, 2. E. C. Mossner, *Life of David Hume* (Edinburgh, 1954), *passim*, for further illustrations of this concern.

[8]For the background and analysis of the lectures; V. M. Bevilacqua, "Adam Smith's Lectures on Rhetoric & Belles-Lettres," *Studies in Scottish Literature*, **3** (July 1965), 42–45ff.

[9]R. M. Schmitz, *Hugh Blair* (New York, 1948), *passim*.

[10]Blair, *Lectures on Rhetoric & Belles-Lettres* (Edinburgh, 1838), 238n.

[11]Quoted in D. Stewart, *Life of Smith, op. cit.*, xvi.

[12]Quoted in J. Rae, *Life of Adam Smith* (London, 1895), 160.

Smith's sources the fact remains that this subject was one of popularity in the eighteenth century. But, before passing to an examination of Smith's own discussion it is necessary to be aware of the context in which the eighteenth century viewed language.

The context was distinctive. First, the theorists of the eighteenth century were. unaware of the "family" of languages; they wrote, by and large, before the discovery of Sanskrit. Instead, the eighteenth century still viewed grammar as a set of rules to be followed; it was, in Jespersen's phrase, "prescriptive" rather than "descriptive."[13] Underlying this view is the conception of Latin grammar as the paradigm of all language and, indeed, the general understanding of language in terms of Aristotle's Categories.[14] This is, as we shall see, of particular importance for Smith because it helps to explain his concern with the different parts of speech and the order in which they were developed. Secondly, the eighteenth century is distinctive because of the sway and dominance of Lockean epistemology, differentiating it from earlier speculation, and "Philosophical empiricism seems to open up a new approach to language for, in accordance with its fundamental tendency, it strives, not to relate the fact of language to a logical ideal, but rather to understand it in its sheer facticity, in its empirical origin and purpose . . . it seeks to know it solely in its psychological reality and function."[15]

Though the eighteenth-century speculation on language is thus distinctively characterized by post-Lockean philosophy and pre-familial linguistics this speculation is not homogeneous. Four approximate "schools" can be identified.[16] The first school we may term the Theological. Its main tenet was that language was a Divine gift to Adam and thereby denied to the brute creation. A corollary of this view was that different languages were to be accounted for by the dispersion of mankind after Babel. This Theological view was upheld by Beauzée in France,[17] Süssmilch in Germany, and Beattie in Scotland.

The second school we may term the Rationalists. The theorists of this school did not accept the Lockean epistemology and, as a result, there are relatively few representatives in the second half of the eighteenth century. To the Rationalists, language was an instrument of logical analysis by which a correlation was, or ought to be, established between thought and speech. The origin of language was ascribed to human invention. Some representatives of this school were Harris in England, Monboddo in Scotland, and the followers of Bullet in France.[18]

[13] O. Jespersen, *Language, its Origin, Nature & Development* (London, 1922), 24.

[14] R. H. Robins, *A Short History of Linguistics* (London, 1967), Chaps. 2 & 3, *passim.*

[15] E. Cassirer, *Philosophy of Symbolic Forms,* trans. R. Mannheim (New Haven, 1953), I, 133.

[16] Cf. the three-fold divisions of R. Wellek: Objective, Emotional, Organic, in *Rise of English Literatary History* (Chapel Hill, 1941); T. Sapir: "Theological, Rational, Naturalist in Herder's 'Ursprung der Sprach'," *Modern Philology, (1907), 109–42;* R. Pascal: "Theological, Ideological, Materialist," *German Sturm und Drang* (Manchester, 1953), Ch. 6.

[17] See his article "Langue" in the *Encyclopédie,* IX, 241ff. R. Hubert, *Les Sciences Sociales dans l'Encyclopédie* (Paris, 1923), Pt. 2, Ch. 8. Cf. P. Juliard, *Philosophies of Language in Eighteenth-Century France* (The Hague, 1970), 23n., for doubts on Beauzée's authorship.

[18] A. LeFlamanc, *Les Utopies Prérevolutionnaires* (Paris, 1934), Ch. 4.

The third school we may term the Organic. This school postulated that language grew alongside the development of mankind and that it had its origin in natural cries. Among representatives of this school we can identify Priestley and Mandeville in England, Condillac and Rousseau in France, and James Dunbar in Scotland. The final school, the Emotionalist, is really a subdivision of the Organic because of a different emphasis that can be distinguished in it. This emphasis was placed on the nature of the origin of language, in which they agreed with the Organic School, whereas the Organicists placed more emphasis on the development of language. Among members of the Emotionalist School were the Scotsmen, Blackwell and Blair.

It must be emphasized that these four schools are not completely exclusive because we find that certain individual's theories exhibit traces of more than one school. For example, Blair has a Theological element in his Emotional theory: Condillac a Rationalist component in his general Organic position; or again certain thinkers, for example, Vico and, especially, Herder, stand apart from any of the schools.

Thus in the general context of eighteenth-century language theory and in our classification we can place Smith squarely in the Organic School. Yet, we can determine more precisely the particular sphere of his interests. To speak broadly, we can identify two general problems, considered by the eighteenth century, relative to the origin of language. The first is put succinctly by Rousseau—"je laisse à qui voudra l'entreprendre la discussion de ce difficile Problème, lequel a été le plus nécessaire, de la Société déjà liée, à l'institution des Langues, ou des Langues déjà inventées, à l'établissement de la Société."[19] A problem that Rousseau thought Condillac had begged and the answer to which Monboddo explicitly directed himself.[20] The second problem was how to account for the presence of the different parts of speech. As previously stated it was this second problem which exercised Smith; he was not concerned with the first problem. Nor, unlike many other thinkers (both Organicists and Emotionalists), was he concerned about the actual origin of language in natural cries[21] or in the role of imitation in the development of language.[22]

Smith, therefore, sets himself a comparatively limited task but due to this limitation his discussion of the particular question of the evolution of the parts of speech is comprehensive. Smith's general theme is to account for the evolution of these parts of speech while circumventing the need for abstraction. The presence of the abstract parts of speech was a problem for the eighteenth-century theorists.

[19]*Discours sur l'origine de l'inégalité parmi les hommes* (Amsterdam, 1754), 60.

[20]*Origin & Progress of Language* (Edinburgh, 1773–93), I, 197.

[21]*Inter alia* Turgot, *Oeuvres*, ed. G. Schelle (Paris, 1913), I, 351; Blackwell, *Inquiry into Life & Writings of Homer* (London, 1735), 37; Blair, *op. cit.*, 64; Priestley, *Lectures on the Theory of Language* (Warrington, 1762), 237–38; Condillac, *Essai sur les connoissances humaines*, in *Oeuvres*, ed. G. LeRoy (Paris, 1947–53), I, 60–62. For a discussion of an aspect of this feature see my "Eighteenth Century Approaches to the Origin of Metaphor," in *Neuphilologische Mitteilungen*, **74** (1973).

[22]*Inter alia* Blair, *op. cit.*, 65; Monboddo, *op. cit.*, I, 191; Condillac, *op. cit.*, I, 61; Herder, "Origin of Language," *Herder on Social and Political Culture*, ed. F. M. Barnard (Cambridge, 1969), 136.

In particular, it was a problem for the Rationalists, since, in the words of Dunbar, the alleged inventors most improbably "must have resolved in imagination all the subtleties of logic and entered far into the science of grammar, before its objects had any existence. Profound abstraction and generalisation must have been constantly exercised."[23] Whereas, in fact, to Dunbar language developed through "the laws of analogy [which] by one gentle and uniform effect superceding or alleviating the effects of abstraction permit language to advance towards its perfection free of the embarrassments which seemed to obstruct its progress."[24] The greatest of these embarrassments was to account for the abstract parts of speech such as prepositions, pronouns, particles, etc.

Smith set about accounting for the evolution of these abstractions or "metaphysical" elements in a manner consistent with the alleged mental ability and state of primitive man (savage). He opens by declaring: "The assignation of particular names to denote particular objects . . . would probably be one of the first steps towards the formation of language."[25] In time, "those words . . . would each of them insensibly become the common name of the multitude"[26] and this seems "to have given occasion to the formation of those classes and assortments (in language),"[27] namely, those seemingly metaphysical and abstract grammatical categories. The next development in language are adjectives and prepositions, that is, words expressing "quality" and "relation."

Smith illustrates how "quality" was conceived: "The quality appears in nature as a modification of the substance, and as it is thus expressed in language, by a modification of the noun substantive."[28] This correspondence between what is "natural" and what occurs in the development of language forestalls the need for abstraction; that is, new adjectival words are not invented, but, instead, the endings of existing nouns substantive are changed. The question of "relation" Smith believes to be even more abstract than that of "quality" but again the same procedure operates so that, in practice, there is no need for abstraction. For example, the relation of possession is expressed by the development of the genitive case and it is only as man develops that abstract words, such as "of," are developed. It is in this way that the absence of particles and prepositions in Latin and Greek is accounted for: they are older languages, which alter the endings of words in order to express the same meaning as prepositions, etc.

Though Smith declares noun substantives to be the first elements of speech in parts he also states that "verbs must necessarily have been coeval."[29] The first verbs Smith believes were impersonal and hence his argument is that there has been a development from impersonal to personal verbs. The rule governing this development is that the verbs grow more general as the number of words for subjects increase, that is, the development of verbs is an integral part of the development of language as a whole. Just as nouns incorporated "relation" and "quality" by altering their endings so verbs incorporate number, tense, and mood in the same way. It is a later development in language that the verbs of existence

[23] *Essays on the History of Mankind* (London, 1780), 91.
[24] *Op. cit.*, 90.
[25] *Considerations*, in *Works* (London, 1805), V, 295.
[26] *Op. cit.*, 296.
[27] *Op. cit.*, 298.
[28] *Op. cit.*, 303.
[29] *Op. cit.*, 317.

and possession come to be used as auxiliaries. Smith summarizes his theory of the development of language in a maxim: "the more simple any language is in its composition the more complex it must be in its declensions and conjugations," and vice versa.[30]

This, in outline, is the tenor of Smith's argument. This argument was influential, especially in Scotland where we can cite two examples, Monboddo and Dunbar. Monboddo's general thesis that language is invented is opposed to Smith's, yet he explicitly agrees with Smith on a number of issues. Monboddo allows that Smith's is an "ingenious" theory as is Smith's conjecture that the names of objects were particular before becoming general.[31] Monboddo further agrees that children name themselves instead of employing the pronoun "I"[32] and does, indeed, refer to Smith on several occasions during his own account of the development of the parts of speech.[33]

While Dunbar, our second example, does not elucidate the development of the parts of speech in such detail as Smith there are positive indications that he accepts Smith's broad argument. The most concrete instance of Smith's influence on Dunbar is a Note (on the subject of the development of verbs from impersonal to personal) in which Dunbar expresses his agreement with Smith's argument.[34] In the text Dunbar sketches out how he envisaged the development of verbs. He postulates that the lion and the serpent are, to the savage, the most hostile animals so that "a certain species of terror would be excited by the approach of one: a different modification of the same emotion would be excited by the approach of the other."[35] Given these emotions, and the fact that the other inhabitants of the forest have names, it is then to Dunbar "abundantly natural for the savage to join the term, indicating the dread of the lion or serpent with a proper name in order to notify the approach of any other offensive creature. This term by an easy extension will be transferred from offensive to other creatures: and hence by gradual transition even to inanimate objects, till it is charged at length with a general affirmation and possesses all the power of a verb."[36] That is essentially the Smithian argument (indeed the example of the lion is taken straight from Smith[37]) that verbs develop from the particular to the general.

To appreciate Smith's position more fully we can now take up a number of points he makes and indulge in some short comparisons. First, as we have seen, Smith avows that verbs and nouns are coeval (though he does conjecture that possibly all the first words may have been impersonal verbs[38]) but this question of the priorities of the parts of the speech was the subject of much speculation. Some thinkers assigned very definite priorities. Vico[39] and Priestley[40] both regarded verbs as later developments. Condillac believed verbs were the third part of

[30] *Op. cit.*, 329.

[31] *Op. cit.*, I, 297.

[32] *Op. cit.*, II, 45; Smith, *op. cit.*, 324.

[33] *Op. cit.*, II, Bk. 1, Chs. 8–10.

[34] *Op. cit.*, 107. Blair agrees with Smith on this point: *op. cit.*, 101.

[35] *Op. cit.*, 81.

[36] *Op. cit.*, 82.

[37] *Op. cit.*, 319.

[38] *Op. cit.*, 318.

[39] *New Science*, trans. T. Bergin and M. Fisch (Ithaca, 1948), 137.

[40] *Op. cit.*, 56.

speech to be developed: after nouns substantive, first (also Priestley's position[41]), and adjectives, second, but before pronouns, fourth.[42] Herder, on the other hand, believed verbs to be the first part of speech to be developed, a consequence of his belief that hearing is the *Lehrmeister;* that it constitutes the "proper gateway to the mind" so that "Verba developed into nomina but not from them. A child does not call the sheep a sheep but a bleating creature, and this changes the interjection into a verb."[43]

This quotation leads on to a second general point raised by Smith's analysis since it was a feature of eighteenth-century discussions of the origin of language, as testified to by Herder in that quotation, that attention was paid to the speech patterns and behavior of children. Thus Vico and Priestley both support their position on the order of the development of the parts of speech by citing as evidence the fact that children tend to omit verbs when they speak.[44] Smith, too, regards the experience of children to be relevant. We have already referred to one occasion of this in the context of the pronoun "I" but there is another instance. He substantiates his point that terms develop from specific reference to become "the common name of a multitude" by the fact that "A child that is just learning to speak, calls every person who comes to the house its papa, or its mama; and thus bestows upon the whole species those names which it had been taught to apply to two individuals."[45] The experience and behavior of children was of course used at length by Condillac to explain the generation of language.[46]

The significance of this recourse to children by the eighteenth-century theorists was the belief that the growth of language in children was thought to be analogous to its growth in mankind (hence the importance attached to imitation in many theories). Added to this was the further belief or presupposition that (extant) primitive peoples (Smith's "savages") exhibit the same processes as children. This is stated clearly by Dunbar at the close of his discussion, where he justifies his own theory as being "consonant to the probability of things, to the experience of early life, and to the genius and complexion of ruder ages."[47]

To take up another point in Smith's analysis, his argument that the simplification of the structure of language was occasioned by the growth of "particulars" was given, in addition to the "logical" argument, an historical expression.[48] That is, this process of increasing complexity in the composition of language was brought about "in consequence of the mixture of several languages with one another, occasioned by the mixture of different nations."[49] Smith con-

[41]*Op. cit.*, 50.

[42]*Op. cit., Essai . . .* , Vol. I Pt. 2, Sect. 1, Chaps. 9–10.

[43]*Op. cit.*, 142. Cf. Turgot's argument that the names of animals in primitive (unmixed) languages are onomatopoeic in origin, *op. cit.*, I, 353.

[44]Vico, *loc. cit.;* Priestley, *op. cit.*, 56.

[45]*Op. cit.*, 296–97.

[46]*Op. cit.*, I, *Essai . . .* , Pt. 2, Sect. 1, Ch. 1. Also Blair, *op. cit.*, 90, and esp. C. de Brosses, *Traité de la Formation Méchanique des Langues* (Paris, 1801), I, 200ff.

[47]*Op. cit.*, 96.

[48]Cf. Wellek, *op. cit.*, 93 who accuses Smith of inconsistency on this point.

[49]*Op. cit.*, 326. Note that the full title of the *Considerations* is . . . *and the Different Genius of Original and Compounded Languages.*

jectures that from the mixing of two languages those ignorant of the intricacies of the other language would "naturally" in the case of declensions, for example, supply prepositions instead, and so on.[50] Again this part of Smith's argument was not lost on Dunbar[51] and, indeed, many writers[52] acknowledged the influence of one language upon another through either conquest or contiguity or both.

Yet another feature of Smith's theory that needs noting is his concluding argument. This argument is really a lament since he believes the increasing simplification of languages only serves to render them less perfect. He produces three reasons for this imperfection: simplified language is prolix, constrained, and monotonous.[53] The languages most at fault, it follows from Smith's earlier analysis, are the most modern, with English, because it is the most simplified (the most mixed), by implication the worst offender. This aspect of Smith's theory needs to be placed in its original context, that is, lectures on rhetoric.[54] In these lectures, in fact, Smith continues by investigating the remedies for these defects in English,[55] and discoursing at length on the correctness of style. Of course, this concern related to the contemporary Scottish concern with "correct" language as mentioned above. On the more precise question of rhetoric it was something of a commonplace that the "moderns" could not compete with the great rhetoricians of the past, such as Demosthenes or Cicero, or indeed with their poets. Sentiments with which this aspect of Smith's theory is in perfect accord—"How much this power of transposing the order of their words must have facilitated the composition of the ancients, both in verse and prose, can hardly be imagined"[56]—since this power, which greatly enhances the quality of ancient or classical literature, is non-existent in English, where the words in the sentence are "almost precisely determined."

A final point about Smith's theory also relates to imperfection in language, but, this time, to both classical and modern languages. Smith points out this general imperfection when he remarks that "Alexander walking" or "Alexander ambulat" express one conception, and "the division of this event, therefore, into two parts, is altogether artificial, and is the effect of the imperfection of language, which, upon this, as upon many occasions, supplies, by a number of words, the want of one which could express at once the whole matter of fact that was meant to be affirmed,"[57] this being a state of affairs that contrasts with the earliest condition of language, that is, when impersonal verbs prevailed and which "express in one word a complete event."[58] This was an opinion shared by many of the heorists, for example, Dunbar in passing, and more explicitly in Rousseau, Blair,

[50] *Ibid.*

[51] *Op. cit.*, 94–95.

[52] Priestley, *op. cit.*, 220; Herder, *op. cit.* 167; Turgot, *op. cit.*, I, 358, and especially his article on "Etymologie" in the *Encyclopédie*, VI, 98–111.

[53] *Op. cit.*, 333–36.

[54] O. Funke, *Englische Sprachphilosophie im späteren 18. Jahrhundert* (Bern, 1934), 31.

[55] In Lothian, *op. cit.*, 18–21.

[56] *Op. cit.*, 336.

[57] *Op. cit.*, 318.

[58] *Ibid.* Cf. the letter to Baird, *loc. cit.*, where Smith remarks that verbs are "in my apprehension the original parts of speech, first invented to express in one word a compleat event."

and Monboddo.[59] Smith, however, elaborates the point by saying that these verbs "preserve in the expression that perfect simplicity and unity, which there always is in the object and in the idea . . . [and] with which the mind conceives its nature."[60]

There is a degree of similarity here with a position adopted by Condillac. Condillac believed that in primitive languages every word stood for an idea, and that there was accordingly perfect communication between individuals.[61] This is Condillac when most rationalistic (see above), that is, when he continues the Port-Royal tradition,[62] and it is a corollary of this view that he regards modern language as inferior, since this perfect communication between individuals is no longer realizable. In fact, this perfect language he believes is now only to be found in algebra: "L'algèbre est une langue bien faite."[63]

Thus we have Adam Smith's theory of language as found in the *Considerations.* Though his treatment of the subject is comparatively short in length and limited in scope it is nevertheless not without significance. In Scotland, in keeping with his general "seminal" importance,[64] his theory was taken up by both Blair and Dunbar and, in part, by Monboddo. In the broader terms of the eighteenth century Smith's theory is typical of what we have here designated the Organic School: language is seen as developing in step with man's own (and society's) development. The merits of this theory must be adjudged in eighteenth-century terms,[65] since the total conception of language changed with the work of the Schlegels, Jones, Bopp, and others, at the turn of the century. Perhaps the aspect of Smith's theory that is most characteristic of his age is his explanation in terms of what is "natural"[66]—hence Stewart's dubbing of his essay as Natural or Conjectural History—an explanation that is at once the most economic in its operating principle, the human mind, and most catholic in what it explains, the growth and development of the character and form of language.

University of Glasgow.

[59]Dunbar, *op. cit.*, 82; Monboddo, *op. cit.* I, 360; Blair, *op. cit.*, 89n.; Rousseau, *op. cit.*, 54.

[60]*Op. cit.*, 318.

[61]See his *Langue des Calculs* (1798).

[62]I. F. Knight, *Geometric Spirit* (New Haven, 1968), Ch. 6. For Condillac's rationalism (his retention of Cartesian elements): C. Frankel, *Faith of Reason* (New York, 1948), 51–55.

[63]*Op. cit., Langue* II, 420. For the significance and influence of this idea: H. B. Acton, "Philosophies of Language in Revolutionary France," *Proceedings of the British Academy,* 45 (1959), 204ff.

[64]D. Forbes, "Scientific Whiggism," *Cambridge Journal,* 7 (1954), 643–70.

[65]M. Müller, *Lectures on the Science of Language* (8th edit.; London, 1875), I, 425ff. treats Smith explicitly as a "pre-scientific" theorist.

[66]Girard, *Les Vrais principes* . . . (Paris, 1747), I, 42: "Persuadé de l'avantage qu'il y a à suivre le fil de la Nature dans toutes les choses dont elle est le principe"—of which Smith thought so highly. See T. D. Campbell, *Adam Smith's Science of Morals* (London, 1971), 55–60 for a discussion of Smith's use of the term "nature."

Name Index